P9-CRX-526

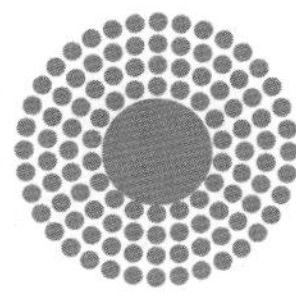

Relationship Selling

third edition

Mark W. Johnston

Greg W. Marshall

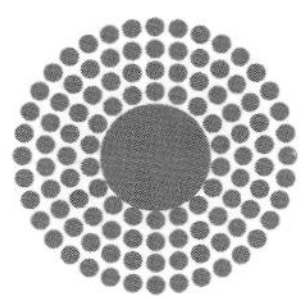

Relationship Selling

third edition

Mark W. Johnston

Greg W. Marshall

Boston Burr Ridge, IL Dubuque, IA New York San Francisco St. Louis
Bangkok Bogotá Caracas Kuala Lumpur Lisbon London Madrid Mexico City
Milan Montreal New Delhi Santiago Seoul Singapore Sydney Taipei Toronto

The McGraw-Hill Companies

RELATIONSHIP SELLING
Published by McGraw-Hill/Irwin, a business unit of The McGraw-Hill Companies, Inc., 1221 Avenue of the Americas, New York, NY, 10020.

This book is printed on acid-free paper.
Printed in China

2 3 4 5 6 7 8 9 0 CTP/CTP 11 10

ISBN 978-0-07-340483-7
MHID 0-07-340483-7

Vice president and editor-in-chief: *Brent Gordon*
Publisher: *Paul Ducham*
Sponsoring editor: *Dana L. Woo*
Developmental editor I: *Sara Knox Hunter*
Associate marketing manager: *Jaime Halteman*
Project manager: *Dana M. Pauley*
Lead production supervisor: *Michael R. McCormick*
Designer: *Matt Diamond*
Media project manager: *Suresh Babu, Hurix Systems Pvt. Ltd.*
Typeface: *10/12 Times Roman*
Compositor: *Laserwords Private Limited*
Printer: *CTPS*

Library of Congress Cataloging-in-Publication Data

Johnston, Mark W.
Relationship selling/Mark W. Johnston, Greg W. Marshall.—3rd ed.
p. cm.
Includes index.
ISBN-13: 978-0-07-340483-7 (alk. paper)
ISBN-10: 0-07-340483-7 (alk. paper)
1. Selling. 2. Relationship marketing. 3. Customer relations. I. Marshall, Greg W. II. Title.
HF5438.25.J655 2010
658.85—dc22 2009000967

www.mhhe.com

To Susie and Grace, thank you . . . for everything.

Mark

To Patti and Justin.

Greg

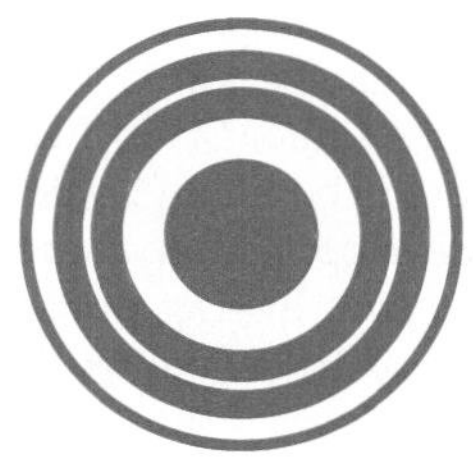

About the Authors

Mark W. Johnston, PhD

Mark W. Johnston is the Alan and Sandra Gerry Professor of Marketing and Ethics at the Roy E. Crummer Graduate School of Business, Rollins College, in Winter Park, Florida. He earned his PhD in marketing from Texas A&M University. Prior to receiving his doctorate he worked in industry as a sales and marketing representative for a leading distributor of photographic equipment. His research has resulted in published articles in many professional journals, such as the *Journal of Marketing Research, Journal of Applied Psychology,* and *Journal of Personal Selling & Sales Management.*

Mark has been retained as a consultant for firms in the personal health care, chemical, transportation, service, and telecommunications industries. He has consulted on a wide range of issues involving strategic sales force structure, sales force performance, sales force technology implementation, market analysis, sales training, and international market decisions. Mark has conducted a number of seminars around the world on a variety of topics, including motivation, managing turnover in the organization, sales training issues, ethical issues in marketing, and improving overall sales performance.

Greg W. Marshall, PhD

Greg W. Marshall is the Charles Harwood Professor of Marketing and Strategy in the Crummer Graduate School of Business at Rollins College, Winter Park, Florida. He earned his PhD in marketing from Oklahoma State University. Greg's industry experience includes 13 years in selling and sales management, product management, and retailing with companies such as Warner Lambert, Mennen, and Target Corporation. When he left Warner Lambert in 1986 to enter academe, he was the manager of the top-performing sales district in the United States. In addition, he has served as a consultant and trainer for a variety of organizations in both the private and public sectors, primarily in the areas of marketing planning, strategy development, and service quality.

Greg is an active researcher in selling and sales management, having published more than 40 refereed articles in a variety of marketing journals, and he serves on the editorial review board of the *Journal of the Academy of Marketing Science, Journal of Business Research,* and *Industrial Marketing Management.* He is editor of the *Journal of Marketing Theory and Practice* and is past editor of the *Journal of Personal Selling & Sales Management,* currently serving on its senior advisory board. Greg is on the board of directors of the Direct Selling Education Foundation, is past president of the Academic Division of the American Marketing Association, and is a fellow and past president of the Society for Marketing Advances. He is president-elect of the Academy of Marketing Science.

In addition to working together on *Relationship Selling,* Mark and Greg are the coauthors of *Churchill/Ford/Walker's Sales Force Management* and *Marketing Management* also published by McGraw-Hill/Irwin.

Preface

Fundamental to the success of any organization is its relationship with customers. Today, the relationship between companies and their customers is in a period of profound change. Technology, globalization, ethical concerns, corporate strategic decisions, and a host of other issues have created a revolution in the selling process. Customers are no longer interested in working with companies that cannot add substantial value to their business. They seek better, more strategic *Relationships* with their suppliers. Changes in the buyer–seller relationship have also led to dramatic changes in the management of salespeople. "Home" and "virtual" offices, communication technology, and demographic changes in the sales force (to name just a few) have created significant challenges for salespeople and their managers. Today's selling model is a very different process than it was even 10 years ago. As a result, any book about selling should fully reflect this new business reality.

This third edition of *Relationship Selling* continues to present a clear and concise portrayal of selling in the contemporary business environment—namely, *relationship* selling with a strong focus on creating and communicating value for customers and on managing the buyer–seller relationship process. It remains the only book to integrate the critical tools of the relationship-selling process with the unique challenges managers face working with salespeople in a highly dynamic competitive environment. Mark Johnston and Greg Marshall, your authors, combine backgrounds in selling and sales management with long established research records and consulting experience in the field.

Why Did We Write This Book?

The idea for writing this book evolved over several years and many conversations with colleagues and sales professionals. There was no single moment of creation, rather a series of conversations that ended with "Gee, I wish there was a book that presents a relevant and current approach to relationship selling, with a value focus, and an integration of managerial issues in buyer–seller relationships."

Our own review of the books in the Personal Selling area revealed no single source for a complete, holistic approach to selling that incorporates not only state-of-the-art sales methodology but also the knowledge base and skill sets necessary to manage such a critical area in the organization. Our colleagues presented us with an exciting challenge: Was it possible to create a book that reflects contemporary relationship selling in a way that maximizes the course's success for both instructors and students? To answer the challenge, our primary goal in writing

Relationship Selling, Third Edition, as in previous editions, was to create a single, comprehensive, and holistic source of information about the selling function in modern organizations, focused on the process of securing, developing, and maintaining long-term relationships with profitable customers—the essence of *relationship selling.* As you read the book, note that our approach links the process of selling (what salespeople do) with the process of managing salespeople (what sales managers do). In order to provide a pictorial representation of this linkage and to create an easily referenced thematic thread, we have developed a Relationship Selling and Sales Management Model that serves as a road map all the way through the book. The model is introduced in Chapter One, and we return to it at the beginning of each subsequent chapter to highlight where that chapter's content fits into the overall model.

In summary, building strong, sustainable customer relationships is no longer optional—it is *required* for long-term business success. As the importance of relationships has grown, the selling function has become assimilated into the rest of the organization. Selling now is truly a "boardroom topic" as companies realize that effective management of the relationship-selling process is a key to gaining overall competitive advantage. Thus, this book incorporates state-of-the-art sales practices and research to develop a comprehensive portrayal of relationship selling today.

Who Is the Audience for the Book?

The overarching theme of this book is securing, developing, and maintaining long-term relationships with profitable customers. As such, the book offers broad appeal and high value added in any Personal Selling course, allowing the instructor to portray a modern, integrative approach to selling in a style that today's students will easily connect with and truly enjoy. In our discussions with colleagues at many colleges and universities we consistently heard a call for a book that offers a fresh, value-driven, integrative approach to relationship selling and also provides important insights into managerial aspects of the buyer–seller relationship. This book addresses those needs.

You may have noticed (as we have) a growing trend in sales-related courses. More and more students who are not majors in marketing (or even in business) are taking courses in Personal Selling. This trend recognizes the inherent value of such courses to the personal growth and success of any student. As such, we believe *Relationship Selling,* Third Edition, serves this emerging market very well by enabling "nonsales majors" wanting a single sales-related course to understand the overall sales field from a modern, application-oriented perspective.

In addition, the book is written to complement and enhance a variety of teaching approaches. Most importantly, this third edition of *Relationship Selling* incorporates a comprehensive role-play model that integrates role-play exercises focused on important relationship selling issues. Role playing is one of the most used training tools by top sales organizations. Our end-of-chapter Role Plays are tied together throughout the book within a common scenario that students will readily and enthusiastically identify with as they progress through the course. Beyond the role plays, a variety of other teaching enhancements are provided within the book. For those interested in a lecture/discussion format an abundance of material is presented in the chapters and reinforced in discussion questions at the end of each chapter. Learning objectives and key terms help focus students on the most important material. Mini Cases and Ethical Dilemmas are also included at the end of each chapter for instructors taking a more case-oriented approach. A variety of other features imbedded within each chapter add value to the students' experience in the course, including boxed features on Leadership, Innovation, and Global Perspective. This third edition updates our popular Expert Advice feature so that each chapter begins with a sales expert giving firsthand advice on some of the key topics in that chapter.

Structure of the Book

As mentioned, the model for relationship selling used by firms today defines the connection between companies and their customers in a new way. We have developed a framework that breaks down the relationship-selling process into three distinct yet interrelated components, reflected by the three parts within the book.

1. **What Is Relationship Selling? (Chapters 1–4)** The book begins with an introduction to relationship selling and the environment in which this process takes place. The opening chapter introduces the model for Relationship Selling and Sales Management and shows how it serves as a road map for the entire book. Next is a comprehensive discussion of two critical precursors to the relationship-selling process—using information to understand sellers and buyers and the concept of value creation and communication, both of which are central to the buyer–seller relationship. Finally the important area of ethical and legal issues within the relationship-selling framework is discussed.

2. **Elements of Relationship Selling (Chapters 5–9).** Each of the elements in the relationship-selling process is identified and examined in detail. These include prospecting and sales call planning, communicating the sales message, negotiating win–win solutions, closing the sale and follow-up, and self-management: time and territory. At the end of each chapter on the relationship-selling process, we conclude with a brief section that links the role of salesperson to the role of his or her manager in a way that is relevant to that chapter's topical focus. As such, students come away with an integrative perspective on how salespeople and their managers relate in order to get the job done.

3. **Managing the Relationship Selling Process (Chapters 10–14).** Key to effectively implementing successful buyer–seller relationships is an understanding of the many managerial issues involved in the relationship-selling process. Fundamental sales management concepts are examined from within the relationship-selling model. The topics addressed include salesperson performance: behavior, role perceptions, and satisfaction; recruiting and selecting salespeople in relationship selling; training salespeople for sales success; salesperson compensation and incentives; and finally, evaluation and rewarding salesperson performance.

Features of the Text

A. Expert Advice—UPDATED Expert Advice is a dialogue with a working professional who has found success in relationship selling by applying aspects of the principles and concepts discussed in the chapter. Designed to be a great chapter kickoff providing a real world perspective, our experts satisfy the desire by both students and instructors to see how people actually use chapter concepts to be successful in business practice.

B. Learning Objectives—Each chapter begins with a set of learning objectives for the students. The objectives guide students as they read and seek to identify the key takeaways from the chapter.

C. Boxed Features—Leadership, Innovation, Global Perspective—NEW AND UPDATED These three boxes are key drivers of relationship selling today—leadership, innovation, and global perspective. Each chapter contains featured boxes that focus on at least one of these concepts. The boxes underscore and provide real world examples related to the material in the chapter. Instructors will benefit from these boxes because they provide excellent discussion starters in class.

D. Key Terms—UPDATED At the end of each chapter key terms are summarized for the students. These terms are also boldfaced the first time they appear in the body of each chapter. As a result, students can use these terms to take a quick check on their level of understanding of the material. They will also find these terms defined in the glossary at the end of the book.

E. Role Play—It is accepted both in field sales training and in the college classroom that role playing is a valuable tool for helping salespeople and students internalize and apply what they are learning. A comprehensive role-play scenario has been developed for *Relationship Selling,* Third Edition, that flows through the various chapters for continuity of learning. It involves a sales district of the "Upland Company," and includes a cast of characters students come to know and empathize with as they move through each chapter's role play. Each part of the role play will enable students to employ aspects of relationship selling they have learned within a particular chapter. In the sales management chapters later in the book the role plays give students maximum opportunity to connect the managerial issues with the relationship-selling topics covered in earlier chapters.

F. Discussion Questions—UPDATED Each chapter contains a set of questions designed to generate classroom discussion of key concepts and ideas from the chapter material, opening vignettes, and boxed features. These questions can also be used by students to enhance their own understanding or by instructors as review questions.

G. Ethical Dilemma—UPDATED Ethical behavior in buyer–seller relationships has never been more important than it is today. Each chapter contains an ethical dilemma designed to place students in realistic scenarios that require one or more decisions. These scenarios can be used as discussion starters in class or assigned to students for reflection and reporting back individually or in groups.

H. Mini Case— UPDATED Cases have consistently been shown to be an effective tool for students in learning and applying material. Each chapter incorporates a mini case that supports chapter subject matter. All the cases are original—written especially for the book and incorporating the latest in relationship-selling issues.

I. Relationship-Selling Math Appendix—NEW AND UPDATED The value proposition provides the basis for the customer's perception of any salesperson's product or service. As part of the value proposition a good salesperson will develop a quantitative analysis to provide concrete evidence of the product's value to a buyer. This appendix to Chapter 3 and the accompanying spreadsheet on the book's Web site (www.mhhe.com/johnston3e) lead students through interactive exercises detailing the process of putting together a financial analysis for a sales proposal and buyer presentation. Many instructors mention the need for better quantitative skills among their students—this feature, updated in the third edition, allows for a class assignment on quantifying the value proposition.

J. Sales Proposal Appendix—NEW AND UPDATED Creating an effective sales proposal is an essential element of a successful sales presentation. The new appendix to Chapter 5 provides a complete template for developing a sales proposal. Along with the Sales Proposal Handbook posted in PowerPoint on the book's Web site (www.mhhe.com/johnston3e), the appendix guides students through the process of professional sales proposal development, linking the required content back to specific chapters and other source material. Instructors who want to assign a sales proposal development project in class will find this new tool exceptionally useful.

K. Videos—A complete set of video material has been included online to support and extend the material in the book. In addition, unique to this book are video segments designed to enhance the role-play exercises.

L. PowerPoint Slides—UPDATED A complete set of PowerPoint slides has been developed to enhance the in-class experience of both instructors and students. The package of slides is flexible enough for instructors to include their own material yet comprehensive enough to stand alone. Links to sales-related sites are imbedded in the PowerPoint presentation to enable the instructor to go directly to relevant Web sites if they are online.

M. Instructor Manual—UPDATED An updated instructor's manual for *Relationship Selling,* Third Edition, provides an overview of each chapter, answers to discussion questions, and a discussion guide to role plays, ethical dilemmas, and mini cases. A comprehensive test bank is included.

N. Ancillary Web Site Materials—UPDATED Instructors and students benefit from a variety of extra materials on the book's Web site. The Web site also contains important additional resources related to the Relationship Selling Math and Sales Proposal appendices.

Acknowledgments

Writing a book is never the result of the authors alone. Many people contribute in a variety of ways to the process. We would like to begin by thanking the many colleagues and sales professionals who inspired us to take on the exciting challenge of creating a text that reflects relationship selling the way it's practiced in contemporary firms. Over many conversations we developed the ideas and concepts you will find in the book. More specifically, we offer a special thank-you to the reviewers who provided valuable insights and guidance through the writing process. They are:

Casey Donoho, *Northern Arizona University*

Gary Ernst, *North Central College*

Todd Saville, *Kirkwood Community College*

John Bing, *Lehigh Valley College*

Amit Mukherjee, *Richard Stockton College of NJ*

Jon Fields, *University of Wisconsin*

Charles Peterson, *University of Connecticut*

Diane Edmondson, *University of South Florida*

Mike Rankin, *Fox Valley Technical College*

Victoria Panzer at the University of South Florida deserves considerable praise for doing an outstanding job of developing the Relationship Selling Math and Sales Proposal appendices. We would also like to thank the great people at McGraw-Hill/Irwin, including Dana Woo, Sara Hunter, and Dana Pauley for their exceptional work and support during the process. Working with professionals who are also fantastic people makes the task much more enjoyable—thanks again to everyone on the McGraw-Hill/Irwin team. Finally, we want to offer a very special thank you to our families and friends. Without their encouragement and support over many months you would not be reading this book. They are special and appreciated. Enjoy the book!

Mark W. Johnston, Rollins College

Greg W. Marshall, Rollins College

March 2009

Relationship Selling is truly unique. It is the first and only text to combine customer value and relationship selling with leadership and sales management. The Model, developed exclusively for the book, provides a great framework for understanding the process of relationship selling (what salespeople do) and the skills necessary to manage a modern sales force (what sales managers do). Chapters contain valuable information on the key building blocks of relationship selling (Leadership, Innovation, and Global) as well as expert advice from sales professionals who have been there and done it. In addition, each chapter includes an ethical dilemma that puts the student in a real world, ethical problem faced by salespeople and managers every day. Also, every chapter has a case to help students learn and apply what they have been studying in the chapter. Finally, a comprehensive set of role plays has been developed for the book that will enable students to *learn by doing,* using one of the most successful sales learning tools.

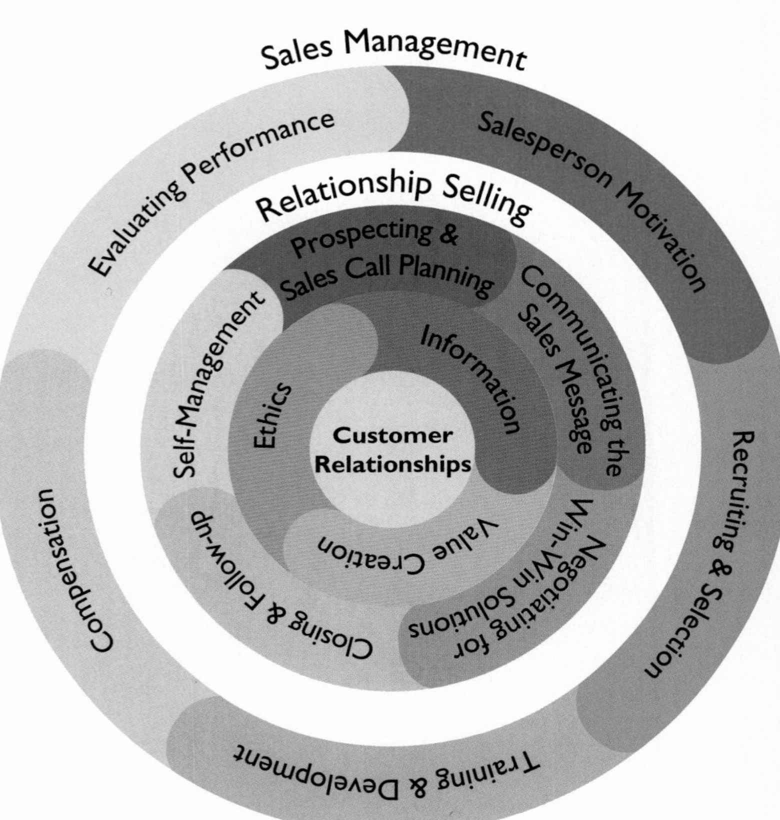

Boxes focusing on Innovation, Global Perspectives, and Leadership are woven throughout the text, using real world examples to emphasize the importance of these key themes in today's selling environment.

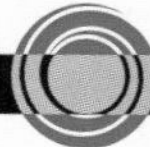

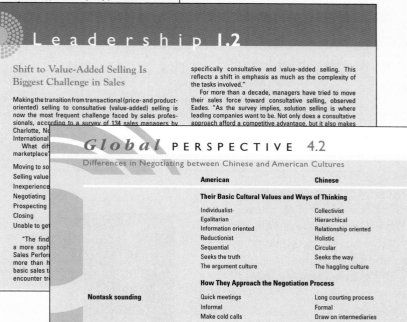

INNOVATION 2.2

Create Your Own Creativity

You don't have to be intellectual or highly educated to come up with good ideas. Although creative people have certain traits that distinguish them from others, such characteristics can be developed with dedication and practice.

Your job becomes easier and you are more productive when you assure no good ideas ever escape you. Almost any process or procedure can be improved upon. If you decide something is perfect as is, you also eliminate considering areas for improvement. This provides a false sense of security at best.

Realize unusual procedures can often solve your most perplexing problems. Good ideas can come from areas where you least expect them. Some of the best ideas ever developed were sparked by investigating in an unfamiliar area of a business.

Tips on getting started in improving creativity.

- *Be accessible.* Since ideas may come from anyone at anytime, you must be available and ready to receive them. If you get the reputation of being hard to reach or

Recognize it is difficult to remember every idea you learn of. Months may pass before a situation arises where it may be put to use.

Benefiting from your creativity. How are some people able to come up with new and unusual approaches to problems when you seldom can do so? In the book *A Whack on the Side of the Head: How You Can Be More Creative* (Business Plus Books), author Roger Von Oech offers these suggestions for getting your mind out of its

Leadership 1.2

Shift to Value-Added Selling Is Biggest Challenge in Sales

Making the transition from transactional (price- and product-oriented) selling to consultative (value-added) selling is now the most frequent challenge faced by sales professionals, according to a survey of 134 sales managers by Charlotte, N
International
What dif
marketplace

Moving to so
Selling value
Inexperience
Negotiating
Prospecting
Closing
Unable to ge

"The find
a more soph
Sales Perfor
more than h
basic sales t
encounter tr

specifically consultative and value-added selling. This reflects a shift in emphasis as much as the complexity of the tasks involved."

For more than a decade, managers have tried to move their sales force toward consultative selling, observed Eades. "As the survey implies, solution selling is where leading companies want to be. Not only does a consultative approach afford a competitive advantage, but it also makes

Global PERSPECTIVE 4.2

Differences in Negotiating between Chinese and American Cultures

	American	Chinese
	Their Basic Cultural Values and Ways of Thinking	
	Individualist	Collectivist
	Egalitarian	Hierarchical
	Information oriented	Relationship oriented
	Reductionist	Holistic
	Sequential	Circular
	Seeks the truth	Seeks the way
	The argument culture	The haggling culture
	How They Approach the Negotiation Process	
Nontask sounding	Quick meetings	Long courting process
	Informal	Formal
	Make cold calls	Draw on intermediaries

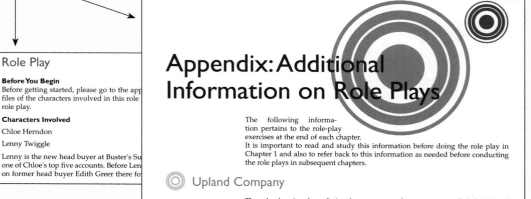

A role play at the end of each chapter gives students the opportunity to put their skills to work practicing the concepts they've just learned. Also, don't overlook the Appendix following Chapter 1, where you'll find instructions and tips on how to get the most out of your role playing experiences.

Role Play

Before You Begin

Before getting started, please go to the app files of the characters involved in this role role play.

Characters Involved

Chloe Herndon

Lenny Twiggle

Lenny is the new head buyer at Buster's Su one of Chloe's top five accounts. Before Len on former head buyer Edith Greer there fo

Appendix: Additional Information on Role Plays

The following information pertains to the role-play exercises at the end of each chapter. It is important to read and study this information before doing the role play in Chapter 1 and also to refer back to this information as needed before conducting the role plays in subsequent chapters.

Upland Company

The role plays involve a fictional consumer products company called the Upland Company. Upland sells a variety of health and beauty aids through supermarkets, drugstores, mass-merchandise stores like Target and Wal-Mart, and similar retail

Ethical Dilemma

Jerry Gutel has been with Step Ahead Publishing for 11 years and witnessed first-hand its technology transformation. When he came to the company, Step Ahead salespeople carried large binders with all relevant information for hundreds of books (sometimes as much as 10 pages on each book). Often he would have to carry two or three of these heavy binders into a bookstore. Meeting with store managers in the Southeast meant that Jerry was frequently on the road, and carrying the books was

Five years ago sales force. Jerry b were no more hea the computer, suc delivery dates. As pany laptops for data. It also wante not as personal pr

Jerry was becor Two years ago he Jerry had little ac the time Jerry ha many nights in a

Questions

1. Should Ben drop Midwest as his account and let it become a second-tier customer?

2. What obligation does a company have to customers who no longer warrant special service or attention?

Mini Case

BestValue Computers

CASE 3

BestValue Computers is a Jackson, Mississippi, company providing computer technology, desktops, laptops, printers, and other peripheral devices to local businesses and school districts in the southern half of Mississippi. Leroy Wells founded BestValue shortly after graduating from college with an information technology degree. Leroy began small but soon collected accounts looking for great value at reasonable prices with local service. When Leroy started his business in Jackson, he believed that anyone could build a computer. In fact, other than the processor and the software that runs computers, many of the components used are sold as commodities.

Leroy initially viewed his company as a value-added assembler and reseller of technology products. This business model was so successful that Leroy decided to expand from Jackson throughout southern Mississippi. To facilitate this expansion,

Following each chapter, students are given an ethical dilemma to consider. These cases can be used within or outside the classroom, and are accompanied by questions to use as an assignment or to help start a classroom discussion. Mini cases at the end of each chapter are also provided for in-class discussion or outside assignments.

The Expert Advice boxes at the beginning of each chapter show how real working professionals apply the concepts of relationship selling and sales management every day to help them succeed.

Expert: Michael T. Bosworth
Company: Cofounder, CustomerCentric Systems, L.L.C.
Business: Mike is one of the top consultants and authors globally in the field of selling. His best-selling book, *Solution Selling,* literally created the modern genre of consultative selling that pervades today's organizations. His new book *Customer-Centric Selling,* written with John R. Holland, breaks exciting new ground by establishing a dynamic process for effective buyer–seller relationship building. (Visit Mike at www .customercentricsystems.com.)

The idea of being customer-centric is very much at the core of both your new book and your approach to working with firms. What's the essence of what it means to be customer-centric?

Customer-centric means you think about your customer's use of your products or services to achieve their goals and solve their problems when you design and market your offerings. It also means allowing your customers to buy from you the way they want to as opposed to being subjected to *your* presentation, *your* proposal, *your* cost justification, and so on. People love to buy and hate to feel "sold." Customer-centric selling empowers buyers to achieve *their* goals, solve *their* problems, and satisfy *their* needs

problem. This approach fundamentally changes the way we sell, as well as the buyer/seller relationship overall. Students of selling today need to be prepared for more than simply walking through the traditional steps of a sales call—they must be able to act as valued consultants to their clients and work toward achieving win–win solutions.

Where do you see the relationship between sales and marketing headed over the next several years in most businesses?

Now that customers are able to gain so much knowledge about companies and their offerings before they ever contact the company, marketing and sales need to be in sync

Expert: Meenakshi A. Hirani, Esq
Company: Meenakshi A. Hirani, P.A
Business: Attorney
Education: LLB, MCL, MBA, JD

What do you see as the most important ethical issues facing salespeople in the 21st century?

With a highly competitive market place, immediate access to information, and demanding customers, there are few boundaries or barriers for salespeople. This has created a lot of new market opportunities; however, this also exposes salespeople to local, state, national, even international laws, regulations, and customs. The cliché, everything legal

manager. It is important for the sales manager to practice the company's code of ethics before asking the salesperson to follow it, as the manager should teach by example. While being a friendly advisor and mentor to salespeople, the manager has to be sensitive to the salesperson's own ethical beliefs while communicating and employing the highest ethical standards set forth by the company. At the same time, the sales manager must be aware of the highly competitive environment in which some companies adopt a

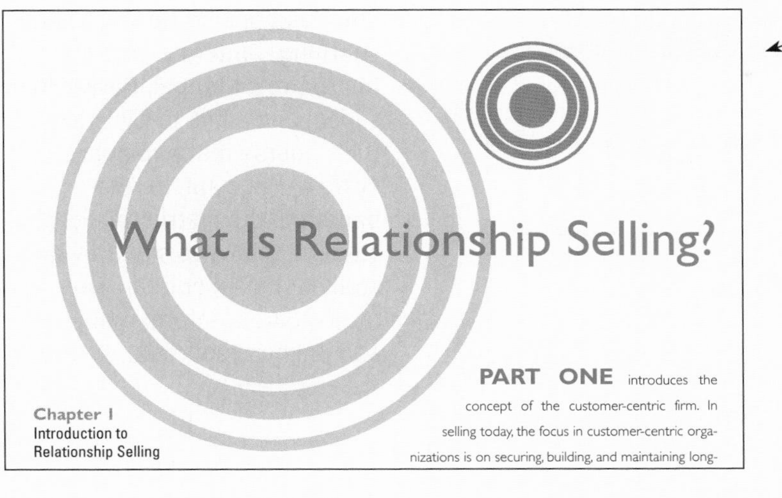
What Is Relationship Selling?
PART ONE introduces the concept of the customer-centric firm. In selling today, the focus in customer-centric organizations is on securing, building, and maintaining long-
Chapter 1
Introduction to Relationship Selling

The Online Learning Center contains everything you need to help you teach your course, including the Instructor's Manual, written by the authors themselves, the Test Bank, and the PowerPoint presentations. Visit www.mhhe.com/johnston3e.

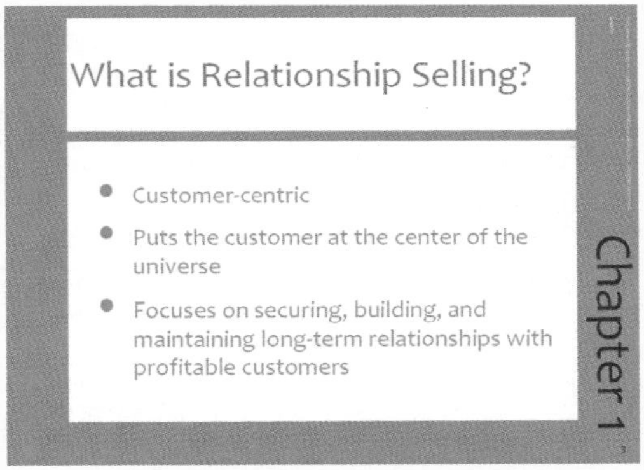

What is Relationship Selling?

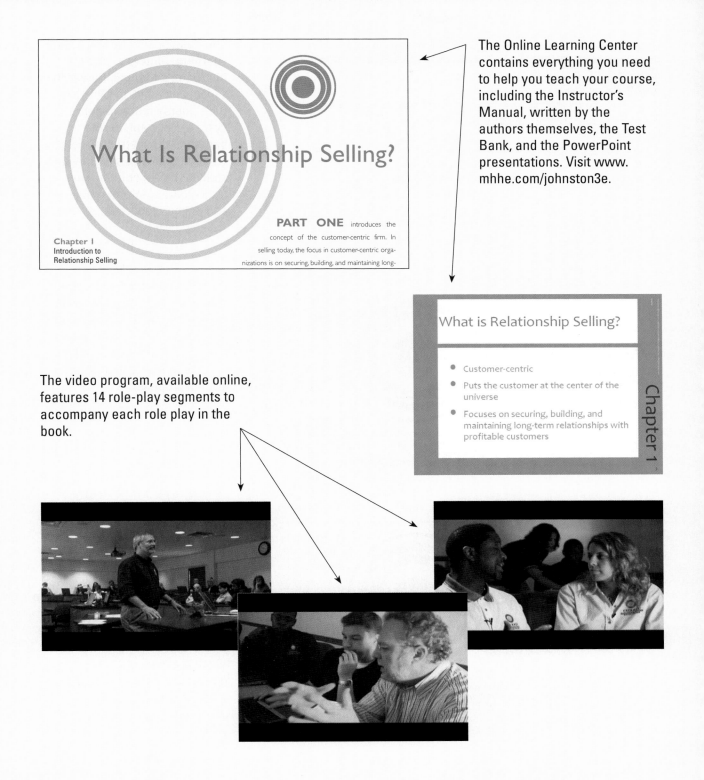

- Customer-centric
- Puts the customer at the center of the universe
- Focuses on securing, building, and maintaining long-term relationships with profitable customers

Chapter 1

The video program, available online, features 14 role-play segments to accompany each role play in the book.

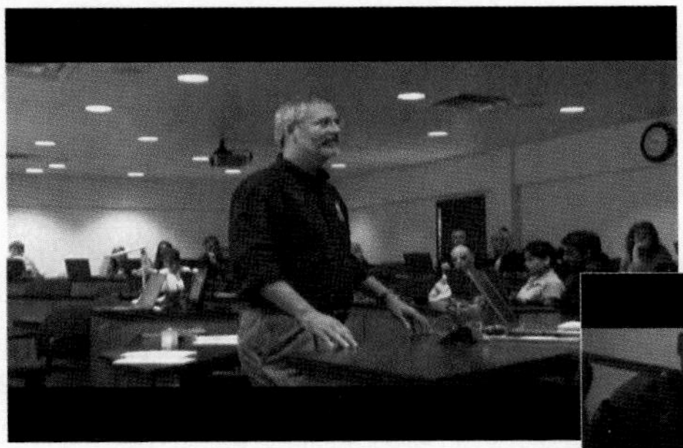

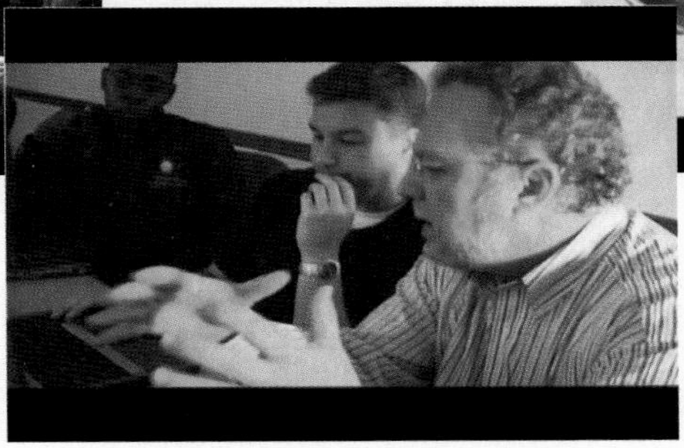

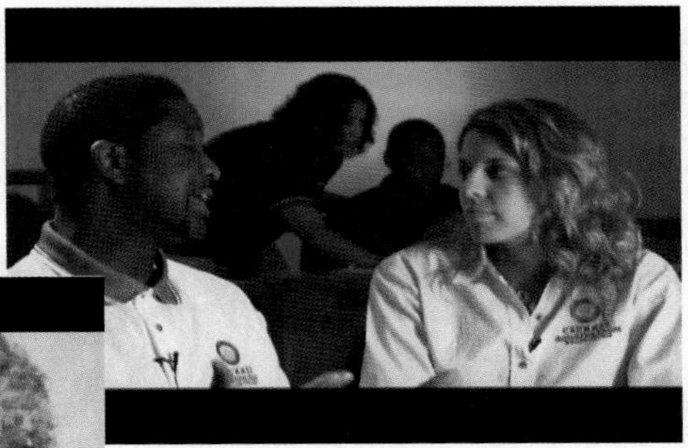

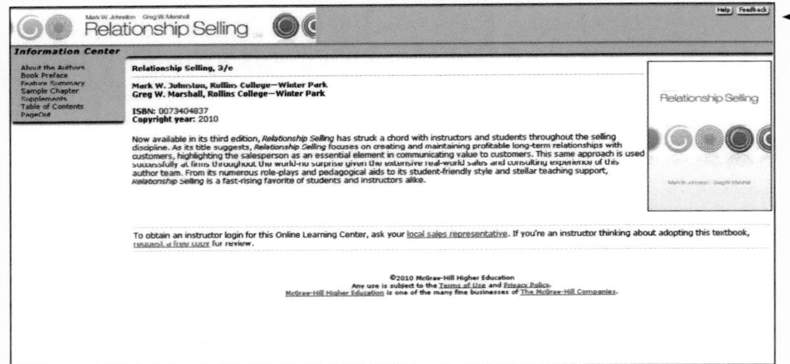

The Relationship Selling Online Learning Center houses the Instructor's Manual, PowerPoint slides, and a link to McGraw-Hill's course management system, PageOut, for the benefit of the instructor. For the student, this Web site provides study outlines, quizzes, key terms, career information, and online resources.

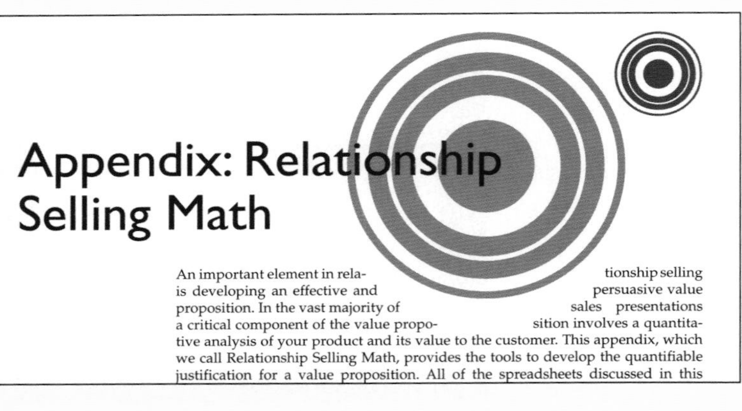

Appendix: Relationship Selling Math

An important element in relationship selling is developing an effective and persuasive value proposition. In the vast majority of sales presentations a critical component of the value proposition involves a quantitative analysis of your product and its value to the customer. This appendix, which we call Relationship Selling Math, provides the tools to develop the quantifiable justification for a value proposition. All of the spreadsheets discussed in this

Combined with online interactive exercises, the Appendix at the end of Chapter 3, "Relationship Selling Math," will walk you through the process of putting together a financial analysis for a sales proposal.

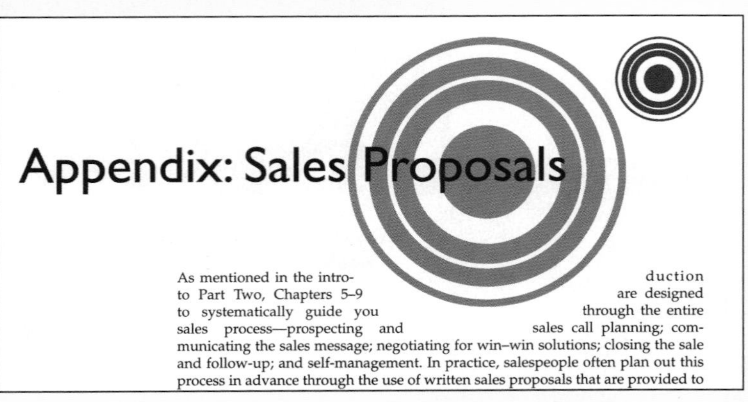

Appendix: Sales Proposals

As mentioned in the introduction to Part Two, Chapters 5–9 are designed to systematically guide you through the entire sales process—prospecting and sales call planning; communicating the sales message; negotiating for win–win solutions; closing the sale and follow-up; and self-management. In practice, salespeople often plan out this process in advance through the use of written sales proposals that are provided to

Following Chapter 5 an Appendix, Sales Proposals, provides a template for developing a sales proposal. The Appendix links specific chapters and other source material to the sales proposal template. Check out the Web site for the Sales Proposal Handbook which provides even more information on the process.

Brief Table of Contents

Table of Contents

Chapter 7
Negotiating for Win–Win Solutions 201

Chapter 8
Closing the Sale and Follow-up 223

Chapter 9
Self-Management: Time and Territory 253

What Is Relationship Selling?

Chapter 1
Introduction to Relationship Selling

Chapter 2
Using Information to Understand Sellers and Buyers

Chapter 3
Value Creation in Buyer–Seller Relationships

Chapter 4
Ethical and Legal Issues in Relationship Selling

PART ONE introduces the concept of the customer-centric firm. In selling today, the focus in customer-centric organizations is on securing, building, and maintaining long-term relationships with profitable customers. In Chapter 1 we introduce the concept of relationship selling and provide a pictorial model for Relationship Selling and Sales Management. The discussion in Chapter 1 follows along with our model, working from the inside out.

Success in relationship selling requires using information to gain a good understanding of sellers and buyers, the topic of Chapter 2. On the selling side, this includes the key drivers of change in relationship selling and sales management today, aspects of selling as a career, key success factors in relationship selling, selling activities, and types of selling jobs. On the buying side, important questions include who participates in the organizational buying process, what are the stages in the buying decision process, and what are the different organizational buying situations.

Value creation is a central theme in most business models today. Chapter 3 takes a close look at the concept of value, how sales organizations and salespeople can create value for customers, and how salespeople can effectively communicate and deliver on that value proposition for their customers.

Finally, no business topic has received more attention recently than companies' ethical and legal behavior. Chapter 4 provides insight into the importance of ethics in relationship selling and sales management, outlines a variety of key ethical concerns in the field, and gives guidance on legal issues that are particularly relevant for salespeople and their managers.

selling environment

Sales Management

Salesperson Motivation

Recruiting & Selection

Training & Development

Compensation

Evaluating Performance

Relationship Selling

Prospecting & Sales Call Planning

Communicating the Sales Message

Negotiating for Win-Win Solutions

Closing & Follow-up

Self-Management

Information

Value Creation

Ethics

Customer Relationships

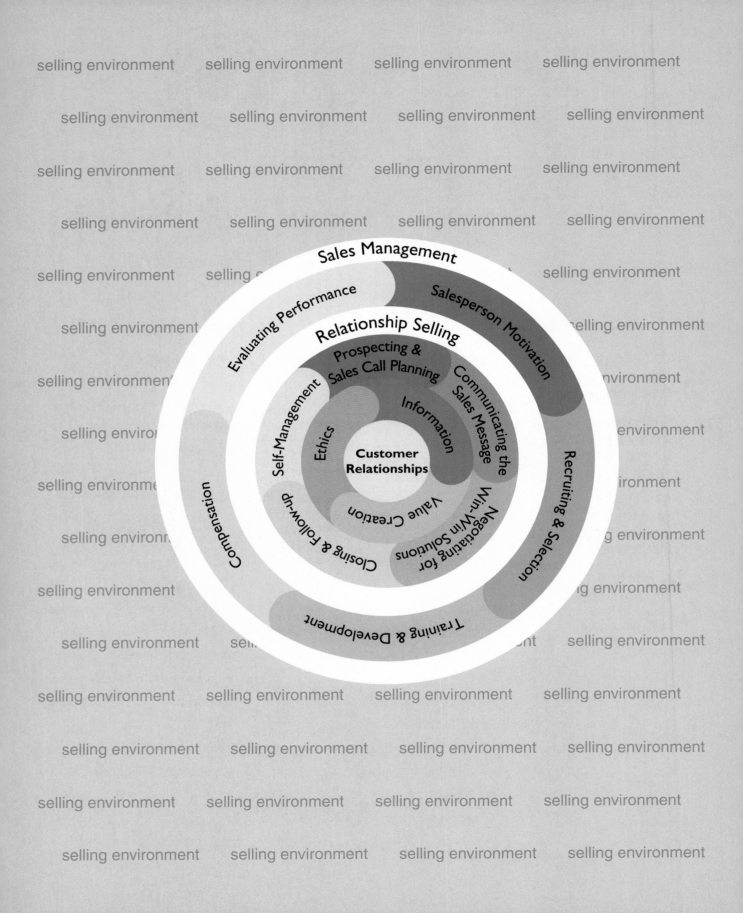

1

chapter

Introduction to Relationship Selling

Learning Objectives

Selling has changed. The focus of much selling today is on securing, building, and maintaining long-term relationships with profitable customers. To accomplish this, salespeople have to be able to communicate a value proposition that represents the bundle of benefits their customers derive from the product being sold. This value-driven approach to selling will result in customers who are loyal and who want to develop long-term relationships with a salesperson and his or her firm. This chapter provides an overview of the book by way of an integrative model for Relationship Selling and Sales Management. After reading the chapter, you should be able to

- Identify and define the concept of relationship selling.
- Understand the importance of a firm being customer-centric.
- Explain why value is a central theme in relationship selling.
- Identify the processes involved in relationship selling.
- Identify the elements in managing relationship selling.
- Discuss and give examples of the components of the external and internal environment for relationship selling.

expert advice

Expert: Michael T. Bosworth

Company: Cofounder, CustomerCentric Systems, L.L.C.

Business: Mike is one of the top consultants and authors globally in the field of selling. His best-selling book, *Solution Selling,* literally created the modern genre of consultative selling that pervades today's organizations. His new book *Customer-Centric Selling,* written with John R. Holland, breaks exciting new ground by establishing a dynamic process for effective buyer–seller relationship building. (Visit Mike at www.customercentricsystems.com.)

The idea of being customer-centric is very much at the core of both your new book and your approach to working with firms. What's the essence of what it means to be customer-centric?

Customer-centric means you think about your customer's use of your products or services to achieve their goals and solve their problems when you design and market your offerings. It also means allowing your customers to buy from you the way they want to as opposed to being subjected to *your* presentation, *your* proposal, *your* cost justification, and so on. People love to buy and hate to feel "sold." Customer-centric selling empowers buyers to achieve *their* goals, solve *their* problems, and satisfy *their* needs.

The notion of selling solutions, not products, has always been important to you. Why does a student in a selling class need to understand this distinction?

The new paradigm of selling—employing a consultative approach to the job—is helping customers achieve goals and solve problems through the use of what you are offering. When you present product information, you are requiring that the customer be smart enough to figure out how they would use your product in their environment. Some can, but at best this group makes up 20 percent of your market. For the other 80 percent you have to build a case for how your product or service will solve a customer's problem. This approach fundamentally changes the way we sell, as well as the buyer/seller relationship overall. Students of selling today need to be prepared for more than simply walking through the traditional steps of a sales call—they must be able to act as valued consultants to their clients and work toward achieving win–win solutions.

Where do you see the relationship between sales and marketing headed over the next several years in most businesses?

Now that customers are able to gain so much knowledge about companies and their offerings before they ever contact the company, marketing and sales need to be in sync on what product information they are making available to the Web surfer. Marketing needs to feature product usage information rather than product features and salespeople need to extensively prepare themselves in advance of a sales call so they can jump right into a discussion about what the buyer is trying to accomplish when they first arrive at the client's office. Unfortunately, most salespeople today are prepared only to talk about the product itself and are not especially adept at discussing how the product would be used by individuals in the client firm across many job titles to achieve each user's specific goals or solve his or her specific problems. Marketing has an obligation to enable the sales force so they can accomplish this task. The value proposition needs to be very clear.

Introduction to Relationship Selling

Mike Bosworth's Expert Advice calls attention to several important lessons in today's selling environment. First, no matter what you sell, selling primarily based on having the best price is no way to build long-term clients. Low prices are very easy for competitors to match, and fickle buyers who are focused only on price will drop you as soon as a competitor beats your price. Second, the concept of creating value for your customers is an important way to get around the problems associated with price selling. **Value** represents the net bundle of benefits the customer derives from the product you are selling. Often this is referred to as your **value proposition.** Certainly low price may enhance value, but so do your expertise, your quality, and your service. Value creation in buyer–seller relationships is the subject of Chapter 3. Finally, firms must focus on keeping customers coming back again and again. This idea of building **customer loyalty,** giving your customers many reasons not to switch to competitors, is central to successful selling today.

This book is not about just selling—it is about **relationship selling,** whose central goal is securing, building, and maintaining long-term relationships with profitable customers. Relationship selling is oriented toward the long term. The salesperson seeks to keep his or her customers so satisfied with the product, the selling firm, and the salesperson's own level of client service that they will not switch to other sources for the same products. The book is also about **sales management,** meaning the way the various aspects of relationship selling are managed by the salesperson's firm.

In modern organizations, relationship selling and sales management is quite an integrated process.[1] The managers in the sales organization have taken time to think through the most efficient and effective way to manage the customer side of the business. This might include using all sorts of technologies, gathering information to make decisions on customer strategies, employing different selling approaches for different kinds of customers, and having a system in place that connects all this together. Such a system is often called **customer relationship management (CRM),** which refers to an organizationwide customer focus that uses advanced technology to maximize the firm's ability to add value to customers and develop long-term relationships. The role of CRM, and information in general, in relationship selling will be discussed in Chapter 2.

A Model for Relationship Selling and Sales Management

A firm that is **customer-centric** puts the customer at the center of everything that happens both inside and outside the firm. Customers are the lifeblood of any business! They are the center of your business universe. Without them you have no sales, no profits, ultimately no business. The starting point for learning about relationship selling, and ultimately sales management, is the customer. The model for Relationship Selling and Sales Management serves as a road map for this book and for your course. Like customer-centric firms, the model places the customer firmly in the center of everything you will read about in this book.

Firms that are customer-centric have a high level of **customer orientation.** That is, they

1. Instill an organizationwide focus on understanding customers' requirements.

EXHIBIT 1.1 Test Your Customer Mindset

External Customer Mindset	Internal Customer Mindset
I believe that . . . • I must understand the needs of my company's customers. • It is critical to provide value to my company's customers. • I am primarily interested in satisfying my company's customers. • I must understand who buys my company's products/services. • I can perform my job better if I understand the needs of my company's customers. • Understanding my company's customers will help me do my job better.	I believe that . . . • Employees who receive my work are my customers. • Meeting the needs of employees who receive my work is critical to doing a good job. • It is important to receive feedback from employees who receive my work. • I focus on the requirements of the person who receives my work.

Score yourself from 1 to 6 on each item. 1 = strongly disagree and 6 = strongly agree. The higher your total score, the more of a customer mindset you've achieved.

Source: Karen Norman Kennedy, Felicia G. Lassk, and Jerry R. Goolsby, "Customer Mind-Set of Employees Throughout the Organization," *Journal of the Academy of Marketing Science* 30 (Spring 2002), pp. 159–71. Reprinted by permission.

2. Generate an understanding of the marketplace and disseminate that knowledge to everyone in the firm.
3. Align system capabilities internally so that the organization responds effectively with innovative, competitively differentiated, satisfaction-generating products and services.[2]

What does customer orientation mean to the individual salesperson? One way to exhibit a customer orientation is through a **customer mindset,** which may be defined as a salesperson's belief that understanding and satisfying customers, whether internal or external to the organization, is central to doing his or her job well. It is through this customer mindset that a customer orientation comes alive within a sales force. Exhibit 1.1 provides example descriptors of a customer mindset both in the context of people you sell to (external customers) and people inside your own firm you need to deal with to get the job done (internal customers). Score yourself to see how much of a customer mindset you have.

Throughout this book, time and again we will come back to this notion of the customer at the center of the business universe. The concentric circular style of the model for Relationship Selling and Sales Management was created to visually portray the notion that in relationship selling and sales management, everything builds outward from a customer focus. The next sections describe the rest of the model from the inside out and lay the groundwork for future chapters, which focus in detail on each component of the model.

The Customer

As mentioned, the customer is in the center of the model to connote a customer-centric organization. The idea of a customer mindset is at the heart of this circle.

What kinds of behaviors comprise a customer mindset? One way to address this is to learn what behaviors are *not* customer friendly. Innovation 1.1 provides some excellent examples of behaviors salespeople should avoid, as they all tell a buyer that you are not engaged in a long-term relationship building form of selling.

The four key relationship selling mistakes in Innovation 1.1 provide great insight into many of the things we will be learning throughout this book. Fundamentally, the onus is on the salesperson to ensure that each sales call results in a meaningful, relationship-building exchange. When problems occur—and they are bound to occur—in things like shipping, billing, out-of-stocks, after-sale service, or anything else, the salesperson must stand ready (and must be personally empowered) to work with the buyer to solve the problem. In fact, as Mike Bosworth mentions in the Expert Advice feature that opens the chapter, the crux of relationship selling is taking a consultative approach with buyers—working together to develop solutions to their business problems.

On the buyer's side, sales organizations must calculate how much time, money, and other resources should be invested in a particular customer versus the anticipated return on that investment. This ratio, often called the **return on customer investment,** is central to our discussion of value creation in Chapter 3 and is also relevant to the information used in prospecting and planning (Chapter 5). More broadly, the customer's long-term value to the sales organization is referred to as the **lifetime value of a customer.**

To summarize, the customer is at the core of today's organizations and therefore is at the center of our model for Relationship Selling and Sales Management, and the topic of customers permeates all the chapters in the book. We will now touch on the other elements of the model: using information, value creation, ethics, relationship selling, and sales management. These topics comprise the remaining chapters in the book.

Information

Think of information as the engine that drives a salesperson's success in securing, building, and maintaining long-term relationships with profitable customers. Technology plays a major role in using information to manage customer relationships. The term customer relationship management has come to signify a technology-driven organizationwide focus on customer. CRM began primarily as a software package designed to collect and mine data. But it has evolved into an overarching organizational philosophy of doing business. (Good places to go to learn more about CRM are the Web sites of leading CRM providers such as Salesforce.com, Siebel.com, Teradata.com, and the highly informative forum for CRM, Customerthink.com.) Chapter 2 provides insights on the use of information and technology in relationship selling and introduces the roles of sellers and buyers in the organizational market place.

Value Creation

Value creation is the second major topic within the customer core circle of the model for Relationship Selling and Sales Management. Earlier we described value as the net bundle of benefits the customer derives from the product you are selling. A more direct way to explain value is as a "give–get" ratio. What does each party "get out of a sale" compared to what they invest? This investment might

INNOVATION 1.1

Want to Think Like a Customer? Mistakes to Avoid *Always*

1. Don't waste their time. If there was one theme that pops up over and over it is this: We have less time to do our job than ever before. So, you better not waste any part of it. In other words, don't come into a customer's business unprepared. Have something of value to share or don't come.

Buyers need to see some value in the time they share with salespeople, every time they see them, or they won't see them. Don't waste their time with idle chitchat, don't take longer to do something than you need to, don't be unprepared, and don't waste the time of the buyer's staff, either. If a salesperson doesn't have something important to do or something valuable to bring, don't visit.

And when they do visit a buyer, the salesperson must make sure he or she has all the answers. Know what the product does or doesn't do, know what the pricing and terms are, and be prepared to answer all their questions.

2. Lack of empowerment to handle things *now*. Customers don't appreciate the "salesperson as a victim." This refers to the salesperson that spends time explaining how the truck broke down, or the manufacturer back-ordered the product, or it was recalled, or whatever. All of these were seen as the salesperson saying, "It wasn't our fault. We're the victims of someone else's mistakes." Customers aren't concerned with whose fault something was, nor are they concerned with the reasons why something wasn't as it was supposed to be.

Ultimately, buyers only want solutions. The Ritz Carlton hotel authorizes its room staff to spend up to $2,000 to make a customer happy; a salesperson calling on an organizational buyer should be able to resolve a problem over a $50-can of paint without several phone calls and days of approvals.

Bottom line, good service means that the salesperson could solve the problem immediately, on the spot.

3. Not knowing the buyer's business. Don't waste the time or insult the intelligence of a buyer by presenting products or services he or she can't use. It is reasonable to expect salespeople to know what their customers' processes are, what their goals and strategies are, and the limitations of their facilities, budgets, and timetables, and then take all of that information into consideration before presenting some product or program. The best salespeople are like extensions of a buyer's own business.

4. Bringing problems, not solutions. Customers do not want to discover after the fact that a purchase will be back-ordered or shipped incomplete. Find the problems before the buyer experiences them, and then bring solutions in advance. Telling what the options are let the buyer decide what to do. That is a professional and respectful approach to relationship selling.

The salesperson who says after the fact, "I'm sorry about last week's back order," is certainly not practicing relationship selling. Say instead, "Next week we're going to be able to partially ship this order. If you need the balance right away, we can do any of three things to help. Here are your options . . . (1), (2), (3). What would you like to do?"

Remember these seven strategies of highly effective salespeople.

1. Look to the customer for the solution—although product knowledge is important, it's only a baseline.
2. Be committed to presentation improvement.
3. Embrace new ideas.
4. Focus on helping. Helping is the overarching strategy—the hallmark—of the highly effective salesperson.
5. Possess a vision and attitude focused on customer *relationships.*
6. Think of themselves as marketers.
7. Pull customers ever closer to a partnership model in business.

Sources: Dan Kahle, "How Well Are Your Salespeople Serving Your Customers?" *American Salesman,* February 2007, p. 11; and John R. Graham, "The Seven Strategies of the Highly Effective Salesperson," *American Salesman,* July 2008, p. 12.

be money, time, labor, production, or any other resources used up in moving the sale forward. For many years, organizations gave little consideration to using value creation to build relationships with customers. Instead, they were content to simply conduct business as a series of discrete transactions. This approach to selling has come to be called **transactional selling.**

EXHIBIT 1.2 Transactional Selling versus Relationship Selling

Transactional Selling

Transactional selling is the set of skills, strategies, and sales processes that meets the needs of buyers who treat suppliers as a commodity and who are mainly or exclusively interested in price and convenience. From the customer's point of view, in the transactional sale there are no additional benefits the seller can bring to the party beyond price.

Transactional selling *reduces* resources allocated to selling because customers don't value or want to pay for the sales effort. So transactional selling creates its value by stripping cost and making acquisition easy, with neither party making much investment in the process of buying or selling.

Relationship Selling

Rackham and DeVincentis distinguish between two forms of relationship selling: consultative selling and enterprise selling. The difference hinges largely on the importance of the customer and the willingness of both firms to invest in more of a strategic partnership.

Consultative Selling Consultative selling is the set of skills, strategies, and processes that works most effectively with buyers who demand, and are willing to pay for, a sales effort that creates new value and provides additional benefits outside of the product itself. Consultative selling depends on having salespeople who become close to the customer and who have an intimate grasp of the customer's business issues. It involves a mutual investment of time and effort by both seller and customer. Listening and gaining business understanding are more important selling skills than persuasion; creativity is more important than product knowledge. In the consultative sale, the sales force creates value in three primary ways:

- It helps customers understand their problems, issues, and opportunities in new or different ways.
- It helps customers arrive at new or better solutions to their problems than they would have discovered on their own.
- It acts as the customer's advocate inside the sales organization, ensuring the timely allocation of resources to deliver customized or unique solutions that meet the customer's special needs.

Because these are demanding skills, good consultative salespeople are hard to find. Diagnostic tools, sales processes, and CRM and other information systems can help "ordinary mortals" perform well in the increasingly sophisticated consultative selling role.

Enterprise Selling Enterprise selling is the set of skills, strategies, and processes that work most effectively with strategically important customers who demand an extraordinary level of value creation from a key supplier. Both the product and the sales force are secondary. The primary function of the enterprise sale is to leverage any and all corporate assets of the sales organization to contribute to the customer's strategic success. No single salesperson, or even a sales team, can set up or maintain an enterprise relationship. These sales are initiated at a very high level in each organization. They are deeply tied to the customer's strategic direction, and they are usually implemented by cross-functional teams on both sides.

Enterprise selling requires continuous redesign and improvement of the boundary between supplier and customer. Frequently, hundreds of people from each side are involved in the relationship and it's impossible to tell where selling begins and ends. Because enterprise selling is a very expensive process, firms must be selective in implementing this approach to relationship selling.

Source: Neil Rackham and John DeVincentis, *Rethinking the Sales Force: Redefining Selling to Create and Capture Customer Value* (New York: McGraw-Hill, 1999), pp. 25–27. Reprinted by permission of the McGraw-Hill Companies.

Neil Rackham and John DeVincentis developed a convenient way of distinguishing between transactional approaches to selling and those more focused on developing long-term relationships.[3] They refer to the relationship-oriented approaches as **consultative selling** and **enterprise selling.** The basis of their approach is segmenting the sales effort by the type and amount of value different customers seek to derive from the sales process. Exhibit 1.2 highlights Rackham and DeVincentis's approach to this issue.

Basically, transactional selling works to strip costs and get to the lowest possible sales price. In contrast, relationship selling works to add value through all possible means. **Value-added selling** changes much of the sales process. Exhibit 1.3 illustrates the major differences in how a salesperson's time is best invested in the two types of selling. Relationship selling requires the salesperson to spend more time developing an understanding of the buyer's needs, which results in a more "front-loaded" selling process. Information, analysis, and communication become much more important to success with the customer. In contrast, in transactional selling focused on price, much more time and energy must be put into closing the sale.[4]

Shifting to value-added selling is not easy. In fact, a recent survey by Sales Performance International indicates it is the challenge most often faced by sales professionals. Leadership 1.2 presents the results of this survey and insights on how to foster value-added selling. The issue of value creation in buyer–seller relationships is the central topic of Chapter 3.

Ethics

In the model for Relationship Selling and Sales Management, the third major topic within the customer core circle is ethics. **Ethics** are moral principles and standards that guide behavior. According to a *Sales & Marketing Management* magazine/Equation Research survey, 83 percent of 220 respondents said they train their salespeople to sell their companies' ethics and integrity along with their products and services. Nearly 70 percent said they believe their clients consider a company's ethical reputation when deciding whether to make a purchase. And while

EXHIBIT 1.3 Time Investment in Each Stage of the Sale: Transactional versus Value-Added Selling

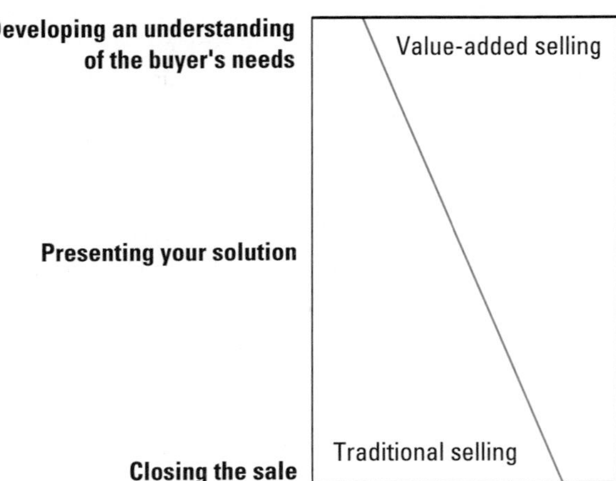

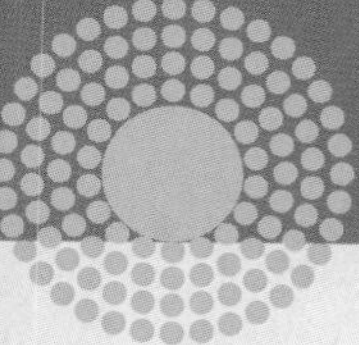

Leadership 1.2

Shift to Value-Added Selling Is Biggest Challenge in Sales

Making the transition from transactional (price- and product-oriented) selling to consultative (value-added) selling is now the most frequent challenge faced by sales professionals, according to a survey of 134 sales managers by Charlotte, North Carolina, consultants Sales Performance International.

What difficulties do your salespeople have in the marketplace?

Moving to solution-type sell	69%
Selling value	67%
Inexperience	63%
Negotiating	58%
Prospecting	55%
Closing	55%
Unable to get to decision maker	51%

"The findings suggest today's sales organization has a more sophisticated focus than a few years ago," said Sales Performance International CEO Keith Eades. "While more than half of respondents still cite frustration with basic sales techniques, like prospecting and closing, more encounter trouble at the higher end of the sales process, specifically consultative and value-added selling. This reflects a shift in emphasis as much as the complexity of the tasks involved."

For more than a decade, managers have tried to move their sales force toward consultative selling, observed Eades. "As the survey implies, solution selling is where leading companies want to be. Not only does a consultative approach afford a competitive advantage, but it also makes for a more honorable seller. The salesperson becomes a problem solver and builds a better relationship with the customer."

But organizations find consultative selling a major challenge, Eades explained. "The accepted dogma is don't push product on customers—address their business problem and show value. Frequently, however, sellers have to deal with customers who need to be in control, want to define what they need, and seek the best price. And when all else fails, the seller falls into old habits and ends up shaving the price to win the deal."

A mistake made by management is to see consultative selling just as a technique, said Eades. "Effective solution selling requires a culture change, top-to-bottom engagement, and an organizationwide commitment. Otherwise, the organization doesn't speak a common language and gives out different messages."

Source: *American Salesman,* "Consultative Selling Now Seen as Biggest Challenge," September 2006, p. 29.

48 percent said their companies haven't changed their emphasis on ethics and values recently, another 48 percent said they recently have placed somewhat more or much more emphasis on ethics.[5]

The values of a society affect relationship selling and sales management in a variety of ways. They set the standards for ethical behavior. Ethics is more than simply a matter of complying with laws and regulations. A particular action may be legal but not ethical. For instance, when a salesperson makes extreme, unsubstantiated statements such as "Our product runs rings around Brand X," he or she may be engaging in legal puffery to make a sale, but many salespeople (and their customers) view such little white lies as unethical.

Two sets of ethical dilemmas are of particular concern in relationship selling and sales management. The first set arises from the interactions between salespeople and their customers. These issues involve the sales manager only indirectly because the manager cannot always directly observe or control the actions of every salesperson. But sales managers have a responsibility to establish standards of ethical behavior, communicate them clearly, and enforce them vigorously. Managers must be diligent in smoking out unethical practices by their salespeople when dealing with customers.

The second set of ethical issues relates to the sales manager's dealings with the salespeople. Issues include fairness and equal treatment of all social groups in hiring and promotion, respect for the individual in supervisory practices and training programs, and fairness and integrity in the design of sales territories, assignment of quotas, determination of compensation and incentive rewards, and evaluation of performance.

Chapter 4 provides insight into a wide variety of ethics topics related to the salesperson–buyer and salesperson–sales manager relationships. In addition, at the end of each chapter you will be challenged by an Ethical Dilemma to solve, related to topics in that chapter.

Relationship Selling

In the model for Relationship Selling and Sales Management, the second circle outside the customer core represents the various process elements of relationship selling: prospecting and sales call planning, communicating the sales message, negotiating for win–win solutions, closing and follow-up, and self-management. These five relationship selling processes are represented by Chapters 5–9 which is Part Two of the book. The following sections provide an overview of these important topics.

Prospecting and Sales Call Planning. In any business, today's customers weren't always customers. Chances are they started out as **prospects**—a set of potential customers you or your firm identified as *very likely* future customers. Building a business involves being on the lookout for great prospects, for it is a pipeline of prospects that ensures a growing, thriving customer base. Salespeople sometimes look at identifying and developing prospects as a "necessary evil" in selling—that's an unfortunate (and unproductive) attitude to take. Nowadays, CRM systems and other technology-driven tools have the capability to provide a wealth of information to salespeople about potential customers if the systems are properly implemented and utilized. Chapter 5 provides insights on how to systematically and successfully go about identifying and developing prospects, and then details how to prepare in advance for the first sales call once you have qualified a prospect as a potentially good future customer.

Communicating the Sales Message. Selling involves **persuasive communication.** When you persuade, you hope to convince someone to do something. In transactional selling, the focus is on communicating a hard sell message. This is because by definition in transactional selling there is no real relationship. Buyers and sellers are likely to be adversarial, little trust exists between them, and they are not working for long-term or win–win solutions.

In relationship selling, communication is handled differently. First, multiple media are now available that have nearly unlimited access (e-mail and cell phones, for example). Second, the hard sell has been replaced by a communication approach of mutual problem solving. The salesperson acts as a consultant or problem solver for buyers and sells value-added solutions. Mike Bosworth, whom you met in the Expert Advice at the beginning of this chapter, popularized the term **solution selling,** in which the salesperson's primary role is to move the buyer toward visualization of a solution to his or her problem (need).[6] Today, almost all of us seem to be selling "solutions," as opposed to "products," whether our wares are cell phones, financial services, computer software, or just about any other product or service (even college courses in selling) that solves a problem or fulfills some buyer's need. Chapter 6 explores the issue of communicating effectively when selling solutions, solving buyer problems, and managing long-term relationships.

Negotiating for Win–Win Solutions. Even when buyers have been doing business with you for a very long time, they will develop **objections** to various aspects of your proposed solution. An objection is simply a concern that some part of your product offering (solution) does not fully meet the buyer's need. The objection may be over price, delivery, terms of agreement, timing, or myriad other potential elements of a deal. Even though typical buyer–seller interactions in a relationship selling environment are far from adversarial, negotiation still must take place. Chapter 7 includes details on planning for, recognizing, and handling common objections from buyers and strategies for negotiating win–win solutions.

Closing and Follow-Up. One of the joys of relationship selling is that the rapport, trust, and mutual respect inherent in a long-term buyer–seller relationship can take some of the pressure off the "close" portion of the sales process. In theory, this is because the seller and buyer have been openly communicating throughout the process about mutual goals they would like to see fulfilled within the context of their relationship. Because the key value added is not price but rather other aspects of the product or service, the negotiation should not get hung up on price as an objection. Therefore, in relationship selling, closing becomes a natural part of the communication process. (Note that in many transaction selling models, the closing step is feared by many salespeople—as well as buyers—because of its awkwardness and win–lose connotation.)

Remember that relationship selling has the central goal of securing, building, and maintaining long-term relationships with profitable customers. In selling, we tend to spend much of our time working on the "securing" and "building" part of this definition. However, we must also develop strategies to maintain customers over the long run as viable, profitable, need-satisfied clients. A big part of this process is **follow-up,** which includes service after the sale. Effective follow-up is one way that salespeople and their firms can improve customer perceptions of service quality, customer satisfaction, and customer retention and loyalty. These issues are central to successful relationship selling, and they will be discussed in detail at various points throughout the book.

Many salespeople try to "underpromise and overdeliver," a catchphrase that reminds salespeople to try to deliver more than they promised in order to pleasantly surprise the buyer. Managing customer expectations is an important part of developing successful long-term relationships. **Customer delight,** or exceeding customer expectations to a surprising degree, is a powerful way to gain customer loyalty. Overpromising can get the initial sale and thus may work once in a transactional selling environment, but a dissatisfied customer not only will not buy again but also will tell many others to avoid that salesperson and his or her company and products.[7]

Innovation 1.3 makes some important points about the power of effective follow-up and customer retention strategies. Chapter 8 provides a variety of ideas on how to move customers toward closure in relationship selling and presents key issues in effective follow-up after the sale.

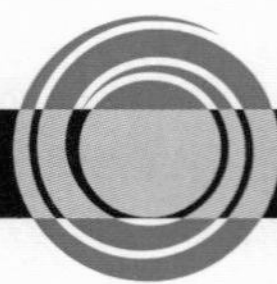

INNOVATION 1.3

The Power of Follow-Up in Customer Relationship Building

The most important thing in sales and marketing is to attract and retain your most profitable business customers. In order to accomplish this feat, you must devise and implement a customer strategy that builds, fosters, nurtures, and extends relationships with your customers. Your company profits only when the earnings from retained customers exceed the costs to acquire and to service customers over time.

There is a strong correlation between long-term business success and long-term customer relationships. Successful businesses capitalize on every stage of the customer life cycle—from customer selection, to customer acquisition, customer retention, and customer growth. Once a certain level of trust and comfort has been established, most customers prefer to remain loyal to companies and their products.

Customer selection and acquisition is just the beginning of the customer relationship life cycle. Ideally, your company should target only high value and low attrition-risk prospects. The cost to acquire a new customer is much greater than the cost to retain an existing customer. Depending on the industry, experts indicate that it is five to ten times more costly to acquire a new customer than it is to keep and develop an existing customer.

In the retention stage of the customer's life cycle, a company retains its customers by delivering on its value proposition. This ensures that the customer needs to look no further; that is the rationale for providing the highest quality of service. When your customer relationship is based on trust, cooperation, and collaboration, the customer is more willing to listen to your new ideas, try your new products/services, and considers you as a long-term, trusted partner.

A savvy business owner/executive understands that it pays to nurture existing customer relationships. If a good working relationship has been established, then it is easier to up-sell and cross-sell your products/services to this existing customer. If your customer's business is growing, there is a good possibility that there will be an increased need for your products/services.

In the growth stage of the customer's life cycle, increasing the value of each existing customer is the ultimate objective. Many organizations think in terms of the "lifetime value" of a customer. Customer growth strategies generally focus on increasing the share of each customer's expenditures by expanding its company's range of products/services.

It is crucial, however, not to lose sight of the importance of continually acquiring new customers. In other words, if your company becomes too dependent on any one or only a few existing customers, then the future growth of your company could be in jeopardy. So, be cautious that the growth in purchases by one or a few customers does not represent too large of a proportion of your company's total sales. Striking this balance, between servicing existing customers and acquiring new customers, is imperative.

Creating and managing this balance can be a major challenge to management. However, Customer Relationship Management (CRM) applications offer solutions to this challenge. CRM is the process of tracking and managing all aspects of a company's interaction with its customers, including prospecting, sales, and service.

Here are just a few customer touchpoints that you can use to strengthen your relationships and keep your customers informed and engaged:

- *E-mail messages, newsletters, and surveys:* Provide product/service updates, promote goods and services, and communicate news/events.
- *Feedback:* Ask for, capture, and act on your customer's input.
- *Insight:* Research your customers' markets, strategies, and goals.
- *Customer loyalty:* Implement loyalty, affinity, and rewards programs.
- *Relationship building:* Talk and listen to customers in order to maintain a dialogue and to build a trust-based relationship.
- *Be accessible:* Make it easy for customers to reach you.
- *Customer satisfaction:* Implement a customer satisfaction policy that provides a way to resolve/remedy problems and issues.
- *Involvement:* Engage customers in product development/enhancement, via beta tests, focus groups, and pilots.
- *Anticipate customer needs:* Learn their business, their purchasing patterns, and their requirements for effective proactive solutions.
- *Become an indispensable resource:* Look for ways to add value, to be a real partner, and to help your customers achieve results.
- *Help lines:* Provide support, service, advice, and information.

In building customer relationships, remember to value the "personal touch." Make an effort to get to know your customer "as a person." You will be surprised at how much you may have in common. Establishing personal bonds goes a long way toward building lasting relationships.

Your efforts will be rewarded with repeat business, referrals, and satisfied, loyal customers.

Source: Terry H. Hill, "How Do You Sustain and Grow Your Customer Relationships?" *American Salesman,* October 2007, p. 26.

Self-Management. In Chapter 2 you will read about various characteristics of sales jobs that make them unique, challenging, and rewarding. One thing that makes selling an attractive career choice for many people is the **autonomy,** which means the degree of independence the salesperson can exercise in making his or her own decisions in the day-to-day operation of the job. Salespeople today have tremendous autonomy to develop and execute their relationship selling strategies. Chapter 9 presents a host of important self-management issues, including organizing the job, designing and routing the sales territory, classifying and prioritizing customer potential, using technology to improve efficiency, and exercising good time management skills.

Sales Management

In the model for Relationship Selling and Sales Management, the third circle outside the customer core is about managing salespeople engaged in relationship selling: motivation, recruiting and selection, training and development, compensation and incentives, and evaluating salesperson performance. These five sales management processes are discussed in Part Three of the book, Chapters 10–14.

Motivation. Psychologists classically view **motivation** as a general label referring to an individual's choice to (a) initiate action on a certain task, (b) expend a certain amount of effort on that task, and (c) persist in expending the effort over a period of time.[8] Thus, for clarity let's consider motivation as simply the amount of **effort** a salesperson chooses to expend on each activity or task associated with the job. This includes all the components of securing, building, and maintaining long-term relationships with profitable customers. This general view of motivation is based on **expectancy theory,** which holds that a salesperson's estimate of the probability that expending effort on a task will lead to improved performance and rewards. The expectancy theory of motivation provides the framework for our discussion of motivating salespeople in Chapter 10.

Recruiting and Selection. With the shift in focus from transactional to relationship approaches, the various skills and knowledge components required to successfully perform the sales role have shifted accordingly. Identifying these **key success factors** in relationship selling is the first step in recruiting and selecting new salespeople. Whereas in the past these success factors tended to be related to fairly traditional selling activities (prospecting, overcoming objections, closing, etc.), nowadays they have broadened substantially. A survey of 215 sales managers across a wide variety of industries identified the following seven success factors as the most important to sales managers interviewing prospective salespeople. Each supports the relationship selling approach:[9]

1. Listening skills
2. Follow-up skills
3. Ability to adapt sales style from situation to situation
4. Tenacity (sticking with a task)
5. Organizational skills
6. Oral communication skills
7. Ability to interact with people at all levels of customer's organization

Chapter 2 discusses sales success factors in more detail. Chapter 11 considers the overall process of recruiting and selecting salespeople based on the skills and knowledge needed to succeed in today's relationship selling environment.

Training and Development. Although a salesperson's ability to manage customer relationships generally improves with practice and experience, it is inefficient to expect a rep to gain skills solely through on-the-job experience. Good customers might be lost due to the mistakes of an unskilled salesperson. Consequently, many firms have a formal training and development program to give new recruits some knowledge and skills before they are expected to pull their own weight in calling on customers.

Training generally focuses on building specific skill and knowledge sets needed to succeed in the job. **Development** is more about providing a long-term road map or career track for a salesperson so he or she can realize professional goals. The rapid changes in technology, global competition, and customer needs in many industries have accelerated the need for effective training in sales organizations.

Chapter 12 discusses training and development of salespeople in detail. It explains that salespeople go through a variety of career stages (exploration, establishment, maintenance, and disengagement) and each stage brings a unique set of training and development needs.[10]

Compensation and Incentives. Professional salespeople are very results-oriented. They crave recognition and rewards for a job well done. Their motivation to expend effort on the various aspects of their job is largely a function of the rewards they expect for a given job performance. **Compensation** involves monetary rewards. **Incentives** include a variety of financial and nonfinancial rewards. Nonfinancial incentives include recognition programs, promotions to better territories or to management positions, or opportunities for personal development. Chapter 13 provides insight on these important issues, including ways to put together an effective sales force reward system.

In their book *Compensating New Sales Roles: How to Design Rewards That Work in Today's Selling Environment,* Jerome Colletti and Mary Fiss identify a variety of specific changes in the role of salespeople with the shift to a relationship selling model.[11] One trend is that today's salespeople often work as part of a team assigned to manage a specific client relationship. Team-based selling requires that rewards must be created both for individual and team aspects of the sales job.

For example, the entire relationship selling process at Bristol-Myers Squibb (BMS) is team driven. A Fortune 100 firm, BMS is one of the world's leading makers of medicines and related health care products. BMS, based in New York City, had 2007 net sales of $19.3 billion and employed over 42,000 people. A key account manager serves as a team leader for a major retail account (Walgreens Drug Stores, for example). A category management specialist tracks sales and competitive trends and provides information to the team and the client for decision making about the product line. Also on the team are BMS merchandisers, who work with the various Walgreens regions and stores to ensure the BMS–Walgreens merchandising program is carried out; local BMS salespeople, who make presentations to pharmacists and front-end managers at Walgreens stores in their area; and members of the BMS product management group in New York, who work with the team and client on new-product development and promotion planning for their respective brands. As you might expect, compensation and incentives reward team performance, as well as individual performance.

Evaluating Salesperson Performance. The final aspect of the sales management process is evaluating the performance of salespeople. Team-based approaches to selling and managing customer relationships make it harder for sales managers to evaluate the impact of individual salesperson performance and determine appropriate rewards. Chapter 14 provides insights into linking rewards to the new sales roles defined by relationship approaches to selling. It also discusses the best practices in evaluating today's salespeople.

Issues Outside the Circles: The Selling Environment

In the model for Relationship Selling and Sales Management, the concentric circles exist inside a broader field labeled "Selling Environment." This implies that the process of selling, as well as the process of managing salespeople, takes place not in a vacuum but rather within a dynamic environment that includes issues relevant to and controllable by your own firm (the **internal environment,** or organizational environment) and issues outside the control of your organization (the **external environment,** or macroenvironment). Throughout this book, all the ideas and examples we will discuss about how to succeed in securing, developing, and maintaining long-term relationships with profitable customers must be considered in the context of the internal and external environments facing you and your customers.

Internal Environment

The policies, resources, and talents of the sales organization make up a very important part of the internal environment. Salespeople and their managers may have some influence over organizational factors in the long run due to their participation in making policy and planning decisions. However, in the short run relationship selling initiatives must be designed to fit within organizational limitations. Components of the internal environment can be divided into six broad categories: (1) goals, objectives, and culture, (2) human resources, (3) financial resources, (4) production and supply-chain capabilities, (5) service capabilities, and (6) research and development (R&D) and technological capabilities. These are depicted in Exhibit 1.4.

Goals, Objectives, Culture. Successful management of customer relationships begins with top management's specification of a company mission and objectives that create a customer-centric organization. As the mission and objectives change, customer relationship initiatives must be adjusted accordingly. A well-defined mission, driven by top management's values and beliefs, leads to development of a strong **corporate culture.** Such cultures shape employees' attitudes and actions and help determine the plans, policies, and procedures salespeople and their managers implement.

Periodically, *Sales & Marketing Management* magazine, a major trade publication covering the selling industry, publishes a special report on America's 25 best sales forces. Firms that appear regularly on the list include Baxter International (health care), Cisco Systems (information technology), Charles Schwab (financial services), and General Mills (consumer products), among others. A common thread among these and other top-performing sales organizations is a culture, embraced from top management all the way throughout the firm, that focuses on getting and staying close to customers. Their customer-centric culture is manifest in their missions, goals, and objectives. In the H.R. Chally Group's 2007 World Class Sales

EXHIBIT 1.4 Components of the Internal Environment

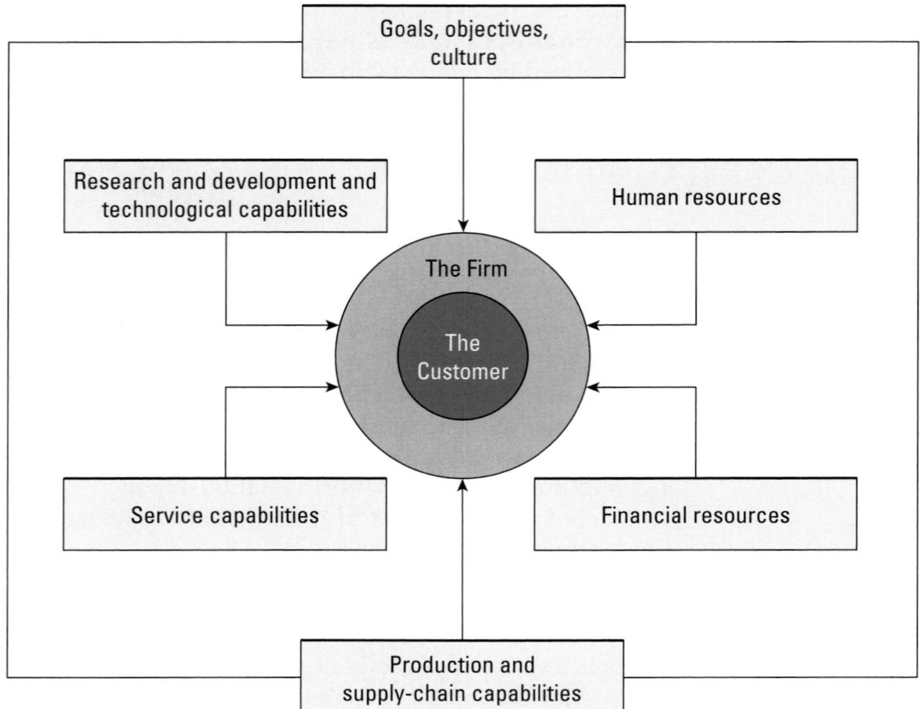

Excellence Research Report, benchmark number 1 for top sales organizations is establishing a customer-driven culture.

We have already mentioned the central role of ethics and legal considerations in selling today. The tone set by upper management and the overall culture of the firm drive ethical behavior in sales organizations.

Human Resources. Modern sales organizations are highly complex and dynamic enterprises, as are their customers' firms. The sheer number of people in many sales organizations, together with the many key success factors needed for relationship selling, creates challenges. Because it takes time to recruit highly qualified people for sales positions and then to train them, it is often difficult to expand a sales force rapidly to take advantage of new products or growing markets. Sometimes, however, a firm can compensate for a lack of knowledgeable employees by hiring outside agencies or specialists on a fee-for-service or commission basis. For example, many companies use distributors when entering new markets, particularly foreign markets, because using preexisting sales forces speeds up the process of market entry.

Financial Resources. An organization's financial strength influences many aspects of its customer relationship initiatives. A tight budget can constrain the firm's ability to develop new value-adding products as well as the size of its promotional budget and sales force. Companies sometimes must take drastic measures, such as merging with a larger firm, to obtain the financial resources necessary to realize their full potential in the marketplace. For example, Procter & Gamble's recent acquisition of Gillette in the highly competitive consumer health products field gave P&G quick entry into the lucrative razor blade market, while benefiting Gillette through P&G's strong supply chain expertise.

Production and Supply-Chain Capabilities. The organization's production capacity, the technology and equipment available in its plants, and even the location of its production facilities can influence the relationship selling initiative. A company may be prevented from expanding its product line or moving into new geographic areas because it does not have the capacity to serve increased demand or because transportation costs make the product's price uncompetitive.

Vendors doing business with Wal-Mart are expected to fulfill orders within 24 hours and to deliver the goods to the Wal-Mart warehouses within a two-hour assigned appointment window. Suppliers who don't meet this requirement pay Wal-Mart for every dollar of lost margin. It is no wonder Wal-Mart's vendors are willing to invest the capital to tie their information systems directly to Wal-Mart's system so the whole ordering and fullfillment process can be handled at maximum efficiency and speed.

As an example of supply-chain efficiency on the e-commerce side, founder Jeff Bezos at amazon.com developed a network of distribution centers nationwide long before Amazon's sales volume could financially support the warehouse capacity, principally because he wanted to ensure seamless distribution and service after the sale and avoid inventory stockouts.

Service Capabilities. We have already mentioned the importance of delivering high service quality in the follow-up stage after the sale. Actually, a sales organization's ability to provide a consistently high level of service is an important source of added value throughout the whole process of relationship selling. This will be discussed further in Chapter 3. For now, be assured that firms committed to providing great service typically enjoy a strong competitive advantage in the marketplace and make it difficult both for (a) other firms to compete for the same customers and (b) customers to switch to competitors even if they offer price advantages.[12]

R&D and Technological Capabilities. An organization's technological and engineering expertise is a major factor in determining whether it will be an industry leader or follower in developing value-adding products and delivering high-quality service. Excellence in engineering and design can also be a major promotional appeal in a firm's marketing and sales programs, as customers are attracted to innovators and industry leaders. When companies are investing heavily in technology, particularly technology that can help meet relationship selling objectives, salespeople can communicate the R&D and technological sophistication to customers as important value-adding aspects of the company and its products. This capability helps avoid the trap of overrelying on price to get the sale.

External Environment

By definition, factors in the external environment are beyond the direct control of salespeople and managers. Companies do try to influence external conditions through political lobbying, public relations campaigns, and the like. But for the most part, the salesperson and sales manager must adapt customer relationship initiatives to fit the existing environment. Exhibit 1.5 groups the components of the external environment in five broad categories: (1) economic, (2) legal–political, (3) technological, (4) social–cultural, and (5) natural.

EXHIBIT 1.5 Components of the External Environment

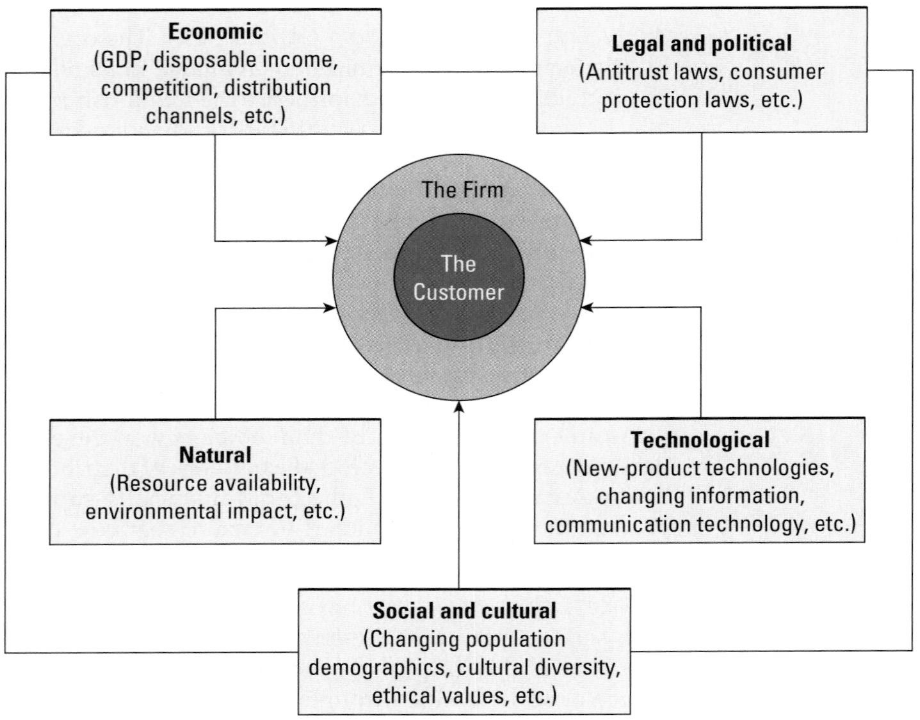

Economic Environment. People and organizations cannot buy goods and services unless they have the money. The total potential demand for a product within a given country depends on that country's economic conditions—the amount of growth, the unemployment rate, the level of inflation, and the gross domestic product (GDP). Sales managers must consider these factors when analyzing market opportunities and developing sales forecasts. Keep in mind that global economic conditions also influence many firms' ability to earn a profit. Companies of all kinds were impacted by the credit crunch created by the general financial and economic crisis that began in 2008, making it difficult to secure capital for investment in growth of products and markets.

A second aspect of the economic environment is the existing distribution structure in an industry. This includes the number, types, and availability of wholesalers, retailers, and other intermediaries a firm might use to distribute its product. Much of a firm's selling effort may be directed to persuading such intermediaries to stock and provide sales and marketing support for the company's products.

A third economic factor is the amount of competition in the firm's industry, both the number of competing firms and the relative strength of each in the marketplace. Ideally, a company's customer relationship initiative should be designed to gain a differential advantage over competitors. For example, rather than trying to compete with the low prices of foreign competitors (such as Komatsu) Caterpillar has succeeded in the heavy construction equipment business by providing superior product quality and excellent service, while charging prices as much as 10 to 20 percent higher than its competitors. A great way to thwart competitive threats is to focus the sales message on value-adding aspects of the product or service rather than price.

Salespeople go head to head with competitors on a daily basis, so they are often the first to observe changes in competitive strategy and activity. One critical issue is getting information from the sales force back to the company so that the firm can act on those observations. CRM systems, discussed in Chapter 2, provide an infrastructure for managing such competitive information (and many other types of customer information).

Legal and Political Environment. Laws and political action affect all organizations. In selling, common legal issues include antitrust, truth in advertising, product liability, issuance of credit, transportation of materials, and product claims, among many others. In addition, differing political administrations at all levels of government can bring changes to the marketplace and sales arena. Sales organizations must always be mindful of laws relevant to doing business and must take laws and political action into account when developing plans and strategies. Also, it is very important that salespeople be trained on the impact of the law on their role.

As discussed earlier in this chapter, ethics is different from the law. Something unethical may not be technically illegal, but it should still be avoided. Many reasons exist for practicing highly ethical behavior in relationship selling and sales management. The ethical environment is the focus of Chapter 4.

Technological Environment. A section under "Internal Environment" discussed the impact of a sales organization's own technological capabilities. Here, we focus on the overall impact of macrolevel technology trends on selling. One obvious impact is the opportunity for new-product development. Technological advances occur faster all the time, and new products account for an increasing percentage of total sales in many industries. For example, historically at 3M Company more than half of the current sales volume is generated by products that did not exist five years ago. And of course at Apple, a few short years back all of their sales came from computers and related items. Today, the bulk of Apple's customers are buying iPods and iPhones.

Most analysts believe new products and services will become even more important to the success of many firms. Rapid development of new products affects many relationship selling activities. New selling plans and messages must be developed, salespeople must be retrained to update technical knowledge, in some cases new salespeople must be hired to augment the sales effort, and new reward and performance evaluation systems must be established that match the new sales roles.

Improvements in transportation, communications, and information management are changing the way customers are targeted, sales territories are defined, salespeople are deployed, and salesperson performance is evaluated in many companies. New communication technologies, together with the escalating cost of a traditional field sales call, are changing how the relationship selling function is carried out. Most relationship selling today is accomplished by a combination of face-to-face communication and electronic forms of communication such as e-mail facilitated by smartphones. Consequently, the nature of many sales jobs, and the role of the sales manager in supervising salespeople and the relationship selling process, have changed dramatically in recent years.

Social and Cultural Environment. The values of a society affect relationship selling and sales management in a variety of ways. Firms develop new products in response to trends in customer tastes and preferences. In the United States, the well-documented demographic trends of aging society, greater influx of minorities as a percentage of total population, two-income households, greater mobility, and ever-increasing desire for more leisure time and more convenience-oriented products all have greatly affected selling.

The attacks of 9-11 provide a vivid example of social–cultural impact. Societal values shifted quickly and sharply toward family, home, safety, and comfort after the attacks. Direct sellers especially saw a resultant change in shopping pattern and intensity. Direct sellers (like Avon, Pampered Chef, Creative Memories, and Mary Kay) typically do business in customers' own homes, where relationships among buyers and sellers are warm, friendly, and high in trust. Most direct sellers, as well as the direct selling industry as a whole, experienced a significant increase in business after the 9-11 attacks as customers gravitated closer to home for many of their purchases.

Natural Environment. Nature influences demand for many products. Of course, natural disasters such as tornadoes and floods increase demand for building products and the like. Hurricane Katrina in Louisiana, Mississippi, and Alabama, in 2005 certainly proved that. But unseasonable weather can either damage or enhance sales, depending on the type of product you are selling. La Niña typically causes an increase in snow for the Northwest, leading cities to boost their orders for road salt. Even a late-season snowstorm or a very cool spring can harm sales for companies that rely heavily on selling in advance of the warm weather. In such conditions, products such as suntan lotion and swimsuits often remain unpurchased on shelves until substantial markdowns are taken.

The natural environment is an important consideration in the development of relationship selling approaches. It is the source of all the raw materials and energy resources needed to make, package, promote, and distribute a product. Since the 1970s, firms in many industries—among them cement, steel, aluminum, wood, plastics, and synthetic fibers—have periodically encountered resource or energy shortages that have forced them to limit sales. You might think salespeople could take things pretty easy under such circumstances, letting customers come to them for badly needed goods. But the sales force often has to work harder during product shortages, and at such times well-developed customer relationships become even more crucial for the firm's success.

During periods of shortage, a company may engage in **demarketing** part or all of its product line. In such cases, the sales force often helps administer rationing programs, which allocate scarce supplies according to each customer's purchase history. Shortages are usually temporary, though. So sellers must be sensitive to their customers' problems in order to retain them when the shortage is over. Salespeople must treat all customers fairly, minimize conflict, and work hard to maintain the customer relationship as well as the firm's competitive position for the future.

Recently, oil prices have skyrocketed globally. Most outside salespeople depend on automobiles or commercial airlines to travel from customer to customer. Gasoline and jet fuel prices have upped the costs of travel substantially. As the trend toward higher energy costs continues, look for sales organizations to find more creative ways of securing, building, and maintaining customer relationships while reducing physical travel by salespeople.

Growing social concern about the impact of products and production processes on the natural environment also has important implications for selling. For instance, countries in the European Union have passed legislation requiring manufacturers to take back—and either reuse or recycle—materials used in packaging and shipping their products.

Summary

Relationship selling is focused on securing, building, and maintaining long-term relationships with profitable customers. Firms that practice relationship selling are customer-centric. They place the customer at the center of everything that happens both inside and outside the organization. This focus on long-term customer relationships requires value-added selling, in which a salesperson communicates a broad range of benefits the customer can achieve by doing business with his or her firm. Value-added selling changes much of the sales process. It especially aids in moving purchase decisions away from simply price.

Information is the engine that drives a salesperson's ability to engage in effective relationship selling. Many firms have implemented technology-driven information systems designed to support the process of managing customer relationships. This type of system is called customer relationship management (CRM).

The model for Relationship Selling and Sales Management is a road map for this book and for your course. This first chapter provided a brief introduction to each element of the model, which will be developed in much greater detail in later chapters.

Key Terms

value
value proposition
customer loyalty
relationship selling
sales management
customer relationship management (CRM)
customer-centric
customer orientation
customer mindset
return on customer investment
lifetime value of a customer
transactional selling
consultative selling
enterprise selling
value-added selling
ethics
prospects
persuasive communication
solution selling
objections
follow-up
customer delight
autonomy
motivation
effort
expectancy theory
key success factors
training
development
compensation
incentives
internal environment
external environment
corporate culture
demarketing

Role Play

Before You Begin

Each chapter in *Relationship Selling* has a role-play exercise at the end. These role plays are designed to provide you the opportunity to work with one or more other students in your class to put into practice, or "act out," some of the important learning from that chapter.

All the role plays involve a cast of characters from a fictional firm, the Upland Company. You will need to know some basic information about Upland and its customers, as well as meet each of the characters you will be asked to role play, before you begin. The appendix to this chapter provides the company and character profiles you need to get started preparing your role play. It also provides valuable tips on how to get the most out of a role-play exercise and specific instructions on how to put your role play together.

Before attempting to go further with this first role play, please refer to this chapter's Appendix.

Characters Involved

Bonnie Cairns

Chloe Herndon

Alex Lewis

Rhonda Reed

Abe Rollins

Justin Taylor

Setting the Stage

Rhonda Reed, sales manager for District 100 of the Upland Company, has called an early morning meeting of all five salespeople in her district. Within a few weeks, Rhonda must work with each salesperson to set goals for the upcoming year. The purpose of this meeting is to discuss any external environmental factors that are likely to affect sales next year. Upland sells a variety of health and beauty aid products through supermarkets, drugstores, mass-merchandise stores such as Target and Wal-Mart, and other similar retail environments. Example products include shampoo, hair spray, deodorant, and skin lotion.

Rhonda Reed's Role

Rhonda's objective is to stimulate discussion about the full spectrum of external environmental factors that are likely to impair Upland's industry/business during the next year. Of course, this also implies she wants to discuss the factors that will affect Upland's customers' business. She will systematically solicit her salespeople's views on the potential impact of changes/issues in each of these elements of the external environment: economic (including the competition), legal–political, technological, social–cultural, and natural. She must be sure that each person has the opportunity to contribute to the discussion and that the impact on Upland's customers is discussed.

Others' Roles

The five members of District 100 will soon be working with Rhonda to develop their sales goals for next year. This meeting is important to everybody, since if there are any external factors that are likely to affect Upland's sales and the sales of Upland's customers, those factors must be taken into account when the annual goals are developed. Much of the income earned by Upland's salespeople comes from the percentage accomplishment against annual goals. Therefore, each of the five salespeople is eager to share his or her best ideas about the potential impact of these external factors on next year's business.

Assignment

First, each student in the class should develop a list of the key issues within each external environmental factor that are likely to affect Upland and its customers.

Once the individual lists are developed, break into groups of six to act out the role play as described above. Allow about 15 minutes for the meeting. One student from each group (other than the student playing Rhonda) will take notes. After all role plays are complete, these students will share their findings with the full class.

Discussion Questions

1. Think about the general concept of a relationship, not necessarily in a business setting, but just relationships in general between any two parties. What aspects of relationships are inherently favorable? What aspects tend to cause problems? List some specific ways one might work to minimize the problems and accentuate the favorable aspects.

2. What is *value*? In what ways does a relationship selling approach add value to your customers, to you the salesperson, and to your sales organization?

3. Southwest Airlines is famous for placing its employees at the center of the organization. Unlike our model for Relationship Selling and Sales Management, Southwest has its employees in the center circle instead of customers. Former Southwest chair Herb Kelleher's vision has always been that if a firm treats its people as though they are the center of the universe, they are bound to provide outstanding customer care. Judging from Southwest's track record, it seems to be working. Can this model be extended beyond Southwest Airlines to other firms and industries? Why or why not? What factors would allow an organization to repeat Southwest's success with such a model?

4. When a firm shifts from traditional selling to a value-added approach, a number of changes have to take place in the way a salesperson approaches customers as well as his or her own job. List as many of these changes as you can and explain why each is important to making value-added selling work.

5. Has transactional selling gone the way of the dinosaur? That is, are there ever any situations in which a transactional approach to selling would be an appropriate approach today? If so, what are the conditions and *why*?

6. Why is it important to talk about selling *solutions* instead of products or services? How does selling solutions further the success of a relationship selling approach?

7. The chapter mentions negotiating for win–win solutions. Think of a time when you negotiated with someone over something and one of you "lost" and the other "won." How did that happen? Why didn't you work toward a win–win solution? If you could do it over again, what might you do to promote a win–win approach?

8. Another salesperson in your company says to you: "Closing techniques today are moot. We know all our customers and their needs too well to have to employ 'closing' techniques on them. Doing so would ruin our relationships." How do you respond to this? Is the person correct, incorrect, or both? Why?

9. Think about the various courses you have taken during your college career. What *motivates* you to work harder and perform better in some courses than others? Why? What rewards are you seeking from your college experience?

10. Sales managers ranked success factors for sales recruits as "listening skills" first, "follow-up skills" second, and "ability to adapt sales style from situation to situation" third. Why do you think managers find these particular success factors so important? How does each contribute to a relationship selling approach?

11. Like all firms, Apple operates within an external environment of factors beyond its immediate control. Consider the various aspects of the external environment portrayed in the chapter. What specific external factors have the most impact on Apple's ability to practice successful relationship selling? Why is each important?

Ethical Dilemma

Ted Gaitlin has been an insurance agent with All Star Insurance for 13 years. He has enjoyed success with the company and won a number of sales awards. In addition, he has developed a reputation as an honest agent who works hard for his clients.

Over the last several years, however, the insurance market in his area became extremely competitive. Even though he was working harder than ever, he was not performing as well as he had during the 1990s. Management was beginning to wonder if Ted would be able to continue as an agent with the company.

Two months ago a sales contest was announced. Ted saw it as an opportunity to reestablish his position. The company wanted to drive new business in the last quarter of the fiscal year, and the contest was based on submitting new insurance policies for underwriting. Ted worked hard to write new business during the period and his efforts yielded good results. Now, as the contest entered its last month, he was concerned about winning. Biweekly results of all the agents across the country showed the contest was down to Ted and two other agents.

This morning Ted got a call from a friend, also an agent with All Star, who encouraged him to go all out to win the contest and suggested Ted submit proposals that would most likely be rejected by underwriters but count during the contest period. Ted dismissed the strategy during the phone call. Although many agents engaged in this practice, Ted had never booked insurance business unless he was confident the underwriter would accept it.

After the phone call, however, Ted began to think about the contest and his future with All Star. Technically, he would not be violating the rules of the contest, since it was based solely on generating new policies for underwriting. He had been working hard the last few years, and he felt it was not his fault that business was down all across his area. Finally, he was sure that winning the contest would improve his standing with management. On the other hand, he knew that writing policies that will be rejected is not in the best interest of the customer or the company. The booked customers would be upset because they could not get the insurance they counted on, and having underwriters review policies that could not be approved wastes the company's money.

Questions

1. What should Ted do? Why?
2. What conflicts do salespeople run into when they try to balance the needs of the company and their customers?
3. Is it OK for Ted to violate the spirit of the contest so long as he does not violate the letter of the contest rules?
4. Who bears more of the ethical responsibility: management (for creating a contest with poorly written rules) or Ted?

Mini Case

CASE 1

Creekside Outdoor Gear

Creekside Outdoor Gear is a Philadelphia-based company that produces and markets clothing sold exclusively in retail stores specializing in apparel for outdoor enthusiasts. The product line includes shirts, pants, jackets, ski-suit bibs and jackets, hats, gloves, and underwear. The stores also sell equipment for mountain climbing, kayaking, skiing, snowboarding, canoeing, and hiking, items for which Creekside's products are a natural complement. Creekside is known throughout the Northeast for high quality. Joe Edwards, Creekside's founder and owner, often tells his employees, "If you provide a quality product, people will want to buy it from you." However, Joe is beginning to detect some changes in his business and is wondering how those changes will affect his company.

One change that Joe has noticed is that the customers visiting the retailers that carry his products look younger and younger. As a member of the baby boomer generation, Joe realizes that his peers are getting older. The group of customers that has spurred his company's growth since its founding in 1978 will likely be a smaller piece of his business in the future. Joe has also noticed the growth in extreme sports. Not only are the people who participate in these sports youngsters, but they also have unusual (to Joe) buying habits. They seem to want what Joe would describe as a sloppy look and attractive color schemes at the same time.

Such customer desires take advantage of new, high-tech materials that provide greater warmth with lighter materials, which support the increased mobility needed to participate in extreme sports. Joe has never used these new materials and he wonders how they would work in his production process. Finally, Joe is concerned about the buying power of this new group of potential customers. Do people in their late teens and early 20s have enough income to purchase Joe's products, which typically command premium prices?

Another concern is geographic expansion. To help offset the impact of some of the trends described above, Joe would like to sell his products in stores in Colorado, Utah, Wyoming, Oregon, and Washington. However, Joe has always been a regional producer (Northeast U.S.), and such an expansion will require a significant investment. Establishing distribution channels and developing relationships with buyers is both expensive and time consuming. Furthermore, Joe doesn't employ a sales force. His operating philosophy has always been that a good product will sell itself. Consequently, he's wondering how best to represent his product to outdoor store buyers in those Western states.

One factor that keeps weighing on Joe's mind as he thinks about these issues is that he believes in developing relationships with his retail partners. Joe has read some information about transactional selling and relationship selling, but he's not at all sure how either one of these methods is actually implemented. Nor does he know how to decide which method of selling will better meet his objectives for sales in the Western states. Needless to say, Joe has much to consider as he decides whether or not to pursue expansion. If he does decide to expand, he needs to determine how best to set up his sales force.

Questions

1. Identify and explain aspects of the internal environment that are affecting Creekside Outdoor Gear's business. What external environmental factors are especially important to Creekside Outdoor Gear and the decisions that Joe faces? Why?
2. If Joe interviewed two different candidates for a sales position, one who has been using a transactional approach to selling and the other who has been using a relationship selling approach, how would he recognize the difference between the two?
3. Should Joe hire a sales manager and allow him or her to hire a sales force, or do other options exist? Why?

Appendix: Additional Information on Role Plays

The following information pertains to the role-play exercises at the end of each chapter. It is important to read and study this information before doing the role play in Chapter 1 and also to refer back to this information as needed before conducting the role plays in subsequent chapters.

Upland Company

The role plays involve a fictional consumer products company called the Upland Company. Upland sells a variety of health and beauty aids through supermarkets, drugstores, mass-merchandise stores like Target and Wal-Mart, and similar retail environments. Example products include shampoo, hair spray, deodorant, and skin lotion. The sales force follows a relationship approach to selling and calls on headquarter buying offices for retail chains as well as some larger independent stores. Competition in this industry is fierce, and salespeople must find ways to add value beyond just low price.

Upland is organized into 45 sales districts in the United States and Canada. Sales outside North America are handled by various international subsidiaries. Each district has a district manager and four to seven account managers (salespeople) who have geographically defined territories. Each district manager reports to one of four regional managers; regional managers report directly to the VP of sales.

Each district manager also has direct selling responsibility for a few large or particularly complex accounts. Districts have two-digit numbers with a third number representing the territory number tacked onto the end. The district of interest in our role plays is District 10, managed by veteran Upland sales manager Rhonda Reed. The next section provides a profile of each person currently working in District 10.

Profiles of District 10 Personnel

District 10: Rhonda Reed, District Manager. Age 38. Married with three children. Five years' experience as district manager with Upland, always in District 10. Previously had seven years' experience as account manager with Upland in another district out of state; three years' experience with another consumer health product firm. Has a BS degree in business administration, marketing major. Is working on an MBA with tuition support from Upland. Would like to move up to a regional manager position with Upland someday.

Territory 101: Bonnie Cairns, Account Manager. Age 23. Single. Upland is first professional job; she was hired right out of college. Has BS in psychology with a minor in business. Has been on the job two weeks. Completed first week-long Upland initial sales training program at the home office. Previous account manager in this territory, Gloria Long, was recently promoted to district manager out of state.

Territory 102: Alex Lewis, Account Manager. Age 41. Married with two children. Has been in current position for 18 years. Previously spent two years as a customer representative with a major bank. Has a BA in communications. Spouse holds a professional position locally and neither wants to move.

Territory 103: Justin Taylor, Account Manager. Age 28. Married with one child (infant). Has been in current position four years. Previously spent two years with Upland's leading competitor. Worked in a supermarket to put himself through college. Graduated with honors with a BS in business administration, dual major of marketing and MIS. His goal (and Upland's) is for him eventually to move into management.

Territory 104: Chloe Herndon, Account Manager. Age 31. Single. Has been in current position for three years. Previously was in the buying office of one of Upland's customers (Doug's Drug Stores Inc.) for five years. Has BS in general business.

Territory 105: Abe Rollins, Senior Account Manager. Age 55. Married with four grown children (one still lives at home and is in college locally). The "senior" designation in his title is reserved for account managers who have chosen not to pursue management positions but who are long-term contributors to Upland's sales success and who manage particularly high volume territories. Served in the army right out of high school, then completed BA degree in economics in college while working full-time as an assistant manager at a motel to support his family. Has been with Upland 27 years, but has moved twice with the company for better sales territories.

Territory 106: Currently vacant. Rhonda needs to recruit for this position. Previous Territory 106 account manager Rocky Lane lasted 15 months before deciding he wanted to pursue a different career track from sales. He left two weeks ago.

Additional Information

On each role play, you will need additional information to fill in some gaps and to prepare and act out the role play. This may involve various customers of Upland, recruits for the open position, compensation background, or many other possibilities. This information will be provided with each role play as needed. Think of the process as building the story or plot as we go along from chapter to chapter.

Tips on Preparing Role Plays

Role-play exercises are fun and provide a great learning opportunity. The following tips will prove useful as you get the hang of doing them. Most importantly, it is unlikely that anyone in your class is a professional actor, so don't worry about how well you come across as a thespian. Simply follow the instructions for the role play, prepare the script, rehearse as needed, and then enjoy acting out your part and receiving feedback.

Tip #1: Take the Role Plays Seriously but Have Fun

These role plays expose you to various aspects of successful relationship selling and sales management and put you into the action by giving you a part to play. Role plays are an excellent surrogate for real on-the-job experience. Topics come off the page from your book and into a real exchange of dialogue among the role players. You will want to do good preparation and take the task you are assigned seriously, but remember that the role play itself should be fun!

Tip #2: Follow These Steps

Each role play is inherently different. However, following some important general steps will enhance your experience with each.

1. **Team up.** Under the direction of your instructor, you will need to team up with one or more students to complete each role play. Although the characters in the role plays are gender identified, if your role-play partner or group does not have sufficient gender distribution to fill each male part with a male and each female part with a female you can certainly have one gender play another.
2. **Prepare a script.** The role-play partners or groups should collaborate to prepare a proper script that fulfills the goals of the role play. *Important: There is no one right way to portray any given role play!* Follow instructions, be open and creative, and incorporate the input of everyone who will be part of your script.
3. **Rehearse the role play.** Except for Chapter 1, all the role plays require rehearsal prior to presentation. Carefully stay within the suggested time parameters for each.
4. **Present the role play.** Your instructor may have you present your role play live in front of the class. Or he or she may ask you to videotape your role play as an outside assignment and bring it to class to turn in or play for the full class. Either way, you want your preparation to result in a professional looking and sounding presentation.
5. **Receive and provide feedback.** The role-play experience is not over when you complete your presentation. One of the best learning opportunities with role play is the chance to receive feedback from your instructor and the other students and for you to provide the same for others. The important thing to remember here is that your feedback should always be *constructive* (not critical) and focused on the relevant issues in the role play.

Tip #3: Broaden Your Learning

As you work on your own role-play exercises, and especially as you witness other presentations, you have a golden opportunity to broaden your learning about relationship selling and sales management. Take good notes, be open to ideas and suggestions from others, and integrate what you learn from the role plays with the remainder of the material in this book. This process will teach you valuable skills and knowledge that will help you succeed at securing, building, and maintaining long-term relationships with profitable customers.

selling environment

Sales Management

Evaluating Performance

Salesperson Motivation

Recruiting & Selection

Training & Development

Compensation

Relationship Selling

Prospecting & Sales Call Planning

Communicating the Sales Message

Negotiating for Win-Win Solutions

Closing & Follow-up

Self-Management

INFORMATION

Value Creation

Ethics

Customer Relationships

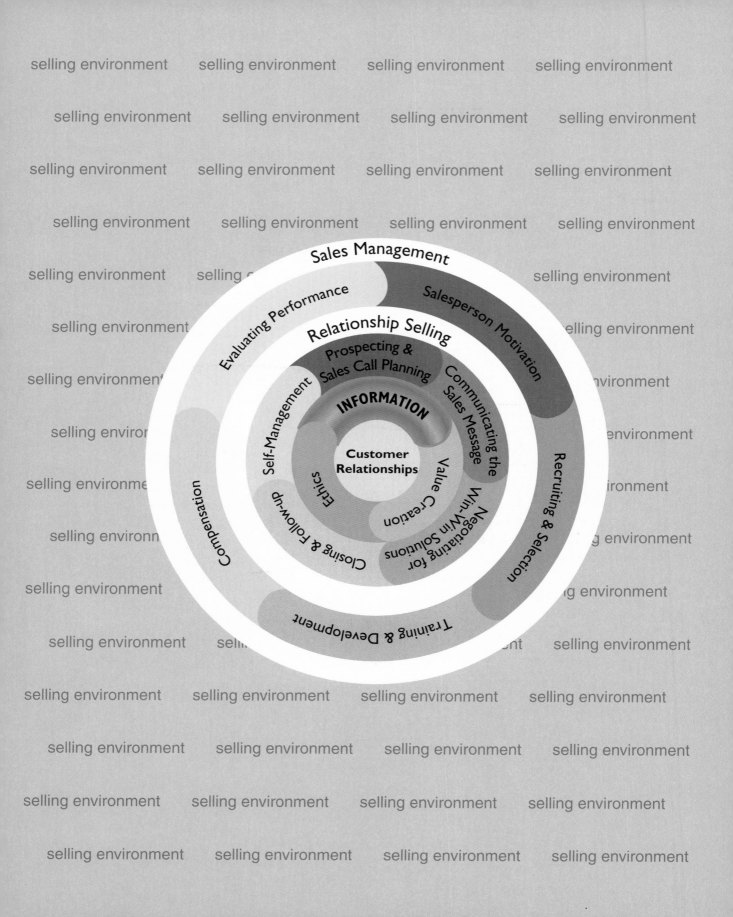

2 chapter

Using Information to Understand Sellers and Buyers

Learning Objectives

This chapter focuses on using information to better understand the roles of sellers and buyers in today's organizational marketplace. Many factors are driving professional selling toward a relationship-based approach. This transformation has created a challenging yet invigorating and rewarding environment in which to pursue a career in selling.

First, aspects of sales careers are introduced. Then perspectives are provided from both a seller's and organizational buyer's points of view. Information is what drives the engine of relationship selling, and customer relationship management (CRM) is introduced as a systematic process a salesperson can use for information management.

After reading this chapter, you should be able to

- Explain the historical basis for stereotyped views of selling in society.
- Point out a variety of reasons why sales jobs can be highly satisfying.
- Identify and explain key success factors for salesperson performance.
- Discuss and give examples of different types of selling jobs.
- List and explain the roles of various participants in an organizational buying center.
- Describe the relationship between buying centers and selling centers and the nature of team selling.
- Outline the stages in organizational buyer decision making.
- Distinguish among different organizational buying situations.
- Understand the concept of CRM and how it serves to help salespeople manage information.

expert advice

Expert: Timothy J. Trow, Region Sales Manager

Company: Tennant Company, San Antonio, TX (www.tennantco.com)

Business: A world leader in designing, manufacturing, and marketing floor maintenance equipment, outdoor cleaning equipment, coatings, and related products that are used to clean factories, office buildings, airports, hospitals, schools, warehouses, shopping centers, parking lots, streets, and more.

Education: MEd Adult Education, University of Minnesota; BA Psychology, University of Oklahoma.

From your experience in working with successful salespeople at Tennant, what are the most important success factors you see that separate great salespeople from good salespeople, and why?

1. Recognizing and capitalizing on opportunities. Top sales performers recognize sales and marketing opportunities and take the appropriate steps to capitalize on those opportunities to continually increase sales, profitability, and market share.

2. Acting as sales consultants. Top sales performers make sound recommendations, present their conclusions and recommendations in a persuasive manner, and create an environment of openness to convey to our customers, and potential customers, that they understand the customers' industry and business and can draw on a variety of resources to add value.

3. Developing strategic partners. Top sales performers identify potential businesses that can benefit from, and contribute to, a working relationship with Tennant Company and have the potential to become strategic partners with us.

4. Maintaining strong business expertise. Top sales performers approach their business from a consultant's perspective.

- They understand the business climate, economic indicators, market potential, and opportunities of their territory.
- They develop strong and effective resource networks (internal and external) and teams, and use them effectively to bring exceptional value to customers.
- They anticipate obstacles, competitive solutions, and internal and external threats and then modify or adjust recommended solutions to be in a preferred position.

What three things about selling at Tennant have changed the most over the past few years? How have these changes affected your salespeople?

- Communication-related technology has evolved and significantly improved sales reps' ability to access and communicate with customers and prospects.
- Downsizing and elimination of middle-management positions have affected who sales reps call on.
- Product knowledge, knowledge of the industry, and knowledge of each company are no longer enough to make sales. Sales reps must understand how to propose integrated solutions that are unique, creative, and relevant to current customer issues.

Buyers are changing too. What three changes in the nature of the buyers your salespeople call on have most affected the way Tennant sells?

- CRM has taken on a new emphasis and drives the selling process.
- Customer buying processes are changing and the purchasing functions are becoming more influential in all buying decisions. Technology is making it easier for everyone to get crucial information that influences purchasing decisions.
- Customers are asking more of fewer suppliers. They want to deal with salespeople who are knowledgeable about their business and recommend solutions rather than just products.

Why Is Information So Important in Relationship Selling?

In Chapter 1 we said that information is the engine that drives a salesperson's success in securing, building, and maintaining long-term relationships with profitable customers. And of course, the myriad technology available today plays a major role in facilitating the effective use of information.

This chapter provides you with important insights to better understand the world of relationship selling. First, you will have the opportunity to take an objective look at selling as a potential career path, including its many attractive aspects as well as some classic stereotypical misconceptions. Leadership 2.1 highlights six business trends that are impacting the sales role today. Then, you will learn about factors that can make one salesperson more successful than another, as well as what activities salespeople perform and different types of sales positions.

Next, we turn the tables and you get to see what organizational buying is all about. Finally, the theme of information in relationship selling is tied together through the introduction of customer relationship management (CRM) as a systematic way to manage information in relationship selling.

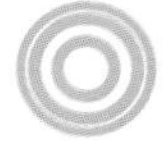

Overview of Selling as a Career

The Expert Advice from Tim Trow at Tennant shows that well-run relationship selling initiatives can produce enthusiasm and job satisfaction for salespeople. Yet recruiting and keeping excellent salespeople can be very difficult. Many college students hold some negative attitudes toward selling as a career. This is due to stereotypes based on old styles of selling where salespeople used hard-sell techniques to get buyers to do things they didn't really want to do and buy products they didn't really need.

The old style of selling is embodied in icons of American media from a classic play, a classic television show, and two classic movies. In his Pulitzer Prize–winning play *Death of a Salesman,* Arthur Miller immortalized old-style selling through the play's principal character, Willie Loman (as in "low man" on the totem pole of life). Poor Willie left for long sales trips on the road at the beginning of every week, returned a tired and disheartened peddler at the end of every week, and worked his customers based "on a smile and a shoeshine." His family was collapsing in his absence, his self-esteem was at rock bottom, his customers were defecting to other vendors at an alarming rate, and there seemed to be no hope of improvement for Willie on any front. This awful image, while certainly dramatic, has emblazoned on every schoolkid who ever read or acted in the play a sad, demoralizing image of selling.

Then in 1978 came the TV show *WKRP in Cincinnati,* about a lovable cast of characters employed at a third-rate rock-and-roll radio station. One character who was arguably not so lovable was sales manager Herb Tarleck. Herb was played as a back-slapping, white-shoe-and-polyester-suit-wearing buffoon who exhibited questionable ethics and made sales only through pure luck. The show was a top draw during much of its four-year run, and Herb's image has never vanished from view because of reruns on cable channels.

Two classic movies also reinforce negative stereotypes. David Mamet's Pulitzer Prize–winning play *Glengarry Glen Ross,* which came out as a film adaptation in 1992, featured a stellar cast, including Al Pacino and Jack Lemmon. It has become a cult favorite as a rental. In the movie, times are tough at Premier Properties, a boiler-room real estate sales company. Shelly "The Machine" Levene and

Leadership 2.1

Six Business Trends Every Salesperson Must Know

Every industry and profession goes through changes, and the sales profession is no different. Just because a certain sales technique or mindset worked in the past doesn't mean it works today. To be a top-performing salesperson, today and in the future, you must continually adapt to both market and social conditions.

With this in mind, there are six new business trends taking place—all of which affect salespeople in every industry. Understand what the trends are and how to maximize them so you can reap the rewards of a successful sales career.

Trend No. 1: Your past success will increasingly hold you back.
People who are in sales long-term tend to be successful. Realize, though, that success is your worst enemy. When you're at the top and doing well, you're really just trying to keep up and meet demand. Having so many sales knocking at your door lulls you into a false sense of security. As such, you're not looking at enough future opportunities because you're too busy reaping the rewards of current business. You're not sowing the seeds of future success, and this sets you up for a fall.

An old saying goes, "If it ain't broke, don't fix it." In today's world we need to rework this statement to be: "If it works, it's obsolete." For example, if you just bought the latest laptop, is the next newer and better version already in existence and about to be released to the public? You bet. Remember that rapid obsolescence isn't just about products. It's about how we do our business, too.

Trend No. 2: Technology-driven change will dramatically accelerate.
It's human nature to protect and defend the status quo. However, you must understand technology is changing the future, your customers' behavior, and your company's reality. This means if you don't change, you'll be soon out of a job. As a salesperson, you must embrace change and make it your best friend rather than fight it and hold tight to the way things were.

How do you make rapid change your best friend? Consider where the changes impacting you and your customers are going. Remember that change causes uncertainty in customers' minds. You can bring certainty to your customers when you are confident in where change is going. You can lead your customers through the change, causing them to view you as more than just a salesperson but as a solutions provider and trusted advisor.

Trend No. 3: Time is increasing in value.
Time is becoming increasingly important to people. Why? We have an aging demographic in the United States, with 78 million baby boomers. And time gets more valuable as you get older because you have less of it. Additionally, the world has become more complex with much more for people to do with their time. Today we have iPods, cell phones, the Internet, and a host of other technologies that didn't exist when baby boomers were infants.

There's so much more going on and we're connected in so many more ways that everyone is strapped for time. With this in mind, the last thing you want to do in sales is seem like you're taking someone's time. Instead, you want to be giving them time. You want your customers to feel that talking to you is actually saving them time.

Think about all the time-wasters your customers might experience: long wait times for service, long hold times on the phone, long delivery times for products. The list is virtually endless. Such time-wasters hurt your sales and profits. Therefore, make sure you have the processes in place to keep customers from wasting time. When you can prove you're a time-saver, people will consistently choose you over the competition.

Dave Moss are veteran salesmen, but only Ricky Roma is on a hot sales streak. Sales leads for the new Glengarry property development could turn everything around, but the front office is holding the leads back until the "losers" prove themselves on the street. Then someone decides to steal the Glengarry leads and leave everyone else wondering who did it. The verbal exchanges among these men desperate to make sales are riveting, and pretty scary to someone interested in sales as a possible career.

In 2000's *Boiler Room,* an overly ambitious group of schemers operates an illegal stockbrokerage. They cold call prospects from the telephone book, trying to get "pigeons" to invest in mostly bogus stocks. The characters' "success at any

Trend No. 4: We are shifting from the information age to the communication age.
Many salespeople rely on marketing tools such as company Web sites, flyers, and sales letters. But all these things are static; they merely inform people. Hopefully your sales messages entice prospects to call, but it's still a one-way interface. A better way is to have your sales messages create action.

One way to do this is to engage prospects with your sales and marketing efforts. A supplier, for example, could encourage people to visit its Web site to enter a contest. So instead of just saying you want distributors to buy your new promotional popcorn, for instance, you can tell them to go online to vote for the next new flavor. Now you get them involved in your product.

The key is to generate communication, engagement, and involvement through your sales and marketing efforts. If you talk to prospects without creating dynamic dialogue, then you're really just giving information. You want to give people consultative advice. You want to listen and speak and create dialogue. Only then do you truly capture your prospects' interests and convert them into paying clients.

Trend No. 5: Solutions to present problems become obsolete faster.
Almost every salesperson has been told to be proactive, which means to be taking positive action. How do you know if a certain action is positive? You wait and see. This sounds like a crap shoot with bad odds.

Therefore, you need to be preactive to future known events. To determine preknown events, look at your customers and identify what types of events they will likely experience soon. Then focus your actions on what will be happening rather than on what is happening.

Being preactive also means changing the way people think. For example, if you unveil a new product or service and hope it catches on, you'll quickly learn that it can take a long time because you're not actively changing the way people think about how the product can be used or how it might change their lives. Therefore, constantly educate customers on the value you and your products and/or services offer so they begin to rethink the results they can achieve and the value you provide.

Trend No. 6: The value you bring today is forgotten faster.
Most salespeople sell the current benefits they offer, but your customers already know these benefits. One of the reasons customers leave for a competitor is that you haven't cemented the future benefit you can bring them. Your goal as a salesperson should be to establish a long-term, problem-solving relationship with customers rather than a short-term transaction.

Your most profitable customer is a repeat customer. Therefore, you want customers to see the benefit you can give them over time, not just in the present. You want to show how the products and services you offer will evolve with their needs. In other words, you want to sell the evolution of your products or services.

Unfortunately, most salespeople don't know their future benefit. Therefore, you and your fellow salespeople must create a list of future benefits that you can provide for customers. Also, talk to the people developing the products and services and get an idea of where they're taking them. You're more likely to deliver future benefits if you can think of them ahead of time. As a side benefit, this kind of dialog will also help internal communications within the company.

More Sales in Your Future
Successful salespeople know they must keep abreast of trends and changes in their industry in order to stay on top. Only then can they stand out and be true solutions providers for their prospects and customers. Therefore, the more you understand and adapt to today's current business trends, the better your sales will be—today and in the future.

Source: Daniel Burns, "Six Business Trends Every Salesperson Must Know," *American Salesman,* February 2008, p. 15.

price" mentality and lifestyle redefine the notion of ill-gained wealth and unethical behavior.

These images of salespeople have become embedded in American culture. Even in other countries, people harbor similar images of American salespeople. The image is not entirely undeserved, as some unprofessional and unethical salespeople always have existed and always will exist (just as unprofessional people exist in any profession—witness the crisis in accounting and in the executive suites of companies such as Enron, WorldCom, and Arthur Andersen early in this decade). In selling, we seem to have to prove our value to society just a little more than in other professions. But the effort is worth it to those who love the profession, because there's no doubt about it—sales jobs are important to society, they're challenging to those who occupy them, and they are also potentially one of the most rewarding career tracks available.

Why Sales Jobs Are So Rewarding

For most professional salespeople, it is precisely the complexity and challenge of their jobs that motivate them to perform at a high level and give them a sense of satisfaction. A number of surveys over the years have found generally high levels of job satisfaction among professional salespeople across a broad cross-section of firms and industries. Even when these surveys do find areas of dissatisfaction, the unhappiness tends to focus on the policies and actions of the salesperson's firm or sales manager, not on the nature of the sales job itself.[1]

Why are so many professional salespeople so satisfied with their jobs? Attractive aspects of selling careers include the following:

1. *Autonomy.* Freedom of action and opportunities for personal initiative.
2. Multifaceted and challenging activities (these *sales activities* will be addressed later in this chapter).
3. Financial rewards. Salespeople hired right out of college tend to start at higher salaries than most other professions and tend to keep up well during their careers with the compensation of their peers outside of sales (due to sales compensation being linked directly to performance).
4. Favorable working conditions—often via telecommuting with a virtual office, and with less minute-to-minute direct supervision than most other careers.
5. Excellent opportunities for career development and advancement.

Each of these advantages of professional selling jobs will now be discussed in more detail.

Job Autonomy. A common complaint among workers in many professions is that they are too closely supervised. They chafe under the micromanagement of bosses and about rules and standard operating procedures that constrain their freedom to do their jobs as they see fit. Salespeople, on the other hand, spend most of their time working directly with customers, with no one around to supervise their every move. They are relatively free to organize their own time and to get the job done in their own way as long as they show good results.

The freedom of a selling career appeals to people who value their independence, who are confident they can cope with most situations they will encounter, and who like to show personal initiative in deciding how to get the job done. However, with this freedom comes potential pressures. Salespeople are responsible for managing their existing customer relationships and developing new ones. Although no one closely supervises their behavior, management usually keeps close tabs on the *results* of that behavior: sales volume, quota attainment, expenses, and the like.

To be successful, then, salespeople must be able to manage themselves, organize time wisely, and make the right decisions about how to do the job.

Job Variety. If variety is the spice of life, sales jobs are hot peppers. Most people soon become bored doing routine tasks. Fortunately, boredom is seldom a problem among professional salespeople, whose work tends to be high in *job variety.* Each customer has different needs and problems for which the salesperson can develop unique solutions. Those problems are often anything but trivial, and a salesperson must display insight, creativity, and analytical skill to close a sale. Many sales consultants expect creative problem solving to become even more important to sales success in the future. Innovation 2.2 provides ideas on developing a creative approach to selling.

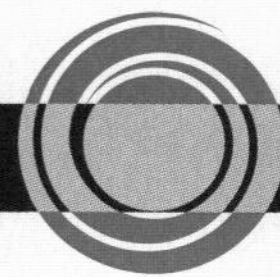

INNOVATION 2.2

Create Your Own Creativity

You don't have to be intellectual or highly educated to come up with good ideas. Although creative people have certain traits that distinguish them from others, such characteristics can be developed with dedication and practice.

Your job becomes easier and you are more productive when you assure no good ideas ever escape you. Almost any process or procedure can be improved upon. If you decide something is perfect as is, you also eliminate considering areas for improvement. This provides a false sense of security at best.

Realize unusual procedures can often solve your most perplexing problems. Good ideas can come from areas where you least expect them. Some of the best ideas ever developed were sparked by investigating in an unfamiliar area of a business.

Tips on getting started in improving creativity.

- *Be accessible.* Since ideas may come from anyone at anytime, you must be available and ready to receive them. If you get the reputation of being hard to reach or in a hurry much of the time, it's probable others will not go out of their way to pass along their ideas.
- *Promote creativity and innovation.* You may receive a lot of impractical suggestions. But don't let that deter you from helping people come up with ideas. Even reticent and introverted co-workers may offer them. Learn to put aside the unworkable ones graciously and tactfully so you don't turn people off.
- *Study each idea carefully, regardless where it originated, including yourself.* Take your time and avoid snap judgments. Quick judgments are usually based on overall assumptions and intuition—seldom on detailed analysis. Too often excellent ideas are prematurely rejected simply because time wasn't taken to check them thoroughly.
- *Keep an open mind.* Since big ideas have a habit of growing out of little ones, avoid passing off something that appears to be minor. Be alert for ideas that are not usable immediately. With some slight modification, they may be usable somewhere else or in the near future.
- *Check details.* Maybe a small error was made in developing or presenting an idea. The idea may be usable when that is corrected. Also, close examination might reveal you can use a part of the idea for solving an entirely different problem.
- *File ideas and suggestions.* Today's unworkable procedure may be appropriate and applicable tomorrow. Recognize it is difficult to remember every idea you learn of. Months may pass before a situation arises where it may be put to use.

Benefiting from your creativity. How are some people able to come up with new and unusual approaches to problems when you seldom can do so? In the book *A Whack on the Side of the Head: How You Can Be More Creative* (Business Plus Books), author Roger Von Oech offers these suggestions for getting your mind out of its mental rut:

- *Don't always look for the one right answer.* "We are taught to look for the one right answer. Actually, it's the second, third, or tenth right answer that solves the problem in an innovative way," Von Oech says.
- *Try to not always think logically.* Logic is appropriate when you're evaluating ideas. But when you're searching for ideas, Von Oech observes, logic can short-circuit creativity.
- *Avoid being too practical.* When faced with a question or problem, ask yourself, "What if . . ." and explore the thought in ways that might not normally be followed.
- *Stop thinking you're not creative.* One of the big differences between creative people and noncreative people is the former pay attention to their small ideas, knowing they could lead to a substantial breakthrough. "Believe in the worth of your ideas and have the persistence to build on them," Von Oech advises.

Using your imagination to advantage. Many successful people feel their imagination contributed greatly to their getting ahead. In business, imagination is an important skill to develop because it helps you see every side of a problem. It also enables you to find the most effective solutions.

How can you tell if your imagination makes you more innovative, and what steps can you take to further your progress? Here's how to handle it:

- *Approach every project and task you undertake with a critical eye.* If you think there's a better way to do a job, do it.
- *Be generally receptive to new ideas.* Check them thoroughly before rejecting them.
- *Use your imagination to explore as many alternative solutions as possible when you have to solve a problem.*
- *Welcome the opportunity to tackle new jobs and different ways of doing things.*
- *Participate in your company's suggestion program.*

Improving procedures. While you may need innovative methods to solve difficult problems and make good decisions, you need them also to improve the procedures that achieve your organization's goals. Art Cornwell, author of *Freeing the Corporate Mind: How to Spur Innovation* in Business (Execu-Press) offers the following creativity-generating tips:

- *Change your daily routine.* "Each of us has a routine we follow in the morning," he says. "These are so well-established we really don't have to think at all before we get to work. Your mind is basically asleep. If you eat breakfast at home, periodically eat out. If you follow a particular route to work, find another one. Do something different to get your mind moving earlier."
- *Use your ingenuity to think of unique ways to improve work procedures—even if they don't seem to be faulty.* Look around your office or plant for an operation or job that could be done better. Think about it during the day, and try to reach a conclusion. Then take on another challenge the next day. This practice will not only boost your creativity, but can also give you a sense of accomplishment.
- *Become an expert at something.* "Innovative ideas aren't produced at random from some unknown stockpile of data. They're actually a merger of ideas from dissimilar fields of experience. A person with more interests tends to be more creative; he or she has a larger knowledge base from which to work. Select a field in which you're already interested and invest your time in learning more."
- *Practice.* "Thinking creatively," says Cornwell, "is much like learning long division. When your teacher first described the process, you wanted to avoid it entirely. But soon, you began following instructions. Through constant repetition, you learned how to do it." The same is true of being creative.

Source: W. H. Weiss, "Demonstrating Creativity and Innovation," *American Salesman,* October 2006, p. 19.

To make the sales job even more interesting, the internal and external environments are constantly changing (as we learned in Chapter 1). Salespeople must frequently adjust their sales presentations and other activities to shifts in economic and competitive conditions. Tim Trow at Tennant mentioned several important external changes that have impacted their sales role including reliance on CRM, rapidly evolving technology, and pressure on suppliers to sell solutions, not just products.

Opportunities for Rewards. For many people in the selling profession, variety and challenge are the most rewarding aspects of their jobs. These aspects help develop a sense of accomplishment and personal growth. As we will see in Chapter 10, they are important sources of **intrinsic rewards** (rewards inherent to satisfaction derived from elements of the job or role itself), as opposed to **extrinsic rewards** (rewards bestowed on the salesperson by the company).

Make no mistake, though—selling can be a very lucrative profession in terms of extrinsic rewards as well! More importantly, a salesperson's earnings (particularly one who receives a large proportion of incentive pay) are determined largely by performance, and often no arbitrary limits are placed on them. Consequently, a salesperson's compensation can grow faster and reach higher levels than that of employees at a comparable level in other departments.

Favorable Working Conditions. If the stereotypes of sales jobs addressed earlier were true, salespeople would be expected to travel extensively, spend much of their time entertaining potential clients, and have little time for home and family life. Such a situation represents a lack of balance between work life and family life such that work is encroaching on family—**work/family conflict.** But it is not an accurate description of the working conditions of most salespeople. Some selling jobs require extensive travel, but most salespeople can be home nearly every night.

Leadership 2.3

When the Boss is Based Far, Far Away

More and more leaders are finding themselves in virtual boss/direct report relationships. Separated in space and often in time (zones), they struggle to communicate effectively, stay aligned, and achieve desired goals. It's all too easy for difficult-to-close gaps to open up when you are working virtually—in assessments, priorities, and expectations. Keeping this from happening is the central challenge of remote leadership.

Dictionaries list two quite distinct definitions for the word *remote,* both of which can apply to the challenge of dealing with a virtual boss. One meaning is "operating effectively from a distance," for example, using a remote control. This is of course the primary objective in a virtual boss-subordinate relationship: to have coordination and control work as well from a distance as it does up close.

The other, less benign, meaning of *remote* is "distant" or "unapproachable." Sometimes the black-hole boss is the problem. Try as you might, you really can't pin her down and get direction from her—in person or electronically.

More commonly, though, it's the direct report who doesn't make enough effort to make communication work across the distance. Particularly at risk for falling into this trap are those leaders who have a strong independent streak and a burning desire to prove themselves. They relish the opportunity to operate remotely and to chart their own course. So they don't put out the effort they should to get feedback and direction from their distant bosses.

This is, unfortunately, akin to sailing by dead reckoning when you are out of sight of land (in the days before GPS, naturally). You may navigate effectively and end up at the desired destination. But if you lack a reference point and get off course, it could take a long time to figure it out, and you may have a lot of distance to make up when you finally do.

What does it take to make remote leadership work? Here are some basic guidelines:

1. **Find a way to spend some face time with the new boss early on.** As soon as you know you are taking on a new role with a virtual boss, secure a significant block of time on his calendar. Regardless of how far away you are and how much you feel you need to do back home, force yourself to spend some time in the same room. Because there is no way you can make a personal connection and lay the foundation for a strong working relationship solely through electronic means.
2. **Discipline yourself to choose the right modes of electronic communication.** E-mail and instant messaging have revolutionized business communication, but they can never convey the sorts of contextual cues and emotional subtleties that are exchanged in conversation. Bias yourself toward electronic conversation and away from messaging in virtual relationships. Pick up the phone more than you would if you were located nearby. If you can't talk in real time, make more use of voice mail.
3. **Find windows of opportunity to check in with your boss.** You and your boss are both busy and it's all too easy for an "out of sight, out of mind" dynamic to creep in. So take the time to figure out your boss's routines and identify times when she is more likely to be available. One accomplished virtual manager I recently spoke with described how he arranged calls when his boss was in the car on the way to or from work.
4. **Discipline yourself to make the connection.** Think of yourself as having 100 percent responsibility for making the relationship work with your virtual boss. Force yourself to take the initiative to reach out regularly. Put reminders to do so into your calendar. Above all, keep in mind that the consequences of getting disconnected, and going off course as a result, will mostly be borne by you.

Source: Michael Watkins, "Remote Leadership," *BusinessWeek* Online, July 20, 2007, accessed October 1, 2008 at http://www.businessweek.com/print/managing/content/sep2007/ca20070918_304769.htm.

Indeed, with the increasing use of computer networks, e-mail, video conferencing, and the like, the trend for over a decade has been toward **telecommuting.** More and more salespeople work from a remote or **virtual office,** often at home, and seldom even travel to their companies' offices.[2]

Telecommuting offers many advantages for salespeople and efficiency and cost savings to the sales organization, but virtual offices do create a challenge for sales managers. They must keep the sales force fully socialized to the culture of the organization. Leadership 2.3 provides important suggestions on how to make a remote leadership arrangement work successfully.

EXHIBIT 2.1 From Salesperson to CEO

As companies focus on customer satisfaction and building long-term relationships with customers, they are increasingly tapping the sales and marketing ranks to fill CEO positions. Here are five steps you can take to place yourself in that swanky corner office.

- *Understand the whole business.* Sales and marketing people can become quite focused on just sales and marketing. Customer relationships are vital, but make sure to learn how the rest of your company works. No executive can be CEO without being able to talk the talk about every aspect of the company.
- *Take on extra responsibilities.* To understand other parts of your business, spend time with other departments. Learn what it's like to be a factory worker or a researcher. Not only will this give you overall insight, but it will undoubtedly get you respect throughout the organization.
- *Show you want it.* Knowledge and experience are important for attaining the top spot, but proving your desire is vital. Let the people above you know your aspirations and constantly prove to them why you're qualified.
- *Gain self-awareness.* No CEO can lead without fully understanding his or her strengths and weaknesses. Ask for honest assessments from your employees, your bosses, and your customers. Process that knowledge and improve with it.
- *Network, network, network.* You have to know the top people to become one of them. It may feel like a game sometimes, but no executive can get the head job unless he or she continuously has meaningful conversations with top brass.

Source: Eilene Zimmerman, "So You Wanna Be a CEO," *Sales & Marketing Management,* January 2000, p. 33.

Ability to Move Up in the Organization. Given the wealth of knowledge about a firm's customers, competitors, and products—and the experience at building effective relationships—that a sales job can provide, it is not surprising that CEOs like Sam Palmisano at IBM and A. G. Lafley at Procter & Gamble often come up through the sales ranks into the executive suite. Jeff Immelt spent more than 20 years in various sales and marketing positions at General Electric before being named the successor to Jack Welch as CEO. Anne Mulcahy, Chairman and CEO of Xerox, spent most of her 30 years at the company in sales. She advises that those who climb the corporate ladder from the sales rung need to be willing to take on nonsales-oriented assignments along the way to broaden their experience. Exhibit 2.1 advises aspiring salespeople on how to improve their odds of one day becoming CEO.

Although salespeople are sometimes reluctant to give up their high-paying jobs to move into managerial positions, most firms recognize the importance of good managerial talent and reward it appropriately, particularly as a person reaches the top executive levels of the sales organization. Total compensation of over $250,000 a year is not unheard of for national sales managers or vice presidents of sales in large firms.

Of course, many managerial opportunities are available to successful salespeople at lower levels of the corporate hierarchy as well, most obviously in sales management, product or brand management, and general marketing management. A survey of human resource managers found that sales professionals are among the most sought-after employees.[3] Exhibit 2.2 shows several possible career tracks for salespeople.

Promoting top salespeople into management can sometimes cause problems. Successful selling often requires personal skills and abilities that are different

EXHIBIT 2.2 From Salesperson to CEO

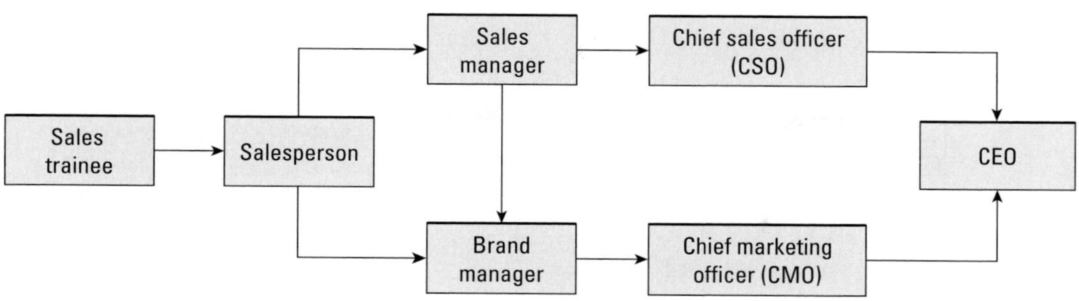

from those required for successful management. There is no guarantee that a good salesperson will be a good sales manager. Also, successful salespeople have been known to refuse promotion to managerial positions because they enjoy selling, or they can make more money in sales than in management, or both. Finally, recent trends toward corporate downsizing, flatter organizational structures, and cross-functional selling teams have changed the number and nature of managerial opportunities available for successful salespeople. The sales manager of the future is more likely to be a coach or team leader than an authority figure isolated in the upper reaches of a corporate hierarchy. We will explore these ongoing changes in the nature of the sales manager's job in more detail in Part Three of the book.

Key Success Factors in Relationship Selling

Although many career advancement opportunities are available to successful salespeople, not all sales recruits turn out to be successful. Some are fired, others quit and seek different careers, and some simply languish on the lower rungs of the sales hierarchy for years. Not everyone possesses the key success factors needed to make it in selling. What personal traits and abilities are related to successful sales performance? This question is somewhat difficult to answer because different types of sales jobs require different key success factors. The factors sales managers consider critical to success in managing customer relationships are different from those required in the transactional approach to selling. Knowing what sales managers look for when hiring a salesperson is very useful for anyone thinking of selling as a career.

One study asked 215 sales managers from a variety of industries to rate the importance of 60 key success factors developed from interviews with salespeople and sales managers.[4] The top 20 factors are presented in Exhibit 2.3. Let's examine the top 10 in more detail.

Listening Skills

The top-rated item is listening skills. Other research has found that buyer–seller relationships are significantly strengthened when salespeople consistently employ effective listening skills.[5,6] Good listeners pay close attention to the buyer, carefully

EXHIBIT 2.3 Success Factors for Salespeople

Success Factors	Mean	S.D.
Highest level of importance		
Listening skills	6.502	0.683
Follow-up skills	6.358	0.772
Ability to adapt sales style from situation to situation	6.321	0.687
Tenacity—sticking with a task	6.107	0.924
Well organized	6.084	0.889
Verbal communication skills	6.047	0.808
Proficiency in interacting with people at all levels of a customer's organization	6.000	0.991
Demonstrated ability to overcome objections	5.981	1.085
Closing skills	5.944	1.109
Personal planning and time management skills	5.944	0.946
Proficiency in interacting with people at all levels of an organization	5.912	0.994
Negotiation skills	5.827	0.975
Dresses in appropriate attire	5.791	1.063
Empathy with the customer	5.723	1.074
Planning skills	5.685	0.966
Prospecting skills	5.673	1.209
Creativity	5.670	0.936
Ability to empathize with others	5.549	1.105
Skills in preparing for a sales call	5.526	1.219
Decision-making ability	5.502	1.023

Note: All items were scaled as follows: 1 = of no importance at all in hiring decisions, 7 = of the utmost importance in hiring decisions. S.D. = Standard Deviation.

Source: Reprinted from *Journal of Business Research* 56, by Greg W. Marshall, Daniel J. Goebel, and William C. Moncrief, "Hiring for Success at the Buyer–Seller Interface," pp. 247–55, Copyright 2003, with permission from Elsevier.

assessing his or her needs. Ironically, selling courses and sales training seminars almost always focus more on teaching salespeople to speak and write than to listen.

Follow-Up Skills

As we learned in Chapter 1, a key difference between transactional and relationship selling is the effort devoted to the ongoing maintenance of the relationship, especially in between face-to-face encounters with the customer. EMC Corporation, a computer storage company, has a reputation for being obsessed with follow-up. Its sales and service teams work hard to anticipate and fix trouble before the client even recognizes a problem. Anything from a toppled storage system to a change in the storage room's temperature causes the boxes to beam home warning messages and activate a response from EMC reps, often before the client is aware of the situation. Locations in 24 countries position their more than 250 individuals and teams to quickly follow up in person if necessary. In fact, CEO Mike Ruettgers responds in person within eight hours in the case of a severe service failure.

Ability to Adapt Sales Style from Situation to Situation

Adaptive selling is the altering of sales behaviors during a customer interaction or from one situation to another based on information the sales rep gathers about the nature of the selling situation.[7] Adaptive salespeople, like nimble firms, are better at relationship selling, since understanding customers' needs and problems lets them provide solutions that add value.

Tenacity—Sticking with a Task

Nurturing customer relationships is a long-term proposition. The objective is not to simply close a sale with one client and then move on to the next. The process of managing relationships requires patience and the willingness to work with a client, often over very long periods, before the potential benefits of the relationship to both parties are realized. Along the way setbacks often occur that must be overcome. Great salespeople always keep the big picture in mind while working on the details. This perspective facilitates tenacity and yields results that are worth the wait.

Well Organized

As the content and responsibilities of sales jobs have increased in complexity and buying organizations have become more complicated for salespeople to navigate, the ability to skillfully prioritize and arrange the work has become a more important success factor. Good organization is a component of effective time and territory management. These and other aspects of self-management are covered in detail in Chapter 9.

Verbal Communication Skills

Salespeople must be great communicators, especially of their value proposition. Communicating the sales message is the topic of Chapter 6. Note that talking skills, while obviously critical to sales success, *are* rated lower in importance than listening skills.

Proficiency in Interacting with People at All Levels of a Customer's Organization

Relationship selling often involves communication and interaction with many people within the client's firm besides the purchasing agent. Later in this chapter we will identify individuals in other roles within customers' firms that may be just as important to the sales rep as the actual buyer.

Demonstrated Ability to Overcome Objections

As mentioned in Chapter 1, customers often have a number of concerns about any given purchase that the salesperson must work to overcome. Objections are a natural and expected part of any sales process. The sales rep can minimize them by developing a trusting relationship with the client over the long run and by working to negotiate win–win solutions. Chapter 7 takes up the topic of customer objections in more detail.

Closing Skills

Closing is of paramount importance, but a win–win approach to negotiating makes closing a much less arduous process for a salesperson. In Chapter 8 you will learn about a variety of different approaches to closing a sale.

Personal Planning and Time Management Skills

Like being well organized, being good at personal planning and managing your time will serve you well in a sales career. Nowadays, both these success factors are aided substantially by technology, including smartphones, laptop computers, and e-mail. Chapter 9 addresses a variety of self-management topics.

Selling Activities

Given what you have learned so far about the complexities of relationship selling, as well as the key success factors sales managers believe are important, you will not be too surprised to learn that salespeople who develop client solutions for Tennant and other firms spend much of their time *collecting information* about potential customers and then using that information to plan and coordinate the activities of other functional departments, service existing customers, and make sales calls. It is difficult to specify the full range of activities in which salespeople engage because they vary greatly across companies and types of sales jobs.

However, in one extensive study, 1,393 salespeople from 51 firms rated 121 possible activities on a seven-point scale according to how frequently they performed each activity during a typical month. These responses were examined statistically to identify the underlying categories of various activities. Ten different job factors were identified.[8] These factors are shown in Exhibit 2.4, along with examples of the specific activities each involves.

One obvious conclusion from Exhibit 2.4 is that a salesperson's job involves a wide variety of activities beyond simply calling on customers, making sales presentations, and taking orders. While the first two factors in Exhibit 2.4 are directly related to selling and order taking, factors 3 and 5 focus on activities involved in servicing customers after a sale is made (follow-up). Similarly, factors 4, 6, and 7 incorporate a variety of administrative duties, including collecting information about customers and communicating it to sales and marketing executives, attending periodic training sessions, and helping to recruit and develop new salespeople. Factors 8 and 9 focus on physically getting to customers and on entertaining them with meals, sports events, and other social interactions. Finally, some salespeople also expend a good deal of effort helping to build distribution channels and maintain reseller support (factor 10).

EXHIBIT 2.4 Sales Job Factors and Selected Associated Activities

1. **Selling function**
   Plan selling activities
   Search out leads
   Call on potential accounts
   Identify decision makers
   Prepare sales presentation
   Make sales presentation
   Overcome objections
   Introduce new products
   Call on new accounts
2. **Working with others**
   Write up orders
   Expedite orders
   Handle back orders
   Handle shipping problems
   Find lost orders
3. **Servicing the product**
   Learn about the product
   Test equipment
   Supervise installation
   Train customers
   Supervise repairs
   Perform maintenance
4. **Managing information**
   Provide technical information
   Receive feedback
   Provide feedback
   Check with superiors
5. **Servicing the account**
   Stock shelves
   Set up displays
   Take inventory for client
   Handle local advertising
6. **Attending conferences and meetings**
   Attend sales conferences
   Attend regional sales meetings
   Work at client conferences
   Set up product exhibitions
   Attend periodic training sessions
7. **Training and recruiting**
   Recruit new sales reps
   Train new salespeople
   Travel with trainees
8. **Entertaining**
   Entertain clients with golf, etc.
   Take clients to dinner
   Take clients out for drink
   Take clients out to lunch
   Throw parties for clients
9. **Traveling**
   Travel out of town
   Spend nights on the road
   Travel in town
10. **Distribution**
    Establish good relations with distributors
    Sell to distributors
    Handle credit
    Collect past-due accounts

Source: Adapted from William C. Moncrief III, "Selling Activity and Sales Position Taxonomies for Industrial Sales Forces," *Journal of Marketing Research* 23 (August 1986), pp. 261–70. Reprinted by permission of The American Marketing Association.

Another study was conducted to update this list of selling activities based on changes in relationship selling and sales management (as described in Chapter 1). Six activities dropped off and 49 new activities entered, which are organized in a matrix in Exhibit 2.5. The activities in the matrix are grouped by either technology or nontechnology activities and by five key content catagories of communication, sales, relationship, team, and database. Most new activities center on the use of technology in communication and non-technology-driven activities in the sales process.[9]

Several important conclusions can be drawn from Exhibit 2.5. First, salespeople have experienced rather substantial **job enlargement** over the past decade.

EXHIBIT 2.5 Matrix of New Selling Activities

	Communication	Sales	Relationship	Team	Database
Technology	E-mail Dictaphone Internet Laptop (CD-ROM) Voice mail Fax Cellular phone Pager Web page* Newsletters Audiovideo conference Provide technical info Overnight services Maintain virtual office	Set up appointments Script sales pitch from database Use software for customer background Laptop for presentation* VCR for presentation Provide technology ability to customers	Web page*	Conference calls	Collect new information from database Enter information/ data on laptop* Update customer files
Nontechnology	Practice language skills	Adaptive selling Conduct research at customers' business Avoid potential litigation Plan for multiple calls to close deal Sell value-added services Respond to referrals Write thank-yous* Target key accounts Pick up sales supplies Consultative sales Listen Ask questions Read body language Sell unique competencies	Bring in vendor/ alliance Develop relationship Hand-hold customer Write thank-yous* Purchase dealers Call on CEOs Build rapport with buying center Network Build trust Train brokers	Mentor Make sale and turn it over to someone else Coordinate with sales support	

*Appears in more than one cell.

Source: Greg W. Marshall, William C. Moncrief, and Felicia G. Lassk, "The Current State of Sales Force Activities," *Industrial Marketing Management* 28 (January 1999), pp. 87–98.

That is, the sales role today is broader and contains substantially more activities. Let's hope the efficiencies gained from the technological advances help offset the sheer number of additional activities salespeople perform today. Second, sales organizations need to ensure that all salespeople receive proper training and

EXHIBIT 2.6 How Salespeople Spend Their Time

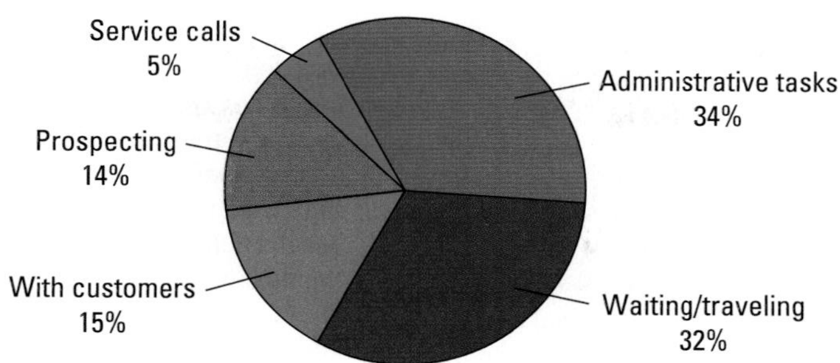

support so they can accept and use the available technology. Finally, performance management systems (appraisals, rewards) must be updated to reflect the dimensions and activities of sales positions today so that salespeople are not evaluated and rewarded based on an out-of-date model of their jobs.

The increasing number of nonselling and administrative activities means that many salespeople spend only a small portion of their time actually selling. Exhibit 2.6 shows the results of a survey of salespeople in a variety of industries. The survey found that, on average, sales reps devote less than half their time to direct contact with customers, either selling or servicing.[10] In firms that sell complicated or customized products or service systems to large customers, the proportion of selling time may be even lower.

The increasing involvement of salespeople in nonselling activities is one major reason why the **average cost of a sales call** has risen consistently in recent years. A rep must perform many nonselling activities over a long period of time to successfully practice relationship selling. The average cost of a single sales call is estimated to be over $450, depending on the industry, and this cost is increasing by about 5 percent per year.[11] To make matters worse, another survey found that it took an average of three calls to close a sale with an existing account and seven calls were required to win a sale from a new customer. This means selling expenses might average as much as $3,000 per sale to new accounts.[12]

This rapid escalation of selling costs helps explain the urgent search for new ways to improve sales force efficiency. Using new technologies, reallocating sales effort to customer retention, and purifying the sales job by eliminating nonessential tasks are some of the strategies companies have used to reduce selling costs and increase sales force efficiency.

How Technology Helps Salespeople

Ten years ago a sales presentation using overhead slides was considered high-tech, but times have changed and technology has transformed almost every facet of the sales job, especially the sales presentation. Sales presentations will be discussed in detail in Chapter 6. Today, there are tremendously powerful new technologies available for a salesperson's everyday use. Innovation 2.4 covers several of these technological tools. Let's take a closer look at two—portable computers and wireless communication.

INNOVATION 2.4

Seven Highly Effective and High-Tech Tools for Sales People

Technology and Internet services are booming, which is a good thing. But to the salesperson whose livelihood hangs on staying a step or two ahead of the curve, navigating the ever-expanding tech-universe can be disorienting if not downright scary. Identifying what's essential and what's just distracting takes commitment, objectivity, and a bit of trial and error. But the good news is that as you figure out what you need for your field, there's a good chance someone will have developed the exact niche service designed for your specific need. According to a recent article in AllBusiness.com, entitled, "Seven Must-Have Tech Tools for Today's Salesperson," there are seven new technologies that could help make your life as a serious salesperson a little easier.

1. **Work the Networks.** Social networking is not just for bands on MySpace and teenagers on Facebook. LinkedIn and Plaxo are social networking sites designed for the professional world. LinkedIn boasts 35 million members in over 200 countries, and operates on the basic idea that you share your network with your contacts and they share theirs with you. So if your friend is "linked in" with an exec at a business you've had your sights set on, you can use that connection to turn a cold call into a warm one. Plaxo helps you better manage and keep up with contacts in your network. Like Facebook and other services, the system notifies you of changes in your friends' activities and information, and can even automatically update your address book.
2. **May the Force Be With You.** As your career grows, so will the number of people you know. Gone are the days of the desktop Rolodex or the overcrowded Excel spreadsheet of contact information. Many sales managers insist that their reps use Salesforce.com. This customer relationship management (CRM) tool gives fast access to data—online, offline, and via mobile devices—and links easily to popular tools like Microsoft® Office and Outlook. It has a simple and intuitive user interface, and is a reasonably priced, effective way to store important information about customers, and make sure nothing falls through the cracks. Because when you make better contact, you close better deals.
3. **Less is More.** If you're tired of carrying your laptop around in a clunky briefcase, just put it in your pocket. Ultra-mobile PCs (UMPCs), like Samsung's Q1 and the OQO, offer all the functions of a laptop without the bulk, and the advantages of a PDA without the sometimes uncomfortably small screen and keypad. You can access the Internet wirelessly, create PowerPoint presentations, and do pretty much anything else at home, in the office, or during those unexpected 15-minute downtimes that pop up throughout the day.
4. **The New Old-Fashioned Thank-You Note.** In the age of instant electronic communication, a mailed handwritten

Portable Computer Systems

The laptop computer brought the power of great presentations into the customer's office. No longer could salespeople get away with overhead slides or simple brochures. A combination of fast, powerful computers, sophisticated software packages, and portable projection equipment lets salespeople create a unique sales presentation experience for every customer.[13] However, they need to be careful the technology does not replace the sales message.

Laptop computers are now standard issue for salespeople. More powerful portable systems are available all the time, as demonstrated by the many new products offered by companies such as Dell and HP. It is almost impossible for a sales force to claim superiority in technology because any technological competitive advantage enjoyed by a sales force will not last very long.

Salespeople should match their needs with the available technology, and management should assess those needs carefully. Too many companies buy more technology than they need and are forced into costly upgrades when it quickly becomes obsolete.

note can create an especially meaningful and lasting impression on your business contacts. But now even this tried and true practice has become a little easier and a lot more high-tech. Booked Solid Cards is an online service that scans your handwriting so you can send cards as easily as you type an email. No need to hunt for stamps or matching envelopes anymore—plus it can actually cost less than buying cards at a store and mailing them yourself.

5. **How Smart is Your Phone?** The Blackberry, Treo, and other Smartphones all specialize in integrating almost every technological need imaginable into one product. Since it's usually our phones that we keep closest to us, it helps when they include our address books and have access to the Internet and email—imperatives for the busy salesperson. Smartphones are easier than using a laptop when you're on the road, and make the daily demands of work a little more manageable. You'll also reap the benefits of up-to-the minute information about clients and businesses that matter to you, and will be able to approach conversations and meetings with confidence.
6. **Power-Up PowerPoint.** Don't let your strong pitch be ruined by a weak slide show. Ovation, by Serious Magic, is an application that transforms basic PowerPoint files into sleek, eye-catching presentations. You can still enter the information and create the slide show in PowerPoint, but then drop the file into Ovation and watch as static slides of bullet lists and charts become memorable, cinema-like events for your stunned audience. You can even read your lecture notes teleprompter-style, which allows you to synchronize your words with the charts and graphics everyone else sees.
7. **Out and About.** If you do enough driving, you're bound to lose your way sooner or later. The loss of momentum can be demoralizing at best, and arriving late could even cause you to lose business. And then there are the hazards of driving unfamiliar roads with a big map unfolded in front of your face while talking on the phone—you get the picture, and it's not pretty. A good Global Positioning System (GPS) device will serve you well. Check out products by TomTom or Garmin. You can get a GPS device that provides real-time traffic updates, offers the shortest route based on historical travel times for that day of the week and time of day, and informs you of local gas prices and weather conditions. Voice recognition and step-by-step route instructions mean you don't have to put your life at risk every time you visit a client. Plus these efficient little tools can even enable you to see more prospects throughout the day.

Adapted from "Seven Must-Have High Tech Tools for Salespeople," AllBusiness.com, http://www.allbusiness.com/technology/computer-software-customer-relation/3871184-1.html.

With PowerPoint and even more sophisticated presentation software like Talk-Show, salespeople can create powerful sales presentations with video and sound clips as well as impressive slide graphics. Talk-Show bills itself as "the leading software for creating, managing, and delivering outstanding presentations."[14] But first they need to understand what they want to accomplish in the presentation. If the product is complex or difficult to demonstrate, a well-produced video clip may be an excellent substitute for a real product demonstration. If, on the other hand, a basic slide presentation is all that is needed, a slower laptop with PowerPoint is more cost effective.

Wireless Communication

Being Internet-connected enables the salesperson to tap into the vast resources of the company right from the customer's office during the presentation. Suppose a rep wants to show a customer how to track an order through the company. He or she no longer needs to talk through it or create a demonstration slide in PowerPoint. By connecting to the company's network, the salesperson can, in real time, track an order. Wireless access also means that sensitive data can remain on the company's computers and be used only when needed. Finally, salespeople can download the latest information from the company's computers before the presentation, ensuring that the most current data is available for the customer.

Types of Selling Jobs

Not every salesperson engages in all of the activities listed in Exhibits 2.4 and 2.5, nor does every salesperson devote the same amount of time and effort to the same kinds of activities. Neither do they all employ portable computers or wireless communication equally. The many different types of selling jobs involve widely different tasks and responsibilities, require different types of training and skills, and offer varying compensation and opportunities for personal satisfaction and advancement. Perhaps most importantly, different kinds of selling jobs bring different levels and types of opportunities for managing customer relationships. Two broad categories of selling are business-to-consumer markets and business-to-business markets.

Selling in B2C versus B2B Markets

In terms of sheer numbers, most salespeople are employed in various kinds of **retail selling.** These jobs involve selling goods and services to *end-user consumers* for their own personal use. These salespeople are selling in the **business-to-consumer (B2C) market.** Examples are direct sellers (Avon, Mary Kay, etc.), residential real estate brokers, and retail store salespeople. However, much more relationship selling is accounted for by the **business-to-business (B2B) market** (which used to be called **industrial selling**)—the sale of goods and services to buyers who are not the end users. Business-to-business markets involve three types of customers:

1. *Sales to resellers,* as when a salesperson for Hanes sells underwear to a retail store, which in turn resells the goods to its customers.
2. *Sales to business users,* as when a salesperson for General Electric sells materials or parts to Boeing, which uses them to produce another product; or when a Xerox salesperson sells a copier to a law firm for use in conducting the firm's business.
3. *Sales to institutions,* as when Dell sells a computer to a nonprofit hospital or a government agency.

Sometimes the key success factors and sales activities relevant to B2C and B2B markets and to managing the two types of sales forces are very similar. Success in both types of selling requires interpersonal and communications skills, solid knowledge of the products being sold, an ability to discover customers' needs and solve their problems, and the creativity to show customers how a particular product or service can help satisfy those needs and problems. Similarly, managers must recruit and train appropriate people for both types of sales jobs, provide them with objectives consistent with the firm's overall marketing or merchandising program, supervise them, motivate them, and evaluate their performance.

But B2C and B2B selling also differ in some important ways. Many of the goods and services sold by B2B salespeople are more expensive and technically complex than those in B2C. B2B customers tend to be larger and to engage in extensive decision-making processes involving many people. Therefore, the key success factors and activities involved in selling to business buyers are often quite different from those in retail selling. Furthermore, the decisions made to manage a B2B sales force are broader than those required for a B2C sales force. Although some topics in this book apply reasonably well to both types of selling situations, others apply more directly to the B2B. Overall this book focuses more on the B2B side of relationship selling and sales management.

Note that many sellers work in both the B2C and B2B markets. An insurance agent, for example, sells automobile policies to both individual drivers and company fleet managers.

Types of B2B Sales Jobs

Even within B2B selling, many different types of jobs exist requiring different skills. One of the most useful classification systems for sales jobs identifies four types of B2B selling found across a variety of industries.[15]

1. *Trade servicer.* The sales force's primary responsibility is to increase business from current and potential customers by providing them with merchandising and promotional assistance. The "trade" referred to in the label is the group of resellers, such as retailers or distributors, with whom this sales force does business. A Procter & Gamble rep selling soap and laundry products to chain-store personnel is an example of trade selling.
2. *Missionary seller.* The sales force's primary job is to increase business from current and potential customers by providing product information and other personal selling assistance. Missionary salespeople often do not take orders from customers directly but persuade customers to buy their firm's product from distributors or other wholesale suppliers. Anheuser-Busch does missionary selling when its salespeople call on bar owners and encourage them to order a particular brand of beer from the local Budweiser distributor. Similarly, pharmaceutical company reps, or *detailers,* call on doctors. When Pfizer first introduced Celebrex, an arthritis drug, its salespeople alerted the physicians in their areas to the efficacy of the product, explained its advantages over traditional pain relievers, and influenced them to prescribe it to their patients. Note that Pfizer sales reps normally don't "sell" any product directly to physicians.
3. *Technical seller.* The sales force's primary responsibility is to increase business from current and potential customers by providing technical and engineering information and assistance. An example is a sales engineer from the General Electric jet engine company calling on Boeing. Most technical selling nowadays is accomplished through cross-functional selling teams because many of the products and associated services are so complex that it is difficult for any one salesperson to master all aspects of the sale.
4. *New-business seller.* The sales force's primary responsibility is to identify and obtain business from new customers. In relationship selling terms, this means focusing on securing and building the customer relationship.

Each type of sales job involves somewhat different activities and thus different key success factors.

In order to truly understand the selling process, why successful salespeople do what they do, and how they manage their efforts effectively, you must understand how customers make purchase decisions. After all, in relationship selling, the salesperson and his or her entire organization aim to fulfill customer needs and solve customer problems. The next sections shift the focus of our discussion from the selling side to the buying side. They examine the participants in the B2B buying process, the stages of this buying process, and finally the nature of organizational buying situations.

Participants in the Organizational Buying Process

To make a decision on a technologically sophisticated IT solution from a firm like IBM or Microsoft, a wide variety of individuals in a client firm may participate in the decision process, including computer analysts, customer service reps, procurement personnel, end users, and others. The various participants in a buying process may be grouped into seven categories: initiators, users, influencers, gatekeepers, buyers, deciders, and controllers.[16] Together, the individuals in these roles form the **buying center,** which represents all the people who participate in purchasing or influencing the purchase of a particular product.

American Airlines operates the largest commercial aviation maintenance and equipment base in the United States in Tulsa, Oklahoma. Mechanics there use a wide variety of products purchased by American from hundreds of vendors. A variety of people at American participate in the purchase of these products in one way or another. Participants in that buying process include the following.

- *Initiators* are the people who perceive a problem or opportunity that may require the purchase of a new product or service. They start the buying process. The initiator can be almost anyone at any level in the firm. Complaints from maintenance workers at American Airlines about outmoded and inefficient equipment, for instance, might trigger the purchase of new machinery. Or the decision to replace the equipment might come from top management's strategic planning on how to make the airline more cost efficient and effective.
- *Users,* the people in the organization who must use or work with the product or service, often influence the purchase decision. For example, drill-press operators at American Airlines might request that the purchasing agent buy drill bits from a particular supplier because they stay sharp longer and reduce downtime in the plant. Users also often initiate a purchase, so the same people may play more than one role.
- *Influencers* provide information for evaluating alternative products and suppliers and often play a major role in determining the specifications and criteria to use in making the purchase decision. Influencers are usually technical experts from various departments. They may include users. At American Airlines, for example, flight engineers and pilots often influence purchase decisions based on their experience with various vendor options.
- *Gatekeepers* control the kind and amount of information to other people involved in the purchasing process. A gatekeeper may control information going to the organization's purchasing agents, the suppliers' salespeople, and others on the selling and buying teams. IT people are often gatekeepers because they frequently hold the information that is key to decision making.

There are two types of gatekeepers: *screens* (like secretaries at American Airlines, who decide whose phone call is put through to the executive or purchasing agent) and *filters* (like the American Airlines purchasing agent who gathers proposals from three companies and decides what to tell others in the buying center about each company). The purchasing agent filters information, choosing to pass along some but not all of it to influence the decision.

- The *buyer* is the person who actually contacts the selling organization and places the order. In most organizations, buyers have the authority to negotiate purchases. In some cases, they are given wide discretion. In others, they are constrained by technical specifications and other contract requirements determined by technical experts and top administrators. At American Airlines, the level of authority to buy is determined by the size and type of purchase involved. In many organizations, the decision may be referred to a buying committee, which may either vote or reach a consensus on which vendor to buy from or which product to buy.
- The *decider* is the person with the final authority to make a purchase decision. Sometimes buyers have this authority, but often it is retained by higher executives. When American Airlines buys a complete, systemwide computer installation and upgrade, for instance, the final decision is likely to be made by the chief executive or a top management committee.
- The *controller* is the person who determines the budget for the purchase. Sometimes the budget is set independently of the purchase. For example, the administrative office at American Airlines' Tulsa facility may receive a budget for office equipment set by corporate headquarters in Fort Worth at the start of the fiscal year. If a copier needs to be replaced or some other unexpected high-dollar expense looms, the cost somehow has to fit into that budget. Alternatively, sometimes the controller may be an engineer or a line manager who is trying to keep the cost of the new maintenance procedure within a certain budget.

Three to 12 people are likely to be in the buying center for a typical purchase. Different members of the buying center may participate—and exert different amounts of influence—at different stages in the decision process.[17] At American Airlines, people from engineering, quality control, and R&D often exert the greatest influence on the development of specifications and criteria that a new maintenance product must meet, while the purchasing manager often has more influence when it comes time to choose among alternative suppliers.

The makeup and size of the buying center vary with the amount of risk the firm perceives when buying a particular product. The buying center tends to be smaller—and the relative influence of the purchasing manager greater—when reordering products the firm has purchased in the past than when buying something for the first time or buying something that is seen as risky.[18] **Perceived risk** is based on the complexity of the product and situation, the relative importance of the purchase, time pressure to make a decision, and the degree of uncertainty about the product's efficacy. The buying center is likely to involve more participants when it is considering the purchase of a technically complex or expensive product, such as a computer system, than a simpler or less costly product.[19]

Selling Centers and Buying Centers

Since major customers' buying centers often consist of people from different functional areas with different viewpoints and concerns, those concerns can often be addressed most effectively by a team of experts from equivalent functional departments in the selling firm, or even from different divisions within the company. Recently, companies have begun to use a **selling center** approach that brings together individuals from around the organization (marketing, customer service, sales, engineering, and others) as a team to join the salesperson who has primary responsibility for a customer. Just as customers have buying centers, the selling organization works together to present a unified, well-coordinated effort to the customer.[20]

The key is establishing a **team selling** structure within the sales organization to meet customer needs. One common structure makes the salesperson (account manager) responsible for working with the entire selling team to manage the customer relationship. Often such customer relationship teams include representatives from functional departments like R&D, operations, and finance. Increasingly, customer relationship teams maintain offices in or very near the customer's facilities.

Since different members of the buying center may be active at different stages of the purchase process, an important part of sales planning involves determining whom the sales organization should contact, when each contact should be made, who within the selling team should make each contact, and what kinds of information and communication each buying center member is likely to find most useful and persuasive.

At Siebel Systems, a part of Oracle and the world's largest producer of CRM software, the team for a major account like Marriott is led by a Siebel account executive who has a global team of salespeople as direct reports but can also draw from the full functional resources of Siebel to provide solutions for GM at any location in the world. This approach creates a **matrix organization** of direct reports and supporting internal consultants at Siebel who bring their collective expertise to bear for this major client.

Team selling can present some coordination, motivation, and compensation problems. Lou Gerstner, former Chairman and CEO of IBM, has frequently spoken out publicly on the difficulties of performance management in team selling environments. In fact, it is a key theme in the book Gerstner released after retiring.[21,22]

Team selling is expensive and involves a substantial commitment of human resources, including management. Thus, team-based approaches tend to be most appropriate for the very largest customers (especially those with buying centers) whose potential business over time represents enough dollars and entails enough cross-functional interaction among various areas of both firms to justify the high costs. Such customers are often referred to as **key accounts.** They generally have a senior salesperson as the key account manager (KAM).

Organizational Buying Decision Stages

You have seen that different members of a buying center may exert influence at different stages in the decision process. What stages are involved? One widely recognized framework identifies seven steps that organizational buyers take in making purchase decisions: (1) anticipation or recognition of a problem or need, (2) determination and description of the traits and the quantity of the needed item(s), (3) search for and qualification of potential suppliers, (4) acquisition and analysis of proposals or bids, (5) evaluation of proposals and selection of suppliers, (6) selection of an order routine, and (7) performance evaluation and feedback.[23] These organizational buying decision stages are portrayed in Exhibit 2.7 and described in detail on the next page.

EXHIBIT 2.7 Organizational Buying Decision Stages

STAGE ONE
Anticipation or recognition of a problem or need

STAGE TWO
Determination and description of the traits and quality of the needed item(s)

STAGE THREE
Search for and qualification of potential suppliers

STAGE FOUR
Acquisition and analysis of proposals or bids

STAGE FIVE
Evaluation of proposals and selection of suppliers

STAGE SIX
Selection of an order routine

STAGE SEVEN
Performance evaluation and feedback

Stage One: Anticipation or Recognition of a Problem or Need

Many organizational purchases are motivated by the requirements of the firm's production processes, merchandise inventory, or day-to-day operations. Such demand for goods and services is **derived demand.** That is, needs are derived from the firm's customers' demand for the goods or services it produces or markets. For example, the demand for luggage is derived in part from the demand for air travel. The luggage department at Dillard's Department Store loses customers, and Samsonite (a leading luggage manufacturer) loses customers, when people don't travel. This characteristic of derived demand can make organizational markets quite volatile, because a small change in the market can result in a large (relatively speaking) change in the organization's sales.

Many different situations can lead someone to recognize a need for a particular product or service. Need recognition may be almost automatic, as when the computerized inventory control system at Wal-Mart reports that the stock of an item has fallen below the reorder level. Or a need may arise when someone identifies a better way of operating, as at the American Airlines Maintenance and Equipment Base when an engineer or mechanic suggests a better procedure than the current practice.

New needs might also evolve when the focus of the firm's operations changes, as when top management decides to make a new product line. Procter & Gamble introduced Crest WhiteStrips, which sell for considerably more on the grocer's shelf than most other Crest products such as toothpaste and mouthwash, because P&G wanted to get into the business of more professional products that will raise its average sale and profit per item. In all these situations, needs may be recognized—and the purchasing process initiated—by a variety of people in the organization, including users, technical personnel, top management, and purchasing managers.

Stage Two: Determination and Description of the Traits and Quantity of the Needed Item(s)

In organizational buying settings, the types and quantities of goods and services to be purchased are usually dictated by the demand for the firm's outputs and by the requirements of its production process and operations. The criteria used in specifying the needed materials and equipment must usually be technically precise. Similarly, the quantities needed must be carefully considered to avoid excessive inventories or downtime caused by lack of needed materials. For these reasons, a variety of technical experts, as well as the people who will use the materials or equipment, are commonly involved in this stage of the decision process.

It is not enough for the using department and the technical experts to develop a detailed set of specs for the needed item, however. They must also communicate to other members of the buying center and to potential suppliers a clear and precise description of *what* is needed, *how much* is needed, and *when* it is needed. When the design and marketing groups of Nissan or Hyundai decide to change the specifications of a car's interior and electronic systems, the changes must be communicated effectively to purchasing so that the vendor (often Lear Corporation) can begin changing the parts these important customers rely on to satisfy picky consumers in this market.

Stage Three: Search for and Qualification of Potential Suppliers

Once the organization has clearly defined the type of item needed, a search for potential suppliers begins. If the item has been purchased before, this search may be limited to one or a few suppliers that have performed satisfactorily in the past. (See the section later in this chapter on types of organizational buying situations.) From the seller's perspective, one advantage of relationship selling is that this step is often skipped. The buyer has enough familiarity and trust that it gives the seller the first opportunity to bid on supplying the new products. Historically, many automobile manufacturers have gone with **single-source suppliers** wherever possible to minimize the variation in quality of production inputs. This approach bodes well for Lear whenever a manufacturer announces spec changes on aspects of car models for which Lear supplies parts. If the purchase involves a new item, or if the item is complex and expensive (again, if the product represents a *risky* decision), organizational buyers often search for several potential suppliers and select the one with the best product and most favorable terms.

Stage Four: Acquisition and Analysis of Proposals or Bids

After potential suppliers are identified, the buyer may request proposals or bids from each. When the item is a frequently purchased, standardized, or technically simple product (for example, nails or copier paper), this process may not be very extensive. The buyer may simply consult several suppliers' catalogs or make a few phone calls. For more complicated and expensive goods and services, the buyer may request lengthy, detailed sales presentations and written proposals from each potential vendor. Governmental and other institutional buyers almost always are required to formally solicit bids.

Stage Five: Evaluation of Proposals and Selection of Suppliers

During this stage of the purchasing process, members of the buying center examine the acceptability of the various proposals and potential suppliers. Also, the buying organization and one or more potential vendors may engage in negotiation about various aspects of the deal. Ultimately, one or more suppliers are selected and purchase agreements are signed.

The people in the buying organization's purchasing department (the buyers) usually evaluate offerings and select the supplier. Others in the buying center, such as technical and administrative personnel, may also play a role in supplier selection, especially when the purchase is complex and costly.

What criteria do members of the buying center use in selecting a supplier? Organizational buying is largely a rational decision-making process, so rational criteria are usually most important—the value-added aspects of the product, the service offered, and the like. However, social and emotional factors can also influence this decision. Organizational buyers and other buying center members are, after all, human, just like buyers in the B2C marketplace. Some differences between consumer and organizational buyer behavior are summarized in Exhibit 2.8.

The relative importance of different supplier selection criteria varies across organizations and the types of products or services being purchased. For example, product quality tends to be more important in the purchase of technically complex products, whereas price and customer service are relatively more important for more standardized, nontechnical items or commodity products. Fortunately, relationship selling greatly increases the likelihood that buying firms will not use price as the sole determinant of vendor selection. Instead, because buyers will have much more complete knowledge about you and your products, they will better understand the overall value to their organization of buying from you versus one of your competitors with whom they do not have a long-standing relationship. Chapter 3 considers the issue of value creation in buyer–seller relationships.

EXHIBIT 2.8 Consumer versus Organizational Buyer Behavior

Aspect of the Purchase	Consumer Buyer	Organizational Buyer
Use	Personal, family, or household	Production, operations, or resale
Buyer motivation	Personal	Organizational and personal
Buyer knowledge of product or service	Lower	Higher
Likelihood of group decision making	Lower	Higher
Dollar amount of purchases	Lower	Higher
Quantity of purchase or order size	Smaller	Larger
Frequency of purchase	More	Less
Number of cyclical purchases	Lower	Higher
Amount of negotiation and competitive bidding	Little	Much

Stage Six: Selection of an Order Routine

Until the purchased item is delivered, it is of no use to the organization. Consequently, after an order is placed with a supplier, the purchasing department often tries to match delivery of the goods with the company's need for the product. Other internal activities also must occur when the order is delivered. The goods must be received, inspected, paid for, and entered in the firm's inventory records. These activities represent additional costs that may not be readily apparent to the buying firm. Retailers have become very aggressive in asking vendors to cover these costs by charging sales organizations **slotting allowances,** fees for the privilege of having the retailer set up a new item in its IT system, program it into inventory, and ultimately distribute the item to the stores. Slotting allowances can cost manufacturers thousands of dollars per new item stocked.

Stage Seven: Performance Evaluation and Feedback

When the goods have been delivered, evaluation by the customer begins. This evaluation focuses on both the product and the supplier's service performance. This is a stage where follow-up by the salesperson is critically important. The goods are inspected to make sure they meet the specifications described in the purchase agreement. Later, users judge whether the purchased item performs according to expectations. The supplier's performance can also be evaluated on such criteria as promptness of delivery, quality of the product, and service after the sale.

In many organizations, this evaluation is a formal process, involving written reports from the user department and other persons involved in the purchase. The purchasing department keeps the information for use in evaluating proposals and selecting suppliers the next time a similar purchase is made. Chapter 8 provides tips for sellers on successful ways to follow up after a sale.

Types of Organizational Buying Situations

The steps just described apply largely to (1) a **new-task purchase,** where a customer is buying a relatively complex and expensive product or service for the first time (e.g., a new piece of production equipment or a new computer system), or (2) **modified rebuy** purchase decisions, where a customer wants to modify the product specs, prices, or other terms it has been receiving from existing suppliers and will consider dealing with new suppliers to make these changes if necessary.

At the other extreme is the **straight rebuy,** where a customer is reordering an item he or she has purchased many times (e.g., office supplies, bulk chemicals). Such a **repeat purchase** tends to be much more routine than the new-task purchase or the modified rebuy. Straight rebuys are often carried out by members of the purchasing department (buyers) with little influence from other members of the buying center, and many of the steps involved in searching for and evaluating alternative suppliers are dropped. Instead, the buyer may choose from among the suppliers on a preapproved list, giving weight to the company's past satisfaction with those suppliers and their products.

Purchasing departments are often organized hierarchically based on these different buying situations. For example, at Wal-Mart's buying office, new buyers begin as analysts and assistants, primarily monitoring straight rebuys. New-task purchases and modified rebuys that require more direct vendor contact are handled by more seasoned veterans.

Being an "in" (approved) supplier is a source of significant competitive advantage for a seller, and the process of relationship selling enhances such favored positions with current customers. For potential suppliers not on a buyer's approved vendor list, the selling problem can be difficult. The objective of an **out supplier** is to move the customer away from the automatic reordering procedures of a straight rebuy toward the more extensive evaluation processes of a modified rebuy.

Since, as we've seen, any member of a firm's buying center can identify and communicate the need to consider a change in suppliers, an out supplier might urge its salespeople to bypass the customer's purchasing department and call directly on users or technical personnel. The salesperson's goal is to convince users, influencers, and others that his or her products offer advantages on some important dimension—such as technical design, quality, performance, or cost—over the products the client is currently purchasing. Finding someone to play the role of initiator can be difficult, but it is possible if latent dissatisfaction exists.

Kamen Wiping Materials Co., Inc., in Wichita, Kansas, sells high-quality recycled cloth wiping rags to manufacturers. The business essentially consists of banks of huge industrial-size washing machines. Kamen buys soiled wiping cloths, cleans them, and then resells them to manufacturers in a variety of industries at prices much lower than paper or new cloth rags. CEO Leonard Goldstein is famous for getting Cessna, Beechcraft, and other heavy users of wiping materials to change wiping-cloth vendors (and even change from paper to cloth, which is a big switch) by scouting out who in the company can benefit the most from the change. This person then becomes the initiator. As with most organizational buying decisions, what benefits the company ultimately benefits the members of the buying center (especially the purchasing agent). If buying from Kamen makes certain members of the buying center look like heroes for saving money or being environmentally friendly, Leonard Goldstein knows he has a great chance of getting the sale—and keeping the customer.

CRM: Managing the Information for Relationship Selling

As you have seen, a common theme in this chapter is the importance of information as a driver of sales success. Technology provides the tools to gather, analyze, and use the information to sell to clients more effectively. Years ago, salespeople kept written notes and records on each sales call. At the end of each day they had to summarize these notes into reports sent by snail mail to management. These reports formed their firm's client information base. Today, it's hard to imagine how cumbersome and time consuming the process was! Fortunately for today's salespeople, information gathering is now quite systematic in many firms. A popular term for the overall process is **customer relationship management (CRM).** Sales jobs have been greatly enhanced by CRM and its enabling technology, as CRM provides a systematic way to manage the information needed to do successful relationship selling.

CRM is a comprehensive business model for increasing revenues and profits by focusing on customers. More specifically, CRM refers to "any application or initiative designed to help your company optimize interactions with customers, suppliers, or prospects via one or more touchpoints—such as a call center, salesperson, distributor, store, branch office, Web site, or e-mail—for the purpose of acquiring, retaining, or cross-selling customers."[24] Thus, **touchpoints** represent various means by which a firm has contact with its customers. Clearly, an interaction of a professional salesperson and his or her customer is one of the most important (if not *the* most important) touchpoints.

PricewaterhouseCoopers Consulting defines CRM as "a journey of strategic, process, organizational, and technical change whereby a company seeks to better manage its enterprise around customer behaviors. This entails acquiring knowledge about customers and deploying this information at each touchpoint to attain increased revenue and operational efficiencies."[25] CRM has three major objectives:

1. *Customer retention.* The ability to retain loyal and profitable customers and channels to grow the business profitably.
2. *Customer acquisition.* Acquisition of the right customers, based on known or learned characteristics, focused on driving growth and increasing margins.
3. *Customer profitability.* Increasing individual customer margins, while offering the right products at the right time.[26]

CRM Enhances Relationship Selling

CRM greatly enhances the process of securing, building, and maintaining long-term relationships with profitable customers—which of course is our definition of relationship selling and is the overarching theme of this book. Well-executed CRM offers several advantages to relationship sellers.

- CRM makes it easier to target specific customers by focusing on their needs.
- It helps organizations compete for customers based on service, not price.
- It reduces overspending on low-value clients and underspending on high-value ones.
- It improves use of the customer channel, thus making the most of each contact with a customer.[27]

CRM Is a Philosophy and a Technology

It is important to understand that CRM is both an overarching business philosophy that puts the customer at the center of strategic decision making (the customer-centric enterprise we discussed in Chapter 1) and a programmatic, integrated implementation system (technology/software-driven) involving a variety of channels and providers, all of which interact to contribute to the delivery of customer value.

Today, companies are adopting CRM as a mission-critical business strategy. They are redesigning internal and external business processes and associated information systems to make it easier for customers to do business with them. Because CRM focuses on aligning the organization's internal and external systems to be customer-centric, the sales force becomes a core contributor to the success of CRM by virtue of its expertise on customers and relationships.

Many of the concepts underlying CRM are not at all new. You could open a principles of marketing textbook from 20 years ago and find many of the elements of what we now refer to as CRM, but without the CRM label. What has changed in the environment to allow for modern CRM's integrated approach to customers is *technology.* Sophisticated approaches to data management are key to CRM, yet it is a serious mistake to consider CRM merely software. In fact, many firms are struggling with their CRM initiatives precisely because they have bought the sophisticated software but do not have the culture, structure, leadership, or internal technical expertise to make the initiative successful.

EXHIBIT 2.9 Process Cycle for CRM

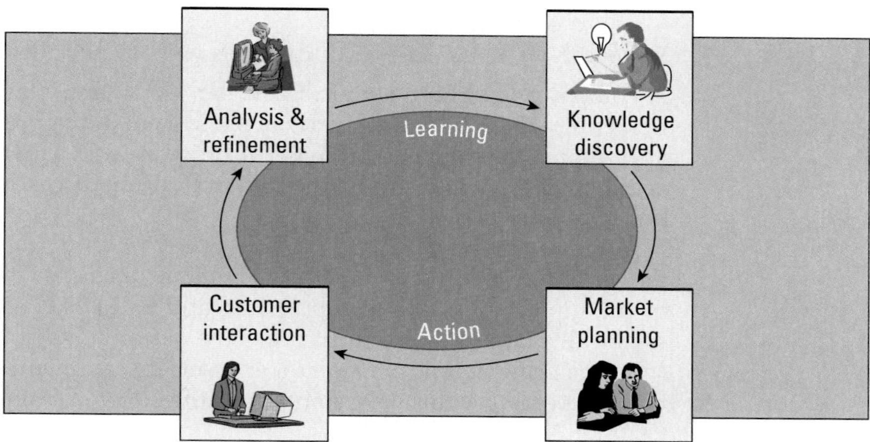

Source: Ronald S.Swift, *Accelerating Customer Relationships: Using CRM and Relationship Technologies*, © 2001. Reprinted by permission of Pearson Education, Inc., Upper Saddle River, NJ.

Process Cycle for CRM

CRM is best thought of as a process cycle, which can be broken down into four elements: (1) knowledge discovery, (2) market planning, (3) customer interaction, and (4) analysis and refinement.[28] They are portrayed in Exhibit 2.9 and discussed next.

Knowledge Discovery. The process of analyzing the customer information acquired through the touchpoints mentioned earlier is called knowledge discovery. These touchpoints might include point-of-sale systems, call center files, Internet accesses, records from direct sales, and any other customer contact experiences. A comprehensive, customer-centric **data warehouse** is the optimal approach to handling the data and transforming it into useful information for developing customer-focused strategies and programs. In a data warehouse environment, marketers combine large amounts of information and then use **data mining** techniques to learn more about current and potential customers. Many software products are available to help manage the knowledge discovery phase.

Market Planning. Customer strategies and programs are developed in market planning, a key use of the output of the knowledge discovery phase. This planning involves the use of the marketing mix, especially the promotion mix, in integrated ways.

Customer Interaction. The customer interaction phase is where the customer strategies and programs are implemented. It includes the personal selling effort, as well as all other customer-directed interactions aimed at any customer touchpoints (channels of customer contact) both in person and electronically.

Analysis and Refinement. Finally, the analysis and refinement phase of the CRM process is where learning takes place based on customer response to the implemented strategies and programs. This *continuous* dialogue with customers is facilitated by all of the inputs for customer feedback. Over time, adjustments made to the firm's overall customer initiatives based on ongoing feedback should yield more and more efficient investment of company resources in securing, building, and maintaining long-term relationships with profitable customers.

Bottom Line: CRM Is Essential to Sales Success

A company's commitment to CRM can go a long way toward successful relationship selling, because it provides a systematic approach to information management. Each element of the CRM process cycle shown in Exhibit 2.9 involves salespeople because they are the most important direct link to customers. They are key touchpoints.

Later as you read Part Two of the book, you will gain an appreciation for the power of information to drive the five elements in the "relationship selling" circle of the model for Relationship Selling and Sales Management—prospecting and sales call planning, communicating the sales message, negotiating for win–win solutions, closing and follow-up, and self-management. Each is critically important to creating value and communicating it to customers. Value is the topic of Chapter 3.

Summary

Relationship selling is a great career path that can also lead to significant upward mobility. Relationship selling bears no resemblance to the stereotyped view of old-style selling. Sales jobs today offer autonomy, variety, excellent rewards, favorable working conditions, and the opportunity for promotion.

The key success factors needed in relationship selling all point to professionalism, strong skills, and broad and deep content knowledge that allow the salesperson to maximize his or her performance (and thus rewards). Quite a few new sales activities have been added in recent years, driven largely by technology and the move from transactional to relationship selling. Understanding the types of selling jobs available will help you decide whether and where to enter the selling profession.

Because customers are the primary focus of relationship sellers, gaining knowledge about the world of organizational buying greatly enhances the effectiveness of a salesperson in his or her role as a customer relationship manager. Many people in a client firm may influence the buyer–seller relationship and the decision of what to buy, and salespeople must study their customers carefully to learn what dynamics are at play within each buying center situation. Selling firms often form selling centers and initiate team selling to better serve buying centers, especially with large and complex customers (key accounts). Of course, salespeople need to fully understand and appreciate the stages of the buying decision process that their customers go through so they can work to add value throughout the purchasing process. Different organizational buying decision situations require different communication between buyer and seller, and the seller must know enough about the nature of each purchase to manage the process properly.

Overall, the more expertise a salesperson has about how his or her own organization operates and how the customer's firm operates, the more likely the salesperson will be able to sell solutions for the customer and add value to both organizations. Effective management of the information needed to accomplish these desired outcomes is critical to the success of any salesperson. CRM provides a systematic process for such information management.

Key Terms

intrinsic rewards
extrinsic rewards
work/family conflict
telecommuting
virtual office
adaptive selling
job enlargement
average cost of a sales call
retail selling
business-to-consumer (B2C) market
business-to-business (B2B) market
industrial selling
buying center
perceived risk
selling center
team selling
matrix organization
key account
derived demand
single-source suppliers
slotting allowances
new-task purchase
modified rebuy
straight rebuy
repeat purchase
out supplier
customer relationship management (CRM)
touchpoints
data warehouse
data mining

Role Play

Before You Begin

Before getting started, please go to the Appendix of Chapter 1 to review the profiles of the characters involved in this role play, as well as the tips on preparing a role play.

Characters Involved

Bonnie Cairns

Rhonda Reed

Setting the Stage

Bonnie Cairns has now been on the job for four weeks, two of which have been in the field beginning to call on her buyers (mostly with the help of Rhonda Reed, her sales manager). The past week or so, she has begun to feel a lot more comfortable in her new position. Rhonda told her yesterday that in about a week she plans to begin doing some campus recruiting at Stellar College, from which Bonnie graduated last year, to look for potential candidates to interview for the open Territory 106. She mentioned that she would like Bonnie, as the newest member of the District 100 sales team, to join her to help tell graduates why careers in relationship selling can be great. The goal is to attract good students to interview for the vacant Upland Company sales territory. Bonnie and Rhonda are meeting for breakfast in a few minutes to discuss this.

Bonnie Cairns's Role

Bonnie has never done any recruiting before, and at age 23 she is only a year older than most of the students she will talk to during the campus visit. She needs to find out what to tell them to convince them that the old stereotypes of selling are not true in professional relationship-selling situations. She wants to use this meeting to get Rhonda to give her ideas on how to "sell" top students on considering a career with Upland.

Rhonda Reed's Role

Rhonda comes to the breakfast meeting to give Bonnie some ideas on how to present relationship-selling careers with Upland Company to students at the Stellar

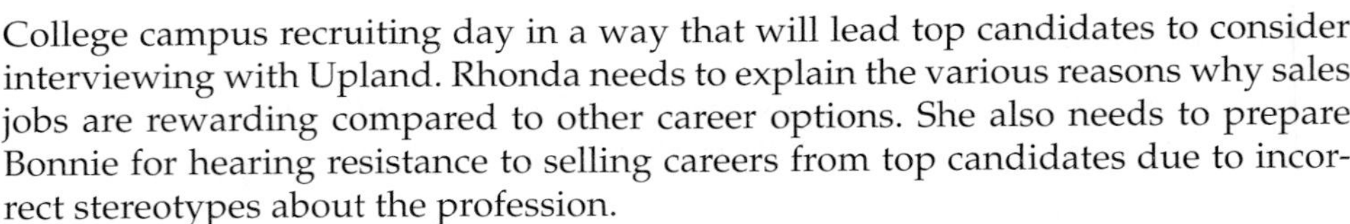

College campus recruiting day in a way that will lead top candidates to consider interviewing with Upland. Rhonda needs to explain the various reasons why sales jobs are rewarding compared to other career options. She also needs to prepare Bonnie for hearing resistance to selling careers from top candidates due to incorrect stereotypes about the profession.

Assignment

Work with another student to develop a five- to seven-minute dialogue on these issues. Be certain to cover both the stereotypical "bad" and the good of relationship-selling careers. Be sure Bonnie is prepared to both convey the many rewarding aspects of relationship selling and to deal with questions about the stereotypes.

Discussion Questions

1. It is often said that successful salespeople today must be "nimble." What does it mean to be nimble as a salesperson and as a sales organization?

2. Take a piece of paper and draw a line down the middle. Write "Pros" on the top left and "Cons" on the top right. Now, from your own perspective, come up with as many issues as you can on both sides regarding relationship selling as a career choice for you. Be sure to note *why* you list each item as you do.

3. Creativity is important to sales success. What is creativity? Give specific examples of several things you have done that you think are especially creative. How might creativity be taught to salespeople?

4. Telecommuting and using a virtual office are major aspects of many professional sales positions. How do you feel about telecommuting and virtual offices? What aspects of them are you most and least attracted to?

5. What aspects of sales jobs do you believe provide a strong foundation for moving up in an organization?

6. Review the top 20 key success factors for relationship selling as listed in Exhibit 2.3. Which of these factors are currently *your* strongest points? Which need the most work? How do you plan to capitalize on your strengths and improve on your weaknesses?

7. Pick the three selling activities presented in Exhibits 2.4 and 2.5 that you would *most* like to perform. Then pick the three you would *least* like to perform. Explain the rationale for your choices.

8. This chapter outlines the roles different members of a buying center play within an organizational buying context. Think of a purchase process you were involved in as an end-user consumer (not an organizational buyer). Can you list people who played these buying center roles in your purchase? Try to connect as many specific people to specific buying center roles as you can.

9. Explain the differences among a new-task purchase, modified rebuy, and straight rebuy. How will each situation alter the way a salesperson approaches a client?

10. How does CRM offer advantages to salespeople in terms of information management? What are some of the problems you could predict for salespeople in firms that do not use CRM?

Ethical Dilemma

Jennifer Lancaster found herself in an uncomfortable situation. Two years ago she graduated from college at the top of her class and took a sales job with Gracie Electronics. Although she had several offers and different career options, Jennifer felt a career in selling offered the best chance to apply her skills while doing something she enjoyed. After an extensive training period, she was given her own territory in Arizona with several large, established clients and great potential for new business.

Jennifer also began volunteering in an after-school program for high-risk teenagers. As part of Gracie Electronics' commitment to employees and local communities, the company supports employees' involvement with local charities and gives them time off to volunteer. Jennifer found her sales work very rewarding but was faced with a significant challenge: balancing the time commitment to her job with her volunteer work in this important nonprofit organization.

At first it was small changes to her schedule. She would choose to call customers from her cell phone on the way home in early afternoon instead of going to their office. Soon, however, her volunteer commitments represented a growing part of each day. She would take off entire afternoons and not report it to the company. She justified it by saying that she was helping needy teenagers and the company did support charity volunteer work. Moreover, she was still on target to hit her performance goals for the year.

Yesterday Jennifer was faced with a difficult choice. Her best customer, Dynamic Manufacturing Systems, asked her to visit its site in Flagstaff. The company is bringing in key suppliers to help plan a new site. This will probably mean a big new contract for Gracie Electronics. Jennifer told the client she would have to check her schedule before committing to the meeting. However, she had recently been named to the board of advisors of the nonprofit, and that day had been set aside for a strategic planning seminar to chart the direction of the organization for the next five years. She had already planned to take the day off. She knew the meeting with Dynamic Manufacturing was important but was seriously considering not going because of her other commitment.

Questions

1. What should Jennifer do?
2. As a salesperson, how would you balance the demands of a sales career with a personal life?
3. Can you identify some other challenges a person might face in balancing a sales career and personal life?

Mini Case

National Agri-Products Company

CASE 2

Sue Wilson, purchasing manager for the Humboldt, Tennessee, plant of National Agri-Products Company, is back in her office reviewing her notes from a meeting she just finished with Tom Roberts, Vicki Sievers, and Greg Runyon. Tom is the plant manager of the Humboldt plant, Vicki is the plant engineer, and Greg the production manager. The four met for the last hour to discuss the equipment National needs to buy to complete expansion of the Humboldt plant.

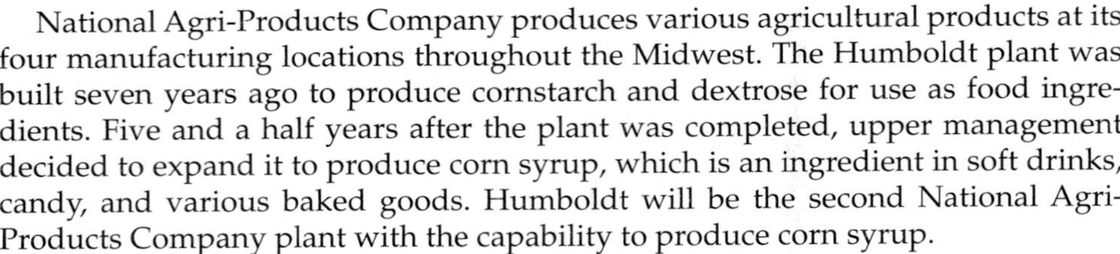

National Agri-Products Company produces various agricultural products at its four manufacturing locations throughout the Midwest. The Humboldt plant was built seven years ago to produce cornstarch and dextrose for use as food ingredients. Five and a half years after the plant was completed, upper management decided to expand it to produce corn syrup, which is an ingredient in soft drinks, candy, and various baked goods. Humboldt will be the second National Agri-Products Company plant with the capability to produce corn syrup.

As Sue reviews her notes, she notices that Tom, Vicki, and Greg have various requirements for the equipment that would be needed to produce the corn syrup. During the meeting, Tom said it was very important to "get everything right" in completing this project. The company already had invested a lot of money in the expansion, and Tom didn't want to risk that investment by installing equipment that would produce syrup inferior to National's standards. Tom said that although he expected to be consulted when needed, he thought Vicki and Greg could handle this assignment without his daily input.

Vicki knew that quality equipment would be needed to produce high-quality corn syrup. She wondered if the plant could meet the deadline National's home office had given of producing corn syrup in six months. Vicki said she was already working on equipment specifications and she would get them to Sue as soon as possible. Greg's main concern was producing the corn syrup efficiently and making sure his maintenance people could "keep the stuff running." Both Vicki and Greg asked Sue to let them know when she had more information about potential suppliers.

After reviewing these notes, Sue knew this was going to be a big job. She has no direct experience buying equipment to produce this type of product line. She decided to call Vijay Sethi, National's VP of purchasing, to discuss a few options. Vijay reminded Sue that National's policy is to get three bids on purchases of this amount and suggested that she start with the storage tanks and tubing since they are the most time-consuming items to fabricate. Vijay also gave Sue the number of Larry McDermott, a salesperson for New Products Steel Company, as a potential supplier. Finally, Vijay asked Sue to keep him up to date on progress, as this was the most expensive expansion project the company was undertaking this year.

After talking with Vijay, Sue decided to call Larry McDermott.

LARRY: "Larry McDermott, New Products Steel. May I help you?"

SUE: "Larry, this is Sue Wilson at the Humboldt, Tennessee, plant of National Agri-Products Company. Vijay Sethi gave me your name as a potential bidder on the stainless-steel tanks and tubing we are installing for our new corn syrup product line."

LARRY: "I'll certainly be glad to help you out with that, Sue. As you may know, we provided similar equipment for your Hawarden, Iowa, plant when they added the corn syrup line there. We worked with Jim Fisher in Hawarden."

SUE: "I didn't know that but I'll certainly give Jim a call. Anyway, our plant engineer will have specs on the equipment available early next week. When can you come in to go over them?"

LARRY: "Next Wednesday around 2:00 looks good to me. How does that sound?"

SUE: "Great. I'll get our team assembled here and we'll look forward to meeting you next Wednesday."

Questions

1. Who are the various members of the buying center that Larry should take time to get to know? What role or roles within the buying center is each person filling?
2. What are the primary *needs* of each member of the buying center? How much influence do you expect each member of the buying center will have on the final decision?
3. Discuss the buying process being followed by National Agri-Products Company. How does this buying process differ from that discussed in the chapter? At what stage of the buying process is it most beneficial for Larry to get involved?

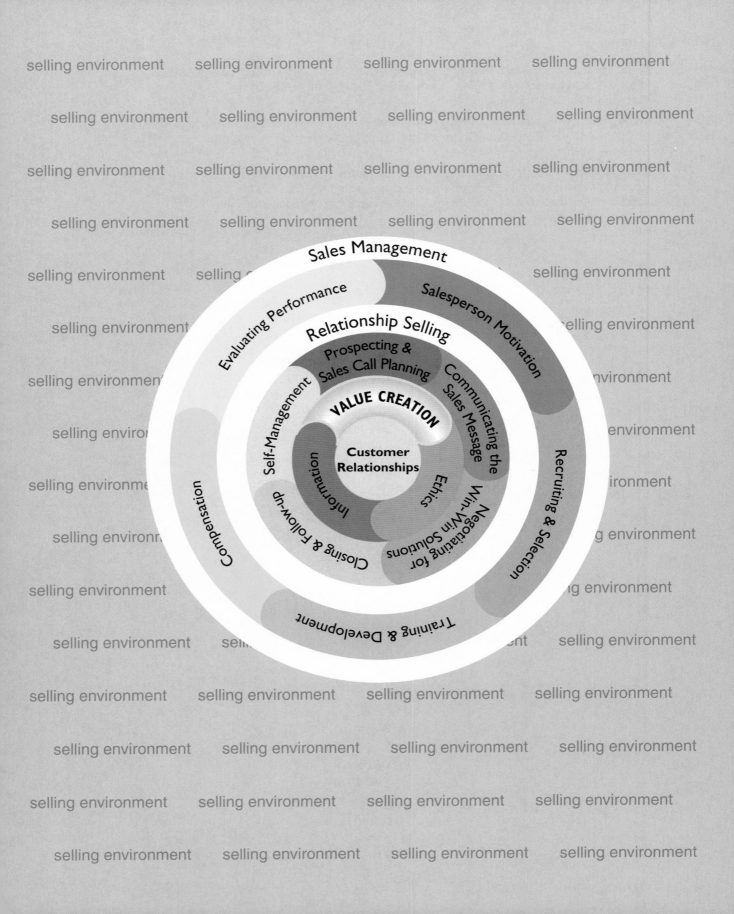

selling environment

Sales Management

Evaluating Performance

Salesperson Motivation

Recruiting & Selection

Training & Development

Compensation

Relationship Selling

Prospecting & Sales Call Planning

Communicating the Sales Message

Negotiating for Win-Win Solutions

Closing & Follow-up

Self-Management

VALUE CREATION

Information

Ethics

Customer Relationships

3 chapter

Value Creation in Buyer–Seller Relationships

Learning Objectives

This chapter focuses on one of the most important concepts in relationship selling: value. Value-added selling sums up much of what securing, building, and maintaining customer relationships is all about. Taking advantage of the opportunity to really understand value and value creation will help you immensely as you move into the selling process chapters in Part Two of the book. After reading this chapter, you should be able to

- Understand the concept of perceived value and its importance in relationship selling.
- Explain the relationship of the roles of selling and marketing within a firm.
- Explain why customer loyalty is so critical to business success.
- Recognize and discuss the value chain.
- Identify and give examples for each category of communicating value in the sales message.
- Understand how to manage customer expectations.

expert advice

Expert: Nat Martin, III

Company: Director, Purchasing and Concept Support, Darden Restaurants, Inc

Business: Operators of Bahama Breeze, Longhorn Steakhouse, Olive Garden, Red Lobster, Seasons 52, and The Capital Grill.

Education: MBA, Rollins College; BA in Law and Society, Purdue University.

In your mind, what is value?

Value is the perceived experience and worth gained from a product or service—*worth* meaning the quality of something that makes it desirable, useful, or valuable. If the value exceeds expectation the customer is highly satisfied. If the value meets expectation the customer is satisfied. If the value falls short of expectation the customer is dissatisfied. The level of the satisfaction experience directly correlates to the prospect of the customer repurchasing the product or service.

When you think of the importance of adding value to the customer, what does that mean to you?

Adding Value to the customer means providing him or her with a product or service (holistically the *relationship experience*) that exceeds the worth expectations. If the customer purchased a tangible product, then the product features and benefits can be enhanced by the relationship experience during the purchase process (resulting in exceeded expectations and higher worth). Of course, the same is true of a service purchase, which can be enhanced when the relationship experience exceeds customers' worth expectancy.

What are some of the most important things suppliers that call on Darden do to add value to your organization?

A vendor truly begins to add value to the Darden enterprise when attitude, commitment (consistency), and organizational relationship building are demonstrated and recognized. When all three behaviors come together a vendor moves from a purely transactional relationship to a strategic partnering relationship.

From your experience, what creates loyalty to one supplier over another? That is, what can a vendor do to keep a client's business over the long run?

The following are critical elements for a supplier to win loyalty from their customers—true "keys to supplier sustainability":

1. Know what's important to the customer.
2. Exhibit a partnering attitude.
3. Invest in organizational relationship building.
4. Commit to continual investment in quality and innovation.
5. Support the initiatives of the client's enterprise.
6. Work proactively with the client in contingency planning.

Adding Value Is "Marketing 101"

In Chapter 1 we defined value as the net bundle of benefits the customer derives from the product you are selling. The salesperson and the firm's other forms of marketing communication ensure the customer perceives these benefits as the value proposition. In transactional selling, the goal is to strip costs and get to the lowest possible sales price. Relationship selling works to add value through all possible means.

Value-added selling changes much of the sales process. As you will see in this chapter, the sources of value (or more properly **perceived value,** meaning that whether or not something has value is in the eyes of the beholder—the *customer*) are varied. Moving to more value-added approaches to selling is not easy, and selling value is the single biggest challenge faced by sales professionals.[1]

Why a chapter focused solely on value? Two simple reasons: (1) The evidence is clear that success in securing, building, and maintaining long-term relationships with profitable customers depends greatly on those customers perceiving that they receive high value from the relationship, and (2) many salespeople have trouble making the shift from selling price to selling value. As you can see from the model for Relationship Selling and Sales Management, value creation is one of only two issues closest to the customer core. This is appropriate, because creating and communicating value are central to success in selling in the 21st century.

Role of Selling in Marketing

A good place to start understanding the role of value is with a brief review of marketing and the role of selling within marketing. For years, introductory marketing textbooks have talked about the **marketing concept** as an overarching business philosophy. Companies practicing the marketing concept turn to customers themselves for input in making strategic decisions about what products to market, where to market them and how to get them to market, at what price, and how to communicate with customers about the products. These **4 Ps of marketing** (product, place or distribution, price, and promotion) are also known as the **marketing mix.** They are the tool kit marketers use to develop marketing strategy.

Personal selling fits into the marketing mix as part of a firm's **promotion mix,** or **marketing communications mix,** along with *advertising* and other elements of the promotional message the firm uses to communicate the value proposition to customers. Other available promotional vehicles are *sales promotion,* including coupons, contests, premiums, and other means of supporting the personal selling and advertising initiatives; *public relations and publicity,* in which messages about your company and products appear in news stories, television interviews, and the like; and *direct marketing,* which might include direct mail, telemarketing, electronic marketing (via Web site or e-mail), and other direct means.[2]

These elements of marketing communications are referred to as a "mix" to emphasize that when developing a strategy and budget for marketing communications, companies must decide how to allocate funds among the various promotional elements.

Several factors may affect the marketing communications mix, as shown in Exhibit 3.1. The number and dispersion of buyers, how much information they need, the size and importance of the purchase, the distribution process, the complexity of the product, and whether postpurchase contact is required all drive decisions about the marketing communications mix.[3]

EXHIBIT 3.1 Factors Affecting the Marketing Communications Mix

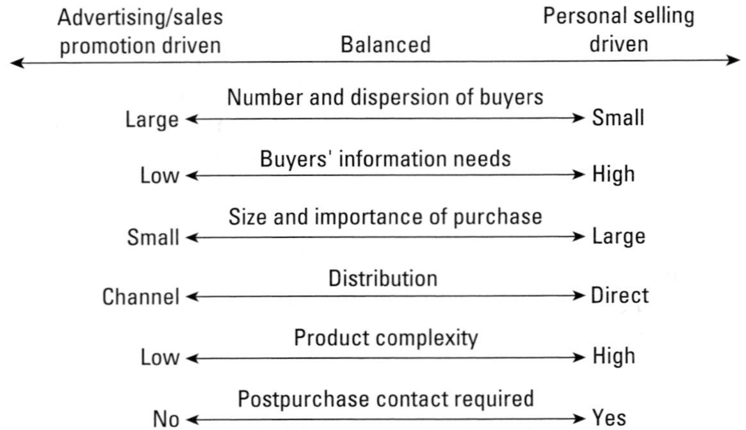

Source: David W. Cravens and Nigel F. Piercy, *Strategic Marketing,* 7th ed. (New York: McGraw-Hill, 2003) pp. 408–09. Reprinted by permission of the McGraw-Hill Companies.

To ensure that the message about a company and its products is consistent, the firm must practice **integrated marketing communications (IMC),** as opposed to fragmented (uncoordinated) advertising, publicity, and sales programs. IMC is very important to relationship selling, as it keeps the message about the value proposition consistent. Key characteristics of effective IMC programs are:

1. IMC programs are *comprehensive.* All elements of the marketing communications mix are considered.
2. IMC programs are *unified.* The messages delivered by all media, including important communications among **internal customers** (people within your firm who may not have external customer contact but who nonetheless add value that will ultimately benefit external customers) are the same or support a unified theme.
3. IMC programs are *targeted.* The various elements of the marketing communications mix employed all have the same or related targets for the message.
4. IMC programs have *coordinated execution* of all the communications components of the organization.
5. IMC programs emphasize *productivity* in reaching the designated targets when selecting communication channels and allocating resources to marketing media.[4]

Dell Computer has been very successful at IMC, in both B2B and B2C markets. Internally, all employees behave as though they have customers. That is, various departments within Dell practice relationship selling among each other. Good **internal marketing** provides a consistency of message among employees and shows that management is unified in supporting Dell's key strategic theme of adding value through a high level of product and service quality. Externally, Dell uses all the elements of the marketing communications mix—advertising, personal selling, sales promotion, public relations/publicity, and various methods of direct marketing. Dell is careful to communicate its value proposition consistently via each element of the mix.

Role of Marketing in Selling

You just saw that personal selling is one important element in the overall marketing communications mix. But how does marketing affect selling? As we discussed, the marketing communications mix (or promotion mix) is one element of the overall marketing mix that a firm uses to develop programs to market its products successfully. Products may be physical goods or services. Some firms market primarily services (such as insurance companies), while others market both goods and accompanying services (such as restaurants).

The marketing mix consists of the famous 4Ps of marketing: product, place (for distribution, or getting the product into the hands of the customer), price, and promotion (marketing communications). Like the elements of the marketing communications mix, each element of the marketing mix plays a large part in forming and communicating the overall bundle of benefits that a customer ultimately will perceive as the value proposition. This is why salespeople benefit from a well-executed marketing mix strategy.

Another important way that marketing contributes to successful relationship selling is through systems that provide needed information for the sales process. In Chapter 2 you learned about CRM, and that discussion provides a framework for understanding marketing's role in managing the acquisition, analysis, retention, and dissemination of customer and market information needed by salespeople.

Clarifying the Concept of Value

Clearly, both personal selling (in its role in the marketing communications mix) and marketing (in its contribution to the salesperson's ability to convey the value proposition) are integral to creating and communicating value for customers. Nowadays, the lines between the functions of selling and marketing are blurring, as exemplified in the opening vignette to this chapter. Especially when cross-functional teams are used to manage customer relationships, marketers (as well as others in the organization, often including top executives) engage directly with customers. Likewise, in successful relationship selling, salespeople effectively convey the value proposition to customers, which means communicating and demonstrating a whole host of value-creating factors associated with the products and the company.

Later in the chapter we will discuss ways value can be created by a firm and communicated by its salespeople. First, however, let's clarify a few issues related to value.

Value Is Related to Customer Benefits

Value may be thought of as a ratio of benefits to costs. That is, customers "invest" a variety of costs into doing business with you, including financial (the product's price), time, and human resources (the members of the buying center and supporting groups). The customers achieve a certain bundle of benefits in return for these investments.

One way to think about customer benefits is in terms of the utilities they provide the customer. **Utility** is the want-satisfying power of a good or service. There are four major kinds of utility: form, place, time, and ownership. *Form utility* is created when the firm converts raw materials into finished products that are desired by the market. *Place, time,* and *ownership utilities* are created by marketing. They are created when products are available to customers at a convenient location, when they want to purchase them, and facilities of exchange allow for transfer of the product ownership from seller to buyer. The seller can increase the value of the customer offering in several ways.

- Raise benefits.
- Reduce costs.
- Raise benefits and reduce costs.
- Raise benefits by more than the increase in costs.
- Lower benefits by less than the reduction in costs.[5]

Suppose you are shopping for a car and trying to choose between two models. Your decision to purchase will be greatly influenced by the ratio of costs (not just monetary) versus benefits for each model. It is not just pure price that drives your decision. It is price compared with all the various benefits (or utilities) that Car #1 brings to you versus Car #2.

Similarly, the value proposition a salesperson communicates to customers includes the whole bundle of benefits the company promises to deliver, not just the benefits of the product itself. For example, Dell Computer certainly communicates the customization and bundling capabilities of its PCs to buyers. However, Dell is also careful to always communicate outstanding service after the sale, quick and easy access to their Web site, and myriad other benefits the company offers buyers. Clearly, perceived value is directly related to those benefits derived from the purchase that satisfy specific customer needs and wants.

For years, firms have been obsessed with measuring **customer satisfaction,** which at its most fundamental level means how much the customer likes the product, service, and relationship. However, satisfying your customers is not enough to ensure the relationship is going to last. In relationship-driven selling, your value proposition must be strong enough to move customers past mere satisfaction and into a commitment to you and your products for the long run—a high level of **customer loyalty.** Loyal customers have lots of reasons why they don't want to switch from you to another vendor. Those reasons almost always are directly related to the various sources of value the customer derives from doing business with you.

Loyal customers, by definition, experience a high level of satisfaction. But not all satisfied customers are loyal. If your competitor comes along with a better value proposition than yours, or if your value proposition begins to slip or is not communicated effectively, customers who are satisfied now quickly become good candidates for switching to another vendor. The reason relationship selling is so crucial to building loyalty is that its win–win nature bonds customer and supplier together and minimizes compelling reasons to split apart. Innovation 3.1 provides insights on how customers have changed in recent years and ways salespeople can foster loyalty with today's customers.

The Value Chain

A famous approach to understanding the delivery of value and satisfaction is the **value chain,** envisioned by Michael Porter of Harvard to identify ways to create more customer value within a selling firm.[6] Exhibit 3.2 portrays the generic value chain. Basically, the concept holds that every organization represents a

INNOVATION 3.1

Customer Loyalty Is Crucial to Business Success

There's a neighborhood hardware store where they never have promotional sales. They don't offer frequent-buyer cards, easy credit terms, or free coffee and doughnuts on Saturday mornings. The shelves are dusty, the parking is terrible, and the salespeople are crotchety. In fact, they seem to violate most of the rules of good customer service. They're nosy. They argue with customers. If a customer is thinking about buying something that is the wrong item for what he or she wants to accomplish, they'll actively voice an alternative opinion.

The store has been at the same location for close to 50 years and it still does a terrific business. There are plenty of other places to buy hardware—the "big box" stores for example—with wider selection and lower prices. So what keeps people coming to this one? It's those crotchety, opinionated salespeople.

These days, many salespeople are polite, efficient and helpful-and utterly anonymous. It's not their fault; they've been trained that way. They sell from a script and never take a chance. You might as well be talking to a robot.

Not so at the corner hardware store. For better or for worse, as a customer you never walk away from the counter without feeling that you've just engaged in a deeply human interaction. Sometimes it's amusing and sometimes it's a little annoying. But in the end, customers keep coming back because they feel somehow connected to the store and its salespeople. It's an institution, and the neighborhood wouldn't be the same without them. *That's* customer loyalty!

Building Loyalty Lots of companies spend lots of money trying to unravel the secret of customer loyalty. They relentlessly measure customer satisfaction on every dimension imaginable: Was the service prompt? Was the salesperson helpful? Could anything have been done to make the buying experience better? The assumption is that most customers defect because they were dissatisfied in some way. So if you can keep customers satisfied, they'll stay loyal.

It turns out that assumption is often incorrect. Customers who say they're satisfied walk away all the time. In fact, a recent study from the Gallup Organization found that customer satisfaction, as it's traditionally measured, does nothing to boost repeat sales. The study found, for example, that "extremely satisfied" bank customers were just as likely to take their business elsewhere as less-satisfied customers. The same pattern emerged among customers of a major supermarket chain. The researchers concluded that customer satisfaction in-and-of-itself "has no real value—none at all." And what about all the money and energy that companies spend to measure and improve it? Wasted, they say.

Not convinced? Take a look at Lincoln-Mercury. According to the American Customer Satisfaction Index, it has the highest customer-satisfaction ratings in the industry-ahead of Honda, BMW, and Toyota. Yet in the past two years, Lincoln-Mercury sales have fallen by 26 percent.

Keeping It Real The Gallup researchers did find something important that is linked to repeat sales: *customer engagement*. That is, a customer's emotional connection with you, your product or service, your company. Think of it this way: Chances are, you're perfectly satisfied with the service you get from your local ATM. But you don't sing its praises to your friends. Or look forward to using it. And if you found another one a half block closer to your home, you wouldn't think twice about using it instead. Compare that with a human teller who smiles and greets you by name, asks about your kids, and chats about the weather while your checks are being processed. Same level of service—same degree of satisfaction—but a world of difference!

In a bigger organization, the equivalent personnel to the salespeople at the hardware store would probably get whisked off to a little room somewhere to get intensive training on selling skills. They'd be reminded to say, "Have a nice day." They'd learn how to meet explicit standards on various dimensions of customer service. If they couldn't get with the program, they'd be replaced-and six months later, some analyst would be wondering why sales had taken a nosedive.

Yes, the hardware clerks at the local store are quirky and cantankerous. But they know their stuff. They take pride in their work. And above all, they're real. That's what keeps customers coming back!

Source: Paul Cherry, "To Keep Buyers Coming Back, Don't Be Nice–Be Real," *American Salesman,* May 2008, p. 13.

synthesis of activities involved in designing, producing, marketing, delivering, and supporting its products. The value chain identifies nine strategic activities (five primary and four support activities) the organization can engage in that create both value and cost.

EXHIBIT 3.2 The Generic Value Chain

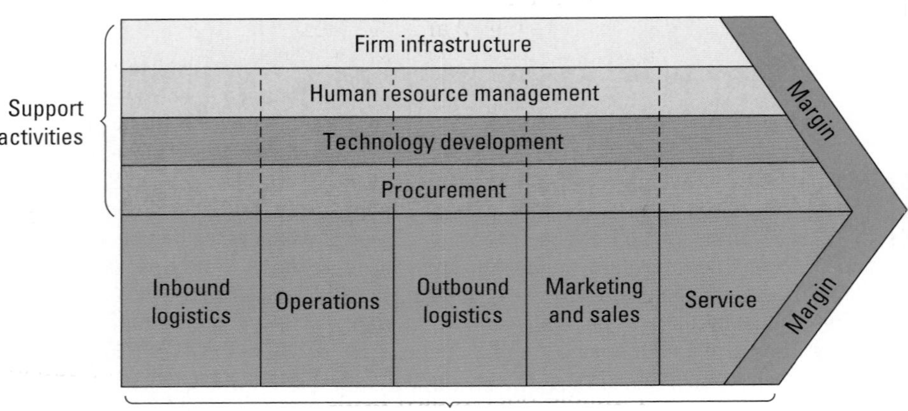

Source: Reprinted with permission of The Free Press, a Division of Simon & Schuster Adult Publishing Group, from *COMPETITIVE ADVANTAGE: Creating and Sustaining Superior Performance,* by Michael E. Porter.

The *primary activities* in the value chain are

- Inbound logistics—how the firm goes about sourcing raw materials for production.
- Operations—how the firm converts the raw materials into final products.
- Outbound logistics—how the firm transports and distributes the final products to the marketplace.
- Marketing and sales—how the firm communicates the value proposition to the marketplace.
- Service—how the firm supports customers during and after the sale.

The *support activities* in the value chain are

- Firm infrastructure—how the firm is set up for doing business. (Are the internal processes aligned and efficient?)
- Human resource management—how the firm ensures it has the right people in place, trains them, and keeps them.
- Technology development—how the firm embraces technology use to benefit customers.
- Procurement—how the firm deals with vendors and quality issues.

The value-chain concept is very useful for understanding the major activities that can create value at the organizational level. CEOs in recent years have been working hard to *align* the various elements of the value chain, meaning that all facets of the company work together to eliminate snags that may impair the firm's ability to secure, build, and maintain long-term relationships with profitable customers.

When the supplier's value chain is working well, all the customer tends to see are the *results:* quality products, on-time delivery, good people, and so on. If the value chain develops just one weak link, the whole process of relationship selling can be thrown off. For example, a glitch in the value chain of one of Wal-Mart's vendors can delay delivery, resulting in stockouts in Wal-Mart stores. If this happens repeatedly, it can damage the overall relationship. To reduce the potential for this happening, Wal-Mart (which is known as a leader in implementing the value chain) requires all vendors to link with its IT system so that the whole process of order fulfillment is seamless.

The Lifetime Value of a Customer

One element depicted in Exhibit 3.2 is **margin,** which of course refers to profit made by the firm. You may have noticed that we've been careful to say that the goal of relationship selling is to secure, build, and maintain long-term relationships with *profitable* customers. If this seems intuitively obvious to you, that's good. It should. In the past, many firms focused so much on customer satisfaction that they failed to realize that not every satisfied customer is actually a profitable one! Today, firms take great care to estimate the **lifetime value of a customer,** which is the present value of the stream of future profits expected over a customer's lifetime of purchases. They subtract from the expected revenues the expected costs of securing, building, and maintaining the customer relationship. Exhibit 3.3 provides a simple example of calculating the lifetime value of a customer.

Selling to this customer is a money-losing proposition in the long run. Firms should not attempt to retain such customers. The analysis raises the prospects of **firing a customer,** which is a rather harsh way to express the idea that the customer needs to find alternative sources or channels from which to secure the products he or she needs. Of course, this assumes that other, more attractive customers exist to replace the fired one.[7] Firms engaged in value-chain strategies who don't pay attention to margin usually don't stay in business long.

On the other hand, for profitable customers, increasing the **retention rate**—meaning keeping customers longer—by increasing loyalty can yield large increases in profits. This is because, as you can see from the calculations in Exhibit 3.3, it is much less costly to retain existing customers than it is to acquire new ones.

EXHIBIT 3.3 Calculating the Lifetime Value of a Customer

Estimated annual revenue from the customer	$ 15,000
Average number of loyal years for our customers	×5
Total customer revenue	75,000
Company profit margin	×10%
Lifetime customer profit	$ 7,500
Cost of securing a new customer	$ 3,500
Cost of developing and maintaining the customer (est. 6 calls per year @ $500 each)	3,000
Average number of loyal years for our customers	×5
Total selling cost	15,000
Estimated costs of advertising and promotion per customer (from marketing dept.)	500
Lifetime customer cost	$ 15,500
Lifetime value of the customer (lifetime profit – lifetime cost)	– $ 8,000

EXHIBIT 3.4 Impact of 5 Percent Increase in Retention Rate on Total Lifetime Profits from a Typical Customer

Industry	Percentage Increase in Profits
Advertising agency	95%
Life insurance company	90%
Branch bank deposits	85%
Publishing	85%
Auto service	81%
Auto/home insurance	80%
Credit card	75%
Industrial brokerage	50%
Industrial distribution	45%
Industrial laundry	45%
Office building management	40%

Source: Reprinted by permission of Harvard Business School Press. From *The Loyalty Effect* by Frederick Reichheld and Thomas Teal. Boston, MA. Copyright 2001 by the Harvard Business School Publishing Corporation, all rights reserved.

Exhibit 3.4 shows the potential impact of customer retention on total lifetime profits in different industries.

Quantifying the value proposition is an important element of relationship selling. At the end of this chapter is an appendix that provides an approach, in spreadsheet format, to quantitative analysis of a product and its value to a customer.

So far, we have looked at important issues of value creation from the perspective of the selling firm via the value-chain concept. In the next section, we identify specific value-creating factors the salesperson can communicate to the customer.

Communicating Value in the Sales Message

In Chapter 6 we will discuss the *process* of communicating the sales message. Now we want to turn our attention to one of the most important *content* issues in relationship selling: selling the value proposition. In Chapter 6 you will learn how to translate the idea of value into specific benefits to the buyer. Now we focus on 12 broad categories from which you can draw these benefits in order to practice value-added selling. Keep in mind that it is customers' *perceptions* of these factors that are relevant. For example, Toyota might have excellent product quality, but if this is not communicated to customers, they may not perceive it as excellent. The twelve categories for communicating value are:

1. Product quality.
2. Channel deliverables (supply chain).
3. Integrated marketing communications (IMC).
4. Synergy between sales and marketing.
5. Execution of marketing mix programs.
6. Quality of the buyer–seller relationship (trust).
7. Service quality.
8. Salesperson professionalism.

9. Brand equity.
10. Corporate image/reputation.
11. Application of technology.
12. Price.

Product Quality

David Garvin has identified eight critical dimensions of product quality that can add value.[8]

- *Performance.* A product's primary operating characteristics. For a car, these would be traits such as comfort, acceleration, safety, and handling.
- *Features.* Characteristics that supplement the basic performance or functional attributes of a product. For a washing machine, they might include four separate wash cycles.
- *Reliability.* The probability of a product malfunctioning or failing within a specified time period.
- *Conformance.* The degree to which a product's design and operating characteristics meet established standards of quality control (for example, how many pieces on an assembly line have to be reworked due to some problem with the output). Conformance is related to reliability.
- *Durability.* Basically, how long the product lasts and how much use the customer gets out of the product before it breaks down.
- *Serviceability.* Speed, courtesy, competence, and ease of repair for the product.
- *Aesthetics.* How the product looks, feels, sounds, tastes, or smells.
- *Perceived quality.* How accurately the customer's perceptions of the product's quality match its actual quality. In marketing, perception is reality.

Channel Deliverables (Supply Chain)

Firms that have excellent **supply-chain management** systems add a great deal of value for customers. A supply chain encompasses every element in the channel of distribution. FedEx is an organization that brings to its clients excellent supply-chain management as a key value proposition. FedEx salespeople, as well as FedEx's overall IMC, constantly communicate this attribute to the marketplace.

Integrated Marketing Communications (IMC)

We have already seen how important integration of the marketing message is in managing customer relationships. When Lou Gerstner, former CEO of IBM, took the job, one of the first things he noticed as he visited various IBM field operations was that the image, message, and even the logo of IBM varied greatly from market to market. Such variance is almost always due to poor IMC. IMC starts with a firm's people accepting its mission, vision, goals, and values. Then the message gets communicated through the internal value chain. Finally, it gets communicated to customers and other external stakeholders through the promotion mix. Clients expect and deserve consistency in the way your value-added message is put forth. With great IMC, salespeople can refer to a well-known message about their firm that is all around to solidify the client relationship.

Synergy between Sales and Marketing

An easy definition of *synergy* is that the whole is greater than the sum of its parts. Sales and marketing exhibit synergy when they are both working together for the greater benefit of customers. The whole concept of our model for Relationship Selling and Sales Management revolves around synergy—seamless organizational processes focused on managing customer relationships. When sales and marketing are out of sync, customers are marginalized and the value proposition is weakened. One way to ensure synergy is with cross-functional selling teams that include members of marketing in key roles.

A vivid example of creating value through synergy is the way Procter & Gamble develops its regular promotion schedule for its brands. Brand management works directly with field sales management to create a schedule and product mix for the promotions that best serve P&G's clients. Thus, when a salesperson presents a new promotion to a customer, he or she can sell the value of the thoughtful planning that took into account the customer's needs and wants in making P&G's promotional decisions.

Execution of Marketing Mix Programs

Firms that do a great job of integrating the marketing mix provide opportunities for value-added selling. Salespeople enjoy communicating with clients about their firm's plans for product changes, new-product development, and the like. And a history of a strong marketing mix program gives salespeople and the firm credibility that helps turn prospects into new customers. Customers have confidence that your firm will support its products through effective marketing mix programs.

Quality of the Buyer–Seller Relationship (Trust)

A key issue in relationship quality is trust. **Trust** is a belief by one party that the other party will fulfill its obligations in a relationship.[9] Obviously, building trust is essential to relationship selling. It represents confidence that a salesperson's word (and that of everyone at his or her company) can be believed. It signifies that the salesperson has the customer's long-term interests at the core of his or her approach to doing business. An atmosphere of trust in a relationship adds powerful value to the process.

Service Quality

Services are different from products. In particular, services exhibit these unique properties:

- *Intangibility.* Services cannot be seen, tasted, felt, heard, or smelled before they are bought.
- *Inseparability.* Unlike goods, services are typically produced and consumed simultaneously.
- *Variability.* The quality of services depends largely on who provides them and when and where they are provided.
- *Perishability.* Services cannot be stored for later use.

These unique properties of services create opportunities for firms to use them to add value to the firm's overall product offerings and for salespeople to communicate this value to customers. Leadership 3.2 provides some valuable insights on how a company can use proficiency in service to be a market leader.

Leadership 3.2

Being a Customer Service Leader

Despite all that has been written about customer service, TARP (an organization that researches the effectiveness of customer service) and the American Customer Satisfaction Index (which ties customer service to profitability) indicate a continual decline in customer service. So what's the problem? Doesn't anybody get it?

"Getting it" requires taking a serious look at how you treat customer service within your organization. Three important considerations are: (1) Customer service is a leadership issue, (2) customer service is a marketing issue, and (3) customer service must be connected to your organization's mission.

A leadership issue Customer service must be thought of as a leadership issue. Employees in their twenties or thirties have probably not experienced much in the way of good customer service. Reading about it, being told about it, even attending training sessions about it, are not the same as personally being on the receiving end of good customer service. So company leaders must make sure good customer service is modeled and rewarded. People grasp what they experience.

One of the leader's most important tasks is to establish an environment of trust. James Copeland, former CEO of Deloitte & Touche LLC, has pointed out that merely talking about trust does little good. "People have to understand that you shoot straight with them and if there's a problem, it has to be talked about honestly and not sugarcoated. If it's a hard solution, that's all right, but you have to deal with that in a way where people would say it reflects the trust they have put in you."

This trust philosophy relates directly to the recovery factor when a customer has been disappointed. Statistics show that when customers are told the truth about a problem and given honest answers and solutions, they not only remain customers but become more loyal. It is a leader's responsibility to model and reinforce this trust.

A marketing issue Customer service is also a marketing issue. It always has been, yet often it is treated as a separate issue. Marketing is, after all, everything you do to reach and keep customers. So any organization that commits to making customer service the focal point of its marketing strategy has an opportunity to add value and gain a great competitive advantage. Today, organizations that understand and deliver effective customer service stand out in customers' minds, especially when so many firms deliver poor customer service.

Start with your mission How do you determine what good customer service is for your organization? Begin with your mission statement. Developing an effective mission statement is a leadership issue. Too many organizations have unrealistic or public relations–oriented mission statements rather than well-developed, realistic, living mission statements. When your mission is genuine, succinctly written, and truly reflective of your organization's core values, it will serve as a valuable document from which to craft operating principles. Take the mission statement from the Ewing Marion Kauffman Foundation, for example: "To help individuals attain economic independence by advancing educational achievement and entrepreneurial success, consistent with the aspirations of our founder Ewing Marion Kauffman."

This mission is so clear it is easy to go into the core of it and define the "who, what, where, when, and how" of each integral part of the mission. As it relates to customer service, for example, when a client of the foundation is dealt with, it would be easy to go into the mission statement and ask, "Did I respond in a manner that will have a lasting impact and did I reinforce that we offer a choice and hope for the future?"

Your mission statement can also help you establish service standards that will be acceptable operating practices for all employees. If, for example, your mission statement says you are to "serve the needs of your members," what standards can be set to ensure you are meeting that part of your mission? What specifically will your employees be expected to do to ensure you are living your mission?

Reevaluating the appropriateness of your mission statement is a good place to start whether you are establishing new policies for delivering customer service or reviewing your current customer service practices.

Make your service standards clear, concise, observable, measurable, and realistic by checking to see if they are aligned with your mission. Once they are established, make sure everyone in your company understands the importance of operating by the standards and monitor them often.

Acknowledge employees who live by the standards and send a strong message to everyone in your organization that you are a leader who is serious about providing good customer service.

Source: Bette Price, "Being a Customer Service Leader," *American Salesman* 47 (October 2002), pp. 6–9. Reprinted by permission of © National Research Bureau, 320 Valley St., Burlington, Iowa 52601.

INNOVATION 3.3

Implementing Value-Adding Services

Value-adding services are everywhere. The dealership where you take your car for servicing now offers free loaner vehicles. The manufacturer of disposable contact lenses now gets them to you via second-day air. Even the theater company in your community has hopped on the bandwagon with a two-for-one deal.

Perhaps you have a few of these programs. Are they working in the way you intended them? Are they bringing in new customers? Helping you hold on to existing ones? Are they giving you a leg up over the competition and helping your salespeople demonstrate your added value? Or are they merely a pain to deliver, draining you of profits and causing complaints from customers who see them not as extras but as givens? To win value-conscious buyers, you need to lead the value-added services race in your industry—and make sure your leadership pays off on the bottom line.

Six Guidelines

Here are six guidelines to use in planning and implementing new services:

1. *Don't confuse your definition of value with that of your customers.* Adding the wrong value is easy to do. It happens all the time. A dangerous prescription might be: Just turn inward and become so involved with your internal processes you forget to ask the customer. The only thing worse than not doing anything to improve your Value Proposition is to move in a direction that takes value away. Instead of adding value, you end up adding something that isn't perceived as such by the customer. It's the leader's role to accurately interpret what the customer's needs are. This can be done through customer surveys, focus groups, and one-on-one interviews.
2. *Figure out what business you're really in.* Smart companies don't compete; they out-think and out-innovate the competition by adding unique value. To do this, you must know what business you're really in. When Merry Maids, the ServiceMaster division, thought through the customer's highest value, it became clear it wasn't clean houses, or more leisure time—it was peace of mind. "Sure, they are paying for the cleaning," says Mike Isakson, Merry Maids president. "But if a prized possession got broken or damaged or stolen, that negated everything." Take time to figure out what business you're in.
3. *Rethink your customer's "highest need."* It's easy to believe the services you assume are important to customers are in actuality not that important at all. As United Parcel Service (UPS) discovered, you can have too much of a good thing. UPS assumed that on-time delivery was the paramount concern of its customers. So the operative word became speed—and rushed drivers.

Because of the unique properties of services, it should not be too surprising that the dimensions of service quality are different from those for goods:

- *Reliability.* Providing service in a consistent, accurate, and dependable way.
- *Responsiveness.* Readiness and willingness to help customers and provide service.
- *Assurance.* Conveyance of trust and confidence that the company will back up the service with a guarantee.
- *Empathy.* Caring, individualized attention to customers.
- *Tangibles.* The physical appearance of the service provider's business, Web site, marketing communication materials, and the like.[10]

In relationship selling, these dimensions of service quality often provide added value for customers. Innovation 3.3 gives some useful examples of how a company can implement them in a value-adding way.

The problem was, UPS wasn't asking the right question. Only when UPS began asking broader questions about service improvement did it discover customers weren't as obsessed with speed as they were with more interaction with drivers. If drivers were less harried and more willing to chat, customers could get some practical advice on shipping. Result: UPS now allows its drivers an additional 30 minutes a day to spend, at their discretion, to strengthen ties with customers.

4. *Develop new ways to listen to your customers.* Norm Brinker, chairman of Brinker International, is one of the country's most respected restaurant gurus. Brinker avails himself of the latest data on changes in what restaurant customers value, but he also has an additional way of taking the pulse. He likes to pose as a confused tourist outside his own and other restaurants. He asks departing patrons if they were happy with their meal. He even visits competitors' restaurants, walking around as if he runs the place, stopping at tables to inquire about the food and service. "You have to listen to customers on an ongoing basis," Brinker says. What Brinker does is what every leader must do: Keep experimenting with new ways to find out what's on customers' minds.
5. *Brainstorm unusual ways to add value.* F.D. Titus & Sons, a City of Industry, California–based distributor of health care supplies and equipment, believes if you're going to develop effective value-adding services you have to first "get out of the box." Titus is referring to the crush of meetings, deadlines, emergencies and other distractions that keep managers from being as creative as possible, and then thoroughly thinking through an idea. Look for ideas you can borrow from other industries, other businesses that are successful in coming out with customer-pleasing programs.
6. *Figure out the lifespan of your proposed value-added service.* A contact lens maker proudly introduced speedier delivery with second-day air service. This gave the firm a big boost, but since then the innovation has been copied by other leading players in that industry.

Before you change or add a new service, anticipate which ones will provide an advantage, and how long you can count on having that advantage before competitors neutralize your service by coming out with one of their own. New services can be expensive initially. Often customers are slow to respond to them.

Creating and implementing value-adding services will sharpen all of your skills as a leader, your sense of where your industry is going and your ability to sell your vision to your people so that they can sell its value to customers.

Source: Robert B. Tucker, "Value Profitability," *American Salesman,* April 2006, p. 28.

Salesperson Professionalism

Your own level of professionalism in the way you handle yourself with customers is a great potential source of value to them. What is professionalism? It includes little things such as clear and concise correspondence, proper dress, good manners, and a positive attitude and can-do demeanor. Part Two of this book covers many aspects of how to exhibit professionalism as you go about relationship selling. For now, read Leadership 3.4 for a meaningful discussion of two of the most important aspects of professionalism in sales—personal values and integrity.

Brand Equity

Brand equity is the value inherent in a brand name in and of itself.[11] Brand equity is a bit like the concept of goodwill on the balance sheet, since if a company liquidated all its tangible assets, a great brand would still add terrific value to the firm. Examples of brands with high equity are Coke, IBM, McDonald's, and Dell.

Leadership 3.4

On the Value of Professionalism

Sales consultant Dave Kahle provides the following words of wisdom about the importance of personal values and integrity in sales.

His eyes were narrow and bloodshot from staying out late and partying too heavily the previous night. A two-day-old stubble framed his face. He was wearing a dark-colored T-shirt, which he hadn't tucked in, a pair of jeans, and scuffed loafers that had probably never seen shoe polish. It was the second day of my Sales Academy seminar, and this participant in the program was complaining to the group that his customers were only interested in low price.

I didn't say this, because I didn't want to embarrass him in front of the group, but I thought it nonetheless: "Do you think your appearance and demeanor have anything to do with your customers' reaction? Do you think that you may give them the idea that you are the lowest rung on the pricing scale? Is it possible that you have inadvertently positioned yourself as the Wal-Mart of the industry?"

I remember, as a child, having a salesperson call on my family. He had an appointment to discuss a correspondence course for one of us. He drove a big Lincoln, dressed richly, spoke articulately, and carried himself with confidence. It wasn't a coincidence that we bought his program without quibbling about the price.

These two scenarios illustrate a powerful and frequently overlooked best practice in the world of sales: Whether you intend to or not, you always create a position in the minds of your customers, and that position influences the customer's attitudes toward you as well as the buying decisions that follow. In other words, if you look like you're the low price, your customers will expect you to be the low price.

It follows, then, that if we are going to be an effective, professional salesperson, we ought to give thoughtful consideration to how we position ourselves in the minds of our customers.

Let's begin by understanding the idea of positioning a little deeper. *Positioning* has long been a term bandied about by advertising mavens and marketing gurus. They define it as the place that your brand or product has carved out in the mind of the customer. It's the pictures that enter the customers' mind when they think of your product, the feelings that your product evokes, the attitudes they associate with you, and the thoughts that they have of you.

Chances are, for example, that the words "Volkswagen Beetle" evoke a set of responses from you that are different than "Chevrolet Corvette." You expect a certain degree of quality, price, and service when you enter a Wal-Mart that is not the same as your expectations upon stepping inside a Saks Fifth Avenue store.

Billions of dollars are spent every year on carefully crafted impressions by businesses anxious to carve out a valuable position in the minds of their customers.

Alas, if only the same thing could be said of many salespeople.

Just like the carefully designed impressions by advertising mediums inexorably chisel a spot into our psyches, so do the repeated visits by a salesperson embed a set of expectations, pictures, and emotions into the minds of our customers. The position you, as a salesperson, occupy is a complex intertwining of the perception of your company, your solutions, and yourself. The most effective salespeople and sales organizations understand that, and consciously work to create a positive position in the minds of their customers.

Creating your position Let's begin at the end. A good starting point is to think deeply and with some detail about what sort of position you want to create. What, exactly, do you want your customers to think of you? Let me suggest two possibilities: the minimum acceptable position, and the ideal position.

At a minimum, I believe your customer should view you as a competent, trustworthy person who brings value to the customer. They believe that you generally know your products and their strengths and weaknesses, that you generally know the customer's issues, and that you can be reliably counted on to do what you say you will do. That's the least acceptable position to which you should work towards. If your customers don't think of you at least in this way, you probably should not be in sales.

At the other end of the spectrum is the ideal position. This builds on the minimum, but adds a specific understanding on the part of the customer of your unique combination of strengths and attributes. It evolves as you have history with the customer until you occupy a position that is totally and uniquely yours and that carries with it the expectation that your strengths in some specific and unique way add value to the time the customer spends with you. The ultimate test of the power of your position is the customer's willingness to see you and the resulting preference for doing business with you.

Here's an illustration. If you were shopping for an automobile, a low-mileage late model Taurus would probably provide you with competent, reliable transportation. So, when you think of that specific automobile, it would evoke a set of ideas in your mind all revolving around competent and reliable transportation. Now, think of a brand new Lamborghini and you would understand it to be transportation, but with a unique flair—something above and beyond just reliable transportation. That flair would be a result of the unique strengths of that particular automobile conveyed in a graphic way to your mind.

So it is with salespeople. You want to position yourself in your customer's mind the equivalent of the Taurus. But if you really want to carve out a unique, memorable position in your customer's mind, you'd want them to think of you as a Lamborghini.

The question then is, how do you want your customers to think of you? Once you articulate a specific picture, you can then start to build that position. Here are four essential steps to help you convey a positive position to your customers.

1. *Soberly assess yourself.* What sort of position are you currently occupying in the customer's mind? Be as objective as possible as you think through each of the issues listed below, and compare yourself to your competitors. How do you stand on your

   - Appearance
   - Product knowledge
   - Understanding of company policies and procedures
   - Competence with basic sales skills
   - Understanding of the customer
   - Bearing and demeanor.

   If you find that you rank below your competitors on any of these issues, then you need to spiff them up so that you are thought of, at least, as a Taurus. Then, you can begin to move toward the Lamborghini position.

2. *Start on the inside.* In my book, *10 Secrets of Time Management for Salespeople,* I propose that you "get grounded." That advice is based on the observation that it is difficult to sustain a false position. It is all a whole lot easier if you portray yourself to be who you are. Integrity, meaning consistency between who you are and who you present yourself to be, is a foundation to a positive position.

   In order to do that, you must clearly understand who you are. That means that you crystallize, in a written document, these three issues:

   - ***Your purpose.*** This really speaks to your spiritual orientation. Why are you here? What is your purpose in life and in this job? Why are you doing this anyway?
   - ***Your vision.*** What would you like to become? What do you see as possible and ideal in your job, your career, and in your life?
   - ***Your values.*** What are the highest priority items in your life and in your job? What are the people, ideas, behaviors and qualities of character that are most important to you?

   Once you have thought deeply about these internal issues, you'll find it much easier to live them. The process of articulating them and putting them on paper keeps you focused and attentive to the deeper issues.

Do a sober assessment of your strengths. If you are going to position yourself in the eyes of the customer as having some combination of uniqueness, you first have to identify what those unique strengths are. What are your personal unique attributes, experiences, and passions as it relates this job? Do you have some special experience? Do you have some unique capabilities? Do you have some unique relationships? Do you have some unusual characteristics? Identify those strengths on a piece of paper, and then add a line or two on how each of those can bring value to the customer.

At this point, you will have done the necessary homework to make the job of building a unique position much easier. You now know who you are and what strengths you can bring to your customers. Now comes the fun.

Continually seek opportunities to convey your brand. *Act in a way that is consistent with your statements of strengths.* For example, if you say that you are good with high tech, don't take notes on a scratch pad. Put them into a PDA. If you say you are personally attractive, don't forget to shave before you make a sales call. Be consistent—act like the person you claim to be.

Find ways to utilize your strengths and emphasize your uniqueness. In one of my sales positions, for example, recognizing that I had some unique talents in speaking to groups, I consistently found ways to organize seminars and workshops for my customers in which I presented to the group. I could have made individual sales calls to six customers, but I found that when I brought all six together in a group, I was more effective. It was just me utilizing my strengths.

Be creative. One of my strengths happened to be my wife, who is a gourmet cook, and extremely good with anything that even looks like food. We collaborated, and as Christmas gifts for my customers, she would make dozens of varieties of homemade cookies and candies, and I'd pack them uniquely for each customer. Within a year or two, everyone looked forward to my arriving with our annual Christmas present.

Develop a reputation by intention. Decide what you want to be known for, and then work to consistently make that happen. One salesperson makes sure, for example, that he doesn't call on a customer unless he has something to share with that customer which he believes that customer will find valuable. As a result, he has no problem getting time with his customers. He's developed the reputation of always bringing something of value.

If you want to be known as the most responsive salesperson, set up a system that allows you to respond to every phone call within an hour or two. If you want to be known as the fountain of product knowledge, make sure that you study every price list and piece of literature on every product you sell. If you want to be known as the specialist in some application, make sure that you know it inside and out.

Consider everything that you do. Question every single aspect of your interaction with the customer, and gradually shape every thing to match the position you want to gain. If you want your customer to think of you as confident and competent, don't drive a dirty 10-year-old car. If you want your customer to think of you as worth an extra couple percentage points in price, then don't come in wearing wrinkled Dockers and a dirty T-shirt. If you want to be known as intelligent and articulate, don't use slang.

Your position in the minds of the customer is a powerful and subtle component of an effective salesperson's approach. Consistently working at building a positive position will pay dividends for years.

Source: Dave Kahle, "Salespeople: Position Yourselves with Power," *American Salesman,* November 2007, p. 14.

In relationship selling, when all else is equal, your job is generally easier if you can sell the value of your brand.

An interesting twist on applying the concept of brand equity in relationship selling is selling yourself to clients. Innovation 3.5 provides insights on how you might brand yourself to help you manage customer relationships.

Corporate Image/Reputation

Closely related to brand equity is the concept of how corporate image or reputation adds value. Some firms that have financial difficulties continue to gain new clients and build business simply based on their reputation. On the other hand, the perils of losing and then trying to regain company reputation are well documented. Enron, WorldCom, and Arthur Andersen have all faced challenges in regaining reputation in the last several years. Selling for an organization with a strong, positive image provides a leg up on competition, and the confidence that image brings to clients can overcome many other issues in making a sale.

Application of Technology

Some firms add substantial value to customer relationships through technology. Fortunately for the salesperson, communicating this value-adding dimension is usually quite straightforward. Pharmaceutical companies like Pfizer and Merck have developed sophisticated software for specific clients. Such activity goes beyond mere relationship selling into the realm of **strategic partnerships,** which are more formalized relationships where companies share assets for mutual advantage.[12]

Price

Now we are back to where we started in this chapter: price. As we said, many salespeople have difficulty transitioning from selling price to selling value. You may be surprised to see price mentioned as a value-adding factor in relationship selling. However, remember the discussion on value as a ratio of benefits to costs. For customers, value is the amount by which benefits exceed their investment in various costs of doing business with you (including the product's price). And one of the ways we pointed out that you can increase value is by reducing costs (in this case, lowering price).

INNOVATION 3.5

Be Your Own Brand

Word of mouth is the most powerful force in business. Who doesn't want to have other people "buzzing" about them? If people respect you, like you and have a good experience with you (or hear about it from someone else) they hire you, promote you, and do business with you. But how do you get people buzzing about you?

Let's look at how big companies do it—Nike, for instance. Everyone recognizes the famous swoosh logo on shoes, hats, shirts, and golf bags. That logo has power. But its power was not the result of a multimillion-dollar marketing effort.

Back in 1971, a graphic design student at Portland State University named Carolyn Davidson was hired to "just do it"—create a logo for the side of a running shoe. She was paid the princely sum of $35. Carolyn had a moment of creative genius! It resulted in a symbol that became ubiquitous on Nike gear. Twelve years later the company gave her a gold Swoosh ring embedded with a diamond, along with a certificate and an undisclosed amount of Nike stock. Today the company reports net revenues of 13.7 billion dollars!

You don't need to have a big budget or a multimillion-dollar ad agency to build a personal brand! It's about focusing on how to communicate effectively—using your wits. A creative, thoughtful approach to delivering the message will get people saying positive things about you. If you and your message are interesting, and if you get out and deliver that message often enough, you are going to develop a powerful personal brand.

Sometimes people try to make it too complicated. A personal brand is really nothing more than a message, and a message is a thought—it's what people think, when they think of you.

What comes to mind when people see you? Or hear your name? That's your personal brand. It's the sum total of what people know about you—what they think of you after you've had a conversation, given a speech, or they've seen you in the public eye in some way.

So every time you speak, you are branding yourself, and it's important to think strategically about what and how you are delivering that message. Your conversations, presentations, e-mails, phone calls and conversations in the hallway all send signals. Are you talking about big ideas? Are you clear, concise, and interesting? Do people appear to sit up and pay attention when you speak?

People have a feeling about others, almost as soon as they meet and work with them. They continue to shape that feeling with the more interactions they have. Pretty soon, they see them walking down the hall, and something registers, positive or negative. It's within your power to make that feeling positive. What constitutes a strong personal brand? There are seven aspects of a powerful personal brand. A personal brand:

- Is instantly recognizable
- Stands for something of value
- Builds trust
- Generates positive word of mouth
- Gives a competitive advantage
- Creates career opportunity
- Results in professional and financial success

Some people have all the tools to create a strong, personal brand—but they just can't get the ball rolling to get their name out there. They've got great ideas, and a semirecognizable name, but there's no buzz about them. So how do you create buzz? One way is to start speaking, in formal and informal settings. Speaking is perhaps the single best way to establish yourself as an expert in any business or industry.

Speaking inside and outside your company or industry positions you as an expert for several reasons:

- Many of your colleagues or competitors don't do it.
- People assume if you are speaking on a topic you are an expert.
- Other people promote your talk.
- You are center stage, which automatically gives you credibility.
- If you give a valuable talk, people remember you.
- If they remember you, you become top of mind—you are the one they think of when they are referring someone for new business, promotions, other speaking engagements, etc.

Some people say, "I don't really have opportunities to speak." But finding opportunities to speak is easier than you think. Here are some tips on finding opportunities:

- If you're a businessowner or entrepreneur, call to ask organizations where you are a member if you can speak.
- Ask all of your local business and community organizations, from the Chamber of Commerce to the Lions Club.
- If you're trying to develop your reputation inside an organization, look for opportunities there. Many companies sponsor brown bag lunches, panels, and have off sites where you can present your ideas. Put your hand up to present in team meetings; by volunteering and putting it on your calendar you automatically create a deadline that forces you to go into action and prepare a great presentation.

In truth, Upland is pretty competitively priced item-to-item versus competitors. However, it is definitely not the lowest-priced supplier, nor would Alex have the discretion to make special prices for Wanda.

Alex Lewis's Role

Alex should begin by expressing his concern about Wanda's overfocus on price as the only added value from Upland. He should be open to any insights Abe can provide from his experience on how to sell Wanda on other value-adding aspects of the relationship.

Abe Rollins's Role

Abe should come into the meeting prepared to give a number of examples of how Alex (and Upland Company) can add value beyond simply low price. (Note: Be sure the sources of added value you choose to put forth make sense in this situation.) Abe uses the time in the meeting to coach Alex on how he might be able to show Wanda that while Upland's products are priced competitively, they offer superior value to the competition in many other ways.

Assignment

Work with another student to develop a 7–10 minute exchange of ideas on creating and communicating value. Be sure Abe tells Alex some specific ways he can go back to Wanda with a strong value proposition on the next sales call.

Discussion Questions

1. Review Nat Martin's Expert Advice at the beginning of the chapter. Which aspects of the 12 categories for communicating value you learned in the chapter do you believe are most relevant for Darden Restaurants? Why are the ones you identified the most important for Darden?

2. What do you think are the most important ways sales can contribute to a firm's marketing and vice versa? Pg. 75

3. Why is it so critical that marketing communications be integrated?

4. What is customer satisfaction? What is customer loyalty? Is one more important in the long run than the other? Why or why not? pg. 76

5. Take a look at Exhibit 3.2 on the value chain. Pick a company in which you are interested, research it, and develop an assessment of how it is doing in delivering value at each link in the chain.

6. Leadership 3.2 provides tips on being a customer service leader. Identify a firm that exhibits many of these qualities of service leadership. How do you think service leadership translates into stronger customer relationships for the firm you selected?

7. Review Leadership 3.4, "On the Value of Professionalism." What does integrity mean to you? How do you know if someone has integrity?

8. Consider the advice in Innovation 3.5, "Be Your Own Brand." Give examples of how these concepts have helped or could help you in your college career. pg. 89

Ethical Dilemma

Ben Lopez has been with Bear Chemicals for seven years and has earned a reputation as one of the best salespeople in the company. Starting as a detail salesperson calling on small specialty companies, he worked his way up to key account manager calling on some of Bear's largest customers.

Today, Ben was faced with a difficult decision. Midwest Coatings, Ben's smallest account, called again this morning wanting him to come out and talk about problems with its new manufacturing operations.

When Ben first started with the company, Midwest was Bear's largest customer. However, over the last few years Midwest has become less competitive and has seen significant declines in its market share, with a corresponding reduction in the purchase of chemicals. Of even greater concern was the trend for foreign competitors to deliver higher-quality products at lower prices than Midwest.

Unfortunately, Midwest still views itself as Bear's best customer. It demands the lowest prices and highest level of service. Its people call frequently and want immediate attention from Ben even though Bear has customer support people (customer service engineers) to help with customer problems and service. For Ben, a growing concern is his personal relationship with several senior managers at Midwest. The chief marketing officer and several top people at Midwest are Ben's friends and their children play with Ben's kids.

After the phone call this morning, Ben called his boss, Jennifer Anderson, to get direction before committing to a meeting. He explained that the problems at Midwest were not Bear's fault and a customer support person should deal with them by phone. Ben was worried that going out there would take an entire afternoon. He did not want to waste his time when a customer service engineer could handle the situation. Jennifer, who knew about the problems at Midwest, suggested it was time for full review of the account. She also told Ben that it might be time to classify the company as a second-tier account, meaning Ben would no longer be responsible for calling on Midwest. While acknowledging the problems with Midwest, Ben is hesitant to lose the account because it might create personal problems for him at home.

Questions

1. Should Ben drop Midwest as his account and let it become a second-tier customer?

2. What obligation does a company have to customers who no longer warrant special service or attention?

Mini Case

CASE 3

BestValue Computers

BestValue Computers is a Jackson, Mississippi, company providing computer technology, desktops, laptops, printers, and other peripheral devices to local businesses and school districts in the southern half of Mississippi. Leroy Wells founded BestValue shortly after graduating from college with an information technology degree. Leroy began small but soon collected accounts looking for great value at reasonable prices with local service. When Leroy started his business in Jackson, he believed that anyone could build a computer. In fact, other than the processor and the software that runs computers, many of the components used are sold as commodities.

Leroy initially viewed his company as a value-added assembler and reseller of technology products. This business model was so successful that Leroy decided to expand from Jackson throughout southern Mississippi. To facilitate this expansion,

Leroy hired Charisse Taylor in Hattiesburg to sell his products to all of south Mississippi, including the Gulf Coast, where a number of casinos were locating.

Before hiring Charisse, Leroy made sure that she had a reputation for developing long-term relationships with her customers and that she was a professional with integrity. Charisse did not disappoint Leroy. She has grown the business significantly in the two years that she has been with BestValue. Charisse credits her success to being honest with customers, which includes explaining exactly what BestValue can provide in terms of software and hardware. That way no one is surprised with the result. In fact, many times customers have remarked to both Charisse and Leroy that they received more than they expected.

Now Leroy has set his sights on the New Orleans and Memphis markets. In addition, many of his initial customers have grown beyond a couple of desktop computers. They are starting to ask Leroy if he can provide and service local area networks (LANs), which allow many computers to share a central server so that workers can share files and communicate much more quickly. Leroy has decided to pursue the LAN business because selling, installing, and servicing LANs seems to be a natural extension of his current business.

However, adding the LAN products and accompanying services to his existing line of business represents a big addition to his current method of operation, which is to provide high-quality, high-value computers and peripheral devices. This new venture into providing more of a service than a product seems somewhat risky to Leroy, but he recognizes that LANs are the wave of the future and that to remain viable he will have to start viewing his company as more of a service provider than a product provider.

To facilitate Leroy's expansion into Memphis and New Orleans, he has hired two new salespeople. They are similar to Charisse in that they are relationship builders who believe providing clients with more than they promised is the key to successful selling today. This attitude is important because the competition in these two markets will be tough. Much larger competitors like Dell, IBM, and Hewlett-Packard have been selling equipment in these areas for a long time, so it will be very important for the sales reps to communicate BestValue's message of great value, including reasonable prices and local service. In fact, Leroy realizes that the only way to compete with the big boys is to be better than they are by providing value over and above what they offer. That philosophy has made BestValue a success so far, and Leroy thinks it will work in these new markets too.

Questions

1. Identify and describe the categories of value creation on which BestValue currently relies most.
2. How can BestValue utilize the service quality dimensions to make sure it is communicating a consistent message of high-quality service and value every time someone from the company interacts with a customer?
3. Even though BestValue provides basically a commodity product, what role can the concept of brand equity play for BestValue's sales reps as they begin contacting customers in the New Orleans and Memphis areas?
4. What is the role of the BestValue sales reps in managing customer expectations? How can they ensure that new customers in the New Orleans and Memphis areas are delighted with their purchases? Be specific and explain.
5. What are some dangers that BestValue must take into account as it moves into the new markets and begins to provide LAN products and services? How will value creation change for it with the addition of LANs?

Appendix: Relationship Selling Math

An important element in relationship selling is developing an effective and persuasive value proposition. In the vast majority of sales presentations a critical component of the value proposition involves a quantitative analysis of your product and its value to the customer. This appendix, which we call Relationship Selling Math, provides the tools to develop the quantifiable justification for a value proposition. All of the spreadsheets discussed in this appendix can be found at the Web site for *Relationship Selling,* 2e (along with other important information). Please go to www.mhhe.com/johnston2e and download the spreadsheets before you continue. Working through the spreadsheets as you read the appendix is the best approach for understanding and applying Relationship Selling Math. In addition, the spreadsheets are interactive so you can create your own scenarios and see how a change in one component of the analysis alters other elements.

Most quantitative analysis involves a spreadsheet and is usually in one of two formats.

- If you are selling a product that is sold to a reseller (for example a retailer), use the *profit margin spreadsheet.*
- If you are selling a product or service that is used in the production of the business, use the *return on investment (ROI) spreadsheet.*

In customer relationship management (CRM) the customer value proposition is ascribed to one of three scenarios: (1) acquisition of new customers, (2) retention of existing customers, or (3) additional profitability (see page 67). When creating a value proposition it is a good idea to identify which of these three is the most important objective in the presentation and create your spreadsheet around that goal. For example, if you were going to sell a new brand of clothing to a department store, you might argue that it would bring in new customers who are loyal current customers of the brand that had not shopped at the store previously. You might also argue it will increase retention by offering existing customers a larger selection which results in their greater satisfaction. Finally, you could argue the addition of the new brand would increase profitability because of the demand for the new product from existing and new customers, which would result in increased sales and profits. Analyzing the customer's needs and then matching the company's products to those needs is essential in choosing the most appropriate objective and spreadsheet model. This is not to say the other advantages should be ignored, just not quantified in the spreadsheet. Let's consider each scenario more closely and give some examples.

Acquisition of New Customers

In a retail purchase situation a customer may have many concerns and questions. Often a critical question in taking on a new product or service is, would the addition of your product or service actually bring new customers to the store? Keep in mind that consumers today are overloaded with product choices and a vast array of convenient purchasing options. When was the last time you went out of your way to find a particular product? Most likely this would occur when the product is a specialty good with high brand recognition. In this selling scenario, you would want to prepare a *ROI spreadsheet*.

Retention or Retaining New Customers

Does the addition of your product or service allow the buyer to have better customer satisfaction? As we have discussed in relationship selling, exceeding customers' expectations results in keeping customers. It is much less expensive to keep existing customers than to attract new ones. How much is this actually worth to the company? It is possible to see the value of retaining particular customers through different kinds of analysis.

- If the goal is to determine the worth of a customer you would use the *lifetime value formula* (Exhibit 3.3 on page 79).
- If the objective is customer retention, you would choose an *ROI spreadsheet* using the lifetime value of the customer offset by the inventory costs of your product.

Profitability

Profit is generated by a reduction in costs or an increase in sales. Questions that are frequently addressed in this selling scenario include: Does the addition of your product or service reduce labor or operational costs? Will the purchase of the product by the reseller increase sales? The information to address these questions can be measured and dealt with in a quantitative analysis.

If the profitability objective is based primarily on reducing costs, you should choose the *return on investment spreadsheet*. The cost savings would be compared to the cost of purchase to see if the ROI is positive. The bottom line of the ROI spreadsheet is the *net savings or return to the company*. If the purchase produces a positive ROI, in other words, if the savings are greater than the costs, it is a good match between the buyer's needs and the seller's product/service. If the purchase would produce a negative ROI—the cost is greater than the savings—it may mean the prospect is not a qualified buyer or the value proposition is not well developed (for example, there are too many product features relative to the cost targets for the customer).

If the value proposition is profitability based on increasing sales, you should choose the profit margin spreadsheet. The revenue from additional sales would be compared to the cost of purchase to project profit margin. The reseller spreadsheet is a simple calculation of costs less discounts, offset by retail price. An actual seller would supply costs and discounts. It is always important to be as accurate as possible in assigning costs and discounts; a thorough analysis of the customer's business and your company's own pricing flexibility is crucial to developing an accurate forecast. All research including interviews with store personnel should be documented and/or presented as evidence in your sales presentation. Let's examine each of these spreadsheet models.

Units	Unit Cost	Total Cost	Quantity Discounts	Co-op Allowance	Net Cost	MSRP	Revenue	Net Profit	Profit Margin/Unit	Markup Up/retail

- The *Units* column indicates the size of the purchase in the multiples in which they are sold. For example, some products are sold only by the case and therefore units would be number of cases. If products were sold individually then it would be the number of individual units.
- *Unit cost* is the wholesale price of the unit. If your unit were a case it would be the price of the case. As stated above, this information would be readily available to you in your industry. It is not easily ascertained outside the company. You might have to find an industry average, ask for a range from an employee, or work backwards from retail price. To work backwards, you could take the retail price less the markup and discover the cost. For example, if you see a product advertised for $100 and you research the industry and discover there is usually 100 percent average industry markup you can deduce that the cost would be $50. Another option would be to check prices at online discounters or cost clubs. They sell closer to wholesale and you could use their numbers as your wholesale cost.
- *Total cost* is number of units multiplied by the unit cost. Be sure you are using concurrent numbers. For example, if you discover the wholesale cost of a bottle of water is .29, but it is sold in cases of 12, you will first need to translate the unit cost to the cost for a case (12 × .29), or break down the number of units from number of cases to number of actual bottles.

Example

Cases	Units per Case	Total Units	Unit Cost	Total Cost
10	6	60	$50	$ 3,000
20	6	120	50	6,000
50	6	300	50	15,000

- In B2B *quantity discounts* are often used to encourage larger purchases. The amount of the discount varies by industry and research can determine an industry standard. Quantity discounts are normally expressed as a percentage of the total cost.
- Another common discount in B2B, especially in heavily advertised brands, is *co-op allowances.* This is money allocated for promotion of the seller's product by the reseller. Co-op discounts are often a percentage of the total cost. These discounts would be offered only if the reseller engaged in advertising that would significantly promote the seller's product. Co-op discounts are not usual for small orders or commodity items.
- *Net cost* would be the result of subtracting all discounts from total cost.

Example

Cases	Units per Case	Total Units	Unit Cost	Total Cost	Quantity Discounts	Co-op Allowance	Net Cost
10	6	60	$50	$ 3,000	$ 0	$ 0	$ 3,000
20	6	120	50	6,000	180	0	5,820
50	6	300	50	15,000	450	750	13,800

- *Manufacturer's suggested retail price (MSRP)* is the price of the product to the end user. It is the price without promotional allowances (markdowns, on sale, clearance, etc.). To find the best MSRP you should go to an actual brick-and-mortar retail location, not a discounter, and research the price at which your product is selling. Online resellers may discount the price and therefore you will not get an accurate MSRP. Manufacturers suggest a retail price to maintain brand equity. If you shop at a reseller location that also maintains strong brand equity you will get a more accurate MSRP.
- *Revenue* is the amount of sales generated by the order. The MSRP would be multiplied by the number of units. Be especially careful that you convert units into individual units because the MSRP will be for one unit. If your total cost was figured by the case, you will need revenue projections that include all the units.

Example

MSRP	Revenue
$100	$ 6,000
100	12,000
100	30,000

- *Net profit,* the bottom line, is revenue minus net cost. The buyer is most focused on this number. You should create a graph showing the increasing levels of profit with increased order size.
- *Profit margin per unit* could be a persuasive indicator. The revenue from the sale of the product or service is reduced by the cost of goods sold to determine profit margin. If the profit margin generated by the unit were significantly higher than the average margin experienced by the buyer, this would be of value. For example, in a grocery store markup on staple items is generally low, often below 30 percent. If your product could generate a pm/unit of more than 50 percent, especially if shelf space needs were low, the purchase would be highly valued.

Example

Net profit	Profit Margin/Unit
$ 3,000	$50
6,180	52
16,200	54

- Markup is the percentage added to the cost of the product to determine the selling price. *Markup based on retail* price should be included if you worked backwards to find the wholesale cost. The formula for markup is Cost / (100% − GM%) = Selling price. You can replace GM in the formula with the average markup to determine cost. Markup could be an industry average if specific numbers are unavailable. Markup is often used to determine if the return on the space your product occupies is worth the investment. For example, retail stores calculate their return on shelf space based on the sales generated from the square footage of selling space available. If your product requires more selling space than the revenue it will generate, it would be a bad purchase decision for the customer.

Understanding the ROI Spreadsheet

	Plan 1	**Plan 2**	**Plan 3**
Expenses			
Daily			
Average number of staff			
Average amount of time			
Labor minutes used			
Labor hours			
Monthly			
Labor hours			
Average hourly wage			
Total monthly cost			
Yearly			
Investment			
Product/service cost			
Additional costs			
Total yearly cost			
Net savings			
Over time . . .			
ROI/month			

The ROI spreadsheet requires a deeper understanding of your buyer's business than the profit margin spreadsheet. It also requires access to sensitive information about the company's operations. If you are selling a product or service that will decrease costs to the customer's business and consequently increase profitability, you need to show your buyer the value of buying/investing in your product. Profitability from the purchase is called the return on investment (ROI). In many cases the main expense is labor costs as in the example. You can use the same format, substituting rows as needed to adapt to the other expenses.

In this example we have chosen to present three options to the buyer with each providing a greater return. It is not always necessary to have numerous options, but it does help illustrate the financial advantage of building the relationship with a long-term contract.

The purpose of the ROI spreadsheet is to persuade the buyer to invest in your product or service. The payoff of their investment, or the return, is the difference between their current expenses and the new purchase.

- The spreadsheet begins by addressing the *expenses.* The buyer will be more comfortable discussing the current situation from this point of view. It is also a good idea to show the need for your product before introducing the price.
- If your product/service is going to reduce labor costs, you first need to know the current labor costs. Begin by determining the current cost of labor associated with the task the sale will impact. If you are selling accounting software, this could be the number of people who will use the software. If you are selling Internet access this would be the number of employees who will benefit from faster connections. In this example we have started with *daily usage* and built into the larger picture. Many buyers will find it easier to think in smaller time blocks. "How many minutes would you estimate you spend waiting on the phone per day?" is much easier to answer than asking the same question for minutes per year.
- *Average amount of time* is the current use of time by the employees included in the staff calculation above. For example, if they use about 30 minutes a day on a task that will now be eliminated or streamlined, that would be put in the cell. Time wasted while waiting on connections or slow computers could also be included.
- *Labor minutes used* are the number of staff members multiplied by the average amount of time worked. This tells us the total usage for the company on a daily basis.
- Since most wages are calculated per hour we need to convert minutes into hours. Thus, *labor hours* are the labor minutes divided by 60.

Example

	Plan 1	**Plan 2**	**Plan 3**
Expenses			
Daily			
Average number of staff	10	10	10
Average amount of time	12	12	12
Labor minutes used	120	120	120
Labor hours	2	2	2

- *Labor hours/month* is calculated to build the bigger picture. Since investments are not made on a daily or even monthly basis, we need to build up to the yearly usage. Labor hours multiplied by 30 gives us the labor hours per month.
- To determine the actual cost of the labor hours we need an *average hourly wage.* Be sure to note that this is an average. In some cases all employees impacted by the investment will be comparable in earnings, in other cases there may be

great disparity between management and staff. This is your best attempt at parity and can be quite easily researched.

- *Total monthly cost* is calculated by multiplying average wage by labor hours/ month. This amount is the cost to the buyer of not buying your product or service.

Example

Monthly

Labor hours	60	60	66
Average hourly wage	$9.00	$9.00	$9.25
Total monthly cost	$540	$540	$611

Most investments in B2B are long term, not merely for 30 days. To calculate the yearly cost of not buying, we would multiply total monthly cost by the number of months in the year.

Example

Yearly	$6,480	$6,480	$7,326

The next section of the ROI spreadsheet is the introduction of the investment or cost to buy your product/service. These costs are usually easy to find as they are the retail price of the good or service.

- *Product/service cost* is the actual amount the business needs to "invest" in the solution. It should be expressed in the total cost for the year to keep our analysis logical.
- *Additional costs* might be installation, training, maintenance, support, compatibility upgrades, etc. In building strong relationships all costs should be discussed. Hidden costs are unethical and do not contribute to long-term relationships.
- The *total yearly* costs are the sum total of the investment for that year. Services are often repeating investments. Many times a discounted price is offered for multiple year contracts. In some buying situations, a large purchase could be amortized over an extended period. All costs should appear when presenting the ROI.

Example

Investment

Product/service cost	$5,000	$6,000	$5,500
Additional costs	1,200	0	0
Total yearly cost	$6,200	$6,000	$5,500

The bottom line of the ROI spreadsheet is the *net savings.* If the purchase produces a positive ROI, in other words if the savings are greater than the costs, it is a good match between the buyer's needs and your (the seller's) product/service. If the purchase would produce a negative ROI—the cost greater than the savings—it may mean the prospect is not a qualified buyer or that price negotiation is needed.

As stated previously, there are often advantages to making a commitment to purchase for more than one year. It is an advantage to the seller to know they will have the repeat business, and an advantage to the buyer to know they have created a relationship with the seller that can provide them benefits from customer service and reduced ordering costs. In the case of some B2B purchases, the one time purchase price is spread out over the life of the product. In both these instances it is important to show the ROI over the life of the contract or product. In the example, we chose to look at the investment over a three-year period. The yearly return for each year is added together to determine the actual return over the three-year life of the investment.

Since many businesses use monthly cash-based accounting methods, it is a persuasive tool to break down the large investment dollars into monthly returns. If you take the three-year ROI and divide by the number of months in the same time period (36) you find the *ROI* per month. As consumers we find $99 per month easier to accept than $1,200. In B2B, the same psychology applies.

Example

Investment			
Total yearly cost	$6,200	$6,000	$5,500
Net savings	280	480	1,826
Over time . . .	840	1,440	5,478
ROI/month	$ 23	$ 40	$ 152

If you are using the ROI spreadsheet to quantify the *acquisition of new customers* a few modifications would be made. You would need to forecast the number of new customers that would be attracted. You would also need a lifetime value for the customer (see Exhibit 3.3). This would determine the revenue stream.

Example

	Minimum	**Average**	**Exceptional**
Acquisition			
Number of new customers	3	4	5
Lifetime value	$ 5,000	$ 5,000	$ 5,000
Revenues	$15,000	$20,000	$25,000

Investment			
Product/service cost	$13,000	$ 17,000	$ 20,000
Additional costs	1,500	1,500	1,500
Total yearly cost	$14,500	$18,500	$21,500
ROI	$ 500	$ 1,500	$ 3,500

The revenues generated would be offset by the cost of the product/service and any related costs. Be sure to include all costs that will be associated with the decision. In this example we are selling advertising space. The additional cost of artwork for the ad design is shown as an additional cost. If you were selling a product that would provide value through *customer retention*, your product cost would be the investment.

The ROI in the acquisition example shows that a $20,000 yearly investment in advertising could return $25,000 in sales revenue and thereby not only recover the expense but actually return $3,500. The spreadsheet also shows that in the worst-case scenario the return on the investment would be $500.

As you work through the spreadsheets it is important to note the challenge of these analyses is not the calculations but, rather, verifying the accuracy of the data. Without valid data the analyses are not very valuable to you as the salesperson, or the customer. Indeed, a poor analysis with invalid data could do more harm than good to the relationship. Mastering the relationship selling process means, in part, becoming comfortable with understanding, creating, and then explaining these kinds of analyses to customers.

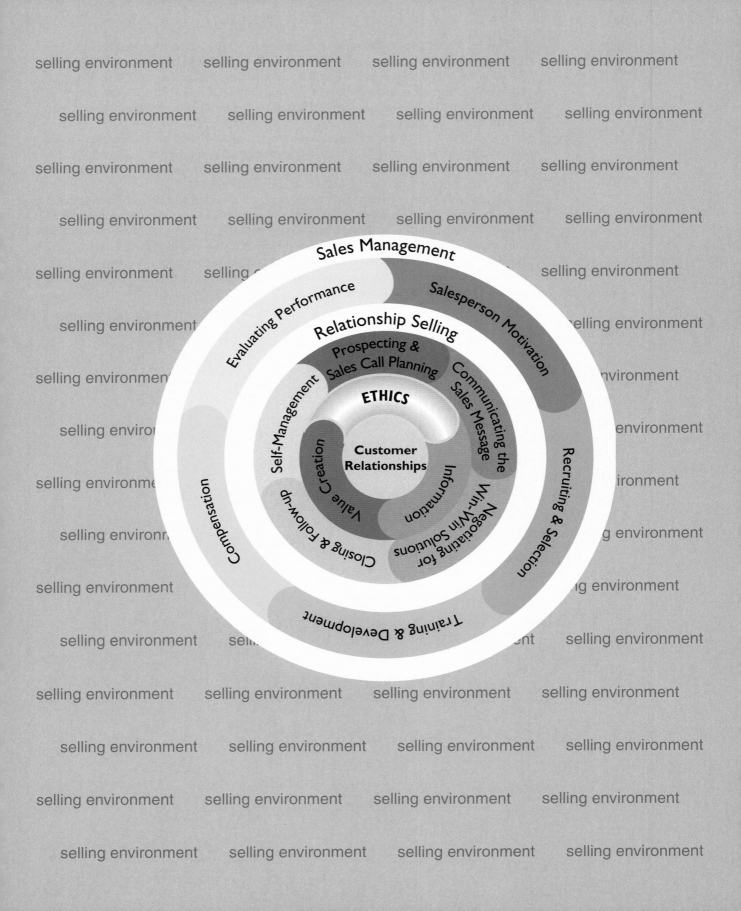

selling environment

Sales Management

Evaluating Performance

Salesperson Motivation

Recruiting & Selection

Training & Development

Compensation

Relationship Selling

Prospecting & Sales Call Planning

Communicating the Sales Message

Negotiating for Win-Win Solutions

Closing & Follow-up

Self-Management

ETHICS

Value Creation

Information

Customer Relationships

4 chapter

Ethical and Legal Issues in Relationship Selling

Learning Objectives

As we have said, ethical relationships are the foundation of relationship selling. Every day salespeople are asked to make ethical judgments. Likewise their managers must make ethical decisions that affect company policies as well as individual salespeople. The events of the last several years have made it clear that ethical behavior cannot be assumed. It needs to be taught and become a fundamental element of the corporate culture. This chapter will explore the many ethical concerns facing salespeople and managers and discuss legal issues that affect sales behavior. The chapter ends with tips on creating a personal code of sales ethics.

After reading this chapter, you should be able to

- Understand the importance of ethical behavior in relationship selling and sales management.
- Identify the ethical concerns facing salespeople as they relate to customers and employers.
- Identify the ethical concerns facing sales managers as they relate to salespeople, company policies, and international sales issues.
- Discuss the legal issues in relationship selling.
- Create a personal code of sales ethics.

expert advice

Expert: Meenakshi A. Hirani, Esq.
Company: Meenakshi A. Hirani, P.A.
Business: Attorney
Education: LLB, MCL, MBA, JD

What do you see as the most important ethical issues facing salespeople in the 21st century?

With a highly competitive market place, immediate access to information, and demanding customers, there are few boundaries or barriers for salespeople. This has created a lot of new market opportunities; however, this also exposes salespeople to local, state, national, even international laws, regulations, and customs. The cliché, everything legal is not ethical, puts a burden on salespeople to learn not only the complicated ever-changing laws of every nation in which their company does business, but to understand and implement the ethical and moral practices in a particular society. What is moral in the United States may not be ethical in Eastern countries due to different religious and social practices. The opposite is also true: What is accepted in Latin America, for example, may be considered unethical, even illegal, in the United States. Therefore, it is difficult for salespeople to come up with a standard code of ethics that is universally acceptable.

Cultural differences among the various groups of people in a given country or region make it practically impossible to create a universal code of ethics. In addition, the Internet enables companies to operate globally with no direct customer contact making it very hard to enforce ethical practices with customers in other countries. Salespeople are put in thorny situations trying to meet the legal and ethical requirement of their company while satisfying the demands of their customers.

What role do sales managers play in creating an ethical environment for salespeople?

Sales managers play a vital, strategic role in creating an ethical environment for salespeople. The company's code of ethics is exemplified, monitored, and enforced by the sales manager. It is important for the sales manager to practice the company's code of ethics before asking the salesperson to follow it, as the manager should teach by example. While being a friendly advisor and mentor to salespeople, the manager has to be sensitive to the salesperson's own ethical beliefs while communicating and employing the highest ethical standards set forth by the company. At the same time, the sales manager must be aware of the highly competitive environment in which some companies adopt a lower ethical standard to generate new business. The sales manager's role in this situation should be to support the company's ethical standards and salespersons. This may mean that the manager needs to accept optimum profits versus maximum profits.

What are the most difficult legal issues salespeople encounter on a regular basis?

The most difficult legal issues faced by salespeople on a regular basis are the laws themselves. There are a plethora of laws at the county, state, national, and international level. Additionally, amendments are constantly being added to existing laws that make legal experts wince. To expect salespeople to know all of these laws, then understand and implement them in their day-to-day profession of selling is a formidable task. Once having overcome the initial difficult task of knowing the law, they must then implement some of the crucial legal issues. Safeguarding client's privacy rights, discrimination laws, antitrust laws, health and safety laws, laws related to the Uniform Electronic Transactions Act, the Uniform Computer Information Transaction Act, deceptive trade practices in warranties and product liability, and securities act issues are the tip of the iceberg that salespeople have to be mindful of on a regular basis.

The Importance of Ethics in the 21st Century

All of us are faced with decisions that test our ethical principles every day. For example, what do you do when the clerk at the grocery store gives you too much change? When your classmate asks you for an answer during a test? What principles guide you as you make decisions about ethical dilemmas?

Given the unique nature of their jobs, it is not surprising that salespeople face ethical issues all the time. As shown in the model for Relationship Selling and Sales Management at the beginning of the chapter, ethics is a core principle of the buyer–seller relationship. Without a commitment to ethical behavior, it is impossible to have a successful long-term relationship with buyers. However, salespeople encounter pressure from a variety of sources, including their managers, customers, and other outside parties (family, friends).[1] Making the right decision for one can mean disappointing another, which complicates the decision even more. For example, refusing to sell a long-term service contract to a customer who doesn't really need it may be in the customer's best interests but is not the most profitable decision for the company.

Also, ethical norms change over time. This can lead to anxiety as salespeople get caught in the middle of changing corporate policies and customer demands. For example, the nature of relationship selling today often means buyers and sellers share sensitive information about manufacturing and pricing. However, many companies are still wary of sharing too much information about sensitive topics with customers.

Unfortunately, defining ethical behavior is difficult. Our focus is on **business ethics,** which comprises moral principles and standards that define right and wrong and guide behavior in the world of business.[2]

Renewed Emphasis on Ethical Practices

In recent years, business ethics has become front-page news as companies like Enron have engaged in unethical, and in some cases illegal, activities. Whether or not salespeople in these companies were directly involved in illegal activities, they suffered as a result of management's ethical lapses.

One outcome of these scandals has been a renewed interest in ethics at every level in the organization. From the board of directors to the lowest level, employees have become more aware of their company's ethical practices. Many large companies have published their code of conduct or values (there are many phrases), which defines the way they do business. Leadership 4.1 is a summary of Dell Computer's code of conduct.

Not surprisingly, one of the areas most affected by the focus on ethics is selling. The relationship between buyer and seller is based on mutual trust. Any ethical lapse by the seller can severely damage the customer's trust. A recent survey of sales managers reported that 70 percent of their clients consider a company's ethical reputation when making purchase decisions.[3] Ethics will play an increasingly important role in the sales decision process for both buyer and seller.

The focus on ethics is not limited to the United States. Around the world, companies are reacting to and in many cases proactively dealing with ethical problems by establishing worldwide ethical policies. This is difficult because ethical

Leadership 4.1

Code of Conduct Dell Computer

Dell's higher standard Dell's success is built on a foundation of personal and professional integrity. We hold ourselves to standards of ethical behavior that go well beyond legal minimums. We never compromise these standards and we will never ask any member of the Dell team to do so either. We owe this to our customers, suppliers, shareholders, and other stakeholders. And we owe it to ourselves because success without integrity is essentially meaningless.

Our higher standard is at the heart of what we know as the "Soul of Dell"—the statement of the values and beliefs which define our shared global culture. This culture of performance with integrity unites us as a company that understands and adheres to our company values and to the laws of the countries in which we do business. Just as the Soul of Dell articulates our values and beliefs, the following Code of Conduct provides guidance to ensure we meet our higher standard and conduct business the Dell Way—the right way, which is "Winning with Integrity." Simply put, we want all members of our team, along with our shareholders, customers, suppliers, and other stakeholders, to understand that they can believe what we say and trust what we do.

Our higher standard includes several key characteristics that both underpin the Soul of Dell and provide the foundation for our Code of Conduct:

- **Trust.** Our word is good. We keep our commitments to each other and to our stakeholders.
- **Integrity.** We do the right thing without compromise. We avoid even the appearance of impropriety.
- **Honesty.** What we say is true and forthcoming, not just technically correct. We are open and transparent in our communications with each other and about business performance.
- **Judgment.** We think before we act and consider the consequences of our actions.
- **Respect.** We treat people with dignity and value their contributions. We maintain fairness in all relationships.
- **Courage.** We speak up for what is right. We report wrongdoing when we see it.
- **Responsibility.** We accept the consequences of our actions. We admit our mistakes and quickly correct them. We do not retaliate against those who report violations of law or policy.

Source: Dell's Code of Conduct. Reprinted by permission of Dell Corporation.

practices vary by region and even from country to country. What is acceptable behavior in Latin America may be against the law in the United States or Europe. For example, offering bribes or payments to enhance the probability of success is often seen as part of doing business in parts of Latin America and the Middle East but is illegal in the United States. As we will explore later in the chapter, internationalizing ethical practices and policies is not easy for any company, no matter where it is from originally.

Companies Take the Lead in Social Responsibility

Beyond the question of ethical behavior is a larger question that companies face on a daily basis. What are my **social responsibilities** as a corporate citizen? As Enron demonstrated, lost shareholder wealth and thousands of layoffs are only two of the consequences of poor ethical judgments. Those decisions, which hurt thousands of people in many ways, are prime examples of bad corporate citizenship. Companies have a responsibility to many groups. Certainly they have a responsibility to their customers. They also have employees (who count on continued employment), shareholders (who invest their money for a financial return), and a host of other entities (among them suppliers, government, and creditors) who expect the company to act in an ethical manner. Exhibit 4.1 details the best corporate citizens, as identified by *Business Ethics* magazine.

EXHIBIT 4.1 The Best Corporate Citizens

For the last eight years, *Business Ethics* magazine has published an annual list of the 100 best corporate citizens. The study highlights companies that balance social responsibility with traditional financial returns. Peter Asmus, a writer at the magazine, summarizes the list like this:

"Service to the environment, to employee well-being, to suppliers, and to the community—these are the kinds of actions that help companies win spots among the 100 Best Corporate Citizens. As we at *Business Ethics* define it, that's precisely what corporate citizenship means: service not just to stockholders but to a variety of stakeholders. Using social ratings compiled by KLD Research & Analytics, Inc., of Boston—plus a financial measure of total return to shareholders—our list ranks companies according to service to eight stakeholder groups: stockholders; the community; minorities and women; employees; the environment; non-U.S. stakeholders; customers and governance."

In putting together the list of 100 best corporate citizens, KLD Research examines information in the following areas:

Environment looks at positive programs in place (such as pollution reduction, recycling, and energy-saving measures), as well as negative measures (such as level of pollutants, EPA citations, fines, and lawsuits).

Community relations looks at philanthropy, any foundation the company runs, community service projects, educational outreach, scholarships, employee volunteerism, and so forth.

Employee relations looks at wages relative to the industry, benefits paid, family-friendly policies, parental leave; team management, employee empowerment, and so forth.

Diversity looks at percentage of minority and women employees, managers, and board members; any EEOC complaints; diversity programs in place; lawsuits, and so forth.

Customer relations might include quality management programs, quality awards won, customer satisfaction measures, lawsuits, and so forth.

Ranked in order, the top 15 corporate citizens in 2007 were as follows:

1. Green Mountain Coffee Roasters, Inc
2. Advanced Micro Devices, Inc.
3. Nike, Inc.
4. Motorola, Inc.
5. Intel Corporation
6. International Business Machines Corporation
7. Agilent Technology, Inc.
8. Timberland Corporation
9. Starbucks Corporation
10. General Mills Incorporated
11. Salesforce.com, Inc.
12. Applied Materials, Inc.
13. Texas Instruments, Inc.
14. Herman Miller, Inc.
15. Rockwell Collins

For a more complete discussion of the 2007 Top 100 Corporate Citizens, go to www.business-ethics.com and click on "Top 100 Corporate Citizens."

Source: "100 Best Corporate Citizens." www.business-ethics.com/node/75, October 2008.

Ethical Concerns for Salespeople

EXHIBIT 4.2 Ethical Concerns for Salespeople

Customers	Employers
Dishonesty	Cheating
Gifts, entertainment, bribes	Misuse of company resources
Unfair treatment	Inappropriate relationships with employees and customers
Breaking confidentiality	

This section discusses the ethical issues salespeople deal with as they interact with customers and their own companies. As you will see, these issues can be complex, and much of the time there is a great deal riding on the salesperson's decision.

Exhibit 4.2 summarizes the ethical concerns for salespeople.

Issues with Customers

There are four primary ethical concerns for salespeople in their relationships with customers. They are dishonesty, gifts (entertainment, bribes), unfair treatment, and confidentiality leaks. We will explore each in detail.

Dishonesty. Salespeople sell. That is their job, and as part of that job they are expected to present their products to customers in the best possible light. It is perfectly acceptable for a salesperson to be passionate about products and services; however, there is a line between enthusiasm and illegal, dishonest behavior. Under no circumstances is it acceptable to be **dishonest** and provide false or deliberately inaccurate information to customers. However, what happens when the customer asks if the company can meet certain shipping deadlines for a product and the salesperson is *not sure* if recent delays in manufacturing could severely push back the requested shipping dates? The question here is not legal but ethical. How does a salesperson ensure that enthusiasm does not become poor ethical judgment? This is a question salespeople face almost every day.

The adage that defined the 20th century sales model was **caveat emptor** (Let the buyer beware). It was generally considered the buyer's responsibility to uncover any untruths in the seller's statements. Even in 21st century-relationship selling, the salesperson must decide how much information to give the customer. If successful relationship selling is based on mutual trust and ethical behavior, the salesperson cannot hold back information or tell half-truths.[4] When customers become aware of such half-truths (as they always do), the long-term damage to the relationship can be far worse than any short-term pain caused by being honest.[5] Dishonesty not only harms the customer relationship but can lead to legal action (which we will discuss later in this chapter) and huge financial judgments against the company.

The salesperson who chooses to provide complete information even when it presents the company in a less than favorable light can create a high degree of credibility with the customer. Cisco, for example, instructs its salesforce to be totally open and honest with customers, to present the most accurate information available even if the information is not positive. Interestingly, the mere fact that the company states this policy has had a positive effect with customers.

Gifts, Entertainment, Bribes. A **gift** is a nonfinancial present. A **bribe** is a financial present given to a buyer to manipulate the purchase decision.

Meeting a customer for lunch is an accepted business custom. Historically, it has been a way for the buyer and seller to build a more personal relationship while getting work done. The vast majority of salespeople take their customers to lunch at least occasionally. But what about taking them to dinner or a nightclub? Does it make a difference if the lunch cost $15 per person or $75? These are the kinds of questions salespeople must answer on a regular basis.

Why do some salespeople offer bribes or illegal gifts to customers? Unfortunately, the answer is it works. Research suggests that gifts can affect whether or not the order is given and the size of the order.[6] Customers often place salespeople in an almost impossible situation. Even if the salesperson desires to be ethical, a customer may ask for "special consideration" in getting the order.

To deal with these difficult ethical questions, many companies on both sides of the buyer–seller relationship have established policies for handling gifts and entertainment. On one hand, companies like Hewlett-Packard tell their salespeople explicitly that under no circumstances should they offer gifts of any kind to secure an order. On the customer side, companies like Target and Home Depot significantly limit the scope of gifts (pencils, coffee mugs) and type of interaction (they must meet at corporate offices) between their purchasing agents and salespeople.

Unfair Treatment. By their very nature, each customer is different. Some customers buy more or have greater potential for new business. It is quite appropriate to offer special pricing or better terms to them. However, salespeople need to be aware of ethical concerns when customers ask for more than is reasonably expected in the course of business.

There are several problems associated with unfair treatment. First, providing special treatment to customers is costly and may not be a good use of the salesperson's time. Consider, for example, the established customer who expects a busy salesperson to drop off orders. Diverting the salesperson away from his or her primary focus could lead to lower productivity. Second, providing special services to some customers will almost surely lead other customers to feel as though they are not important enough to warrant special treatment, which will lead to a weaker relationship with those customers.

Confidentiality Leaks. A key element of the trust between buyer and seller is **confidentiality,** which is the sharing of sensitive information. Salespeople learn critical facts about their customers all the time. At a minimum they know how much, at what price, and when shipments of their own products will be purchased by their customer. Today their knowledge often goes much deeper. For example, in working with customers they may learn about the development and introduction of new products. They can also learn a great deal about the pricing structure and strategy of existing products. This information would be useful to the customer's competitors, some of whom could be the salesperson's customers already.

It is essential for the credibility of a salesperson and his or her company that any information shared by the customer be held in the strictest confidence. Divulging sensitive information to others, even to nonessential employees in the salesperson's company, is one of the surest ways to lose a customer. Customers have long memories in these situations and do not easily forget or forgive any salesperson who shares confidential information with individuals or organizations not authorized by the customer.

Issues with Employers

Not all of a salesperson's ethical concerns deal with the customer relationship. Three ethical concerns related to the salesperson's employer are (1) cheating, (2) misuse of company resources, and (3) inappropriate relationships with other employees. Let's look at each issue more closely.

Cheating. Salespeople work, for the most part, away from their employer, so the company relies on their honesty and integrity. More importantly, the salesperson is the primary (if not the only) source of direct communication with the customer, and companies must have confidence in that information in order to make sound business decisions. Salespeople report on things like the number of sales calls, expenses, and even how sales are recorded to the company and this information is assumed to be true and accurate.

Unfortunately, when salespeople do not make enough sales calls, want to win a sales contest by booking orders within a certain period of time, or any of hundreds of other situations they can be tempted to cheat. For example, if a salesperson is evaluated on the number of sales calls he or she makes each week but has not made that number, is it ethical to list a sales call with a customer *this* week that he or she intends to contact by phone *next* week? What would you do in a similar situation?

Misuse of Company Resources. Salespeople need a number of resources to do their jobs effectively, so it is expensive to equip and maintain a sales force in the field. Among the resources are technology (smartphones, computers) and transportation (cars, air travel). Legitimate business expenses include taking a customer to lunch, for which the salesperson is entitled to be reimbursed. Salespeople are often given direct control of some resources, such as cell phones and computers. For other expenses, such as travel, they submit expense reports and are reimbursed by the company. In still other situations, salespeople are given a budget for items like a car and submit a report at the end of the year detailing how they used the money.

If salespeople misrepresent their business expenses to generate additional income, they cross the ethical line. Often this happens when the salesperson believes the compensation is not adequate or company policies are not sufficient to cover legitimate business expenses. Sadly, this practice is not uncommon. A study by the Department of Commerce estimated employee theft in the United States at $60 billion. Another study reported that 30 percent of all business failures are caused by employee theft. More specifically, 60 percent of sales managers said they had caught one of their salespeople cheating on an expense report.[7]

It may be true that the company compensation plan is inadequate and policies regarding reimbursement of expenses are not fair, but this does not justify illegal or even unethical behavior. We'll discuss in the section on ethical concerns for management the wisdom of having plans and policies in place that are fair to salespeople.

A good rule of thumb is to adopt your own standard of living when you are incurring business-related expenses. Companies should not ask their salespeople to have a lower standard of living on business than at home, but salespeople should not use the opportunity of business travel to live a more lavish lifestyle than they do at home either.

It is not always clear whether the use of business resources for personal use is unethical. Some companies permit the personal use of business assets. Consider the company cell phone. After business hours, is it unethical for a salesperson to use the cell phone for personal use when it does not interfere with business activities? Companies almost always have a stated policy on the personal use of business resources, and the salesperson needs to become familiar with that policy. Violating it can have serious implications for a salesperson's continued employment with the company.

Inappropriate Relationships with Other Employees and Customers. In today's workplace, men and women work closely together in a variety of situations, as members of the same organization (peers and co-workers), or as buyer and seller. For the most part, men and women work in an environment of mutual respect and professional business behavior. However, occasionally these relationships become more personal and intimate, which can be dangerous for everyone involved. In a survey, 57 percent of respondents had personally witnessed romantic relationships between salespeople in their companies but only 15 percent of the companies had a stated policy on personal relationships between employees.[8] This creates a gap between what individuals in the organization are doing and company policy on such behavior.

The biggest ethical issues for individuals are the potentially negative implications of the relationship on them, their loved ones, and the company. What happens when the relationship ends? Might the company be charged with sexual harassment? If the relationship is with a customer, how will it affect the business relationship between the two companies? These are tough questions that involve not only business but personal decisions.

While a number of companies do not expressly prohibit personal relationships among co-workers, it is important to realize there are serious implications crossing the line into a personal, nonprofessional relationship. Simple common sense can help you avoid such compromising situations. For example, always keep the conversation professional and on business topics. Even joking about sexual matters or personal business can give someone the wrong impression. Also, don't put yourself in a situation that could be misinterpreted. Taking a co-worker to dinner alone after business hours could give that person the wrong idea.

Ethical Concerns for Management

Salespeople are not the only members of the sales force who face ethical concerns. Management must address significant ethical issues with (1) salespeople, (2) company policies, and (3) international customers and policies. Let us explore each of these issues in greater detail.

Exhibit 4.3 summarizes the ethical concerns for management.

Issues with Salespeople

Sales managers face a number of ethical questions with their employees. If companies expect their salespeople to behave ethically, they must behave ethically as well. Management has a significant role in setting the overall culture of ethical behavior for the sales force.[9] In their relationship with salespeople, managers most often deal with three ethical issues: (1) sales pressure, (2) deception, and (3) abuse of salespeople's rights.

Sales Pressure. Pressure is part of the selling profession. Salespeople are evaluated all the time on how much they have sold, how profitable the order is, and

EXHIBIT 4.3 Ethical Concerns for Management

Salespeople	Company Policies	International Ethics
Sales pressure Deception Abusing salesperson rights	Unethical climate Unfair corporate policies	Cultural differences Differences in corporate selling policies

the configuration of the sales order, among other issues. However, when **sales pressure** is applied unfairly or too forcefully, management may be crossing the line into unethical behavior. Professional salespeople expect management to define clear sales goals without threatening undue pressure.

Unfortunately, some managers do exert unfair pressure for sales results and set goals they know their salespeople cannot attain. Setting unrealistic goals can, over time, demotivate people, especially if they feel that there is nothing they can do to reach sales targets. It can also cause salespeople to consider unethical practices. Setting sales targets and holding salespeople accountable for hitting those targets are part of the manager's job, but it is important to set realistic goals that motivate salespeople.

Deception. **Deception,** the practice of misleading or misrepresenting something, has no place in the manager–salesperson relationship. However, managers are often in situations when being totally honest has negative consequences. Consider, for example, what happens when a salesperson is forced to leave the company. What does the manager tell a prospective employer asking for a reference? Should the manager be honest and say the employee was a consistent poor performer and has no future in sales? In today's legal environment, being totally honest can lead to expensive lawsuits. In general, though, honesty is still the best policy.

In dealing directly with salespeople, managers must be honest and clear in their discussions. For example, when a salesperson is performing poorly and the future is not bright, it serves no purpose to put him or her in an impossible situation (for example, assigning a poor-performing territory or customers with little business potential) to force the salesperson out of the company. While confrontation is not easy, misleading the person is more harmful in the long run.

Abuse of Salespeople's Rights. All employees have certain rights, which managers must be aware of to avoid legal and ethical problems. These rights cover a variety of employment matters, including (1) following the policies and procedures related to termination, (2) maintaining the confidentiality and security of personal information, (3) creating a work environment free of any form of discrimination or bias (for example, race or gender bias), and (4) following established policies and rules regarding performance appraisals, compensation, and benefits. Essentially, they involve doing the right thing when you say you are going to do it.

Many problems arise when managers do not follow established company policies and procedures. For example, not reporting instances of bias or discrimination is not only unethical but illegal (as we shall discuss later in this chapter). Terminating salespeople without proper notification and not following established procedures is also unethical and potentially illegal. Frequently, managers' mistakes result from omission (not knowing the appropriate procedures) rather than commission (deliberately abusing the rights of the salesperson). It is critical that managers aggressively protect and defend the rights of their salespeople.

Issues with Company Policies

A primary role for any sales manager is to delineate, implement, monitor, and enforce the procedures and policies of the organization as they relate to the sales force. In the vast majority of instances, these policies are fair and ethical. Unfortunately, some company policies create significant ethical challenges for managers and salespeople. We will examine two such examples: unethical climate and unfair corporate policies.

Unethical Corporate Culture. Every organization has a **corporate culture,** a set of unwritten norms and rules that influence the behavior of its employees. On one hand, companies like CNL Investments follow a strong code of personal and corporate ethics. The climate at CNL encourages people to behave in an ethical manner. It is based on the personal beliefs of senior management, conveyed in the Core Values statement and other documents and demonstrated as a matter of management practice.

On the other hand are companies like Enron, which in the late 90s exhibited a consistent and profound lack of moral and ethical judgment beginning with senior management. The problem for many frontline sales managers is that the corporate culture is the result of many things beyond their control. Specifically, senior management style (do their actions match their words?), the established culture of the organization, and external pressures (like customer dissatisfaction) can create a climate where unethical or even illegal behavior is tolerated, even encouraged. At Enron, salespeople perceived that unethical behavior was acceptable because they could see that was the company culture.

Managers need to create a climate in which ethical behavior is considered the norm, not the exception. Encourage open communication so that salespeople can be honest with management without fear of negative consequences. Generate an atmosphere of mutual respect that will not tolerate discrimination of any kind. Research suggests that an ethical climate can improve salespeople's job satisfaction, organizational commitment, and willingness to stay with the company.[10]

Unfair Corporate Policies. Often managers do not make corporate policies and procedures, but they must enforce them. Company policies are developed from a variety of areas inside the organization. In matters of hiring, termination, work rules, expense reimbursement, grievance procedures, and performance appraisals, the human resources department almost always approves company policies. Its focus is not necessarily on the sales force. Sometimes policies and procedures that work fine for the rest of the organization create a problem in the sales area. For example, a company might require that employees submit business expenses once a month, but a salesperson who travels a high percentage of the time can face an unfair financial burden while waiting for reimbursement.

Managers must be flexible enough to consider the unique situation of salespeople when they enforce company policies and procedures. Most of the time salespeople operate outside the company, spending their time with customers, which makes it difficult to follow all the company rules. Good managers understand the importance of applying corporate policies in a fair manner to their sales force.

International Ethical Issues

The buyer–seller relationship does not end at the U.S. border. Complex relationships between companies and their customers extend around the world, and ethical challenges follow customers no matter where they are located. Customers operating in other countries pose unique ethical concerns for salespeople and management, especially in (1) cultural differences and (2) differences in corporate selling policies.

Cultural Differences. Culture has a considerable influence on everyone's perception of the world. Every culture creates its own set of norms, accepted behaviors,

Global PERSPECTIVE 4.2

Differences in Negotiating between Chinese and American Cultures

	American	Chinese
	Their Basic Cultural Values and Ways of Thinking	
	Individualist	Collectivist
	Egalitarian	Hierarchical
	Information oriented	Relationship oriented
	Reductionist	Holistic
	Sequential	Circular
	Seeks the truth	Seeks the way
	The argument culture	The haggling culture
	How They Approach the Negotiation Process	
Nontask sounding	Quick meetings	Long courting process
	Informal	Formal
	Make cold calls	Draw on intermediaries
Information exchange	Full authority	Limited authority
	Direct	Indirect
	Proposals first	Explanations first
Means of persuasion	Aggressive	Questioning
	Impatient	Enduring
Terms of agreement	Forging a "good deal"	Forging a long-term relationship

Source: Reprinted from Harvard Business Review, John L. Graham and N. Marklam, "The Chinese Negotiation," October 2003, pg. 4.

and beliefs that manifest themselves as **cultural differences.** For example, the American culture places a high value on individualism, while many Asian cultures value more group consensus. Even countries next door to one another can have different cultural systems. The German and French cultures, while very close geographically, have evolved very differently.

Global Perspective 4.2 highlights the differences in negotiation strategies between the Chinese and American cultures. Notice the major differences in the critical selling step in the relationship selling process. Salespeople must understand these differences in order to avoid breaching local business custom.

As companies work with customers around the world, cultural differences can dramatically affect ethical business decisions. One of the most profound examples is the use of money payments or bribes to facilitate the purchase decision. As we discussed earlier, the American business culture views bribes as unethical and illegal. However, in some Asian and Latin American cultures, it is not only acceptable but sometimes expected to give bribes or gifts to assist buyers in their purchase decision.

Consider also the use of entertainment as a business tool. Many American companies severely restrict this aspect of the buyer–seller relationship. Yet in Asian cultures, salespeople are expected to spend time with customers in social situations before the purchase. These culture clashes can create personal ethical dilemmas for salespeople and by extension for management.

Differences in Corporate Selling Policies. The "one size fits all" approach does not work when you are selling to customers in the United States, Germany, and China. Companies have adjusted their selling policies to different countries. But these policies can become so inconsistent they affect customer relationships. For example, many Middle Eastern cultures do not let women take a leadership role in business. Even the most talented saleswoman will not be readily accepted by many Middle Eastern customers. The company must decide whether to send the best person, potentially a woman, or one who fits the cultural norms of the customer. Companies like General Electric encourage their salespeople to be receptive to local business customs in dealing with customers and try to match salespeople with customers' cultural sensitivities.

It's a challenge for managers to balance corporate ethics rules with the business practices of cultures around the world. American companies face a particularly tough challenge because ethics rules in the United States tend to be much tougher than in many parts of the world. The Foreign Corrupt Practices Act (1977) forbids U.S. companies to bribe foreign officials. In 1998 the law was amended to allow for small payments that are consistent with cultural norms.[11] When corporate policies conflict with local cultural practices, salespeople are in a difficult position. If they follow corporate policy, they may lose the business, but if they follow local business customs, they may violate company ethics policies. As you can see, it is critical for members of management to be aware of their salespeople's customer experiences and to impart company policies clearly to avoid ethical problems. Even highly ethical salespeople and managers find themselves faced with very difficult choices. Recent research suggests that salespeople are much more comfortable making tough ethical decisions when their companies have a defined and consistently applied code of conduct, reinforce ethical principles in their training, and enforce corporate ethical policies.[12]

Legal Issues in Relationship Selling

So far we have focused on ethical sales standards and behavior. Society also sets legal standards that define and direct the behavior of sellers and buyers. While almost every country has its own laws, our focus is on United States laws and their effect on selling.

Over the years a number of laws have been enacted at the federal, state, and local levels that either directly or indirectly influence the buyer–seller relationship. Salespeople (or managers) who violate these laws put their companies and their personal reputations at great risk.[13] As a result of recent scandals, new laws have been enacted and existing laws strengthened to mandate large financial penalties as well as jail time for people who break them.

Uniform Commercial Code: The Legal Framework for Selling

We have talked a lot already about buyers, sellers, and a host of other important concepts in a successful sales relationship. But if someone asked you the legal definition of a sale, would you be able to tell them? What are the legal obligations of the salesperson and the buyer? What is the difference between an express and an implied warranty? These are all important terms, and salespeople must understand the legal implications of what they say and do with customers.

The **Uniform Commercial Code,** the most significant set of laws affecting selling, defines these terms (as well as many more). The UCC consists of nine articles and is modified by each state. It sets out the rules and procedures for almost all business practices in the United States. The most relevant section of the UCC for selling is Article 2, titled simply "Sales." It defines terms related to selling and spells out legal obligations for buyers and sellers. Exhibit 4.4 summarizes some of the key terms in selling.

The UCC is the most fundamental legal framework for selling and influences almost all transactions, so salespeople and managers need to become familiar with it. A mistake can cost the company a lot of money and the salesperson his or her job. The salesperson has significant legal responsibilities, which can be summarized as follows:

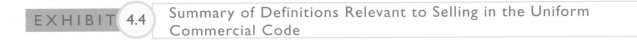

EXHIBIT 4.4 Summary of Definitions Relevant to Selling in the Uniform Commercial Code

As you read the definitions, some will seem amazingly simple (salesperson, buyer), while others are more complex (express and implied warranties). Each term has legal meaning, and the UCC defines literally hundreds of terms. Some of the most significant terms for selling are defined here using the language of the UCC. The section where the definition is located is also identified.

1. **Salesperson**—a person who sells or *contracts* to sell *goods* (Section 2-103)
2. **Buyer**—a person who buys or *contracts* to buy *goods* (Section 2-103)
3. **Sale**—consists in the passing of title from the seller to the *buyer* for a price (Section 2-401).
4. **Contract for sale**—includes both a present sale of goods and a *contract* to sell goods at a future time.
5. **Goods**—all things (including specially manufactured goods) that are movable at the time of identification to the *contract for sale* other than the money in which the price is to be paid, investment securities (Article 8), and things in action. "Goods" also includes the unborn young of animals and growing crops and other identified things attached to realty, as described in the section on goods to be severed from realty (Section 2-107).
6. **Person in the position of a seller** includes as against a principal an agent who has paid or become responsible for the price of *goods* on behalf of his or her principal or anyone who otherwise holds a security interest or other right in goods similar to that of a *seller* (Section 2-707)
7. **Express warranties** by the seller are created as follows (Section 2-316):

   (1) a. Any affirmation of fact or promise made by the *seller* to the *buyer* that relates to the *goods* and becomes part of the basis of the bargain creates an express warranty that the goods shall conform to the affirmation or promise.

   b. Any description of the *goods* that is made part of the basis of the bargain creates an express warranty that the goods shall conform to the description.

   c. Any sample or model that is made part of the basis of the bargain creates an express warranty that the whole of the *goods* shall conform to the sample or model.

   (2) It is not necessary to the creation of an express warranty that the *seller* use formal words such as "warrant" or "guarantee" or that he or she have a specific intention to make a warranty, but an affirmation merely of the value of the *goods* or a statement purporting to be merely the seller's opinion or commendation of the goods does not create a warranty.

8. **Implied Warranty**
   (1) Unless excluded or modified (Section 2-316), a warranty that the *goods* shall be merchantable is implied in a *contract* for their sale if the *seller* is a *merchant* with respect to goods of that kind. Under this section the serving for value of food or drink to be consumed either on the premises or elsewhere is a sale.
   (2) *Goods*, to be merchantable, must be at least such as
      a. pass without objection in the trade under the *contract* description; and
      b. in the case of fungible *goods*, are of fair average quality within the description; and
      c. are fit for the ordinary purposes for which such goods are used; and
      d. run, within the variations permitted by the *agreement*, of even kind, quality, and quantity within each unit and among all units involved; and
      e. are adequately contained, packaged, and labeled as the *agreement* may require; and
      f. conform to the promise or affirmations of fact made on the container or label, if any.
   (3) Unless excluded or modified (Section 2-316), other implied warranties may arise from course of dealing or usage of trade
9. **Exclusion or Modification of Warranties (Section 2-316)**
   (1) Words or conduct relevant to the creation of an express warranty and words or conduct tending to negate or limit warranty shall be construed wherever reasonable as consistent with each other; but subject to the provisions of this Article on parol or extrinsic evidence (Section 2-202) negation or limitation is inoperative to the extent that such construction is unreasonable.
   (2) Subject to subsection (3), to exclude or modify the implied warranty of merchantability or any part of it the language must mention merchantability and in case of a writing must be conspicuous, and to exclude or modify any implied warranty of fitness the exclusion must be by a writing and conspicuous. Language to exclude all implied warranties of fitness is sufficient if it states, for example, that "There are no warranties which extend beyond the description on the face hereof."
   (3) Notwithstanding subsection (2)
      a. unless the circumstances indicate otherwise, all implied warranties are excluded by expressions like "as is", "with all faults" or other language which in common understanding calls the *buyer's* attention to the exclusion of warranties and makes plain that there is no implied warranty; and
      b. when the *buyer* before entering into the *contract* has examined the *goods* or the sample or model as fully as he desired or has refused to examine the goods there is no implied warranty with regard to defects which an examination ought in the circumstances to have revealed to him; and
      c. an implied warranty can also be excluded or modified by course of dealing or course of performance or usage of trade.
   (4) Remedies for breach of warranty can be limited in accordance with the provisions of this Article on liquidation or limitation of damages and on contractual modification of remedy (Sections 2-718 and 2-719).

1. *Representing the company.* Since a salesperson is a legal representative of the company, his or her words carry a legal obligation for their employer. Quite simply, salespersons are speaking for the entire company when they are in front of the customer. Any statement, promise, or action is technically a statement from the company and is a legal commitment.
2. *Oral versus written commitments.* The UCC considers an oral commitment from a salesperson legally binding to the company. Any sale over $500 does require a written agreement; however, salespeople need to know that statements made in front of the customer carry just as much weight as a written agreement.
3. *Implied and express warranties.* Products and services often come with express warranties that assure the buyer the product will perform as represented by the company. However, salespeople need to be careful because statements they make regarding product/service performance, even if they are not consistent with company materials, can constitute an implied warranty. This is especially important in relationship selling. If the salesperson, after learning about the customer's needs, presents the product as a solution, there is an implied warranty the product will do the job.

Unlawful Business Activities

In addition to the Uniform Commercial Code, a number of federal laws have been passed over the years that affect selling. The laws include but are not limited to the Sherman Antitrust Act, Clayton Act, and Robinson-Patman Act. State and local municipalities have also adopted similar statutes and in many cases passed new laws that directly affect selling. For example, every state has its own set of real estate laws, which influence the sale of real estate in that state.

While there are a number of unlawful activities, this section summarizes the most significant: collusion, restraint of trade, reciprocity, competitor obstruction, defamation, and price discrimination. Exhibit 4.5 provides recommendations to help management create company policies that encourage legal behavior.

Collusion. When competing companies get together and fix prices, divide up customers or territories, or act in a way to harm a third party (often another competitor or customer), they are engaged in **collusion.** One example of this kind of activity occurs when two companies fix prices to force a third competitor into an unprofitable or uncompetitive position. Any activity between two competitors that serves to lessen competition is illegal.

Restraint of Trade. It is not uncommon with today's complex distribution systems to find companies that exert powerful influence over their channel of distribution. However, it is illegal for any company to engage in **restraint of trade,** which is forcing a dealer or other channel member to stop carrying its competitors' products as part of its arrangement with the dealer.

Reciprocity. The practice of suppliers buying from one another is called **reciprocity** and is not illegal per se. A company buys from a supplier and then turns around and sells it another product or service. However, if the arrangement effectively shuts out other competitors, it is illegal and must be stopped.

Competitor Obstruction. It is illegal for salespeople or their companies to actively participate in **competitor obstruction,** which is the practice of impeding competitor access to a customer. For example, altering a competitor's products or marketing

EXHIBIT 4.5 Sales Management Policies to Encourage Legal Behavior

1. Provide detailed instructions on relevant laws and legal guidelines in training for beginning salespeople and follow-up sessions for experienced salespeople.
2. Update salespeople on new judicial and statutory developments as they relate to customer relationships, reporting procedures, and interactions with other employees.
3. Develop incentive compensation packages that reward salespeople for avoiding or effectively managing potentially illegal situations.
4. Review performance to identify quickly and decisively salespeople who engage in illegal or potentially illegal activities.
5. Manage by example. Always follow both the letter and the spirit of the law. Hold no salesperson to a standard higher than you hold yourself.

Source: Karl Boedecker, Fred W. Morgan, and Jeffrey J. Stoltman, "Legal Dimensions of Salesperson's Statements: A Review and Managerial Suggestions," *Journal of Marketing* 55, no. 1 (January 1991), pp. 70–80. Reprinted by permission.

communications clearly interferes with the competitor's right to do business and is illegal. A good rule is steer clear of your competitors' products when you encounter them with a customer.

Competitor Defamation. While direct competitor obstruction happens occasionally, a much more common problem for salespeople is **competitor defamation.** It is illegal to harm a competitor by making unfair or untrue statements about the company, its products, or the people who work for it. Unfair statements are statements that are difficult to prove (or disprove) and put the competitor at a disadvantage in the marketplace while untrue statements are deliberate falsehoods. Among the remedies open to the injured party are cease-and-desist orders, which effectively force the guilty company to stop or face several penalties. It can also take the offending party to court and pursue other remedies (financial compensation).

There are two basic types of defamation:

Slander is unfair or untrue *oral* statements (for example, a salesperson making false statements during a presentation) that materially harm the reputation of the competitor or the personal reputation of anyone working for the company.

Libel is unfair or untrue *written* statements (for example, a salesperson writing unfair statements in a letter or sales proposal) that materially harm the reputation of the competitor or the personal reputation of anyone working for the company. Examples of statements that defame a competitor:

- "That company has not met any target delivery dates for new products in the last five years" (untrue statement about the competitor's ability to meet contractual obligations).
- "I heard they were going to lay off a lot of people due to poor sales over the last four quarters" (untrue statement about the company's financial condition).
- "You know, the salesperson for that company is not very knowledgeable about their products and services" (unfair statement about the personal qualifications of a legal representative of the company).

Not only is defamation illegal, but it is also a bad idea. Disparaging the competition is bad selling and will not help build a strong customer relationship. While factual comparisons between your products and competitors' are accepted sales practice, it is always best to focus on your product rather than belittle your competition.

Price Discrimination. Put simply, it is illegal to discriminate based on price. While the original law, Robinson-Patman, focused on interstate commerce, most states have passed legislation that provides the same protection to intrastate business transactions. **Price discrimination** is the practice of giving different prices or discounts to different customers who purchase the same quality and quantity of products and services. Of course, companies are legally allowed to charge different prices if (1) they reflect differences in the cost of operations (manufacturing, sale, or delivery), (2) they meet, in good faith, competitor pricing to the same customer, or (3) they reflect differences in the quality or quantity of the product purchase. It is perfectly legal, for example to charge a lower price to a customer who buys more (quantity discount) or has received a better price from a competitor. At the end of the day the issue is the fair treatment of customers.

A Code of Sales Ethics

What are the rules that govern your life? How do you make ethical decisions? We all grow up learning a sense of right and wrong that, over time, becomes our **code of ethics.** We use our personal code to guide us in life; regrettably, it is often tested by situations and people that force us to either reaffirm or compromise our code of ethics. As we examined the many ethical concerns and issues salespeople and managers face, you saw how difficult it can be to make the right ethical decision. Let's examine how a code of ethics can be helpful for salespeople as they face ethical issues every day.

Corporate Code of Ethics

Salespeople (indeed, all employees) make ethical decisions using two ethical frameworks, their own personal code of ethics and the company's ethical code. Not all companies have a written code of ethics, but all companies have a culture that defines acceptable and unacceptable ethical behavior.

Corporate codes of ethics are important for three reasons. First, they are—or at least should be—the framework for the company's approach to doing business. Second, by defining the company's values, corporate ethical codes can serve as a point of reference for individual employee behavior. Third, a strong corporate code of ethics can have a positive effect on customers and other organizations that interact with the company.

As we saw earlier in the chapter, companies like Dell have a code of conduct that defines what they believe and how they expect employees to conduct the company's business. A corporate code of ethics, like a personal code of ethics, does not define what to do in every possible ethical situation. Rather, it identifies certain key traits to help direct the salesperson's decision making. "Integrity. We do the right thing without compromise. We avoid even the appearance of impropriety" tells customers clearly that Dell salespeople will do the right thing in every situation. This is a powerful tool for salespeople who know the company will support them as long as they act with integrity.

Of course, it is essential that the values and behaviors spelled out in the code of ethics (or whatever it is called) are actually part of the company's corporate culture. Companies like Adelphia embraced ethics in their codes but *key senior managers* behaved in an unethical and illegal manner anyway. Senior management, in particular, must not only "talk the talk" but "walk the walk" and actually support an ethical business climate.

Individual Code of Sales Ethics

Everyone has his or her own code of ethics, which influences the decisions that a person makes in certain situations. Unfortunately, in some cases salespeople make unethical choices. The vast majority of salespeople and managers, however, are ethical and seek direction in making the difficult decisions we have examined in this chapter.

A personal code of sales ethics can be a valuable tool for everyone in selling. It provides a framework for evaluating situations and helps individuals coordinate their own personal values system with their corporate ethics code and established guidelines for ethical sales behavior. The process begins with your own definition of what is right and wrong. Very early in life we develop a value system that is learned from our parents and reinforced by religious or moral beliefs. We also learn from our company's code of ethics and accepted business practices. Research suggests salespeople are generally more successful when their personal code of ethics is consistent with those of the company and management.[14]

It can be helpful to evaluate the current circumstances and possible decisions against a code of sales ethics. One example is provided by the Sales and Marketing Executives Institute (a leading professional organization for salespeople and managers). Exhibit 4.6 is the SMEI Sales and Marketing Creed. Many salespeople subscribe to this and other codes that delineate ethical conduct in selling.

EXHIBIT 4.6 SMEI Sales and Marketing Creed

Your pledge of high standards in serving your company, its customers, and free enterprise

1. I hereby acknowledge my accountability to the organization for which I work and to society as a whole to improve sales knowledge and practice and to adhere to the highest professional standards in my work and personal relationships.
2. My concept of selling includes as its basic principle the sovereignty of all consumers in the marketplace and the necessity for mutual benefit to both buyer and seller in all transactions.
3. I shall personally maintain the highest standards of ethical and professional conduct in all my business relationships with customers, suppliers, colleagues, competitors, governmental agencies, and the public.
4. I pledge to protect, support, and promote the principles of consumer choice, competition, and innovation enterprise, consistent with relevant legislative public policy standards.
5. I shall not knowingly participate in actions, agreements, or marketing policies or practices which may be detrimental to customers, competitors, or established community social or economic policies or standards.
6. I shall strive to ensure that products and services are distributed through such channels and by such methods as will tend to optimize the distributive process by offering maximum customer value and service at minimum cost while providing fair and equitable compensation for all parties.
7. I shall support efforts to increase productivity or reduce costs of production or marketing through standardization or other methods, provided these methods do not stifle innovation or creativity.
8. I believe prices should reflect true value in use of the product or service to the customer, including the pricing of goods and services transferred among operating organizations worldwide.
9. I acknowledge that providing the best economic and social product value consistent with cost also includes:
   - (a) recognizing the customer's right to expect safe products with clear instructions for their proper use and maintenance.
   - (b) providing easily accessible channels for customer complaints.
   - (c) investigating any customer dissatisfaction objectively and taking prompt and appropriate remedial action.
   - (d) recognizing and supporting proven public policy objectives such as conserving energy and protecting the environment.
10. I pledge my efforts to assure that all marketing research, advertising, and presentations of products, services, or concepts are done clearly, truthfully, and in good taste so as not to mislead or offend customers. I further pledge to assure that all these activities are conducted in accordance with the highest standards of each profession and generally accepted principles of fair competition.
11. I pledge to cooperate fully in furthering the efforts of all institutions, media, professional associations, and other organizations to publicize this creed as widely as possible throughout the world.

Source: Sales and Marketing Executives Institute Web site (www.smei.org), October 2008.

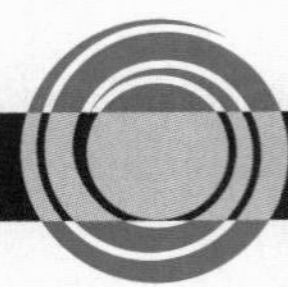

INNOVATION 4.3

Ethical Checklist

		Circle the appropriate answer on the scale; 1 = not at all; 5 = totally yes				
1.	**Relevant Information Test.** Have I/we obtained as much information as possible to make an informed decision and action plan for this situation?	1	2	3	4	5
2.	**Involvement Test.** Have I/we involved all who have a right to have input and/or to be involved in making this decision and action plan?	1	2	3	4	5
3.	**Consequential Test.** Have I/we anticipated and attempted to accommodate the consequences of this decision and action plan on any who are significantly affected by it?	1	2	3	4	5
4.	**Fairness Test.** If I/we were assigned to take the place of any one of the stake-holders in this situation, would I/we perceive this decision and action plan to be essentially fair, given all of the circumstances?	1	2	3	4	5
5.	**Enduring Values Test**. Does this decision and action plan uphold my/our priority enduring values that are relevant to this situation?	1	2	3	4	5
6.	**Universality Test.** Would I/we want this decision and action plan to become a universal law applicable to all similar situations, even to myself/ourselves?	1	2	3	4	5
7.	**Light-of-Day Test.** How would I/we feel and be regarded by others (working associates, family, etc.) if the details of this decision and action plan were disclosed for all to know?	1	2	3	4	5
8.	**Total Ethical Analysis Confidence Score.** Place the total of all circled numbers here.					

How confident can you be that you have done a good job of ethical analysis?	
7–14	Not very confident
15–21	Somewhat confident
22–28	Quite confident
29–35	Very confident

Source: Used with permission from copyright holders: Doug Wallace and Jon Pekel, Twin Cities-based consultants in the Fulcrum Group. Do not copy without reference to copyright owners. Not to be used for commercial purposes.

It also helps to use a checklist to walk through the ethical issues. One such checklist (and there are many) is Innovation 4.3, which allows you to quantify your ethical analysis and determine how well you have assessed the situation.

The goal of these analyses is to help each salesperson make the best ethical decision. The time to think about ethics is not in the middle of a difficult ethical situation but before you get caught up in the circumstances. This is one reason corporate and personal codes of ethics are important; they give salespeople greater confidence in their final ethical decisions.

Summary

Ethics is a core principle of successful relationship selling. This chapter examined the ethical and legal issues of salespeople and managers. Salespeople are placed in difficult ethical situations every day, and the decisions they make affect not only themselves but their companies. Management also faces a number of ethical challenges.

The last few years have brought a new focus on the importance of ethical behavior and decision making. As a result of recent scandals, salespeople and, by extension, their managers confront customers who demand integrity and honesty and evaluate their suppliers on their business practices. There is also a growing emphasis on demonstrating social responsibility in the community (whether it is the local, national, or even global community). Companies understand that being ethical also means being a good corporate citizen.

Salespeople face two fundamental ethical arenas. First, they encounter a number of ethical challenges with their customers: dishonesty; gifts, entertainment, and bribes; unfair treatment; and confidentiality leaks. Dishonesty should never be an accepted business practice, and salespeople will find it impossible to have a strong relationship with any customer after engaging in dishonest behavior. It is appropriate to offer small tokens of appreciation and take customers to business lunches; however, at some point gifts and entertainment cross a line and become unethical and even illegal. Not all customers are equal, but it is unethical to provide unfair or unwarranted treatment to customers. Some customers demand unfair service as part of the terms of business. In these situations, salespeople must be supported by their companies. Finally, in light of today's complex selling relationships, salespeople need to maintain the confidentiality of their customers. There is no better way to destroy a good customer relationship than to betray a confidence.

A second area of ethical issues for salespeople involves their employer. There are three basic issues a salesperson needs to be aware of: cheating, misuse of company resources, and inappropriate relationships with other employees. Cheating (as in giving false information) as it relates to employers is grounds for dismissal and never tolerated in any company. Likewise, misusing company resources (as in misrepresenting expenses) is unethical. In effect, it's stealing from the company—no matter how unfair company policies may be. Finally, the highly interactive nature of selling places salespeople in contact with many co-workers and customers. Developing inappropriate relationships is dangerous and not in the salesperson's or the company's best interests.

Management must also deal with three areas of ethical concern: salespeople, company policies, and international ethics. Management should avoid putting too much pressure on salespeople to hit sales targets, which can create a climate that encourages or at least condones unethical behavior. Just as companies expect their salespeople to be honest, it is unethical for management to practice deception on salespeople. Finally, salespeople deserve certain rights in working with management. The company should follow established policies for termination and performance appraisals and create an environment free from discrimination. Managers who violate company policies in working with salespeople are behaving unethically.

All companies have a business climate or culture, which is a set of unwritten rules and policies that influence salespeople's behavior. Management should create a climate that encourages salespeople to make ethical decisions. It should also create (when possible) and enforce fairly company policies and procedures that directly affect the sales force. It is wrong to punish salespeople with company policies that do not consider the unique aspects of their job (such as having to wait for expense reimbursement).

International ethics is a final ethical concern for managers. Cultural differences can produce profound ethical challenges for salespeople dealing with customers around the world. One example is the use of gifts or bribes to influence the sales decision, which is much more accepted in some cultures than in the United States. This leads to a second issue: Differences in corporate selling policies need to be monitored so salespeople can effectively manage their many relationships with large, multinational customers in different countries. If company policies are vastly different, customers become confused and salespeople can be put in a difficult situation.

In addition to ethics, laws at the local, state, and federal level define and place limits on sales activities. The most fundamental set of laws affecting sales is the Uniform Commercial Code which legally defines business practices in the United States and, more specifically, the responsibilities of a salesperson. Illegal business activities include collusion, restraint of trade, reciprocity, competitor obstruction, competitor defamation, and price discrimination.

A code of ethics can be a useful tool in helping salespeople work through difficult ethical situations. Most salespeople use two codes in making ethical decisions. A personal code of ethics is their own definition of right and wrong. The company's code of ethics defines conduct for all employees in the organization.

Key Terms

business ethics
social responsibility
dishonesty
caveat emptor
gifts
bribe
confidentiality
sales pressure
deception
corporate culture
cultural differences
Uniform Commercial Code
collusion
restraint of trade
reciprocity
competitor obstruction
competitor defamation
slander
libel
price discrimination
code of ethics

Role Play

Before You Begin

Before getting started, please go to the appendix of Chapter 1 to review the profiles of the characters involved in this role play as well as the tips on preparing a role play.

Characters Involved

Chloe Herndon

Lenny Twiggle

Lenny is the new head buyer at Buster's Supermarkets, a chain of 20 stores that is one of Chloe's top five accounts. Before Lenny started at Buster's, Chloe had called on former head buyer Edith Greer there for about eight years (three representing

Upland Company and five representing a competitor of Upland's) and had an outstanding professional relationship with Edith and Buster's. Edith left to take a position with another supermarket chain out of state.

Setting the Stage

While meeting with another account this morning, Chloe received a voice mail from Lenny Twiggle, the head buyer at Buster's Supermarkets, asking her to stop by there to see him at 4:30 P.M. today. Lenny has been on the job for about three months. Chloe has made four calls on him during that time and has been generally pleased with the business she has received from the account. It is a little unusual for his office to summon her in between regular appointments and very unusual for Lenny to call personally instead of his assistant. When she calls back to confirm that she can make it, she attempts to find out the agenda for the meeting. But Lenny just says, "We'll talk when you get here." Puzzled but not concerned, Chloe heads for Lenny's office.

Lenny closes the door and says, "Chloe, I have been pleased with your service and with Upland so far. I want to give you a chance to really perform. What I need are some special concessions from you. If you can get me what I want, I will increase your orders next quarter 20 percent over last year."

Chloe Herndon's Role

Chloe has been in her job for three years. Before that she worked for a competitor for five years. She has had buyers ask for all sorts of inappropriate things during her career. Tempting as Lenny's offer might be, she knows she cannot succumb to the temptation, as his expectations of special favors will only escalate over time and eventually she (and Upland Company) will be the big loser. She must formulate a response right now that lets him know where she stands on this sort of thing but also lets him know she wants to do business with him legitimately.

Lenny Twiggle's Role

Lenny is looking for a variety of what he calls "special concessions": gifts, entertainment, extra merchandise for free, unauthorized lower prices, even a dinner date with Chloe if he can get it (he's single). Basically, he is trying to see how far he can push her to give him things that enhance his professional position with Buster's as well as his personal situation. He is quite insistent and proposes several ideas for how she might meet his request. He will back down only when he understands that losing Upland Company as a vendor would severely impair his performance as perceived by management.

Assignment

Work with another student to develop a 7- to 10-minute dialogue on the issues that might occur in Lenny's office. Chloe must be firm in her unwillingness to behave unethically but at the same time keep her reasons for not doing what he asks on a professional (not personal) level. Lenny should start out nearly contemptuous in attitude, but if Chloe does a good job fending off his various requests he should end up agreeing to the value of continuing to do a healthy legitimate business with Upland.

Discussion Questions

1. Much has been made of the scandals at Enron and other large companies. What effect do you think these scandals have had on the salespeople who work for these companies? Do you think it makes their jobs easier or harder? Why?

2. Companies talk a lot about being socially responsible. What do you think that means for a company like General Electric or IBM? As a salesperson, would you incorporate your company's social responsibility into your presentation. If so how?

3. The chapter talks about the business practice of "caveat emptor," or let the buyer beware. Do you think this philosophy is consistent with relationship selling? Why or why not?

4. As a sales manager, how would you handle this situation? One of your salespeople (not a top performer but one who consistently comes close to hitting sales objectives) has turned in a receipt for a very expensive dinner with a client that is above the company's stated guidelines for customer entertainment expenses. When questioned, the sales rep says the customer is thinking of giving the company a large order and the salesperson was looking to close the deal. However, it's been three weeks and there's no contract. Other salespeople have heard about the dinner and are questioning why this employee was allowed to spend that much entertaining the customer. What do you do?

5. A large customer has just told you it expects to introduce a new product over the next 45 to 60 days. This product will definitely enhance this customer's position in the market. Your company also sells to this customer's major competitors. While you have none of these companies as customers, this information would be helpful for salespeople working with these other companies. Should you share with them?

6. As part of a mid-year cost reduction effort, your company has reduced your bonus for achieving annual sales targets. This is widely perceived as unfair; even your manager declares the company should not have instituted this policy. At the same time, the company has a very flexible expense reimbursement policy that allows salespeople to claim mileage. Historically, you have been very conservative in submitting mileage for reimbursement. However, talking with a group of sales colleagues the other night, you heard that several of them are going to start inflating the mileage to their expense reports since the company has unfairly cut their bonuses. What will you do?

7. You are a district sales manager for a high-tech company selling IT services in the Southeast. Sales have been down in the last year and senior management is putting significant pressure on you to hit the sales targets for the rest of the year. Your superior, the eastern regional manager, implied that if the Southeast does not achieve sales numbers, your job may be in jeopardy. How will you deal with this pressure from management? What kind of pressure will you apply to your sales force?

8. You are head of sales for a large company with operations around the country. The top-performing saleswoman in your western region has come to you with a sexual harassment complaint. She says her immediate boss, a 20-year veteran with the company who is well liked and in line for a promotion to regional vice president, has made improper comments and touched her inappropriately. He denies everything and says she is upset because her performance has been slipping over the last two years. What do you do?

9. How would you create an ethical business climate?

10. You travel a lot for your company and fly at least twice a month, accumulating thousands of frequent flyer miles with your airline of choice. Is it ethical to keep the miles even though you earned them traveling on business for your company?

11. As a sales manager, how would you educate your sales force about the Uniform Commercial Code? Go to www.law.cornell.edu/ucc and review the UCC. What topics do you think are most relevant for salespeople?

12. A salesperson is giving a sales presentation to a customer purchase committee. At the end, the head of purchasing looks at her and asks, "You know our specific requirements. Can your product do the job?" The salesperson responds, "Yes." Has she just offered an implied warranty?

13. What policies and procedures can a company use to discourage salespeople from discriminating on price with certain customers? As a manager, how would you deal with the problem of price discrimination?

14. Develop a personal code of sales ethics using the ethical checklist in Innovation 4.3 as a guide.

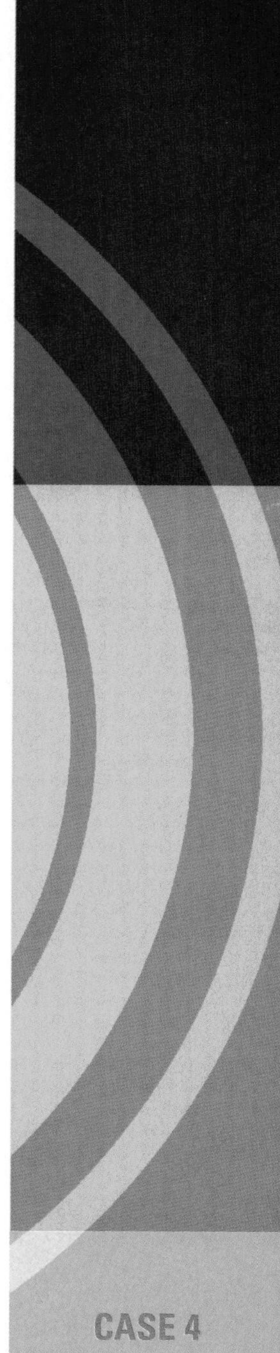

Ethical Dilemma

Your company gets a call from a large company that is based in Latin America and has operations around the world. It is the industry leader in this region of the world. The vice president of sales for your company has been trying to enter the Latin American market for several years with no luck and considers this a tremendous opportunity.

The VP calls you into her office to tell you that you have been chosen to explore the potential for a relationship with this company. After several visits over the next six months, you realize the customer is impressed with your company's reputation for quality and is seriously considering giving you a substantial contract. This contract will open up all of Latin America for your company.

At the final meeting with the potential new customer, you expect to sign the contract. However, the company's CEO suggests it would be very helpful if you (and your company) make a substantial contribution to the company's "retirement fund." The CEO is not specific about the fund, but you have a pretty good idea that your contribution is a bribe.

Questions

1. What do you do?

2. If you were the vice president of sales, what would you tell your salesperson when he contacts you for advice?

Mini Case

Health Sense Pharmaceuticals

CASE 4

Karen Simmons awoke early one cold winter morning because she had almost 70 miles to drive to begin her day as a pharmaceutical sales representative with Health Sense Pharmaceuticals. Karen knew the trip might take a little longer that day because the forecast called for about three inches of snow and a high temperature of 35 degrees, the ideal conditions for a very sloppy day. Even though most of the trip was on the interstate highway, Karen didn't want the snow to make her late for any of her 10 appointments scheduled that day. Karen has worked for Health Sense for almost three years and enjoyed much success during that time—often outselling more senior representatives in nearby territories. She attributes her success to dedication and the desire to "give the company a full day's work for a full day's pay." As Karen looked out her bedroom window, she realized that for once, the weatherman had gotten it right.

After making all of her sales calls for the day, Karen attended a social gathering sponsored by the local chapter of Sales Representatives International (a worldwide trade association dedicated to the advancement of the sales profession). There she ran into Mike Johnson and Lisa Wright, two Health Sense Pharmaceuticals reps with territories that border Karen's.

MIKE: "Hi, Karen. How's it going?"
KAREN: "Pretty good. Today's weather was kind of bad, wasn't it? I had to go all the way up to the northern end of my territory, and you know how people drive in the snow."
MIKE: "I wouldn't know. I got this really cool golf game for my computer over the weekend, so when I saw today's weather I decided to play golf! I did a little paperwork this afternoon but the golf game works really well. I guess I'll have to make up a few calls on doctors just to fill my day."
LISA: "Why does it always have to snow or rain on Mondays? When I saw that snow I decided to go to the mall—at least it's indoors. I did make it to my 2:00 appointment though, because I had been trying to get in to see that doctor for quite a while."
KAREN: "Well, you two had interesting days. Hey, there's Dave. I think I'll go say hi. You both take care and I'll see you at the next meeting."

Dave is a sales rep for Midtown Copiers. Karen met him in a doctor's office two weeks ago while they were both waiting to see the same doctor, Karen to discuss pharmaceuticals and Dave to sell the doctor a new copy machine for his practice.

DAVE: "Hi, Karen. How's business?"
KAREN: "Pretty good. I had a good day today. You know, customers seem to really appreciate you making the effort to keep your appointments in bad weather. Did you ever get that doctor to buy a new copy machine? I've been hearing the office workers complaining about the copier."
DAVE: "Well, the office workers may be complaining, but that doctor didn't think he needed a new copier. In fact, he still thought his copier was under warranty and that the manufacturer could fix any problems."
KAREN: "So, was the copier still under warranty?"
DAVE: "Yeah, I think so. That manufacturer offers five-year warranties and the machine in that office is only four years old. However, the nice thing is that he doesn't have the invoice any longer and the dealer for that machine is out of business now. I was able to convince him that without a local dealer, he wouldn't be able to get service—even though the manufacturer maintains a service center 50 miles away in Springfield."
KAREN: "I guess you sold him a new copier then?"
DAVE: "I sure did, but the nice thing is that I got him to hold off on placing the order until this week. That way the order will count toward a sales contest our firm is holding over the next two months. Waiting until March to place the order will put me on the path to winning a trip to Cancun, Mexico."
KAREN: "Well, good luck with that, Dave."
DAVE: "Hasta la vista, Katarina."

Questions

1. Discuss the ethical situation faced by Mike and Lisa. What did they do that was unethical? Pretend that you are the manager of Mike, Lisa, and Karen. How could you find out if Mike and Lisa acted unethically? What would you do about it?
2. What do you think of Dave's behavior in selling the doctor a new copier? Did Dave act unethically at all? If you believe that Dave acted unethically, how did he do so and what should his manager do about it? Finally, how will Dave's actions affect his relationship with this doctor?

Elements of Relationship Selling

PART TWO describes the process of buyer–seller interchange that is the heart and soul of relationship selling. Chapter 5 discusses two important tasks that must be done before meeting with a customer—prospecting and sales call planning, including a preapproach.

Once you have an appointment scheduled with your customer, preparing and delivering a great sales presentation becomes key. In Chapter 6 you will learn about ways to make a good first impression, strategies for approaching the customer for the first time, and characteristics of different types of sales presentations. Then you will learn how to use the sales presentation to build the relationship and convey the value proposition to your customers. Chapter 7 gives you tips on keeping the buyer–seller dialogue focused on win–win solutions, and provides specific negotiation strategies to get there.

Closing is about achieving the goals set for a specific sales call. Chapter 8 provides several approaches to closing, as well as ideas for dealing with rejection and maintaining a professional attitude. Also in Chapter 8 you will learn how to recognize buying signals and avoid several classic mistakes in closing, as well as how to do great follow-up after the sale.

The final chapter in Part Two, Chapter 9, provides a bridge from relationship selling to sales management. It covers the importance of good time and territory management to salespeople and their managers, including a number of tips on efficient and effective self-management.

In order to directly connect the sales process to sales management, each chapter in Part Two concludes with a section on the sales manager's role in the element of the sales process covered in that chapter.

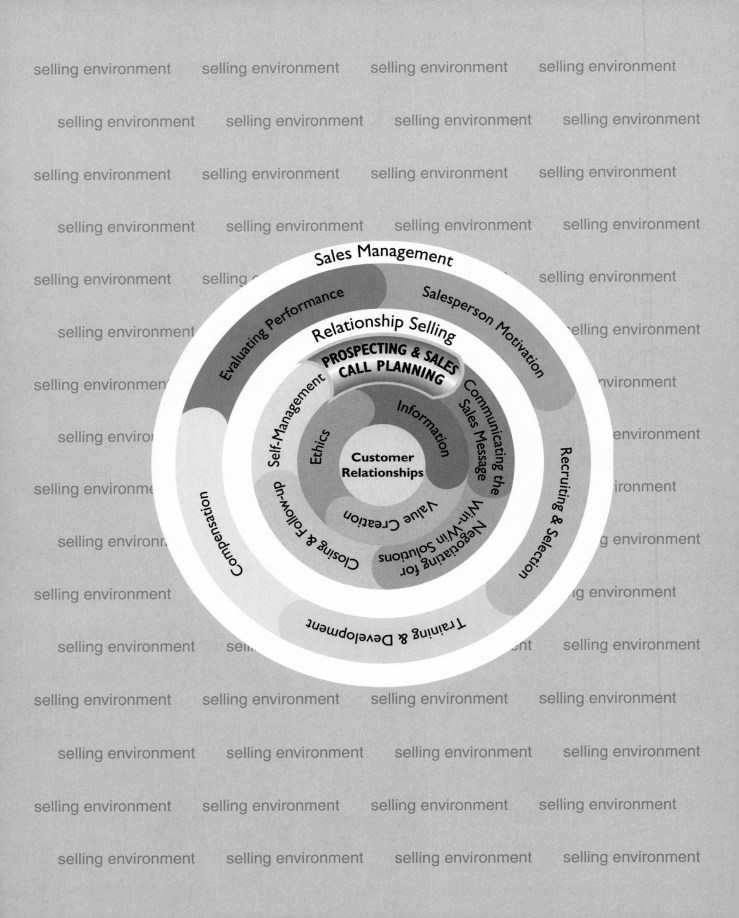

selling environment

Sales Management

Evaluating Performance

Salesperson Motivation

Recruiting & Selection

Training & Development

Compensation

Relationship Selling

PROSPECTING & SALES CALL PLANNING

Communicating the Sales Message

Negotiating for Win-Win Solutions

Closing & Follow-up

Self-Management

Information

Value Creation

Ethics

Customer Relationships

5 chapter

Prospecting and Sales Call Planning

Learning Objectives

This chapter explores important issues in how salespeople successfully prospect and plan for a sales call (the preapproach). These important activities in advance of a sales call set the stage for success in relationship selling. After reading this chapter, you should be able to

- Describe how to qualify a lead as a prospect.
- Explain why prospecting is important to long-term success in relationship selling.
- List various sources of prospects.
- Prepare a prospecting plan.
- Explain call reluctance and point out ways to overcome it.
- Describe elements of the preapproach and why planning activities are important to sales call success.
- Understand the sales manager's role in prospecting and sales call planning.

expert advice

Expert: Jack Gillespie
Company: Founder and Broker, South Bay Brokers, Inc., Manhattan Beach, CA
Business: Second largest residential real estate brokerage firm in the South Bay area of Los Angeles. Presently employs 110 agents.
Education: BS in Political Science, California State University Northridge

Where do most of your new clients come from? That is, what brings them to South Bay Brokers instead of somewhere else?

South Bay Brokers is unique in that our company was founded within the communities from which our business thrives. We have the distinct ability to fully concentrate on branding our name and expertise in our neighborhoods without bring restricted to a broad national identity. Our intimate knowledge of the area and quality of expertise in the field are keys to creating a solid first impression; however, our propensity to *exceed expectations* is what keeps our clients loyal, and keeps the referrals coming. These new and existing clients, buyers and sellers alike, also respond to our company's consistent market presence, which is reinforced by the volume of property listings that feature our signs and our informative advertising in our community publications.

Winning new clients and then ultimately fostering loyalty and repeat business from those clients is the lifeblood of a successful real estate brokerage firm. How do you go about keeping customers loyal to your firm?

We concentrate on maintaining relationships within our spheres of influence; mainly our affiliations, our clients, and the community in which they live. By supporting the fundraisers, events, and campaigns of our neighborhoods, schools, and charity organizations, we better our community and demonstrate that our realm of business extends beyond just the real estate transaction. Such personal attention makes our clients more inclined to use us as a resource for anything real estate related—from valuations for financial planning to contractor referrals for property maintenance. Besides traditional forms of real estate marketing, one exclusive form of personal correspondence our company offers is a bimonthly e-newsletter that emphasizes the latest market area information and statistics as well as useful community information links. Each agent can monitor "clicks" on various articles presented in the newsletter and use that feedback to anticipate the needs and interests of his or her client. Ultimately, it is our ethics, honesty, and willingness to serve that keeps our clients loyal to South Bay Brokers.

Are there any specific customer groups that you have targeted as especially high potential prospects?

An adept knowledge of multiple property types and a diverse clientele are the core of our business. To overly target one segment of the marketplace would limit our proficiency and longevity. Our clients, both buyers and sellers alike, come to us with many different yet specific needs. For example, we need to be prepared to meet the requirements of a first time home buyer as well as an extremely savvy investor. "Farming" a specific clientele—that is, focusing on cultivating a particular client group—is one way for a salesperson to gain recognition and garner sales. But over the long run, in our business the best approach is a well-rounded perspective on prospecting due to the unpredictability of market conditions.

Prospecting: Customers Don't Start Out as Customers

We have talked a lot about customers. It is now time to realize an important aspect of selling that has not yet come up in our discussion: today's customers didn't start out as your customers at all. Somehow, your company, through its various selling and marketing efforts, brought them to you, you to them, or both.

Your customers have probably gone through a series of stages with you. The process may start out with a **lead,** which is the name of someone who *might* have the potential to buy from your company. Leads come from many places, and later in the chapter we will review those sources. Many (if not most) leads never make it past that stage to become **prospects.** Unlike mere leads, prospects have to meet certain criteria to be considered potential customers. Prospects are considered a *very likely* set of potential customers. The process of analyzing a lead to see if it meets the criteria to be a prospect is called **qualifying the prospect.**

Qualifying the Prospect

The criteria applied to qualify potential prospects vary somewhat from company to company, but several standard qualifications exist for leads to be considered full-fledged prospects. Here are five key qualifying questions.

1. *Does the potential prospect appear to have a need for your product or service?* This criterion is fundamental. You have already learned that relationship-building approaches to selling don't involve arm-twisting, hard-sell techniques. You want to do business over the long run and eventually gain referrals (leads) from current happy customers about potential new customers. Thus, success in relationship selling depends on understanding that what you sell can satisfy a potential buyer's needs.
2. *Can the potential prospect derive added value from your product in ways that you can deliver?* This criterion is closely related to #1. In Chapter 3 you saw a number of ways beyond price and the product itself that a seller can add value for customers. To answer this question accurately, you must analyze the different ways you might do this with a potential customer. The more ways you can add value, the more likely you have a good prospect.
3. *Can you effectively contact and carry on communication/correspondence with the potential prospect?* Contact and communication with potential customers might seem easy, but this is actually a very important point. Some customers look good on paper but are not really accessible. The potential customer's geographic location and your ability to get an appointment with him or her fall within this criterion. Consider what type of contact is needed to develop the relationship. If access and communication lines are significant barriers, then it may be wise to move to another prospect.
4. *Does the potential prospect have the means and authority to make the purchase?* Quite often, as you learned in Chapter 2, a wide variety of people contribute to the ultimate purchase decision. The salesperson must determine (a) if the person being considered as a potential prospect can and will make a purchase and (b) how much effort and investment might be needed to see the purchase through to completion. Xerox pioneered a sales training package in the 1960s called Xerox PSS (for Professional Selling Skills). One of its classic training role plays partners a salesperson with a buyer to try to make a sale. The script

Leadership 5.1

Four Classic Categories of Prospects

It happens over and over again. The sales representative delivers an outstanding presentation to the prospect. She not only knew all the facts about her product, but also about all of her competitors. Her vocal skills were impeccable, and she portrayed professionalism and confidence. Her close was strong and affirmative.

But her prospect—a very prominent physician—said he would "consider" using her product if it became "appropriate." He may as well have said, "No." What went wrong?

While it is true that everyone is different and unique, it's also true that people tend to fall into four basic behavioral types when it comes to buying a service or product. The success (or failure) of the sales call is dependent upon the sales representative being able to distinguish the correct behavioral type of the prospect, the sales message and also the appropriate communication style. For example, a sales representative cannot sell the same way to Donald Trump as he can to Richard Simmons, and vice versa. The product is the same in both sales calls, but in order to close the sale effectively, the approach and the message would (or should) be different to each of the four categories.

1. **The Donald Trump—The Direct Type.** This buyer is usually a Type A personality—think "Donald Trump." They are usually in a hurry and tend to be very direct in their conversation. Direct Type buyers are often blunt and even interrupt the sales representative constantly. They state their opinions as fact. They are impatient and demanding, wanting to get to "the bottom line" quickly.

   While you want to be direct and specific, provide alternatives so that the Direct Type buyer can make the decision to buy. Let this buyer speak and you listen. Do not go into all the details or try to control the situation. Ensure he/she "wins." You must act quickly, because this buyer type decides fast. Whatever happens, don't take issues personally.
2. **The Richard Simmons—The Interpersonal Buyer.** This buyer is very friendly and excitable, often animated—think "Richard Simmons." They cannot focus on details and jump from subject to subject. Because they don't always have the ability to listen for long periods, they may ask the same question several times. Interpersonal buyers are more interested in forming a relationship than they are in buying.

   Schedule time for chatting and let this buyer speak, giving recognition as appropriate. Talk about people and feelings. As you converse with this buyer type, move closer and maintain a positive atmosphere. You want to show how your product will help to achieve popularity and recognition. Focus on the people aspects. Do not fail to socialize. Also, do not set hard restrictions, unless absolutely necessary.
3. **The "Aunt Bee"—The Safety or Status Quo Type.** These buyers usually appear calm and do not get easily excited; imagine speaking with "Aunt Bee" from the old *Andy Griffith* show. They listen carefully and ask specific questions. Completely new ideas/things make these buyers uncomfortable.

   It is key to slow down your presentation and build trust. Provide the necessary information that this buyer needs logically, and secure commitment piece by piece. Ask specific questions to find out true needs, and then provide support. It is also advantageous to provide precedents or examples of previous success to reduce uncertainty. Be sincere and do not dominate.
4. **The Albert Einstein—The Contemplative Buyer.** These buyers are usually very quiet. They focus on details and ask questions. The "Albert Einstein" characters of the world study specifications and other information carefully. In fact, they may have even done some research on your product or service prior to your sales call.

   When selling to this type, patiently provide facts and plenty of detailed information. Go slowly and do not invade his or her private space. Avoid talking about personal issues or small talk. Listen carefully, and then answer questions calmly and carefully. Be thorough; remember to include all relevant information, utilizing written supporting documentation. Find out what the key issues are and focus on them. Don't move too fast, move too close, or lose patience in providing all the requested information. Also, don't expect decisions right away.

In order to be successful, sales representatives must tailor their approaches and messages very differently to each Buyer Behavioral Type. Let's examine the differences below:

As the numbers suggest, sales representatives who try to use the same "canned" message will be effective only 25 percent of the time because the approach and message will be effective only for the buyer behavior type it was designed for. The ability to recognize the various behavior types and adapt the sales call appropriately takes training and practice.

Also, just as buyers fall into one of each of these buying types, so do sellers. More times than not, sales representatives will have to learn (and train) themselves on how to adapt their own behavioral type to the specific prospect they're calling on. Success in the sales arena will increase exponentially by training sales representatives on how to properly identify the behavioral type of their prospect, and how to adapt the sales approach and message appropriately.

Source: Alan G. Bayham, "Do You Know Who You're Selling to?" *American Salesman,* April 2008, p. 7.

(each player reads only the script for his or her role) gives the person playing the salesperson the task of making initial entry into the buyer's firm to present a new product. Unfortunately, the person role playing the buyer is told in the script that he or she has no authority to buy and cannot do anything to further the relationship until the salesperson starts to ask questions relevant to means and authority to make the purchase. Most salespeople participating in the role play never solve the dilemma. Sadly, this is a common problem in qualifying prospects.

5. *Does the potential prospect have the financial capability to make the purchase?* This issue is directly related to #4. Obviously, little is to be gained by pursuing a potential customer who does not have access to the money needed to buy what you sell. Thus, an important criterion is determining the prospect's financial status. The credit department of your firm may perform this role, or you may have to personally investigate the prospect's financial strength. It is far better to determine in advance that a prospect cannot afford to buy than to waste time pursuing someone who ultimately will not become your customer for this very straightforward reason.

Qualifying prospects effectively is fundamental to success in selling. It often involves ranking leads according to their attractiveness. *A prospects* might be most attractive and most worthy of pursuit by the sales force, *B prospects* next, and *C prospects* last. Prioritizing customers is discussed in more detail in Chapter 9. Leadership 5.1 provides insights on four categories of prospects and how a salesperson might best prepare for each.

The overall process of moving from leads to prospects to customers is best portrayed as an upside-down triangle (see Exhibit 5.1). There are many, many leads, fewer leads that can be successfully qualified as prospects, and ultimately many fewer customers.

A CRM system as described in Chapter 2 can be of great help in tracking and qualifying leads and ultimately ensuring that prospects really are likely customers. The database aspect of CRM provides bountiful information on potential customers that is readily available to anyone with a laptop computer. By definition and design, a CRM system tracks the very information necessary for making these decisions.

In the past, salespeople had to rely on others in their company to perform customer analysis and provide reports for use in qualifying prospects, but today more and more salespeople are being trained to do their own data mining and analysis.

EXHIBIT 5.1 From Leads to Customers

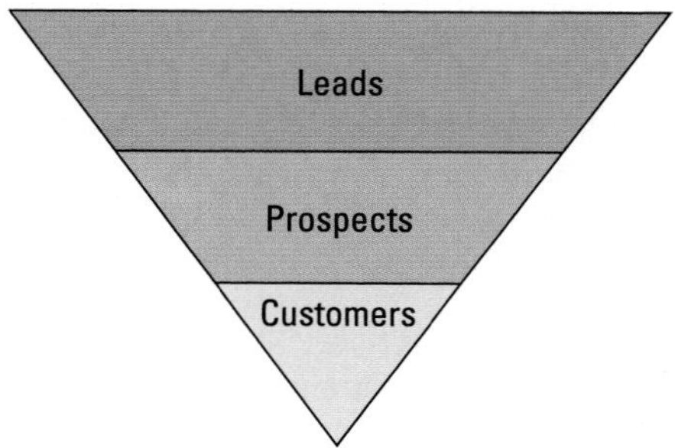

In fact, to be successful today in relationship selling, you must be able to use to full advantage the information technology tools available. This important trend plays well into a later section of this chapter that explores various sources of leads. But first, let's ensure we understand *why* prospecting is so important to success in relationship selling.

Why Prospecting Is So Important

Think of **prospecting,** pursuing leads that you hope will develop into customers, as a way to fill your pipeline of future business. Today's business generated by current customers is well and good, but a salesperson always has to be thinking ahead to where business will come from next week, next month, and even next year. Prospecting is not a haphazard or part-time process in selling. Truly great salespeople are always engaged in prospecting in one form or another. They always have their sights set on where tomorrow's business is coming from.

Now you may be thinking, if we truly are engaged in *relationship* selling, shouldn't we be able to relax some on prospecting? After all, doesn't developing long-term relationships with our customers ensure they will stay loyal and provide business to us over and over for years? Why do we need to worry about getting new customers all the time? These are good questions with important answers. Yes, of course developing long-term relationships with your customers goes a long way toward sustaining your business. But all sales organizations are continually working to find new clients, take customers away from competitors, and build their market share. The lifeblood of business success is *growth,* from both existing customers and new ones.

Beyond this general growth perspective, several specific circumstances may make prospecting for new customers an even higher priority.

- A *customer gets into financial difficulty or goes out of business entirely.* This can be quite unpredictable, as with a number of financial institutions during the credit crunch and mortgage bust that began in 2008. If you have developed a long-term vendor relationship with a firm that is in financial trouble and have not been engaged in prospecting, you may find yourself in as much trouble as your client.
- *Your main contacts in the client firm leave or change positions.* This may result in a change in the relationship. If the result is not favorable for you, ongoing prospecting can buffer any business losses from that client.
- *Your firm needs to increase revenues to pay for expansion or other items.* In such cases, the compensation and rewards system of your firm may be altered so that salespeople are paid more for prospecting and securing new customers than for developing and maintaining existing ones. Chapters 13 and 14 discuss linking sales force rewards with desired outcomes.
- *A customer moves to a new location outside your area of sales responsibility.* In this case, the business may simply move to another salesperson in your company, but you will need to find replacement business for yourself. Prospecting ensures a ready pool of potential new customers.

In sum, prospecting is a key activity of successful relationship selling. How leads are developed from which prospects (and ultimately customers) are derived is the topic of the next section.

Sources of Prospects

Leads for potential prospects come from a variety of sources. Some sources involve activities initiated by the salesperson; others involve activities initiated at the sales organization level for which the salesperson can follow up. In Chapter 3, you learned that personal selling is but one element of the promotion mix of a firm. The other elements are advertising, public relations and publicity, sales promotion, and direct marketing.[1] One function of these other promotion mix elements is to secure leads for the sales force and even to stimulate prospects to make contact with the salesperson. Exhibit 5.2 summarizes various sources of prospects.

Loyal Customers

What better source of leads than existing customers, those who are loyal to you and your company and who are satisfied with your products and the service they have been receiving from you? Sometimes a loyal customer may give you a lead without being asked. More often, however, you will need to ask. This is a normal process of communication with your customers and you should not feel uncomfortable asking. This process is called getting a **referral** because the customer is referring more business your way. One study found that about 80 percent of customers are willing to provide a referral, but only about 20 percent of salespeople ask for one.[2]

An idea currently receiving much attention in relationship selling is how to turn loyal customers into "advocates" for you and your business. **Customer advocacy** means that a customer is satisfied, loyal, and willing to spread the word that he or she is pleased with you. Satisfied customers are an important source of **word-of-mouth** advertising—a powerful source of leads that have a strong chance of resulting in qualified prospects.

Customer referrals and advocacy are among the best sources of leads. These prospects are likely to meet your qualification criteria.[3]

Endless Chain Referrals

In an **endless chain referral,** the salesperson asks an open-end question during each customer contact, such as "Ms. Buyer, who else do you know who would

EXHIBIT 5.2 Sources of Prospects

Loyal customers
Endless chain referrals
Networking

- Friends and relatives
- Centers of influence
- Bird dogs
- Civic and professional groups

Directories
Trade shows
Conferences
Internet

- Social networking Web sites (Myspace, Facebook, LinkedIn, etc.)
- E-mail

Telemarketing
Written correspondence
Cold calls
Prospecting by others in your firm
Other forms of prospecting

Sources: *Accelerating Customer Relationships: Using CRM and Relationship Technologies,* by Ronald S. Swift, © 2001. Reprinted by permission of Pearson Education Inc., Upper Saddle River, NJ.

benefit from our products?" When the question is phrased this way, the buyer is free to recommend as many potential prospects as possible. Later, when contacting these leads, the salesperson should use the buyer's name.

> "Mr. Prospect, I was talking with one of my clients recently, Ms. Buyer, and she mentioned to me that you might have a need for our products."

This method is best used when the person giving the referral is in a long-term customer relationship with you, but it can be used even when the referrer is a prospect who doesn't buy from you. The point is to always ask for suggestions of potential new customers.

Networking

All salespeople have a variety of contacts. Using these contacts to develop leads is referred to as **networking.** Network relationships between salespeople and those with whom they interact can take several forms.

Friends and Relatives. A primary network involves your friends and relatives. Northwestern Mutual Life Insurance Company encourages new agents to start their networking with this group. The idea is to think of friends and relatives as a core circle of potential leads for prospects and use an endless chain approach to work concentrically out from the core. Northwestern Mutual has shown that after a few years, successful agents have developed an entirely new set of customers and prospects who are not even directly connected to the core of friends and relatives. But starting with that core group is fundamental to success.

Centers of Influence. People are **centers of influence** if they are in a position to persuade a salesperson's potential customers. For example, a salesperson selling sporting equipment to a school system might visit with coaches, trainers, and sports medicine experts to try to win influence over a purchasing agent. These people are analogous to the group we called influencers in the buying center (discussed in Chapter 2).

Bird Dogs. No, not the canine kind! In selling, **bird dogs** (also often called "spotters") are people who come into contact with an unusually large number of people in the course of their daily routine. Salespeople can use bird dogs as their eyes and ears in the marketplace. For example, a tour operator might ask a bellman at a resort hotel for referrals of promising clients or even compensate the bellman for mentioning the tour guide's services to guests as they settle into their rooms. Some bird dogs work in client firms. Receptionists tend to hear much of what goes on in an organization. A long-standing rule of selling is to cultivate a rapport with anyone in a firm who is in a position to provide information about the potential for gaining business.

Civic and Professional Groups. One highly useful way of forming networks is to join groups. New agents with State Farm Insurance are encouraged to join Rotary International, Kiwanis, and the like, especially when they enter a new community. The friendships developed there are a terrific source of leads for the agents, and the agents' membership provides a source of strong goodwill for State Farm in the community. Likewise, if you are engaged in B2B selling, seek out primary prospects in professional groups that represent the industry you are targeting.

However, a note of caution is in order. Salespeople have been known to overdo it when joining organizations. Some become so tied up in leadership roles with groups that they lose too much valuable time from their core job of selling. Be careful to network selectively, targeting civic and professional groups that you believe will return the most leads for your time and effort invested. Leadership 5.2 provides additional tips on networking.

Leadership 5.2

Networking 101

So you've decided to do some networking. You attend an after-hours event, arriving early with a stack of business cards. By the end of the evening you've met a lot of people and exchanged a lot of business cards. On the way home, the faces are all a blur. You're stressed out—all "networked out."

A few days later, in a better frame of mind, you call each person you met, working your way through the stack of cards you collected. You ask each one if they need your product or service. Most say they do not. You're exhausted again.

This could give networking a bad name.

But is this what networking is all about? Does it have to be a nerve-racking, enervating process that leaves you with an empty feeling? No, it doesn't have to be. In fact, it can be a fun, fulfilling process.

"Fun?" you ask. "Walking into a room full of strangers is your idea of fun?" Trust me, it can be fun, but first you'll have to make a paradigm shift, move beyond networking into what I call the "R-Zone"—the "R" stands for "relationships"—to a place where you're not really networking so much as building relationships.

Here comes the simple, unadorned truth: One of the most effective ways to build a relationship is to help the other person get what he or she wants first.

This "give first" approach will turn everything you've ever known about networking on its ear.

And it's very simple: Just go into a room full of strangers telling yourself, "All I'm here to do is to help each person I meet get what they want." Obviously, that requires that you first find out what they're looking for, and that you actively listen and ask questions that help you understand their needs. Also, that you be resourceful when it comes to coming up with contacts and possible options for your new contact.

When you're in the R-Zone, you're not talking to people about high school reunions or past jobs. You're not searching to find names of people you know in common. You're not discussing current movies. You're not even being witty. You're focused on only two things: What the other person is looking for and how you're going to help them find it. When you come up with the name of someone they can call—even if it's only someone who can point them in the right direction—it's amazing how they'll warm to you.

There's an old adage, "It's not what you know, but who you know that counts." While the statement is true, it also oversimplifies. For, as many will tell you, simply knowing an important or powerful person is no guarantee your calls will be returned. The other person must perceive you as worth knowing. That's what gets calls returned. And, there's no faster way to be perceived as someone worth knowing than to give first.

Here are some other thoughts that can guide you as you develop your ability to work in the R-Zone.

- Do less better. One reason so many people find networking exhausting: They get frantic. They feel obligated to meet everyone at a given meeting. They have to "work the room." Leave working the room to the professionals. Go into a networking event with limited objectives. Just tell yourself, "I'll count this as a good experience if I can have five quality conversations with five quality contacts." And after you meet five, don't feel obligated to hang around and meet more . . . unless you want to. Pace yourself and do less better.
- Speak with confidence. Don't be shy when it comes to telling new contacts about what you can do for them. Speak with calm conviction. Project confidence. Believe in yourself. If you don't believe what you're saying, no one else will.
- Prepare a memorable introduction. In a quiet moment, reflect on why clients or customers like to do business with you. Then, write down what you would like to say that sets you or your business apart—the benefits more than the features. The introduction should begin with your name followed by your business name. Then it should tell them, from their point of view, why they should want to do business with you—in 20 seconds or less. Practice saying your "introduction" in front of a mirror. You don't have to repeat it word for word each time. Feel comfortable with the general concepts and phrases. Then begin saying your introduction to new contacts.
- Join a contact group. Whether it be an industry association, a charitable organization's board, or a religious group, make an effort to put yourself in situations where you meet new people.
- Tell people what you want. Although in this article I've focused mainly on helping other people get what they want, when building a relationship you should be clear about what you're looking for, as well. When you give first, it's amazing how quickly people look for ways to help you find what you need. An effective strategy is to tell people what you're looking for right after your introduction—something like, "And this week I'm looking for someone who can introduce me to . . ." or "This week I'm looking for companies who need . . ." naming a specific person or need.
- Practice putting yourself in the R-Zone. When meeting new people, make an effort to really listen to what they're saying. As much as possible, find out what they want. Put yourself "at source" to help them find it.

Networking really isn't enough because it's not enough just to make contacts. To be effective, we must build relationships, something that sounds easier than it is. It takes genuine caring and listening skills that make you a valuable asset in any work situation. Don't always assume that a person you meet at a networking event is looking for a new client or a job. The person may really be looking for a golf instructor, an electrician, a PC technician, a new car . . . or even a friend! Be there for them. And stay in the R-Zone.

Source: Debbie Mrazek, "How to Evolve beyond Networking into the "R-Zone," *American Salesman,* December 2007, p. 27.

Social Networking Web Sites. Especially when prospecting for younger customers, social network Web sites such as MySpace, Facebook, and LinkedIn can be very effective. LinkedIn is particularly good at connecting businesses and salespeople with both customers and others the need to interact with to be successful. It can help promote events and also provide a highly convenient means for ongoing business relationship building.[4]

Directories

A variety of **directories** are available that can serve as lead generators. These directories may be print copies, or more likely nowadays they are accessed online or via CD-Rom. The usefulness of directories depends heavily on the type of business you are in and the types of clients you are targeting as customers. Many industry groups have their own directories, often published by trade associations and made available to salespeople for a fee. Also available are many general directories, such as *Moody's Industrial Manual,* the *Dun & Bradstreet Reference Book, Standard & Poor's Corporation Record Service,* and the *Thomas Registry of American Manufacturers,* to name only a few. Of course, the good old Yellow Pages and the R. L. Polk city directories (criss-cross phone books) are valuable resources.

Many listings formerly available only in hard copy are now available online. Go to any search engine and type in the word "directory." You will be overwhelmed with sources of information on businesses and individuals. Whether online or in hard copy, a variety of specialty directories and listings are for sale. For example, a local medical society might sell a mailing list or database of all the physicians practicing in a particular geographic area for use by pharmaceutical reps.

Internet

In the age of Google, the Internet is obviously one of the richest (and most convenient) sources of leads. The Internet is used for lead generation in two primary ways. First, salespeople use it to research potential clients and their industries, with a focus on answering as accurately as possible the five qualifying questions for prospects presented earlier.

The second main way companies use the Internet for prospecting is by using their own Web site to generate inquiries from prospects. They either solicit information on a prospect's needs or make special offers to individuals who respond (probably by e-mail) to a pop-up, banner ad, or other promotional offer or mechanism on the Web site. Again, social networking Web sites can greatly facilitate these processes. Smartphones have opened the door for Web surfing and e-mail virtually anywhere, anytime.

One potential problem with this approach is that, to this day, not everyone has access to the Internet on a regular basis. This necessitates providing alternate means of contact (such as phone or fax) for prospects who do not regularly use the Internet. Another problem is that customer inquiries or requests must be responded to rapidly. If the firm does not have a well-designed way to contact these prospects quickly, it can do more harm than good, since prospects are expecting a prompt response but do not receive it. Yet another problem is the growing consumer backlash against aggressive and invasive pop-ups, which are often viewed as detracting from the usefulness of the Internet. Finally, security concerns still overwhelm all other consumer issues surrounding e-commerce. Prospects may want to provide contact information online but ultimately fail to do so because of privacy concerns.

E-mail. E-mail prospecting is a subset of using the Internet. It typically involves outward communication from the sales organization to the prospect. Usually the firm buys an e-mail list and sends an unsolicited communication to members of the list, with a means for the prospect to reply (by return e-mail, going to a designated Web site, etc.) The proliferation of e-mail prospecting has led to a growing concern about **spam,** or junk e-mail messages. Many e-mail users (especially business users) filter the spam out of their e-mail inboxes before they even have a chance to view the messages. Legislation against e-mail spam seems almost inevitable.

Overreliance on technology in general in prospecting can be a problem, as evidenced by Innovation 5.3.

Telemarketing

Many firms support their salespeople through **telemarketing. Outbound telemarketing** involves unsolicited phone calls to leads in an attempt to qualify them as prospects. This approach has come under increasing scrutiny by the federal government and many state governments. Strict guidelines and regulations have been adopted about when telemarketers can call. Opt-out lists are available to ensure prospects do not receive such calls at all. The Federal Trade Commission (FTC) is the key agency regulating telemarketing. The FTC Web site provides up-to-date information on telemarketing regulations. The declining reputation of outbound telemarketing, the resultant regulation and litigation, and especially the new opt-out lists have drastically reduced the effectiveness of outbound telemarketing as a prospecting tool.

Often salespeople, especially in B2B markets, prospect by phone themselves rather than relying on mass telemarketing. This approach has the distinct advantage of allowing the salesperson to hear potential prospects' responses, both favorable and unfavorable, firsthand. It also helps minimize the time and information gap between prospect identification and initial sales call.

Inbound telemarketing holds promise for prospecting. Like Web sites, inbound telemarketing gives prospects a way to receive more information from a sales organization. As with other approaches, the key to success with this method is to ensure timely response to customer inquiries, ideally by the salesperson who will be calling on the prospect when he or she becomes a customer.

Written Correspondence

Salespeople may choose to prospect via written correspondence with potential customers. This may be a personalized effort using a letter, proposal, samples, or a personal note. Or it may be part of an unsolicited mass direct-mail

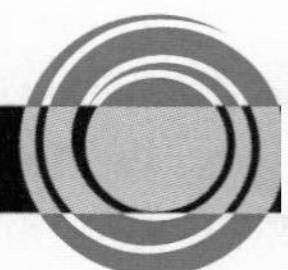

INNOVATION 5.3

When Technology Is a Prospecting Crutch

Many salespeople are relying too heavily on technology today as a sales tool to:

- Contact new prospects
- Maintain contact with current customers
- Handle after sales service issues
- Cultivate relationships with customers

Although technology is a wonderful tool and has made it possible for salespeople to save time and stay in touch—it is at what cost? Relationships, especially sales relationships, are about people. People want and need human contact. This e-mail tip is a wonderful way to stay in touch with my clients and prospects, but it will never replace a personal visit or telephone call.

- How often have you sent an e-mail versus picking up the phone?
- How often have you sent a fax versus setting an appointment with a customer to discuss the issue?

Yes—technology lets you get more done easier and is often faster (I mean, I am sitting at my computer in my home-office with a glass of wine while I write this, and who knows where you are or what you will be doing when you read this.) I love technology, but I also enjoy talking with my friends, visiting with clients and getting to know people on a personal basis—face to face. Nothing can ever replace that—not the fastest computer, glitziest Web site or smallest handheld device.

Why not try the following for the next 30 days (if you can stand the high-tech withdrawal):

- Call 1 friend every day.
- Call 5 clients every day just to say hi.
- Call a relative to say you were thinking about him/her.

No e-mails except when absolutely necessary to send critical information. I know it will be hard, but, hey, they might enjoy hearing from you.

Be careful not to assume that everyone is as technologically advanced or competent as you are.

Source: Tim Connor, "Are You Using Technology as a Crutch," EnzineArticles.com, October 6, 2006, accessed at http://ezinearticles.com/?Are-You-Using-Technology-As-A-Crutch&id=319978, October 3, 2008.

campaign by the firm. The former has the benefit of the personal touch, but it means that the salesperson may be spending too much time writing instead of selling. The latter, often called **junk mail,** is less personal but has the advantage of volume. It takes large numbers of bulk mailings to generate large numbers of leads.

Trade Shows

Most people are familiar with **trade shows,** major industry events in which companies doing business in a particular industry gather together to display their new products and services. Such events are usually held annually or semiannually. Examples include the annual housewares show in Chicago and the annual consumer electronics show in Las Vegas.

Trade shows provide leads in several ways. First, the listing of participants can be quite rich in terms of developing potential prospects. Second, networks can be developed and enhanced through contacts made at trade shows. And finally, there are opportunities to actually sell as customers come by your booth to view and learn about your new products.

Exhibit 5.3 shows the results of research conducted with 457 executives on the top 10 categories of prospect generation. They rated trade shows second.[5]

EXHIBIT 5.3 Trade Shows Rank High in Prospect Development

Prospecting Approach	Percentage of Firms Using
Direct marketing	73%
Renting a booth at a trade show	71
Print advertising	69
E-mail marketing	63
Speaking engagements	48
White papers/sponsored research	30
Radio advertising	20
Outdoor advertising	14
TV advertising	14
Other	16

Sources: Jennifer Gilbert, "The Show Must Go On," *Sales & Marketing Management*, May 2003, p. 14.

Conferences

Some sales organizations create their own **conferences** or other events to provide a forum for prospecting. Typically such conferences combine information sessions with social outings, and they are usually held in attractive locations.

Cold Calls

Making **cold calls,** also referred to as canvassing, means telephoning or going to see potential prospects in person, without invitation. Historically, salespeople dislike cold calling. In many industries it is discouraged nowadays because it is very expensive to call on individuals whose likelihood of purchase is unknown.

This is not to say that if you find yourself in a remote city with some extra time, a personal visit cold call on an interesting prospect company might not be worthwhile as a fact-finding mission. Such junkets often provide invaluable information (and sometimes surprises) that can lead to the development of a business relationship. Likewise, if you have some spare time at home or on the road, it might be fruitful to cold call by phone. Innovation 5.4 gives excellent strategies for improving your success with telephone cold calls to potential prospects and their gatekeepers.

Prospecting by Others in Your Firm

Chapter 2 highlighted the trend toward the use of cross-functional teams in selling and Chapter 3 discussed the intertwined roles of selling and marketing in modern organizations. These trends bring to light an important issue—prospecting by people in your firm *other than salespeople.* To the extent various support personnel, engineers, design people, and especially marketers and executives are out in the marketplace interacting with customers, they can employ the same approaches to lead generation and prospecting as salespeople. For this approach to provide any benefits, the firm must have a formal mechanism in place by which prospecting information collected by nonsales personnel can be recorded and disseminated to the sales force. Typical CRM systems allow for easy entry of such information into a database.

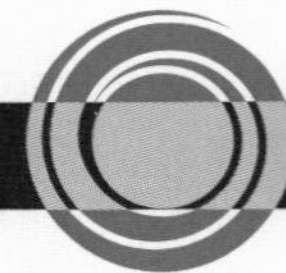

INNOVATION 5.4

The Art of the Cold Call

As energy prices continue to skyrocket and the cost of travel dramatically increases, companies large and small are once again turning to the telephone. Though it continues to be one of the most cost-effective tools in the sales arsenal of business outreach tools, as anyone who has ever been in sales will tell you, "cold calling" is one of the most intimidating and difficult tasks you can undertake. I have seen former chief financial officers (CFOs), and chief executive officers (CEOs), sweat beading on their foreheads, hands trembling, as they made call after call, only to fail miserably.

What many fail to realize is that using the telephone effectively is a cultivated skill. Experience does not replace expertise and unless an individual has made the investment in understanding and developing this highly specialized communication skill, it is unreasonable to expect that they can succeed using it.

By far the greatest common denominator for failure is fear. No one wants to admit it, but even seasoned sales professionals cringe at the idea of cold calling prospects. So what is it about cold calling that strikes such fear in us? We all fear what we don't understand. The first step is developing a methodology that allows us to control, and even overcome, the irrationality that fear can often become. But how do you turn fear into confidence and failure into success? How do you master the one sales effort that can make a pivotal difference in the overall success of an entire company? Like any skill, using the telephone requires practice, knowledge, and above all patience.

At this point it is important to distinguish the difference between telemarketing and actual telephone prospecting. The concept of telemarketing is based on the use of scripts; repetitive, marginally successful predigested dialogue that often is written by people that don't understand the basics of successful telephone usage themselves. It is also, for the most part, perceived to be numbers driven. Unfortunately what works for basic "widget" sales significantly changes when you cross the widget boundary into the world of large, complex, and often protracted business relationships.

Successful telephone prospecting is not driven solely by the number of calls you make, but rather, the number of effective calls you make. In fact, making too many calls should be the first red flag that you're not making the right kind of calls. Any telephone effort that is not "results" driven instead of numbers (or task) driven will almost assuredly fail. Likewise the value of the true telephone professional and what they can accomplish should never be underestimated, or undervalued, particularly by the company for whom they work.

Harnessing the energy of fear and converting it into the synergisms of success lies in developing techniques that remove the elements of the unknown, changing them into a step-by-step approach with a clear and unfettered view of what you want to accomplish.

The following is a step-by-step approach to the techniques, that when applied to the individual talents of the seasoned telephone professional, transforms the common telephone into one of the most viable and effective tools in the first offensive line of any company.

As with any business the selling cycle of your particular company is unique and my intention is not to imply that all business outreach criteria are the same, but there are universal aspects to the process. It is important that you realize that you still have to do the heavy lifting yourself; this is only a methodology to get you there.

Before Making the Call

1. *Market Understanding.* Before making the first call it is important to make adequate preparations. It begins with product knowledge and understanding your market, and how your product or service fits into that landscape.
2. *Focus.* Create a master plan. Set up your target prospects. Both time and momentum are lost when you have to stop to determine who to call next.
3. *First Five Seconds.* The first five seconds of a call will determine how an entire relationship is defined. Introductions should be fluid and concise and your voice should be relaxed and succinct. Remember the most important element of a successful call, is telling the recipient what they need to hear, not what you want to tell them. As with all sales initiatives, it's also about listening, not only to what a prospect says, but also the way he or she says it. Knowledge is always the driver, but emotions are the vehicle it moves on.
4. *Practice Talking Points.* I am not an advocate of canned scripts, but having fluid and concise talking points and practicing them until they become second nature is extremely important. It is easy to fall into the mindset that sophisticated rhetoric implies professionalism. It doesn't. We all think and remember in three-second intervals so making statements simple and concise tend to get the message across more effectively, without sounding pretentious. Stumbling verbally is the surest way to imply a lack of expertise and you risk losing control of the call.
5. *Familiarization.* Use the Internet to familiarize yourself with your prospect. If the Internet is not available there are various publications that will give you

a quick overview of your prospects and how they can best use your product or service. Use the same to find out the names of various individuals within the organization. Mentioning familiar names or market specific trends in a conversation implies a common history. Mentioning names within the organization, particularly management names, will imply that you have multiple contacts and will significantly lessen the tendency of some lower-level individuals to try to shut you down prematurely.

6. *Names.* Practice pronouncing difficult names. If a name is particularly difficult, write it out phonetically and put it in your notes for easy reference. The fastest way to ruin the illusion of an implied history is to mispronounce a name. I will often call the CFO's office just to be referred to a particular person or office. "I just spoke with Bob Peterson's office and it was suggested that you would be the best person to talk to." The more you know about your business and the various players, the more you will be able to overcome the obstacles that can suddenly pop up.
7. *Gatekeepers.* Secretaries have an ever-evolving responsibility as "gatekeepers." They should always be referred to as "assistants" and they can make a huge difference in your success. Always use their names when talking to them and always have the sound in your voice that you already know them. People respond unconsciously to a warm voice that sounds familiar.
8. *The Power of a Question.* Again the first five seconds of a call are critical. Even before giving your initial introduction, try asking a question using that person's name. "Sarah, can you help me I'm not sure I'm in the right place." This stops the initial qualifying that we all do and focuses the individual on helping you rather than trying to size you up. Thanks to telemarketers we are all increasingly sensitive to being cornered by unwanted sales calls.
9. *Call Business Plan.* Every call requires a business plan. Before you call, you should already know what you want to accomplish. Make an outline of all the information variables that you will need to make the deal happen. Questions are the key to understanding any opportunity. Take time to consider the questions you need to ask and how you will ask them. You can often lead a sales process just by asking questions and how those questions are answered will often tell you how serious your prospect really is. Determine the decision makers from the decision influencers. How many deals have been lost just because the wrong people were involved?

Positioning

Positioning is one of the finer nuances of telephone sales and perhaps one of the most critical. In a way, positioning is like an acting job, sounding as if you are on the same level as your prospect, whether it be a manager or a director, or even a CFO. This does not mean you should try to mimic these levels, but you should have the same tonal comfort and familiarity in your conversation. People are more relaxed and typically more honest when they perceive that they are talking to a colleague.

As you begin to develop this technique of "Implied Same Status," keeping your voice relaxed and friendly also requires "balance." It is easy for "friendly" to become "gushy" or worse, pretentious, and once that boundary is crossed, it is very hard to go back.

I once had a trainee listen to my calls to better demonstrate how these concepts work. At the end of the day she said to me, "This was helpful, but tomorrow, can we call people who don't already know you?" I looked at her, "We already did." The truth was every call I made that day was to people I didn't know. The illusion was not perceptible, even to someone who was looking for it.

So why does the sound and intonation of your voice make such a difference? We all have an unseen "Body Language" to the way we speak. At least 60 percent of what we communicate when we talk is nonverbal. If your speech pattern is uneven, or laced with nervous breaks, or you unconsciously use a reverse inflection (ending sentences with a rise making them sound questioning) it sounds as if you are unsure of what you are saying, or worse, untruthful. If you also sound anxious, your prospect unconsciously will become anxious as well. We transfer what we project. Even a smile can be heard and felt.

Also when you're talking to people, listen for responses better known as "vocal receipts." If you hear responses, even if it's nonverbal, it means they are listening, if not, there is a good chance they aren't. You never want a person to stop listening before you stop talking. If you sense this is happening, ask a question. Soliciting a response is a good way to regain control.

Understanding these basic personality links and how they reflect in our speech patterns also helps us understand the motivations and needs of others, particularly prospects. The way to best develop this skill is to listen to yourself. Using a tape recorder is one way, but the best way I've found is to call my own voice mail and leave a message. When you do this, you will hear things that you never heard before and ultimately, you will never sound believable to others, if you don't first sound believable to yourself.

Source: Kim Michael, "Conquering the Fear of Cold-Calling," *American Salesman,* August 2008, p. 7.

In truth, many salespeople accomplish some of the preapproach activities in the process of prospecting. At least, they lay the groundwork for the preapproach based on the research they have done in identifying the target prospect. Think of preapproach activities as the things you focus on between qualifying a lead as a definite prospect and picking up the phone to make the appointment. The preapproach is a planning step. You are doing research, thinking about the potential client and how to approach him or her with your value proposition, and examining the best way to contact the client to make the appointment. A terrific amount of groundwork is laid during the preapproach that pays off during the actual sales call and beyond. The work you do here ensures that you make a good first impression on the prospect on the phone and/or face to face.

The preapproach includes the following elements.

1. Establish goals for the initial sales call.
2. Learn all you can about the prospect.
3. Plan to portray the right image.
4. Determine your approach.
5. Prepare a sales proposal.

These tasks do not need to be accomplished in order. In practice, you will likely be working on them simultaneously.

Establish Goals for the Initial Sales Call

It is amazing how many salespeople call on clients without setting specific goals for what they want to accomplish in the call. This is not professional, nor does it make good use of your client's valuable time. Like goals for prospecting, goals for the sales call must be specific, measurable, and attainable. They must take into account your firm's goals, your own goals as a salesperson, and the client's goals.[7] Use your judgment as to how much you can accomplish in one sales call—especially the first one, where you and the customer are just getting to know each other. Salespeople tend to map out in advance goals across several planned sales calls with a client. The nature and scope of your goals will vary depending on your business and the client. Some sample goals for a first sales call might be

- To have the prospect agree to a demonstration of your product.
- To have the prospect agree to contact several of your references.
- To have the prospect initiate the process in his or her firm to allow your company to be set up as a vendor.
- To set up another appointment to address specific issues brought out in the initial sales call.

Note that none of these goals involves actually making a sale. If getting an order on the first sales call is realistic, then by all means set that goal. As time goes by and your relationship with a customer blossoms, you and the client can work together on mutual goal setting to build each other's business.

Learn All You Can about the Prospect

If you are engaged in B2B selling, you must pay attention to both professional and personal aspects of the potential customer. Some of the sources used in your prospecting research can serve you well here. You can turn to the Internet for more information on the professional (company) side. Other sources of information on the prospect and his or her company are noncompeting salespeople in your network who have been calling on the firm and members of the firm's buying center whom you can contact comfortably before the sales call. Exhibit 5.4 lists sample items you can research before making an initial sales call.

The idea is to obtain enough information to match yourself and your company to your prospect's situation and needs right from the very first sales call. It is also important to avoid mistakes such as mispronouncing a buyer's name or not knowing the client firm is going through a merger. Missing such major personal or professional aspects gives a very poor first impression.

Plan to Portray the Right Image

Image is important in forming a good first impression. In most cases, the first real impression you make on a prospect occurs when you meet him or her in your first face-to-face sales call. You can lay the groundwork for an excellent impression by sending written materials in advance along with a professional letter, or by being very professional when you set up the sales call appointment by phone. Planning the right image includes two key aspects: deciding what type of presentation to prepare and deciding what to wear for the sales call. Chapter 6 provides more on first impressions and image in the discussion about the approach.

Type of Presentation. Chapters 6 and 7 provide considerable detail about how to get ready for a great presentation as well as various sales presentation strategies. For now, you need to know that you actually decide what type of presentation you want to make at the preapproach stage. Here are some key issues to consider.

- How much technology should I employ, and what types (PowerPoint, laptop, etc.)?
- How formal should the presentation be?

EXHIBIT 5.4 Sample Items to Research before the Sales Call

Information on the Person	Information on the Company
Name Personal interests Personal goals Attitude toward salespeople in general Impression of your company and its products Any history of dealings with your company How rewarded/compensated by the firm Receptivity to socializing with salespeople	Size of firm Types of products offered Other vendors currently used Corporate culture How decisions are made (buying center or otherwise) Purchasing history of competing products General policies on buying and vendor relations Any unusual or especially relevant current circumstances

- How long should I allow for the presentation? How long for Q&A?
- What materials should I send the prospect in advance and what should I bring with me?

To answer these questions, you must learn as much as you can, in advance, about the prospect's preferences. If you have trouble determining critical answers from your research, it is perfectly acceptable to query the prospect or his or her gatekeeper about preferences, either by phone (perhaps when you make the appointment), by follow-up letter, or by e-mail.

Your goal at the preapproach stage should be to ensure you can show up at the prospect's office with the confidence of knowing that what you have prepared will be comfortable for the prospect, be a good fit to his or her style, and have the highest possible likelihood of gaining a favorable reaction. Bottom line: a great first impression!

Grooming and Attire. Grooming, or general personal cleanliness and professional appearance, is a given in professional selling. You *must* look the part of a competent, trusted business partner to succeed in relationship selling. Visible tattoos and body piercings, unclean fingernails, unkempt hair, and the like tell the prospect you are not playing in the professional leagues. People with poor grooming habits or attention-grabbing skin art or piercings will *not* be successful in sales.

Attire is less dogmatic than grooming for several reasons. Of course you don't want your clothing to appear sloppy and unkempt, and you don't want unusual jewelry or accessories to distract from your sales message. However, many firms have shifted to business casual all the time, so you can choose whether to match that attire or dress up to a more professional image. Here are a few tips:

- If the client suggests dressing in business casual, do so.
- When in doubt, dress up to business attire.
- When you do the preapproach, ask the prospect or gatekeeper about the dress code.
- *Never* dress down below the client's level of attire.

Following these simple rules will ensure your first impression is enhanced, not hurt, by the way you are dressed.

Determine Your Approach

The approach means how you are going to contact the prospect initially to set up an appointment and begin the dialogue. Part of the preapproach is assessing options for the approach itself. Often the telephone is used, although other viable options include e-mail, letter, or even an initial in-person interview. Your preapproach research should help you determine which of these is most appropriate for use with your particular prospect. Chapter 6 provides more information on making the approach.

Prepare a Sales Proposal

An excellent way to plan out the sales process in advance is through the use of written sales proposals. A sales proposal formalizes much of what we have learned in this chapter and focuses on the value proposition. It provides an effective means to approach the prospect. The appendix at the end of this chapter guides you through the development of a sales proposal. The research, time, and energy you put into this preparation at the preapproach stage will pay off in multiple ways during the sales call.

 The Sales Manager's Role in Prospecting and Sales Call Planning

Given the critical importance of the tasks to be performed by a salesperson prior to the first meeting with a customer, sales managers often find themselves serving as a key resource to salespeople engaged in prospecting and sales call planning. As we have learned, prospecting sometimes can be a bit intimidating, and the best sales managers carefully monitor the progress their salespeople are making on their prospecting plan.

It is important for the manager to be especially sensitive to the potential for sales call reluctance. One highly effective way to coach and mentor salespeople on prospecting activities is through ongoing "work-withs" by the sales manager, in which he or she spends a day or so periodically traveling with the salesperson on visits to customers. In cold calls, the sales manager can occasionally reverse roles and actually do the selling while the salesperson observes, in order to provide an example. Besides the opportunity to observe a salesperson in action, work-withs also provide ample time while traveling in between sales calls for general discussion between salespeople and their managers about prospecting, as well as two-way constructive debriefing of calls after they have taken place.

The sales manager can be a terrific source of ideas and information for the preapproach. Often, he or she will have direct access to more or different information that would help the salesperson better prepare for making the sales call. The salesperson can share a draft of a sales proposal or presentation materials with the manager beforehand to solicit input and ideas. And, importantly, sales managers are in the very best position of any manager in a company to ensure that the company's standards of professionalism, image, and branding are upheld consistently by the sales force through their interaction with the company's customers.

Summary

Prospecting is important to building new and future business. Leads must be qualified as prospects based on criteria established by the salesperson and his or her firm. Numerous approaches to prospecting exist. One of the most effective is referrals from loyal customers. A prospecting plan can ensure that salespeople do a thorough and systematic job of prospecting. If a salesperson suffers from call reluctance, the sales manager should provide training support to help the rep overcome it.

The preapproach (the planning stage just before the sales rep approaches the prospect) is one of the most important aspects of relationship selling. The preapproach is the salesperson's opportunity to prepare a presentation that will make a strong first impression. Good preparation during the preapproach also builds confidence that comes across in the sales call.

Key Terms

lead
prospect
qualifying the prospect
prospecting
referral
customer advocacy
word of mouth
endless chain referral
networking
centers of influence
bird dogs
directories
spam
telemarketing
outbound telemarketing
inbound telemarketing
junk mail
trade shows
conferences
cold calls
call reluctance
preapproach

Role Play

Before You Begin

Before getting started, please go to the appendix of Chapter 1 to review the profiles of the characters involved in this role play, as well as the tips on preparing a role play.

Characters Involved

Bonnie Cairns

Abe Rollins

Setting the Stage

Abe Rollins has just received a referral from a fellow Rotarian that Budget Beauty Biz (BBB) is going to open a new store in District 10, its first store in the area. BBB is a major chain that sells discount hair products, and several of Upland Company's products in the hair care category (shampoo, conditioner, creme rinse, hair spray, mousse, gel, and hair color) sell very well in BBB's stores. Upon further inquiry, Abe finds out the new store will be in Bonnie Cairns's sales territory. This will be the first new account Bonnie has opened, and Rhonda Reed (the district manager) asks Abe to help Bonnie develop her preapproach.

Bonnie Cairns's Role

Bonnie schedules a meeting with Abe to discuss preparing for making contact with the new customer. At this point, nothing is known about the new BBB store except that it will open in about six months and the buyer, José Reynaldo, will be in town in about a month to begin meeting with vendors for initial inventory orders. Bonnie needs to discuss with Abe the entire set of issues regarding the preapproach. She prepares a list of questions for Abe about what she should accomplish during the preapproach.

Abe Rollins's Role

Abe has a wealth of experience over the years in calling on new customers. He also enjoys helping Rhonda by coaching new salespeople. He is delighted to meet with Bonnie and prepares in advance an outline of the things she needs to accomplish during the preapproach on BBB.

Assignment

Work with another student to develop a 7- to 10-minute exchange about what Bonnie needs to accomplish during the preapproach stage with BBB. Both parties should come to the table prepared with extensive lists of preapproach issues, and the role play should be used to make decisions on specifically what Bonnie should do before calling José for that first appointment.

Discussion Questions

1. Someone says: "Our firm focuses on maintaining long-term relationships with our customers. We don't have to do any prospecting." Evaluate this statement.

2. List three or four criteria you could use to qualify a lead as a likely prospect. How would you find out if the lead meets these criteria?

3. What are some reasons a potential prospect might not be readily accessible? How far should you go to try to overcome such an accessibility problem before you move to the next lead?

4. Pick any three of the sources of prospects discussed in the chapter and pick a product or service you like. Develop several ideas for how you would use each source to locate leads for the product or service you are interested in selling.

5. Who is currently in your own network that you could use for prospecting? How might you add to your network?

6. Why do you think a salesperson might experience call reluctance? How can it be overcome?

7. The chapter provides sample goals for an initial sales call on a prospect. (a) What other goals can you come up with that might be appropriate for an initial sales call? (Try for three or four more.) (b) Develop three or four goals that would be appropriate for a sales call on an *established* customer.

8. Why are grooming and attire so important in relationship selling? How do you know if you are dressed appropriately for a customer?

Ethical Dilemma

We have seen in the chapter how important telemarketing can be in generating prospective customers. Recently the U.S. Congress passed and the president signed the "Do Not Call" law. After several court challenges, the register is now in place.

The national Do Not Call Registry (www.donotcall.gov) offers individuals the opportunity to register their phone number with the federal government. (Many state governments have similar registries.) Telemarketers must check the list and are prohibited from calling any phone number on it. Fines are high at $11,000 per infraction, so telemarketers have a real motivation to follow the law.

There are exceptions to the prohibition. Companies that have had a business relationship with the individual in the last 18 months, telephone surveyors conducting a phone survey, and political organizations can still call numbers on the list. However, everyone agrees this should cut down on the ability of telemarketers to make unsolicited phone calls.

Telemarketers argue, and modern selling practices suggest, that although abuses occur, telemarketing is a valid method for making prospective customers aware of new products and services. In addition, the telephone is one of the best methods for reaching certain target markets, such as senior citizens. Finally, fundamental questions about free speech and the ability to make a living are called into question if people are prohibited from engaging in a legal form of communication.

Questions

1. Should marketers be prohibited from using the telephone to solicit prospective customers? Why or why not?

2. If you worked for a company that used telemarketing to help generate new prospects, how would you feel about losing this source of customers?

Mini Case

CASE 5

Strong Point Financial Services

Rafael Sanchez is about to begin his career as a financial investment representative with Strong Point Financial Services, a national company specializing in investment opportunities for individuals. Strong Point provides its customers with the ability to trade and own individual stocks and bonds. It also helps them manage Individual Retirement Accounts (IRAs) and 401(k) accounts.

Strong Point emphasizes a conservative investment philosophy of "buy and hold" and seeks clients who have the same philosophy. It differs from investment firms that encourage account holders to execute stock or bond trades often, thus creating commissions for the investment representative. The target market for Strong Point includes small business owners, empty nesters (people whose children have grown up and left home), two-income households with no children, and retired people. Strong Point's investment reps have had much success targeting this group of customers, and Rafael is eager to get started.

Rafael has just finished a seven-week training program for Strong Point's new investment representatives. He learned about the products and services Strong Point provides, who is included in the company's target market, how to identify potential customers, and how to represent and sell financial services. Now that Rafael is back in his company-assigned territory of southeast San Diego, he has been assigned a company mentor to help him through his first two years of employment with the company. Rafael's mentor, John Green, has been with the company for 11 years and has been extremely successful. In their first meeting, Rafael and John discuss how Rafael can begin to develop a list of prospects that will generate some clients for his new investment practice.

JOHN: "Rafael, what do you plan to do to begin generating clients for your business?"
RAFAEL: "Well, at training, they said there is no substitute for knocking on doors and introducing myself to people. I'll start doing that tomorrow. I already have a couple of neighborhoods picked out—places where a lot of retired people live."
JOHN: "That sounds like a good idea, and it looks as though you've picked the right neighborhoods. How many prospects do you plan to see in a day?"
RAFAEL: "I want to make at least 20 contacts, which as you know means getting their name, address, and phone number so I can follow up with them later. If I can get other information, such as whether they are already invested in the stock market or what their investment philosophy is, that will be great. But right now, I'll settle for an OK to contact them later with information about a potential investment in which they may be interested. If I reach my goal of 20 contacts per day, by the end of four weeks I'll have 400 names and addresses in my database. It'll require a lot of work and shoe leather, but I got into this business to be successful and that's what I plan to be."
JOHN: "That sounds great. What else do you have planned?"
RAFAEL: "Well, I've contacted the local chamber of commerce. They keep a listing of all businesses owned by individuals and a separate list of businesses employing fewer than 50 people. I figure this will be a good source of information to begin targeting small business owners. They're sending me the lists and I should have them by the end of the week. Another thing I'm considering is having a booth

at the local home show—you know, the one where home builders and building products suppliers display their home plans and products. I hear they get a big attendance at the show and I should be able to make some contacts there. What do you think?"

JOHN: "Those both sound like great ideas, especially the chamber of commerce lists. I'm not sure what your success will be at the home show, but it's worth a shot. In a couple of months you should consider putting on a seminar on one of the topics the company has provided, such as the difference between stock and bond investing. The last person I mentored, Maria Santiago, found that many of her current clients were people who had attended one of her seminars."

RAFAEL: "Thanks for the tip. I'll keep the seminar idea in mind and start thinking about an appropriate topic. As you can tell, I'm eager to get started."

JOHN: "That's great. I'll touch base with you later in the week to see how things are going. Good luck."

Questions

1. Which methods of prospecting discussed in the chapter has Rafael decided to use? Are they the most appropriate for his situation?
2. As Rafael continues to develop his client base, what other sources of prospects do you recommend he try? Why do you think these methods may be successful for him?
3. Assume you are Rafael's mentor, John Green. What recommendations would you make to help Rafael get the most out of his prospecting efforts?

Appendix: Sales Proposals

As mentioned in the introduction to Part Two, Chapters 5–9 are designed to systematically guide you through the entire sales process—prospecting and sales call planning; communicating the sales message; negotiating for win–win solutions; closing the sale and follow-up; and self-management. In practice, salespeople often plan out this process in advance through the use of written sales proposals that are provided to clients prior to making a sales call. Preparing a sales proposal accomplishes two important functions: (1) It forces the salesperson to formalize much of the advanced planning discussed in this chapter—the things that need to be done *before* going face-to-face with a buyer; and (2) it focuses the dialogue between buyer and seller on the *value proposition* from the very beginning, thus laying the groundwork for an effective long-term buyer–seller relationship. Sales proposals are an exceptionally professional way to approach the job of relationship selling.

In the course, your instructor may have you prepare a sales proposal and also role play a complete presentation with a buyer (perhaps played by one of your classmates, by the instructor, or by someone else). On the Web site for this book (www.mhhe.com/Johnston3e) you will find a Sales Proposal Handbook, which includes a complete set of instructions and accompanying templates for a sales proposal assignment. In the handbook, the required content of the sales proposal is cross-referenced to the chapters in your book that contain information you will need to prepare each of the parts of the proposal. For now, let's briefly take a look at the four key components of a professional sales proposal.

- *Seller Profile.* Includes introductory information on you as the salesperson, your firm, and the products you foresee ultimately discussing with the buyer.
- *Critical Questions to Be Addressed.* You will learn in Chapter 6 that a great way to establish initial communication with your buyer is through the use of well-reasoned, insightful questions. Asking the right questions will show the buyer that you have done your homework and are prepared for the sales call. One approach to using effective questions is a technique called SPIN selling, which will be described further in Chapter 6.
- *Outline the Features, Advantages, and Benefits (FAB) of the Product.* Buyers today are very busy and pressed for time. They appreciate succinct, to-the-point information about sellers' offerings. One convenient way to provide what they need is through the FAB approach, which is also described in Chapter 6.
- *Provide a Value Analysis in Financial Terms.* In Chapter 3 and its appendix you learned about the importance of conveying a strong value proposition in

relationship selling. A key part of a sales proposal is quantifying the value of doing business with you to the buyer.

In this chapter, we built a strong case for the importance of taking time to do good prospecting and a thoughtful preapproach. The groundwork laid during these activities ensures a strongly favorable first impression with a buyer and pays off by getting the overall relationship off to a great start. Think of a sales proposal as a natural bridge between the prospecting/preapproach and the actual approach to the buyer. A sales proposal formalizes what you have learned during the analysis stage and presents an initial inquiry to a buyer in a way that will hopefully lead to the opportunity to meet with him or her in person. The next chapter prepares you for that in-person sales call.

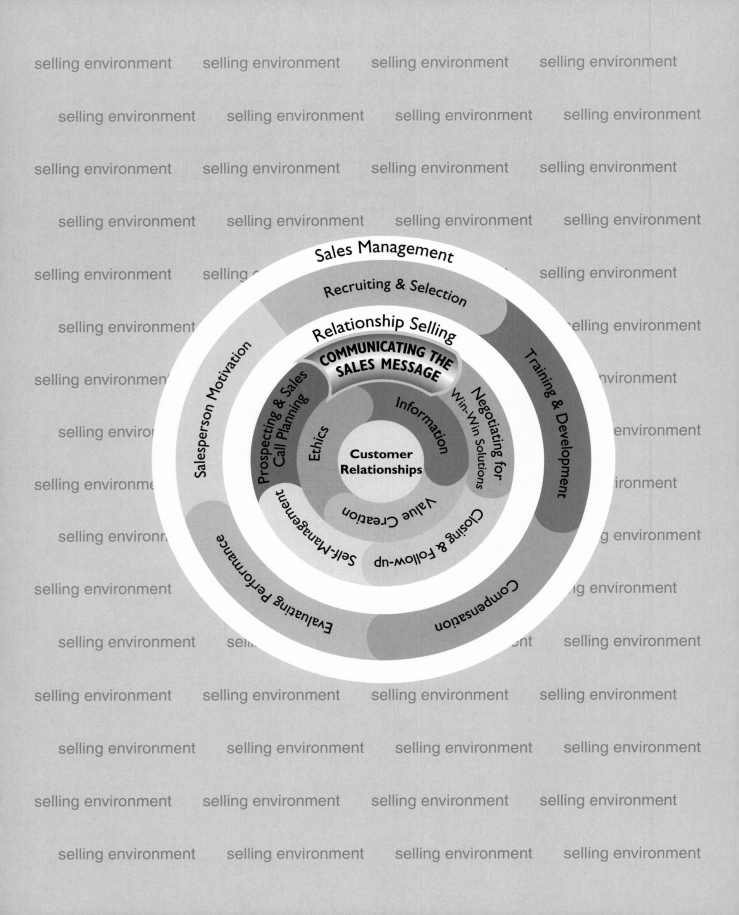

selling environment

Sales Management

Recruiting & Selection

Training & Development

Compensation

Evaluating Performance

Salesperson Motivation

Relationship Selling

COMMUNICATING THE SALES MESSAGE

Negotiating for Win-Win Solutions

Closing & Follow-up

Self-Management

Prospecting & Sales Call Planning

Information

Value Creation

Ethics

Customer Relationships

6 chapter

Communicating the Sales Message

Learning Objectives

Read the Expert Advice for Chapter 6 and you will see how difficult and important it is to deliver a great sales presentation. Sales presentations are complex and require different skill sets for almost every situation. Successful salespeople know that building strong customer relationships depends in large part on their ability to do a good job presenting their products and services to customers.

In this chapter, you will learn about the building blocks of a sales presentation. The chapter will discuss how to prepare for the sales presentation and what specific information you need to get ready. It will also talk about the initial contact with the customer (the approach). Finally, the sales manager's role in the sales presentation will be discussed. While the salesperson is ultimately responsible for the presentation, the manager helps prepare the salesperson and does everything possible to ensure his or her success.

After reading this chapter, you should be able to

- Understand the characteristics of a sales presentation.
- Identify sales presentation strategies.
- Discuss the steps in preparing for the sales presentation.
- Discuss the steps involved in approaching the customer.
- Understand how to apply your sales knowledge to the customer's needs.
- Understand how important product demonstrations are in the presentation.
- Define the keys to a great sales presentation.
- Understand the role sales managers play in sales presentations.

Leadership 6.1

Never Underestimate the Power of Your First Impression

It seems obvious to most of us, but there are still some salespeople out there who do not grasp the importance of their first impression on a prospect. Communicating a positive first impression will heighten your sales performance as well as your sales success. Here are eight tips to improve the way you first meet your prospects.

1. Above all, portray a confident but not superior manner. A lack of self-confidence is readily apparent, and if you don't seem to believe in yourself, how is your prospect supposed to believe in you and your product or service? At the same time, don't cross the subtle line between confidence and arrogance.
2. A clean, neat appearance is essential to making a positive first impression. Showing up in wrinkled or dirty clothes and unkempt hair suggests a lack of respect for your prospect. Do your best to dress slightly above (never below) the type of prospect you are calling on.
3. Another simple but important tip is to smile. Smiling fosters a positive atmosphere, which is exactly what you want if you hope to persuade a prospect to work with you.
4. When conversing with your prospect for the first time, try to use his or her name. That tells the prospect he or she is important enough for you to remember the name. However, be sure to pronounce the name correctly. Mispronouncing it can cause a fatal setback to the new relationship.
5. Showing that this meeting is important to you is key to creating a positive first impression. A casual or nonchalant attitude will make the prospect wonder if you are serious about the value of your product or service. He or she may also wonder how important fulfilling needs, solving problems, or filling wants really is to you.
6. Don't apologize for taking your prospect's time. Extensive apologies simply raise questions regarding your confidence in yourself and your product or service. If you think it is necessary to apologize for taking up a prospect's time, you must not think your product or service is worth the time.
7. Be comfortable and relaxed. If you exude discomfort when meeting your prospect for the first time, you are sure to inspire the same feeling from the prospect. You want your prospect to feel at ease talking to you about his or her wants and needs. The first step in establishing a comfortable relationship is for you to be comfortable yourself.
8. Finally, position yourself through everything you say and do. The first encounter can set the stage for the rest of your professional relationship with your prospect. If you make antagonizing or distracting comments, you jeopardize the positive feelings needed for the relationship to flourish.

Yes, first impressions really are lasting impressions. Too many salespeople forget this simple truth. Following these eight tips will help you establish positive, fruitful relationships with your prospects from the very start. All sales relationships begin with the salesperson's first impression on the prospect, so don't ruin your chances from the beginning. Remember, people pay attention to those whom they perceive as having something important to say, and they often make that assessment in the first 30 seconds. You might win or lose the sale right there. It's up to you!

Source: Bill Brooks, "The Power of First Impressions," *American Salesman,* April 2006, pp. 3–6. Reprinted by permission of © National Research Bureau, 320 Valley St., Burlington, Iowa 52601.

Greeting the Customer. As we said earlier, the first few minutes of a presentation are critical to success.[4] Keep a few basic rules in mind as you create that first impression. First, make sure your overall look is appropriate. You may want to take a moment and freshen up. Second, make sure all wireless communication devices are turned off or put in silent mode. Having your cell phone go off just as you reach to shake hands will not start the meeting off on a good note. Third, be organized. Cause a minimum of disruption as you enter the customer's office. Walking in with stacks of paper or your laptop open sends a negative impression of your overall organizational skills.

If the customer extends his or her hand, shake it firmly. If you are unfamiliar with the surroundings, look for a place to sit. In a conference room, if the customer sits at the head of the table, sit to one side close to the head. If the customer sits at a long side of the table, look for a chair across from him or her.

Most of the time, however, you meet customers in their office. The customer will give you verbal or nonverbal cues about where to sit. If there is a desk with chairs on the other side, move there immediately after greeting the customer. In large offices the customer may have a separate seating area (sofa and chairs with a coffee table) and you should follow his or her lead. If no cues are forthcoming, you may want to ask, "Where would you like me to sit?"

The First Three Minutes. The period just before the approach varies depending on your personal style, the customer's personal style, and the environmental situation at the time of the presentation. It's often helpful to spend some time developing a personal rapport with the customer.[5] Noncontroversial topics like the weather or sports (of course, depending on how the local team is doing, this may or may not be controversial) are the best subject choices. The key is to know when to make the transition from customer greeting to customer approach. Spend too long in small talk, and the customer will perceive you are wasting time. Be too abrupt, and you'll create an awkward moment. Initially, you may find these transitions difficult. However, in time you will develop a sense of the right moment to make the transition. Always remember the customer knows why you are there and it will not come as a surprise when you launch into the presentation.

Approach Strategies

The **approach** is what sales professionals call the first part of the sales presentation. It is a transition point from the greeting to the main body of your presentation where you will deliver the primary sales message to the customer. While you may have spoken by phone or e-mail, most customers clearly prefer a face-to-face presentation. A well-executed approach can set up the rest of the presentation so you can move the buying process much more efficiently and effectively. The customer approach has two objectives: (1) get the customer's attention and (2) create enough interest in you, your company, and its products and services that you can continue the presentation.

The five common approach strategies are shown in Exhibit 6.3.

Referrals. One of the best ways to approach the customer is to be referred by a third party (often a satisfied customer). The **referral** is effective because of the third party's external endorsement of the company and by extension the salesperson as well. Research suggests the referral increases the credibility of the salesperson's points during the presentation and reduces customer anxiety about their validity.

A number of customers, however, do not wish to be used as referrals. There are many reasons for this reluctance. The relationship between the company and customer may deteriorate while the customer is being used as a referral with other prospective customers. Or the salesperson may also be calling on the customer's competitors.

Customer Benefit. Customers want to know how your products will benefit them, so telling them is a good way to begin a sales presentation. By starting the presentation with a solution to at least one of the customer's problems, you create an instant win–win situation. One caveat: It is essential that you be well prepared

EXHIBIT 6.3 Approaches to the Sales Presentation

- **Referral**
  Mr. Render, my name is Charlie Smith. I am with Xentury Business Machines and you will remember we spoke by phone several times. Our networked copiers and printers offer great value and performance for businesses like yours. Indeed, you know Ms. Ferrino with Avalon Products and she suggested I give you a call. Ms. Ferrino has been a customer for five years and is very satisfied with our products and service.
- **Customer benefit**
  Ms. Santorum, your company needs reliable and cost-effective trucks to deliver your flowers every day. This new Ford van has the lowest costs per mile of any full-size van in the market, and our quality ratings (show appropriate studies) are among the highest in the industry. The new Ford van will not only get your flowers to their customers every day but will do so for the lowest cost of any full-size van.
- **Question**
  Our company can offer you a bundle of services that is the best in the industry. Are you interested in hearing more about them?
- **Assessment**
  Ms. Yeaple, as a successful businesswoman you want to be sure you are maximizing your current assets. I would like to evaluate your investment portfolio. There is no cost to you for this evaluation. If you would take a few moments to complete this short financial questionnaire, I will prepare an analysis of your current portfolio. Thank you.
- **Product demonstration**

and have a thorough understanding of your customer's current situation, problems, and needs. Otherwise, this approach strategy could actually do more harm than good. The customer might be annoyed by your misperceptions.

Question. There are two advantages to the question method. First, getting the customer involved in the presentation is always a positive, and asking questions in the approach involves the customer right from the start. This goes a long way toward establishing customer buy-in to your sales message. Second, by getting customer feedback you are positioning yourself for success in the presentation. Ask questions that can focus the customer on the problem and help you gain greater acceptance; then structure the questions so they will lead into the presentation.

The risk of the question approach is that you may get an answer that will effectively end the presentation. If the customer answers yes, you are in an excellent position to transition into your presentation. But if the customer answers no, you will have to reestablish a point of contact or end the presentation.

Assessment. One technique that salespeople in certain industries (IT, insurance, financial services) have found effective is the assessment approach. You ask the customer to complete a set of questions. Then you collect the data, analyze the information, and make a presentation to the client based on your analysis.[6] The assessment approach is really a part of a larger problem-solving presentation strategy in which you put together a solution for the customer based on his or her feedback.

This approach can be effective for several reasons. First, it is relatively nonthreatening. You are not actually asking the customer to buy anything but simply requesting information that you will use to provide additional feedback. Second, the end result is generally an assessment that you can go over with the customer. Financial planners, for example, often ask prospective clients for a summary of their financial history. Based on the responses, the planner/salesperson prepares a financial plan for the customer. At the end of the presentation, the financial planner offers suggestions on how his or her company can help meet the customer's needs.

Product Demonstration. We will discuss the product demonstration in greater detail later in the chapter. Some salespeople find it an effective approach strategy. With certain products, such as automobiles, demonstrating the product is crucial to the presentation. Laptop computers and sophisticated graphics software let salespeople demonstrate products that are difficult to exhibit in a customer's office (security systems, for example).

Once you start the product demonstration, it is important to move quickly into the rest of the presentation, including the buying process. Salespeople often use the product demonstration in conjunction with another approach, such as the question, to get customer involvement while demonstrating the product.

The Sales Presentation: Building the Relationship

Once the approach has established a relationship with the customer, it is time to move into the sales presentation. You did much of this work as you prepared for the sales meeting—but every salesperson will tell you there are always surprises. The customer might convey a new, critical piece of information, pose a new problem, disagree with your value proposition, or any one of hundreds of other challenges that a salesperson faces during a sales presentation. However, at the heart of the presentation is a simple process of identifying the customer's needs and applying your knowledge in a way that will solve the problem, add value to the customer's business (and your company), and build a successful relationship (Exhibit 6.4). Let's begin with identifying the customer's needs.

Identify Customers' Needs

How important is identifying the customer's needs? Very. Research suggests that being able to focus on customers and correctly identify their needs is one of the key characteristics that distinguish high-performing salespeople. Indeed, of all the

EXHIBIT 6.4 The Sales Presentation

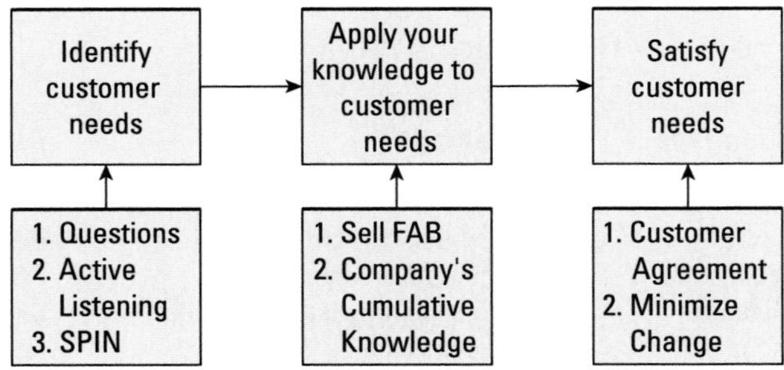

elements in a sales presentation (approach, handling objections, and closing) the single factor shown to differentiate successful salespeople from the rest of the pack was their ability to discover the customer's need(s). Relationship selling is based, in large part, on the salesperson's ability to identify those needs and develop win–win solutions that benefit both the customer and the company.

The need identification process really begins before the first customer meeting as you study the customer's business and get ready for the sales presentation. By learning about the customer, you will develop an initial assessment of needs. This will change as you talk with the customer and go through the need identification process. Even after the presentation, as you move forward in the relationship, you should continue to assess and update your understanding of the customer's needs.

Questioning Drives a Great Presentation. Identifying the customer's needs is not a complicated process, but it does require salespeople to perform several tasks very well. The first skill is asking the right questions at the right time. This may seem easy but, as we saw earlier, high-performing salespeople are significantly better at it than low performers. Asking questions and listening (which we will discuss shortly) are not easy for many people, especially in stressful situations like a sales presentation. Many inexperienced salespeople believe (incorrectly) that they should be talking and in control of the presentation.

A second and sometimes more difficult problem is the potential struggle within the customer. In the course of the presentation, he or she may become threatened by your questions. The customer may perceive that your proposed solutions could place him or her in jeopardy (if the presentation uncovers inefficiencies that are the customer's responsibility). In addition, remember that salespeople are change agents. By definition they are asking the customer to change by buying their product. Change creates conflict for the customer. What if you are wrong and the customer is blamed for buying your product? What if you are right and the customer fails to buy your product? As you can see, asking tough questions is threatening to both salesperson and customer. The basic categories of questions salespeople can ask during the presentation are summarized in Exhibit 6.5. Let's examine each type more closely.

Unrestricted/restricted questions. Encouraging the customer to open up and share information, unrestricted questions impose few limitations. Often referred to as open-ended or nondirected questions, they draw out information by allowing the customer to frame the answer. Restricted questions, on the other hand, require yes/no or very short answers. They direct the customer to a specific, very short response.

EXHIBIT 6.5 Categories of Questions

Question Type	Advantage	Disadvantage
Unrestricted	Encourages customer to speak	Is time consuming
Restricted	Gets specific information	Discourages dialogue
Data collection	Uncovers relevant data	Wastes customer time
Investigation	Helps uncover customer needs	Difficult to manage responses
Validation	Provides customer buy-in	Can derail presentation

Most of the time salespeople will use both types of questions. Unrestricted questions encourage the customer to speak more freely and allow the salesperson to develop a richer, more complete understanding of the customer's issues. Restricted questions provide specific information the salesperson can use to shape the presentation. Indeed, it is common to move from one question type to the other. It is a good idea to get the customer more involved by asking unrestricted questions, but asking too many of them will almost certainly create time pressure on other parts of the presentation. There are particular pieces of information the salesperson may need during the presentation, and restricted questions are the most efficient way to get the information.

Data collection questions. These questions gather basic data about issues related to the customer's current business or historical perspective. While the information can be helpful, salespeople should limit data collection questions in a presentation for several reasons. First, customers may provide information that interferes with elements of the presentation. Given the access to information today, it is the salesperson's responsibility to be familiar with as much of the customer's business as possible. A general rule is to ask data collection questions that verify existing knowledge. Second, if a salesperson asks too many data collection questions, the customer may perceive a lack of preparation, and wonder, "Why doesn't this person already know this about my business?"

Inexperienced salespeople may incorrectly assume that asking customers questions about their business is the same as identifying their needs. This is not true; customers expect salespeople to know about their business before the presentation even begins. Data collection questions can be useful, but use them sparingly and do the customer homework before the presentation so that you don't waste time asking unnecessary questions.

Investigation questions. These questions probe for information about problems, opportunities, or challenges in the business. The answers are often critical in correctly identifying the customer's needs. By encouraging the customer to talk about current issues and concerns in the business, salespeople gain valuable insight. Successful salespeople use these questions to assess the customer's current state of mind.[7]

Validation questions. At various critical points in the presentation, you want to validate something with the customer. You might reaffirm the customer's needs or some key fact that came out of the investigation questions asked earlier in the presentation. Validation questions are important for two reasons. First, they help get agreement from the customer and move him or her through the buying process. Validating the customer's needs eliminates a point of disagreement later in the presentation. Second, they keep the customer involved in the presentation. Even if the response is simply yes or no, the customer is mentally engaged.

Keep in mind a few basic rules as you ask questions. First, go over them before the presentation. Poorly worded or inappropriate questions will do more harm than good. Second, always anticipate the answers. This is not to say you script the answers, but asking questions for which you have no general idea of the response can lead to real problems if you are surprised by a customer's response. Face-to-face time with the customer is limited, and fumbling for a response to an unexpected statement will not instill confidence in your abilities. Third (and most importantly), once you ask the question, listen to the customer's answer.

Leadership 6.2

The SPIN Selling Approach

Situation Questions: Finding facts about the customer's existing situations.

- Are used more in failed sales calls.
- Are overused by inexperienced salespeople.

Problem Questions: Learning about the customer's problems, difficulties, or dissatisfaction.

- Are used more in calls that succeed (especially for smaller sales)
- Are asked more by experienced salespeople.

Implication Questions: Learning about the effects, consequences, and implications, of the customer's problems

- Are strongly linked to success in larger sales.
- Build up the customer's perception of value.
- Are harder to ask than situation or problem questions.

Need Payoff Questions: Learning about the value or usefulness of a proposed customer solution

- Are strongly linked to success in larger sales.Increase the acceptability of your solution.
- Are particularly effective with influencers who will present your case to decision makers.

Source: Anthony Sigrorelli, "Transition to Consultative Selling," *American Salesman,* 46(1), January 2001, 11–16. "SPIN Selling," Neil Rackham (McGraw-Hill, NY; 1988). Used with permission from Huthwaite, Inc.

SPIN to Customers' Needs. Based on research conducted by Huthwaite, Inc. (and company founder Neil Rackham), the **SPIN** strategy is a comprehensive selling approach based on a series of questions about: **s**ituation, **p**roblem, **i**mplication, and **n**eed payoff.[8] This approach works very well with large, important sales. A number of multinational companies have adopted the SPIN selling approach, including UPS and Bank of America. Leadership 6.2 summarizes the SPIN selling approach.

Situation questions. These questions provide basic information about the customer's circumstances. Often they are broad questions designed to substantiate information the salesperson already knows. You don't want to overuse these questions, since customers may tire of answering them. Situation questions suffer from the same problems as the data collection questions we discussed earlier, but they do offer a format for establishing rapport with the customer.

Problem questions. Based on his or her own research and responses to the situation questions, the salesperson moves on to more specific problems. Asking directed questions gets the customer concentrating on particular problems and issues. An effective tool when used by experienced salespeople, problem questions are much more useful in identifying the customer's needs than situation questions.

There are two goals for problem questions. First, the customer's responses offer critical information the salesperson will use in discovering the customer's needs. Second, in answering a carefully planned set of questions, customers will (if all goes well) admit they have a problem. While problem questions are valuable, the salesperson must continue to ask questions that will help the customer see the full effect of the problem.

Implication questions. Once a problem has been defined, the salesperson must help the customer recognize its implications for his or her business. Implication questions help customers realize the seriousness of the problem and begin to search for solutions. You *must* get agreement on the problem before asking implication questions. These questions are instrumental in moving the customer closer to the value proposition you will offer in the presentation. As the customer comes to recognize the full implications of the problem, he or she becomes less concerned with the cost of the solution (your products and services) and more interested in solving the problem.

Need payoff questions. The transition from problem identification and clarification to problem solution begins with need payoff questions. It is not enough to make the customer aware of a problem, nor to define its scope and potential ramifications. At some point the salesperson must move the customer to the solutions offered by the company. While problem and implications questions focus on establishing the customer's problem, need payoff questions directly connect the problem with the value proposition. If the customer agrees to the need payoff questions, the salesperson is in a strong position to successfully complete the sale. Conversely, if the customer disagrees, the salesperson has not yet established a significant problem for the customer to act on.

Listen

Should salespeople be better talkers or listeners? Many people unfamiliar with selling would probably say talking is more important, but the idea that salespeople are fast-talking individuals not really interested in customer's opinions is far from accurate. Listening, really listening, to customers is a vital trait of successful salespeople.

Despite its importance, most people (even those in selling) listen actively only 25 percent of the time. That means people don't really hear what is being said three-quarters of the time. Not surprisingly, the likelihood of correctly identifying a customer's needs if you are listening to only one quarter of what he or she says is pretty small. Interestingly, people can listen more effectively than they speak. Research suggests that most people can hear up to 800 words per minute but speak around 140 words per minute. The slowness of speech leads too many listeners to become distracted.

Active listening involves a commitment by the listener to focus on the speaker, concentrate on what is being said without thinking about other things, and take in nonverbal as well as verbal messages.[9] People speak with their voices, but they also speak nonverbally. Facial expression, arm and hand movements, body positioning, and eye contact all communicate just as much as the spoken word. Active listeners focus not just on what is being said but *how* it is being communicated. (We will talk more about nonverbal communication later in the chapter.)

Exhibit 6.6 summarizes recent research on how to enhance your active listening. When salespeople take the time to change from passive to active listening, they notice changes in the way customers react to them. Little things like providing nonverbal cues to a customer who is speaking (nodding your head, making direct eye contact) and clarifying or rephrasing information can make the customer much more responsive. In turn, that customer is more likely to pay attention when you are speaking.

EXHIBIT 6.6 Guidelines for Active Listening

1. *Listen patiently to what the other person has to say, even though you may believe it is wrong or irrelevant.* Indicate simple acceptance, not necessarily agreement, by nodding or perhaps injecting an occasional "mm-hmm" or "I see."
2. *Try to understand the feeling the person is expressing, not just the intellectual content.* Most of us have difficulty talking clearly about our feelings, so it is important to pay careful attention.
3. *Restate the person's feeling briefly but accurately.* At this stage you simply serve as a mirror. Encourage the other person to continue talking. Occasionally make summary responses such as "You believe our product does not add value" or "You feel you are not getting good service." Keep your tone neutral and try not to lead the person to your pet conclusions.
4. *Allow time for the discussion to continue without interruption and try to separate the conversation from more official communication of company plans.* Focus on sales presentation and not smaller, less vital company issues.
5. *Avoid direct questions and arguments about facts.* Refrain from saying, "That is just not so," "Hold on a minute, let's look at the facts," or "Prove it." You may want to review evidence later, but a review is irrelevant to how a person feels now.
6. *When the other person touches on a point you want to know more about, simply repeat his or her statement as a question.* For instance, if he remarks, "Your company is the most expensive in the industry," you can probe by saying, "So, you believe my company is the most expensive in the industry." With this encouragement, he will probably expand on his previous statement.
7. *Listen for what is not said, evasions of pertinent points or perhaps too-ready agreement with common clichés.* Such an omission may be a clue to a bothersome fact the person wishes were not true.
8. *If the other person genuinely appears to want your viewpoint, be honest in your reply.* In the listening stage, try to limit the expression of your views since they may influence or inhibit what the other person says.
9. *Do not get emotionally involved yourself.* Try simply to understand first and defer evaluation until later.
10. *BE QUIET.* Let the other person talk. Actively listen to what he or she has to say.

Source: Dan Sharp, "Guidelines for Active Listening and Reflection," October 2008, www.salesconcepts.com. Reprinted by permission.

Apply Your Knowledge to Customer Needs

While identifying the customer's needs is essential in communicating the sales message, that's just the beginning of the salesperson's task. It is now time to take your knowledge of your company's products and services and apply it to the customer's needs. Providing solutions that solve customer problems is the essence of a salesperson's role in the relationship-selling process. You are the critical link between what the company has to offer the customer and the customer's needs.

Sell FAB. Good salespeople are very knowledgeable about their company's products and services. They know product performance characteristics, service turnaround times, and a host of other important features. These facts are important, but customers do not buy features. They buy solutions to their problems. So you need to link your knowledge of company products and services facts to solutions that meet customers' needs. This process is often referred to as **FAB** (features, advantages, and benefits).

By applying the FAB approach, salespeople can make the company's products and services relevant for the customer. A **feature** is any material characteristic or specification of the company's products and services (say, antilock brakes on a car). An **advantage** is a particular product/service characteristic that helps meet the customer's needs (antilock brakes stop the car faster and in a more controlled fashion). A **benefit** is the beneficial outcome to the buyer from the advantage found in the product feature (the car will provide greater safety for the driver and passengers).

Let's examine the FAB approach in greater detail.

Features. All products and services are the sum total of physical characteristics and specifications. Consider the purchase of a new laptop computer. The buyer will learn the processor speed, hard disk drive size, screen size, and a host of other product **features,** or characteristics. Go to the Hewlett-Packard Web site at www.hp.com and click on home/home office. Then go to the Notebooks hyperlink. Several models are listed and their product features are described.

By themselves, however, product features are not very persuasive. Indeed, most customers will never even see the processor or hard drive in a new computer. No matter what the buying situation, customers do not buy product features. They buy product benefits that meet their needs.

Advantages. Customers want benefits, but they also want to know how your product is better. What makes it better? Why should I buy your product/service over one of your competitors'? In short, they want to see the **advantages** of your product.

If you return to the HP Web page, click on through to a technical presentation of the notebooks. There you will see various product features such as versatile performance and mobility. Clicking on one of those boxes takes you to a specific model that lists the various processors. The Processor box describes the various Intel and AMD chips used in those models. HP highlights the product advantages using phrases that speak to the Pavilion, "powerful processors . . . [that] enhance gaming, digital music; digital photography, and video editing." This translates the features of the Intel or AMD chips into advantages customers will understand.

Unfortunately, most salespeople get a lot of training on the features of products and services but little training on the advantages and benefits. Remember, the task here is to apply your knowledge of the company's products and services to the customer needs you identified earlier in the sales presentation. Simply knowing the product's physical characteristics and specifications is not enough; understanding the product's advantages for your customer is good but still probably not enough to get a commitment. Ultimately, the customer must see how those advantages benefit him or her directly.

Benefits. Extending the application from product features to product advantages and ultimately to product benefits answers one of the most fundamental questions customers have in the relationship-building process: "What's in it for me?" Ultimately, there will be no relationship if you cannot answer that question.

Customers need to understand specifically how your product benefits them, solves their problem, or meets their needs.

Often, your customer will be comparing your product with at least one competitor. In the highly competitive, information-rich world of today, customers expect salespeople to have a thorough knowledge of their competitors' products and their benefits.

If you go back to the HP Web page one more time, notice it does not describe the benefits of a long-life battery. Why not? Because the company wants salespeople to do that. By phone call or visit, an HP rep (direct salesperson or distributor's agent) will identify the particular customer's needs and then define the most relevant product advantages as benefits.

For example, engineers for a manufacturing company would find the high-speed Intel or AMD processor's ability to process the latest graphic-intensive software an advantage because it allows them to work sophisticated engineering programs while they are traveling. It is the salesperson's job to recognize the key customer issue (ability to work while traveling) and translate the product features into advantages (long battery life) and benefits (no more downtime while traveling).

This is an example of the synergy companies seek between their marketing communication (such as the HP Web site) and the salesperson calling on the customer. While the Web site is outstanding at presenting product features and even identifying basic product advantages, direct contact with a salesperson (either inside or outside sales) is needed to connect the advantages to benefits for a given customer.

Collect the Company's Cumulative Knowledge. Salespeople are on the front line meeting customers and giving presentations. However, everyone in the organization supports them in one way or another. The support of areas like product development, customer service and support, and manufacturing is indispensable as salespeople apply the organization's cumulative knowledge to meeting the customer's needs. It is always helpful and often mandatory to tap into the knowledge base of the sales firm.

If a customer needs modifications to a product or has special service requirements, the salesperson calls in people from product development and manufacturing to get a true understanding of the issues and costs involved in making changes to existing products. When the customer has tight delivery and scheduling deadlines, it is important to contact the right people in the company to get the best, most up-to-date answers quickly.

Team selling is based in part on the premise that no one individual can successfully develop and manage large customer relationships. Applying your knowledge to the customer's needs really means applying the company's cumulative knowledge to those needs.

Satisfy Customer Needs

The ultimate goal of the presentation is to satisfy the customer's needs by identifying them, applying your knowledge to them, and creating a plan of action for the customer that incorporates your products and services to address them. Although the relationship-selling process certainly is not finished after the sales message is communicated (as you'll see over the next two chapters), every sales presentation should focus on customer satisfaction. No matter how much negotiating remains, no matter how tough it is to close the sale or build that long-term relationship, the customer should receive some satisfaction as a result of the sales presentation.[10]

Get Customer Agreement. As you have undoubtedly noticed, a sales presentation is based on interaction with the customer. Through a prescribed process of preparation and customer communication, the salesperson comes to learn the customer's needs and develops a plan of action for solving the customer's problems. At every step in the presentation, it is important to get customer agreement.

This agreement can take many forms. Sometimes you ask a question. "Do you agree that my product provides the best value for your business?" Sometimes you make a statement. "We agree you need a product that offers great value and specific performance characteristics, and I have demonstrated how our product offers the best combination of performance and lowest cost of any product in the market." Often agreement can be a simple yes or no.

Customer satisfaction in the presentation is not a single event. It builds as a series of agreements during the presentation. When you secure agreement at many steps in the presentation, the customer will be much more compelled to agree to the purchase at the appropriate time. As you will see in Chapter 8, closing the sale is a process that begins at the start of the presentation.

Minimize Change Conflict. As we discussed earlier, the sales presentation can create more stress for the customer than for the salesperson. The presentation is based on the assumption that you have a better solution than the customer is currently using, and customers can react negatively to your presentation even if (sometimes because) they find your product superior to their current choice.

One key to leaving a customer satisfied at the end of the presentation is to minimize change conflict. To help customers feel less conflict about the purchase, you can manage their expectations. Clearly explain the specifics of your value proposition and then deliver exactly what you promise. Overpromising and under-delivering is one of the surest ways to destroy a buyer–seller relationship. Also, make sure that details of the purchase agreement are known to everyone in the sales organization and all relevant individuals in the customer's company. Misunderstandings between other people often lead to disappointment later in the relationship.

Establish the Relationship. It is critical to build the buyer–seller relationship with every presentation, indeed every customer interaction. Sales presentations are big events. Salespeople need be sure that no matter what happens to the potential sale on the table, the relationship is not damaged. Phone calls and e-mails are everyday occurrences, but getting face to the face with the customer raises the stakes for you and your company.

Most of the time a sales presentation is the best opportunity for a company to forge a new relationship. Keep in mind the basic elements of relationship selling: Focus on creating value for the customer and always conduct business with the highest ethical standards.

Keys to a Great Sales Presentation

Successful sales presentations don't just happen. They require preparation and a lot of hard work. This section examines ways to turn a good presentation into a great one.

EXHIBIT 6.7 Demonstration Checklist

- Justify the need for a product demonstration.
  - Does this sales presentation need a product demonstration?
- State the objective of the demonstration.
  - What do I want to accomplish with the product demonstration?
- Design the demonstration.
  - What will the demonstration look like?
- Rehearse the demonstration.
  - Can I deliver the product demonstration effectively and efficiently?
- Plan for unforeseen circumstances.
  - Have I identified key times or events when unforeseen events could disrupt the demonstration (power failure, lack of proper display facilities in the room, disruptions for the customer)?

Demonstrations

Have you ever heard the phrase "talk is cheap"? This cliché highlights a basic concept behind product demonstrations: At some point the salesperson must prove the claims and statements in the sales presentation. There are few selling tools more effective at proving the worth of a product than a product demonstration.[11] The product demonstration is not without risk (which we will discuss shortly), but when properly planned and executed, it offers three distinct benefits to the salesperson.

First, a successful buyer–seller relationship is based on trust and credibility. Fundamental to that trust is the customer's belief that your product will perform as promised in the sales presentation. Product demonstrations are an excellent tool that can *build credibility with customers.* When you prove the sales presentation with a product demonstration, the customer is more likely to accept you.

Second, seeing the product in action *creates a greater connection between the customer and the product.* Consider the last time you went shopping for clothes. By trying them on, you were demonstrating the product to yourself. If you liked the outfit, the demonstration worked and your probability of buying it increased dramatically. If you went into a clothing store and were told you could not try on that suit or dress, you would probably not purchase the product or even shop at the store. The same is true in all buying situations. Allowing the customer to interact with the product and see it in action can generate a strong affiliation between the customer and product. The product becomes more than words on a page or facts in a brochure.

Third, product demonstrations can *enhance the effectiveness of your communication.* People can process nonverbal information much faster than spoken words. By demonstrating the product, you are presenting information in a format that is probably more interesting and memorable for the customer.

Think about your own experiences. Would you rather have someone describe the horsepower, torque, and six-speed transmission of a new Porsche or experience it for yourself by test driving one? If you are choosing a new printer for the office,

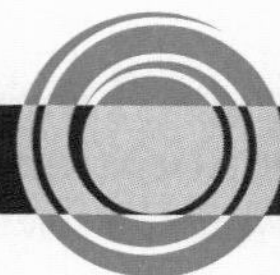

INNOVATION 6.3

How to Be a Better Communicator

Good communication skills have to be learned. Most people are poor communicators. It's not that they don't try, but without proper training and practice it is difficult to listen or communicate effectively. Debra Condren, a business psychologist and president of Humaninvestment.com in New York, offers seven tips to help salespeople become better communicators.

1. *Focus on listening.* This lets the other person know you are paying attention to his or her thoughts and expertise.
2. *Ask for clarification.* Making sure you've heard the person correctly goes a long way toward keeping communication clear. Asking for clarification gives the person you are speaking with a chance to confirm exactly what he said or refine what she wants to convey.
3. *Be brief.* Deliver your sales message in as few words as possible. The less you say, the more likely you are to be heard.
4. *Don't repeat yourself.* Even if you don't get an acknowledgment that the customer agrees, don't try to drive your point home by saying it again a different way. Say it once and move on.
5. *Periodically ask, "Am I making sense?"* Asking for feedback as you are speaking lets others know you are more interested in their reaction and creative input than in being right.
6. *Have an open-door policy.* When customers feel that you are approachable, they are more likely to keep the lines of communication flowing.
7. *Use self-deprecating humor.* Research shows that the ability to laugh at oneself is a key indicator of emotional intelligence (the ability to connect well with other people). Connecting and listening are two key skills of good communicators.

As you can see, good communicators need many skills.

Source: Craig Harrison, "Tip Sheet: A Failure to Communicate Should not Be an Option When Doing Business," *PR News,* August 21, 2006, p. 1, and "How to Be a Better Communicator," *Sales & Marketing Management,* February 2003, p. 46. © 2003 VNU Business Media. Used with permission.

what do you think will be more effective: (1) a brochure detailing the pages per minute, 256 color combinations, and networking capabilities or (2) a file sent to your printer that is printed automatically in full color? Demonstrating the product makes all other communication during the presentation more effective. Once the customer sees the printer in action, the brochure the salesperson leaves takes on more meaning.

Innovation 6.3 talks about the importance of good communication. Keep those points in mind as we examine product demonstrations more closely.

Prepare for a Successful Demonstration. Clearly, the demonstration is an effective tool in the sales presentation—when it works. But when it fails or does not meet the customer's expectations the negative effect is significant. This is why it is so important to prepare for the presentation.

Exhibit 6.7 is a checklist of things to consider as your prepare for a product demonstration. Not all items are appropriate in every situation, but in general, when you have completed the checklist you should be ready to give a successful demonstration. There are three key points to keep in mind as you prepare for a demonstration: develop objectives, get customers involved, and practice.

First, *develop' objectives for the demonstration.* We spoke earlier about the importance of setting presentation objectives, and the same is true for product demonstrations. Most products have many characteristics that could be incorporated into a demonstration. Consider the specific customer's needs and develop a demonstration that shows how the product will address those needs. If the customer for a copier is interested in speed, the demonstration could focus on pages printed per minute. The objective could be, "The customer will know how fast and dependable the copier is as a result of the product demonstration."

Second, *get customers involved in the demonstration.* Imagine looking at a new car and not being allowed to test drive it. It's the same principle in any product demonstration. The more involved the customer is in the demonstration, the more he or she will connect to the product and your presentation. Be sure the customer knows how to use the product. There are few things more dangerous in a product demonstration than a customer who does not know how to use the product correctly.

Third, *practice, practice, and practice the demonstration.* You generally have only once chance to be successful in a product demonstration. You must be absolutely comfortable with the product and the specific characteristics you are demonstrating and know how to do deal with unforeseen problems (which will almost surely appear at some point in time). Practice not only the demonstration itself but also your words and actions during the demonstration. Since you will be talking and showing the product at the same time, you need to know both very well. One benefit of practice is that it builds confidence. When you have mastered a demonstration, indeed an entire presentation, you are more confident in front of the customer.

The Demonstration: More than Just the Product. Is the product itself the best demonstration tool? Yes. Is it the only tool available to demonstrate the product's features, advantages, and benefit? No. Sometimes it is not possible to demonstrate the actual product in front of the customer, and you'll need to find other tools to help in the product demonstration. Evaluate the best possible format to demonstrate the product.

Many other tools can enhance the demonstration or even substitute for a live product display. In some cases, the product has not even been produced. Consider architects bidding on a big construction project. They have no product to show, so they must rely on models and drawings to demonstrate their vision of the final product (the building itself).

Another situation, often found in technology, is the demonstration of something that cannot be seen. How can a salesperson for HP demonstrate how the Pavilion actually processes information faster than the competition? One way is to compare a set of prescribed functions using a competitor or older model with a new Pavilion. The demonstration should show the same functions being performed faster on the new machine. You don't really see the product working, but you see the results of the faster processor. Another tool might be charts that highlight the relative speed differences between the competitors and the Pavilion.

A powerful tool commonly used in education and business is Microsoft's Office Suite of business software. Incorporating Excel, Word, and PowerPoint software into a presentation can enable the salesperson to convey a great deal of information. PowerPoint and programs like it can graphically display many elements of a product demonstration. Through the use of graphics software, embedded video, and other tools, the salesperson can develop a successful demonstration without actually having the product in front of the customer. Almost every computer manufacturer sells portable projectors. Among the more popular are Dell and Mitsubishi. With them, salespeople can take very sophisticated demonstrations right into the customer's office.

The Value Proposition

You remember the discussion on value creation in Chapter 3. We talked about the importance of value in the relationship-selling process. Creating value for their customers is really why companies are in business. However, customers must see the value of the company's products and services. The sales presentation is where that value is conveyed to the customer.

Chapter 3 highlighted many ways a company can create value for its customers. The job of salespeople is to identify their customers' needs and apply their knowledge of their company and its products to satisfy customers. Critical to that process is the **value proposition,** which is the summary of the value the customer receives based on the expected benefits and costs.

A realistic assessment of benefits and costs can be a persuasive tool to support the claims of the company's products and services. Customers today are often looking for a strong business case to justify the purchase decision. They ask a valid question, "How is your company adding value to my business?" Refer to the appendix to Chapter 2 (Relationship Selling Math) for an in-depth discussion of building a financial business case in relationship selling.

A value proposition should be part of every presentation. Assessing the value proposition for your customer should be part of your preparation. Of course you will learn more about the customer's needs during the presentation, but by assessing the customer value of your company's products before the presentation, you can anticipate objections. As we shall examine in Chapter 7, many customer objections deal with the value added by your company's products. If the price is too high (a common objection), the customer is really saying he or she has not been convinced the value of your product exceeds the cost. The customer does not believe your value proposition. Defining the customer value of your company's products and services and communicating it are essential to success in relationship selling.

Nonverbal Communication

Nonverbal communication is the single most important element in the communication process. Research suggests that over half of all communication is a result of things we see or feel. These include but are not limited to facial expressions, posture, eye contact, gestures, and even dress. Surprisingly, less than 10 percent of communication is based on the actual words we speak in a conversation. The remainder (about 40 percent) of what we take in is the result of *how* we hear the communication (vocal clarity, pitch, tone of voice).

Given the importance of nonverbal communication to the total communication process, salespeople need to know how to interpret their customers' nonverbal communication. They also need to know how to use nonverbal signals to communicate. How you sit, what you wear, even the amount of space between you and the customer sends a message. Let's examine nonverbal communication more closely.

Customer Nonverbal Communication. We spoke earlier about active listening and how important it is to focus intently on the customer. Customers, indeed all of us, speak volumes in the way we move. We communicate with almost every part of our body. Our hands, legs, facial expressions, even the way we hold our body (slumped over, sitting straight up) all convey a message. A person who has arms open and palms extended is sending a much different message than a person with folded arms and legs.

Face. The face is the single most important feature of nonverbal communication. Without saying a word, a customer can convey acceptance or rejection, anger or amusement, understanding or confusion, with a facial expression. We all know the meaning of a smile or a scowl, but the face can convey many subtle messages as well.

"The eyes are the window to the soul" is a famous saying. Watching a customer's eye contact can tell you a lot about what he or she thinks of your sales presentation. A customer who stares blankly at the presentation is not really interested. Yet the more intently the customer stares, the greater the likelihood he or she is reacting negatively. When people are really focused on oral communication, they usually look down or up to enhance their concentration. Turning away indicates the customer believes the presentation is over—or wishes it were.

Arms and hands. Arms open, palms extended is one of the clearest signals the customer is open to the communication. Conversely, folded arms with closed hands indicate he or she is not receptive to what is being said.

Many gestures have different meaning around the world. Gestures and hand movements that are accepted in one culture can have very different meanings somewhere else. It is always helpful to know the customer's culture before interpreting these kinds of signals—or attempting to send them.

Body language. When a customer leans forward in the chair, he or she is showing interest, while leaning back indicates a lack of concentration in the presentation. Quick movements indicate something has changed in the customer's mind. He or she may have a question, want you to conclude the presentation, or even feel bored.

No single customer movement or action should be taken out of context. People lean back in their chair for many reasons besides boredom. Without thorough knowledge of the customer's behavior patterns, it would be dangerous to infer too much from a specific gesture or even a single meeting.

Salespeople need to balance what they are seeing (nonverbal communication) with what the customer is saying (oral communication). When the presentation is going well and the customer accepts the information, verbal and nonverbal communication will likely be consistent. When the two forms of communication are inconsistent, the customer's comments may not express his or her true feelings about the presentation.

Salesperson Nonverbal Communication. Just as customers convey a great deal through nonverbal communication, so do salespeople. Literally hundreds of nonverbal signals are conveyed in every sales presentation, and salespeople need to be aware of their own nonverbal communication. Customers watch salespeople for nonverbal messages. Slight movements (looking away from the customer, glancing at the clock) can convey a message that was not intended. Here are some critical nonverbal cues.

The space between you and the customer. We all operate with concentric circles of space around us. The concept of territorial space is based on research that suggests that people have varying levels of space around themselves that they do not want people to enter without permission. Have you ever met someone and felt crowded? When their space is violated, people become uncomfortable. A salesperson should never violate a customer's space.

There are four levels of space around a customer. The most accessible is **public space** which is at least 12 feet away. Almost anyone is welcome in this space, and this is often the distance between a salesperson and the group in a public presentation. **Social space** is from 4 to 12 feet and is often the space between customer and salesperson in a personal sales presentation. Think of it as the desk between the customer and salesperson in the customer's office. In this space, keep in mind your position relative to the customer. Standing while the customer is seated can be uncomfortable for the customer when you are this close. **Personal space** is two to three feet and should not be violated except for a handshake. Even then, the salesperson should be careful not to suffocate the customer. Finally there is **intimate space** (up to two feet). This space is reserved for family and close friends. Violating it is rude and even offensive.

Body movements. When you look down or appear ill at ease, it suggests to the customer that you are not confident in the presentation. If the customer senses a lack of confidence or preparation, the presentation will probably not be successful, no matter what you say. You need to communicate confidence in your facial expressions and body movements. An open, accepting demeanor conveys a positive message to the customer before you have even said a word.

It is helpful to study your customers and match their style. Some people have a more conservative style than others, and being too gregarious or entering the customer's personal space can send negative nonverbal messages.

One caveat in nonverbal communication: Do what comes naturally. Don't try to be something you aren't. You'll just confuse and alienate customers. The key is to blend basic rules of nonverbal communication with your own communication style. Practice your nonverbal communication in front of a mirror or have a friend watch as you run through your presentation. Too often practicing a presentation consists of going over the words and PowerPoint slides without taking the time to practice the nonverbal messages you are sending the customer.

What to Do When Things Go Wrong

No matter how much planning and hard work you put into it, you can't control every aspect of the sales presentation. Indeed, most presentations offer at least one obstacle. Successful salespeople realize that even when they have created the right setting for the presentation, things still come up to distract the customer. It is wise to consider what to do in difficult situations *before* they happen. While every situation introduces unique challenges, we will focus on three: interruptions during the presentation, inappropriate sales presentation environment, and a failure of technology.

Interruptions during the Presentation. Most of the time you are presenting at the customer's business, which means you do not control the environment. Of course it helps when the customer tells the staff to hold all calls, but that is no guarantee there will be no interruptions. Cell phones, pagers, and superiors can still find the customer when necessary.

What do you do when the customer is disturbed during the presentation? First, assess the nature of the call. If it's confidential, withdraw to give the customer space to deal with the issue in private. Second, consider any interruption an opportunity to assess the progress of the presentation and plan where you want to go from here.

Third, be patient and allow the customer to refocus attention on you before proceeding. Perhaps the customer needs to make some notes after the interruption or simply take a few moments to collect his or her thoughts. Don't proceed without first getting some indication that the customer is now focused again on you and the presentation. Fourth, briefly restate the key points you have covered in the presentation. You might validate where you left off with the customer by asking a question. "I believe we were talking about the benefits of our extensive product inventory to your manufacturing needs, is that correct?" Wait until you have the customer fully engaged before proceeding with the rest of the presentation.

Inappropriate Environment. Another issue for a salesperson meeting at the customer's place of business is the location of the presentation. A personal office or conference room with all the necessary equipment and privacy is ideal, but it's not always available. In pharmaceutical sales, for example, salespeople often meet with the doctor between patient visits and have only five to ten minutes.

The key for dealing with less than ideal conditions for a presentation is preparation. Be knowledgeable and confident enough in your presentation that you can improvise in a difficult environment. If you have a 30-minute presentation and the customer says he or she has to leave in 15 minutes, make the necessary adjustments and go for it. Customers often appreciate salespeople who can accommodate unforeseen challenges in their presentation.

Technology Failure. In the high-tech world of today's selling environment, where PowerPoint and video are part of many presentations, salespeople need to be prepared when (not if) technology fails. What do you do when the computer crashes, the projector bulb burns out, or the customer wants the presentation in a room with no technology capabilities? As we have discussed already, technology can certainly enhance a presentation, however, it is not the basis for the presentation.

The solution is simple. Always have a backup plan when technology fails. If your presentation is in PowerPoint, bring a set of overhead transparencies and a hard copy of the presentation just in case. Even when the computers are down, you can usually get access to an overhead projector. The customer can follow your hard copy even if you cannot project it on screen. You should always bring a copy of the presentation anyway to leave with the customer.

Many companies now are equipping their sales force with portable projectors to use when the customer does not have the proper equipment. This gives salespeople a great deal more flexibility in location. They are no longer dependent on the customer to set up for a computer-generated presentation. The key in these situations is to develop a plan of action to deal with any possible technology glitch. A good rule of thumb is to expect the unexpected.

The Sales Manager's Role in the Sales Presentation

Ultimately, the salesperson is responsible for the presentation. Yet salespeople do not operate alone. As part of their company's sales force, they are supported by hundreds (even thousands) of other employees. The sales manager plays a significant role in the overall success of a sales presentation. As the salespeople's immediate supervisor, he or she is responsible for providing all the tools they need. Let's examine the sales managers' role in more detail.

Managers Are Essential to a Great Presentation

Salespeople operate in the customer's environment, and they rely on the sales manager to support their efforts back at the office. Without that support they would be unable to sustain an effective presence with customers in the field. The two basic roles for the sales manager are mentor and salesperson.

Many managers come out of the sales ranks, and every manager is expected to work with salespeople to enhance their effectiveness during the presentation. Most organizations consider the role of **mentor** very important. Helping salespeople improve their skills is part of the job description.

The second role is that of salesperson. Yes, even sales managers have sales responsibilities. Customers, especially large customers, expect to see the manager as part of the sales presentation. The manager's presence makes customers feel important. Also, customers, at certain levels in their organization expect to negotiate with a sales manager.

We will discuss these roles in much greater detail in Part Three.

Providing the Tools for Success

The manager needs to equip salespeople for success. First, the salesperson needs the proper training to get the job done. Sending a salesperson in front of a customer without sufficient training will ensure failure. (We will discuss training in Chapter 12.) Second, the manager needs to provide the equipment for success. Today that means computers (laptop or desktop), mobile communications (cell phones), and other technologies the salesperson needs to deliver a persuasive message to customers. Third, the manager needs to develop and manage effective reward and compensation systems to ensure a highly motivated and satisfied sales force. (A detailed discussion of this topic is found in Chapter 13.)

While we will explore the manager's tasks and responsibilities to the sales-person later in the book, it is important to recognize now that managers do play an important role in the salesperson's success during presentations.

To develop this role play, Alex will need to identify and present to Tracy some features, advantages, and benefits (FABs) of Happy Teeth related to both (a) end users of the product (shoppers in Max's Pharmacies) and (b) Tracy's (Max's) business (what's in it for them). Benchmark what you learn about Crest Whitestrips to come up with these FABs. Assume that Upland will be introducing Happy Teeth at a 10 percent price advantage over Crest Whitestrips, that Happy Teeth has been shown through clinical testing to get teeth whiter faster than Crest Whitestrips, and that the whiteness provided by Happy Teeth lasts longer than that provided by Crest Whitestrips. Beyond that, make up any other reasonable FABs you like for use in the presentation.

Tracy Brown's Role

Tracy has been a customer of Alex's for 12 years, and a high level of trust exists in the business relationship. Although Tracy will have some questions and minor concerns/objections about the new product (you can make these up in advance as well as come up with some during the actual presentation), ultimately Tracy will agree to the purchase without giving Alex too much trouble.

Alex Lewis's Role

Alex must prepare and present a maximum 10-minute presentation to Tracy about Happy Teeth. He wants her to stock the product in the front end of each Max's Pharmacy and to feature Happy Teeth in an upcoming newspaper ad at a special price of $5 off, for which Upland will compensate Tracy in promotional "push" monies. Alex would like to sell three dozen per store for a total order of 24 dozen. He needs to use the elements of a good "need satisfaction" presentation and incorporate all other relevant presentation tips provided in the chapter.

Rhonda Reed's Role

In the call itself, Rhonda should only briefly greet and engage in pleasant conversation with Tracy before and after Alex's presentation. Her key role is to observe Alex's presentation carefully during the sales call. Afterward, Alex and Rhonda will leave Tracy's office and Rhonda will give Alex at least five minutes of constructive feedback/coaching about his performance. The feedback should cover both verbal and nonverbal aspects of his presentation.

Assignment

Work together to orchestrate the sales presentation, buyer responses, and manager feedback/coaching encounter. Limit the sales call to 10 minutes and the manager feedback/coaching discussion to five minutes.

Discussion Questions

1. As a customer, think back to a recent sales presentation that you felt went well. What made it good? What did the salesperson do (or not do) that most impressed you? Did you buy the product or service? What did the salesperson do that convinced you to buy from him or her?

2. Imagine you are working for a company that sells teleconferencing equipment. Draft a value proposition for selling your equipment to a sales manager who has 10 salespeople traveling two weeks a month to visit customers all over the country.

3. Identify three selling situations where a memorized sales presentation may be appropriate. Explain why they would be appropriate.

4. You are the sales manager for a company selling components to companies in the auto industry and are considering upgrading computer equipment for the sales force. Draft a document detailing the specifications for the new computer system. Your reps need access to a great deal of product information and run a simulation detailing the functions of the product. They need a computer that can handle a sophisticated simulation program.

5. Identify the five objectives of a sales presentation and develop an example of how a sales presentation would accomplish each one.

6. Pair off in class and practice a salesperson's approach to a customer. Develop an approach that lasts three minutes and includes a greeting.

7. Select two of the approach strategies and develop each one into a one-page dialogue between you and a customer.

8. You are a salesperson working for American Airlines calling on the vice president of a large manufacturing company. Many of the company's people travel all over the world, and you would like them to sign an agreement to use American Airlines exclusively. Develop a SPIN approach for this customer.

9. Choose a product and sell it using the FAB methodology.

10. You are a salesperson for the local cell phone company presenting to the sales manager of a company considering adopting a companywide cell phone provider. Develop a five-minute product demonstration of any cell phone provider in your area.

Ethical Dilemma

Jerry Gutel has been with Step Ahead Publishing for 11 years and witnessed firsthand its technology transformation. When he came to the company, Step Ahead salespeople carried large binders with all relevant information for hundreds of books (sometimes as much as 10 pages on each book). Often he would have to carry two or three of these heavy binders into a bookstore. Meeting with store managers in the Southeast meant that Jerry was frequently on the road, and carrying the books was always cumbersome.

Five years ago Step Ahead management began to integrate technology into the sales force. Jerry began using the laptop as his only sales tool and was happy there were no more heavy binders. There was a great deal of sensitive information on the computer, such as individual book sales, wholesale prices, and new-product delivery dates. As a result, the company had a strict rule against the use of company laptops for personal use. It didn't want any outsiders gaining access to the data. It also wanted salespeople to view the laptop as strictly for company use and not as personal property.

Jerry was becoming increasingly dependent on computers in his personal life. Two years ago he bought a computer for his family. With two teenagers, however, Jerry had little access to the computer at home. Compounding the problem was the time Jerry had to work on personal matters while traveling and spending many nights in a hotel. He thought the company's policy was wrong, and other salespeople told him they used their laptops for personal business all the time. They even told him about software that would protect company files using secure passwords and encoding key data.

Today Jerry stopped by his bank to find out how to do all his banking online. All he needed was financial software like Quicken on his computer and a phone

selling environment

Sales Management

Evaluating Performance

Salesperson Motivation

Recruiting & Selection

Training & Development

Compensation

Relationship Selling

NEGOTIATING FOR WIN-WIN SOLUTIONS

Closing & Follow-up

Self-Management

Prospecting & Sales Call Planning

Communicating the Sales Message

Information

Value Creation

Ethics

Customer Relationships

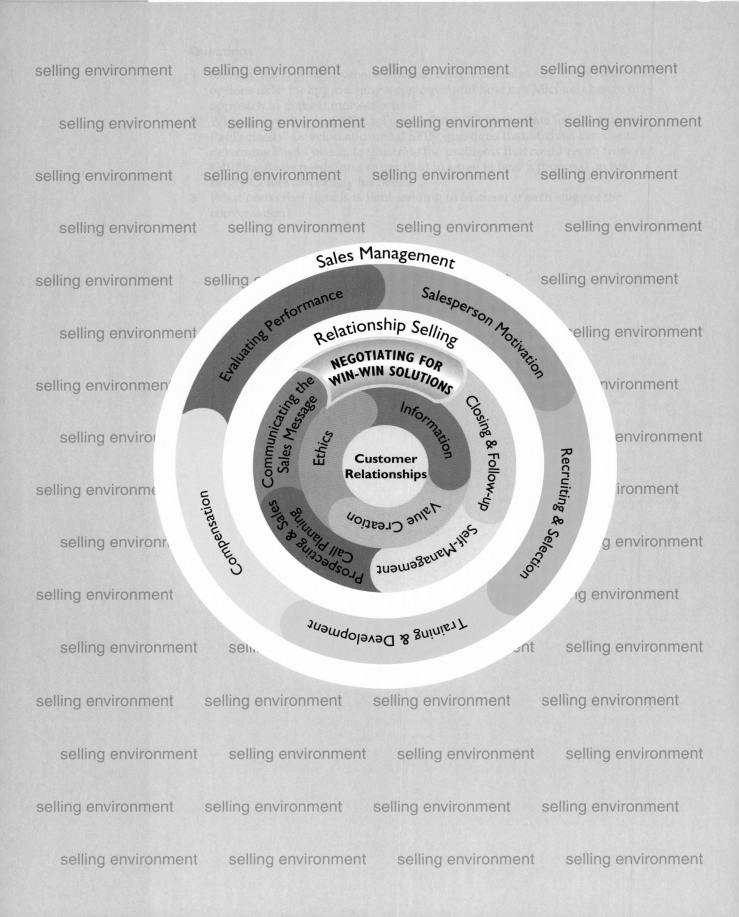

7 chapter

Negotiating for Win–Win Solutions

Learning Objectives

No matter how well you prepare, no matter how well you present your material to the customer—indeed, despite everything you do—the customer will seldom, if ever, buy the product based solely on your presentation. Does this mean you should not prepare the best sales presentation possible? Of course not. The presentation is the starting point for a successful buyer–seller relationship. But negotiating and working with customers to develop a win–win solution to their problems are at the heart of the relationship-selling process. There are many occasions when the customer will have legitimate, specific questions or objections about the nature of your material. Negotiations are the process whereby customer objections and questions are resolved.

This chapter explores the process of negotiating with customers. We will identify customer objections and how you can learn to respond successfully when customers raise objections about your product. It describes specific negotiating strategies designed to help you work through customer concerns. Finally, it discusses the sales manager's role in negotiating win–win solutions.

After reading this chapter, you should be able to

- Understand the process of negotiating win–win solutions.
- Know the common objections most salespeople encounter working with customers.
- Know the basic points to consider in negotiating with customers.
- Understand the specific negotiating strategies.
- Understand the sales manager's role in negotiating win–win solutions.

expert advice

Expert: David Yeaple, Vice President of Sales

Company: Odyssey Software, Rochester New York

Business: Odyssey Software develops applications that allow mobile workers to travel freely, directly accessing and interacting with critical data and business systems transparently while maintaining the security of intellectual assets.

Education: Bachelors Degree (Electrical Engineering), Rochester Institute of Technology, MBA, Oregon State University.

What is the most significant customer concern you face? How do you address that concern?

While the quality of Odyssey Software's products is excellent and we've been extremely successful, customers will sometimes express a concern about Odyssey Software's size (less than 20 people). Obviously a C-level executive at a Fortune 1000 company isn't interested in licensing a product to use in their enterprise that will be obsolete and/or unsupported in a few years.

We've created a 3-element approach to deal with this concern.

- First, all of our products are standards based, meaning that we've eliminated the need for proprietary interfaces. This means that customers can often support our products themselves (because knowledge about how to work with standards-based products is widely available) and they are very comfortable that they haven't bought into a proprietary technology that will soon be obsolete.
- Second, we've partnered with industry leaders (e.g., Microsoft), and that underscores the value of our products and validates for the customer that choosing our products is a "safe bet." It adds a great deal of credibility when your company is making joint sales calls with industry leaders and your company is certified with their credentials (e.g., Microsoft Gold Partner).
- Third, we can offer our customers a "software escrow" which entitles the customer to access the source code for the product(s) that they've licensed in the unlikely event that something catastrophic should happen to Odyssey Software. This provides assurance that they can provide business continuity, even in a worst-case scenario.

Provide an example of a customer who felt Odyssey's software was too expensive and how you handled that situation?

For some customers, the Internet has created an impression that "all software is free," which means that *any* price greater than zero is too high. Early in any customer engagement we try to quickly assess (i.e., qualify) a customer to see if this is their perception. In some cases, we'll make the decision to pursue other opportunities. However, in most cases it's a classic question of how much value do they really place on the functionality that Odyssey Software's products are able to provide. For this reason, we've constructed our flagship product using a modular architecture for functionality that enables a customer to license only the specific functionality they need and value. In other words, they can start out by licensing a very basic configuration and then enhance it over time—as dictated by the needs of their business. Interestingly, in almost every case where license price is stated to be a concern, a customer will start out by specifying only some very basic functions, and will then end up licensing the entire product suite!

What guidelines do you use in dealing with customer concerns and objections?

The nature of Odyssey Software's products requires a highly technical sale, and many potential vendors' specifications all look roughly the same on paper. In addition, many customers have been "burned" by great (highly controlled) conference room product demonstrations, only to find out that the product doesn't really live up to the proclaimed capabilities in a real-life scenario. To deal with this, we highly encourage customers to try our software products on an extended basis (e.g., 30 days or 60 days) in their own, real environments. Our best advocates (influencers) in any sale are typically the customer's own technical personnel who have utilized our products in their own environment and found them to be extremely valuable.

Negotiating Win–Win Solutions

"Obstacles are those frightful things you see when you take your eyes off your goal," Henry Ford observed. Dealing with customer objections is an element of the relationship-building process that many salespeople do not enjoy. However, as Ford pointed out, it is critical to keep your eyes on your goal: building the buyer–seller relationship. When a customer shares objections, it gives the salesperson an opportunity to strengthen the relationship. Read the Expert Advice to see how one successful company approaches customer objections and negotiates win–win strategies.

The objections customers raise during the sales presentation are one reason salespeople are so important to the relationship-building process. If customers readily accepted the presentation, the company could just mail them a brochure or send them to the company's Web site to view a PowerPoint presentation. It is salespeople and their unique ability to answer customer objections that enables the company to sell products to customers.

This chapter examines the delicate process of negotiating win–win solutions. It is not particularly difficult to understand the basics of negotiation, but doing it well requires training, practice, and experience. By the end of the chapter you will have the tools to negotiate successfully with customers. The chapter also examines the role managers play in supporting the salesperson during the negotiating process.

Negotiations: The Heart of the Win–Win Solution

Many books on personal selling speak to the issue of "customer objections" and how salespeople should deal with them. They seem to think that objections are a problem that salespeople need to manage. The relationship-selling process considers customer objections an opportunity for the salesperson to create a win–win solution, and that is the goal to focus on during the presentation. Refer to the model of Relationship Selling at the beginning of the chapter to see where we are in the process.

Too often salespeople believe that when the customer wins, they lose. Or the customer believes he or she has lost and the salesperson has won. They think there can be only one winner. Presenting customer concerns as problems suggests that if salespeople can somehow develop a scheme to win, they are successful. This is simply not the case in relationship selling.[1] If either the buyer *or* the seller loses, both have lost. An unhappy buyer is likely to seek out other suppliers, and the relationship will suffer. If, on the other hand, the seller is forced into an unprofitable contract, the customer will ultimately bear the cost through less service, poorer-quality products, or some other problem. In either case, there is no winner.[2] Successful buyer–seller relationships are based on both parties being satisfied with the customer's purchase.

Webster's dictionary defines **negotiation** as the act of "conferring with another so as to arrive at the settlement of some matter" and to "arranging for or bringing about through conference, discussion, and compromise."[3] Notice the definition speaks about discussion and compromise with the customer. It does not include words like exploitation and manipulation. We have spoken about the importance of building relationships based on mutual respect and customer value. Negotiating through customer objections is a critical element in that process.

Common Customer Concerns

Casual observation may suggest there are many different customer concerns; however, when you look closely, it is clear the anxieties fall into five areas. Note that customers may mask their true concern with general anxieties. Successful salespeople know that when they hear a customer objection, they need to clarify and determine its true nature. Exhibit 7.1 is a summary of the five main customer concerns.[4] Let's examine them.

Do I Need *Your* Product?

Customer objections regarding the product fall into two broad areas that require different approaches to deal with the customer's concern.

Product Need. First, the customer may not be convinced that there is a need for the product. This is especially true if the customer has never used a product like it. He or she may simply not see the value in buying the product or the need that it satisfies. This view can be summarized as, "We've always done it one way. Why should we start something new now?"

Consider the Apple Newton. When it was introduced in 1993, the Newton was one of the original personal digital assistants (PDAs) and ahead of its time. Unfortunately, many corporate customers could not see the need for a personal organizer and thought of it as an expensive calendar and meeting organizer. Corporate buyers asked why they should spend $500 for a calendar. Where Apple failed, companies like Palm succeeded by demonstrating these were really little computers capable of many things besides being a calendar. Today, PDA functions are built into cell phones or other mobile wireless devices like the iPod Touch. The Newton lives, but only with a group of enthusiasts, as Apple discontinued the product in 1998.[5]

Ultimately, customers must see a clear and convincing reason to buy the product. If they don't, you shouldn't be surprised if they choose not to buy. Keep in mind that customers are not usually risk takers. With new products they are likely to wonder if the technology is too new or unproven. They may also question if it is significantly better than their current solution. The fundamental question is "Do I really need your product?" Key to the answer is a well-conceived value proposition that explains clearly how the product will benefit the customer and how it will be better than the existing solution.

Your Product Need. A much more common concern regarding product is whether the customer needs *your* product. Perhaps the configuration of your product is different or your competition's product has features that aren't on yours (or vice

EXHIBIT 7.1 Summary of Customer Concerns

- Do I need *your* product?
  - Product need
  - *Your* product need
- Do I trust *your* company?
  - Unease about your company
  - Loyalty to existing supplier
- I don't really know you.
- I need more time to consider your product.
- Is this your best price?

versa). Almost anything about your product may be of concern to the customer. Careful preparation is critical in dealing with questions about your product's superiority. This is why you must have a thorough knowledge of your competitor's products and services.

Since the customer has been using your competitor's products, he or she knows their configuration, terminology, and product benefits very well. You must clearly define your product's Features, Advantages, and Benefits so the customer will understand the value proposition of your company's products over your competition. Again, change is not easy, and buying your product means the customer will have to learn a new product, so your value proposition must consider the cost of change. Put simply, your product cannot be just as good as the competition because that will not be sufficient reason for the customer to change. Your product must be demonstrably better.

Do I Trust *Your* Company?

If a customer asked, "Why should I trust your company?" would you be able to answer? As we have discussed, relationship selling is based in part on mutual respect and trust between buyer and seller, including trust between the buyer's company and your company. In most cases customers already have a supplier. They may not be totally satisfied with that supplier, but they're familiar with them. They know whom to call to get a problem resolved. They are also familiar with that company's policies and procedures. You must overcome the customer's reluctance to change suppliers.

There are two types of customer objections regarding the salesperson's company. Often these two issues work together to create a formidable concern for the customer.

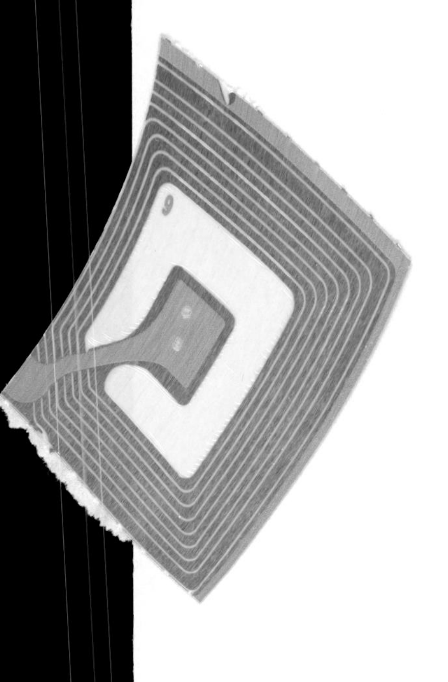

Unease about Your Company. If customers are not aware of your company, they may simply be concerned about your ability to deliver when, where, and what they need. This is a legitimate concern, as they are putting their company at some risk by choosing you as a supplier. They need to know that you will do what you promise in the presentation. Refer to the Expert Advice to see how one successful sales professional deals with this concern.

Customers can be concerned about your company for many reasons. If you are small, they may be apprehensive about whether you can deliver what they need or whether you are even going to be in business in two years. If you are big, they may fear they will not be a valued customer. These objections can be difficult to overcome. How can you prove to the customer that your company will be around in two years? How can you demonstrate you will deliver what the customer needs when and where it's wanted, every time? Perhaps the customer has read or heard something negative about your company. For example, the accounting problems at KPMG made it difficult for account executives to overcome the negative perceptions in the marketplace.

Loyalty to the Existing Supplier. A customer who has objections about your company may be showing loyalty to or satisfaction with the current supplier. The customer may say, "I have been buying from Mr. McAllaster at Steadfast for years and they have been excellent. I never had a problem they didn't fix." In those situations it is not that your company has done anything wrong; rather, your competitor has done things right. This problem must be handled carefully, or you will anger the customer and lose the opportunity to build the relationship.

Directly confronting the customer with negative comments about the supplier will almost surely fail. Remember, customers don't like change, and speaking critically about someone they have had a relationship with for a time will not endear you to them. The best approach is to stay focused on your product and company.

I Don't Really Know You

Customers may be concerned about the ability of a new, inexperienced salesperson to learn their business or their commitment to the company. (Is the salesperson going to be there for a while?) The salesperson has to earn the customers' respect. When salespeople are new, customers may ask to see their supervisor or want someone more experienced to handle their business. In these situations, it is important to be very prepared and demonstrate knowledge of the customer's value proposition. The salespersons shouldn't become defensive about their education or qualifications. Rather they should use the concerns as an opportunity to build the relationship and ask those customers to put them to the test. The salesperson is asking for a chance at their business.

Selling is a people business, and occasionally your personality will not be compatible with the customer's. Keep in mind Henry Ford's quote: Stay focused on the goal. While you and the customer may not be friends or even get along, what matters is the relationship between your companies. Of course, you should notify your manager of the problems and seek his or her help on how to address personal compatibility issues. (We will talk about this later in this chapter when we examine the manager's role in negotiations.)

Even experienced salespeople run across personality conflicts when they take on a new account. Customers often develop a relationship with a salesperson as well as the selling company. When a salesperson is replaced, the new person and customer will naturally go through a period of getting to know one another. During this period, the salesperson should be supported by management so the customer understands the company has complete confidence in the new person. Some companies rotate the sales force to prevent this situation from developing with customers. The focus should always be on the relationship between the *company* and the customer, not the salesperson and the customer.

I Need More Time to Consider Your Product

Every day salespeople hear "I need more time to think about your proposal." Customers have a legitimate concern about making a purchase decision too quickly. If the purchase involves several parts of the company (for example, the decision to build a new plant or develop a new product), there will most likely be a committee involved in the purchase process. In some industries (defense, airlines), the decision to purchase may take a year or more. Lockheed Martin, one of the leading defense contractors with over $35 billion in sales, is typical. Its F/A-22 aircraft literally took years to develop, test, and market to the Department of Defense. When a customer says he or she needs more time to think about the purchase, it may be true.

However, customers frequently ask for more time because they wish to delay or **stall** the final decision for several reasons. First, customers may be reluctant to make a decision because of the uncertainty of something new. You are asking them to trust you, your company, and your solution to their problem. While you may know it to be the best solution to their problem, they may be anxious.

INNOVATION 7.1

Tips for Negotiating Price

1. **Understand the buyer's biggest value.** Purchasing agents are rewarded for "the lowest price" contact and it is important to remember that the buyer's personal success is a huge driver in price negotiations. Salespeople need to help the purchasing agent deliver on the value message inside his or her own company.

2. **Understand the buyer's fear.** Choosing a new vendor takes the buyers outside their "comfort zone." In addition, higher than expected costs tied to increased functionality may seem reasonable to the salesperson but create anxiety for the buyer as they will ultimately bear the responsibility of presenting the rationale for a decision to management. It is important to minimize concerns that feed the buyers' fear of change.

3. **Focus on the lowest TOTAL cost.** Buyers tend to focus on the initial purchase price when the TOTAL cost of the purchase includes vendor reliability (can they deliver on time), customer service, product quality, and reduced down time. Salespeople must focus on the TOTAL cost instead of getting caught in the "lowest price" trap.

4. **Utilize questions to uncover what the buyer values.** It is important for the salesperson to clearly understand what is important to the customer. Buyers will say "lowest price" because they don't want to address the specific issue. Successful salespeople go beyond "lowest price" to find out what really drives the customer's decision.

Source: Paul Cherry, "Disarming the Price-Squeezing Customer: Six Ways to Eliminate Price Concerns," *American Salesman* 52(12), December 2007, pp. 9–14.

The second (and more likely) scenario is that you have failed to prove the value proposition. The customers do not see the benefits of your product over their existing situation. It is important to realize, however, they are not saying no. They are indirectly asking you to build a stronger case for your product. Again, this is an opportunity to build the relationship. Go back into your presentation and ask questions to ascertain the source of the customers' anxiety. Summarize the value proposition to reinforce the positive results from a purchase decision.

Is This Your Best Price?

Salespeople will consistently tell you price is the concern they hear most often. This concern is voiced in many ways: "Your price is too high," "I don't have the budget right now," "I'd like to purchase your product but not at that price," "I can't justify that price for your product." In many cases, the customer has legitimate objections about the price of your product. Many customers, especially professional buyers, are directed to buy the lowest-cost product. Often they are evaluated and rewarded on their ability to drive down the price of the products they purchase. Professional buyers at Wal-Mart are trained to negotiate the lowest price possible. Innovation 7.1 offers some insights into how to negotiate price.

However, while price is a legitimate customer concern, a more likely explanation is that the customer has not accepted the value proposition. Remember that value is a function of price and perceived benefits. A customer who does not perceive that the product benefits exceed the price will not be inclined to purchase the product. You are left with two options to make the sale. Lower the price until it is below the product's perceived benefits, or raise the perceived benefits until they exceed the price. A customer who says your price is too high is really saying the benefits I perceive for buying your product are not greater than the price you are currently charging. Here are some guidelines to follow in dealing with the price concern.

selling environment

Sales Management

Evaluating Performance

Salesperson Motivation

Recruiting & Selection

Training & Development

Compensation

Relationship Selling

CLOSING & FOLLOW-UP

Self-Management

Prospecting & Sales Call Planning

Communicating the Sales Message

Negotiating for Win-Win Solutions

Information

Ethics

Value Creation

Customer Relationships

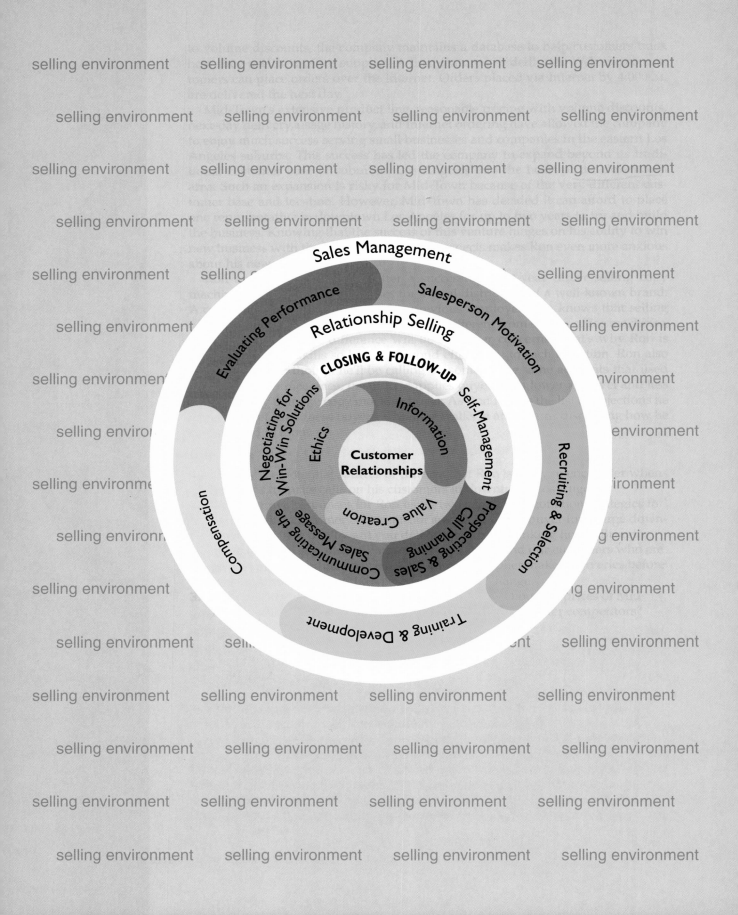

8 chapter

Closing the Sale and Follow-up

Learning Objectives

This chapter completes our journey through the relationship-selling process by examining closing the sale and following up to enhance customer relationships. In relationship selling, closing is a natural progression of the process. Because we are building toward win–win solutions with customers, closing simply connotes that both parties recognize the value-added of doing business with one another. Postsale follow-up presents a marvelous opportunity to add even more value to clients through problem solving and service.

After reading this chapter, you should be able to

- Define closing and explain how closing fits into the relationship-selling model.
- Understand different closing methods and provide examples of each.
- Discuss the concept of rejection and ways to deal with it.
- Identify various verbal and nonverbal buying signals.
- Know when to trial close.
- Recognize and avoid common closing mistakes.
- Explain aspects of follow-up that enhance customer relationships.
- Understand the sales manager's role in closing the sale and follow-up.

expert advice

Expert: James A. Decker, CMP, Sales Manager, Resort Sales and Marketing
Company: Universal Orlando Resort
Business: Represents three hotels located at Universal Orlando Resort: Loews Portofino Bay Hotel (750 rooms), Hard Rock Hotel (650 rooms), Loews Royal Pacific Resort (1,000 rooms). These properties have over 250,000 square-feet of meeting and event space.
Education: MBA, Rollins College; BS, Pennsylvania State University.

From your experience working with lots of high powered clients who are seeking the right resort for their meetings, why is being a great listener so important in sales?

The key to working in sales in any industry is the ability to listen to your clients. The hospitality industry caters to a demanding clientele set in a highly competitive market. If you don't listen to your client, you could miss discovering the key elements that are vital to creating a successful program for them, and could instead end up trying to sell them on something they actually view as a negative! "Feature dumping"—that is, verbally dumping all your product's features on them without first knowing what they are actually interested in—can be detrimental to a sale, and makes it obvious to a client that you aren't listening. Clients may *think* they know what they want, but until you obtain their history and truly understand what their needs are, you will not be able uncover and focus on the finer details essential to producing the most successful program for them.

What about times when something unexpected goes wrong after a sale? What is your advice on how to do effective service recovery?

The sale should never truly be considered over or complete. Too many variables can impact the group's overall experience, making it critical that you partner with all staff and departments who will ultimately impact the group (for example, the food and beverage department). Without their support and partnership through teamwork, you cannot have success with your clients. When a challenge arises, the best advice is to be honest with the client and get an answer as to what went wrong. Ask them directly if they feel that they are comfortable with the service recovery. It is very easy to lose a client's trust if they do not see that you are working toward their best interests. Do not make excuses, but always stand by your product.

What other tips can you give about the importance of serving the client between the time the contract is signed and when their event takes place?

People buy from friends, and the best compliment you can get is when your client refers you to another, or they give you another piece of business themselves. Always treat your clients like they are your friends. It is always fun to be in business with friends, so stay in touch with them after the contract is finalized—before, during, and after their meeting. Also contact your clients to recognize important personal events such as their birthday, their child's big football game, and other special occasions.

Selling is fun, relationships with clients are meaningful, and being a salesperson is rewarding. Take advantage of the sales profession and enjoy the job!

What Is a Close?

For anyone engaged in relationship selling, **closing the sale** means obtaining a commitment from the prospect or customer to make a purchase. Even long-time customers still need to be closed on specific orders or transactions. Also, as you learned in Chapter 6, a salesperson should always enter a call with specific goals for that call. Closing connotes the achievement of those sales call goals.

Closing the sale should not be viewed as a discrete event that takes place at the end of a sales call. Such a perspective leads to much anxiety on the part of perfectly capable salespeople by focusing on a single element in developing the client relationship. Chapter 1 introduced the concept of closing the sale in the context of our overall model for Relationship Selling and Sales Management:

> One of the joys of relationship selling is that the high level of rapport, trust, and mutual respect inherent in a long-term buyer–seller relationship can take some of the pressure off the "close" portion of the sales process. In theory, this is because the seller and buyer have been openly communicating throughout the process about mutual goals they would like to see fulfilled by a particular sales transaction. Because the key added value is not price but rather other aspects of the product or service, the negotiation should not get hung up on price as an objection. Therefore, in relationship selling, closing becomes a natural part of the communication process.

Selling Is Not a Linear Process

The components of successful relationship selling you have learned so far throughout this book liberate you from the need to use clever, tricky, and manipulative closing approaches with your prospects and customers. Note that our guiding model for Relationship Selling and Sales Management is not linear. That is, it doesn't show "steps" of selling progressing one after another in order. This is because relationship selling usually is decidedly nonlinear. In relationship selling, the various components of the selling process take place simultaneously, always focused on the customer at the core, with adding value and performing ethically as guiding central themes. The layout of our model connotes this, and the visual of the process as emanating from the customer at the center is important to an understanding of how relationship selling works.

At no place in the selling process is understanding the nature of the model for Relationship Selling and Sales Management more relevant than in closing the sale. Closing as a selling function is actually appropriate at *any point* in the relationship-selling process—not just at the end of a lengthy sales presentation. In this chapter, we advocate learning different approaches to closing, because knowing different ways to communicate to buyers the need to gain commitment to the goals of the sales call is a fundamental skill in seller–buyer communication. However, we also strongly advocate that these closing skills be used at the appropriate point in the dialogue with the customer—*not just at the end.* The salesperson must watch for **buying signals,** verbal and nonverbal cues that the customer is ready to make a commitment to purchase.

If a salesperson has done the job well on the tasks described so far in this book—understanding the buyer, creating and communicating value, behaving ethically, using information for prospecting and sales call planning, communicating the

3. *Don't automatically assume that you are the problem.* The prospect may be an intimidating, self-serving individual with some deep personal problems that cause the behavior you see. The prospect may be just having a bad day or may be like that all the time. You are not to blame for any of these possibilities.
4. *Positively anticipate the possibility of rejection and it will not overwhelm you.* Expect it, but don't create it. That is, think in advance what your response to rejection will be if it occurs. (Note: This does not conflict with an assumptive close approach.)
5. *Consider the possibility that not buying is a rational decision because of underlying reasons.* Possible reasons are bad timing, shared decision making, or budget constraints that truly do prevent purchase. The prospect may not feel comfortable revealing these reasons to you.[4]

The preparation you learned in Chapter 7 for anticipating and handling buyers' objections will help buffer you against taking rejection personally. If you do a great job during the preapproach of researching reasons a customer might not buy and then planning appropriate responses for dealing with the objections, at the end of the day if the customer does not buy you can look at yourself in the mirror and say "I did everything I could." This is a sign of professionalism in selling.

Excellence in call preparation yields a confidence and professionalism that cannot be equaled. This is why sales executives often call the preapproach the single most important stage in the relationship-selling process. (Interesting, isn't it, how this runs counter to the stereotype that the most important step is the close?) If despite your preparation and presentation the customer still doesn't buy, know when to pack up graciously and leave the door open to sell to this client another day.

Attitude Is Important

Books on successful closing agree that a critical determinant of whether or not a salesperson closes customers is attitude.[5,6] **Attitude** represents the salesperson's state of mind or feeling with regard to a person or thing. Everything else being equal, salespeople who believe in themselves and their product or service, show confidence, exhibit honest enthusiasm, and display **tenacity** (sticking with a task even through difficulty and adversity) will close more business than those who don't.

In a survey 215 sales managers across a wide range of industries were asked which success factors are the most important in their salespeople. Tenacity (sticking with a task/not giving up) ranked fourth out of over 50 key success factors.[7] Successful salespeople are successful in large measure because they don't give up easily. They stick with the process of developing customer relationships and moving customers to closing the sale. They aren't distracted from this core mission of selling, and they don't feel rejected when they don't make a sale.

Attitude is infectious. Customers pick up on a salesperson's attitude and outlook on life right away. Innovation 8.1 gives a rousing picture of the value of honest enthusiasm in our daily lives.

One important way to approach closing involves envisioning a successful outcome with the buyer. Sit back and mentally rehearse how a positive outcome might unfold. Think about all the steps needed to close the sale. This exercise helps solidify the road map toward closing the sale. It also feeds your positive attitude and confidence before you actually engage in the close.

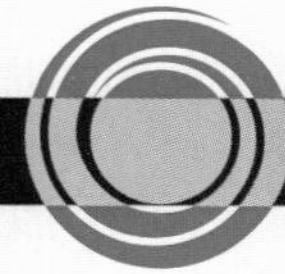

INNOVATION 8.1

The Essence of Enthusiasm

It is rare that one can find more up's and down's in a career than you'll find in the selling profession. A prosperous month and life is good. A down month and job *dis*-satisfaction reigns supreme. It is so very common that one's job satisfaction is tied directly to their production. It's hard not to experience some of this as a professional salesperson—after all, how many vocations have a measuring stick as clear and defined as monthly sales production?

Sales organizations would do well to look around their sales forces for these signs of trouble:

- Negativity
- Call reluctance—avoidance of prospecting or making calls
- Lack of motivation/action
- Good month/bad month swings in production
- Lack of ownership/professionalism in their work
- (And here's the biggie that can bring down the house)
- Lack of *enthusiasm* for their work

Many salespeople let their production (the destination) dictate their job satisfaction instead of letting their daily activities (the journey) provide them the purpose and fulfillment they seek. It's a trap that causes inconsistent production, sporadic motivation, and in the end—burnout!

So what's the solution to creating a long-term, successful sales career?

Answer: LIVE YOUR BLISS!

Your bliss is that activity or experience that when doing it, you feel truly alive. Time slows down and you find real meaning and purpose in what you are doing. When you find your bliss and incorporate it into the practice of your work, you've just discovered the secret to passion and high performance. Everyone has their personal bliss that excites and motivates them. When we are engaged in these activities we find it easy to commit to the practice. Discipline and willpower are not a struggle because we love what we are doing. Are there actual salespeople who live their bliss and excel in the sales profession? Yes, they are called "Specialists."

The generalists are the majority; they do what most others do and get similar results. Of the 80/20 rule they make up the 80 percent who produce the 20 percent. When the market for the generalists' product or service is not in high demand they tend to experience a drop off in production, which in turn can cause stress and if it lasts too long, they may be forced to exit the company or industry all together.

Specialists have developed a creative approach to their profession. Specialists enjoy top of mind awareness, are the highest paid salespeople in the world, and exhibit a natural passion for their work. When we encounter a person who is passionate about the part they play in their work, we are witnessing vocation excellence. Think about it, enthusiasm is contagious and in a time of similar pricing and products, enthusiasm often makes the difference.

A salesperson that wants to experience a dramatic shift in passion and performance should try these tips:

Tip One: Find your bliss—utilize the 20-10-5 rule.

Twenty. List 20 things you love to do most and gain enjoyment from. Is it baking, golfing, smoking cigars, swimming, fantasy sports, coaching, public speaking, sailing, technology, running, lifting weights, bowling, pottery, event planning (you party hound!), skiing, gardening/harvesting, playing music, wine tasting, dancing, yoga—we can add to this list ad infinitum.

Ten. Choose the top 10 that fit the following criteria:

1. Could these activities be incorporated into the practice of my selling activities (prospecting, presenting, closing, follow-up, client retention, etc.) and have a positive impact on production?
2. Could I see myself doing it week in and week out with enjoyment, said another way, could I find it easy to commit to the practice and make it my specialty?

This is where we really need to think outside the box and be open-minded in developing a creative approach. Here are just a few examples of what top producing specialists have incorporated into their work:

- One salesperson loved to cook and bake, so she put her bliss to work and would bake treats of all kinds and deliver them to prospective offices in need of her company's services. As an add-on bonus she would teach prospective clients some helpful hints on cooking/baking free of charge.
- Another salesperson loved to exercise. A self-proclaimed gym rat, she used her joy of working out to share nutritional information and even train many of her prospects and later clients a few times a month as a free add-on service to her core business product.
- One guy incorporated public speaking into his prospecting activities and found various forums to speak on behalf of his industry as well as his products/services. In a very short time he built credibility and a large book of business because of his bliss.
- A golf enthusiast helped his clients with their golf swing.

There are probably some clubs/organizations that get together and share a similar bliss as you do or other places to practice your bliss and develop relationships. The only limit here is one's own creativity and imagination.

Five. Narrow the list to the top five that you love to do most and start enjoying your work! The Key: Get Creative!

Tip Two: Declare yourself a specialist.

Using one or more of your top five, develop a creative brand message and deliver it effectively. Examples:

- The Technology Lady to the (fill in the blank) industry
- The Friendly Fisherman for your financial peace of mind

Tip Three: Commit to the "musts" of your job.

Company requirements such as attendance at all meetings, completed paperwork turned in on time, parking in designated employee parking, and so on are examples of the "musts." The professional salesperson is the one who complies with the requirements of his/her employer. Prima donnas abound the requirements of their employer. Prima donnas abound in the sales profession. Don't be one of them. Selling is one of the most time flexible professions available—this is good news and a major benefit to this vocation. In a 40-hour week, it's possible that your musts may only require 5 to 10 hours of your time, leaving 30 hours or more to "live your bliss."

Let's recap:

1. Utilize the 20-10-5 rule.
2. Declare yourself a specialist.
3. Commit to the "musts" of your job.

The real bottom line of these three tips is this: Do what you love to do and be of service while doing it. Service to others will make you successful in any endeavor you choose. So now, get creative and enjoy the daily journey. Before long you'll be searching for ways to slow your business growth. Not a bad problem to have!

Source: Steve McCann, "Find Your Sales Bliss," *American Salesman,* May 2007, p. 3.

Identifying Buying Signals

As we mentioned, a close does not necessarily happen at the very end of a presentation. It can happen any time. The timing is driven by the buyer's readiness to commit—not the salesperson's need to cover a certain amount of material, present all the available features and benefits, or make it to the end of the presentation. Many salespeople, especially new ones, experience problems in closing because they ignore or are insensitive to buying signals, those verbal and nonverbal cues that the customer is ready to make a commitment to purchase.

Verbal Buying Signals

A buyer may not come right out and say "I'm ready to buy," at least not in those words. However, salespeople should look out for the following verbal signals, which essentially communicate the same message.

- *Giving positive feedback.* The most overt buying signal is a positive comment or comments from the buyer about some aspect of your product. Or the buyer may reinforce something you have said. Examples:
    - "I like the new features you described."
    - "Those extended credit terms really help me out."
    - "You certainly are right that our current vendor can't do that."
- *Asking questions.* When buyers become more engaged, they tend to ask more questions. Buyer questions come in many types, and not all signal a readiness to buy. But watch for questions that seem to open the door to close. Examples:
    - "When will it be available to ship?"
    - "What colors does it come in?"

    - "How much is it?" (Note: A price question may be a signal to close, or it may represent the beginning of an objection.)
    - "Can you explain your service agreement?"
- *Seeking other opinions.* Buyers usually don't ask for opinions about your product or company unless they are seriously considering purchase. This may involve someone else in their company, or it may involve asking you for references or even your own opinion about you versus the competition. Examples:
    - "Let me get Bob from our engineering department in to look at your specs."
    - "Who are some other firms that have bought your product recently?"
    - "Give me your honest opinion about how your product stacks up against your competitors."
- *Providing purchase requirements.* Watch for the point where a buyer begins to become very specific about his or her needs. Often these relate to relatively minor points, not the key attributes of your product or company. This signals acceptance of the major points. Examples:
    - "My orders must be split among four warehouses."
    - "The only way I can change vendors is if you are willing to train my people to use your equipment."

Nonverbal Buying Signals

Often nonverbal communication tells as much or more about the buyer's readiness to buy as words. Watch closely for nonverbal signals that indicate it's time to close.

- *The buyer is relaxed, friendly, and open.* If the buyer moves to this mode during the call, it likely signals he or she is comfortable with what you are selling.
- *The buyer brings out paperwork to consummate the purchase.* A purchase order, sales contract, or other form is a sure signal to close.
- *The buyer exhibits positive gestures or expressions.* Head nodding, leaning forward in a chair, coming around the desk to get a better look at a sample, significant eye contact, and similar nonverbal signals connote interest and potential commitment to the purchase.
- *The buyer picks up your sample and tests it or picks up and examines your literature.* The more involved your customer is in your presentation, the more likely he or she is ready for a close.

Trial Close

When you detect one or more buying signals, it's time to engage in a **trial close.** "Trial" suggests that the buyer may or may not actually be ready to commit. A trial close can involve any of the closing methods discussed earlier. Often a trial close elicits a negative response from the prospect because he or she still has some objections you must overcome. By nature, a trial close can be used at any time during the sales process. In fact, if you walk into a sales call and get a strong buying signal immediately, go ahead and do a trial close. If the customer commits, great. Never feel compelled to deliver a presentation to a buyer who is already sold! A trial close that works becomes *the* close.

Common Closing Mistakes

You have already learned that in relationship selling, closing the sale should not be viewed as an end in and of itself but rather as a part of the overall process of securing, developing, and maintaining long-term relationships with profitable customers. Over the long run, there will always be some orders you don't get and some deals you don't close. A number of potential problems in closing have been identified. Avoiding them will improve your success in closing. The following are some classic closing errors.

- *Harboring a bad attitude.* We established earlier that salespeople who believe in themselves and the product, show confidence, exhibit honest enthusiasm, and display tenacity will close more business than those with a different attitude. A positive approach to life (as exemplified in Innovation 8.1) is infectious and carries over to your relationships with customers.
- *Failure to conduct an effective preapproach.* The preapproach stage is where you do the advanced research and planning needed to arm yourself with the knowledge to give the sales presentation, handle objections, and ultimately provide win–win solutions to customers. This "behind the scenes" part of relationship selling is very important, and failure to plan for the sales call usually leads to poor results in closing. Well-prepared salespeople exude confidence; ill-prepared salespeople come across as—well, ill prepared.
- *Talking instead of listening.* Listening is key to understanding your buyer, getting to know his or her needs, uncovering objections, catching buying signals, and knowing when to trial close.
- *Using a "one size fits all" approach to closing.* Closing methods must be carefully selected and customized to fit a particular buyer and buying situation. In relationship selling, you certainly do not want to come across as a "closing robot" who uses the same techniques every time. Practice and experience will raise your comfort level in applying multiple closing methods to different situations.
- *Uncertainty about what to do after the close.* Sometimes salespeople will hang around and keep talking about the sale after the buyer has already committed. Would you believe that this behavior can talk a buyer out of a sale? It's true! Once commitment is received, it's fine to firm up details (delivery, timing, support staff, etc.). But *never* linger and postmortem the sale with the buyer.

At the end of this chapter is an appendix, "Checklist for Using Effective Closing Skills." Its extensive set of questions will help you identify what aspects of your closing skills are going well and what areas need more work. Especially for new salespeople, this checklist provides considerable insight into the complexity of issues in closing sales and is a source of ideas for use in closing.

Follow-up Enhances Customer Relationships

In Chapter 3 on value creation in buyer–seller relationships, many foundation issues were developed that lead to long-term relationships with customers. Central to nurturing these relationships are how the sales organization creates value for customers and how salespeople communicate that value proposition through actions and words. One of the most important ways to add value is through excellent service after closing the sale, often referred to as **follow-up.**

During this follow-up, the various dimensions of service quality described in Chapter 3 really come into play. Recapping, those are:

- *Reliability.* Providing service in a consistent, accurate, and dependable way.
- *Responsiveness.* Readiness and willingness to help customers and provide service.
- *Assurance.* Conveyance of trust and confidence the company will back up the service with a guarantee.
- *Empathy.* Caring, individualized attention to customers.
- *Tangibles.* The physical appearance of the service provider's business, Web site, marketing communication materials, and the like.[8]

The above descriptors of good service refer not only to salespeople but also to their whole organization. Often salespeople rely heavily on support people to aid in postsale service. Customer care groups, call centers, technicians, and many others frequently represent a firm during the follow-up process. But no matter who else has contact with your customer, ultimately *you*—the client's primary salesperson—are the person your customer views as the main contact with your firm. So you must understand and involve yourself directly in follow-up activities with customers.

Customer Expectations and Complaint Behavior

During the sales process, you and your firm set certain expectations that customers have a right to believe you will meet. These expectations relate to all phases of your product and service. When customer expectations are not met, customers perceive a **performance gap** between what you promised and what you delivered. Performance gaps result in **customer complaints.**

Customer complaints are not something to be dodged or avoided. In fact, customers should be encouraged to share their postsale concerns. Otherwise, how will the sales organization ever know that a problem exists that needs to be corrected? Leadership 8.2 provides a number of ideas on how salespeople and their firms can best use complaints to their advantage.

The following performance gaps are among the most common sources of postsale complaints.

- *Product delivery.* Classically, when problems go wrong with product delivery, it is due to a service failure outside the direct control of the salesperson. However, you must not give excuses, blame someone else, or act as though delivery is not your problem. Your customer expects *you* to research and solve delivery problems.
- *Credit and billing.* Again, this problem is usually not due to some direct action or lack of action by the salesperson. Regardless, you are the customer's main contact person. If problems occur on the invoice, you should shepherd your credit department toward solving the problem and keep your customer in the communication loop during the process.

Leadership 8.2

Using Customer Complaints to Your Advantage

Most salespeople view the job of fielding customer complaints as an arduous chore, just one of those unpleasant realities of sales life. After all, who in their right mind wants to listen to someone complain?

The truth is listening—really listening—to a customer complaint could affect your sales bottom line for the better. Here are five suggestions for dealing with customer complaints and for transforming ill feelings into customer loyalty:

1. It's all in how you take it. One of the least understood realities about customers is that they generally do not complain where there is a problem with a product or service. Instead, in most cases, if a customer for one reason or another is dissatisfied with a salesperson or their product, they simply do not purchase from them again. In fact, past studies have shown that 96 percent of dissatisfied customers don't complain. But although they may not complain, you won't hear from most of them again, either. Sixty-three percent of these silent dissatisfied customers will not buy from you again. Fifteen percent of all customers who switch product brands do so because a complaint was not handled to their satisfaction.

A successful salesperson is one who is genuinely interested in what their customer is thinking as well as saying. Try to encourage feedback from your customer to discover what he or she is thinking about your product or service.

Be specific without making your customer feel uncomfortable. Don't accuse, but make sure your customer understands your intent is to fix a problem, not to assess any blame.

Make sure all bases are covered by examining each phase of the sales process with your customer by asking questions such as these: "Did you feel pressure when ordering?" "Do you feel your order was processed quickly and efficiently?" "Was delivery of your order handled to your satisfaction?"

2. Is this a bona fide complaint? After you have received a complaint from a client or a prospective client the first order of business is to determine whether or not the complaint is justified. Is the product defective? Was the service rendered unprofessionally? Be honest with yourself as well as your customer. You will both sleep better for it.

If the complaint is justified, offer to solve the problem. Be careful not to give away the farm, but frequently, solving a problem, even at a loss to you and your company, will pay valuable rewards in the form of future sales saved.

Perhaps there is no problem at all but a misunderstanding of what was expected. These problems can frequently be dealt with easily by reviewing order forms and merchandise with the client.

3. Consider the source. While it's generally a good philosophy to try to keep everyone happy, sometimes that works better in theory than anywhere else. As they say, you can please some of the people some of the time, but . . . you get the point.

What position does the complainer occupy, and can they affect this or future sales? Be careful how you answer and deal with this. Just because a complainer is not responsible for sales doesn't mean they don't have the ear of someone who is.

Be careful also who you write off. The fellow that is a "nobody" today could be your customer tomorrow. The point is to determine your priorities. It's always nice to solve someone's complaint, but if you are pressed for time and the complainer is a relative nobody, either delegate the handling of that complaint to a subordinate or consider the complaint something to be handled at a less busy time.

4. Address the problem immediately. Once you understand the nature of a complaint, look into it immediately. Nobody likes to feel their problem is being ignored. On the other hand, if a complaint is going to take time to solve, let your customer know when they can expect a resolution.

One sales professional I know has a unique way of viewing customer complaints: He considers complaints as invitations for more business. "Whenever I get complaints from a customer," he told me, "I consider that an open invitation. It's like saying, this is what you can do for me if you want to make me a happy customer. They're begging you to make them happy, and I'm there to do just that."

5. Observe and report. We have all heard the old saying, "If you want something done right, do it yourself." Sometimes it's very true. When it comes right down to it, if a customer doesn't see their complaint being resolved, who is it they see? *You.* Wouldn't it be nice to say to your customer you have personally looked into their complaint and found a solution? Everyone knows it takes skill and understanding to solve a problem. The person whose only concern is making the sale is just an order taker. Even if the resolution is not in their favor, a customer will hold you in high regard for investing your time in solving a problem and letting them know you did your best.

When a customer takes the time and trouble to complain about your product or service, it should be considered an opportunity to serve. The chances are good when a customer extends that invitation, the salesperson that takes it not as a complaint, but as an opportunity to extend good service, will maintain a cherished relationship with that customer for a long time to come.

Source: Michael W. Michelson, Jr., "Fielding Customer Complaints," *American Salesman,* December 2005, p. 22.

- *Installation of equipment.* If a delay occurs on a promised installation, or if something goes wrong with the installation, a customer can quickly become frustrated. Sometimes you must travel in person to the installation site to display empathy and responsiveness to the customer—even if you don't have the technical expertise to contribute to the installation itself.
- *Customer training.* Promising that your firm will train a client's users of your product is very common. If a breakdown occurs somewhere in this process, you must become involved in straightening out the mess.
- *Product performance.* A gap between a customer's expectations of your product's performance and its actual performance may evoke the most severe of complaints. While other complaint issues are relatively transient, problems with the product itself get at the core value the customer expected from the purchase. Guarantees and warranties can go a long way toward appeasing customers with product performance problems, but any customer would prefer to have a product that works right in the first place. Hence, the salesperson should work hard to communicate with the customer during a period of malfunction, and also help the customer find alternative solutions during a period of repair.

Communicating with Customers about Complaints. Salespeople are not absolved from communicating with customers just because they've closed the sale. In fact, properly handled complaints are strong opportunities for salespeople to show customers that they have the customers' long-term best interests at heart. Well-handled follow-up to customer problems—**service recovery**—can be a powerful solidifier of long-term customer relationships.

Here are a few guidelines for salespeople to follow in communicating with customers about problems after the sale.

1. *Listen carefully to what the customer has to say.* Especially if he or she is upset, let the customer vent. Use active listening skills and good body language (eye contact, nodding in agreement, etc.). If the correspondence is by phone, interject verbally occasionally to let the customer know you are listening and you understand.
2. *Never argue.* Never get emotionally charged about the problem. Simply evaluate the complaint and work with the customer to formulate viable solutions.
3. *Always show empathy.* Understand the customer's point of view about the problem.
4. *Don't make excuses.* Don't say, "Your order was late because our truck broke down." Focus on *fixing* the problem. And never, ever make negative remarks about or blame other people inside your company.
5. *Be systematic.* Work with the customer and your company to develop specific goals for solving the problem, including a timetable, action steps, and who will do what. Don't set unrealistic expectations for solving the problem. That will only widen the gap between your performance and the customer's expectations.
6. *Make notes about everything related to the complaint.* Keep the notes updated as things progress.
7. *Express appreciation.* Sincerely thank the customer for communicating the complaint and show by your words and actions that you value his or her business.

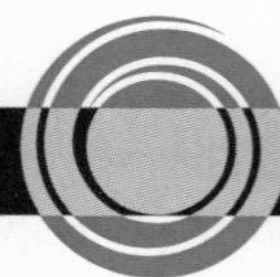

INNOVATION 8.3

E-mail Etiquette in Client Follow-up

E-mail correspondence is the fastest-growing communication medium in the world. The average businessperson sends and receives about 90 e-mail messages daily. In 2005, e-mail usage exceeded 5 billion messages per day.

Although e-mail is certainly powerful and popular, it's not always the most effective way to get your ideas across to clients. Between the limitations of ASCII text, odd line breaks inserted by mail servers, clients who use bizarre terms, spamming, never-get-to-the-point authors, tedious e-mail lists, and hard-to-decipher unsubscribe routines, it's amazing anything gets communicated electronically at all.

To use e-mail effectively in customer follow-up and make sure customers read and understand your messages, stick with the six simple guidelines here.

1. *Always include a detailed subject line.* Because e-mail messages don't go through a screening process or gatekeeper, many people use the subject line to determine which messages get read and which get instantly deleted. Even if your message is important for the recipient, if you make the subject line vague or leave it blank, there's a good chance the message will never get read. Be sure your subject line reflects the message's content. Trying to trick recipients with "sensational" subject lines will only make them wary of future correspondences from you. Keep your subject line brief; most e-mail programs display only the first seven to ten words. The more concise and truthful your subject line is, the greater the chance your recipient will read your message (and future messages from you).
2. *Allow ample time for a response.* Nearly everyone regards e-mail as "instant communication" and expects an immediate response to every message. But immediate responses are not always feasible. Depending on your recipient's workload, log-on habits, and time constraints, responding to your message may take several days. The general rule is to allow at least *three days* for a response. If you don't receive a reply, resend the original message and insert "2" into the subject line. So if your original message subject lines reads, "product information you requested," the resent subject line will read, "product information you requested—2." If your second attempt doesn't get a response, consider calling your recipient and alerting him or her to your message.
3. *Know when and when not to reply to a sender.* One challenge with e-mail is that everyone wants to have the last word. As a result, an e-mail trail can continue for days without the new messages adding anything. Consider this typical e-mail exchange:

Person 1: *"Let's meet at 3 P.M. in the conference room."*

Person 2: *"That works for my schedule, too. See you then."*

Person 1: *"Great. Looking forward to it."*

Person 2: *"Me, too. Talk with you later."*

Person 1: *"Okay. See you at 3:00."*

Don't Wait for Complaints to Follow Up with Customers

Although handling postsale problems and complaints is an important aspect of follow-up, successful salespeople are *proactive* in their follow-up. The very idea of relationship selling implies that the seller and buyer will communicate regularly to build each other's business. Many salespeople develop a communication plan with customers between sales calls that includes touching base by phone, mail, and e-mail. A particularly effective approach is to check with the customer right after delivery of an order just to ensure everything is as expected. Usually the customer will simply say everything is fine. But when a problem has occurred, the correspondence ensures the salesperson can deal with it quickly.

The greatly increased use of e-mail for customer follow-up has created the need to educate salespeople about its effective use (and potential abuse). Innovation 8.3 explains basic e-mail etiquette in client follow-up. Following these rules will ensure that this outstanding communication tool enhances your relationship with the customer rather than detracting from it.

On and on the exchange continues, simply because neither person can resist the temptation to reply. Such correspondences not only waste time but take up bandwidth space on the server and add to people's frustration as their e-mail boxes fill. If your intended reply does not add anything to the original message's objective, don't send it.

On the other hand, know when you definitely should send a response. If someone e-mails you a document to review, a simple acknowledgment that you received it and are reviewing it is sufficient. Don't force people to wait in limbo, unsure of the status of their request. Give a brief confirmation when you receive important messages, similar to the order acknowledgments you receive from online retailers.

4. *Use your reply button properly.* All e-mail programs have a "reply" and a "reply to all" option. Using the wrong one could cause you undue embarrassment. Clicking the "reply" button sends your message to the original sender only. In contrast, the "reply to all" button sends your message to the original sender and to all the other addresses listed in the original message's To, CC (carbon copy), and BCC (blind carbon copy) fields. Unless you want all these people to read your message, it's wise to simply use the "reply" button. Since the BCC addresses are not revealed to you, there's no way of knowing just who will receive your "reply to all" message. When in doubt, use the "reply" option.
5. *Set up your reply features apropriately.* When you set up your e-mail program's reply preferences, you have many options to choose from. To make replies easy for you and your recipient, set your new message to appear as the first block of text, above the original message. Placing your reply message below the original can confuse your recipient, who may not scroll all the way down and may think you did not add any new information. If the original message is lengthy, start a new e-mail rather than replying. All the additional text could slow the transmission. Finally, if you are replying to a series of questions, either restate the question before each answer or type "See answer below" at the top of your reply, then go back into the original message and type your answers there. Use this second approach only if you can easily distinguish your answers via different colored or styled text.
6. *Ask permission to add clients to your message list.* Because of the sheer number of e-mails your customers receive daily, always ask permission before you automatically put someone on your daily message list. While you may enjoy receiving jokes, photos, and silly cartoons throughout the day, others may not appreciate such items taking up space on their server. You don't always know what kind of technology your customer has, so your 250 KB photo may take your recipient over an hour to download with old technology.

Source: Dana May Casperson, "Your Most Coherent Communication Tools," *American Salesman,* September 2004, p. 10. Reprinted by permission of © National Research Bureau, 320 Valley St., Burlington, Iowa 52601.

Other Key Follow-up Activities

After the sale, companies have the opportunity to focus on several other important customer-building activities.

- *Customer satisfaction.* Sales organizations need an ongoing program to measure and analyze customer satisfaction—to what degree customers like the product, service, and relationship. Although the marketing department usually leads this initiative, the sales force often participates in the process. It certainly benefits from the information by altering sales approaches to better serve customer needs.
- *Customer retention and customer loyalty.* After the sale is a good time to work on building customer loyalty and retention rate. One reason periodic measurement of customer satisfaction is important is because a dissatisfied customer is unlikely to remain loyal to you, your company, and its products over time.

Importantly, however, the corollary is not always true: Customers who describe themselves as satisfied are not necessarily loyal. Indeed, one author estimates that 60 to 80 percent of customer defectors in most businesses said they were "satisfied" or "very satisfied" on the last customer survey before their defection.[9] In the interim, perhaps competitors improved their offerings, the customer's requirements changed, or other environmental factors shifted. The point is that businesses that measure customer satisfaction should be commended—but urged not to stop there. Satisfaction measures need to be supplemented with examinations of customer behavior, such as measures of the annual retention rate, frequency of purchases, and the percentage of a customer's total purchases captured by the selling firm.

- *Reexamine the value added.* Customers should be analyzed regularly to ensure that your value proposition remains sufficient to retain their loyalty. Review the various sources of value discussed in Chapter 3 to determine if you are maximizing the added value for your customers. Gaining feedback from customers after the sale has been institutionalized in many sales organizations. IBM, for example, includes such feedback as a formal part of its performance evaluation process for everyone who interacts directly with a client. This is part of a concept called "360-degree feedback," and it will be discussed further in Chapter 14.

- *Reset customer expectations as needed.* This topic was discussed in Chapter 3 but is well worth visiting again. Many salespeople try "to underpromise and overdeliver." This catchphrase encourages salespeople not to promise more than they can deliver and reminds them to try to deliver more than they promised in order to pleasantly surprise the buyer. Overpromising can get the initial sale and may work *once* in a transactional selling environment, but a dissatisfied customer will not buy again—and will tell many others to avoid that salesperson.

  Managing customer expectations is an important part of developing successful long-term relationships. Customer delight, or exceeding customer expectations to a surprising degree, is a powerful way to gain customer loyalty. The follow-up stage is a great time to overdeliver and delight customers, as well as to close any lingering gaps between customer expectations and the performance of your company and its products.

CRM and Follow-up

All CRM systems allow for managing your business with any customer through all aspects of the relationship. As described in Chapter 2, CRM systems use underlying data warehouses into which information about customers is entered at all touchpoints, or places where your firm interacts with the customer.

The follow-up activities in relationship selling should all be documented in a CRM system. Among the analyses such documentation makes possible are

- Tracking common customer postsale problems, sharing these problems with others in your firm, and creation of viable solutions.
- Sharing postsale strategies among all members of the sales organization.
- Documenting and comparing levels of satisfaction, retention, and loyalty across customers.

- Developing product and service modifications, driven by customer input.
- Tracking performance of individual salespeople and selling teams against customer follow-up goals.

The Sales Manager's Role in Closing the Sale and Follow-up

Very early in a salesperson's career an opportunity should be provided for him or her to learn and practice good listening skills. Then, these skills should be modeled and practiced periodically through role play—hopefully during sales manager work-withs—including sensitizing the salesperson to both verbal and nonverbal buying signals.

The onus is on sales managers to create a healthy environment for closing—an environment that recognizes the win–win nature of relationship selling, not one that allows a high potential customer relationship to be thrown offtrack by inappropriate, pushy closing techniques. Such a culture is created by training, and by everyone in the company (especially managers) practicing what they preach on a day-to-day basis. You know from reading this chapter that salespeople should not translate the failure to get an order or close a deal into a personal rejection. The sales manager is in the best position of anyone in the firm to promote a healthy "can-do" attitude among his or her salespeople. When a sale is missed, the manager must work with the salesperson to debrief the sales process so that together they can come up with approaches that are likely to be successful with the next customer—or in future contacts with the customer who failed to close.

Finally, sales managers need to fully realize the power of follow-up after a sale to strengthen customer relationships, and then actively encourage their salespeople to invest in follow-up activities. Ideally, an assessment of how well salespeople engage in follow-up with customers should be a part of their performance review process and they should be rewarded accordingly. Evaluating salesperson performance is the topic of Chapter 14.

Summary

In relationship selling, closing the sale should not be a traumatic experience for either the salesperson or the customer. Because the goal all along has been to work toward value-adding win–win solutions that benefit both parties and lead to a long-term relationship, closing is a natural outcome of the seller–buyer dialogue.

It is important for salespeople to become familiar with many closing methods so they can apply the best methods to different situations. Successful salespeople know that not getting an order is not a personal rejection. They understand the importance of learning from such experiences but not basing their self-worth on them. Attitude is very important to successful closing. Salespeople who believe in themselves and the product and show confidence, honest enthusiasm, and tenacity will close more business than those who don't. Empathy with customers and their needs is central to successful closing.

Good salespeople recognize a variety of verbal and nonverbal buying signals and respond appropriately with a trial close. It behooves salespeople, especially

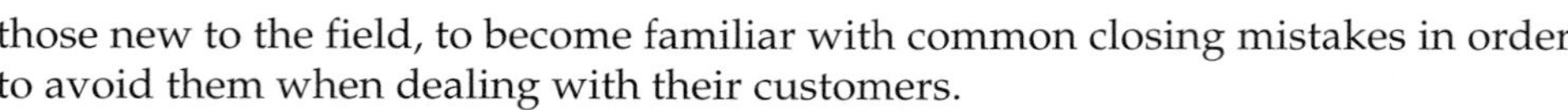

those new to the field, to become familiar with common closing mistakes in order to avoid them when dealing with their customers.

Postsale follow-up with customers is an excellent time to add considerable value to the client and the relationship. Excellent salespeople provide follow-up not just to handle customer problems and complaints but proactively to ensure customer satisfaction and loyalty.

Key Terms

closing the sale
buying signals
empathy
active listening
silence
assumptive close
minor point close
alternative choice close
direct close
summary-of-benefits close
balance sheet close
buy-now close
rejection
attitude
tenacity
trial close
follow-up
performance gap
customer complaints
service recovery

Role Play

Before You Begin

Before getting started, please go to the appendix of Chapter 1 to review the profiles of the characters involved in this role play, as well as the tips on preparing a role play. This particular role play requires that you be familiar with the Chapter 6 and 7 role plays.

Characters Involved

Alex Lewis

Rhonda Reed

Setting the Stage

Assume all the information given in the Chapters 6 and 7 role plays about Alex's sales call on Tracy Brown (Alex's long-time buyer at Max's Pharmacies). Again assume you are at the meeting between Alex and Rhonda a few days prior to Max's sales call and that the goal now is to brainstorm several potential closing approaches that Alex might use in the upcoming sales call on Tracy to present Happy Teeth. Again, Rhonda wants to role play a buyer–seller dialogue with Alex about these potential closing approaches so he will have a chance to practice them *before* making the actual sales call on Tracy.

Alex's Role

Work with Rhonda to develop a list of specific closing methods likely to be relevant in the Happy Teeth call on Tracy. Develop a specific dialogue for the role play in which Tracy (role played by Rhonda) responds differently to the different closing approaches—sometimes accepting, sometimes expressing concerns/objections, and sometimes neutral or nonresponsive. Develop dialogue that allows Alex to respond properly to each reaction expressed by Tracy. Refer to the sample buyer/seller dialogues in the section on closing methods for ideas on developing the list and the role-play dialogue.

Rhonda's Role

Work with Alex on the above.

Assignment

Present a 7–10 minute role play in which Alex plays himself in a mock sales call on Tracy (Rhonda gets to role play Tracy). Focus only on the *closing* part of the sales dialogue. Use as many of the closing methods in the chapter as you find appropriate to the situation. Vary Rhonda's responses so that Alex can use different approaches to moving the sale forward after each. In some cases Rhonda should come up with concerns/objections after the trial close so that Alex can demonstrate proper negotiation techniques to overcome the concern and then try to close again. At the end of the mock sales call, Rhonda should take no more than five minutes to provide constructive feedback/coaching to Alex on how well he used the closing methods.

Discussion Questions

1. What images of "closers" did you have before reading this chapter? List as many negative stereotypes of closing as you can. What is it about relationship selling that changes the role of closing the sale?

2. Why is attitude so important to successful closing? What are some aspects of a positive attitude that you believe contribute to success in closing (and in relationship selling in general)?

3. Once a salesperson sees one or more buying signals from a prospect, he or she should trial close. What happens if the prospect doesn't close at that point? Why is this outcome actually favorable for continuing the dialogue with the buyer and moving toward closing?

4. Why is it important to be able to use different closing methods in different situations?

5. A sage of selling once said: "Your job as a salesperson is to do 80 percent listening and 20 percent talking." Do you agree? Why or why not?

6. Review the list of common closing mistakes in the chapter. Give specific examples of how each might affect your success in a sales call.

7. What is it about postsale follow-up that makes it one of the most important ways to enhance long-term customer relationships? What specific things can you do in follow-up to accomplish this?

8. Consider the statement: "Customer complaints are customer opportunities—but only if we know about them." Do you agree or disagree? Why?

9. How do CRM and the use of databases in selling enhance closing and follow-up?

Ethical Dilemma

Jeff Hill of Southeast Distributors has a decision to make and not much time to make it. As senior account manager for the Ronbev Technologies account, Jeff has a very good relationship with Ron Yokum, CEO and founder of Ronbev. In the four years since Jeff began managing the account, sales have increased 50 percent.

Ronbev has been a customer of Southeast for more than six years and the two companies have a close working relationship. Several years ago (after much hard work on Jeff's part), Ron signed an agreement to make Southeast his exclusive supplier, thereby ensuring price stability and enhanced service. Neither Southeast nor Ronbev has been disappointed in the relationship.

Despite the strong relationship between the two companies, Ron (CEO) and Hugh Jacoby (head of purchasing) insist that they personally initiate every order. While overall sales are worked out in strategic planning meetings every year, the configuration of each order and specific characteristics of product size, quantity, and delivery dates vary a great deal. As a result, Ron feels it is important for either Hugh or himself to sign off on every order to be sure it meets Ronbev's needs. Jeff often sits in on the strategic planning meetings and knows Ronbev's purchasing patterns quite well.

Today he sits in his office considering a difficult decision. It's the last day of month and he is reviewing the Ronbev account. He knows that a big order is overdue, but Ron and Hugh are both out of town on vacation and aren't due back for another week. Jeff is also quite aware that today is the last day for sales to be counted in a sales contest that offers salespeople and their customer support teams the opportunity for a big bonus. Jeff's team of three support staff and two salespeople have worked hard on the Ronbev account all year, and the results have been very positive. He feels they deserve to win the award and the bonus.

Unfortunately, he is well aware of Ron's standing request to personally initiate orders. He has spoken to Ronbev often about creating a CRM system that would allow him to make assumptions about the order based on past history and feedback. Jeff knows that such a system would save Ronbev time and money. However, as he sits in his office today contemplating the situation, it is not in place.

Questions

1. Should Jeff go ahead and place the order he knows is coming and win the contest while risking the anger of Ron Yokum?

2. How much latitude should a salesperson assume in closing the sale when he or she has an established relationship with a customer?

Mini Case

CASE 8

St. Paul Copy Machines

Paula Phillips arrived back at her office at St. Paul Copy Machines around 4:00 on Tuesday afternoon. As she sat behind her desk looking dejected, her sales manager, Jeff Baker, showed up to ask how that afternoon's sales call had gone.

Paula had been scheduled to meet at 2:00 P.M. with a few representatives from Direct Mailers Inc. to finalize their purchase of a high-speed, multifunction copy machine. Direct Mailers uses these high-end machines to copy direct-mail pieces it sends out for a wide array of clients. The pieces are typically coupons that companies pay to have sent to local residents in an effort to entice customers to visit their businesses and begin to buy their products or services. Because Direct Mailers' clients require high-quality reproductions of their coupons, Paula has already made several sales calls on buying center members at Direct Mailers to get to know their operations and their specific requirements for a copy machine.

At today's meeting, Paula had planned to present to the Direct Mailers' representatives the copy machine that would fulfill all of their needs, resulting in an order for a new machine. However, once Jeff saw the look on her face, he knew that things had not gone as planned.

JEFF: "Hi, Paula. How did it go at Direct Mailers today?"
PAULA: "You don't want to know. I'm not sure we'll be able to salvage this sale."
JEFF: "Why don't you tell me what happened and we'll see if there's anything that can be done to give us another shot at the sale."
PAULA: "Well, it started when I first walked in there. You know how things have been sort of rough with me lately. I haven't made a sale all month, so I probably didn't have the best attitude going in. Nevertheless, I made my presentation and it seemed to be going great."
JEFF: "What kind of questions did they ask?"
PAULA: "The standard questions about warranty, when the copier could be delivered and installed, purchase price, annual operating cost, and how much more productive they can be with this new machine versus what they currently own. I handled all of these questions and they still were reluctant to make a decision today."
JEFF: "What closing technique did you use?"
PAULA: "The one I always use—the balance sheet method. This method has worked for me in the past and I've used it on dozens of buyers. Not all of them buy from me, of course, but hey, you can't have success all of the time, can you? Plus, I get enough buyers that I make my quota most years. I mean, what else can I do?"
JEFF: "How many items did you end up with on both sides of the balance sheet?"
PAULA: "On the 'reasons for buying' side I had six items and on the 'remaining questions' side I had three items. I know that sounds like quite a few remaining questions, but at least the reasons for buying were greater. They were going along with the proposal pretty well at this point in the presentation. In fact, I'm pretty sure that they had decided to purchase the copier. It had gotten to the point where we were standing around chitchatting about various things."
JEFF: "What kinds of things?"
PAULA: "You know, things like how much their business could improve with a new copier and how much more efficient they could be from an operational standpoint. You know the feeling and the look of how people relax when they have made a decision. We had reached that point and I thought it was done. I waited about 15 more minutes to pull out the contract for them to sign because they seemed to be having a good time talking about these issues among themselves."
JEFF: "What do you suppose made them change their mind?"
PAULA: "In the conversation, someone mentioned all of the money they had just spent on supplies to operate their current machine—copy toner and stuff like that. Before I knew it, they had decided that too much money had been sunk into those supplies and they couldn't justify a new copier. Having spent money on supplies for the current machine wasn't even on the balance sheet list of 'remaining questions.' It just came out of the blue and then I was stuck."
JEFF: "It's obvious that you're tired. Why don't you use the rest of today to finish your paperwork and make sure you have everything you need to see your clients tomorrow. We'll talk about this some more when you get into the office tomorrow afternoon."

As Paula finished her paperwork and checked her schedule for Wednesday, Jeff pondered what their conversation would include the next day.

Questions

1. What are some of the common closing mistakes that Paula made in her sales call with the representatives from Direct Mailers Inc.?
2. Why do you think Paula's closing method did not work? What could she have done differently to give it a better chance to work? What *other* closing methods might have worked better in her attempt to get this sale? Write a brief script for what Paula could have said using one of the closing methods you just identified.
3. What do you recommend Paula do now? Are there any key follow-up activities she should undertake to get another opportunity to make this sale with Direct Mailers?

Appendix: Checklist for Using Effective Closing Skills

For some strange reason, many salespeople who can present a flawless case for their products or services and calmly overcome the toughest of objections suddenly flounder at the point of asking for the order. Yet asking for the order is the logical conclusion of everything that has preceded it, from qualifying the prospect to giving the presentation. Since few prospects volunteer their order, salespeople seldom ring up a sale without asking for it.

This extensive set of questions will help you determine where you stand in using closing skills effectively. The idea is to get you to think about where you might need some coaching and practice in the important area of closing the sale.

1. Do you ask for the order several times during the course of your presentation?
2. Do you try for a close on the first call?
3. Do you regularly ask prospects which alternative (models, payment plans, delivery schedules, etc.) they prefer rather than whether they are interested?
4. Is your presentation enthusiastic and positive, suggesting that you fully expect to get the order?
5. If necessary, can you usually give compelling, plausible reasons for buying immediately?
6. Do you avoid giving the impression of high pressure in your requests for the order?
7. If the prospect hesitates, do you tactfully try to determine the reasons for his or her reservations, then answer them fully and persuasively?
8. Failing to get an explicit yes, do you proceed to try to get your prospect to do something (get figures, call in an assistant for backup information, show you where the display would be placed) that may be interpreted as approval of your proposition?
9. Do you unobtrusively introduce your order form early in your presentation?
10. Are you usually prepared to meet the standard objections to your product or service?
11. Have you the tools for an order at hand, ready to use (catalog, spec sheets, order form, etc.)?
12. Do you ever arrive armed with the order form already filled out (based on an intelligent estimate of the prospect's needs) and requiring only a signature?

13. If you've dealt with the customer before, are you familiar with his or her buying patterns, idiosyncrasies, pet peeves, and complaints?
14. Do you usually have a fairly accurate idea of the prospect's credit rating?
15. Before calling on the person with authority to buy, do you ever visit other departments or buying center members to determine the firm's needs and otherwise gather "selling ammunition"?
16. Can you describe three good ways any prospect is losing out by not buying your product immediately?
17. Are there any tax advantages to your proposition that might make it more appealing to your prospects?
18. How do you handle the buyer who seems impressed by your offer but hesitates, explaining, "I'll have to discuss it with my partner (boss, committee, spouse, etc.)"?
19. Are you ever guilty of behaving in a manner that tells your prospect, "I don't really expect an order now"?
20. Conversely, are you ever so obviously elated by the possibility of getting the order that the customer backs away?
21. Are your presentations benefit oriented so the prospect is continually aware of what he or she will gain by buying?
22. Do you always maintain control of your sales calls—or does the prospect frequently control the agenda?
23. Have you ever been so afraid of being turned down that you did not ask for the order?
24. Do you keep some reserve ammunition for the end of your presentation—some benefit or advantage tucked away in your back pocket that you can use in a final attempt to get the prospect to buy?
25. Do you always know in advance your product is right for the prospect?
26. When you fail to close, do you get out of the prospect's place of business quickly but not abruptly?
27. When you do close, do you get out of the prospect's place of business quickly but not abruptly?
28. Suppose you feel your price is the one thing standing in the way of a sale. How can you make it more palatable to the prospect (delayed billing, financing help, trade-ins, leasing plans, etc.)?
29. How can you convince a prospect who says "I want to think it over" that any delay in the purchase of your product is unwise?
30. Do you demonstrate your product to prospects?
31. Do you usually manage to get the prospect to participate in the demonstration in some way, by handling something, examining, reading, operating, or testing it?
32. Do you tend to assume a prospect will never buy from you if he or she says no on your first call?
33. How often do you call on a prospect before giving up?
34. Do you keep up to date on personnel changes in the firms you already deal with on the assumption that the next buyer is, for all practical purposes, a brand-new prospect?

35. Do you keep in touch with prospects who have turned you down to find out if circumstances have changed in your favor?
36. In a typical presentation, how many times do you ask for the order?
37. A prospect turns you down, claiming satisfaction with the present supplier. How, in terms of personal service, can you break through this loyalty barrier?
38. Describe three ways you can ask for the order without literally asking for it (e.g., "Shall we bill you this month or next?").
39. How is your product unique? That is, how is it genuinely different from all the competition?
40. Can you name the person with the authority to buy in three of your largest prospects' offices?
41. When was the last time you simply gave up on a sale, convinced that pursuing it any further was a waste of time? Think. Has anything (business conditions, your line, your price, the prospect's needs, etc.) changed since then that may provide a reason for trying again?
42. You ask for the order from an out-of-town prospect who tells you he or she prefers to buy locally. Your answer?
43. The prospect puts you off with, "I have a reciprocal arrangement with your competition." What's your answer to that one?
44. When you run into an objection that you cannot answer, do you make it your business to find a convincing answer that you can use the next time you encounter it?
45. You sense the prospect isn't saying yes because of doubts about his or her own judgment. How do you go about changing his or her mind?
46. The prospect tells you that she needs a little more time to decide and suggests that you call back in a few days. When you do make that phone call, how do you ask for the order this time?
47. When was the last time you reassessed your customer's needs (by talking to him or her or an associate, taking stock of what he or she has on hand, projecting future growth, etc.)?
48. In your presentations, are you fully aware of your prospect's biggest problem and prepared to show how buying from you will solve it or alleviate it?
49. How will your product help your prospect become more competitive?
50. With three specific prospects in mind, what are the best times of the year in each case to ask for the order? Why?
51. Similarly, what are the least promising times of year to ask for the order in each case. Why?
52. If you can somehow help a prospect use or sell more of your product profitably, it follows that he or she will buy more. How can you help your two toughest prospects get more profit out of your product?
53. What literature (sales, product, research, news items, etc.) is currently of help in closing sales?
54. Are you using that literature with all of your prospects to the best possible advantage?
55. If your product is part of a full line, do you regularly try for tie-in sales?

56. Do you check back on former customers who, for one reason or another, have stopped buying from you?
57. What percentage of your sales calls do you turn into actual sales?
58. On which call are most of your initial sales made (first, second, third, fourth)?
59. Which of your prospects do you think are ripe for a close this week?
60. When, specifically, are you going to ask them for their orders?

Closing is a natural and expected part of a client relationship. As a challenging and rewarding part of a salesperson's professional activities, it deserves your best efforts.

Source: Ted Pollock, "How Good a Closer Are You?" *American Salesman,* June 2003, pp. 18–23.

selling environment

Sales Management

Evaluating Performance

Salesperson Motivation

Recruiting & Selection

Training & Development

Compensation

Relationship Selling

SELF-MANAGEMENT

Prospecting & Sales Call Planning

Communicating the Sales Message

Negotiating for Win-Win Solutions

Closing & Follow-up

Information

Value Creation

Ethics

Customer Relationships

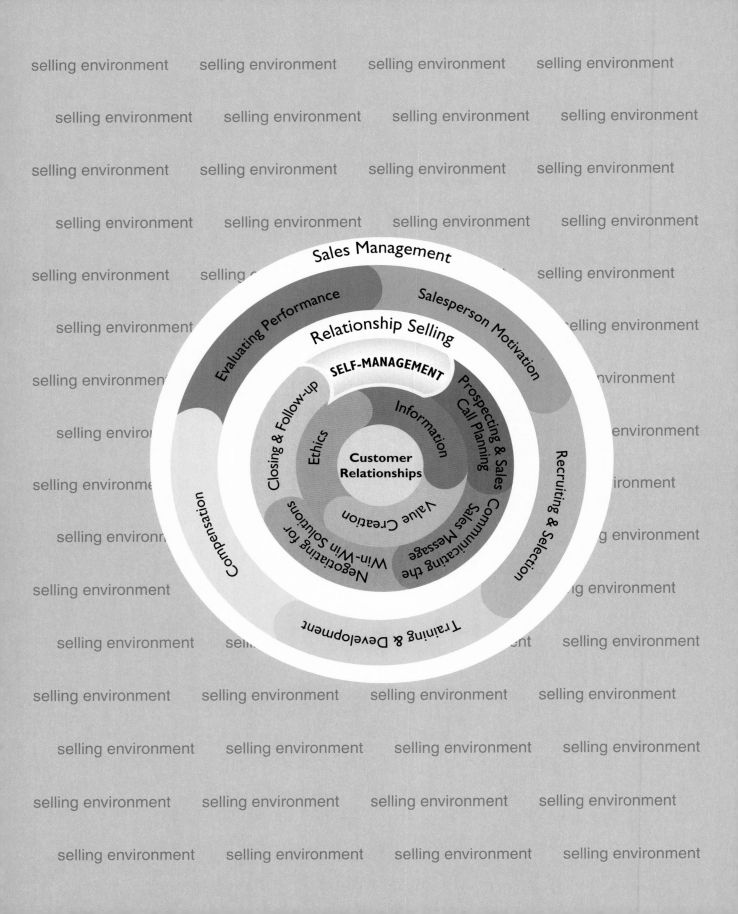

9 chapter

Self-Management: Time and Territory

Learning Objectives

To salespeople, time is literally money, and managing their territory and time well is critical to long-term success in relationship selling.

After reading this chapter, you should be able to

- Understand salespeople's role in time and territory management.
- Explain efficient time management tools for salespeople.
- Discuss territory management techniques.
- Describe the sales manager's role in time and territory management.
- Determine how salespeople should allocate their time.
- Design an effective sales territory.
- Measure sales territory performance.

expert advice

Expert: Sean Allen, Territory Manager

Company: Cargill, Inc., Minneapolis, Minnesota

Business: Cargill, Inc., is an international provider of food, agricultural, and risk management products and services. With 142,000 employees in 61 countries, the company is committed to using its knowledge and experience to collaborate with customers to help them succeed. Cargill Salt produces, packages, and ships salt for the following five major market segment applications: agriculture, food, water conditioning, and industrial and packaged ice control. Cargill makes over 1,000 different salt products/package sizes and markets national and regional brands, including Diamond Crystal® branded household consumer food and water softener salt products; Champions Choice® branded agricultural Cargill Salt is a business unit of Cargill, Incorporated.

Education: Bachelor's Degree, Morehouse College (Atlanta, Georgia)
M.B.A., Rollins College

Does effectively managing your time increase your productivity? How?

Effective time management skills are an important tool to improve productivity, especially in a field sales position. As a senior solutions manager for Cargill Salt, my responsibility includes the states of Florida and Georgia. I manage over 250 active customer accounts and prospect relationships, participate in selling administrative activities and contribute to several cross-functional teams. In order to accomplish my goals and become successful in each area it is essential I manage my time efficiently.

Since there are only so many things you can do in each given day, it is critical to plan in order to maximize your productivity. I begin by looking at my calendar in three-month intervals and then listing the key activities to be completed during that time frame. The activities include: (a) accounts I need to call and (b) deliverables for my cross-functional team activities (reports, presentations, recommendations). Next, I prioritize the list, and finally, I evaluate how much time should be allocated to each activity and schedule it into my calendar.

Do you think effective time management improves your relationships with clients? How?

No question, effective time management does improve my relationship with clients. A key element in building successful customer relationships is the quality of the time spent with them. By managing time effectively, I can identify and segment my customers appropriately and spend additional time creating relationships with those customers that demand extra effort.

Effective time management also helps to build trust between you and the client by saying to the customer; I will do what I promise to do. For example, when the customer has a request and you deliver in the specified time frame, you are building trust with your customer and improving the relationship. In the salt business, a highly competitive industry where the end product can be commoditized, this means identifying more opportunities for the customer.

Another area where effective time management improves customer relationships is better sales presentation preparation. By preparation, I mean doing the necessary homework on the client's business, key contact(s), and the purpose of each interaction with the customer. By being prepared I can spend my time proactively uncovering new customer opportunities rather than always reacting. As a territory manager, my biggest asset is my time and effectively managing it so that I am spending the right amount of time with each customer, which really allows me to improve relationships with key accounts.

What guidelines can you offer for effective time management in selling?

Plan, prioritize, and use the Pareto Principle. It is easy to be inefficient with your time when you try to do everything for or be everything to everyone. Plan your day, the week, even the next month and quarter. I would also understand and use the Pareto Principle, or the 80/20 rule. That is, of the things you do during your day, only 20 percent really matter. That 20 percent produces 80 percent of your results. Try and use this principle to your advantage in managing your time. Finally, I would prioritize my accounts and activities. What tasks are important? Which ones are urgent? What tasks are not so important but seem to consume a lot of your time? To borrow a principle from Steven Covey, try to spend as much time as possible addressing things that are important but not urgent. This will allow you to be more proactive and also a more effective salesperson.

The Importance of Time and Territory Management

In Part Two of this book, we have been discussing the relationship selling process. Part Three will focus on the issues and activities of the sales manager. However, this chapter is about an activity in which salespeople and their managers both play critical roles: time and territory management. Salespeople are in the field and responsible for managing their time and territory effectively, but without careful management design and monitoring, they cannot tap the full potential of the territory. The Relationship Selling model at the beginning of the chapter highlights the time and territory management area.

How important is time management in selling? Go to Google at www.google.com and type in "time management and sales." You will find dozens of companies offering courses and seminars in time and territory management for salespeople.[1] For further proof, visit Amazon at www.amazon.com or Barnes & Noble at www.barnesandnoble.com and type in "time management." The search engine will identify dozens of books dedicated to helping salespeople manage their time more effectively.

A simple calculation will help demonstrate the importance of time management. Suppose a salesperson works 47 weeks a year (subtracting vacation and other miscellaneous time off) for 8 hours a day. That gives a total work time of 1,880 hours in a year. However, a salesperson has many responsibilities, including traveling, completing reports, researching and dealing with customer concerns, and a host of other activities designed to build successful customer relationships. These activities total, on average, 67 percent of the salesperson's time. In our example that totals 1,260 hours for the year, which leaves only 620 hours—14 hours a week—of face-to-face selling time with customers. If a salesperson produces $500,000 in sales per year, that means for every hour in front of the customer he or she must generate $806.45. Time is precious, and the ability to manage time and territory is essential to success for both the salesperson and sales manager.

Specific reasons why salespeople and managers care about time and territory management are detailed in Exhibit 9.1.

Reasons for Salespeople

Salespeople's ability to manage their time and territory is essential for three reasons. Salespeople who are efficient time and effective territory managers (1) increase productivity, (2) improve customer relationships, and (3) enhance personal confidence. Let's examine each result more closely.

EXHIBIT 9.1 Why Time and Territory Management Is Important

Reasons for Salespeople	Reasons for Sales Managers
1. Increase productivity.	1. Ensure territory and customer coverage.
2. Improve customer relationships.	2. Minimize sales expenses.
3. Enhance personal confidence.	3. Assess sales performance.
	4. Align company policies with customer expectations.

Increase Productivity. The more effective and efficient salespeople are in managing their territory and time, the more productive they are in the job. Management designs territories so that salespeople must exert maximum effort to reach the territory's full sales potential. If a salesperson is not efficient in managing time and effective in managing the customers in the territory, he or she will not hit the sales targets set by the company.

At the same time, salespeople have many duties to accomplish in relatively little face to face time with customers. Time management makes sure that every minute with customers is productive. This is especially true in territories that require a lot of travel, where salespeople must manage time and territory so they can focus on relationship building.

Improve Customer Relationships. One of the most constructive tools salespeople use to build customer relationships is effectively managing customer time. Wasting the customer's time never leads to a better relationship. When the salesperson is on time, deals with customer concerns, and makes maximum use of the customer's time, the customer relationship often improves. Remember, customers don't see the entire organization. They see the salesperson. When the salesperson is efficient and effective, it raises the customers' opinion of the entire organization. Building successful customer relationships means the salesperson knows when to see customers and what to say (and not say) while with them. Time and territory management are critical to that process.

Enhance Personal Confidence. What makes people confident? The answer is certainly complex and varies by individual. However, research suggests that capable time and territory management skills go a long way toward improving salespeople's confidence that they can get the job done. Having the time to prepare properly for each customer enhances the salesperson's comfort level and confidence and reduces stress.

Reasons for Sales Managers

Good sales managers know that skillful time and territory management is essential to (1) ensure territory and customer coverage, (2) minimize sales expenses, (3) assess sales performance, and (4) align company policies with customer expectations. Creating relationships that both satisfy customers and motivate salespeople depends in large part on helping salespeople manage their time and territory.

Ensure Territory and Customer Coverage. The single most effective way to make sure the company has the right relationships with its customers is to create territories that define where and how customers will interact with the company. Clearly, not all customers will be treated the same; however, defining the customer relationship and creating territories (which we will discuss later in this chapter) is vital to ensure that all customers have a salesperson (or sales team) to build the relationship.

In today's selling environment, territory and customer coverage is much more difficult and demanding. Unique customer relationships may require salespeople to move between established territories. Some argue that this makes territories less important, but in fact the opposite is true. Not all customers warrant special treatment. Territory management ensures the company aligns the sales force appropriately with various customers.

Minimize Sales Expenses. Running a sales force is expensive, and a territory structure helps manage sales expenses. Creating territories eliminates duplication and maximizes salespeople's face-to-face customer time while minimizing nonselling time. Few management activities have greater potential to reduce sales expenses than designing, creating, and monitoring the performance of sales territories.

Assess Sales Performance. How well is a product selling in Kansas? Why hasn't our best customer, Gracie Incorporated, been buying as much from us in the last six months? Why are sales so high in our upstate New York territory? Sales managers ask questions like these every day, and territory management is critical to getting answers. By investing in a territory management system, managers can evaluate individual territories, districts, regions, or even countries to identify problems before they get too big and positive trends in time to capitalize on them.

Align Company Policies with Customer Expectations. As we discussed in Chapter 5, the ability to collect data by product, customer, and territory, analyze it, and make decisions based on it helps managers make better decisions about recruiting, training, compensation, and a host of other key management activities. In addition, specific customer feedback provides a consistent, organized mechanism for managers to hear the customers' needs and align company strategy with those needs. For example, salespeople can be hired with explicit qualifications (experience, background) to fit into specific territories or certain salespeople can receive training based on territory analysis and need identification.

Salespeople's Role in Time and Territory Management

We began the chapter talking about the roles played by the salesperson and sales manager in time and territory management. Managers analyze customers and design territories to put together the most efficient and effective territory structure (as we shall see in the next section). However, once management identifies the basic territory requirements (customers, call frequency, call duration, nonselling time), salespeople have the flexibility—indeed, the responsibility—to manage their time and territory effectively. Two key questions drive salespeople in time and territory management:

- What is the most efficient use of my time?
- What is the most effective way to manage my territory?

Note that although we are focusing on salespeople assigned to territories, all salespeople need to be good time and territory managers. In some industries, such as insurance, companies do not assign specific territories; they allow salespeople to prospect for customers in a large geographic area. For example, if you go to the State Farm Insurance Web site (www.statefarm.com), click on "Insurance," then click on "Find an Agent," you will see methods for identifying the nearest agent. Type in your zip code and you will see a number of agents who are close to you. Even salespeople in these situations need to be good time managers.

Efficient Time Management

Time—everyone seems to need more of it, but unfortunately there is only so much to go around. Given the demands on their time, salespeople must become efficient time managers if they wish to be successful. For years people have examined the backgrounds and characteristics of successful salespeople, and good time management is one strength they list consistently. To manage their time efficiently,

EXHIBIT 9.2 Priority Checklist

Personal	Life	Family	How important is my family?
		Life goals	Do I live to work or work to live?
		Personal wealth	How important is personal wealth?
	Career	Goals	What are my career goals?
		Ambition	Would I do anything to succeed?
		Trade-offs	What trade-offs am I prepared to make to be successful? (Example: Would I take a job if it meant moving my children to a new location?)
Professional	Account	Sales volume	Is the customer buying more now than last year?
		Satisfaction	Is the customer satisfied with my company/me?
		Sales potential	What is the potential for new business with this customer?
	Activity	New sales calls	How many new sales calls have I made this year?
		New customers	Am I finding new customers or relying on existing customers?
		Sales/expense ratio	What is my ratio of sales to expenses compared to last year?

salespeople must (1) identify their personal and professional priorities and (2) develop a time management plan.

Identify Personal and Professional Priorities. What's important to you? That is a critical question in time management. People spend time doing what they want to do or they spend time on things they don't want to do, which eventually makes them less productive, frustrated, and even unhappy. Does this mean that you will enjoy every minute of being a salesperson (or whatever career you choose)? Of course not. However, it does mean that successful salespeople are successful in part because selling is consistent with their life and career goals.[2] Exhibit 9.2 shows the relationship between your personal and professional (sales) priorities.

Choosing priorities falls into two broad categories: personal and professional. Salespeople must identify their goals for each of these priorities. First, they must make choices about their personal priorities in life and career. **Life priorities** deal with basic choices in life. For example, is your family important to you? Most people would say yes, but just how important has a big effect on the choices you make in a career. Salespeople travel a lot, and those with children may not want to be away from their family. Complicating the decision is that people often begin with one set of priorities but as life changes (they get married or have a baby or get divorced), their priorities change. Life priorities need to be reevaluated every so often to make sure that career and professional priorities are consistent (refer to Leadership 9.1 for a discussion on the importance of priorities).

Career priorities deal with what kind of sales career you want to have over time. Historically, there are two basic choices: (1) a sales career, leading to a position as a senior account or key account executive or (2) sales management. But there are other concerns too. For example, do you want to work for the same company (which usually means moving to new locations over time)? Or is your home more important (which means you may change companies over time)?

Professional priorities concern the sales task at hand and fall into two areas. **Account priorities** relate to goals and objectives for individual customers, such as increased sales or greater customer satisfaction year over year. Often these are the primary measures of individual sales performance (which we talk about in

Leadership 9.1

Take Control of Your Life

One result of today's "connected world" is that time has become a very valuable commodity. This is particularly true for salespeople who must manage a variety of relationships including customers, company, and family. People often focus on being more efficient, getting more "stuff" done. As a result, time management is more about efficiency—doing more things faster—than effectiveness—doing the right things better. However, efficiency is not always the answer and misses the point. Consider that doing the incorrect things more efficiently does not make that person a good time manager. It is possible, even likely the individual feels good because more activities are getting done but, at the end of day, he or she may not have accomplished the things needed to make their life better.

In that context time management becomes life management. Put another way, to be a better time manager, salespeople, indeed everyone, need to prioritize better. Identify what is really important and focus on those activities. Establishing priorities enables an individual to spend time on what is important increasing both efficiency and effectiveness. How does this happen? Learn to effectively manage your:

- Goals
- Priorities
- Focus
- Conversation
- Expectations
- Technology
- Organization
- Mind and Emotions

Source: Michael Guld, "Effectively Manage Hour Multi-Tasking Day," *American Salesman* 53(7), July 2008, pp. 25–29.

Chapter 14). **Activity priorities** include goals such as number of new accounts, number of sales calls per week or month, and sales-to-expense ratio. These objectives are often identified by management or by management working with the salesperson to set specific performance goals for a given period of time.

Develop a Time Management Plan. Once you have identified personal and professional priorities, the next step is to develop a **time management plan.** The basic steps in a time management plan are not difficult to understand. The problem for most people is implementing the steps and sticking with the plan over time. The real benefits of a time management plan come when you incorporate behavioral changes into your everyday thinking.[3] A good time management plan has three basic elements.

1. **Daily event schedule.** What are you going to do today?
2. **Weekly/monthly planning calendar.** What are you going to do this week? This month?
3. **Organization of critical information.** How do you control the information you need to be a good time manager?

Daily event schedule. Creating a daily to-do list is a time management tool almost everyone has tried at least once. The process involves sitting down in the morning or the previous evening, thinking about the specific tasks you want to accomplish, and prioritizing them. There are variations on this process, but all time management counselors, such as Franklin Covey, advise taking control of events and prioritizing what you need to accomplish every day. It is important to write them down either on a piece of paper or in a cell phone because writing down the tasks affirms their importance. A schedule you keep in your head is too easily changed because often things that come up during the day seem to be more important at the time.

The second component of a territory management plan is communication. Salespeople know that successful territory management involves using technology to maximize their effectiveness. Customers want answers to questions now and often will not wait until the next scheduled visit, so salespeople use e-mail and wireless technologies to deal with customer and company issues quickly. But immediate communication does not preclude face-to-face customer time. Customer questions can be answered in an e-mail or phone call, but sales presentations and relationship building require one-on-one time with the customer.

Provide Territory Feedback to Management. Managing a sales territory is not a static procedure. Managers develop territories based on the best available information at the time, but conditions change literally overnight. Customers, competitors, and the general environment are changing all the time. Salespeople bring in new customers, existing customers move to different suppliers, and many other events can change the dynamics of a territory.

It is imperative that salespeople provide feedback to management on what is happening in the sales territory. Management does receive a great deal of information in the sales analysis (coming up in the next section), but salespeople are working in the territory and often develop an understanding that extends beyond the numbers. Analyses of customer, product, or territory sales cannot convey nuances in the customer relationship. For example, management changes at a customer can signal potential changes in purchasing patterns. This information would be known to the salesperson but not necessarily show up in current sales numbers.

This kind of feedback is important for two reasons. First, management needs to know this information so it can be aware of any potential problems or opportunities before it is too late. Second, salespeople can benefit from a shared information community. Once a feedback system is created, salespeople in one territory can hear about insights (or problems) from other salespeople around the country. Such information sharing can be extremely helpful for salespeople in the field.

Sales Managers' Role in Time and Territory Management

While salespeople bear ultimate responsibility for how they use their time, sales managers play a critical role in designing and creating territories that enable salespeople to be effective and efficient. Essentially there are two activities sales managers must do well to maximize the efficiency of salespeople's time and the potential of sales territories.

- Design the most effective sales territories.
- Measure the sales performance of the company's products, customers, and territories.

Design the Most Effective Sales Territories

Sales managers strive to make all **sales territories** roughly equal with respect to the amount of sales potential they contain and the amount of work it takes a salesperson to cover them effectively. When the sales potential is basically the same across all territories, it is easier to evaluate each salesperson's performance and to compare salespeople.

EXHIBIT 9.3 Stages in Territory Design

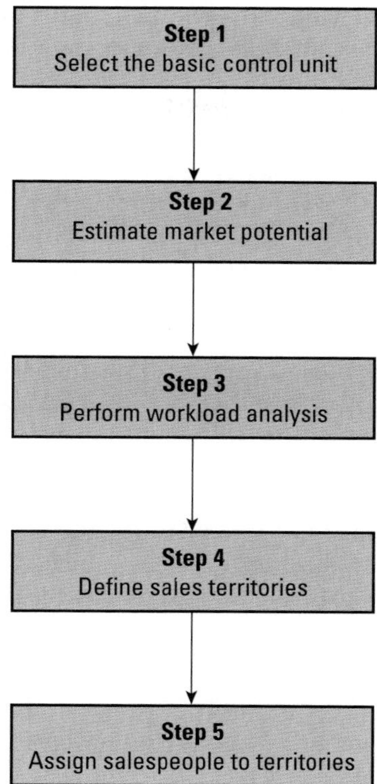
Step 1
Select the basic control unit
Step 2
Estimate market potential
Step 3
Perform workload analysis
Step 4
Define sales territories
Step 5
Assign salespeople to territories

Equal workloads also tend to improve sales force morale and diminish disputes between management and the sales force. Sales managers should also consider the impact of particular territory structures and call frequencies. It is difficult (if not impossible) to achieve a perfect balance with respect to all these factors.

Sales managers should do their best to ensure fairness and equity in territory design. Salespeople do not perform well when their managers fail to consider the long-term effects of poor territory design. While, managers should design territories based on rules and company priorities, and not for specific salespeople, they should consider personal issues. As we discussed, people's priorities change over time, affecting their relationship with customers and their territory. The five steps in territory design are illustrated in Exhibit 9.3.

Step 1: Select the Basic Control Unit. The first step is for the manager to identify what is called the **basic control unit.** This is the fundamental geographic area used to form sales territories (county or city, for example). As a general rule, small geographic control units are preferable to large ones because low-potential accounts may be hidden by their inclusion in areas with high potential. This makes it difficult to pinpoint the true market potential, which is a primary reason for forming geographically defined sales territories in the first place. Also, small control units make it easier to adjust sales territories when conditions warrant. It is much easier to reassign the accounts in a particular county from one salesperson to another, for example, than it is to reassign all the accounts in a state.

The size of the basic control unit depends on many factors. Small, growing companies with a national distribution can manage the entire country with a relatively small number of salespeople. Odyssey Software (from Chapter 7) is a good example of a small company with national distribution and very few salespeople. Business-to-business companies generally have fewer customers who are often concentrated in a limited number of areas (the automobile industry around Detroit, technology companies in Silicon Valley and the northeastern United States), which makes delineating basic control units easier. Business-to-consumer companies face a more difficult challenge, as they need a large sales force to cover a very large market area like the United States.

Getting the size and configuration of the territory correct is difficult and requires constant monitoring. Too small and the company will not maximize the full potential of the sales force (and increase sales expenses). Too large (the more common dilemma) and the organization can create problems in customer coverage and salesperson performance. As salespeople are asked to spread themselves over more customers (or geography) they may not be able to satisfy the requirements of each customer. In addition, they may not be able to discern important from less critical customers because of territory call demands. Performance can suffer and customers become dissatisfied.

While there are a number of basic control units, such as states and trading areas, we will focus on those most commonly used, which include counties, cities or metropolitan statistical areas (MSAs), and zip code areas.

Counties. Counties are probably the most widely used basic geographic control unit. They permit a more fine-tuned analysis of the market than do states, given that there are over 3,000 counties and only 50 states in the United States. One dramatic advantage of using counties as control units is the wealth of statistical data available by county. The *County and City Data Book,* published biennially by the Bureau of the Census, is a great source of information on such things as population, education, employment, income, housing, banking, manufacturing output, capital expenditures, retail and wholesale sales, and mineral and agricultural output.[6] It is available at the Census Bureau Web site. Another advantage of counties is that their size permits easy reassignment from one sales territory to another. Thus, sales territories can be altered to reflect changing economic conditions without major upheaval in basic service.

The most serious drawback to using counties as basic control units is that frequently they are still too large, especially in metropolitan areas. Los Angeles County, Cook County (Chicago), Dade County (Miami), and Harris County (Houston), for example, may require several sales representatives and must be divided into even smaller basic control units.

Metropolitan statistical areas. Historically, when most of the market potential was within city boundaries, the city was a good basic control unit. But now that the surrounding area often contains more potential than the central city, companies employ broader classification systems to help them identify and organize their territories. Developed by the Census Bureau, the control unit is called an **MSA (metropolitan statistical area).** MSAs are integrated economic and social units with a large population nucleus. Any area that qualifies as an MSA and has a population of one million or more can be recognized as a CMSA (consolidated metropolitan statistical area). Exhibit 9.4 ranks the 10 largest population centers in the United States by size based on the most recent data (2000 census).

EXHIBIT 9.4 Ten Largest CMSAs in Decreasing Order of Size

Rank	Area	2007 Population (in thousands)
1	New York–northern New Jersey–Long Island, NY–NJ–PA	18,815,988
2	Los Angeles–Long Beach–Santa Ana, CA	12,875,587
3	Chicago–Naperville–Joliet, IL–IN–WI	9,524,673
4	Dallas–Fort Worth–Arlington, TX	6,145,037
5	Philadelphia–Camden–Wilmington, PA–NJ–DE–MD	5,827,962
6	Houston–Sugar Land–Baytown, TX	5,628,101
7	Miami–Fort Lauderdale–Pompano Beach, FL	5,413,212
8	Washington–Arlington–Alexandria, DC–VA–MD–WV	5,306,565
9	Atlanta–Sandy Springs–Marietta, GA	5,278,904
10	Boston–Cambridge–Quincy, MA–NH	4,482,857

Source: "Estimated Ten Largest CMSA/MSAs in Decreasing Order of Size," U.S. Bureau of the Census Web site: www.census.gov.

The heavy concentration of population, income, and retail sales in MSAs explains why many firms are content to concentrate their field selling efforts in those areas. Such a strategy minimizes travel time and expense.

Zip code and other areas. In really large metropolitan areas when the city or MSA boundaries are too large, companies use zip code areas as basic control units. The U.S. Postal Service has defined more than 36,000 five-digit zip code areas. An advantage of zip code areas is that they are likely to be relatively similar in age, income, education, and other socioeconomic data and to even display similar consumption patterns (unlike residents within an MSA).

Although the Census Bureau does not publish a lot of data by zip code area, an industry has developed to tabulate such data by arbitrary geographic boundaries. The *geodemographers,* as they are typically called, combine census data with their own survey data or data they gather from such administrative records as motor vehicle registrations or credit transactions to produce customized products for their clients.

Typically geodemographers analyze census data to identify homogeneous groups that describe the American population. Claritas, the first firm to do this and still one of the leaders in the industry, uses over 500 demographic variables in its PRIZM system when classifying residential neighborhoods.[7] This system breaks the population of the United States into 15 groups and over 60 specific market segments based on consumer behavior and lifestyle. Each type has a name that endeavors to describe the people living there: Urban Gold Coast, Shotguns and Pickups, Pools and Patios, and so on.

Claritas and its competitors will do a customized analysis for whatever geographic boundaries a client specifies. Or a client can send a list of the zip code addresses from its customer database, and the geodemographer will attach the cluster codes. For more information about PRIZM, visit the Claritas Web site at www.claritas.com. These analyses are expensive, but they give companies, especially B2C organizations, tremendous insight into specific market segments.

Step 2: Estimate Market Potential. Step 2 in territory design involves estimating **market potential** by considering the likely demand from each customer and prospect in a basic control unit. This works much better for B2B products than for B2C goods because B2B customers are typically fewer in number and more easily identified. Furthermore, each typically buys much more product than a B2C buyer. This makes it worthwhile to identify at least the larger prospects by name, estimate the likely demand from each, and add up these estimates to produce an estimate for the territory as a whole.

In B2C markets, historical data and market research results are combined with feedback from salespeople to estimate market potential in a given territory. Companies seek precise figures, but market potential is just an estimate and subject to change for a variety of reasons.

Step 3: Perform Workload Analysis. The next step is to determine how much work is required to cover each territory. Ideally, managers like to form sales territories that are equal in both potential and workload. Although step 2 should produce territories roughly equal in potential, they will probably require a decidedly unequal amount of work to cover adequately. In this step, managers estimate the amount of work involved in covering each territory and try to match the sales potential with the workload of each salesperson.

Account analysis. Typically, the **workload analysis** considers each customer in the territory, emphasizing the larger ones. The analysis is often conducted in two stages. First, the manager does an **account analysis** to estimate the **sales potential** (the share of total market potential a company expects to achieve) for each customer and prospect in the territory. Then the sales potential estimate is used to decide how often each account should be called on and for how long. The manager determines total effort required to cover the territory by considering the

- Number of accounts.
- Number of calls to be made on each account.
- Duration of each call.
- Estimated amount of nonselling and travel time.
- *Criteria for classifying accounts.* Sales potential is only one of several criteria for determining an account's attractiveness to the firm. In addition, the factors that affect the productivity of an individual sales call are likely to change from firm to firm. Factors likely to affect the productivity of the sales call include
  - Competitive pressures. How many competitors are actively targeting the account?
  - Prestige. Is the account a market leader, or does it influence other companies in the industry?
  - Size. How big is the account?
  - Number and level of buying influences. How many individuals are responsible for buying decisions inside the account?[8]

Leadership 9.3

Account Planning Guide

Account potential	Competitive strength: Strong	Competitive strength: Weak
High	**Opportunity** Account offers good opportunity. It has high potential and sales organization has a differential advantage in serving it. **Strategy** Commit high levels of sales resources to take advantage of the opportunity. 1	**Opportunity** Account may represent a good opportunity. Sales organization must overcome its competitive disadvantage and strengthen its position to capitalize on the opportunity. **Strategy** Either direct a high level of sales resources to improve position and take advantage of the opportunity or shift resources to other accounts. 2
Low	**Opportunity** Account offers stable opportunity since sales organization has differential advantage in serving it. **Strategy** Allocate moderate sales resources to maintain current advantage. 3	**Opportunity** Account offers little opportunity. Its potential is small and the sales organization is at a competitive disadvantage in serving it. **Strategy** Devote minimal resources to the account or consider abandoning it altogether. 4

Source: *Churchill/Ford/Walker's Sales Force Management,* 9th ed., by Mark Johnston and Greg Marshall (New York: McGraw-Hill, 2009), p. 161. Reprinted by permission of the McGraw-Hill Companies.

Determining account call rates. Once the specific factors affecting the productivity of a sales call have been isolated, they can be treated in various ways. Customer accounts can be divided along two dimensions that reflect (1) the customer's sales potential and (2) the company's ability to capitalize on that potential (competitive advantage or disadvantage). Each account is then placed in the account planning guide matrix in Leadership 9.3. The guide uses account potential and the firm's competitive account advantage (disadvantage) to classify accounts into four cells that require different call frequencies. The heaviest call rates in the sample matrix depicted in Leadership 9.3 would be on accounts in cells 1, 2, and possibly 3, depending on the firm's ability to overcome its competitive disadvantages. The lowest planned call rates would be on accounts in cell 4.

Determining call frequencies account by account. Accounts do not have to be divided into classes and call frequencies set at the same level for all accounts in the class. Instead, the firm might want to determine the workload in each tentative territory on an individual account basis. One popular approach is to estimate the likely sales to be realized from each account as a function of the number of calls on that account. There are many methods for doing this. In one common approach, someone in the sales organization (typically the salesperson serving the account but sometimes the sales manager) estimates the sales-per-sales-call function to determine the optimal number of calls to make on each account. Much of this work is now done by sophisticated programs that optimize call frequencies and even design sales territories (refer to our earlier discussion on TerrAlign). CRM systems like those from Oracle provide a wealth of opportunity for data collection toward estimating future sales based on calls on particular customers.

Determine total workload. When the account analysis is complete, a workload analysis can be performed for each territory. To determine the total amount of face-to-face contact (direct selling time), multiply the call frequency of each type of account by the number of such accounts. Combine the amount of direct selling time with estimates of the nonselling and travel time required to determine the total amount of work involved in covering that territory.

Step 4: Define Sales Territories. Step 4 in territory planning defines the boundaries of the sales territories. While attempting to balance potentials and workloads across territories, the analyst must keep in mind that the sales volume potential per account changes over time. It is also likely to vary with the number of calls made. Computer call allocation models such as TerrAlign consider this. However, many sales managers rely on personal intuition or historical data, which do not take workload changes into account.

Clearly there is a relationship between account attractiveness and account effort. **Account attractiveness** affects how hard the account should be worked. At the same time, the number and length of calls affect the sales likely to be realized from the account. Yet these relationships are not directly recognized in many managerial decisions used to determine territory workloads. The firm needs a mechanism for balancing potentials and workloads when adjusting the initial territories if it is not using a computer model. Critical customer relationships will certainly affect account attractiveness and may necessitate adjustments to the overall territory configuration.

Step 5: Assign Salespeople to Territories. After territory boundaries are established, the analyst determines which salesperson to assign to which territory. In the past, these assignments ignored differences in abilities among salespeople and in the effectiveness of different salespeople with different customers. At this stage in territory planning, the analyst should consider such differences and attempt to assign each salesperson to the territory where he or she can contribute the most to the company's success.

Unfortunately, the ideal match cannot always be accomplished. Changing territory assignments can upset salespeople. It would be too disruptive to an established sales force with established sales territories to change practically all account coverage. If the firm is operating without assigned sales territories, then the realignment might be closer to the ideal. However, a firm with established territories typically must be content to change assignments incrementally and on a more limited basis.

The assignment of salespeople to sales territories also incorporates personal considerations. The firm may not want to change call assignments for particular accounts because of the potential for lost business. It may not want to reduce sales force size even if the analysis suggests it should because of morale problems associated with downsizing. Even increasing sales force size can be disruptive. More salespeople means more sales territories, which means redrawing existing boundaries, changing quotas, and disrupting potential for incentive pay. In sum, sales managers want to consider the people involved when they redraw territory boundaries and minimize disruptions to existing personal relationships between salespeople and customers.

Measure Sales Territory Performance

Once the territories have been developed and the salespeople assigned to them, it is important for the manager to monitor how well sales are doing. This is different from evaluating a salesperson's individual performance (which we will examine in Chapter 14). Here we are looking at how well the product, customer, or territory itself is doing relative to its potential. The process may be a relatively simple one of comparing company sales in two time periods or it may involve detailed comparisons of all sales (or sales-related) data among themselves, with external data, and with like figures for earlier time periods.

The major advantage of even the most elementary sales analysis is the ability to identify those products, customers, or territories in which the firm's sales are concentrated. A heavy concentration is very common. Often 80 percent of the customers or products account for only 20 percent of total sales. Conversely and more significantly, the remaining 20 percent of the customers or products account for 80 percent of the total sales volume. This is often called the **80:20 rule,** or the concentration ratio.[9]

The same phenomenon applies to territories. A few of the company's territories often account for most of its sales. The 80:20 rule describes the general situation (although, of course, the exact concentration ratio varies).

Managers who wish to undertake a sales analysis must decide the (1) sources of information and (2) types of information they wish to focus on in the analysis. Exhibit 9.5 provides an overview of the nature of these decisions.

Sources of Information for Sales Analysis. A key decision for sales managers is what sources of information to use in the analysis. The firm first must determine the types of comparisons that it wants to make to determine how well customers, products, and territories are doing. A comparison with sales in other territories will require less analysis than a comparison against market potential or quota or against the average sales in the territory for the last five years.

The firm also needs to decide the extent to which preparing the sales report should be integrated with preparing other types of reports. These may include inventory or production reports or sales reports for other company units such as other divisions.

EXHIBIT 9.5 Key Decisions in Sales Analysis

Sources of Information	Types of Aggregation
Sales invoice	Geographic region
Salesperson call reports	Salesperson territory
Salesperson expense reports	Customer
Warranty cards	Customer size
Store scanner data	Customer location
CRM system	Product size and category
ERP system	Size of order
	Customer industry classification

The document with the most information is usually the sales invoice. From this, the following information can usually be extracted:

- Customer name and location.
- Product(s) or service(s) sold.
- Volume and dollar amount of the transaction.
- Salesperson (or agent) responsible for the sale.
- End use of product sold.
- Location of customer facility where product is to be shipped and/or used.
- Customer's industry, class of trade, and/or distribution channel.
- Terms of sale and applicable discount.
- Freight paid and/or to be collected.
- Shipment point for the order.
- Transportation used in shipment.[10]

Other documents provide more specialized output. Some of the more important of these are listed in Exhibit 9.6. As you have learned, CRM systems facilitate the capturing of customer information, which can be analyzed and applied to particular sales analysis questions.

Software that links processes such as bid estimation, order entry, shipping, billing systems, and other work processes is called an **enterprise resources planning (ERP)** system. Boeing uses an ERP system to price out airplanes.[11] Each airline and private customer fits out each jet differently, so the salesperson's proposal has to account for each different item in order to derive a price. Also, commission has to be paid on the sale, parts have to be ordered for manufacturing, delivery has to be scheduled. The ERP helps manage all of these functions. As with CRM, the information generated through enterprise software is an invaluable resource in sales analysis. Firms like Oracle and IBM market ERP systems that are integrated throughout the companies and cost millions of dollars to install and maintain.

Types of Information Aggregation for Sales Analysis. The second major decision managers must make when designing a sales analysis is what they want to study (products, customers, territories). The most common and instructive

EXHIBIT 9.6 Sources of Information for Sales Analysis

Cash register receipts
Type (cash or credit) and dollar amount of transaction by department by salesperson

Salespeople's call reports
Customers and prospects called on (company and individual seen; planned or unplanned calls)
Products discussed
Orders obtained
Customers' product needs and usage
Other significant information about customers
Distribution of salespeople's time among customer calls, travel, and office work
Sales-related activities: meetings, conventions, etc.

Salespeople's expense accounts
Expenses by day by item (hotel, meals, travel, etc.)

Individual customer (and prospect) records
Name and location and customer number
Number of calls by company salesperson (agent)
Sales by company (in dollars and/or units by product or service by location of customer facility)
Customer's industry, class of trade, and/or trade channel
Estimated total annual usage of each product or service sold by the company
Estimated annual purchases from the company of each such product or service
Location (in terms of company sales territory)

Financial records
Sales revenue (by products, geographic markets, customers, class of trade, unit of sales organization, etc.)
Direct sales expenses (similarly classified)
Overhead sales costs (similarly classified)
Profits (similarly classified)

Credit memos
Returns and allowances

Warranty cards
Indirect measures of dealer sales
Customer service

Source: *Churchill/Ford/Walker's Sales Force Management*, 9th ed., by Mark Johnston and Greg Marshall (New York: McGraw-Hill, 2009), p. 167. Reprinted by permission of the McGraw-Hill Companies.

EXHIBIT 9.7 Sales Reports in a Consumer Food Products Company

Report Name	Purpose	Report Access*
Region	To provide sales information in units and dollars for each sales office or center in the region as well as a regional total	Appropriate regional manager
Sales office or center	To provide sales information in units and dollars for each district manager assigned to a sales office	Appropriate sales office or center manager
District	To provide sales information in units and dollars for each account supervisor and retail salesperson reporting to the district manager	Appropriate district manager
Salesperson summary	To provide sales information in units and dollars for each customer on whom the salesperson calls	Appropriate salesperson
Salesperson customer/product	To provide sales information in units and dollars for each customer on whom the salesperson calls	Appropriate salesperson
Salesperson/product	To provide sales information in units and dollars for each product that the salesperson sells	Appropriate salesperson
Region/product	To provide sales information in units and dollars for each product sold within the region. Similar reports would be available by sales office and by district	Appropriate regional manager
Region/customer class	To provide sales information in units and dollars for each class of customer located in the region. Similar reports would be available by sales office and by district	Appropriate regional manager

*Salespeople were assigned accounts in sales districts. Salespeople were assigned one or, at most, a couple of large accounts and were responsible for all the grocery stores, regardless of geography, affiliated with these large accounts, or they were assigned a geographic territory and were responsible for all the stores within that territory. All sales districts were assigned to sales offices or sales centers. The centers were, in turn, organized into regions.

Source: *Churchill/Ford/Walker's Sales Force Management,* 9th ed., by Mark Johnston and Greg Marshall (New York: McGraw-Hill, 2009), p. 170. Reprinted by permission of the McGraw-Hill Companies.

procedure is to assemble and tabulate sales by some appropriate groupings, such as these:

- Salesperson territories divided by state, county, MSA, or zip code.
- Customer or customer size.
- Product or package size.
- Size of order.

The kind of information a company uses depends on things like its size, diversity of product line, geographic extent of sales area, number of markets, and customers it serves. Different people in the organization may want different analyses. Product managers will focus on territory-by-territory sales of their products. On the other hand, sales managers will likely be much more interested in territory by salesperson or customer analyses and only secondarily interested in the territory sales broken out by product. Exhibit 9.7 summarizes sales analysis reports for a major B2C food products company.

Summary

One of the most important activities for both salespeople and sales managers is the efficient and effective management of time and territory. Salespeople who are good time and territory managers can increase productivity, improve customer relationships, and enhance their confidence. Sales managers also benefit by ensuring territory and customer coverage, minimizing sales expenses, assessing the sales performance of customers and products, and aligning company policies with customer expectations.

Salespeople have two fundamental questions to answer in time and territory management: What is the most efficient use of my time? What is the most effective way to manage my territory? Salespeople should identify their personal and professional priorities and develop a time management plan. They should also develop a territory management plan and provide territory feedback to management.

Sales managers have two fundamental tasks to complete in time and territory management. First, they must design the most effective sales territories. The overall success of a salesperson in any territory is based in part on how well management designs the territory. The second major task is measuring the sales performance of the company's products, customers, and territories. Territories are the fundamental unit of measure for evaluating various critical aspects of the company's business, such as the success of various products, how well customers are doing compared to other customers, or historical purchasing patterns.

Key Terms

life priorities
career priorities
professional priorities
account priorities
activity priorities
time management plan
daily event schedule
weekly/monthly planning calendar
organization of critical information
call frequency
territory management plan
routing schedule
sales territory
basic control unit
metropolitan statistical area (MSA)
market potential
workload analysis
account analysis
sales potential
account attractiveness
80:20 rule
enterprise resources planning (ERP)

Role Play

Before You Begin

Before getting started, please go to the appendix of Chapter 1 to review the profiles of the characters involved in this role play as well as the tips on preparing a role play.

Characters Involved

Rhonda Reed

Any one of the five account managers you would like to include in the role play.

Setting the Stage

Upland has asked all district managers to assist each of their account managers in developing a personal plan for continuous improvement in time and territory management. Rhonda has decided that the best way to approach this task is to ask each of her people to develop a page of bullet points for discussion and then meet individually to debrief the plan and provide input and ideas. To prepare these notes, each salesperson will follow the guidelines from the chapter sections on efficient time management and effective territory management.

Rhonda Reed's Role

Rhonda will meet with whichever account manager the other role play partner chooses to be. Rhonda will listen as the account manager goes over the key bullet points for improving his or her time and territory management. Ultimately, Rhonda will provide advice and suggestions on the plan and (with the account manager) come to an agreement on what steps to implement.

Account Manager's Role

Choose one of the five account managers to prepare the plan and meet with Rhonda. Pick a manager you think will be the most interesting character for this role play. Then develop the list of time and territory management improvement items. You may use leeway in fleshing out specific personal and job issues for discussion points in the meeting. Just be sure to thoroughly cover the key points from the chapter sections on efficient time management and effective territory management.

Assignment

Work together to develop and execute the role-play discussion on improving time and territory management between Rhonda and one of her account managers. Limit the meeting to 12–15 minutes. Be sure to agree on a plan for the account manager to put into practice.

Discussion Questions

1. Suppose you are a salesperson working 50 weeks per year, five days a week, eight hours a day. You want to make $50,000 per year, which is based on a 10 percent commission of gross sales. How many hours of face time with customers can you expect in any given year? How much will you have to generate in sales per hour to make $50,000?

2. As sales manager, you realize your salespeople need to be more efficient and effective in managing their time and territory. As you deliver the opening comments at an all-day seminar on time and territory management, your best salesperson stands and asks why this is so important. How do you respond?

3. You are vice president of sales for your company and are speaking with your sales managers from around the country. You have been asked by the CEO to prepare a five-minute presentation on why time and territory management is so important to the company. What do you say?

4. Complete the priority checklist in Exhibit 9.2. What do your responses to the checklist tell you about your career choices?

5. You are sales manager for an office supply distributor in a large metropolitan area. What do you use as your basic control unit in creating territories? Why?

6. What are the criteria used for estimating the total effort required by a salesperson to cover a territory?

7. You are sales director for a company with 1,125 customers generating $30 million in sales. Calculate the number of customers and sales generated using the 80:20 rule.

8. What is the most useful source of information on customers generated by any company? Identify all the possible data available on that source.

9. What are the primary ways data is aggregated in sales analysis?

10. Identify five types of sales reports a consumer products company might generate. Specify the purpose of such a report and who should have access.

Ethical Dilemma

Frank Lay, vice president of sales for Red Dot Graphics, faces a difficult decision. The company specializes in high-quality, difficult graphic printing and has a number of national clients.

Business is very good in the Nashville district and Red Dot management decided a new territory was needed to maximize the area's sales potential. After meeting with the local district sales manager, Larry Van Dyke, Frank selected the area that would be carved out for a new territory. It would include several high-volume existing clients and a number of large prospective customers (in other words, it would be a territory with high potential). Frank knew the area well since he had been the district sales manager in Nashville just prior to being promoted to vice president of sales. Company policy dictates that local district managers select which salespeople fill a particular territory.

Frank thinks Jim Henderson should be assigned that territory. Jim has been with the company for many years. While his performance has diminished in recent years, Frank feels this opportunity will reenergize Henderson. After all, it's not Henderson's fault that several large clients in his territory moved to different locations. Finally, Frank and Jim have been friends for many years. They both started at Red Dot about the same time. Last night Jim called to tell Frank he really wanted the opportunity to show what he could do in this new territory.

Van Dyke, on the other hand, believes Sylvia Beckett is the best candidate. She has been with the company only one year but has demonstrated an ability to increase business with her clients and exceeded her sales goals. Despite her short tenure, her performance justifies a promotion to a new, more challenging territory. Van Dyke thinks this opportunity would give her the chance to be a real star with the company.

As Frank sits at his desk, he is trying to decide whether to violate company policy and overrule Larry Van Dyke's decision to put Beckett in the new territory. Frank believes that Henderson deserves this chance to prove he can still perform at a high level, but he knows this move could have a negative effect on both Van Dyke and Sylvia Beckett.

Questions

1. What would you do with a salesperson who had been a high performer in the past but was currently not performing well?

2. Should Frank Lay give the new territory to Jim Henderson?

3. If you were Larry Van Dyke, what would be your reaction to Frank Lay's decision to put Jim Henderson in the new territory?

Mini Case

CASE 9

Diagnostic Services Inc.

Diagnostic Services Inc. (DSI) is a new company. It has been in business for only one year, offering diagnostic services to physicians in the Tampa/St. Petersburg, Miami, and Orlando markets. DSI carries the latest technology, including magnetic resonance imaging (MRI) machines, computerized tomography (CT) scanners, and electron beam tomography (EBT) scanners. The EBT scanners are the state of the art in medical diagnostic equipment, and DSI is one of only three locations in each market to have them. DSI executives are particularly excited about having the EBT scanners in all three locations because these machines detect potential health problems much earlier than previous medical tests could. The EBT scanners are very flexible. They can perform individual organ scans (for example, a heart scan, a lung scan, or a spleen scan) or they can perform a full-body scan. DSI plans to use the machines to expand its market base and brand awareness in the markets in which it operates.

DSI has operated for the past 12 months with six sales representatives, two for each metropolitan area. Until recently, the company has not had a sales manager. Company executives, all of whom are medical doctors, thought the motivation of each sales representative would be enough to make the company successful. However, after disappointing results in the first year of operation, the management team decided to hire a sales manager to bring some order and direction to the sales force's efforts.

DSI recently hired Lydell Washington as the sales manager. Lydell has 15 years of sales and sales manager experience with a pharmaceutical company. For the last two years his district finished second in sales productivity for the entire company. DSI management told Lydell his mission is to increase the sales force's productivity and name recognition throughout the three-market area by using the new EBT technology.

In his first month with the company Lydell spent a day with each sales rep making sales calls. By the time Lydell met with the sixth rep, Cindy Minnis, he already knew how to increase the sales force's productivity. He had noticed consistency across the sales force to his questions about their workdays. Cindy's responses were no different from the others. When Lydell asked which doctors she called on, she replied: "I call on all types of doctors. Wherever I find an office I'll stop in and talk to them. I don't care if they are pediatricians, obstetricians, or cardiologists. I'll talk to anyone who will see me."

After Lydell suggested that the physicians most likely to use the company's diagnostic equipment were cardiologists, oncologists, neurologists, and internists, Cindy said, "Really? No one ever told me that."

Next Lydell asked Cindy how many doctors she called on per day. "Only about five, sometimes six. My territory is so large I can't seem to get around to very many offices in a day. Sometimes I run into Mike, the other DSI rep in this area, at an office. There should be something we can do to prevent us from showing up at the same office on the same day." Lydell knew 10 calls per day is the industry standard and many times reps can do more.

Finally, Lydell asked Cindy what kind of information she provided back to the home office about her activity in the field. She answered, "Not much really. I keep some notes on who I've talked to and what we discussed but until now I haven't had anyone to send them to. I guess that will change now that you're onboard."

After his visit with Cindy, Lydell returned to his office and began to design a plan to increase the company's sales productivity.

Questions

1. What are some of the problems that DSI's salespeople have experienced as a result of not having had the direction of a sales manager for the first 12 months?
2. Describe the process Lydell should follow to design territories for the six sales reps currently employed by DSI. What sources of information are available for Lydell as he designs these territories?
3. What types of information should Lydell use to conduct a sales analysis of his reps' territories? Why?

Managing the Relationship-Selling Process

PART THREE

To this point we have focused on the roles of salesperson and customer in the relationship-selling process. As we have observed, building a successful buyer–seller relationship is a complex process involving a lot of hard work by the salesperson. However, there is another key player in the relationship-selling process—the sales manager. In this section we will explore the difficult task of managing the sales force. We will focus on the five critical components of managing the relationship-selling process.

Chapter 10 examines salesperson performance from both the salesperson's and sales manager's perspective. It discusses role perceptions and motivation, which are both key elements in the model. Sales force recruitment and selection are investigated in Chapter 11, while the objectives of sales training and a variety of training techniques are examined in Chapter 12. Chapter 13 focuses on how rewards are incorporated into effective sales compensation and incentive programs. Finally, Chapter 14 explores a critical management function in relationship selling: evaluation.

selling environment

Sales Management

SALESPERSON MOTIVATION

Relationship Selling

Evaluating Performance

Recruiting & Selection

Training & Development

Compensation

Closing & Follow-up

Self-Management

Prospecting & Sales Call Planning

Communicating the Sales Message

Negotiating for Win-Win Solutions

Information

Value Creation

Ethics

Customer Relationships

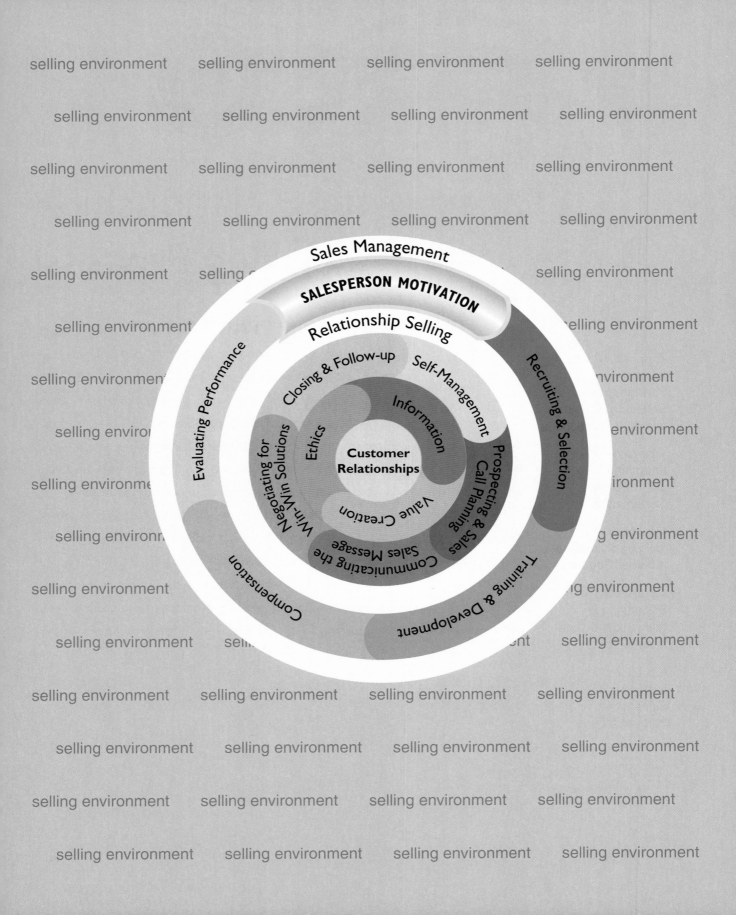

10 chapter

Salesperson Performance: Behavior, Motivation, and Role Perceptions

Learning Objectives

How a salesperson performs is the result of a complex interaction among many factors, including the individual's personal characteristics, motivation, and perceptions of the job. Sales managers must have a clear understanding of salesperson performance to maximize the performance potential of their people. This chapter will present a model of salesperson performance and lay the groundwork for Chapters 11 through 14. It also focuses on a key element in the model: the salesperson's role perceptions.

As the Expert Advice suggests, a number of factors can affect a salesperson's performance. Sales managers must motivate and direct the behavior of sales reps toward the company's goals, so they must understand why sales reps behave the way they do. This chapter offers a model for understanding salesperson performance.

After reading this chapter, you should be able to

- Understand the model of salesperson performance.
- Identify the various components that make up the model.
- Discuss the role perception process.
- Understand why salespeople are susceptible to role issues.

expert advice

Expert: Mr. Nick Hanna, General Sales Manager

Company: Parker Boat Company, Orlando, Florida

Business: Parker Boat Company is a retail boat store selling boats, service, and parts since 1927. It is the second oldest boat dealer in the United States and the oldest dealer in the state of Florida. The company carries SeaRay, Boston Whaler, and Triton Saltwater fishing boats. It is consistently rated very highly by customers and has achieved Master Dealer status by SeaRay.

Education: Bachelor of Arts in Physical Education and Health, Cumberland College

What do you think, are good salespeople born or made?

I believe they are both. God gives us all gifts, and some of us were born to sell. Others may have been given different gifts, but learn to sell anyway. Some of the best salespeople in the world are those who worked hard to learn all they could and have the "energy" to do their best at their line of work. They often are better than those who are "gifted," but don't try to improve as time goes on.

At the end of the day, a good salesperson must enjoy people. This does not mean that they are necessarily a "people person" but, rather, they like to interact with people. Successful relationship selling involves interacting with people to meet their needs (find the right boat for their life situation). Someone who doesn't want to be around people will find it much more difficult to build a relationship with the customer.

What do you believe is the single most important characteristic a salesperson needs to have in order to be successful selling boats?

The most important characteristic has to be honesty. It doesn't matter whether its boats or anything else, if you don't treat people as you would want to be treated, then you will fail in the long run. You cannot improve your skills if you are wasting time trying to figure our how to take advantage of someone instead of helping them make the right decision. Also, you will almost always keep a customer and gain repeat business when you are honest. The customer will feel you are interested in him or her through the process, instead of simply trying to make a sale.

Honesty is critical in building trust with the customer and trust is essential to a long-term relationship. We have loyal customers who buy several boats from the same salesperson over a period of years because they believe the salesperson is honest and, consequently, they trust that individual. Customers are very perceptive and they can tell when a salesperson is being honest (or dishonest).

How do you define the salesperson's role in working with customers in selling a boat?

Their role here at Parker Boats is to be a "friend" first and a salesperson second. In every situation the salesperson should first seek to learn about customers before they try to sell them a boat. Sometimes this is hard, but 9 out of 10 people appreciate the attention they are getting and it makes them feel at home with us. Our top salespeople all have made great friends with many of their customers over the years. Many customers call or stop by and speak with their salesperson because of the experience they had while shopping and buying a boat from us.

How do you influence the performance of your sales-people?

I see my role as a teacher first and a "closer" second. As the teacher I provide new information in our weekly sales meetings that will increase their sales effectiveness. When they forget to put the customer first I remind them who it is that really writes our paychecks and try to coach them into focusing more on the customer. As a "closer," it sometimes takes a second voice to reinforce what the salesperson and customer have already discussed. If the salesperson has been totally honest and done a good job in their sales presentation then the customer is going to hear the same things from me. It usually works to our favor as well as the customers.

I also encourage my people to have a positive outlook on life and that means to leave your troubles outside the door when you come to work or, if needed, let's talk about a problem and move past it. We try to allow a higher power to lead us every day and when we let "Him" lead, it usually works out for the good of all. I coach our salespeople that we are there to serve the customer and my job is to give them the tools they need to be successful. Their job is to match the training and tools we have given them with their own ability and experience to identify the customers' needs and then exceed their expectations.

Why Is It Important for Management to Understand Salesperson Performance?

Understanding the model of salesperson performance is extremely important to the sales manager because almost everything the sales manager does influences sales performance. For example, the way the sales manager organizes and deploys the sales force can affect salespeople's perceptions of the job. How the manager selects salespeople and the kind of training they receive can affect their aptitude and skill. The compensation program and the way it is administered can influence motivation and overall sales performance.

As our focus changes to managing the sales force, refer back to the model for Relationship Selling and Sales Management at the beginning of the chapter and note the shift from relationship selling to sales management. This chapter will concentrate on salesperson performance (motivation).

Salesperson Performance

A salesperson's performance is a function of five factors: (1) role perceptions, (2) aptitude, (3) skill level, (4) motivation, and (5) personal, organizational, and environmental variables.[1] These factors are shown in Exhibit 10.1. The success of any salesperson is a complex combination of these forces, which can influence his or her performance positively or negatively.

EXHIBIT 10.1 The Determinants of Salesperson Performance

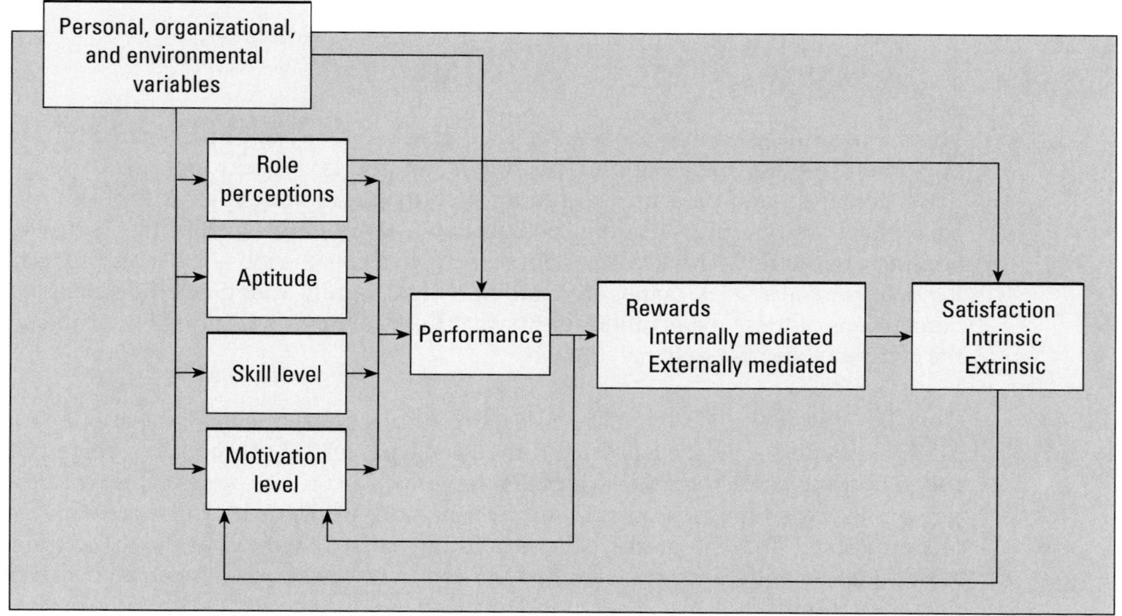

Source: *Churchill/Ford/Walker's Sales Force Management*, 9th ed., by Mark Johnston and Greg Marshall (New York: McGraw-Hill, 2009), p. 200. Reprinted by permission of the McGraw-Hill Companies.

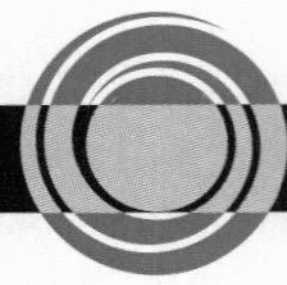

INNOVATION 10.1

Test Your Sales Management Skills

Let's assess your sales management skills. Answer the questions below; all are True/False. Check your answers at the end of the Discussion Questions.

1. If you monitor expenses regularly and your salespeople know that you are checking their expense reports, it is still necessary to have a written expense policy and procedures document.
2. Sales incentive programs should always focus on financial compensation.
3. Require salespeople to get permission for job-related travel.
4. When performance does not meet company expectations the sales manager should confront the salesperson directly.
5. Salespeople should not allow family responsibilities to conflict with work during regular business hours.
6. Promotion is not the long-term goal of a salesperson.
7. Sales training should focus on delivering critical product updates and company information.
8. Good salespeople are born with the inherent abilities to be good.
9. There should be one set of rewards applied across the entire sales organization.
10. Sales managers are responsible for making sure the salesperson understands company performance expectations.

Although not pictured in the model, the determinants interact with each other. For example, if the salesperson has native ability and the motivation to perform but lacks understanding of how the job should be done, he or she will likely perform at a low level. Similarly, a salesperson who has the ability and accurately perceives how the job should be performed but lacks motivation will likely perform poorly. As you can see already, understanding and improving salesperson performance is challenging. Take the short quiz in Innovation 10.1 and see how well you would do as a sales manager.

Role Perceptions

The *role* of a salesperson is the set of activities or behaviors to be performed by any person occupying that position. This role is defined largely through the expectations, demands, and pressures communicated to the salesperson by his or her role partners. These partners include people both outside and within the firm who have a vested interest in how the salesperson performs the job—top management, the salesperson's sales manager, customers, and family members. Salespeople's perceptions of these expectations strongly influence their definition of their role in the company and behavior on the job.

Defining Role Perceptions. The role perceptions component of the model for salesperson performance has three dimensions: perceived role conflict, perceived role ambiguity, and role inaccuracy. **Perceived role conflict** arises when a salesperson believes the role demands by two or more of his or her role partners are incompatible. Thus, he or she cannot possibly satisfy them all at the same time. A salesperson suffers from perceptions of conflict, for example, when a customer demands a delivery schedule or credit terms the salesperson believes will be unacceptable to company superiors.

Perceived role ambiguity occurs when a salesperson believes he or she does not have the information necessary to perform the job adequately. The salesperson may be uncertain about what some role partners expect in certain situations, how he or she should satisfy those expectations, or how his or her performance will be evaluated and rewarded.

Role inaccuracy is the degree to which the salesperson's perceptions of demands from his or her role partners—particularly company superiors—are not accurate and is different from role ambiguity in that the salesperson feels certain about what should be done. However, the salesperson's belief is wrong. It differs from role conflict in that the salesperson does not see any inconsistencies because the rep does not realize his or her perceptions are inaccurate.

Why Are Role Perceptions Important? How salespeople perceive their roles will have significant consequences for them. Role perceptions can produce dissatisfaction with the job. They can also affect a salesperson's motivation.[2] These effects can increase sales force turnover and hurt performance. However, role stress (role conflict and ambiguity) does not necessarily imply a negative job outcome (quitting). Believe it or not, a certain degree of role conflict and ambiguity enables salespeople to make creative decisions that can be beneficial to the customer and the organization.

Because they spend so much time out of the office and with customers, industrial salespeople are particularly vulnerable to role inaccuracy, conflict, and ambiguity. Several personal factors (such as traveling, work demands) and organizational factors (such as infrequent meetings with their supervisor) can affect people's role perceptions. Fortunately, many of these factors can be controlled or influenced by sales management policies and methods, so sales managers can help their salespeople perform better.[3]

Sales Aptitude: Are Good Salespeople Born or Made?

Stable, self-sufficient, self-confident, goal-directed, decisive, intellectually curious, accurate—these are personal traits one major personnel testing company says a successful salesperson should have. Sales ability has sometimes been thought to be a function of (1) physical factors such as age and physical attractiveness, (2) aptitude factors such as verbal intelligence and sales expertise, and (3) personality characteristics such as empathy and sociability. However, there is no proof that these types of broad aptitude measures, by themselves, affect sales performance. It's an open question whether the presence or absence of such traits is determined by a person's genetic makeup and early life experiences or whether they can be developed through training, supervision, and experience after the person is hired for a sales position. In other words, the question is, are good salespeople born or made?

Many sales executives seem unsure about what it takes to become a successful salesperson. When forced to choose, a majority of managers say they believe good salespeople are made rather than born. By a margin of seven to one, the respondents in a survey of sales and marketing executives said training and supervision are more critical determinants of selling success than the rep's inherent personal characteristics.[4] But many of those respondents also described someone they knew as "a born salesperson," and a minority argued that personal traits are critical determinants of good sales performance.

Leadership 10.2

Personal Traits That Lead to Sales Success

Are good salespeople born or made? As we have seen, this question is difficult to answer. However, leading sales managers agree all good salespeople possess at least a few basic personality traits. Recently, managers and sales experts identified the following five traits of successful salespeople.

Optimistic. Have you ever noticed how the best reps tend to look on the bright side? Optimism may also determine how resilient a salesperson will be.

Flexible. Being able to adjust to difficult situations is key to success in sales. "A salesperson needs to be able to accept 15 no's before you get a yes."

Self-motivated. Most experts and managers believe motivation cannot be taught. Whether it's being driven by money or recognition or simply pride, the best salespeople tend to have an inherent competitive drive.

People person. Simply put, you can't sell if your customers don't like you. Being friendly and sociable is a hallmark of salespeople who network and maintain long-term customer relationships.

Empathetic. This intuitive, perceptive ability underlies virtually all other emotional intelligence skills because it involves truly understanding the customer. Empathetic salespeople tend to have good listening and communication skills.

Thus, while most managers believe the things a firm does to train and develop its salespeople are the most critical determinants of their success, many also believe that certain basic personal traits—such as a strong ego, self-confidence, decisiveness, and a drive to achieve—are requirements. Most likely both sets of factors play crucial roles in shaping a salesperson's performance. Leadership 10.2 highlights five traits considered critical for sales success.

Sales Skill Levels

Role perceptions determine whether the salesperson knows what to do in performing a job, and aptitude determines whether the individual has the necessary native abilities. Skill levels are the individual's learned proficiency at performing the necessary tasks.[5] They include such learned abilities as interpersonal skills, leadership, technical knowledge, and presentation skills. The relative importance of each of these skills, and the need for other skills, depends on the selling situation. Different kinds of skills are needed for different types of selling tasks.

Aptitude and skill levels are thus related constructs. Aptitude consists of relatively enduring personal abilities, while skills are proficiencies that can improve rapidly with learning and experience. A salesperson for Cisco Systems selling multimillion-dollar network switching equipment needs different skill sets from someone selling BMWs to consumers.

The salesperson's past selling experience and the extensiveness and content of the firm's sales training programs influence skill level. While American companies spend large amounts of money on sales training, very little is known concerning the effects of these training programs on salespeople's skills, behavior, and performance. We will discuss training the sales force in much greater detail in Chapter 12.

Motivation

Motivation is how much the salesperson wants to expend effort on each activity or task associated with the job. These activities include calling on existing and potential new accounts, developing and delivering sales presentations, and filling out orders and reports.

Defining Motivation. The salesperson's motivation to expend effort on any task seems to be a function of the person's (1) expectancies and (2) valences for performance. **Expectancies** are the salesperson's estimates that expending effort on a specific task will lead to improved performance on some specific dimension. For example, will increasing the number of calls made on potential new accounts lead to increased sales? **Valences for performance** are the salesperson's perceptions of the desirability of attaining improved performance on some dimension(s). For example, does the salesperson find increased sales important?

A salesperson's valence for performance on a specific dimension, in turn, seems to be a function of the salesperson's (1) instrumentalities and (2) valences for rewards. **Instrumentalities** are the salesperson's estimates that improved performance on that dimension will lead to increased attainment of particular rewards. For example, will increased sales lead to increased compensation? **Valences for rewards** are the salesperson's perceptions of the desirability of receiving increased rewards as a result of improved performance. Does the salesperson find increased compensation attractive enough to put in the time calling on more prospects?

Why Is Motivation Important? Sales managers constantly try to find the right mix of motivation elements to direct salespeople to do certain activities, but rewards that motivate one salesperson may not motivate another. The manager of a leading consulting company in Chicago gave his top performer a new mink coat. The only problem was that the individual was opposed to wearing fur. Rewarding the salesperson was a great idea, but the form of the reward led to problems for the sales manager.

A salesperson's motivation is not directly under the sales manager's control, but it can be influenced by things the sales manager does, such as how he or she supervises or rewards the individual.[6] Since motivation strongly influences performance, the sales manager must be sensitive to the way various factors affect each rep. Innovation 10.3 explores ways to motivate and retain your star salespeople.

Organizational, Environmental, and Personal Factors

It is difficult to separate organizational, environmental, and personal variables. The sales performance model in Exhibit 10.1 suggests that they influence sales performance in two ways: (1) by directly facilitating or constraining performance and (2) by influencing and interacting with the other performance determinants, such as role perceptions and motivation. Many questions remain unanswered concerning the effects of these factors on sales performance.

Organizational and Environmental Variables. Organizational factors include the company marketing budget, current market share for products, and the degree

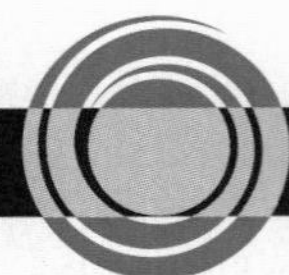

INNOVATION 10.3

Motivate Your Star Salespeople for Free

Most sales managers believe that it costs a lot of money to motivate and retain your best salespeople. They think that financial rewards are the only way to keep those stars from leaving the company. However, consider five ways to motivate your star salespeople for practically nothing.

1. *Understand personal difference.* What motivates one rep may leave another cold. Get to know your salespeople and their likes and dislikes.
2. *Encourage balance.* Successful people need to juggle work along with family and friends. Respect their personal lives.
3. *Praise good work.* Find salespeople doing something worthwhile, like sharing leads, and notice it.
4. *Get out.* Be supportive, visible, and available. Don't hide in your office.
5. *Don't play favorites.* Even a hint of favoritism can undermine a sales team.

of sales force supervision. There is an indirect and direct relationship between performance and environmental factors like territory potential, the salesperson's workload, and the intensity of competition.

When you look at sales territory design (remember the discussion from Chapter 9), a salesperson's performance increases as he or she becomes more satisfied with the territory's design and structure. Including salespeople in the territory design process may seem intuitive, but managers sometimes find it difficult to balance the needs of the organization with the input of the salespeople. Sales managers have learned, however, that including them in the decision-making process on key issues such as territory design may increase their performance over time.[7] As we discussed in Chapter 9, computer territory mapping software helps sales managers and salespeople work together to create the most profitable and efficient territory configurations.[8] In the long term this can lead to less role ambiguity and more job satisfaction, as well as better performance.

Personal Variables. Personal and organizational variables (such as job experience, the manager's interaction style, and performance feedback) affect the amount of role conflict and ambiguity salespeople perceive. In addition, their desire for job-related rewards (such as higher pay or promotion) differs with demographic characteristics such as age, education, family size, career stage, and organizational climate.[9]

As the role of salespeople has evolved into building and maintaining customer relationships, they have been asked to engage in a whole range of activities that can be described as being good corporate citizens. These behaviors are called **organizational citizenship behaviors** and encompass four basic types of activity: (1) sportsmanship, (2) civic virtue, (3) conscientiousness, and (4) altruism. Sportsmanship is a willingness on the salesperson's part to endure less than optimum conditions (like slow reimbursement of expenses or reduced administrative support) without complaining to superiors or other salespeople. Civic virtue is a proactive behavior that includes making recommendations to management that will improve the overall performance of the organization (e.g., providing feedback from customers even when it is not complimentary). Conscientiousness is the willingness to work beyond the normal expectations of the job (late at night or on weekends). Altruism refers to helping others in the organization (for example, mentoring younger salespeople).

There is a growing understanding that salespeople who engage in these activities perform better on both outcome-based measures (sales volume) and behavior-based measures (customer satisfaction). Measuring and evaluating salesperson performance will be discussed in Chapter 14. Engaging in activities that enhance the overall organization becomes even more important as the focus shifts to relationship selling.

Rewards

Exhibit 10.1 indicates that performance affects the salesperson's rewards. However, the relationship between performance and rewards is very complex. For one thing, a firm may choose to evaluate and reward different dimensions of sales performance. A company might evaluate its salespeople on total sales volume, quota attainment, customer satisfaction, profitability of sales, new accounts generated, services provided to customers, or some combination of these. Different firms use different dimensions. Even firms that use the same performance criteria are likely to have different emphases.

A company can also bestow a variety of rewards for any given level of performance. There are two types of rewards—extrinsic and intrinsic. **Extrinsic rewards** are those controlled and bestowed by people other than the salesperson, such as managers or customers. They include such things as pay, financial incentives, security, recognition, and promotion. **Intrinsic rewards** are those that salespeople primarily attain for themselves. They include such things as feelings of accomplishment, personal growth, and self-worth.

Satisfaction

The **job satisfaction** of salespeople refers to all the characteristics of the job that salespeople find rewarding, fulfilling, and satisfying—or frustrating and unsatisfying. Satisfaction is a complex job attitude, and salespeople can be satisfied or dissatisfied with many different aspects of the job. There are seven dimensions to sales job satisfaction: (1) the job itself, (2) pay, (3) company policies and support, (4) supervision, (5) co-workers, (6) promotion and advancement opportunities, and (7) customers. See Exhibit 10.2 for a summary. Salespeople's total satisfaction with their jobs is a reflection of their satisfaction with each element.[10]

Like rewards, the seven dimensions of satisfaction can be grouped, into intrinsic and extrinsic components. *Extrinsic satisfaction* is based on the extrinsic rewards bestowed on the salesperson, such as pay, company policies and support, supervision, fellow workers, chances for promotion, and customers. *Intrinsic satisfaction* is based on the intrinsic rewards the salesperson obtains from the job, such as satisfaction with the work itself.

Salespeople's satisfaction is also influenced by their role perceptions.[11] Salespeople who perceive a great deal of conflict in job demands tend to be less satisfied than those who do not. So do those who experience great uncertainty in what is expected from them on the job.

Finally, a salesperson's job satisfaction is likely to affect his or her motivation to perform, as suggested by the feedback loop in Exhibit 10.1. The relationship between satisfaction and motivation is complex and varies by individual.

EXHIBIT 10.2 Job Satisfaction Dimensions

Job satisfaction consists of the following dimensions.

1. The job itself.
2. Pay (all forms of financial rewards, including salary and commission).
3. Company policies and support (procedures such as expense polices, reports, paperwork).
4. Supervision (immediate sales manager, senior sales management in the company).
5. Co-workers (other salespeople, people on the sales team, staff).
6. Promotion and advancement (opportunities to move up in the company).
7. Customers (friendliness, ease of working with people).

How Salespeople Influence Performance

Clearly, the salesperson has the most significant effect on his or her own performance. Two areas that influence performance in relationship selling are the salesperson's role perceptions and the many factors that influence those perceptions. As we have seen, the salesperson's role is complex and has conflicting demands.

The Salesperson's Role Perceptions

Role perceptions have important implications for sales managers and affect salesperson performance in many ways. For example, feelings of ambiguity, conflict, and inaccurate role perceptions can cause anxiety and stress, which can lead to lower performance. Fortunately, the sales manager can minimize the negative consequences of role perceptions by the kind of salespeople that are hired, training methods, the incentives used to motivate them, criteria used to evaluate them, and the way they are supervised.

What makes understanding and managing role perceptions even more complicated is that not all the consequences of role ambiguity, role conflict, and role accuracy are negative. Eliminating all ambiguity and conflict would reduce the challenge for a salesperson and can actually limit long-term performance. The sales manager's job is to create an environment that will stimulate and motivate salespeople while reducing the negative effects of role stress that are a natural part of selling. The salesperson's role is defined through a three-step process:[12] Role partners communicate expectations, salespeople develop perceptions, and salespeople convert these perceptions into behaviors.

Stage 1: Role Partners Communicate Expectations. First, expectations and demands concerning how the salesperson should behave, together with pressures to conform, are communicated to the salesperson by people with a vested interest in how he or she performs the job. These people include the rep's immediate superior, other executives in the firm, customers and members of customers' organizations, and the salesperson's family. They all try to influence the person's behavior, either formally through organizational policies, operating procedures, and training programs or informally through social pressures, rewards, and sanctions.

The salesperson's family members can have a significant effect on job perceptions. Their demands are much more likely to differ from one salesperson to the next than the expectations of customers or management. So no matter what the company expects in hours of work, customer relationships, travel, and the like, a substantial number of salespeople are likely to be in conflict with their families' expectations. That is becoming an increasingly serious problem for today's workers, as Global Perspective 10.4 indicates.

Stage 2: Salespeople Develop Perceptions. The second part of the role definition process involves salespeople's perception of the expectations and demands of those around them (sales manager, customers, loved ones). Salespeople perform according to what they think these individuals expect, even when their perceptions of those expectations are not accurate. To really understand why salespeople perform the way they do, it is necessary to understand what they think the members of the role set expect.

At this stage of the role definition process, three factors can wreak havoc with a salesperson's job performance and mental well-being. As Exhibit 10.3 shows, the salesperson may suffer from role ambiguity, role conflict, or role inaccuracy.

Stage 3: Salespeople Convert Perceptions to Behaviors. The final step in the role definition process involves the salesperson's conversion of role perceptions

EXHIBIT 10.3 Sales Perception of the Job

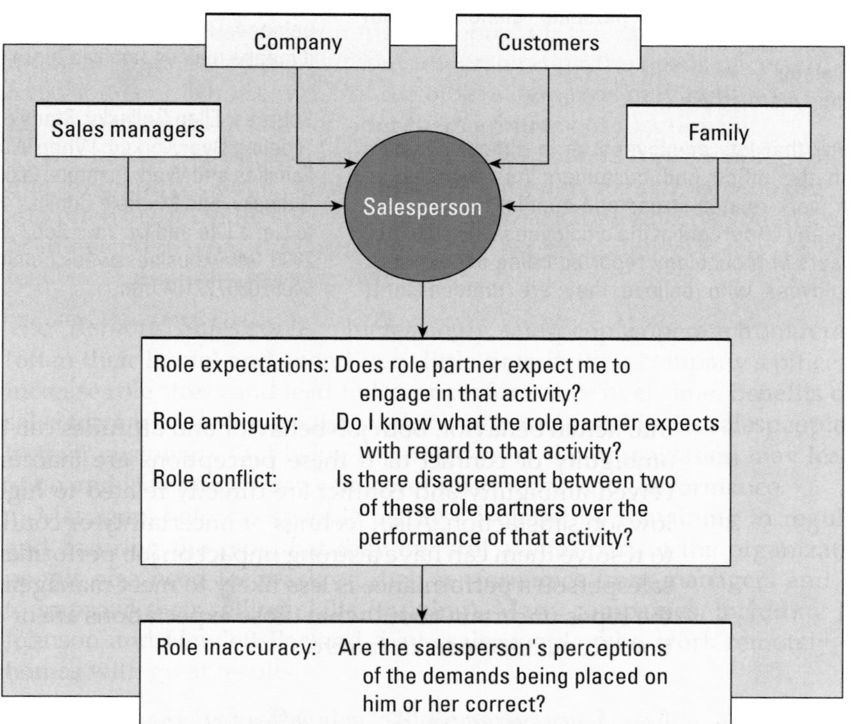

Source: *Churchill/Ford/Walker's Sales Force Management*, 9th ed., by Mark Johnston and Greg Marshall (New York: McGraw-Hill, 2009), p. 210. Reprinted by permission of the McGraw-Hill Companies.

the firm's revenue. The specific design of a product and the delivery and credit terms quoted by the salesperson directly affects people in the engineering, production, and credit departments, for example. All these people may hold definite beliefs about how the salesperson should perform the job and may pressure the individual to conform to their expectations.

The large number of people from diverse departments and organizations who depend on the salesperson increases the probability that at least some demands will be incompatible. It also means the salesperson's perceptions of some demands will be inaccurate and he or she will be uncertain about others.

Selling in a Team. The complex nature of the relationship between company and customer has created a need for salespeople to work in teams that include specialists from many parts of the company (technical, manufacturing, logistics, and others). As we have discussed, the role of salesperson has evolved from selling to customers to managing the relationship between the company and customers. Companies as diverse as Sun Microsystems, 3M, Siemens, and Sony have created sales teams managed by salespeople. Inside salespeople and customer service reps create additional contact with the customer that often requires greater coordination with the field representatives. This may create role conflict as salespeople deal with the expectations and demands of many individuals in the sales team and the organization as a whole.

Innovative Role. Salespeople are frequently called on to produce new, innovative solutions to nonroutine problems. This is particularly true when they are selling highly technical products or engineered systems designed to customer's specifications. Even salespeople who sell standardized products must display some creativity in matching the company's offerings to each customer's particular needs. With potential new accounts, this is an extremely difficult but critical task.

As a result of their innovative roles, salespeople tend to experience more conflict than other employees because they must have flexibility to perform at a high level. They must also have the authority to develop and carry out innovative solutions. This need for flexibility often brings the salesperson into conflict with standard operating procedures of the firm and the expectations of co-workers who want to maintain the status quo. The production manager, for example, may frown on orders for nonstandard products because of the adverse effects on production costs and schedules—although marketing (especially the salespeople) desires flexible production schedules and the ability to sell custom-designed products.

Workers with innovative roles also tend to experience more role ambiguity and inaccurate role perceptions because they face unusual situations where they have no standard procedures or past experience to guide them. Consequently, they are often uncertain about how their role partners expect them to proceed. Their perceptions are more likely to be inaccurate because of the nonroutine nature of the task. The flexibility needed to fulfill an innovative role can have unforeseen negative consequences.

How Managers Influence Performance

While salespeople are most responsible for their own performance, sales managers also play a critical role. Managers affect all elements in the model of sales performance, though in this section we focus on two: role perceptions and motivation. (Chapters 11–14 will look at how managers influence other factors in the model.)

Role Perceptions

Given that role conflict and ambiguity produce mostly negative consequences for salespeople, the question is: Can sales management do anything to reduce conflicts and ambiguities or help salespeople deal with them when they occur? Yes. There are many things management can do to manage salesperson conflict and ambiguity.

Role Conflict. Experienced salespeople perceive less conflict than less-experienced representatives. Perhaps salespeople who experience a great deal of conflict become dissatisfied and quit, whereas those who stay on the job do not perceive as much conflict.

Also, successful sales representatives also learn with experience how to deal with conflict. They learn that demands that initially appear to conflict can turn out to be compatible or perhaps they find out how to resolve conflicts so they are no longer stressful. They build up psychological defense mechanisms to screen out conflicts and ease tension. Sales training programs can prepare salespeople to deal with job-related conflicts and teach them to do their job better.

When their sales managers structure and define their jobs, salespeople seem to experience more conflict. Perhaps too close supervision decreases a salesperson's flexibility in dealing with the diverse role expectations with which salespeople must contend (customers, management, and family). Peter Sowden, vice president of business development for Polytex Fibers, puts it this way: "Most salespeople love autonomy and flexibility. I find the greatest compliment is to be left alone to run my territory as if it were my own business."[14] Another way to reduce role conflict, then, is to give salespeople a greater voice in what they do and how they do it.

Role Ambiguity. There are also things management can do to reduce role ambiguity. Since it too depends on experience, training should help salespeople cope with it. More importantly, it also depends on the manager's supervisory style. Close supervision may actually reduce ambiguity, though salespeople should have some influence over the standards used to control and evaluate their performance. Closely supervised salespeople are more aware of their supervisors' expectations and demands, and inconsistent behaviors can be brought to their attention more quickly.

Similarly, salespeople who have input in determining the standards by which they are evaluated are more familiar with these standards, which tends to reduce role ambiguity. Another way to reduce ambiguity is by reducing the number of people who report directly to the sales manager. An increase in the number of people who report to a manager also increases a salesperson's perceived role ambiguity. Reducing it allows closer supervision, and tends to make job-related issues clearer to salespeople.[15]

As you can see, close supervision can be a two-edged sword. While it can reduce ambiguity, it can increase role conflict and job dissatisfaction when salespeople feel they don't have enough latitude to deal effectively with customers or enough creative input to service their accounts. The problem is particularly acute when sales managers use coercion and threats to direct their salespeople.[16] Sales managers must walk a very fine line in how closely and by what means they supervise their sales force.

Leadership 10.5

Secrets of Motivation

Sales managers must overcome a number of challenges to successfully motivate their sales force. Often the challenges are easy to identify, although they may difficult to address, such as compensation. However, some problems are less easy to recognize although their impact on sales force motivation can be dramatic. Let's look at two of those issues.

A persistent perception held by many sales managers is that salespeople can learn how to become successful on their own. In other words salespeople have an innate ability to identify what they need to know, learn it, and then be able to apply to their own situation. For the top 5 percent of sales performers, that is true, but what about the other 95 percent? The reality is that the vast majority of salespeople don't know what they don't know. Most salespeople invest very little in their own sales education and most sales managers fail in providing useful skills. Success-oriented sales managers value a "best practices" approach to selling, searching for skills and information that benefit their salespeople then creating an environment for salespeople to learn and practice those skills. The result is a more confident, motivated salesperson. Incorporating "best practices" throughout the sales force raises the performance and motivation for everyone, not just the top 5 percent.

Another widely held perception is that sales performance mediocrity must be tolerated. The theory often used in those situations is, "it's better to have somebody in that territory than no one." The "solution" may be to reassign the individual to a less desirable territory (usually in an attempt to force the individual to leave the company) or engage the individual in discussion to identify and address the problem.

While those ideas may work for that individual, most sales managers, unfortunately, fail to consider the effect mediocre performance has on the rest of the sales force. The belief that performance issues are person-specific can inflict serious damage on the motivation of the entire sales force. Sales managers need to address performance issues directly seeking regular, meaningful input on what is working (and not working), what motivates each individual, and what can be done to improve their performance. In a very real sense sales managers need to consistently focus on improving performance individually and across the entire sales force.

Source: Dave Kahle, "Are There Best Practices for Salespeople?" *American Salesman* 53, 2, *February 2008,* pp. 11–15 and Paul Cherry, "How to Motivate Your Sales Team to Achieve Next-Level Selling," *American Salesman* 52, 11, *November 2007,* pp. 8–12.

Motivation

Through company policies, the sales manager can directly facilitate or hinder a salesperson's motivation. They may also influence salespeople's performance indirectly, however, by affecting their interest in company rewards and the size and accuracy of their expectancies and instrumentalities. How do sales executives motivate their sales forces? Check out Leadership 10.5.

Motivation and Managerial Leadership. One well-regarded theory of leadership suggests that managers can attain good performance by increasing salespeople's personal rewards and making the path to those rewards easier to follow—by providing instructions and training, reducing roadblocks and pitfalls, and increasing the opportunities for personal satisfaction.[17]

Effective leaders match their style and approach to the needs of their sales force and the kinds of tasks they must perform. When the salesperson's task is well defined, routine, and repetitive, the leader should seek ways to increase the intrinsic rewards, perhaps by assigning a broader range of activities or giving the rep more flexibility to perform tasks. When the salesperson's job is complex and ambiguous—as is the case in most selling situations—he or she is likely to be happier and more productive when the leader provides more guidance and structure.

Take Joe Torre, manager of the Los Angeles Dodgers who is widely regarded as one of the best managers in baseball. His style is simple. "I try to understand what motivates other people." He does not focus on mistakes but rather seeks to build confidence and trust. He is constantly meeting one on one with his players to find ways to make them better. Judging by his long-term success with the Yankees and now the Dodgers, his approach works.[18]

The more accurate salespeople's role perceptions are, the more motivated they're likely to be. Salespeople work at the boundary of their companies, dealing with customers and other people who may make conflicting demands. Salespeople frequently face new, nonroutine problems. However, closely supervised salespeople can learn more quickly what is expected of them and how they should perform their job. On the other hand close supervision can increase role conflict since it can reduce flexibility in accommodating and adapting to customers' demands.

Another factor is how often salespeople communicate with their managers. The more frequent the communication, the less role ambiguity salespeople are likely to experience and the more accurate their expectancies and instrumentalities are. Again, too frequent contact with superiors may increase a representative's feelings of role conflict.

Incentive and Compensation Policies

Management policies and programs concerning rewards, such as recognition and promotion, can influence the desirability of such rewards in the salesperson's mind. If, for example, a large proportion of the sales force receives some formal recognition each year, salespeople may think such recognition is too common, too easy to obtain, and not worth much. If very few representatives receive formal recognition, however, recognition may not motivate simply because the odds of attaining it are so low. The same kind of relationship is likely to exist between the proportion of salespeople promoted into management each year (the **opportunity rate**) and the importance salespeople place on promotion.[19]

Another issue is preferential treatment for stars. The goal of recognition and other forms of incentives is to motivate people to do better, but what happens when one star demands and receives much more than the average or even much more than the company's other top performers? A few years ago, baseball player Alex Rodriguez (A-Rod) was on the market to the highest bidder. One of the teams recruiting Rodriguez was the New York Mets. However, the Mets withdrew from consideration when they realized that while they could afford Rodriguez, the effect on team morale would be negative. General manager of the Mets at the time, Steve Phillips said, "It's not about an individual. It's about 25 players that join together as a team. When that is compromised, it becomes difficult to win." The same is true for a sales force. A company's policies on the kinds and amounts of financial compensation paid to "star" salespeople are also likely to affect their motivation. When an individual is basically satisfied with his or her pay, money become less important and the value of that reward to that person is reduced.

Finally, the reward mix offered by the firm is a factor. **Reward mix** is the relative emphasis placed on salary versus commissions or other incentive pay and

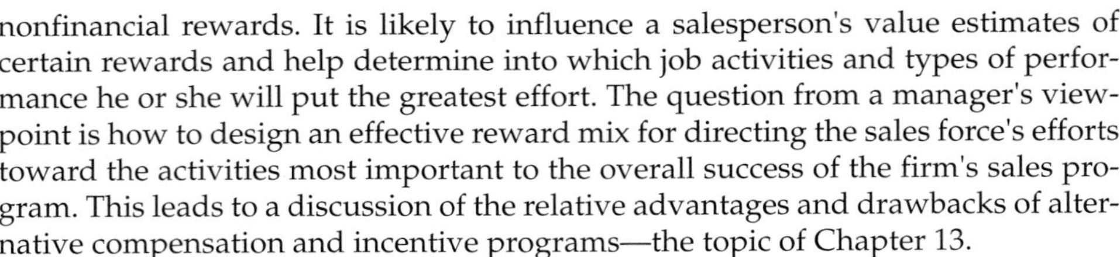

nonfinancial rewards. It is likely to influence a salesperson's value estimates of certain rewards and help determine into which job activities and types of performance he or she will put the greatest effort. The question from a manager's viewpoint is how to design an effective reward mix for directing the sales force's efforts toward the activities most important to the overall success of the firm's sales program. This leads to a discussion of the relative advantages and drawbacks of alternative compensation and incentive programs—the topic of Chapter 13.

Summary

This chapter, the first on managing the sales program, presents a model (Exhibit 10.1) for understanding the performance of salespeople. It examines the first component of the model, the salesperson's role perceptions.

A salesperson's performance is a function of five basic factors: (1) role perceptions, (2) aptitude, (3) skill level, (4) motivation, and (5) organizational, environmental, and personal variables. There is substantial interaction among the components. A salesperson who is deficient in any one may perform poorly.

Salespeople's role perceptions are defined largely through the expectations, demands, and pressures communicated by role partners (people both within and outside the company who are affected by the way they perform the job). The role of salesperson is defined through a three-step process: (1) Role partners communicate expectations and demands concerning how the salesperson should behave in various situations, together with pressures to conform. (2) The salesperson perceives these expectations and demands. (3) The salesperson converts these perceptions into actual behavior.

The three major variables in role perception are role accuracy, ambiguity, and conflict. Role accuracy is the degree to which the salesperson's perceptions of his or her role partners' demands are accurate. Role ambiguity occurs when the salesperson does not believe he or she has the information to perform the job adequately. Role conflict arises when a salesperson believes the demands of two or more of his or her role partners are incompatible.

Salespeople's performance affects the rewards they receive. There are two basic types of rewards: extrinsic rewards, which are controlled and bestowed by people other than the salesperson, and intrinsic rewards, which are those that people primarily attain for themselves.

The rewards received have a major impact on a salesperson's satisfaction with the job and the total work environment. Satisfaction is also of two types. Intrinsic satisfaction comes from the intrinsic rewards the salesperson obtains from the job, such as satisfaction with the work and the opportunities it provides for personal growth and a sense of accomplishment. Extrinsic satisfaction comes from the extrinsic rewards bestowed on the salesperson, such as pay, promotion, and supervisory and company policies.

The salesperson's role is affected by many factors. They work on the boundary of the organization between the company and customer. Much of the time they are working away from the office and interact with many diverse individuals. Finally, the role of salesperson is one of the most innovative in the company.

The manager plays an important part by having a profound influence on role perceptions (conflict, ambiguity). In addition managers affect a salesperson's motivation through reward and compensation plans and other company policies.

Key Terms

perceived role conflict
perceived role ambiguity
role inaccuracy
motivation
expectancies
valences for performance
instrumentalities
valences for rewards
organizational citizenship behaviors
extrinsic rewards
intrinsic rewards
job satisfaction
opportunity rate
reward mix

Role Play

Before You Begin

Before getting started, please go to the appendix of Chapter 1 to review the profiles of the characters involved in this role play as well as the tips on preparing a role play.

Characters Involved

Alex Lewis

Abe Rollins

Setting the Stage

Over the past couple of years, Alex Lewis's children (a 12-year-old boy and 14-year-old girl) have become more and more involved in sports and other extracurricular activities that require frequent travel to other cities for competition, sometimes road trips 100 miles or more away from home. A parent must accompany the child on each trip. Alex's wife, Sonya, holds a professional position that involves overnight travel three or four nights per month. Alex's sales territory involves only minimal overnight travel (an occasional night here and there, generally not more than two or three nights per quarter). Thus, he often plays Mr. Mom at home when his wife is on the road. Sometimes both he and Sonya have to be out of town at the same time. Sonya's parents live in the area and can watch the children when that happens.

Although Alex's job performance has consistently been quite good, the stress of the family work conflict is beginning to take its toll. Unless something changes, he expects the stress to increase in the next few years until his children get their drivers' licenses.

Alex knows that Abe Rollins went through a similar situation back when his four children were teenagers and somehow Abe survived with both marriage and career intact. Like Sonya, Abe's wife is employed in a professional position, but unlike Sonya, Kate does not travel for work. Alex wants to visit with Abe to get some ideas on how to balance the various roles required to be successful at Upland and at home. He calls Abe and sets an appointment to meet over lunch.

Alex Lewis's Role

Alex is to meet with Abe and lay out his concerns about the role requirements of his job and the role requirements of his family. He needs to listen more than talk, as Abe has a lot of insight on how to strike a successful role balance and how to prioritize roles successfully.

Abe Rollins's Role

Abe will play the role of the trusted, experienced senior account manager. He needs to come to the lunch meeting prepared to discuss all aspects of role conflict, role ambiguity, role stress, job satisfaction, and especially family work conflict. Basically Abe needs to help Alex develop a game plan to put balance back into his work and family life, and especially to ensure that Alex continues to be motivated to do a good job. The elements needed to prepare for this discussion are all in the chapter.

Abe should ask relevant questions and provide appropriate advice. Abe will do most of the talking in the role play, with Alex sharing information and listening. Alex should end up with a game plan to follow to continue his record of good performance and at the same time maintain a healthy family life.

Assignment

Work together to develop and execute the role-play dialogue surrounding the issues described. Limit the lunch meeting to 12–15 minutes. Be sure to end up with an agreed-upon, specific plan for change that will reduce Alex's role stress. In addition to changes Alex can make, some of the changes may involve recommendations to make to Rhonda later regarding Alex's territory. Assume that both Rhonda and Upland want their account managers to have high motivation and satisfaction and low role stress.

Discussion Questions

1. A salesperson's past and present performances affect his or her expectations for future performance. After experiencing several failures, many new salespeople quit their sales job within a few months because they assume that selling is not for them. What role can a sales manager play in such situations?

2. The president of Part-I-Tyme, manufacturer of salty snack foods, is dismayed over the dismal sales results for the past six months. A new product, a deluxe cookie, had been taste tested and consumers' responses were very positive. Part-I-Tyme's sales force consists of over 5,000 truck-driver distributors who have excellent reputations with their customers. Part-I-Tyme's president is convinced that the sales force enthusiastically supports the new product line, but it's obvious that something is wrong. How would you determine the nature of the problem? Can you use the model of salesperson performance in this situation?

3. Although many aptitude tests exist, their ability to predict sales performance has been weak. How do you account for this?

4. Frequently, sales managers use contests and recognition rewards to motivate the sales force. If sales managers understand salesperson performance, why is it necessary to employ these additional techniques?

5. "I want sales representatives who can stand on their own. Once they have been through training and show how to apply their knowledge, it shouldn't be necessary for me to constantly tell them how they are doing. The stars always shine; it's the other reps who need my attention." Comment on this statement. Do you agree or disagree?

6. A sales representative for Lead-In Technologies is faced with a demand from an important customer that is in direct conflict with company policies. The customer wants several product modifications with no change in price. What can the sales rep do to handle this conflict?

7. Salespeople for the Ansul Company, a manufacturer of fire prevention systems for industrial applications, have been told they will now have to sell small fire extinguishers to the retail market. The salespeople have never sold in the retail market before and have no background in this area. What role problems are likely to occur?

8. Maria Gomez-Simpson, a customer service rep with Mar-Jon Associates, spends considerable time traveling to various customer offices. As a result, she often arrives home late. Maria asked her manager if she could rearrange her Thursday work schedule to attend an evening class at a local college. Which of the following statements best reflects how to manage the conflict created by Maria's request?

a. "Since we're talking about only one night, go ahead, sign up for the course, and we'll work out the details."

b. "We need to discuss this first to see if you can be back most Thursdays in time for your course and still get the job done."

c. "We know that you get home late on certain days, but it's part of the job. Maybe you can take the course some other time."

Answer Key for Innovation 10.1

Scoring Key

1. True
2. False
3. True
4. False
5. False
6. True
7. False
8. False
9. False.
10. True.

Ethical Dilemma

Due to increasing reports of unethical behavior on the part of its sales force, top management of PrimeTech industries recently held a meeting to denounce the alleged practices. Ron Yeaple, CEO and founder of the company, said these activities are never tolerated and anyone found violating company policies was subject to immediate dismissal.

Frank Harris has been a salesperson with PrimeTech for 10 years. In the past he has performed at or above the average and received sales awards from time to time. However, his recent performance has been less than what both he and the company had hoped. Recently, Frank learned his future with the company was being reevaluated by management. He knew his performance over the next few months was critical.

Two months ago Frank began calling on a large potential new customer, First Line Manufacturing. The potential with this company was very big and it seemed receptive to Frank's company and products. Frank believed obtaining a large contract with this company would secure his job, so he provided gifts (a DVD player, an expensive bottle of wine) charging them against his expense account disguised as other expenses. However, after hearing Mr. Yeaple's remarks, he realizes that his actions have violated company policy.

Questions

1. What should Frank Harris do?
2. Can you be ethical and still violate company policy on ethical practices?
3. If you were Ron Yeaple, would you fire Frank Harris?

Mini Case

CASE 10

Ace Chemicals

Dave Parrett, sales manager for Ace Chemicals, is wrestling with the issue of how to get Kay Powers back on track. Kay has been with the company 20 years. Historically, she had been one of the company's top salespeople, but her performance has fallen off during the past three or four years.

That concerns Dave because Kay calls on some of Ace's largest accounts. She earned each of those assignments. When she joined Ace Chemicals, Kay turned heads with her performance. She secured business in companies the firm had never previously served. Customers were extremely pleased with the service she provided. Ace received more unsolicited compliments on how she serviced her accounts than on any other salesperson. Her call reports indicated she made more calls in a week than almost any other salesperson with the company, and her sales showed it. She regularly exceeded the quotas she was assigned.

All this has changed in the last few years. Kay has developed very few new accounts. Complaints from customers, while not the highest in the sales force, have shown a marked increase. Kay seems to start later and quit earlier than she used to. She makes fewer calls most weeks than most of the other salespeople. She has barely met her quota in three of the last five years and fell short of it once. Yet she is still a good enough salesperson that her annual income (salary and commissions) exceeds six figures.

Senior management is pushing to increase productivity. Several younger salespeople are eager to move into larger, more demanding accounts. Dave contemplated the future and considered his next move.

Questions

1. Attempt to discern why Kay's performance has deteriorated and offer training and assistance to help improve her performance.
2. If you were Dave Parrett, what would you do in this situation?
3. What do you with a salesperson who is no longer great?

selling environment

Sales Management

RECRUITING & SELECTION

Relationship Selling

Training & Development

Compensation

Evaluating Performance

Salesperson Motivation

Self-Management

Prospecting & Sales Call Planning

Communicating the Sales Message

Negotiating for Win-Win Solutions

Closing & Follow-up

Information

Value Creation

Ethics

Customer Relationships

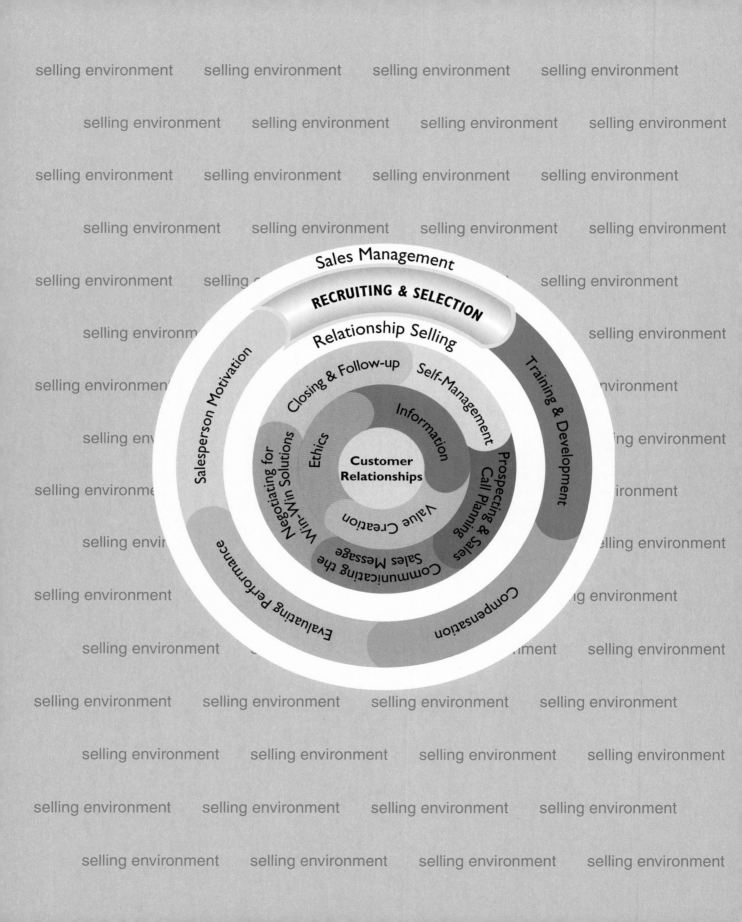

11 chapter

Recruiting and Selecting Salespeople

Learning Objectives

Perhaps more than any other function of the sales manager, successfully recruiting new salespeople into the company is critical to the long-term success of the organization. As markets expand both domestically and internationally, companies seek qualified new candidates to fill sales positions. At the same time, talented people inside the company are being recruited by competitors. Competition for talented candidates is fierce and the direct and indirect costs of poor recruiting are high. For all these reasons, recruiting and selecting salespeople has become a very important part of the sales manager's job. This chapter describes the process of recruiting new salespeople into the organization.

After reading this chapter, you should be able to

- Understand the key issues that drive the recruitment and selection of salespeople.
- Identify who is responsible for the recruitment and selection process.
- Understand a job analysis and how selection criteria are determined.
- Define the sources for new sales recruits.
- Explain the selection procedures.
- Describe salespeople's role in the selection process.

expert advice

Expert: Jean Sheehan, Manager of Technical Services Division

Company: Burns Personnel, Inc.

Business: One of the largest, highest performing privately owned staffing firms in the United States. The company's expertise ranges from the disciplines of highly specialized engineering and information technology to administration, manufacturing, light industrial, and customer service. Their service offerings include temporary, contract, temporary to direct and direct hire staffing, vendors on premise, and on-site consultants.

Education: BS Management, St. John Fisher College

What are the key criteria you look for in successful salespeople and why are these important?

When I am evaluating candidates for a new sales position I look at several key factors. First, it is important for salespeople to have good communication skills. There is a misperception that having good communication skills means being a good speaker and it is important to speak clearly and be understood. However, good communication also involves effectively listening to the customer and adjusting the responses given to the customer's statements and needs.

A second quality I look for is persistence. Salespeople must be patient and stay connected to their customers. Follow-up is critical to increasing our customers' satisfaction and getting new business. Finally, salespeople must be willing to "think outside the box" and get creative in developing solutions to customer problems. A salesperson who takes the first "no" as the final answer will not be successful. Overcoming objections and creatively dealing with customer concerns is an important skill in today's competitive environment.

What is the process for recruiting and selecting salespeople at Burns Personnel, Inc.?

At Burns Personnel we use a variety of recruiting methods in the selection process. First, the job is posted on the company Web site and job boards which generates inquiries from interested candidates. At the same time, a notice is sent out to employees and staff announcing the open position and asking them to refer interested candidates who might qualify. Once a pool of applicants has been identified, the vice president of Sales does an initial screening looking for a small, qualified (at least on paper) list of candidates to include in the interview process.

The first interview takes place over the phone. As discussed earlier, good communication skills are important and the phone interview provides an initial sense of the applicant's abilities to communicate effectively in an interactive environment. The VP of Sales or the hiring manager conducts the phone interview and, if successful, the candidate is asked to come in for a personal interview. Our interview process is fairly structured. The candidates meet with the hiring manager and team members. We want to assess the applicant's skill in dealing with questions, motivation to sell, and basic knowledge of the industry and products to determine their overall potential for sale success. The hiring manager will narrow the search and bring in the top two or three candidates for a second interview with themselves, the VP of Sales, and at least one other member of the Executive Team. While interviewing, the candidate will take a personality/behavioral assessment. Afterwards, the interview team will meet and make a final decision.

What advice would you give someone looking for a selling position?

First, meet people and never miss an opportunity to network. Find out if you or anyone you know has a contact at the company you are interested in and if they do, follow up, and make contact with that person. Second, do your research and learn as much as possible about a company before an interview. There is no second chance in an interview and it is important to be well prepared.

Third, your résumé makes the first impression and gets you in the door so it is important to build your résumé around your "sales" experience. Your résumé is a critical "sales tool" so do not use a "generic" résumé, rather, create each résumé for the specific job for which you are applying. Fourth, take the time to investigate your interests and get to know yourself. What are your selling strengths and weaknesses? Sell your strengths in an interview.

Fifth, even if you are not sure you even want to work at the company, take the interview. It never hurts to practice interviewing. You also may find out something at the interview that changes your mind. Always leave the interview on good terms. Thank the company and follow up by sending an e-mail or a card. Follow up in a timely manner on any items requested of you. Stay in appropriate contact with the company throughout the hiring process. Finally, and this is important, be creative and don't be afraid to take a risk.

Recruitment and Selection Issues

Sales managers must resolve a number of important issues when recruiting and selecting new salespeople for relationship selling. Refer to the Relationship Selling model to see where we are.

To better understand the recruiting and selection process for salespeople, refer to Exhibit 11.1. The decision process has four stages: establishing policy, analyzing the job, attracting applicants, and evaluating applicants.

The first decision concerns who is responsible for hiring new salespeople. While it is common to assign this responsibility to field sales managers, top sales executives or human resources departments play a more active role and bear more of the burden for this important function in some firms, such as Ritz-Carlton.

Regardless of who is responsible for recruiting salespeople, certain procedures should be followed to make sure they have an aptitude for the job and the potential

EXHIBIT 11.1 The Decision Process for Recruiting and Selecting Salespeople

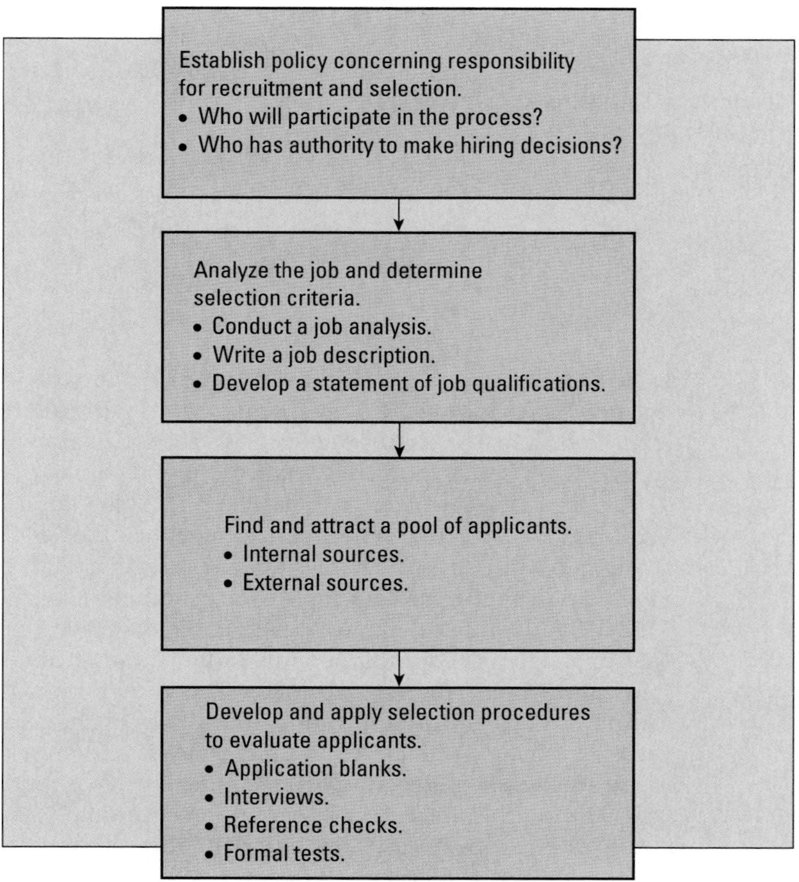

Source: *Churchill/Ford/Walker's Sales Force Management,* 9th ed., by Mark Johnston and Greg Marshall (New York: McGraw-Hill, 2009), p. 286. Reprinted by permission of the McGraw-Hill Companies.

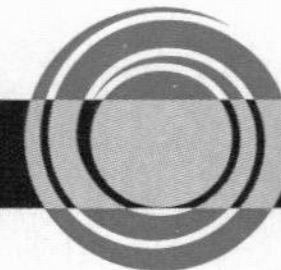

INNOVATION 11.1

The Hiring Quiz

Managers are always searching for tools that will help them make better hiring decisions. Here is a quiz that helps define the right candidate.

1. Are you in an industry with
   a. Relatively few well-known competitors and few changes in relation to new products and service (1 point)
   b. New competition entering the market and rapid changes to products and services introduced (2 points)
2. What category fits your product?
   a. Capital equipment (1 point)
   b. Consumer (2 points)
   c. Service (3 points)
3. If your product is technical in nature, what is your level of technical sales support?
   a. Strong (1 point)
   b. Average (2 points)
   c. Weak (3 points)
4. How do you market your product?
   a. Heavily (1 point)
   b. Very little (2 points)
   c. Rely on sales staff to do it (3 points)
5. Are you interested in
   a. The development of additional business within existing accounts (1 point)
   b. The management of an existing line of business within mature accounts (2 points)
   c. The promotion of a new product to prospective customers (3 points)
6. How much time can you afford to hire and train new sales staff before receiving a return on your investment?
   a. 30–90 days (1 point)
   b. 91–180 days (2 points)
   c. 181 days or more (3 points)
7. Will your sales staff work in an office where
   a. Direct supervisor is present (1 point)
   b. No direct supervisor is present (3 points)

to be successful. As discussed in Chapter 10, there do not seem to be any general characteristics that make some people better performers across all types of sales jobs. Therefore, the recruitment process should begin with a thorough analysis of the job, a job description, and a statement of the qualifications for a new hire.

The next step is to find and attract a pool of job applicants with the right qualifications. The objective is not to maximize the number of applicants but to attract a few good applicants. This is because there are high costs involved in attracting and evaluating candidates. One large industrial services firm spent more than $750,000 for want ads, employment agency fees, psychological tests, and the time sales managers spent interviewing and evaluating candidates in order to hire 50 new salespeople. And it cost another $1 million to train those new recruits.

The final stage in the hiring process is to evaluate each applicant through a review of their personal history, interviews, reference checks, and formal tests. The purpose is to determine which applicants have the traits and abilities for success. During this stage, managers must be especially careful not to violate equal employment opportunity laws and regulations. The recruiting process is complex and involves many criteria. Test your skills at hiring in Innovation 11.1 and see what kind of candidate you would choose for a sales position.

8. Will your sales staff
   a. Rely on other sales personnel to prospect and qualify potential customers (2 points)
   b. Qualify prospects themselves (0 points)
9. How much time will you spend training your new hire?
   a. More than 80 hours (1 point)
   b. 41–80 hours (2 points)
   c. 0–40 hours (3 points)
10. How much time will you spend coaching and counseling your new sales staff?
   a. More than 20 hours per week (1 point)
   b. 11–20 hours per week (2 points)
   c. 0–10 hours per week (3 points)

How to score

1. Add your total points from questions 1–10.
2. Match your point total to the corresponding point totals following.
3. Your ideal candidate will possess the characteristics indicated for the point total.

Primary characteristic of salesperson

13 points or less	Tenacity, rapport building, work standards, oral communication, ability to learn
14–18 points	Leadership, planning and organization, job motivation, presence
19–28 points	Persuasiveness, negotiation, analysis, initiative, written communication

Secondary characteristic of salesperson

13 points or less	Planning and organization, listening, job motivation, initiative, written communication
14–18 points	Analysis, tenacity, oral communication, written communication, rapport building
19–28 points	Independence, listening, oral communication, presence, planning

Source of sales recruits

13 points or less	New college graduate or hire from within
14–18 points	Hire from within or competitive hire
19–28 points	Competitive hire

Source: Walt Shedd, "Ten Steps to Top Sales Professionals," www.sellingpower.com.

Establish Responsibility

An MBA student at the authors' school was recently recruited for a sales job with a major software company. She was interviewed extensively, not only by the sales manager (her prospective supervisor) but also by higher-level executives in the firm, including a regional vice president of marketing. All this attention from top-level managers surprised the candidate. She asked, "Is it common for so many executives to be involved in recruiting new salespeople?"

The student's question raises the issue of who should have the primary responsibility for recruiting and selecting new salespeople. The way a company answers this question typically depends on the size of the sales force and the kind of selling involved. In firms with small sales forces, the recruitment and selection of new people is a primary responsibility of the top-level sales manager. In larger, multilevel sales forces, however, attracting and choosing new recruits is usually too extensive and time consuming for a single executive. Authority for recruitment and selection is commonly delegated to lower-level sales managers or staff specialists.

When a firm must be more selective in choosing new recruits with certain qualifications and abilities, a recruiting specialist may assist first-level managers in evaluating new recruits and making hiring decisions. These staff positions are usually filled by sales managers who are being groomed for higher-level executive positions.

In some firms, members of the human resources department (or outside HR specialists) instead of the sales management staff assist and advise sales managers in hiring new salespeople. This approach helps reduce duplication of effort and avoids friction between the sales and HR departments. One disadvantage is that HR specialists may not be as knowledgeable about the job to be filled and the qualifications necessary as a sales manager. Even when the HR department or outside specialist helps attract and evaluate applicants, the sales manager typically has the final say in whom to hire.

Finally, when the firm sees its sales force as a training ground for sales and marketing managers, either HR executives or other top-level managers may participate in recruiting to make sure the new hires have management potential. This was the situation in the firm that interviewed our MBA student. Although it offered her "just a sales job," company executives saw that job as a stepping-stone to management responsibilities.

Analyze the Job and Determine Selection Criteria

Research relating salespeople's personal characteristics to sales aptitude and job performance suggests there is no single set of traits and abilities sales managers can use to help them decide which recruits to hire. Different sales jobs require different activities, and people with different personality traits and abilities should be hired to fill them. The first activities in the recruitment and selection process thus should be the following:

1. Conduct a **job analysis** to determine what activities, tasks, responsibilities, and environmental influences are involved in the job to be filled.
2. Write a job description that details the findings of the job analysis.
3. Develop a statement of **job qualifications** that describe the personal traits and abilities a person should have to perform the job.

Most companies, particularly larger ones, have written job descriptions for sales positions. Unfortunately, those job descriptions are often out of date and do not accurately reflect the current scope and content of the positions. The responsibilities of a given sales job change as the customers, the firm's account management policies, the competition, and other environmental factors change. When this happens, companies need to conduct new analyses and update descriptions to reflect those changes. When firms create new sales positions new tasks also need to be identified.

Consequently, a critical first step in the hiring process is for management to make sure the job to be filled has been analyzed recently and the findings have been written out in great detail. Without a detailed, up-to-date description, the sales manager will have difficulty deciding what kind of person is needed and prospective recruits will not really know what is expected of them.

Job Analysis and Determination of Selection Criteria. In some firms, someone in sales management analyzes and describes the sales job. In other firms, the task is assigned to a job analysis specialist, who is either from the company's HR department or an outside consultant. Regardless of who is responsible, that person should collect information about each selling job's content from two sources: (1) the current occupant of the job and (2) the sales manager who supervises that person.

Current job occupants should be observed and/or interviewed to determine what they actually do. Sales managers at various levels should be asked what they think the job occupant should be doing in view of the firm's strategic sales program and account management policies. It is not uncommon for the person who analyzes a job to discover the salespeople are doing extra work that management is not aware of and slacking off on some activities management believes are important. Such misunderstandings and inaccurate role perceptions illustrate the need for accurate, detailed job descriptions.[1]

Job Descriptions. **Job descriptions** written to reflect a consensus between salespeople and their managers can serve several useful functions. In addition to guiding the firm's recruiting efforts, they can guide the design of a sales training program that will provide new salespeople with the skills to do their job effectively and improve their understanding of how the job should be done. They can also serve as standards for evaluating each salesperson's job performance, as discussed in Chapter 14.

In many companies there are a variety of sales positions. Some may not even include the word "sales" in the job title. Exhibit 11.2 presents the job descriptions for two sales positions at Dell Corporation. Note that each description spells out many of the items identified below. The two sales positions require different skills and experience. This kind of detailed job description tells both the company and the potential salesperson exactly what the expectations are before employment, which vastly increases the rep's chances of success.

Good **job descriptions** of sales jobs typically identify the following dimensions and requirements:

1. The nature of product(s) or service(s) to be sold.
2. The types of customers to be called on, including policies concerning how often calls are to be made and the personnel within customer organizations who should be contacted (e.g., buyers, purchasing agents, plant supervisors).
3. The specific tasks and responsibilities to be carried out, including planning tasks, research and information collection activities, specific selling tasks, other promotional duties, customer servicing activities, and clerical and reporting duties.
4. The relationships between the job occupant and other positions within the organization. To whom does the job occupant report? What are the salesperson's responsibilities to the immediate superior? How and under what circumstances does the salesperson interact with members of other departments, such as production or engineering?
5. The mental and physical demands of the job, including the amount of technical knowledge the salesperson should have concerning the company's products, other necessary skills, and the amount of travel involved.
6. The environmental pressures and constraints that might influence job performance, such as market trends, the strengths and weaknesses of the competition, the company's reputation among customers, and resource and supply problems.

EXHIBIT 11.2 Dell Job Descriptions

Systems Consultant III—Austin, TX

Description

Individual contributor role based in Austin/Round Rock, TX, the Systems Consultant role provides in depth technical and architectural sales expertise in enterprise opportunities. Provides leadership to ensure that the Dell enterprise solutions are comprehensive, achieve customer expectations and meet customer business needs. Builds trust with customers and owns technical side of customer relationships. Focused on delivering a positive customer experience according to Dell standards. Ensures the Dell Account Executive understands and meets customers' on-going enterprise needs. Meet or exceed quarterly enterprise sales objectives by providing technical sales consulting in a diverse set of end users computing environments. Takes a lead role on the technical side of the sale to ensure that the Dell solutions are comprehensive, achieve customer goals, and provide an outstanding customer experience. Works with our enterprise third party partners and the appropriate customer technical personnel to build relationships, and ensure Dell sales team understands the customer's on-going enterprise needs.

Qualifications

Identifies appropriate enterprise solutions to meet the full range of customer needs. Identifies cost effective and practical "solutions" to maximize Dell's opportunity while meeting customer's needs. Skillfully negotiates with others to achieve desired results/meet customer needs. Explains where enterprise products and services fit into customer's IT structure. Must have a thorough understanding of, and experience with, server, storage, layer 3 networking and enterprise software. Intermediate level of NAS and SAN storage system experience is required. Candidate must demonstrate working knowledge in Microsoft and Linux systems software, layer 3 networking, and server/storage management and IT consolidation principles. The candidate must be able to work independently, with strong written and oral communication skills. Basic selling skills and good time management skills required. A minimum of 5 years pre-sales technical work experience and IT certifications is needed. 75% travel required.

Job Outside Sales—System Consultant

Primary Location North America-US-TX-Round Rock

Schedule Full-time

Corporate Accounts—Account Executive (Dev)—Minneapolis

Description

Responsible for development and retention of named accounts in Minnesota. Develop partnership between Dell and accounts through the coordination of sales, services, technical and internal sales and support teams. Responsible for increasing account penetration, customer satisfaction, and sales growth for long term results. Develop and execute sales strategies in market/territory for growth of Dell's portfolio of products and services. Must have experience using a team and consultative selling approach while managing the entire sales cycle. Strong knowledge of technology industry products, services and sales tactics. Strong organizational planning, teamwork and customer support skills are critical to success.

(continued)

EXHIBIT 11.2 Dell Job Descriptions (concluded)

Qualifications

Candidate should have at least a 4-year college degree and 4-6 years of outside sales experience is a plus. Previous experience that includes selling high-end enterprise solutions, services, enterprise software, tape back-up solutions, SAN and/or NAS, client products and software/peripherals experience is preferable. Proven track record exceeding sales quota selling business solutions with expertise in negotiating and closing.

Job Outside Sales—Account Executive

Primary Location North America-US-Minnesota

Schedule Full-time

Determining Job Qualifications and Selection Criteria. Determining the qualifications of a prospective employee is the most difficult part of the recruitment and selection process. The sales manager, perhaps with assistance from a planning specialist, should consider the relative importance of all the personal traits and characteristics discussed previously. These include physical attributes, mental abilities and experience, and personality traits.

The problem is that nearly all these characteristics play at least some role in choosing new salespeople. No firm, for instance, would actively seek sales recruits who are unintelligent or lacking in self-confidence. At the same time, not many job candidates will possess high levels of *all* desirable characteristics. The task, then, is to decide which traits and abilities are most important for which job and which are less critical. Also, some thought should be given to trade-offs among the qualification criteria. Will a person with a deficiency in one important attribute still be considered acceptable if he or she has outstanding qualities in other areas? For example, will the firm want someone with only average verbal ability and persuasiveness if that person has a great deal of ambition and persistence?

Deciding on Selection Criteria. Simply examining the job description can assist decision makers looking for key qualifications in new salespeople. If the job requires extensive travel, for instance, management might prefer applicants who are younger, have few family responsibilities, and want to travel. Similarly, statements in the job description concerning technical knowledge and skill can help management determine what educational background and previous job experience to look for when selecting from a pool of candidates. For example, in Exhibit 11.2, the systems consultant requires extensive travel *and* work experience. Criteria like these often limit the number of candidates.

Larger firms go one step further and evaluate the personal histories of their existing salespeople to determine what traits differentiate between good and poor performers. This analysis seldom produces consistent results across different jobs and different companies. It can produce useful insight, however, when applied to a single type of sales job within a single firm. The assumption is that there may be a cause-and-effect relationship between such attributes and job performance. If new employees have attributes similar to those of people who are currently performing the job successfully, they may also be successful.[2]

Another compelling reason to analyze personal history is to validate the selection criteria the firm is using, as required by government equal employment opportunity regulations. Besides comparing the characteristics of good and poor performers in a particular job, management might also try to analyze the unique characteristics of employees who either quit or were fired. One study found that salespeople who fail often have the following traits.

1. Instability of residence.
2. Failure in business within the past two years.
3. Unexplained gaps in the person's employment record.
4. Recent divorce or marital problems.
5. Excessive personal indebtedness (for example, bills could not be paid within two years from earnings on the new job).

Based on whatever information the company deems relevant for the specific job, a written statement of job qualifications should be prepared that is specific enough to guide the selection of new salespeople. These qualifications can then be reflected in the forms and tests used in the selection process,[3] such as the interview form in Exhibit 11.3.

Find and Attract Applicants

Some firms do not actively recruit salespeople. They simply choose new employees from applicants who come to them and ask for work. Although this may be a satisfactory policy for a few well-known firms with good products, strong positions in the market, and attractive compensation policies, today's labor market makes it unworkable for most companies.

Firms that seek well-educated people for sales jobs must compete with other occupations in attracting such individuals. To make matters worse, people with no selling experience often have negative attitudes toward sales jobs. Also, people who do seek employment in sales often do not have the qualifications a firm is looking for, particularly when the job involves relatively sophisticated selling, such as technical or new-business sales. Consequently, the company may have to evaluate many applicants to find one qualified person.

This is one area where some firms are "penny wise but pound foolish." They attempt to hold down recruiting costs in hopes that a good training program can convert marginal recruits into solid sales performers. Unfortunately, several determinants of sales success are difficult or impossible to change through training or experience. Therefore, spending the money and effort to find well-qualified candidates can be a profitable investment. In certain industries and when environmental conditions make the job market tight, finding enough qualified individuals can be a challenge. For example, the life insurance industry reports that it must interview 60 to 120 people to find one good hire.[4]

In view of the difficulties in attracting qualified people to fill sales positions, a well-planned and well-implemented recruiting effort is usually a crucial part of the firm's hiring program. The primary objective of the recruiting process should not be to maximize the total number of job applicants. Too many recruits can overload the selection process, forcing managers to use less thorough screening and evaluation procedures. Intel, for example, receives thousands of applications every day. Besides, numbers do not ensure quality. The focus should be on finding a few good recruits.

EXHIBIT 11.3 Applicant Interview Form

Business Division
Applicant Interview Form

Applicant name: ______________________ Date: ____________

Interview with: Time:

1. ______________________ ____________
2. ______________________ ____________
3. ______________________ ____________
4. ______________________ ____________

Directions: Check square that most correctly reflects characteristics applicable to candidate. An outstanding candidate would score 95 to 100.

	1	2	3	4	5
General appearance					
1. Neatness, dress					
2. Business image					
Impressions					
3. Positive mannerisms					
4. Speech, expressions					
5. Outgoing personality					
6. Positive attitude					
Potential sales ability					
7. Persuasive communication					
8. Aggressiveness					
9. Sell and manage large accounts					
10. Make executive calls					
11. Organize and manage a territory					
12. Work with others					
13. Successful prior experience					
14. Potential for career growth					
Maturity					
15. General intelligence, common sense					
16. Self-confidence					
17. Self-motivation, ambition					
18. Composure, stability					
19. Adaptability					
20. Sense of ethics					

General comments: ______________________

Overall rating (total score): ____________

Would you recommend this candidate for the position? ____________

Why or why not? ______________________

Source: *Churchill/Ford/Walker's Sales Force Management*, 9th ed., by Mark Johnston and Greg Marshall (New York: McGraw-Hill, 2009), p. 294. Reprinted by permission of the McGraw-Hill Companies.

Therefore, recruiting should be the first step in the selection process. Self-selection by prospective employees is the most efficient means of selection, so the recruiting effort should discourage unqualified people from applying. For example, many companies recruit via the Internet. Companies like Cisco Systems and IBM have a screening procedure by which candidates can provide certain key pieces of data about themselves and the company will search its job openings to look for a match.

Recruiting communications should point out both the attractive and unattractive aspects of the job to be filled, spell out the qualifications, and state the likely compensation. This will encourage only qualified and interested people to apply for the job. Also, recruiting efforts should focus only on sources where fully qualified applicants are likely to be found.

Internal Sources. Sales managers go to a number of places to find recruits or leads on potential recruits. **Internal sources** are people already employed by the firm, while external sources include people in other firms (who are often identified and referred by current members of the sales force), advertisements, recruiting agencies, educational institutions, and the Internet.

Different sources are likely to produce candidates with somewhat different backgrounds and characteristics. Therefore, while most firms seek recruits from more than one source, recruiting should concentrate on sources that are most likely to produce the kinds of people needed. When the job involves technical selling that requires substantial product knowledge and industry experience, firms focus more heavily on employees in other departments within the company and on personal referrals of people working for other firms in the industry.[5]

People in nonsales departments within the firm, such as manufacturing, customer service, engineering, or the office staff, sometimes have latent sales talent and are a common source of sales recruits. Surveys suggest that more than half of U.S. manufacturers hire at least some of their salespeople from other internal departments.

Recruiting current company employees for the sales force has distinct advantages.

1. Company employees have established performance records, and they are more of a known quantity than outsiders.
2. Recruits from inside the firm should require less orientation and training because they are already familiar with the company's products, policies, and operations.
3. Recruiting from within can bolster company morale, as employees become aware that opportunities for advancement are available outside of their own department or division.

To facilitate successful internal recruiting, the company's human resources department should always be kept abreast of sales staff needs. Because HR staffers are familiar with the qualifications of all employees and continuously evaluate their performance, they are in the best position to identify people with the right attributes to fill available sales jobs.

Internal recruiting has some limitations. People in nonsales departments seldom have much selling experience. Also, it can cause animosity within the firm if supervisors of other departments think their best employees are being pirated by the sales force.

External Sources. Although it is a good idea to start with internal sources when recruiting new salespeople, most of the time there will not be enough qualified internal candidates to meet the needs of a firm's sales force. As a result, the vast majority of companies must expand the search to include **external sources** like people from other firms, ads, professional recruiting agencies, educational institutions, and the Internet.

All of the recruiting issues faced by sales managers are magnified as companies expand globally and seek to hire salespeople in new international markets. Cultural differences, language barriers, and legal restrictions create additional concerns about hiring the right people for the sales position. The key is for a company to do its homework and research each new market before deciding to enter it. For example, in many European countries it is much more difficult to terminate an employee than in the United States, so it's even more crucial to hire the right people. It is important for a company to understand the legal requirements of hiring new salespeople.

Referral of people from other firms. In addition to being potential sales employees themselves, company personnel can provide management with leads to potential recruits from outside the firm. Current salespeople are in a good position to provide leads to new recruits. They know the requirements of the job, they often have contacts with other salespeople who may be willing to change jobs, and they can do much to help "sell" an available job to potential recruits. Consequently, many sales managers make sure their salespeople are aware of the company's recruiting needs. Some companies offer bonuses as incentives for their salespeople to recruit new prospects. Referrals from current employees must be handled tactfully to avoid hard feelings if the applicant is rejected later.

Customers can also be a source of sales recruits. Sometimes a customer's employees have the kinds of knowledge that make them attractive as prospective salespeople. For instance, department store employees can make good salespeople for the wholesalers or manufacturers who supply the store because they are familiar with the product and the procedures of store buyers. Cosmetics companies such as Estée Lauder and L'Oreal recruit from the ranks of department store personnel.

Customers with whom a firm has good relations may also provide leads concerning potential recruits who are working for other firms, particularly competitors. Purchasing agents know what impresses them in a salesperson, they are familiar with the abilities of the sales reps who call on them, and they are sometimes aware when a sales rep is interested in changing jobs.

The question of whether a firm should recruit salespeople from its competitors is controversial, however. Such people are knowledgeable about the industry from their experience. They may also bring along some of their current customers when they switch companies. This does not happen frequently, however, since customers are usually more loyal to a supplier than to the individual who represents that supplier.

On the other hand, it can be difficult to get salespeople who have worked for a competing firm to unlearn old practices and conform to their new employer's account management policies. Also, some managers think recruiting a competitor's personnel is unethical. They believe it is unfair for firm B to recruit actively someone from firm A after A has spent the money to hire and train that person. It would also be unfair for that person to divulge A's company secrets to B. Consequently, some firms refuse to recruit their competitor's salespeople, although whether such policies are due to high ethical standards, the expense of retraining, or fear of possible retaliation is open to question. Leadership 11.2 highlights the pros and cons of hiring salespeople from the competition.

Leadership 11.2

Pros and Cons of Hiring Salespeople from Competitors

Competitors are often used as a source for new salespeople. In considering competitor salespeople for a new position, it is important to understand the pros and cons. Let's take a closer look at the advantages and disadvantages.

Pros

Reduce the learning curve. Competitor salespeople take less time to get up to speed and selling for the company. For example, they already know the industry and are frequently familiar with the company's products having sold against them in the past.

External motivator. There is nothing like an external competitor to get your existing salespeople motivated. Quite often hiring salespeople from competitors motivates your current salespeople to demonstrate they are better than the new hire.

Knowledge base. Someone who knows the customers, products, and market environment has a distinct advantage over an "outsider." The more experienced a competitor's salesperson, the less they need to learn and the more value they can add to the company immediately. In addition, much of the knowledge experienced salespeople bring to the table is not easily trained; rather, it is the result of spending time in the field.

Cons

Square peg in round hole. The single biggest concern in hiring salespeople from competitors is assimilating those individuals into the company culture and getting them to learn the policies and procedures. It can be difficult for a salesperson trained in one sales culture to "unlearn" what they currently know and successfully adapt to a new culture. The real problem occurs when those salespeople interact with customers, the resulting culture class can spill over into the customer relationship.

Customer trust. It is unsettling for a customer who has seen a salesperson marketing one company's products suddenly switch companies and argue that these new products do a better job of meeting the customer's needs. If it is not handled properly customers question the honesty of the salesperson. By extension they also may question the honesty of the company. Again, these types of circumstances can do significant harm to the customer relationship.

Short-term versus long-term strategy. Hiring competitor salespeople does offer some short-term benefits (lower training costs, reduced learning curve) but at a price. There is evidence to suggest these salespeople are less loyal and have the potential to create greater cultural conflict that younger, less experience salespeople trained in the company culture, policies and procedures. The question becomes, "does the company want to take a long- or short-term approach to building the sales force?" Younger, less experienced salespeople will take longer to become profitable in the field but may be a better investment long term.

Advertisements. A less selective way to attract job applicants is to advertise the position. When a technically qualified or experienced person is needed, an ad might be placed in an industry trade or technical journal. More commonly, ads are placed in the personnel or marketplace sections of local newspapers to attract applicants for less demanding sales jobs that don't require special qualifications. A well-written ad can be very effective for attracting applicants—though that is not necessarily a good thing. When a firm's ads attract large numbers of applicants who are unqualified or only marginally interested, the firm must engage in costly screening to separate the wheat from the chaff.[6]

If a firm does use newspaper ads in recruiting, it must decide how much information about the job to include in its ads. Many sales managers argue that *open ads,* which disclose the firm's name, product to be sold, compensation, and specific job duties, generate a more select pool of high-quality applicants, lower selection costs, and decreased turnover rates than ads without such information. Open ads also avoid any ethical questions concerning possible deception.

However, for less attractive, high-turnover sales jobs like door-to-door selling, some sales managers prefer *blind ads,* which carry only minimal information—sometimes only a phone number. These maximize the number of applicants and give the manager an opportunity to explain the attractive features of the job in a personal meeting with the applicant.[7]

Professional recruiting agencies. While employment agencies are sometimes used to find recruits, often for more routine sales jobs like retail sales, relationship selling usually requires more sophisticated outside professionals. These agencies specialize in finding applicants for more demanding sales jobs. When the company clearly understands the demands of the job and knows the kind of candidates it is looking for, these organizations can be helpful.

Some sales managers have had unsatisfactory experiences with employment agencies. That is often the company's fault for not understanding the agency's role and not providing sufficient information about the kinds of recruits it is seeking. When a firm carefully selects an agency with a good reputation, establishes a long-term relationship, and provides detailed descriptions of job qualifications, the agency can perform a valuable service. It locates and screens job applicants and reduces the amount of time and effort the company's sales managers must devote to recruiting.

Educational institutions. College and university placement offices are a common source of recruits for firms that require salespeople with high intelligence or technical backgrounds. Most educational institutions allocate resources to "career management" departments that help graduates develop their careers. Educational institutions are an effective source when the sales job is viewed as a first step toward a career in management. Good grades are at least some evidence the person can think logically, budget time efficiently, and communicate reasonably well.

But college graduates generally have less selling experience and are likely to require extensive orientation and training in the basics of salesmanship. Also, college-educated sales recruits tend to "job hop" unless their jobs are challenging and promotions are rapid. One insurance company stopped recruiting college graduates when it found that they did not stick around very long. Such early turnover is sometimes more the fault of the company than of the recruits. When recruiters paint an unrealistic picture of the demands and rewards of the job, or when they recruit people who are overqualified, high turnover is often the result.[8]

Junior colleges and vocational schools are another source of sales recruits that has expanded rapidly in recent years. Many such schools have programs explicitly designed to prepare people for selling careers. Firms that recruit from such programs do not have to contend with the negative attitudes toward selling they sometimes encounter in four-year college graduates.

The Internet. Increasingly companies are seeking applications over the Internet. Indeed, as Exhibit 11.2 shows, companies like Dell are posting jobs and requesting candidates to submit their applications online. Younger candidates are as comfortable submitting applications over the Internet as they are filling them out on paper. In high-tech industries, the Internet application process demonstrates a comfort level with technology. Finally, by targeting the Internet application to specific job postings, the company can direct the information to the right people very efficiently. For example, Internet applications to Dell include a unique job reference and number so that the information can be sent to the right people at a specific geographic location.

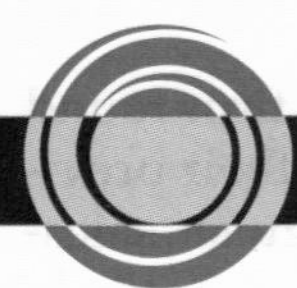

INNOVATION 11.3

Personal Interviews: An Important Test for Selecting Salespeople

Personal interviews are both the most commonly used method of selecting salespeople and the one sales managers consider most helpful. But assessments of evaluations based on personal interviews across a variety of occupations suggest they are disappointing predictors of future job performance. One analysis found that evaluations based on interviews have a low correlation with candidates' subsequent performance. Other research offers a more favorable view of the personal interviewing process and suggests that interviews are more useful when several different people interview the candidate.

Sales managers often take a more pragmatic view. One regional sales manager focuses on the candidate's *presentation* and suggests, "See how prepared they are. Do they bring visual aids or give interesting anecdotes to set themselves apart?" *Personality* can also be assessed in the personal interview. A technology sale executive looks for candidates willing to take risks and tells of an applicant who was doing well until the critical Q&A time. The applicant's questions focused entirely on benefits and safety nets. The executive noted that salespeople overly concerned with security demonstrate a red flag that they're not going to be out there putting it all on the line.

Finally, experience is valued by managers. Many companies seek a match between the applicant's cultural orientation and the company's own culture. Also, managers ask open-ended questions to get candidates thinking on their feet.

It is clear the sales manager should play an active role in interviewing prospective salespeople. The interview should seek to draw out a candidate's basic skills, such as product knowledge, as well as presentation and oral communication skills. It is also important to note that while interviews are important, they work best when used with other assessment tools that provide additional insights on the individual. One metaphor of the job candidate is that he or she is like an iceberg, with only 10 percent of the individual visible during a standard interview. Things like education and skill sets are easier to evaluate, however, critical skills like problem solving and decision making represent the 90 percent that is hidden making it more difficult to assess but more important to consider.

Techniques like these can help assess a candidate's character and selling skills, but they should be only one part of the interview. Sometimes sales managers become so obsessed with finding the "one best way" to assess candidates that they allow interviewing gimmicks to get in the way of real communication. After all, another purpose of job interviews is to provide candidates with information about the job and company so they will be interested in taking the job. Gimmicky interviewing techniques may cause the applicant to lose interest in working for the firm.

Regardless of what interviewing techniques are used, more managers rely on interviews than any other selection tool to evaluate sales candidates. Yet there is evidence that evaluations based on personal interviews are among the least valid predictors of job performance. Does this mean many firms are doing a less than optimal job of evaluating and selecting new salespeople? Are there ways to improve the accuracy of impressions gained from interviews? These questions are explored in Innovation 11.3.

Requirements for interviews and applications. Because it is illegal to discriminate in hiring on the basis of race, sex, religion, age, or national origin, a firm should not ask for such information on its job application forms or during personal interviews. It is wise to avoid all questions in any way related to such factors. Then there will be no question in the applicant's mind about whether the hiring decision was biased or unfair. This is easier said than done, however, because some innocent questions can be viewed as attempts to gain information that might be used to discriminate against a candidate. Exhibit 11.4 offers guidelines

EXHIBIT 11.4 Illegal or Sensitive Questions to Eliminate from Employment Applications and Interviews

Nationality and Race

Comments or questions relating to the race, color, national origin, or descent of the applicant—or his or her spouse—must be avoided. Applicants should not be asked to supply a photo of themselves when applying for a job. If proficiency in another language is an important part of the job, the applicant can be asked to demonstrate that proficiency but cannot be asked whether it is his or her native language. Applicants may be asked if they are U.S. citizens but not whether they—or their parents or spouse—are naturalized or native-born Americans. Applicants who are not citizens may be asked whether they have the legal right to remain and work in the United States.

Religion

Applicants should not be asked about their religious beliefs or whether the company's workweek or the job schedule would interfere with their religious convictions.

Sex and Marital Status

Except for jobs where sex is clearly related to job performance—as in a TV commercial role—the applicant's sex should not enter the hiring discussion. Applicants should not be asked about their marital status, whether or not their spouse works, or even whom the prospective employer should notify in an emergency. A woman should not be asked whether she would like to be addressed as Mrs., Miss, or Ms. Applicants should not be asked any questions about their children, baby-sitting arrangements, contraceptive practices, or planned family size.

Age

Applicants may be asked whether they are minors or age 70 or over, because special laws govern the employment of such people. With those exceptions, however, applicants should not be asked their age or date of birth.

Physical Characteristics, Disabilities, Handicaps, and Health Problems

In view of the Americans with Disabilities Act, all such questions are best avoided. However, once an employer has described the job, applicants can be asked whether they have any physical or mental condition that would limit their ability to perform the job.

Height and Weight

While not illegal, such questions are sensitive since they may provide a basis for discrimination against females or Americans of Asian or Spanish descent.

Bankruptcy or Garnishments

The bankruptcy code prohibits discrimination against individuals who have filed bankruptcy.

Arrests and Convictions

Questions about past arrests are barred. Applicants can be asked about past convictions, but the employer should include a statement that the nature and circumstances of the conviction will be considered.

Source: Adapted from C. David Shepherd and James C. Heartfield, "Discrimination Issues in the Selection of Salespeople: A Review and Managerial Suggestions," from *Journal of Personal Selling & Sales Management*, Fall 1991, p. 71. Copyright © 1998 Pi Sigma Epsilon, Inc. Reprinted with permission of M. E. Sharpe, Inc.

concerning the kinds of illegal or sensitive questions managers should avoid when conducting employment interviews and designing application forms.

References. If an applicant passes the face-to-face interview, a reference check is often the next step. Some sales managers question the value of references because "they always say nice things." However, with a little resourcefulness, reference checks can be a valuable selection tool.

Checking references can ensure the accuracy of factual data about the applicant. It is naive to assume that everything a candidate writes on a résumé or application form is true. Facts about previous job experience and college degrees should be checked. The discovery of false data on a candidate's application raises a question about basic honesty as well as about what the candidate is trying to hide.

References can supply additional information and opinions about a prospect's aptitude and past job performance. Calling a number of references and probing them in depth can be time consuming and costly, but it can also produce worthwhile information and protect against expensive hiring mistakes.[14]

Psychological Tests. A final set of selection tools used by many firms consists of tests aimed at measuring an applicant's mental abilities and personality traits. The most common tests are intelligence, aptitude, and personality tests. Within each category, there are a variety of different tests used by different companies.

Intelligence tests. Intelligence tests are useful for determining whether an applicant has sufficient mental ability to perform a job successfully. Sales managers tend to believe these are the most useful tests for selecting salespeople. General intelligence tests are designed to measure overall mental abilities by examining how well the applicant comprehends, reasons, and learns. The Wonderlic Personnel Test is a common general intelligence test. It is popular because it is short; it consists of 50 items and requires only about 12 minutes to complete.

When the job to be filled requires special competence in one or a few areas of mental ability, a specialized intelligence test might be used to evaluate candidates. Tests are available for measuring such things as speed of learning, number facility, memory, logical reasoning, and verbal ability.

Aptitude tests. Aptitude tests are designed to determine whether an applicant has an interest in, or the ability to perform, certain tasks and activities. For example, the Strong Interest Inventory asks respondents to indicate whether they like or dislike a variety of situations and activities. This can determine whether applicants' interests are similar to those of people who are successful in a variety of different occupations, including selling. Other tests measure abilities, such as mechanical or mathematical aptitude, that might be related to success in particular selling jobs.

One problem with at least some aptitude tests is that instead of measuring a person's native abilities, they measure his or her current skill level at certain tasks. At least some skills needed for successful selling can be taught, or improved, through a well-designed training program. Rejecting applicants because they currently do not have the necessary skills can mean losing people who could be trained to be successful salespeople.

Personality tests. Many general personality tests evaluate an individual on numerous traits. The Myers Briggs Personality Type, for instance, measures 16 traits such as extroversion, sensing, thinking, and judging. Such tests, however, contain many questions, require substantial time to complete, and gather information about some traits that may be irrelevant for evaluating future salespeople.

More limited personality tests have been developed in recent years that concentrate on only a few traits thought to be directly relevant to a person's future success in sales.[15] The Multiple Personal Inventory, for example, uses a small number of "forced-choice" questions to measure the strength of two personality traits: empathy with other people and ego drive.

Concerns about the use of tests. During the 1950s and early 1960s, tests—particularly general intelligence and sales aptitude tests—were widely used as selection tools for evaluating potential salespeople. However, due to legal concerns and restrictions posed by civil rights legislation and equal opportunity hiring practices, use of these tests was cut back until recently. Current evidence suggesting that properly designed and administered tests are a valid selection tool has spurred an increase in their popularity.[16]

Despite the empirical evidence, however, managers continue to be wary of tests, and many firms do not use them. There are a number of reasons for these negative attitudes. For one thing, despite the evidence that tests are relatively accurate, some managers continue to doubt their validity for predicting the success of salespeople in their specific firm. No mental abilities or personality traits have been found to relate to performance across a variety of selling jobs in different firms. Thus, specific tests that measure such abilities and traits may be valid for selecting salespeople for some jobs but invalid for others.

Also, tests for measuring specific abilities and characteristics do not always produce consistent scores. Some commercial tests have not been developed using the most scientific measurement procedures, so their reliability and validity are questionable. Even when a firm believes a particular trait, such as empathy or sociability, is related to job performance, there is still a question about which test should be used to measure that trait.

A related concern, particularly in the case of personality tests, is that some creative and talented people may be rejected simply because their personalities do not conform to the test norms. Many sales jobs require creative people, especially when they are being groomed for future management responsibilities. Yet these people seldom fit an average personality profile because the "average" person is not very creative.

Another concern about testing involves the reactions of the subjects. A reasonably intelligent, test-wise person can fudge the results of many tests by giving answers he or she thinks management wants rather than answers that reflect the applicant's feelings or behavior. Also, many prospective employees view extensive testing as a burden and perhaps an invasion of privacy. Therefore, some managers fear that requiring a large battery of tests may turn off candidates and reduce their likelihood of accepting a job with the firm.

Finally, any test that discriminates between people of different races or sexes is illegal. Some firms have abandoned the use of tests rather than risk getting into trouble with the government. Exhibit 11.5 outlines some guidelines for the appropriate use of tests.

Salespeople's Role in Recruitment

Our discussion has focused on managers' role in the recruitment and selection process. However, salespeople also have responsibility in this process. For both the company and the prospective salesperson, decisions about employment have significant long-term effects. In many respects the candidate's role is even more important since decisions here influence his or her career and income potential. Prospective salespeople have two tasks in this process.

EXHIBIT 11.5 Guidelines for Using Tests

1. *Test scores should be a single input in the selection decision.* Managers should not rely on them to do the work of other parts of the selection process, such as interviewing and checking references. Candidates should not be eliminated solely on the basis of test scores.
2. *Applicants should be tested only on those abilities and traits that management, on the basis of a thorough job analysis, has determined to be relevant for the specific job.* Broad tests that evaluate a large number of traits not relevant to a specific job are probably inappropriate.
3. *When possible, tests with built-in "internal consistency checks" should be used.* Then the person who analyzes the test results can determine whether the applicant responded honestly or was faking some answers. Many tests ask similar questions with slightly different wording several times throughout the test. If respondents are answering honestly, they should always give the same response to similar questions.
4. *A firm should conduct empirical studies to ensure the tests are valid for predicting an applicant's future performance in the job.* Hard evidence of test validity is particularly important in view of the government's equal employment opportunity requirements.

The first task is to determine whether or not selling is the best career choice and if it is, what kind of sales position is best for them. There is no point in seeking a sales career if your skills and career goals are directed at another profession. In addition, there are many different careers in relationship selling. Choosing the right one can go a long way toward giving an individual the best chance for success. There are a number of career assessment tools available and many schools provide career assessment instruments in their career management office. Companies like Career Leader offer standardized career assessment tests that offer tremendous insights into your personality and the types of careers for which you have the highest probability of success.

The second task is preparing for a successful interview. Amazingly, many people enter an interview without a really good understanding of the company or the job. Prospective salespeople (and for that matter, anyone interviewing for a job) have the responsibility to research the company and learn about the job and industry in which the company operates. Salespeople recruited from competing firms will already know the industry and probably a lot about the company as well, but it is always helpful to study the company and the specifics of the position. Remember, interviewing is your most important sales job because you are selling yourself.

Summary

This chapter reviewed the recruitment and selection of new salespeople. The issues discussed ranged from who is responsible for these tasks to the impact on selection procedures of federal legislation barring job discrimination.

Two factors are primary in determining who is responsible for recruiting and selecting salespeople: (1) the size of the sales force and (2) the kind of selling involved. In general, the smaller the sales force, the more sophisticated the selling task. The more the sales force is used as a training ground for marketing and sales managers, the more likely it is that higher-level people, including the sales manager, will be directly involved in recruitment and selection.

After responsibility is allocated, recruitment and selection is a three-step process: (1) job analysis and description, (2) recruitment of a pool of applicants, and (3) selection of the best applicants from the available pool.

The job analysis and description phase includes a detailed examination of the job to determine what activities, tasks, responsibilities, and environmental influences are involved. This analysis may be conducted by someone in the sales management ranks or by a job analysis specialist. That person must prepare a job description that details the findings of the job analysis. The job description is used to develop a statement of job qualifications, which describes the personal traits and abilities an employee should have to perform the tasks involved.

The pool of recruits can come from a number of sources, including (1) people within the company, (2) people in other firms, (3) advertisements, (4) recruiting agencies, (5) educational institutions, and (6) the Internet. Each source has its own advantages and disadvantages. Some, such as ads, typically produce a large pool. The key question for the sales manager is which source or combination of sources is likely to produce the largest pool of good, qualified recruits.

Once the qualifications necessary to fill a job have been determined and applicants have been recruited, the final task is to determine which applicant best meets the qualifications and has the greatest aptitude for the job. To make this determination, most firms use some or all of the following tools and procedures: (1) applications, (2) face-to-face interviews, (3) reference checks, and (4) intelligence, aptitude, and personality tests. Although most employers find the interview and then the application most helpful, each device seems to perform some functions better than the others do. This may explain why most firms use a combination of selection tools.

Salespeople also play an important role in the recruiting and selection process. First, they should know what career and job are best suited to meet their own personal goals and objectives. Second, a candidate should prepare for an interview by learning as much as possible about the industry and company.

Key Terms

job analysis
job qualifications
job description
internal sources
external sources
selection procedures

Role Play

Before You Begin

Before getting started, please go to the appendix of Chapter 1 to review the profiles of the characters involved in this role play as well as the tips on preparing a role play. This particular role play requires that you be familiar with the Chapter 2 role play.

Characters Involved

Rhonda Reed

Another student in the class, who will role play himself or herself as a job candidate for the vacant Territory 106 in Rhonda's district at Upland Company.

Setting the Stage

Back in the role play in Chapter 2, new hire Bonnie Cairns met with district manager Rhonda Reed to prepare for doing some campus recruiting at Stellar College, which is Bonnie's alma mater. his was necessary because Territory 106 is currently vacant. Rocky Lane, who was the account manager in Territory 106 for 15 months, left a few weeks ago because he came to the conclusion that sales was not the right career track for him. Since then, Rhonda has corresponded with Rocky's most important customers to determine what needs to be done while the territory is vacant. Despite Rocky's decision to leave sales, the customers have told Rhonda that they were mostly happy with Rocky and Upland's service. Rhonda is relieved that the new person hired for Territory 106 will not be inheriting a mess.

The campus interviews Rhonda and Bonnie conducted at Stellar College went very well, and Rhonda has a short list of seven candidates she wants to visit within a more formal setting. Below is the general process Upland follows when recruiting from colleges and universities.

1. The district manager (possibly accompanied by an account manager) gets on the list to conduct brief (15–20 minute) informational interviews with students on campus.
2. Top candidates from the campus visit are called back and invited to interview with the district manager in a more formal setting.
3. Remaining finalists are assigned to spend a "typical day" working with an Upland Company account manager. At the end of the day, the district manager and account manager take the candidate to dinner to debrief the experience and determine if the candidate still holds a strong interest in pursuing a position with Upland.
4. A final interview is then conducted. Each remaining candidate is asked to participate in an impromptu role play sales call on a client.
5. A hiring decision is made, references are checked, and an offer is made contingent on the candidate passing a physical examination.

With regard to the Territory 106 position, Rhonda is at stage 2 of the process and needs to conduct the first in-depth interview with each of the seven candidates who emerged from the campus visit. An appointment has been set for one candidate.

Rhonda Reed's Role

Before the interview, Rhonda must analyze the job and determine the selection criteria. To do this, follow the process outlined in the chapter. You may exercise some leeway in developing the content for this assignment, but be sure the various criteria seem to be a good fit for sales positions such as those at Upland. Prepare a one- or two-page typed summary of this information. Rhonda will need to review the candidate's résumé again prior to the interview and develop some questions for a structured job interview. She will want to ask good questions to determine whether or not to keep this candidate in the finalist pool. Remember to use good active listening skills and let the candidate do much of the talking.

Job Candidate's Role

The other student involved in this role play will play himself or herself as the actual job candidate. Develop a one- or two-page résumé for yourself targeted toward an account manager job at Upland Company. If your actual résumé does not qualify you for the position, you can fictionalize your qualifications for purposes of this role play. Also, assume you are about to graduate and could start the job in the next month or so. Rhonda can share with you in advance the job description and other relevant information that a candidate would likely have before arriving at an interview. Prepare for the interview by coming up with some good questions to ask that will help you decide whether you want to pursue the position further. Use good active listening skills during the interview.

Assignment

Work together to develop and execute the role play of the job interview. Although interviews of this type are usually 45–60 minutes, here do a shortened version of about 15 minutes. At the end of the interview, leave it that the candidate remains interested and Rhonda will call him or her after completing the other first-round interviews (probably within the next week).

Discussion Questions

1. The sales manager for one of the nation's largest producers of consumer goods has identified eight factors that appear to be related to effective performance. The manager of human resources, who is concerned about high turnover rates among the sales force, would like to use this information to improve the company's recruiting and hiring process. The key factors are

Setting priorities
Initiative and follow-through
Working effectively with others
Creativity and innovation
Thinking and problem solving
Leadership
Communication
Technical mastery

How could these factors become part of the company's recruiting and hiring process? How would you define these factors and determine if applicants for sales positions possess them?

2. In a recent discussion on the use of the Internet to generate applications, the following quote was made.

"The Internet doesn't care whom you know, what kind of suit you're wearing, or whether you have a firm handshake. Salespeople looking for a job may soon have to face their toughest interview yet—with a computer." Do you agree or disagree? Why?

3. What are the advantages of using the Internet to conduct preliminary job interviews?

What problems is a company that uses computer-aided interviewing likely to encounter?

4. College recruiters were discussing some of the students they had interviewed one day. One interviewer described an applicant with excellent credentials as follows: "She looked too feminine, like she would need someone to take care of her, and she was not all that serious about a sales job with us." When asked to explain her comments, the interviewer said, "Under her jacket she wore a flowery blouse with little flowing sleeves and a lace collar." The other recruiter countered, "What do a flowery blouse, flowing sleeves, and a lace collar have to do with performance?" Comment.

Ethical Dilemma

Craig McMillan faced a difficult choice. His company, Cutting Edge Logistics, had experienced significant growth in the last five years, and as vice president of sales he had been one of the key people in watching the company grow from just under $100 million to over $500 million in sales. Based in Chicago, the company had hired experienced salespeople from competitors to help grow quickly and had used generous financial packages to keep them motivated and loyal.

However, as McMillan reviewed the sales for the last four quarters, he noticed a disturbing trend. Many of these salespeople were older and performance had begun to drop off. He knew he needed to hire new salespeople, but he was unsure if he should use the old model (experienced salespeople from competitors) or a new model of hiring less-experienced salespeople fresh out of college who could communicate with younger buyers and decision makers at the client companies. The old model had been hugely successful and he was afraid that a new one would alienate salespeople who had been with the company for years. McMillan was afraid that changing the hiring model could destroy morale, yet he knew the sales force needed greater diversity.

Question

1. Craig McMillan has called you for advice. What would you tell him?

Mini Case

CASE 11

Right Times Uniform

Steven Zhang, regional director of sales for Right Times Uniform Company, is reviewing the résumés and applications and his own notes on three job candidates he interviewed for a vacant sales position in the Salt Lake City area. In a few minutes, Steven will meet with Peggy Phillips, regional sales trainer, and Tony Brooks, district sales manager, to choose whom to hire for the vacancy in Tony's district.

Right Times Uniform provides uniforms to a variety of businesses throughout the country. The professional-looking uniforms allow the businesses' employees to present a consistent, professional appearance to their customers. Like other companies in this industry, Right Times Uniform provides its customers' employees enough uniforms to use for an entire week. At the end of the week, a Right Times Uniform customer service driver picks up the dirty uniforms and leaves clean ones for all employees for the next week.

The sales process for Right Times involves a salesperson visiting a prospect, determining if the prospect is a candidate for Right Times' services, and selling that prospect on the advantages of using Right Times Uniforms. Whether or not a company is a prospect for Right Times depends on the number of employees it has and the importance of their presenting a professional image to the public. The range of customers Right Times Uniforms serves is vast, from Joe's Mechanic Shop with five employees all the way to some of the nicest downtown hotels with over 200 employees.

STEVEN: "Let's talk about our final three candidates for this position. I have an application, résumé, and my interview notes for David, Kathy, and Tim. Do we have any more information on these three people?"

TONY: "No, we don't. We all have the same information. One thing you and Peggy may not know is how these people became aware of this job opening. David is the cousin of Richard, one of the reps in my district working down in Provo. Kathy saw our ad in the local newspaper and Tim found out about the opening from our Web site. The local newspaper and our company Web site are the only places where we published the job opening."

STEVEN: "I'm worried about Tim as a potential employee. He comes from New Orleans, where a high percentage of the population is Catholic. If he's Catholic, how will he fit into our community here in Salt Lake?"

PEGGY: "I asked him his religion. He looked sort of uncomfortable about the question but said he has lived in several places around the country and he didn't see any special problems with fitting in here."

TONY: "Tim is not the one I'm concerned about. David is the one who indicated on his application that he was convicted of a felony. I asked him and he said there was a DUI on his record from 10 years ago, when he was 20 years old. Richard never said anything about this when he recommended David. Evidently David learned his lesson because he finished college and has several years of good sales experience with an office supplies company. However, do we want a felon on our payroll?"

STEVEN: "I think David's record and his lack of a repeat incidence in the last 10 years speak for themselves. What about Kathy?"

PEGGY: "Did you notice that engagement ring on Kathy's finger? She's obviously in the middle of a very big life change and likely will be distracted by that for some time. I asked her when the wedding is and she said in six months. Her fiancé is a software engineer who may or may not be staying in Utah for the long term. His family is in Seattle and we all know there are plenty of job opportunities for people in his line of work there. Plus, Kathy's likely to want to have children soon. I asked her about those plans. She hesitated but finally said that while they want to have children, they haven't set a deadline for that yet. However, she's 33 years old and the clock is ticking. I'm guessing she'll be out on maternity leave sooner rather than later."

STEVEN: "We have a lot to consider. What do you say we look at their sales experience and see if we can come to some conclusion?"

With that comment, the conversation steered toward the sales experience of the three candidates and their potential to perform the job at hand. After a discussion of about 30 minutes, a decision on whom to offer the job to was made and the meeting ended. One last decision made by the group was that if the person getting the offer didn't take the job, they would try to get another pool of candidates.

Questions

1. Analyze the recruitment and selection process used by Right Times Uniform Company. What was the source of this pool of candidates? What changes, if any, do you recommend to the process?
2. What tests do you recommend the company use to help select its salespeople? Discuss the advantages and disadvantages of such tests.
3. What do you think of some of the questions that were asked of these job candidates? Did the company expose itself to any potential problems by asking them? If so, how?

selling environment

Sales Management

TRAINING & DEVELOPMENT

Relationship Selling

Recruiting & Selection

Compensation

Evaluating Performance

Salesperson Motivation

Closing & Follow-up

Self-Management

Prospecting & Sales Call Planning

Communicating the Sales Message

Negotiating for Win-Win Solutions

Information

Ethics

Value Creation

Customer Relationships

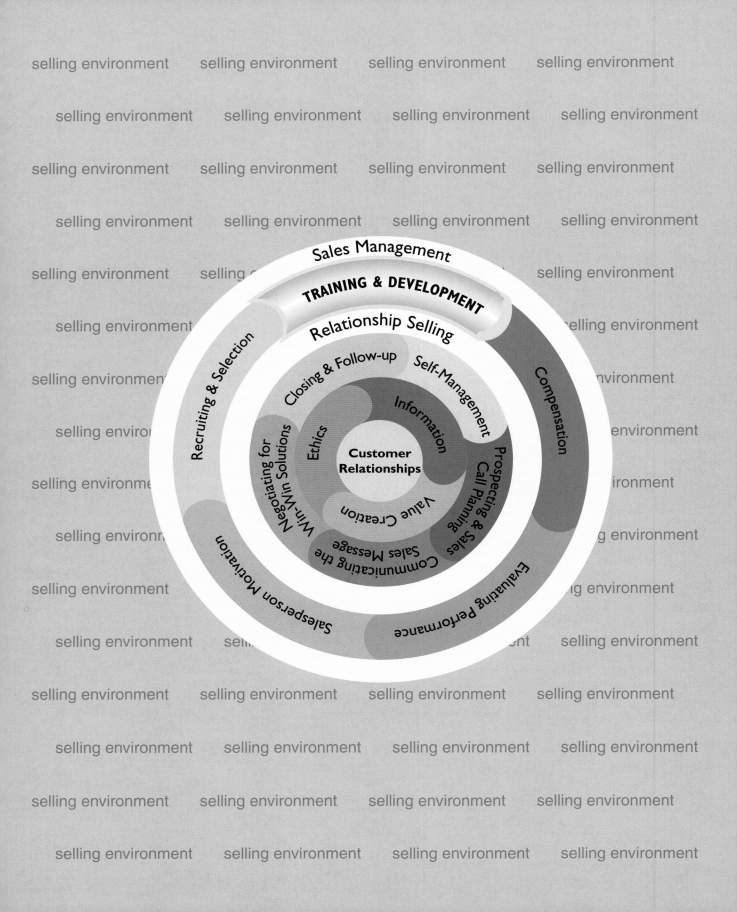

12 chapter

Training Salespeople for Sales Success

Learning Objectives

Salespeople operate in a highly competitive and dynamic environment. New salespeople must assimilate a great deal of information to make them effective with customers sale. A key element in enhancing the success of current salespeople and preparing new salespeople is training. This chapter will examine the objectives, techniques, and evaluation methods for training in the sales force.

After reading this chapter, you should be able to

- Identify the key issues in sales training.
- Understand the objectives of sales training.
- Discuss how to develop sales training programs.
- Understand the differences in training new recruits and experienced salespeople.
- Define the topics covered in a sales training program.
- Understand the various methods for conducting sales training.
- Explain how to measure the costs and benefits of sales training.

expert advice

Expert: Tim Riesterer, CEO, CMM Group

Company: Customer Message Management

Business: The CMM Group provides a proven process, training and practical tools, along with message development and delivery services, to help companies increase the impact of their messaging, marketing, and communications support on selling effectiveness.

Education: University of Wisconsin–Milwaukee

What are the benefits for salespeople and companies from good sales training?

First the sales training has to be good. This means it not only needs to train salespeople on how to construct a sales call or sales cycle—it needs to provide solutions-oriented messaging and support to guide the consultative customer conversation.

The problem occurs when our *sales skills training,* such as solution selling–type training sessions are completely disconnected from our *product training.* It's like building a race car, but not putting the right gas in the tank. We want salespeople to engage in more consultative conversations, but we aren't equipping them with the necessary messaging and sales tools. That creates a disconnect in the sales training.

Companies looking for a competitive advantage and a differentiated market presence need to reorient their product messaging and align it with the consultative sales training approach—which starts with the customer and their business needs, not the product and its features.

Have you found sales training programs need to be different for new versus experienced salespeople? If so, how are they different?

First, all sales training needs to integrate the process with the content. Companies need to take every opportunity to reinforce the desired best-selling practice and demonstrate how the messaging and tools align with—and support—it.

Second, no matter how much salespeople disdain it, all training should include practicing, role playing, and coaching. I've seen some of the most experienced and successful reps struck dumb in these sessions, and they blame it on the fabricated environment. Well, I'm still of the school that you "play like you practice."

Finally, I believe in a level of certification for new hire and new solution training. Salespeople need to be able to demonstrate a level of proficiency on the customer targets, the business needs, the way a company's products and services solve those needs, the value created by the company, and the reference proof points used to validate the story.

What metrics do you think are critical for companies to use in assessing the value of sales training programs?

Metrics belong on a continuum because we want to make sure the steps we take to train for success are followed not skipped. If we only measure the end result, let's say "close rates" for example, we run the risk of not knowing for sure if our sales training programs contributed to that success. In other words, we want to make sure success is happening on purpose—not by accident.

I suggest that each sales rep be tracked for their completion and certification across the various training programs, and then we align those programs with key revenue-generating outcomes.

For example, for new reps this may be: "time to first sale." You can tell a lot about how well your new hire training is doing at equipping sales reps by decreasing the time to first sale, which reduces your costs and maximizes the profitable life of a sales rep.

For existing reps, we can measure close rates, deal size, and deal profitability. These measures are the precise targets and reasons why we conduct consultative selling training in the first place. They will tell us if we are truly creating a differentiated, value-added sales cycle by comparing rep results in these categories to sales training completion and certification.

Issues in Sales Training

Sales training is a critical task for sales managers in the relationship-selling process. Refer to our model of Relationship Selling and Sales Management and see where we are in the sales management process now. Training salespeople is a huge industry. According to the latest data, American companies spent more than $50 billion on training in 2008. It is not surprising then the subject of sales training produces considerable interest among managers at all levels of a company.

Sales managers have a variety of objectives for training. A national account manager wants sales training to provide specific details about certain industries and to teach salespeople how to develop close relationships with customers—a critical issue, especially with large national accounts. A regional market manager, will be interested in teaching salespeople to deal with the complex problems of local customers. Product managers, of course, hope salespeople have expertise in product knowledge, specifications, and applications. Even managers outside the marketing function, such as human resource managers, will have a stake in the sales training process. They know that highly regarded sales training programs enhance the firm's ability to recruit and retain salespeople. A few firms have developed such strong sales training programs that graduates say completing them is like earning a second degree or an MBA.

When determining sales training needs, three issues must be considered.[1]

- *Who should be trained?* (new and/or experienced salespeople?)
- *What should be the primary emphasis in the training program?* (relationship building, product knowledge, company knowledge, customer knowledge, and/or generic selling skills such as time management or presentation skills?)
- *How should the training process be structured?* (on-the-job training and experience versus a formal and more consistent centralized program, field initiatives and participation versus headquarters programs, in-house training versus outside expertise?)

Sales training is an ongoing process. Sales training for new recruits tries to instill in a relatively short time a vast amount of knowledge that has taken skilled sales reps years and years to acquire. Sales training for experienced salespeople may be needed due to new product offerings, changes in market structure, new technologies, competitive activities, and so on, plus a desire to reinforce and upgrade critical selling skills. Although some sales managers think sales training has only one objective—for example, to increase motivation—others identify a variety of objectives. Our Expert Advice talks about how customer messaging is used in sales training.

Objectives of Sales Training

Although the specific objectives of sales training may vary from firm to firm, there is some agreement on the broad objectives. Sales training is undertaken to improve relationships with customers, increase productivity, improve morale, lower turnover, and improve selling skills (like better management of time and territory). Exhibit 12.1 summarizes the objectives of sales training programs.

EXHIBIT 12.1 Objectives of Sales Training

Improve Customer Relationships

As we have discussed, building successful sales relationships is difficult and requires a significant commitment from salespeople and their company. One benefit of effective sales training is continuity in customer relationships. Having the same salesperson call on a given customer for an extended period of time can enhance the relationship between the company and the customer, especially when the salesperson can handle customer questions, objections, and complaints (the topics covered in many sales training programs). Inadequately trained salespeople usually cannot provide these benefits, and customer relations suffer.

Customer message management, as the Expert Advice highlighted, emphasizes training that enhances customer value. In a highly dynamic environment, CMM realizes that if salespeople are not trained on what is important to the customer, competitors will have an opportunity to take business away.

Increase Productivity

An important objective of sales training is giving salespeople the skills they need to improve their performance and make a positive contribution to the firm. In a relatively short time, sales training attempts to teach the skills of successful sales force members. The time it takes for a new salesperson to achieve satisfactory productivity is thus shortened considerably. The productivity of sales training receives strong support from companies like Cisco Systems, which credits much of its success to having the best-trained sales force in the industry. That success has been dramatic; Cisco's revenue rose from $18.9 billion in 2003 to $39.5 billion in 2008.[2]

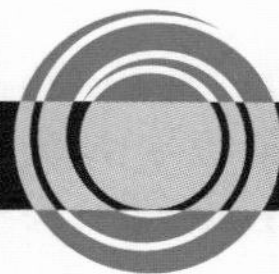

INNOVATION 12.1

Creating a Powerful Sales Training Experience

Many training professionals will tell you salespeople are the toughest audience. Motivational pep talks and PowerPoint presentations that do not provide real tools *now* will anger salespeople and waste money for the company. Salespeople tend to be independent and critical of the information they receive in training. They demand training that is geared toward them and their unique needs.

Experts suggest two key elements in successful sales training. First, link training to the challenges reps face right now. Second, provide specific tools for them to use. Incorporate forms that enable them to organize information.

Above all, sales training cannot be boring. Inordinate amounts of reading and theory will not work with salespeople. They will turn off the trainer, and the training experience will be wasted from the company's perspective. Keep the agenda open so that issues raised by salespeople can be dealt with at the training session. Telling salespeople you will get back with them will not work. They want the information now.

Improve Morale

How does sales training lead to better morale? One objective of sales training is to prepare trainees to perform tasks so their productivity increases as quickly as possible. When sales trainees know what is expected of them, they are less likely to experience frustration that arises from trying to perform a job without adequate preparation. Without training, the salesperson may not be able to answer customers' questions, leading to frustration and lower morale.

Creating the right format for sales training is a very challenging task. Innovation 12.1 describes how to create an effective training experience, which is not based on motivational hype but rather on delivering specific skills and techniques to enhance the salesperson's ability to be successful in the field.[3]

Lower Turnover

If sales training can lead to improved morale, lower **turnover** should result. Young, inexperienced salespeople are more likely to get discouraged and quit than their experienced counterparts. Turnover can lead to customer problems, since many customers prefer continuity with a particular salesperson. When a salesperson suddenly quits, the customer may transfer business to other suppliers rather than wait for a new representative. Sales training can help mitigate such problems.

The pharmaceutical industry has focused a lot of effort on improving its sales training programs. Industry experts estimate that turnover can cost twice as much as a salesperson's compensation package and cite training as the most significant factor in improving the retention rate of high-performing salespeople.[4]

Improve Selling Skills

Many companies believe that improving basic selling skills can lead to improved performance in the field. As we discussed in Chapter 9, time and territory management is a subject of many sales training programs. How much time should be devoted to calls on existing accounts and how much to calls on potential new accounts? How often should each class of account be called on? What is the most effective way of covering the territory to reduce miles driven and time spent? Many sales training programs provide answers to these questions.[5]

Developing Successful Sales Training Programs

There is no doubt that sales training is an important function. However, implementing it creates a number of challenges. For example, top management may not be dedicated to sales training or the training program not adequately funded. Some salespeople resent the intrusion on their time and resist making the changes suggested by training programs.[6]

This pessimistic view of sales training stems from two problems. First, management too often expects training will be a panacea for all of the company's sales problems. If those problems are not resolved, budget cutting often starts with the sales training program. Sales training is viewed as a cost of doing business rather than an investment that pays future dividends.

The second problem is that too many sales training programs are conducted without any thought of measuring the benefits. Evaluation is difficult, but considering the millions of dollars devoted to sales training, it is essential for management to take the time to develop a cost-effective training program that delivers on specific, measurable objectives.

Analyze Needs

The starting point in creating an effective sales training program is to analyze the needs of the sales force (see Exhibit 12.2). An important first step is to travel with salespeople, observing them and asking what they need to know that will help them perform more effectively. Local sales managers are a useful source of information because they are closest to the salespeople. Other sources include company records on turnover data, performance evaluations, and sales/cost analyses. Attitudinal studies of the sales force are also helpful. On the other hand, sending questionnaires to customers is less useful because they either don't have time or are not particularly interested in providing good feedback. The needs analysis should answer three basic questions:

- Where in the organization is training needed?
- What should be the content of the training program?
- Who needs the training?

Determine Objectives

Specific, realistic, and measurable objectives are essential to a sales training program. They may include learning about new products, sales techniques, or procedures. It pays to keep the objectives simple. Management may want a 10 percent sales increase, which then becomes the broad objective of the training program. The specific objective might be to teach sales reps how to call on new accounts, which will help achieve the broad objective.

EXHIBIT 12.2 Analyzing the Training Needs of the Sales Force

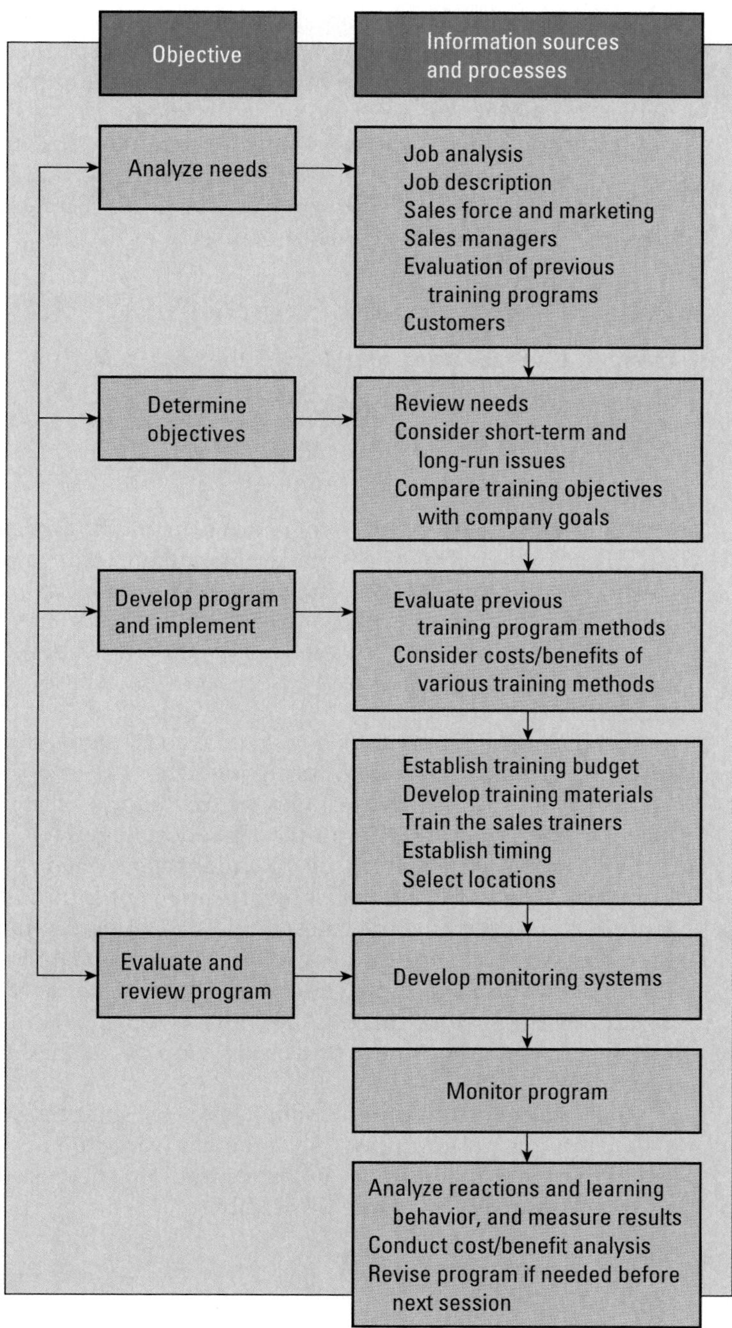

Source: *Churchill/Ford/Walker's Sales Force Management,* 9th ed., by Mark Johnston and Greg Marshall (New York: McGraw-Hill, 2009), p. 320. Reprinted by permission of the McGraw-Hill Companies.

Develop and Implement the Program

At this point, management must decide whether to develop the training program in-house or hire an outside organization. Small companies often use outside training professionals. Large companies develop most of their own programs, though they may employ outside agencies like our experts at the beginning of the chapter to handle specific training topics.

Outside suppliers should be screened carefully. One sales manager was embarrassed when a company he hired put on an "entertaining song and dance routine" that cost $45,000 but failed to have any lasting effect. Outside sources can be cost effective if they meet the company's objectives.

Evaluate and Review the Program

Designing a measurement system is the next step.

- What do we want to measure?
- When do we want to measure?
- How do we measure the training?

Using tests to measure learning is not difficult, but measuring application in the field is. Whether a salesperson learns to demonstrate a product can be evaluated during the training session. But whether the salesperson demonstrates effectively in front of a customer is harder to evaluate. This is why field sales managers are an important link: They provide follow-up and feedback on how well sales reps demonstrate the product and also coach the reps on how to demonstrate the product.

Finally, evaluations of sales performance provide additional proof of the value of training, although such information must be used carefully. Changes in performance, like sales increases, may be due to other factors. To claim they are due solely to sales training may ultimately reflect negatively on the training effort.

Since measurement is crucial, the sales trainer needs to collect data before training starts. The needs analysis provides relevant information about program content. For example, if some salespeople had difficulty managing their sales calls, then observation by the trainer or the field sales manager after the program should provide data on their improvement and thus the value of the training. Call reports are another source of information. Follow-up must continue beyond the initial check since the use of new skills may drop off. If this happens, reinforcement is necessary.

The data collection process should provide sales trainers with information that will justify the program. Top management wants to know if the benefits exceed or equal the costs. Keeping top management informed about the success of training programs contributes to overall credibility.

Training Needs Change with Time

Not everyone in the sales force needs the same training. Certainly newly hired recruits need training on company products and policies. Then when procedures or products change, everyone should receive additional training. However, if certain sales reps are having a sales slump, the training needs to be directed at them specifically. To include the entire force may create problems. Salespeople who aren't in a slump may resent being included and let others know it. As you can see, training needs vary a great deal based on the individuals involved.

New Recruits

Most large and medium-size companies have programs for training new sales recruits. These programs differ considerably in length and content, however. The differences often reflect variations in company policies, the nature of the selling job, and types of products and services sold. Even within the same industry, sales training programs vary in length, content, and technique.

Although a few companies have no preset time for training sales recruits, most have a fixed period for formal training. The time varies from just a couple of days in the office, followed by actual selling and on-the-job coaching, to as long as two or three years of intensive training in a number of fields and skills.

What accounts for this variation? First, training needs vary from firm to firm and even within a firm. One pharmaceutical company has a seven-week program for new recruits who will sell conventional consumer products—and a two-year program for those selling technical products.

Second, training needs vary because of differences in the needs and aptitudes of the recruits. Experienced recruits have less need for training than inexperienced recruits, although most large firms require every new hire to go through some formal training. One industrial firm requires a one-week program for experienced recruits and a two- to three-year program for inexperienced recruits.

A final reason the length of training programs varies is company philosophy. Some sales managers believe training for new recruits should be concentrated at the beginning of their career; others think it should be spread over a longer time and include a large dose of learning by doing. Indeed, many companies promote lifelong learning. General Electric's many companies deliver training throughout a salesperson's career because GE believes the need to learn never ends.

Experienced Salespeople

After new salespeople are assigned to field positions, they quickly become involved in customer relationships, competitive developments, and other related matters. Over time, their knowledge of competitors and market conditions becomes dated. Even their personal selling styles may become less effective. Sales reps also require refresher or advanced training programs because of changes in company policies and product lines. Few companies halt training after the trainee has completed the basics. As discussed previously, most managers agree that the need to learn is a never-ending process and even the most successful sales rep can benefit from refresher training.

Additional training often occurs when a sales representative is being considered for promotion. In many companies, a promotion means more than moving from sales to district sales manager. It can mean being assigned better customers, transferring to a better territory, moving to a staff position, or being promoted to sales management. Whenever salespeople are assigned new customers or new territories, additional sales training helps them assimilate their new responsibilities.

Many companies decentralize the training for experienced salespeople. Black & Decker, IBM, and Cisco are among those companies that deliver training into the field using online, Internet-based computer programs.

Training experienced salespeople provides insurance for a company's major asset—people. Debbie Brady, director of learning and organizational effectiveness at financial services company Edward Jones, notes that the focus on training allows the company to "thrive in the chaos." She states, "By cultivating our next generation of leaders and preserving the company culture, we are allowing our employees to truly learn and grow."[7]

Sales Training Topics

For new trainees, the content of sales training tends to remain constant. Most programs cover product or service knowledge, market/industry orientation, company orientation, and selling skills like time and territory management. Beyond these standard topics is a vast array of subjects. They range from the logical (such as training sales reps how to use the company's new computerized procedures, instructing the sales force how to build relationships, and educating the sales reps in team selling procedures) to some questionable topics such as training sales reps to modify their presentation based on whether the customer is left-brained or right-brained. Exhibit 12.3 identifies the primary topics covered in sales training programs.

Product Knowledge

Although product knowledge is one of the most important topics, knowing when and how to discuss the subject in a sales call is probably even more important. More

EXHIBIT 12.3 Topics in Sales Training

Source: *Churchill/Ford/Walker's Sales Force Management,* 9th ed., by Mark Johnston and Greg Marshall (New York: McGraw-Hill, 2009). Reprinted by permission of the McGraw-Hill Companies.

time is typically spent on product knowledge than any other subject (although the time spent varies with the product sold).

Companies that produce technical products, such as computer and other technology-related companies, spend more time on product knowledge than do manufacturers of nontechnical products. Hewlett-Packard, Intel, and others spend a great deal of time educating salespeople on their products and services because it is critical that the right product or service be applied to each customer's unique application.

Product knowledge involves knowing not only how the product is made but also how it is used—and, in some cases, how it should not be used. One producer of machine tools gives newly hired sales engineers extensive in-plant exposure to technical and engineering matters. Before field assignment, they spend time in a customer's plant where they are taught machine setup and operations under realistic conditions.

Product knowledge is not limited to those products the salesperson will eventually sell. Customers often want to know how competitive products compare with each other on price, construction, performance, and compatibility. They expect salespeople to show them how the seller's products can be coordinated with competitive products, as in a computer installation that involves products made by different manufacturers. One manufacturer that supplies paper towels to industrial firms exposes sales trainees to competitive towel dispensers so they will know which dispensers handle their paper towels.

A major objective in training product knowledge is to enable a salesperson to give potential customers the information they need for rational decision making. As we discussed in Chapter 6, many benefits accrue to salespeople as they acquire product knowledge:

1. Pride and confidence in product quality.
2. Self-assurance emanating from technical knowledge of product makeup.
3. Communication with customers through the use of the operational vocabulary peculiar to the industry.
4. Understanding of product functioning that allows effective diagnosis of customer problems.[8]

All these benefits improve the customer–salesperson relationship.

Market/Industry Orientation

Sales training in market/industry orientation covers both broad and specific factors. From a broad viewpoint, salespeople need to know how their particular industry fits into the overall economy. Economic fluctuations affect buying behavior, which affects selling techniques. Information about inflationary pressure, for example, may be used to persuade prospective buyers to move their decision dates up. If the sales force is involved in forecasting sales and setting quotas, knowledge of the industry and the economy is essential.

From a narrower viewpoint, salespeople must have detailed knowledge about present customers. They need to know their buying policies, patterns, and preferences and the products or services these customers produce. In some cases, salespeople need to be knowledgeable about their customers' customers. This is especially true when they sell through wholesalers or distributors, who often want reps to assist them with their customers' problems. Missionary salespeople are expected to know the needs of both wholesalers and retailers, even though the retailers buy from the wholesalers.

Company Orientation

New salespeople must be aware of company policies that affect their selling activities. Like all new employees, they need to learn the company's policies on such items as salary structure and company benefits.

Salespeople can expect customers to request price adjustments, product modifications, faster delivery, and different credit terms. Most companies have policies on such matters arising from legal requirements or industry practices. Too often, however, avoidable delays and even lost sales result from inadequate sales training in company policies.

Two practices provide salespeople with knowledge of company policies. (1) New salespeople learn about company policies and procedures by working in various departments, such as credit, order processing, advertising, sales promotion, and shipping. (2) Salespeople work inside sales for a time before being assigned to a field sales position. They process customer orders, maintain contact with customers (e-mail, phone), and sometimes serve as the company contact for a group of customers.

Most corporations provide the sales force with manuals that cover product line information and company policies. A well-written sales manual can give a sales rep a quick answer to a customer's question.

Time and Territory Management

As we discussed in Chapter 9, new and even experienced salespeople can benefit from training in how to manage their time and territories. A survey by Learning International suggests that salespeople perceive this as an important problem. Management also considers time management a critical issue. Blue Cross Blue Shield instituted Internet-based learning so salespeople could spend more time with their customers. Dan Goettsch, sales training manager, states, "One of the big issues here is the notion that selling time is a very precious commodity. Any time [out of the field] is costly for sales folks."[9]

Legal/Ethical Issues

You learned in Chapter 4 that statements (or misstatements) made by salespeople have legal and ethical implications. Lapses in ethical conduct have been known to lead to legal problems. Leadership 12.2 describes one industry's response to ethical problems. When major insurance companies allowed sales reps to engage in unethical practices (such as selling whole-life insurance policies as annuities), the legal settlements ran into millions of dollars. National organizations like the Insurance Marketplace Standards Association support ongoing mandatory ethics training for salespeople.

Technology

Laptop computers are standard issue for most salespeople today. Many companies (for example, Procter & Gamble and IBM) are also creating home offices for their sales forces that eliminate the need to go to an office at all. With a high-speed

Leadership 12.2

Training Ethics in the Sales Force

The insurance industry has been plagued by deceptive sales practices for years. Indeed, the industry has suffered from a bad reputation as many salespeople followed unethical (and even illegal) sales techniques. One company, the AXA Financial Corporation (www.AXAonline.com), has created a number of policies and procedures to help ensure that its sales force behaves in an ethical manner.

One of the policies requires all agents and support staff to take an ethics course taught by agency managers. The sales professionals are given study materials on ethics and take an exam.

As stated in the company's policy statement on ethics, AXA wants their salespeople to adhere to the highest ethical standards:

> AXA Financial's reputation for integrity is tested every day by the way you treat clients. Honesty, fairness and keeping commitments must be hallmarks of the way you do business.
>
> - Sell products and services on their merits. Describe them truthfully and without exaggeration.
> - Explain contracts, products, services, and investment opportunities clearly and accurately.
> - Ensure that commitments are honored and that all your clients receive the highest quality service that you can provide.
> - Scrupulously follow compliance procedures applicable to your company. When in doubt consult the compliance department of your company or its legal counsel.

AXA has also joined the Insurance Marketplace Standards Association (IMSA at www.imsaethics.org), an association of companies that promotes high ethical standards in the sale and service of life insurance, annuities, and long-term care products. As of 2008, only a small percentage of more than 1,000 life insurance companies in the United States had been awarded membership in IMSA, yet they represent more the vast majority of all life insurance business. To belong, a company must follow the IMSA code of ethical business conduct. A key component of the IMSA code is training salespeople in the products and services of their company and in techniques for presenting that information in an ethical way.

Sources: Web sites for AXA Financial (www.AXAonline.com) and Insurance Marketplace Standards Association (www.imsaethics.org), October 2008. Used with permission.

network connection, laptop or desktop computer, printer, and cell phone, a salesperson is almost totally self-sufficient. Salespeople use laptops or other mobile devices to plan their call activities, submit orders, send reports, check on inventory, receive both customer and company messages, and present product and service demonstrations. In some cases, the sales rep can access the company's decision support system (DSS) to learn what products have been selling in an area or for a specific customer.

Effective use of technology allows salespeople more face-to-face customer contact time. It also lets them respond much faster to customers. With cell phones, they can be in contact with customers almost all the time. Add to these direct network connections that companies such as General Motors and Ford have with their suppliers, and it's no wonder that many customers report much better communication with the salespeople who call on them. Innovation 12.3 discusses the growing importance of Internet technology in sales training.

Specialized Training Topics

Sales training topics may be very specific. Price objections are common in sales transactions, and sales managers are not pleased if reps offer discounts too quickly. Johnson Controls Inc., a manufacturer of automated control systems based in Atlanta, instituted a training program on price negotiations. The company found

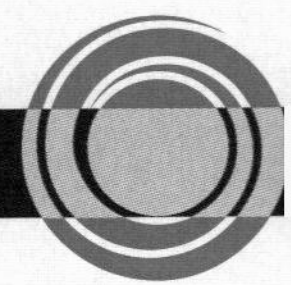

INNOVATION 12.3

E-Commerce Uses E-Sales Training

With the growth of the Internet for delivering sales training, many companies worry that at least some of those dollars will be wasted. To many managers, e-learning means taking sales training manuals and putting them on a Web site—but that is not effective e-sales training.

Consider three key factors when creating an effective e-learning environment:

- Content that captures and maintains salespeople's interest.
- A clear explanation of what the salespeople are expected to learn from the training.
- Continuous practice updates.

Currently, most e-sales training involves providing product knowledge or some other kind of specific data content (price changes, company polices) to salespeople spread all over the country or the world. Companies are just beginning to see the potential of e-sales training to deliver simulations and other people-related training that focuses on decision making and relationship building, not simply memorization and data download.

A rep for a leading consumer products company found the simulation helped her learn how to respond to a particular customer who had been very negative toward her sales presentation. By working with the simulation software, she was able to overcome the customer's objections and make the sale.

The future of e-sales training lies in its ability to provide cost-effective training on people skills rather than data. The ability to efficiently deliver a wide range of different sales scenarios makes e-sales training an effective sales training option for companies.

that many salespeople were more comfortable reducing market price than building value. One solution was to provide salespeople with detailed financial information to help customers see the added value of Johnson's pricing policies.[10]

Many companies, like Caterpillar Inc., spend substantial sums each year on trade shows. Higher costs raised management's concern about the return on their investment. Now Caterpillar salespeople selected to participate in trade shows take part in a training program designed to help them handle such shows' unique features. Most salespeople have the training and experience to make in-depth presentations to specific customers, but they are not necessarily skilled at working trade shows. Specific training helps them to engage and qualify new prospects and handle big crowds.[11]

Sales Training Methods

The most common methods of sales training are **on-the-job training (OJT),** individual (one-on-one) instruction, in-house classes, and external seminars. Recognizing that different subjects require different methods, companies use a variety of techniques. Overlap exists within a given method. On-the-job training includes individual instruction (coaching) and in-house classes held at district sales offices. District sales personnel attend external seminars as well. Leadership 12.4 is another example of how companies use creative ideas to help train their sales force.

The techniques of instruction vary. The most prevalent forms of instruction are videotapes, lectures, and one-on-one instructions. Often companies combine techniques to achieve the best possible balance.

The design, development, and sale of training materials is big business these days. However, the use of outside sources is not without controversy. Companies

Leadership 12.4

Cooking Great Sales Training in the Kitchen

In an effort to build team spirit and foster cooperation, companies have moved sales training to the kitchen. Using cooking classes to get a group of sales people to work together for a common goal has proved a successful recipe for some companies.

In the end the most important thing about the process is not the finished product, which often includes an entire meal for a group. Rather, it is working together as a team to create something new. One of the advantages of using cooking as a way of fostering team building is the fact that it does not require a lot of training to accomplish the task. While it is helpful to have knowledge of cooking, programs are set up for anyone, including individuals who wouldn't know a colander from a blender.

Another advantage is getting people who wouldn't normally interact at the office to get to know each other and work together in a different setting. Programs encourage participants to get to know a more personal side of their colleagues and encourage greater communication, trust, and shared responsibilities than would normally be found in a work environment. People often get into a pattern of communication and thought processes that limits their interaction with fellow employees. This is particularly true in a competitive sales environment where salespeople seek to differentiate themselves through individual performance. Bringing salespeople from a sale district together for a cooking class helps break down walls and creates an "esprit de corps" in the sales force.

Not surprisingly, the key is to make the event fun. Many cooking team building experiences make a night of it that includes a learning program, the cooking experience, and a casual dinner to enjoy the food they worked so hard to prepare. Professional facilitators are trained to reinforce learning objectives during the cooking and dinner components of the team-building seminar. While participants are having a good time cooking and eating, the facilitator is asking questions, providing insights, and motivating participants to consider the learning takeaways.

question whether they should spend money on external sales training sources. Sales consultant Jack Falvey says, "Only if you have lots of discretionary money to spend and don't know what to do with it."

According to Falvey, "Selling is an interactive skill that must be acquired in combination with the knowledge of how both you and your customers do business. It can't be separated out into a generic system that can later be recombined in some way with your business."[12]

Verizon, like many other companies, has established outsourcing partnerships that provide training programs for all types and levels of employees. It hired an outside training company, Acclivus, to improve the problem-solving skills of its sales and customer service staff. However, the outsourcing partnership did not eliminate the training function at Verizon. The net effect was to enhance the company's training capabilities.[13]

On-the-Job Training

The mere mention of on-the-job training sometimes scares new sales recruits. The thought of learning by doing is psychologically troubling for many people, often due to incorrect perceptions of OJT. On-the-job training is not a "sink or swim" approach in which the trainee is handed an order book and a sales manual and told, "Go out and sell."

OJT should be a carefully planned process in which the new recruit learns by doing and, at the same time, is productively employed. A good OJT program contains procedures for evaluating and reviewing a sales trainee's progress. Critiques should be held after each OJT sales call and summarized daily. The critiques cover effectiveness, selling skills, communication of information in a persuasive manner, and other criteria.

On-the-job training is a very effective way of learning for salespeople. Indeed, it is said that three-fourths of all learning at work takes place informally. The Education Development Center identifies five keys for effective on-the-job informal training.

1. *Teaming.* Bringing together people with different skills to address issues.
2. *Meetings.* Setting aside times when employees at different levels and positions can get together and share thoughts on various topics.
3. *Customer interaction.* Including customer feedback as part of the learning process.
4. *Mentoring.* Providing an informal mechanism for new salespeople to interact and learn from more experienced ones.
5. *Peer-to-peer communication.* Creating opportunities for salespeople to interact for mutual learning.[14]

A key aspect of OJT is the coaching new salespeople receive from trainers, who may be experienced salespeople, sales managers, or personnel specifically assigned to do sales training.

When on-the-job training and coaching occur together, it is called one-on-one training. Observation is an integral part of the process. For managers, helping salespeople reach their full potential means spending time with them one on one. One consultant specializing in sales performance states, "Managers play an essential role in cultivating talent. They need to take on a coaching role." Providing individual feedback can lead to greater salesperson satisfaction. One salesperson sums up the benefits of one-on-one feedback this way, "For my entire sales career, my manager went on calls with me at least two days every month. The [sales] classes never would have had an impact without coaching."[15]

OJT often involves job rotation—assigning new salespeople to different departments where they learn about such things as manufacturing, marketing, shipping, credits and collections, and servicing procedures. After on-the-job training, many sales trainees proceed to formal classroom training.

Internet (Online)

The Internet has revolutionized the delivery of training not just in sales but across the entire organization. Indeed, it's now possible for companies to deliver quality learning experiences to their customers online. Companies find the Internet very effective and very efficient in delivering information. Online training is growing at a very rapid rate and companies are literally spending billions on online training methods. Innovation 12.5 highlights one way the Internet is being used in sales training.

IBM invests a great deal of time and resources in the delivery of online training to its sales force of over 300,000 worldwide. Its Internet-based training strategy involves delivering small incremental packets of information on products and customers in time to complete specific projects currently on the salesperson's activity list. Online chat groups help salespeople gather even more information and provide feedback on current activities.

INNOVATION 12.5

Cyberspace Sales Simulation

Real estate companies are experimenting with a variety of Internet-based sales training tools to improve agent performance. One area receiving a lot of attention is sales simulation programs. Align Mark has created a sales simulation that tests salespeople on various Real estate sales tasks.

Using actors and interactive video, the Sales Simulator assesses the agent's ability to deal with customer objections or handle a difficult customer. After watching a video clip, the agent is asked to respond to a menu of possible options. Which option provided the best choice in the situation? Which option was the worst choice? A score is given for each response and the agent performance is evaluated.

Each agent taking the simulation receives a report that gives his or her score as well as an overall assessment of strengths and weaknesses. The report gives the agent feedback in four critical areas:

- Analyzing the customer's needs.
- Active listening.
- Managing the sales process.
- Influencing and closing.

Perhaps most importantly, agents are also given specific tools to improve their performance. Sophisticated, interactive simulations like these are not cheap. Align Mark's Real Estate Sales Simulator starts at $300 per salesperson.

IBM believes online training has led to greater effectiveness in sales and plans to do 35 percent of sales training over the Internet. The key is to deliver the information when and where salespeople can use it most. Nancy Dixon, consultant in corporate learning, says, "People are learning all the time. It's up to the company to make sure they have the tools they need in order to focus that learning on their jobs." Another significant benefit of the program is the cost saving. IBM estimates it will save millions in travel and hotel costs over the next several years.[16]

Classroom Training

For most companies, formal classroom training is an indispensable part of sales training—although very few rely on it exclusively. The Internet now allows much of the information delivered in a classroom to be sent directly to salespeople in the field, yet classroom training still has several advantages. First, each trainee receives standard briefings on such subjects as product knowledge, company policies, customer and market characteristics, and selling skills. Second, formal training sessions often save substantial amounts of executive time because executives can meet an entire group at once. Third, classroom sessions permit the use of audiovisual materials. Lectures, presentations, and case discussions can also be programmed into a classroom setting.

The opportunity for interaction among sales trainees is a fourth advantage. Reinforcement and ideas for improvement can come from other sales trainees. Interaction is so important that many companies divide sales trainees into teams for case presentations, which forces them to become actively involved.

Classroom training also has its disadvantages. It is expensive and time consuming. It requires recruits to be brought together and facilities, meals, transportation, recreation, and lodging to be provided for them. In an attempt to cut costs, sales managers sometimes cover too much material in too short a time. This results in less retention of information. Sales managers must avoid the tendency to add more and more material because the additional exposure is often gained at the expense of retention and opportunity for interaction.

Role Playing

As you already know, **role playing** is an important part of the learning experience. The sales trainee acts out a part, most often a salesperson, in a simulated buying session. The buyer may be either a sales instructor or another trainee. Role playing is widely used to develop selling skills, but it can also test whether the trainee can apply knowledge taught via other methods of instruction. The trainee, the trainer, and other trainees critique the trainee's performance immediately after the role-playing session.

Role playing critiques can be harsh sometimes if the critique is conducted only in the presence of the sales trainee and only by the instructor. When role playing is handled well, most trainees identify their own strengths and weaknesses without input from other trainees.

Other Electronic Methods

While many companies use open delivery systems directly over the Internet, the most dominant form of online training (30 percent) is the internal company network.[17]

Do online training programs work? Can they train salespeople to interact with customers effectively? The answers have not been well documented. As with all methods, salespeople need a great deal of information to do their jobs well. Online training can be very effective in delivering certain kinds of information but will not likely eliminate the need for one-on-one training for salespeople.

Measuring the Costs and Benefits of Sales Training

Sales training is a time-consuming and very costly activity. Is all this effort worth the cost? Does sales training produce enough benefits to justify its existence? If done properly, sales training can be one of the best ways to increase the satisfaction and performance of salespeople. However, as Global Perspective 12.6 discusses, there are many obstacles in the way of a successful training strategy.

Sales training and increased profits have an obscure relationship at best. In the beginning of this chapter, we identified some broad objectives of sales training: improved customer relationships, increased productivity, improved morale, lower sales force turnover, and improved selling skills (like better time and territory management). Unfortunately, pinning down the relationship between sales training and these broad objectives is not easy. Very little research has been done to determine what effect, if any, training has on the sales force. Most organizations simply assume on blind faith that their sales training programs are successful as long as they have high sales and high profits.

Sales Training Costs

Businesses spend millions of dollars each year on sales training in hopes of improving overall productivity. They allocate funds for training with minimal regard for the results. Clearly, measuring the benefits of sales training needs some attention.

Global PERSPECTIVE 12.6

Successful Sales Training Roadblocks

It's 8:30 and 30 minutes into an all-day seminar costing $1,000 per person. The salespeople already know they've heard it all before, which means another day of training with little or nothing to show for it. Companies spend billions on training, yet they find it difficult to determine the real value of it.

Unfortunately, there are many problems associated with the development of effective training programs. Here are nine common problems that inhibit training success in many sales organizations.

1. *Training can't solve the problem.* The real cause of many problems inside the sales force is often something that won't be solved by more training. A training specialist in the Northwest got a call from the head of a manufacturing company asking for training on its new products. Upon investigation the trainer found out the sales force was unhappy because the commission had been cut to 10 percent (it had been 20 percent). The issue was not training but compensation.
2. *Your busy, jaded salespeople are not open to learning new skills.* Salespeople never have enough time. When they are away from their customers, sales performance takes the hit. They want to see results immediately.
3. *Managers don't support the training program.* Not surprisingly, salespeople are reluctant to participate actively in training if management does not support it.
4. *Conflicting methods and philosophies are taught at different sessions.* Everyone should be familiar with previous training so that conflicting information is not presented to the sales force.
5. *The training isn't relevant to the company's pressing needs.* It is crucial to have frontline managers provide at least some input into the content of training programs.
6. *The training format doesn't fit the need.* Many companies fail to match the need with the format. For example, a half-day seminar might work to change salesperson attitudes, but will almost never be successful to provide detailed information about a new product. A common problem is a failure to build in practice time when salespeople can try out what they've learned in the training. If you give them a half-day seminar on new selling skills and then let them go, those skills will probably not work.
7. *E-learning is overused or used in the wrong situations.* While e-learning can be successful, many companies fail to consider whether it is the right way to deliver the training.
8. *There's no follow-up after training.* Companies spend millions on training but don't follow up. The result is that salespeople don't feel compelled to use it.
9. *The trainer can't relate to the sales team.* It is a fact of human nature that if a person is not interesting, people lose interest. A trainer must be able to connect with his or her audience.

Is the measurement process that difficult? After all, if sales training is supposed to lead to better productivity, improved morale, and lower turnover, why not measure the changes in these variables after training has occurred? Some sales managers have done just that. They instituted sales training and shortly afterwards sales increased, so they assumed, sales training was the reason. Right? Wrong!

Unless the research is designed properly, it is hard to say what caused the sales increase. The reason may have been improved economic conditions, competitive activity, environmental changes, and/or seasonal trends, among others. Research must isolate these contaminating effects to identify the benefits directly attributable to training.

Measurement Criteria

If it is important to measure training, what characteristics of sales training should be assessed? Exhibit 12.4 is an evaluation options matrix. A company could single out one method to measure effectiveness, but using several criteria will yield more accurate results. Measuring what participants learned, for example, is not enough

EXHIBIT 12.4 Evaluation Options Matrix

Evaluation level: What is the question?	Information required: What information to collect?	Method: How to collect?
Reaction Did participants respond favorably to the program?	Attitudinal	Evaluation: 1. Surveys 2. Interviews with participants
Learning Did participants learn concepts or skills?	Understanding of concepts, ability to use skills	Before and after tests
Behavior Did participants change their on-the-job behavior?	On-the-job behavior	1. Behavior ratings 2. Before and after critical incident review
Results What personal or organizational results occurred?	Changes in sales, productivity	Cost/benefit analysis

Source: *Sales Force Management,* 9th ed., Mark W. Johnston and Greg W. Marshall (New York: McGraw-Hill 2009), p. 335.

because the obtained knowledge may not produce desired behavior changes. Yet the program might be considered a failure if nothing was learned or if what was learned was not helpful. The solution is to specify the objectives and content of the sales training program, the criteria used to evaluate the program, and the design of the research so benefits can be unambiguously determined.

Measuring Broad Benefits

Broad benefits of sales training include improved morale and lower turnover. Morale can be partially measured by studies of job satisfaction. This approach is feasible with experienced sales personnel. Suppose, for instance, a company measured job satisfaction as part of a needs analysis and found evidence of problems. A follow-up job satisfaction study after the corrective sales training program would determine if morale changed noticeably.

Measuring reactions and learning in sales training is important for both new and experienced personnel. Most companies measure reactions by asking participants to complete an evaluation form either immediately after the session or several weeks later. Enthusiasm may be high right after a session, but sales training effectiveness is much more than a warm feeling.

Measuring what sales trainees learned requires tests. To what extent did they learn the facts, concepts, and techniques covered in the training session? Objective examinations are needed.

Measuring Specific Benefits

Enjoying the program and learning something are not enough. Specific measures are needed to examine behavior and results. The effectiveness of sales training aimed at securing more new customers, for example, is assessed in part, by examining call reports to see whether more new customers are being called on. Results can also be measured by tracking new-account sales to see whether they have increased. If the specific objective of sales training is to increase the sales of more profitable items, the checking on overall sales profitability is a valid measure of training effectiveness. If reducing customer complaints is the objective, then it is appropriate to consider whether customer complaints do in fact decrease.

The measurement of both specific and broad benefits presumes the sales training program is designed to achieve certain goals. The goals should be established before training begins. When specific objectives have been determined, the best training program can be developed to achieve these objectives. Most training programs have several objectives, so multiple measurements of their effectiveness are a necessary part of evaluating their benefits.

Many sales training evaluation measures are simple, consisting primarily of reactions to the program. Meaningful evaluation measures, such as learning, behavior, and results, are not used often enough, while the weakest or easiest-to-collect measures—staff comments and feedback from supervisors and trainees—are used the most.[18]

There is no doubt that evaluating the benefits of sales training is difficult, but it is important. Management must continually seek to find better, more accurate methods for determining the effectiveness of sales training.

A well-designed training program shows the sales force how to sell. It also enables sales managers to communicate high performance expectations through training and equip the reps with the skills they need to reach those levels.

The Salesperson's Role in Sales Training

Whatever form it takes, sales training is directed at the salespeople. Every salesperson has a significant role to play in the training process. Both new and experienced salespeople should understand their role to maximize the benefits of training.

New salespeople come into the job without a knowledge base. At a minimum they are not familiar with company policies. Younger salespeople with little sales experience may require training in many areas, including basic selling skills, competition, and customer needs. They may not even know what they don't know, which means additional time spent learning about the things they are going to cover during training. New salespeople must be open to learning and follow up on assignments to maximize the effectiveness of training efforts.

Experienced salespeople, on the other hand, understand many aspects of the job. Their training, often involves learning new information about the company's products or competitors. Practicing specific selling skills can also enhance their performance. Experienced salespeople are often aware of their training needs and proactive in requesting additional training. Sales managers, as coaches, often rely on experienced salespeople to recognize not only what they are doing well but also what areas need improvement.

An issue for experienced salespeople is being receptive to training. An "I already know this stuff" attitude minimizes the effectiveness of any sales training. Of course, managers must develop effective sales training programs; however, the salesperson's willingness to participate fully is often the difference between success and failure.

Summary

Sales training is a varied and ongoing activity that is time consuming and expensive. Most companies engage in some type of sales training. In fact, most sales managers require it for everybody, regardless of their experience. Some common objectives of sales training are to improve customer relations, increase productivity, improve morale, lower turnover, and teach selling skills (like time and territory management).

Sales training programs vary greatly in length. Industry differences account for variations not only in length but also in program content. Company policies, the nature of the selling job, and the types of products and services offered also contribute to differences in time spent and topics covered.

Product knowledge receives the most attention, followed by market/industry orientation and company orientation. This allocation is the subject of considerable criticism.

As a result of various environmental changes, the content and method of sales training have changed. Standard issue for salespeople today are cell phones and laptops. They are as likely to receive training via the Internet rather than from another person. Most companies use a mix of training methods, including on-the-job training, classroom training, and role playing.

Sales training is very expensive. It's generally considered beneficial, but accurate measurement of the benefits is difficult. It is hard to isolate the effects produced solely by sales training from those that might have been produced by other factors, such as changes in the economy or the nature of competition. Evaluation methods should be designed carefully, and both broad and specific benefits should be measured.

For sales training to achieve its full potential, both new and experienced reps must enter into it wholeheartedly.

Key Terms

turnover

on-the-job training (OJT)

role playing

Role Play

Before You Begin

Before getting started, please go to the appendix of Chapter 1 to review the profiles of the characters involved in this role play, as well as the tips on preparing a role play. In addition, you will need to review the following exhibits and accompanying discussion from Chapter 2: Exhibit 2.4 (Sales Managers' Importance Ratings of Success Factors for Professional Salespeople), Exhibit 2.5 (Sales Job Factors and Selected Associated Activities), and Exhibit 2.6 (Matrix of New Selling Activities).

Characters Involved

Bonnie Cairns

Justin Taylor

Setting the Stage

Bonnie has been with the company only a few weeks. During that time, she spent the first full week at the Upland Company's initial sales training program at the home office. This program is a comprehensive introduction to the company, its products, and the knowledge, skill, and other factors necessary for successful relationship selling at Upland.

After returning home from that first week of intensive training, new Upland account managers spend the second week riding with their district manager, calling on customers together. This allows the district manager to reinforce in the field what the new account manager learned in the training class. During the third and fourth weeks with the company, a new Upland account manager is turned over to a mentor within the district, who is another more experienced account manager. In Bonnie's case, her mentor is Justin Taylor. Rhonda assigned Justin to this role because he is interested in eventually moving into management with Upland, and she believes this experience will be good training for him (as well as for Bonnie!).

During the two weeks of mentorship, the trainer doesn't work with the new account manager every day. Justin and Bonnie will make calls together four days during the two weeks, which represents on-the-job training. This is to allow Bonnie to use the other days to begin to get her feet wet calling on a few customers by herself. In addition to the on-the-job training component of these two weeks, Upland also requires the mentor to work with the new account manager during this time period to identify specific success factors that can be practiced and reinforced through role play between the mentor and the trainee. These may be selling activities, knowledge or skill factors, or other factors important to the job. After identifying these factors, the mentor and trainee work together to develop and execute several role plays over the course of the two weeks to allow the new account manager to build confidence with these key success factors.

Bonnie Cairns's Role

Bonnie needs to work with Justin, with Justin taking the lead, to identify two or three specific factors that she can benefit from practicing through role play. From Chapter 2, Exhibits 2.4, 2.5, and 2.6 and the accompanying discussion provide you with some possible factors and activities that can be the focus of this role-play training. Bonnie and Justin will decide on two or three relevant factors or activities, develop a role-play script to demonstrate effective use of these factors or activities, and then execute the role-play training session. In the role play, Bonnie will play herself.

Justin Taylor's Role

As mentioned earlier, in his role as Bonnie's mentor Justin can both contribute to her training and also contribute to his experience as a trainer in preparation for achieving his goal of being promoted to district manager. He wants to do a very good job of putting together this role play, and will work with her to identify two or three specific factors that Bonnie can benefit from practicing through role play. Once the factors are jointly identified and the script jointly developed, Justin will role play a part that is appropriate to each situation (her buyer, her district manager, or some other appropriate character—these parts can stay the same or change as different success factors are built into the role play). Afterward, Justin should assume his mentor role and provide constructive feedback on how well Bonnie demonstrated the knowledge, skills, or other factors represented by the role play.

Assignment

Work together to develop and execute the role-play dialogue surrounding the issues described above. Limit the overall role play to 12–15 minutes.

Discussion Questions

1. The response from a few of the Marlow Technology sales reps toward the new sales training topic was not encouraging. Geoff Marlow, national sales manager, was dismayed at what he perceived to be a total lack of social graces on the part of the 15-person sales force. He retained a consulting firm that specializes in etiquette training to provide a daylong session on the subject. Frank Casey, one of Marlow's sales trainees, was not pleased. He said, "What's this? Now we have to go to charm school too! Next thing you know, they'll want to teach us how to dress." Are such topics as etiquette and dress appropriate for sales training?

2. How would you evaluate the effectiveness of etiquette training for Marlow?

3. The newly assigned sales representative was perplexed about her inability to learn about customers' needs. She contends her customers are not willing to tell her what problems they are experiencing. After making several joint calls with her, the district sales manager agreed she was not receiving informative responses to her questions. What are the characteristics of good questions? How can sales reps be trained to ask better questions?

4. Experimental design, a subject taught in most marketing research courses, has had limited application in measuring the benefits of sales training programs. Why is this? How would you design an experiment to measure the benefits of a sales training program?

5. One expert contends that sales training is not at all complicated. He predicts that regardless of advances in communication, resources, technology, and training tools, the basic selling skills that trainers teach salespeople will change very little from those that have been successful during the past 50 years. What will change, according to the expert, is how salespeople are trained to use these skills effectively. Do you agree with this prediction?

6. The CEO of the company asks you to justify the 10 percent increase in sales training expenditures for next year. How would you satisfy this request by the CEO?

7. As sales manager for a nationwide electrical products distributor, you are about to roll out a new line of electrical products. What method would you use to train the 500 salespeople in your national sales force on the new products?

8. Sales have been increasing rapidly at your company. The chief financial officer has called you suggesting that next year's training budget be cut because "You don't really need it, things are going so well." What do you tell her?

9. The sales force is getting ready to spend two days learning about improving customer relationships. How would you assess the success or failure of the training?

10. What role do salespeople play in effective sales training?

Ethical Dilemma

Beverly Hart is wondering how to solve the problem that confronts her as she looks out the corner office window at Bottom Line Consulting. As head of worldwide marketing for the company, she is responsible for a sales force of 1,000 consultants around the world. Earlier today she received a phone call from the CEO,

Sarah Klein, who was upset about a conversation she had yesterday with the president of World Mart, a company with huge potential for new business. Bottom Line had obtained only a small contract for a customer analysis study, but both Klein and Hart had targeted World Mart for future growth. Unfortunately, the president told Klein the research conducted by Bottom Line was unacceptable and it was unlikely the company would be receiving any new business from World Mart. After investigating the situation, Klein found that Bottom Line had made some mistakes in the study and the results were not valid.

Klein told Hart the lead account representative for World Mart, Jeff Blake, should be fired for losing the account due to mistakes on the study. After Klein hung up, Hart gave Blake a call. She asked him what happened and how he had made such blunders. Jeff said that while he took responsibility for the errors, he felt he had been poorly prepared for the task. He reminded Beverly his instructions were to get new business, any new business, from World Mart. It was understood that Bottom Line needed to get its foot in the door to build new business opportunities with the company.

He went on to say he had received no training in conducting this kind of research. Contributing to the problem was the fact that World Mart had given him a short window to complete the study and told Blake if Bottom Line was unable to do the job, they would find someone who could. Hart knew he was right. The company had been pressuring him to get new business from World Mart but not really given him the tools to get the job done. Indeed, four customers had asked for similar studies in the last two months, but Bottom Line still did not offer training on marketing research methods. On the other hand, Blake had gone ahead and done the study, making mistakes that invalidated the results.

Hart ponders the fact that both Klein and Blake are right. Mistakes were made in the study; however, Blake was never given the training to get the job done. She realizes that Klein will be unhappy with her if she learns that Blake was not given the training he needed.

Questions

1. What critical management issue does Beverly Hart face as she deals with the current crisis?
2. Did the CEO overreact in telling Hart to fire Jeff Blake?
3. Should Beverly Hart fire Jeff Blake? Why or why not?

Mini Case

House Handy Products

CASE 12

House Handy Products manufactures plastic products and utensils for use in a number of situations. The company produces and sells a vast range of products that can be used in the home (plastic cooking utensils, food storage containers, dish drainers, laundry baskets, etc.), in the garage (garbage cans, workbench and garden tool organizers), and recreationally (coolers, plastic cups, plates and eating utensils, fishing tackle boxes, etc.). The company is extremely innovative and introduces many new products every year. In fact, House Handy's CEO has set the goal to have products introduced in the previous five years account for 65 percent of current-year sales. This goal puts tremendous pressure on the research and development department to design, test, and develop potential new products. It also requires the sales force stay knowledgeable about the new products and work hard to have them stocked by retail partners.

House Handy's products are sold in full-line discount stores, national grocery store chains, and home and garden stores located throughout the United States, Canada, and Puerto Rico. Each representative is responsible for up to 25 retail outlets in his or her territory. Sales reps call on specific department managers (housewares, sporting goods, grocery) in the stores and seek to develop relationships that lead to mutually beneficial results for both the department and House Handy. The relationship-building process includes

1. Managing the inventory of their products in the store and placing orders when inventory needs replenishing.
2. Trouble-shooting any problems (for example, shipping or billing errors) that may occur.
3. Working with the department manager to secure shelf space for the many new products that House Handy introduces every year.
4. Building end-of-aisle and point-of-purchase displays to give the company's products more visibility and enhance the profit potential of House Handy's products for the department.
5. Expediting orders when necessary.
6. Working with store managers when they want to run a promotion that takes their product out of the departments in which it is usually located. For example, at the beginning of spring, during the week before Memorial Day, and around the fourth of July, coolers are moved to a point-of-purchase display near the entrance of each store.

House Handy's sales force consists of both new recruits and more experienced representatives. About 35 percent of the sales force have two years of experience or less with the company. The company recruits most of its new salespeople from universities around the country. It divides the United States into four regions and identifies 12 universities in each region as target universities. They are chosen based on the strength of their academic programs, the student body's work ethic, and the willingness of graduates to relocate to other areas of the region. The Canadian and Puerto Rican locations follow similar strategies adapted for their specific situations.

New recruits are assigned to a sales territory where they will work for a district manager. District managers typically are responsible for 15 to 20 sales representatives. The company assigns a mentor to the each recruit to answer any questions he or she has. Initial training comes in the form of product manuals. Recruits are told, "Walk around the stores and see for yourself what goes on." Training for each new product is also done through product manuals.

Questions

1. What type of training do you recommend that House Handy provide new members of its sales force? How should this training differ from that provided to the company's more experienced sales reps?

2. Discuss the various methods House Handy could use to provide its sales force with ongoing training. What method or methods of training would make the most sense for House Handy's sales force? Justify your response.
3. Suppose House Handy implements a comprehensive training program for not just new recruits but also experienced reps. How can House Handy's VP of sales determine if she is getting any return on the money she invests in training the sales force? What specific items would you recommend she measure to make that determination?

selling environment

Sales Management

COMPENSATION

Relationship Selling

Training & Development

Evaluating Performance

Recruiting & Selection

Salesperson Motivation

Closing & Follow-up

Self-Management

Negotiating for Win-Win Solutions

Prospecting & Sales Call Planning

Communicating the Sales Message

Ethics

Information

Value Creation

Customer Relationships

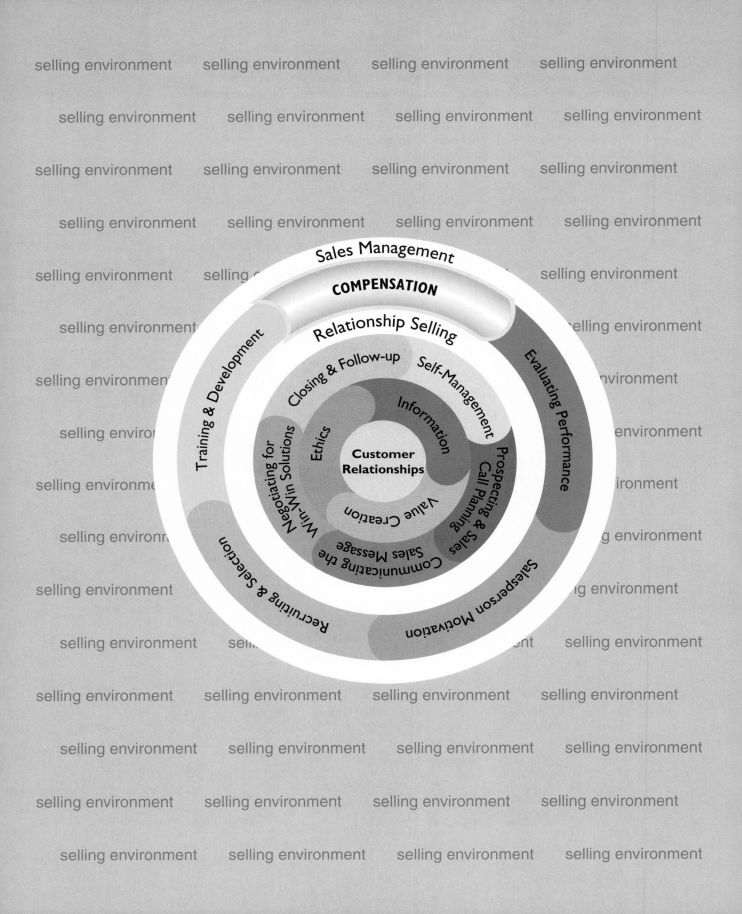

13 chapter

Salesperson Compensation and Incentives

Learning Objectives

This chapter provides an overview of key issues related to compensating salespeople, including the types of compensation, especially incentive forms of compensation available and when to offer each.

After reading this chapter, you should be able to

- Discuss the advantages and limitations of straight salary, straight commission, and combination plans.
- Explain how and why a bonus component to compensation might be used as an incentive.
- Understand the effective use of sales contests, as well as the potential pitfalls of their use.
- Identify key nonfinancial rewards and how and why they might be important.
- Recognize key issues surrounding expense accounts in relationship selling.
- Describe how to make compensation and incentive programs work.
- Discuss making decisions on the mix and level of compensation.

expert advice

Expert: Debra Lacy

Company: Fortune 125 firm offering a wide range of insurance products and services including personal automobile, homeowners, workers compensation, commercial multiple peril, commercial automobile, general liability, global specialty, group disability, assumed reinsurance, fire, and surety.

Business: Sales Director for a sales organization of over 225 salespeople, leads, supervisors, and managers.

Education: MBA, Crummer Graduate School of Business, Rollins College; BS, College of Technology, University of Houston–University Park.

What do you do to make sure a new salesperson in your group understands the values and vision of your company and your group right from the beginning?

Once we've made a commitment to hire a salesperson, it's critical they get off to a great start from day one. We have a strong, employee-friendly culture and value giving each person the opportunity to go as far as they want to go in their career. To help acculturate them to our way of business as quickly as possible, I like to spend some time with each newly hired salesperson. I hold "skip level" meetings (so-called because it puts her as director in front of the people, skipping over the sales manager and sales supervisor levels) with new hires early on. Think of these like focus groups where I can directly connect with the salespeople. Important discussions in these meetings include:

- The value of a high level of employee engagement.
- Why I am drawn to the company myself—what motivates me?
- No matter what impression a customer may hold about us from elsewhere, the highest impact touchpoint is with the salesperson.

I find that well-timed "skip level" meetings create a great bond between the salespeople in my group and me and that we connect on a level that tears down barriers of position and distance. These meetings are a great trust builder, and trust is one of the strongest motivators.

That's a great approach. Once a salesperson is onboard, how do you get your managers and supervisors to carry on this same leadership approach with the salespeople over time?

In my company, we have a strong ethic toward internal customership. That is, our job in management is to treat our salespeople as valued internal customers. My management team and I want to ensure that people feel good about working for the company, and especially working within our group. The more we work to ensure high salesperson satisfaction, the more likely the salesperson is to work toward achieving high customer satisfaction. We hold quarterly business meetings with all salespeople and openly discuss not only how the group is doing but also how the company is doing—everyone needs to know why their part is important to the success of the whole.

I also want to emphasize that it's just as important that my managers and supervisors motivate their top people to continue to excel as it is to remediate underperformers. Those top performers are likely the supervisors and managers of tomorrow—we can't have them leaving because we don't nurture their desire to excel.

Give me a specific example of how the culture, vision, and values of your group get translated into some actual reward opportunity for your salespeople.

Here's one example. Every salesperson fills out a card indicating preferences like favorite foods, "wish list" gifts, preferences for receiving performance recognition (as in, do they prefer to be recognized publicly or one-on-one), and so on. Then, when we decide to run a sales contest we can easily customize the rewards around the specific likes/dislikes of each participant.

How important do you believe nonfinancial rewards are to motivating salespeople?

I see great value in nonfinancial rewards and use them a lot—things like bringing professional development courses right on-site, encouraging salespeople to shadow in other departments, and generally giving people an opportunity to become more valuable on the job. Two of my three current sales managers started out as sales reps. Many of our salespeople have gone from inside sales to outside sales, as well as to different jobs and units throughout the company. Nonfinancial rewards are potentially very powerful motivators.

Overview of Compensation and Incentives

Chapter 10 introduced the concept of rewards. The way the reward structure is implemented in a sales organization is through the **compensation plan.** Three basic questions drive successful compensation plans.

1. Which compensation method is most appropriate for motivating specific kinds of selling activities in specific selling situations?
2. How much of a salesperson's total compensation should be earned through incentives?
3. What is the best mix of financial and nonfinancial compensation and incentives for motivating the sales force?

In most firms, the total financial compensation paid to salespeople has several components, each of which may be designed to achieve different objectives. The core of sales compensation plans consists of a salary and incentive payments. A **salary** is a fixed sum of money paid at regular intervals. The amount of salary paid to a given salesperson is usually a function of that salesperson's experience, competence, and time on the job, as well as the sales manager's judgments about the quality of the individual's performance. Salary adjustments are useful to reward salespeople for performing customer relationship-building activities that may not directly result in sales in the short term, such as prospecting for new customers or providing postsale service. They can also help adjust for differences in sales potential across territories.

Many firms that pay their salespeople a salary also offer additional **incentive pay** to encourage good performance. Incentives may take the form of commissions tied to sales volume or profitability, or bonuses for meeting or exceeding specific performance targets (e.g., meeting quotas for particular products or particular types of customers). Such incentives direct salespeople's efforts toward specific strategic objectives during the year, as well as provide additional rewards for top performers. A **commission** is a payment based on short-term results, usually a salesperson's dollar or unit sales volume. Since a direct link exists between sales volume and the amount of commission received, commission payments are useful for increasing reps' selling efforts.

A **bonus** is a payment made at management's discretion for achieving or surpassing some set level of performance. Commissions are typically paid for each sale; a bonus is typically not paid until the salesperson surpasses some level of total sales or other aspect of performance. The size of the bonus might be determined by the degree to which the salesperson exceeds the minimum level of performance required to earn it. Thus, bonuses are usually *additional incentives* to motivate salespeople to reach high levels of performance, rather than part of the basic compensation plan. Bonuses are almost never the sole form of compensation. Rather, they are combined with other compensation elements.

Attaining a **quota** is often the minimum requirement for a salesperson to earn a bonus. Quotas can be based on goals for sales volume, profitability of sales, or various account-servicing activities. To be effective, quotas (like goals) should be specific, measurable, and realistically attainable. Therefore, bonuses can be a reward for attaining or surpassing a predetermined level of performance on any dimensions for which quotas are set.

In addition to these incentives, many firms conduct **sales contests** to encourage extra effort aimed at specific short-term objectives. For example, a contest might offer additional rewards for salespeople who obtain a specified volume of orders from new customers or who exceed their quotas for a new product during a three-month period. Contest winners might be given additional cash, merchandise, or travel awards.

Finally, a foundation of most compensation plans is a package of **benefits** designed to satisfy the salesperson's basic needs for security. Benefits typically include medical and disability insurance, life insurance, and a retirement plan, among others. The types and amount of benefits in a compensation plan are usually a matter of company policy and apply to all employees. The benefit package a firm offers its salespeople should be comparable to competitors' plans to avoid being at a disadvantage when recruiting new sales talent.

The key forms of financial compensation of salespeople are summarized in Exhibit 13.1.

It is important to know that beyond financial compensation, a variety of **nonfinancial incentives** exist. These might take the form of opportunities for promotion

EXHIBIT 13.1 Components and Objectives of Financial Compensation Plans

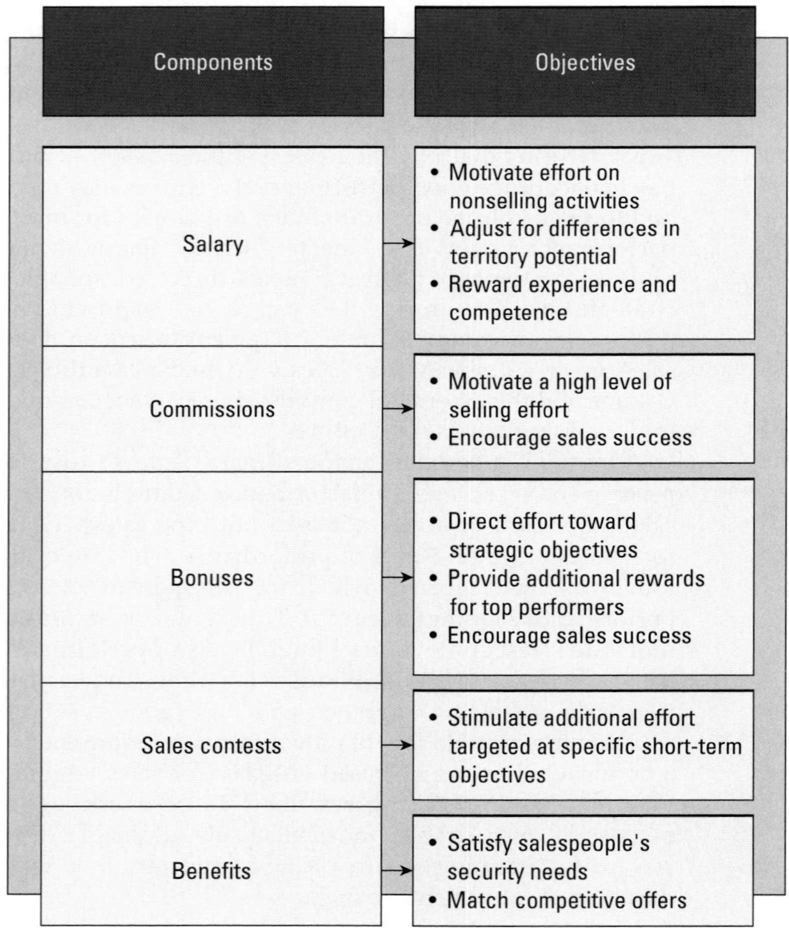

Components
Objectives
Salary
• Motivate effort on nonselling activities
• Adjust for differences in territory potential
• Reward experience and competence
Commissions
• Motivate a high level of selling effort
• Encourage sales success
Bonuses
• Direct effort toward strategic objectives
• Provide additional rewards for top performers
• Encourage sales success
Sales contests
• Stimulate additional effort targeted at specific short-term objectives
Benefits
• Satisfy salespeople's security needs
• Match competitive offers

Source: *Churchill/Ford/Walker's Sales Force Management,* 9th ed., by Mark W. Johnston and Greg W. Marshall (New York: McGraw-Hill, 2009), p. 347. Reprinted by permission of the McGraw-Hill Companies.

or various types of recognition for performance, such as special awards and mention in company newsletters. Nonfinancial incentives will be discussed in more detail later in the chapter.

Straight Salary, Straight Commission, and Combination Plans

The three primary methods of compensating salespeople are (1) straight salary, (2) straight commission, and (3) a combination of base salary plus incentive pay in the form of commissions, bonuses, or both. In recent years, the steady trend has been away from both straight salary and straight commission plans toward combination plans. Today, combination plans are by far the most common form of compensation.

In essence, managers seek to create a "pay for performance" plan that uses both salary and incentive programs to maximize salespeople's performance. Unfortunately, creating such programs is very complex, and companies often choose a program based on convenience or cost effectiveness rather than actual benefits to the company.[1] There is much variety in preferences for rewards among salespeople.

The following sections highlight the three main compensation approaches, along with advantages and disadvantages of each. Exhibit 13.2 summarizes the discussion.

EXHIBIT 13.2 Compensation Methods for Salespeople

Compensation Method (Frequency of Use)	Especially Useful	Advantages	Disadvantages
Straight Salary	When compensating new sales reps; when firm moves into new sales territories that require developmental work; when sale reps must perform many nonselling activities	Provides sales rep with maximum security; gives sales manager more control over sales reps; is easy to administer; yields more predictable selling expenses	Provides no incentive; necessitates closer supervision of sale reps' activities; during sales declines, selling expenses remain at same level
Straight Commission	When highly aggressive selling is required; when nonselling tasks are minimized; when company cannot closely control sales force activities	Provides maximum incentive; by increasing commission rate, sales managers can encourage reps to sell certain items; selling expenses relate directly to selling resources	Sales reps have little financial security; sales manager has minimum control over sales force; may cause reps to provide inadequate service to smaller accounts; selling costs are less predictable
Combination	When sales territories have relatively similar sales potential; when firm wishes to provide incentive but still control sales force activities	Provides certain level of financial security; provides some incentive; selling expenses fluctuate with sales revenue; sales manager has some control over reps' nonselling activities	Selling expenses are less predictable; may be difficult to administer

Source: *Churchill/Ford/Walker's Sales Force Management,* 9th ed., by Mark W. Johnston and Greg W. Marshall (New York: McGraw-Hill, 2009), p. 348. Reprinted by permission of the McGraw-Hill Companies.

Straight Salary

Two sets of conditions favor the straight salary compensation plan: (1) when management wishes to motivate salespeople to achieve objectives other than short-run sales volume and (2) when the individual salesperson's impact on sales volume is difficult to measure in a reasonable time. Because relationship selling may involve both of these conditions, it is not uncommon for sales jobs with heavy customer care to be compensated by straight salary.

Advantages. The primary advantage of a straight salary is that management can require salespeople to spend their time on activities that may not result in immediate sales. A salary plan or a plan with a large proportion of fixed salary is appropriate when the salesperson is expected to perform many customer service or other nonselling activities. These may include market research, customer problem analysis, product stocking, customer education, or sales promotion. Straight salary plans are also common in industries where many engineering and design services are part of the selling function, such as in high technology industries.

Straight salary compensation plans are also desirable when it is difficult for management to measure the individual salesperson's impact on sales volume or other aspects of performance. Thus, firms tend to pay salaries to their sales force when (1) their salespeople are engaged in missionary selling, as in the pharmaceutical industry; (2) other parts of the marketing program, such as advertising or dealer promotions, are the primary determinants of sales success, as in some consumer packaged-goods businesses; or (3) the selling process is complex and involves a team, cross-functional, or multilevel selling effort, as in the case of computers.

Career counselors often advise college students seeking a first job in relationship selling to try to make that first experience heavier in salary component than incentive pay. This gives the new salesperson some time to learn the ropes and hone his or her skills while earning a steady income. Because straight salary plans provide a steady, guaranteed income, they are often used when the salesperson's ability to generate immediate sales is uncertain, as with new recruits in a field training program or when a firm is introducing a new product line or opening new territories.

Finally, straight salary plans are easy for management to compute and administer. They also give management more flexibility. It is easy to reassign salespeople to new territories or product lines because such changes will not affect their compensation (unless the manager chooses to provide a salary increase). Also, since salaries are fixed costs, the compensation cost per unit sold is lower at relatively high sales volume.

Disadvantages. The major limitation of straight salary compensation is that financial rewards are not tied directly to any specific aspect of job performance. Management should attempt to give bigger salary increases each year to the good performers than the poor ones. However, the amount of those increases and the way performance is evaluated are subject to the whims of the manager who makes the decision. Also, salaries do not provide any direct financial incentive for improving sales-related aspects of performance. Consequently, over the long run salary plans appeal more to security-oriented than achievement-oriented salespeople.

Straight Commission

A commission is payment for achieving a given level of performance. That is, salespeople are paid for sales results. Usually, commission payments are based on the salesperson's dollar or unit sales volume. However, it is becoming more popular for firms to base commissions on the *profitability* of sales to motivate the sales force to expend effort on the most profitable products or customers. The most common way is to offer salespeople higher commissions for sales of the most profitable products or sales to the most profitable customers. Such a **variable commission rate** can also be used to direct the sales force's efforts toward other straight sales objectives. For example, the firm might pay a higher commission on a new product line being introduced.

Advantages. Direct motivation is the key advantage of a commission compensation plan, since a clear and direct link exists between how much salespeople sell and how much they earn. Salespeople are strongly motivated to improve their sales productivity to increase their compensation, at least until they reach such high pay that further incremental increases become less attractive. Commission plans also have a built-in element of fairness (assuming that sales territories are properly defined, with about equal potential) because they reward good performers and discourage poor performers from continuing their low productivity.

Commission plans have some advantages from a sales management viewpoint. Commissions are usually easy to compute and administer. Also, compensation costs vary directly with sales volume. This is an advantage for firms that are short of working capital because they do not need to pay high wages to the sales force unless it generates high sales revenues.

Disadvantages. Straight commission compensation plans have some important limitations that have caused many firms, especially those engaged in relationship selling, to abandon them. Perhaps the most critical weakness is management's lack of control over the sales force. When all their financial rewards are tied directly to sales volume, salespeople can be difficult to motivate to engage in relationship-building activities that do not lead directly to short-term sales. Salespeople on commission are likely to "milk" existing customers rather than work to acquire new accounts and build long-term relationships. For example, they may overstock their customers and neglect service after the sale. Finally, they have little motivation to engage in market analysis and other functions that take time away from selling.

Straight commission plans also have a disadvantage for many salespeople. They make earnings unstable and hard to predict. When business conditions are poor, turnover rates are likely to be high because salespeople can't live on the low earnings produced by poor sales. To combat the inherent instability of commission plans, some firms provide a **draw,** or drawing account, that advances money to salespeople in months when commissions are low to ensure they will always take home a specified minimum pay. The amount of each salesperson's draw in poor months is deducted from earned commissions when sales improve. This gives salespeople some secure salary and allows management more control over their activities. A problem arises, however, when a salesperson fails to earn enough commissions to repay the draw. Then the person may quit or be fired, and the company must absorb the loss.[2]

Combination Plans

Compensation plans that offer a base salary plus some proportion of incentive pay are the most popular. They have many of the advantages but avoid most of the limitations of both straight salary and straight commission plans. The base salary provides salespeople with a stable income and gives management some ability to reward them for performing customer service and administrative tasks that are directed more toward relationship building than building short-term sales. At the same time, the incentive portion provides direct rewards to motivate salespeople to expend effort to improve sales volume and profitability.

Combination plans bring together a base salary with commissions, bonuses, or both. When salary plus commission is used, the commissions are tied to sales volume and/or profitability, just as with a straight commission plan. The only difference is that the commissions are smaller in a combination plan. A bonus component typically recognizes the achievement of some specific performance goal(s).

Whether base salary is combined with commission payments or bonuses, managers must answer several questions when designing effective combination compensation plans. (1) What is the appropriate size of the incentive relative to the base salary? (2) Should a ceiling be imposed on incentive earnings? (3) When should the salesperson be credited with a sale? (4) Should team incentives be used? If so, how should they be allocated among members of a sales team? (5) How often should the salesperson receive incentive payments?

Proportion of Incentive Pay to Total Compensation. What proportion of total compensation should be incentive pay? The sales manager's decision should be based on the degree of relationship selling involved in the job. When the firm's primary selling approaches relate directly to short-term sales (such as increasing dollar or unit sales volume, or profitability), a large incentive component should be offered. When customer service and other nonsales objectives are deemed more important, the major emphasis should be on the base salary component of the plan. This gives management more control over rewarding the sales force's relationship-selling activities.

When the salesperson's selling skill is the key to sales success, the incentive portion should be relatively large. However, when the product has been presold through advertising and the salesperson is largely an order taker, or when the sales job involves a large proportion of missionary or customer service work, the incentive component should be relatively small.

If a particular combination plan is not very effective at motivating salespeople, the incentive portion is probably too small to generate much interest. Companies are always challenged to hire and retain the best salespeople. One approach is to open up the incentive component to negotiation on an individual basis. Salespeople who seek greater security can focus on more fixed compensation (salary); risk takers can opt for the potential to earn even higher total compensation by placing more of their compensation in incentive-based rewards.[3] Such individualized approaches must allow a salesperson to change his or her compensation allocation periodically, perhaps annually.

Incentive Ceilings. Should there be a ceiling or cap on incentive earnings to ensure top salespeople do not earn substantially more money than other employees? This issue is dealt with in very different ways across companies and industries. Strong arguments can be made on both sides. Part of the difference in how different firms handle this issue seems to reflect variation in average compensation levels. Firms in relatively low-paying industries are more likely to impose caps than those in higher-paying fields.

One argument in favor of ceilings is that they ensure top salespeople will not earn so much that other employees in the firm (sometimes even managers) suffer resentment and low morale. Ceilings also protect against windfalls—such as increased sales due to the introduction of successful new products—where a salesperson's earnings might become very large without corresponding effort. Finally, ceilings make a firm's maximum potential sales compensation expense more predictable and controllable.

A strong counterargument can be made, however, that ceilings ultimately reduce motivation and dampen the sales force's enthusiasm. Also, some salespeople may reach the earnings maximum early and be inclined to take it easy for the rest of the year.

The issue of incentive ceilings has become a growing problem in relationship selling, especially in a team-selling environment. As team selling brings individuals from around the company to help with a customer, the question becomes how much the sales rep should make in a sale that results from the efforts of many individuals. This problem gets worse as the size of each sale grows larger and is especially relevant with key accounts.

Another problem with incentive ceilings occurs when the customer is a global firm. How much should the sales rep who is servicing the customer's headquarters in his or her territory be compensated for a sale in another part of the world? The solution that many companies have chosen is capping incentive compensation.[4]

Some desired effects of ceilings can be accomplished without arbitrary limits on the sales force's motivation if management pretests any new or revised compensation plan before implementing it. Sales managers can do this by analyzing the sales performance records of selected reps to see how they would have come out under the proposed compensation system. Particular attention should be given to the compensation that the best and poorest performers would have earned to ensure that the plan is both fair and reasonable.

When Is a Sale a Sale? When incentives are based on sales volume or other sales-related aspects of performance, the precise meaning of a *sale* should be defined to avoid confusion and irritation. Most incentive plans credit a salesperson with a sale when the order is accepted by the company, less any returns and allowances. Occasionally, though, it makes good sense to credit the salesperson with a sale only after the goods have been shipped or payment has been received from the customer. This is particularly true when the time between receipt of an order and shipment of the goods is long and the company wants its salespeople to maintain close contact with customers to prevent cancellations and other problems. As a compromise, some plans credit salespeople with half a sale when the order is received and the other half when payment is made.

Team versus Individual Incentives. The increasing use of sales or cross-functional teams to win new customers and service major accounts raises some important questions about the kinds of incentives to include in a combination compensation plan. Should incentives be tied to the overall performance of the entire team, should separate incentives be keyed to the individual performance of each team member, or both? If both group and individual incentives are used, which should be given greater weight? Sales managers must address these questions when designing team-based incentives.

When Should a Salesperson Receive Incentive Payments? One survey of over 500 compensation plans found that 21 percent paid salespeople incentive earnings on an annual basis, 3 percent paid semiannually, 24 percent paid quarterly, and 52 percent made monthly payments. In general, plans offering salary plus commission were more likely to involve monthly incentive payments, while salary plus bonus plans more often made incentive payments on a quarterly or annual schedule.

Shorter intervals between performance and the receipt of rewards increase the motivating power of the plan. However, short intervals add to the computation required, increase administrative expenses, and may make the absolute amount of money received appear so small salespeople are not very impressed with their rewards. Quarterly incentive payments are an effective compromise.

Sales Contests

Sales contests are short-term incentive programs designed to motivate sales reps to accomplish specific sales objectives. Although contests should not be considered part of a firm's ongoing compensation plan, they offer salespeople both financial and nonfinancial rewards. Contest winners often receive prizes in cash, merchandise, or travel. They also receive recognition and a sense of accomplishment.

Successful contests require the following:

- Clearly defined, specific objectives.
- An exciting theme.
- Reasonable probability of rewards for all salespeople.
- Attractive rewards.
- Promotion and follow-through.[5]

Contest Objectives

Because contests *supplement* the firm's compensation program and are designed to motivate extra effort toward some short-term goal, their objectives should be very specific and clearly defined. Equally important, incentive compensation needs to be consistent with stated corporate objectives. Unfortunately, although companies may believe having an objective is important, they do not always create incentives that reflect those objectives.

The time frame for achieving the contest's objectives should be relatively short so that salespeople will maintain their enthusiasm and effort throughout the contest. But the contest should last long enough to allow all members of the sales force to cover their territories at least once and have a reasonable chance of generating the performance necessary to win. The average duration of sales contests is about three months.

Contest Themes

A sales contest should have an exciting theme to build enthusiasm among the participants and promote the event. The theme should also stress the contest's objectives and appeal to all participants. Companies are getting more and more creative about the themes they devise for contests. Popular themes center around the distribution of award travel, sports events, or the products available for contest winners (such as home entertainment centers and other popular consumer electronics).

Probability of Winning

Three popular contest formats are available. In the first, salespeople compete with themselves by trying to attain individual quotas. Everyone who reaches or exceeds quota during the contest period wins. A second form requires that all members of the sales force compete with each other. The people who achieve the highest overall performance on some dimension are the winners, and everyone else loses. A third format organizes the sales force into teams, which compete for group and individual prizes.

Historically, individual sales quotas have been the most popular of the three formats because they allow firms to design contests that focus salespeople's efforts on specific objectives, they don't penalize reps in low-potential territories, and they don't undermine cooperation by forcing salespeople to compete against each other. Whichever format is used, it is essential that every member of the sales force have a reasonable chance of winning an award. If there will be only one or a few winners, many salespeople may think their chances are remote and completely give up on the contest. Average or below average performers may automatically assume the top performers will win the award and not try as hard to hit sales goals. Contests that provide rewards to everyone who meets his or her own quota during the contest period are desirable. Increasingly, companies are focusing on incentive programs, including contests, that seek to reward more rather than fewer salespeople.

Types of Contest Rewards

Contest rewards commonly take the form of cash, merchandise, or travel. A company may vary the kinds of rewards offered from contest to contest. As you heard from Debra Lacy in the Expert Advice at the beginning of this chapter, when deciding on sales contest rewards one size does not fit all. More and more rewards are being tailored to individual reps' hot buttons. Once the dollar value is established, the winner may choose from several rewards. Or the manager may simply ask what kind of reward the salesperson wants. The idea is to find rewards that motivate each salesperson (within budget constraints). One consultant cautions, "Tom, your top salesperson, learns that the reward for achieving success in the new sales contest is a set of MacGregor golf clubs. However, Tom's wife just bought him a new set of Callaways complete with the new Big Bertha driver. Chances are that Tom will not be motivated to win another set of clubs."[6]

An Incentive Federation survey found that on average, 79 percent of respondents found noncash reward programs extremely effective in motivating participants to achieve sales goals.[7] "Cash is great," says a sales and marketing manager for a major insurance company. "But we like to give merchandise so the winner has some boasting rights. And if we award money, the reps generally won't spend it on something for themselves—even if it's something they really want." One of the company's salespeople was awarded a suede jacket for a contest he won recently. "I wear it all the time, and every time I get a compliment, I tell them I won it," he says.

Merchandise also gives management an opportunity to present the reward as part of a ceremony celebrating success. "When you present someone with a watch with all their colleagues around, they can congratulate the winner and, at the same time, see what they can win if they hit their next target," the manager says. And the salesperson agrees: "Merchandise gets me going. A check isn't as tangible as merchandise. You can't really show someone a check—it's not interesting. When you get money, you just mentally lump it in with your paycheck."[8]

INNOVATION 13.1

Today's Incentive Market Demands Simple, Value-Oriented Rewards Plans

In the last few months, several incentive companies have introduced new programs that emphasize simplicity and back-to-basics value. Incentive Logic's new IGNITExpress, Rewards Direct by Maritz, and Altour Incentive Management (AIM)'s Aspire software bundles are all offering companies a formal, but simple, rewards program.

Rewards Direct, announced in early August, serves clients needing rewards fulfillment service only. According to Michael Donnelly, CEO of St. Louis–based Maritz Motivation, the program is targeted at organizations with a "do-it-yourself" approach to incentives.

"They really understand their business and their clients, but on the motivation side, they need the help with awards that really deliver the promise," says Donnelly. He explains that client companies may be strong on the "understanding and enabling" of employee performance, but will want to reach out to a company with Maritz's background to provide a "purposeful choice" to winners. The program aims to fit easily into clients' pre-existing incentive programs, rather than overhaul the whole thing. Similarly, Incentive Logic's platform, IGNITExpress, also aims to help get companies onboard with a formal program, even if it's a modest one.

"It helps companies that really have no internal benchmark for a program and want to try it out, but the full engagement of a customer program is just too much to bite off," says Troy Darling, manager of corporate marketing for Incentive Logic. "What it will tell companies is whether just the fact of having a program will have some impact."

The IGNITExpress platform handles all aspects of a points-based rewards program such as online reward redemption, fulfillment, tracking, and administration.

"We know that if we do the deeper analysis, do the more consulting-oriented work, then we can do a more efficient incentive program," says Darling. "But IGNITExpress is a good way for them to test the water a bit."

In some senses, these programs are a response to the more lean economic times. The simpler, more budget-friendly rewards programs may be desirable for companies trying to keep costs down, but they also offer a solution to clients looking for a boost to productivity that may be new to formal incentive systems.

"If you've got a big program already and you're looking to cut costs, that might be one place you're looking," says Darling. "But if you don't have a program and you're looking to be more competitive, then you're looking at incentive programs. We expect a certain amount of turn, but we also expect to gain a lot of business as well."

Altour Incentive Management (AIM)'s Aspire packages aim for similar ease-of-use to buyers. According to the Mesa, Arizona–based company's president, Rosemarie Christofolo, the packages are targeted to "midtier" companies that are just looking to run the basic functions of an incentive program—"without all the bells and whistles." Instead of customizing the program for each specific company, the Aspire packages work more as off-the-shelf options that will get clients set up with a simple, proven rewards program that they can expand on as needed.

AIM currently is offering three Aspire software bundles: a standard and premium employee recognition program, as well as a sales incentive program. Customers purchasing one of these can add additional custom features as they choose.

Source: Alex Palmer, "Motivation Made Easy: Incentive Houses Go Back to Basics with New Programs," *Incentive,* September 2008, p. 182.

Lexington, Kentucky–based printer manufacturer Lexmark International adjusted its incentive program to allow for changing preferences among its sales staff. Rather than offering a one-size-fits-all reward, Lexmark adopted a points-based program in which salespeople can select gifts from a catalog. So far, the most popular items have been useful products for the home.[9]

Whatever form of reward is used, the monetary value must be large enough to appeal to the participants given their level of compensation. For example, the latest iPhone, Blackberry, or GPS device may be more attractive where the average salesperson makes $40,000 per year than where the average compensation is $100,000.

In today's value-conscious marketplace, firms are turning to incentive programs that are simple yet meaningful. Innovation 13.1 describes several of these rewards programs offered by three popular sales force incentive vendors.

Contest Promotion and Follow-through

To generate interest and enthusiasm, contests should be launched with fanfare. Where possible, firms should announce contests at national or regional sales meetings. Follow-up promotion is also necessary to maintain interest throughout the contest period. Special Web sites where salespeople can access password-protected personal pages facilitate this. Also, as the contest proceeds, salespeople should be given frequent feedback concerning their progress so they know how much more they must do to win. Finally, winners should be recognized and prizes awarded promptly.

Criticism of Sales Contests

Although many sales managers believe contests motivate special efforts from salespeople, contests can cause a few problems—particularly if they are poorly designed or implemented.

Some critics argue that contests designed to stimulate sales volume may produce fleeting results with no lasting improvement in market share. Salespeople may "borrow" sales from before and/or after the contest to increase their volume during the contest. That is, they may hold back orders before the contest and rush orders that would normally not be placed until after it. As a result, customers may be overstocked, causing sales volume to fall off for some time after the contest ends.

Contests may also hurt the cohesiveness and morale of the sales force, especially when they make individual reps compete against each other for rewards and when the number of rewards is limited.

Finally, some firms use sales contests to cover up faulty compensation plans. Salespeople should not have to be compensated a second time for what they are already being paid to do. Contests should be used only on a short-term basis to motivate special efforts beyond the normal performance expected of the sales force. If a firm has to conduct frequent contests to maintain acceptable sales performance, it should reexamine its entire compensation and incentive program.

Nonfinancial Rewards

In her Expert Advice, Debra Lacy emphasized the power of nonfinancial rewards. And Leadership 13.2 emphasizes the fact that it's a mistake to think that a firm's sales force compensation plan is the only way to improve sales performance. In fact, most sales managers consider opportunities for promotion and advancement second only to financial incentives as effective sales force motivators. This is particularly true for young, well-educated salespeople, who tend to view their jobs as steppingstones to top management. One common career path is from salesperson to district sales manager to top sales management. A rep who has been with a firm for several years without making it into sales management may start to believe such a promotion will never happen. He or she may begin to concentrate solely on financial rewards or lose motivation and not work as hard at the job.

Leadership 13.2

Compensation Is Just Part of the Performance Equation

I'm often asked to help a company refine their sales force compensation plans. As a consulting company, that's work that we regularly do. I believe in having a well-designed, effectively managed compensation plan as a fundamental part of any productive sales system.

But, it's a mistake to think that the compensation plan is the entire solution. It's only a part.

The reason that a company will call us to help with the compensation plan is often a deeper issue. Their sales are flat, or even declining. They are casting about to find a solution to their lack of sales effectiveness, and have arrived at compensation as the culprit.

It may very well be contributing to the general malaise. But it's rarely the only issue. Let's consider some other factors commonly contributing to dismal sales numbers.

1. Training. Sales is a sophisticated profession where the skill set of the highest performers is significantly greater than that of the mediocre. And the unfortunate, ugly truth is that most B2B salespeople don't know how to do their jobs well. They have never been instructed in the best practices of the best salespeople. They have struggled to learn on their own, on the job, through trial and error. Some of them have arrived at routines that have been successful for them, but most have not.

You can change the compensation plan all you want, but if you don't instruct the salespeople in how to do the thing that you are paying them to do, your results will be considerably less than spectacular.

Here's an example. Let's say that you want to gain new customers. So, you change your compensation plan to pay a premium for new customers. That's good, and some salespeople will, as a result, put more effort to acquiring new customers.

But, that doesn't mean that any of them know how to do this well. While some will be attracted to the income, the lack of comfort associated with how to do it will be a far greater force, holding them back.

If you pay them a premium to create new customers, and then train them specifically in how to do that, you'll find that your change in sales force compensation will make a dramatic improvement in their behavior.

The same can be said for any specific behavior that you want to encourage through a revised sales force compensation plan. It won't do you much good to emphasize key account penetration, key product line sales, and so on, unless you take the time to show them how to do what you want them to do.

2. Management practices. The practices and routines followed by sales management can have a great impact on the performance of the salesperson. For example, if you change your compensation plan to emphasize acquiring new accounts, and your sales manager never measures the number of new accounts acquired, never measures the various steps in that process, never asks the salesperson about it nor holds him accountable in any way, your change in sales force compensation will be ineffective.

Sales managers need to measure the progress on every performance indicator encouraged by the compensation plan. They need to have regular meetings with each salesperson in which the topic of conversation is dictated by the sales manager, and focuses on specific progress on each performance indicator, and specific plans to achieve greater numbers.

3. Structure. In much of my other writing, I discuss the concept of "sales structure." Briefly, the structure is the set of written and unspoken policies, procedures, and expectations that surround the job of the salesperson. I like to characterize it as everything left in the sales department after you remove all the people. It is larger and more specific than "culture" because it is often codified and institutionalized. Some examples of elements of the structure include:

Sales compensation plan
Job descriptions
Territory definitions
CRM or lack thereof
Call reports, planning itineraries, or lack thereof
Pricing guidelines
Sales process definitions

This is just a small sampling of the list that makes up the "rules"—the way things are done in your company.

The key rule here is that the structure must support the behaviors that you are reinforcing in the compensation plan. For example, if you emphasize the acquisition of new accounts, but several of your salespeople have mature territories with few prospects left, the structure stands in the way of the compensation plan.

Most components of sales structure are vestiges of days gone by. They were created, typically, in response to a crisis some time ago, and became codified. Most companies aren't even aware of many elements of their structure, because they have been so imbedded into the routines of the company that they don't even notice them anymore.

It's not unusual to find elements of the sale structure that present obstacles to the attainment of the compensation behaviors. Not only are they not supportive, they stand in the way.

When you change your sales force compensation plan, look at every single behavior that you want to encourage, and ask yourself "Is there anything in the way we do sales in this company that presents an obstacle to the salesperson performing on this issue?" Be open-minded. You may even ask for some outside input. Remember, many of the elements of your structure are so deeply embedded into your routines that no one even notices them.

When you identify structural elements that are obstacles to sales success, work to eliminate them.

4. People. It is an unfortunate truth that many salespeople, maybe as high as 40 percent of your sales force, should not be in their jobs. While they may have all the product knowledge in the world, they just are not suited to deal effectively with the challenges of the job of the salesperson:

- Constant rejection.
- The need to create positive relationships with everyone.
- The responsibility to effectively manage their time.
- The need to continually learn more about every customer.

Sales is a profession that is growing more sophisticated and challenging by the day. Many of today's salespeople, who were adequate in terms of their aptitude and attitudes in the past, are not up to the rigorous demands of the job today.

You can have the greatest compensation plan in the world, but if your people are just not capable of performing, the plan will be a waste of time.

While I applaud every company's efforts to revise their compensation plans, at the same time I have learned that compensation is only one part of the picture. If you really want to revise your sales efforts, you need to attend to the other issues discussed above as well.

Source: Dave Kahle, "It Takes More than Just Compensation to Unleash a Sales Force," *American Salesman,* October 2007, p. 3.

To overcome this problem, some firms have instituted two career paths for salespeople. One leads to management, the other to more advanced positions within the sales force. The latter usually involves responsibility for dealing with key accounts or leading sales teams. Even if a salesperson doesn't move into management, he or she can still work toward a more prestigious and lucrative position within the sales force. To make advanced sales positions more attractive as promotions, many firms provide extra **perquisites (perks)** including higher compensation, a better car, and perhaps a nicer office.

Recognition Programs

Like contests, effective recognition programs should offer everyone in the sales force a reasonable chance of winning. But if everyone achieves recognition, the program is likely to lose some of its appeal because the winners feel no special sense of accomplishment. Consequently, effective programs often recognize the best performers across several dimensions. For example, winners might include reps with the highest sales volume for the year, the biggest percentage increase in sales, the biggest dollar increase, the highest number of new customers, the largest sales per account, and the best customer retention record.

Recognition is an attractive reward because it makes a salesperson's peers and superiors aware of the outstanding performance. Communicating the winner's achievements through recognition at a sales meeting, publicity in the local press, announcements in the company newsletter, and other ways is an essential part of a good recognition program. Firms typically give special awards that have low monetary but high symbolic value, such as trophies, plaques, or rings. Finally, as Exhibit 13.3 points out, objectivity and good taste are important ingredients of recognition programs (as they are for contests and other incentives).

Expense Accounts

Expense items incurred by sales reps in the field—travel, lodging, meals, and entertaining customers—can be substantial. Although field selling expenses vary across industries and types of sales jobs, nearly $16,000 per year is the average for a salesperson, and the amount may be much higher.[10] The growing trend of creating home offices for salespeople has increased expenses related to technology (laptops, smart phones, fax machines, teleconferencing) but reduced some travel expenses. Expense reimbursement plans, or **expense accounts,** range from unlimited reimbursement for all "reasonable and allowable" expenses to plans where salespeople must pay all expenses out of their total compensation. Obviously, an expense account enhances a salesperson's compensation.

When deciding which form of expense reimbursement to use, sales managers must make trade-offs between tight control aimed at holding down total expenses and the financial well-being—and subsequent motivation level—of salespeople. Some expense items (such as entertainment expenses, club dues, and the costs of personal services while the salesperson is away from home) can be considered either legitimate business expenses that should be reimbursed by the company or personal expenses that the rep should pay. Company policies and reimbursement plans that treat such costs as business expenses increase the salesperson's total financial compensation but also increase the firm's total selling costs.

Three key types of expense plans are direct reimbursement, limited reimbursement, and no reimbursement.

EXHIBIT 13.3 Guidelines for Effective Formal Recognition Programs

Regardless of its size or cost, any recognition program should incorporate the following features:

- The program must be strictly performance-based, with no room for subjective judgments. If people suspect that it is in any way a personality contest, the program will not work. The winners should be clear to anyone looking at the data.
- It should be balanced. The program should not be so difficult that only a few can hope to win or so easy that just about everyone does. In the first case, people will not try; in the second, the program will be meaningless.
- A ceremony should be involved. If rings are casually passed out or plaques sent through the mail, a lot of the glamour of the program will be lost.
- The program must be in good taste. If not, it will be subject to ridicule and, rather than motivate people, it will leave them uninspired. No one wants to be part of a recognition program that is condescending or tacky. The program should make people feel good about being part of the company.
- There must be adequate publicity. In some cases, sales managers do such a poor job of explaining a program or promoting it to their own salespeople that no one seems to understand or care about it. Prominent mention of the program in company publications is the first step to overcoming this handicap.

Sources: *Churchill/Ford/Walker's Sales Force Management*, 9th ed., by Mark W. Johnston and Greg W. Marshall (New York: McGraw-Hill, 2009), p. 358. Reprinted by permission of the McGraw-Hill Companies.

Direct Reimbursement Plans

One popular type of expense reimbursement plan involves direct and unlimited reimbursement of all "allowable and reasonable" expenses.[11] The primary advantage is that direct reimbursement plans give the sales manager some control over both the total magnitude of sales expenses and the kinds of activities salespeople will be motivated to do. If a particular activity, such as entertaining potential new accounts, is an important ingredient of the firm's account management policies, reimbursing all related expenses will encourage salespeople to do it. On the other hand, managers can discourage their subordinates from spending time on unimportant tasks by refusing to reimburse expenditures for such activities.

Thus, company policies concerning reimbursable expenses can be a useful tool for motivating and directing the sales effort. Some firms adjust their expense reimbursement policies according to the differences in the territories covered or the job activities required of different sales reps. For example, some reimburse a broader range and higher levels of expenses for their national account managers than for members of their regular field sales force.

The salesperson must submit receipts or detailed records justifying expense claims, so the processing and evaluation of expense claims add to the firm's sales administration costs in direct reimbursement plans.

Limited Reimbursement Plans

Some firms limit the total amount of expense reimbursement either by setting limits for each expense item (such as a $40 per person maximum for restaurant meals) or by providing each salesperson a predetermined lump-sum payment to cover total expenses. This approach keeps total selling expenses within planned limits—limits that are often determined by the sales expense budget set at the beginning of the year. Budgeted expense amounts may vary among members of the sales force, depending on past or forecasted sales volume or territory requirements.

Unless the budgeted limits are based on an accurate understanding of the costs associated with successful sales performance in each territory, however, limited reimbursement plans can hurt motivation and sales performance. Individual salespeople may believe their ability to do a good job is constrained by tightfisted reimbursement policies. Rather than pay for necessary activities out of their own pockets, they are likely to avoid or cut back on certain expense activities.

No Reimbursement Plans

Some firms require salespeople to cover all of their own expenses. Such plans usually pay higher total financial compensation to help salespeople cover necessary expenses. This is a variation on the predetermined lump-sum approach. No reimbursement expense plans usually accompany straight commission compensation plans involving high-percentage commissions. The rationale is that salespeople will be motivated to spend both the effort and money needed to increase sales volume as long as the financial rewards are big enough.

Like limited reimbursement plans, no reimbursement plans help the firm limit sales expenses or—in the case of commission plans—make them a totally variable cost that moves up and down with changes in sales volume. However, they also sacrifice management control over the motivation and activities of sales reps.

Leadership 13.3

The Perils of Rewarding A While Hoping for B

Steven Kerr coined the phrase "rewarding A while hoping for B" way back in 1975 in an article in the *Academy of Management Review.* His premise was this: "Very frequently, organizations establish reward systems that pay off one behavior even though the rewarder hopes dearly for some other behavior." This concept has strong application in sales force compensation plans, especially in today's complex environment of relationship selling.

Sales managers who wonder why their salespeople's behaviors do not seem to match their organization's goals might ask if their reward systems pay off salespeople for behaviors other than those sought by the firm. In the past, rewarding salespeople was easier. The focus was on individual salespeople approaching customers on a transaction-to-transaction basis. The focus today is on not just the salesperson but the whole organization working together toward developing long-term customer relationships. Do straight commission plans make sense in this environment? Not likely, since they motivate individual sales efforts, not teamwork.

Take hypothetical salesperson Chris. To achieve goals that yield desired results, Chris often has to rely in part on the performance of teammates who represent other functional areas of the firm. Unlike many salespeople of the past, she cannot individually and directly control much of the relationship-selling process. Chris can marshal internal resources and apply them to the relationship-building process and can certainly serve as a point person for managing the relationship, but she *cannot* directly control the actions of the whole team. Clearly, in such a situation standard compensation and incentive systems are inadequate.

Firms cannot expect salespeople to focus on operating effectively within a team or on securing, building, and maintaining long-term relationships with profitable customers if the reward system doesn't recognize and compensate them for these behaviors. That is, "hoping for B" should be matched by "rewarding B." In the relationship selling environment, incentives must be rethought and performance appraisal instruments refashioned to reflect the goals and behavior required for success today.

Steven Kerr had it right in 1975: "For an organization to act upon its members, the formal reward system should positively reinforce desired behaviors, not constitute an obstacle to be overcome."

Kerr's original article was updated and republished as follows: Steven Kerr, "On the Folly of Rewarding A, While Hoping for B," *Academy of Management Executive* 9:1 (1995), pp. 7–14.

Making Compensation and Incentive Programs Work

The many complex issues involved make designing and implementing an effective compensation and incentive program difficult. Many managers wonder whether their company's program is as effective as possible in motivating the kinds and amounts of effort they desire from salespeople. Sometimes, compensation plans get so complicated that they have to be retooled to be understandable to the sales force.

To make matters worse, even well-designed compensation programs can lose their effectiveness over time. As we discussed earlier, relationship selling is different from other approaches to selling, and this fact, along with the changing nature of the market environment, can cause plans to lose their motivational value. As salespeople become satisfied with the rewards offered by a particular incentive plan, for instance, the requirements of the job or the customer may change. Leadership 13.3 describes what may happen when reward systems do not match current job needs.

Recognizing such problems, an increasing number of firms review their compensation and incentive approaches often. Many firms adjust their total compensation levels at least annually and make more substantial adjustments in their programs when circumstances demand. Some firms have established compensation and incentive committees to monitor programs for fairness and effectiveness. Two major issues involve (1) assessing the firm's relationship selling objectives and (2) determining which aspects of job performance to reward.

Assessing the Relationship-Selling Objectives

A major purpose of any sales compensation program is to stimulate the sales force to work toward accomplishing the objectives of securing, building, and maintaining long-term relationships with profitable customers. As a first step in deciding what job activities and performance dimensions a new or improved compensation and incentive program should stimulate, a manager should evaluate how salespeople are allocating their time. On what job activities do they focus? How much time do they devote to each? How good are their current outcomes on various dimensions of performance, such as total sales volume, sales to new customers, or retention of existing customers? Much of this information can be obtained from a company's CRM program and from salesperson performance evaluations.

This assessment of the sales reps' current allocation of effort and levels of performance can then be compared to the firm's specific objectives for relationship selling. Such comparisons often reveal that some selling activities and dimensions of performance are receiving too much emphasis from the sales force, while others are not receiving enough. This situation requires an adjustment in the incentive plan, including an immediate look at the quotas salespeople are working against.

An important sales management function is monitoring whether the compensation and incentive plan, as well as associated quotas, continue to motivate the sales force over time. Remember that to be effective, quotas (goals for attaining some aspect of the sales job) must be specific, measurable, and realistically attainable. And, as indicated in Leadership 13.4, a great quota system must be backed up by a set of sales standards.

Determining Which Aspects of Job Performance to Reward

When a firm's relationship-selling objectives are misaligned with its sales reps' allocation of time, redesigning the compensation and incentive program to better reward desired activities or performance outcomes will motivate the reps to redirect their efforts.

Exhibit 13.4 on page 383, lists specific activities and performance dimensions that can be stimulated by a properly designed compensation and incentive program. Of course, managers would like their salespeople to perform well on all of these dimensions. As we saw earlier in the chapter, different components of a compensation program can be designed to reward different activities and achieve multiple objectives.

It is a mistake to try to motivate salespeople to do too many things at once. When rewards are tied to numerous aspects of performance: (1) It becomes difficult for a salesperson to focus on improving performance dramatically in any one area and (2) the salesperson is likely to be uncertain about how total performance will be evaluated and what rewards can be obtained as a result of that performance. In short, complex compensation and incentive programs may lead to great confusion by salespeople. Instead, compensation and incentive plans should link rewards to only the key aspects of job performance that are consistent with the firm's highest-priority relationship-selling objectives.

Leadership 13.4

Sales Standards for Better Sales Results

The vast majority of sales teams today work without a plan. In a basically hit-or-miss environment, it's amazing when they actually land sales contracts. Even when a sales force is hitting quota, company management often believes that they are operating at a fraction of their potential.

The bottom line is that a sales force often is not the disciplined group of professionals that management wants them to be. Many people attribute this lack of discipline to the "sales personality," and argue that attempting to infuse order and structure into their world would surely result in failure. Management, however, understands that absence of order in the sales team is one of the highest opportunity costs in the organization.

The power of sales standards. Is there a way to put discipline into the sales function without breaking its spirit? Won't discipline kill the motivation of a good sales team?

Good sales people are typically high-energy, relationship-oriented people with a low tolerance for structure. Their talents lie in handling the nuances of multiple relationships in an uncertain and dynamic environment. It's hard to be successful while following strict (and restrictive) rules in a high-stakes game with shifting goals, fierce competition, and multiple layers of decision makers, influencers, and spoilers to navigate.

Sales standards are the answer. Sales standards are not policies and procedures. They are a set of best practices, lessons learned, and minimal operating procedures that help create discipline and that form the baseline for team learning. They offer the right structure for high performance as well as discipline, and also allow the freedom to adapt and improvise as needed.

The seven building blocks of good sales standards. Sales standards can take many forms. To be effective, they have these common sections:

1. **Corporate information.** This section discusses the corporation, areas of business, and strategy. It needs to tie corporate strategy to a compelling "dream" that can really motivate the sales team.
2. **Sales organization.** This section covers "how things work" with topics such as territories, marketing support, team procedures, and performance measurement. "Sales operations rhythm" is a key topic. It defines the timing, tone and objectives of periodic sales meetings. It also includes the manner and method of management spot checks. Another key topic in this section covers coaching to support their continued development. A coaching standard that includes simple forms and steps can ensure that coaching takes place on an ongoing basis.
3. **On-boarding process.** Getting the right people on the bus (and the wrong ones off) is one of the easiest ways to improve the performance of the whole sales force. This section of your sales standards should spell out in detail how you market for new sales positions, what prehire assessments you use, the interview process, structured interview questions for each step of the process, and the hands-on skill demonstration tests candidates must pass.
4. **Tools and technology.** This section outlines the basics of your sales management software system, and is as much about data entry consistency as about instruction. The important items to include here are screenshots and how-to's for entering new prospects into the system, forecasting, contact management, report creation, and any other key system use.
5. **Prospecting.** There is no one right way to prospect; different personality styles are better at different approaches. This section should contain all of the "best practices" your team uses, directly from the people who have been successful using them.
6. **The engagement cycle.** This section should diagram the critical milestones in your engagement or sales cycle. It should also provide guidelines for account management. This helps everyone who touches the customer coordinate with each other in order to win the sale.
7. **Selling tactics.** This section covers how to qualify prospects, position your services, and close business. It should include lists of questions to use at each stage of the sales cycle and for approaching different types of buyers. It should also include "how to" scripts for positioning your products, selling against competitors, as well as closing techniques.

You have them, now use them. When you have completed your sales standards, make the document tangible. Print, bind, and distribute it the "old fashioned" way. Use version numbers with different covers for new iterations, and make sure people destroy or return old copies. People will take the document far more seriously when formal updates are employed. You can have an electronic version on your intranet, but this is not a substitute for the printed document.

When you are ready to launch your sales standards, hold a series of meetings with your team to review the document. Expect resistance, but don't succumb to it. If you don't communicate clearly at this point, no one will take the standards seriously, and you won't establish the discipline you want to achieve.

Refer back to the standards in every meeting. If an issue is not addressed in the standards, add it to the document. If there are loopholes that allow individuals to take advantage of others on the team, close those loopholes. If you have a recurring problem with poor coordination between sales and service, send the team back to the standards the next time the issue comes up. After a while, people will catch on and get in the habit of referring to the standards when resolving issues.

Create a standards review committee that meets at an interval appropriate for your business. Their role is to review and update the standards based on feedback from the sales team. This helps establish the sales standards as the primary repository for best practices and lessons learned.

These tips for creating and using sales standards will go a long way toward decreasing the opportunity cost of an undisciplined sales team. Over time, you will see measurable benefits that provide a clear return on the time and energy spent on this key element of an effective sales force.

Source: Bryan Feller, "Sales Standards for Better Sales Results," *American Salesman,* August 2007, p. 12.

The complex relationship between today's customers and their suppliers means salespeople must cooperate and work with many individuals within their own firm as well as within the customer's business. Many of the performance outcomes in Exhibit 13.4 cannot be achieved unless salespeople cooperate with others. Linking financial compensation programs with the need for salesperson cooperation is critical in building long-term relationships with customers.[12] Oracle's Siebel CRM applications, for example, link sales rep compensation with customer-oriented metrics such as customer satisfaction. However, some firms are reluctant to base rewards on customer satisfaction because of the difficulty of measuring changes in satisfaction over time.

Also, while there is some evidence that strong satisfaction-based incentives improve customer service by salespeople, some managers worry that such incentives may distract sales reps from the tasks necessary to capture additional sales volume in the short term. To offset this problem, some firms combine customer satisfaction–based incentives with bonus or commission payments tied to

EXHIBIT 13.4 Sales Activities and Performance Outcomes That Compensation and Incentive Programs Can Encourage

- Sell a greater overall dollar volume.
- Increase sales of more profitable products.
- Push new products.
- Push selected items at designated seasons.
- Achieve a higher degree of market penetration by products, kinds of customers, or territories.
- Secure large average orders.
- Secure new customers.
- Service and maintain existing business.
- Reduce turnover of customers.
- Encourage cooperation among members of sales or account management teams.
- Achieve full-line (balanced) selling.
- Reduce direct selling costs.
- Increase the number of calls made.
- Submit reports and other data promptly.

Source: *Churchill/Ford/Walker's Sales Force Management,* 9th ed., by Mark W. Johnston and Greg W. Marshall (New York: McGraw-Hill, 2009), p. 363. Reprinted by permission of the McGraw-Hill Companies.

sales quotas or revenue. Unfortunately, such mixed-incentive plans can sometimes confuse the sales force—and even lead to *reductions* in customer service levels.[13]

The bottom line is that although rewarding customer service is an attractive goal, it can present some thorny measurement and design issues that the sales manager will have to work out.

Deciding on the Mix and Level of Compensation

Not all salespeople find the same kinds of rewards equally attractive. Needs and preferences vary depending on personalities, demographic characteristics, and lifestyles. No single reward—including money—is likely to motivate all of a firm's salespeople. Similarly, a mix of rewards that motivates a sales force at one time may lose its appeal as the members' personal circumstances and needs change and as new salespeople are hired. In view of this, a wise first step in designing a sales compensation and incentive package is to determine the reps' current preferences for various rewards.[14]

The decision about how much total compensation (base pay plus any incentives) a salesperson may earn is crucial in designing an effective motivation program. The starting point for this decision is to determine the gross amount of compensation necessary to attract, retain, and motivate salespeople who can manage the firm's customer relationships. This also depends on the specific type of sales job in question, the size of the firm and the sales force, and the resources available to the firm.

Chapter 2 introduced several types of sales jobs, and it is important to note that average total compensation varies substantially across them. In general, more complex and demanding sales jobs, which require salespeople with special qualifications, offer higher compensation than more routine sales jobs. To compete for the best talent, a firm should determine how much total compensation other firms in its industry or related ones provide people in similar jobs. Then the firm can decide whether to compensate its salespeople an average or above average amount relative to these other firms. Few companies consciously pay below average (although some do so without realizing it) because below-average compensation generally cannot attract selling talent.

The decision about whether to offer average or premium total compensation depends in part on the size of the firm and its sales force. Large firms with good reputations in their industries and large sales forces generally offer only average total compensation. Firms like Intel and Cisco can attract sales talent because of their reputation in the marketplace and because they are big enough to offer advancement into management. Such firms can hire younger people (often just out of school) as sales trainees and put them through an extensive training program. This allows them to provide relatively low total compensation because they do not have to pay a market premium to attract older, more experienced salespeople.

In contrast, smaller firms often cannot afford extensive training programs. They may have to offer above-average compensation to attract experienced sales reps from other firms.

Dangers of Paying Salespeople Too Much

Some firms, regardless of their size or position in their industries, offer their salespeople opportunities to make very large amounts of money. The rationale for such high compensation is that it will attract the best talent and motivate sales reps to continue working for higher and higher sales volumes. This leads some sales managers to think there's no such thing as paying salespeople too much, since in their view compensation relates directly to volume of sales.

Unfortunately, overpaying salespeople relative to what other firms pay for similar jobs and relative to what other employees in the same firm are paid for nonsales jobs can cause major problems. For one thing, compensation is usually the largest element of a firm's selling costs, so overpaying salespeople increases selling costs and reduces profits. Also, it can cause resentment and low morale among the firm's other employees and executives when salespeople earn more money than even top management. It becomes virtually impossible to promote good salespeople into managerial positions because of the financial sacrifice they would have to make.

Finally, it is not clear that offering unlimited opportunities to earn higher pay is always an effective way to motivate salespeople to continually increase the selling effort. At some compensation level, the next dollar earned would likely show diminishing returns in terms of motivation.

Dangers of Paying Salespeople Too Little

Overpaying salespeople can cause problems, but it is critically important not to underpay them. Holding down sales compensation may appear to be a convenient way to hold down selling costs and enhance profits, but this is usually not true in the *long run.* When buying talent in the labor market, a company tends to get what it pays for. If poor salespeople are hired at low pay, poor performance will almost surely result. If good salespeople are hired at low pay, the firm is likely to have high turnover, with higher costs for recruiting and training replacements and lost sales.

In the high-flying days of the e-commerce boom of the late 1990s, many technology companies offered low salaries but stock options that promised salespeople (and everyone else in the firm) great wealth when the options were cashed in later. However, as the technology sector fell on more difficult economic times, the value of stock options diminished to the point where many technology companies have gone back to financial compensation as the primary motivator.[15]

This raises a question of cause and effect. Are firms more successful when they create the opportunity for a big payday that does not always happen or when they pay people what they are worth plus an incentive for outstanding performance? Paying what it takes to attract and keep a competent sales force seems a more likely path to high performance in relationship selling than being overly creative with the latest financial gimmicks designed to recruit but not necessarily retain the best people.

Leadership 13.5 provides insights on why sales force incentive plans must also contribute to the success of the overall firm.

Leadership 13.5

Maximizing Incentive ROI

It's the start of a new year, which means sales managers are reviewing last year's incentive programs to determine whether they're worth repeating. And in a climate where businesses are looking for places to trim the fat, managers are likely being asked to justify the expense of even long-standing incentive programs.

"If you haven't been asked to justify your program, consider yourself lucky," says Michelle Smith, vice president of business development for O.C. Tanner, a provider of employee recognition and incentive solutions based in Salt Lake City. Demonstrating return-on-investment (ROI) isn't easy, as increased revenue does not necessarily yield greater ROI. But here are three fundamental steps to ensure you get your money's worth from your programs:

1. Clearly define all program goals. Evaluating an incentive program aimed at increasing sales can prove difficult, because a simple percentage increase is not a good-enough measure; you must know what sales are now, and what is expected. Do you want a 10 percent increase in revenue or in products sold? "Quantify your goal as much as possible," Smith says. An incentive program to boost productivity must also be defined. For instance, in a call center, determine whether your goal is to have customer service reps answer more calls per hour or reduce the time spent on each call.

2. Involve all stakeholders. A sales incentive program encompasses more than just the sales force. In determining who the stakeholders are, ask, "Who can help us achieve our goal and who can hurt us?" Smith says. Should sales support and customer service be involved? How about the sales distribution channel? Can inventory support our goal, or does manufacturing need to be beefed up? How about shipping? Can our suppliers keep up with our growing demand? Without buy-in from all stakeholders, the salespeople may not get the support of the departments that they need, Smith says. Constant communication will also help keep all the stakeholders engaged; having everyone track the progress can keep the stakeholders motivated and involved in the program.

3. Identify potential pitfalls. Anticipating problems can make the difference between a successful program and one that was merely well-intentioned. With a sales incentive, numbers can be skewed by several factors. For example, a sale could have been recorded and entered into the ROI calculation, but then the product may have been returned, or heavy discounts can be eroding your profit margin. Set specific and consistent parameters regarding when a sale is recorded, and institute limits on discounts. Also, take note of the market: If it is unusually strong, set your goal higher; if the trend is downward, make your expectations more realistic.

In addition, make sure that whatever incentives you use—even non-sales incentives, such as productivity incentives—aren't accidentally alienating customers. A decline in product or service quality due to new practices could drive customers to competitors.

Source: Mary Litsikas, "Maximize Incentive ROI: Tips to Keep Your Reward and Recognition Programs in the Black." *Sales & Marketing Management* 158, January/February 2006, p. 16.

Summary

To manage the relationship selling function effectively, sales managers must address the firm's compensation system. Which rewards do salespeople value? How much of each is optimum? How should the rewards be integrated into a total compensation system? This chapter provides insights to these issues.

In determining the most effective form of financial compensation, the firm must decide whether to use (1) straight salary, (2) straight commission, or (3) a combination of base salary and incentive pay such as commissions, bonuses, or both.

Most companies today use a combination approach. The base salary gives salespeople a stable income while allowing the company to reward them for performing tasks not directly related to short-term sales. The incentive portion of a combination plan provides direct rewards to motivate salespeople to expend effort to improve their sales volume or profitability. To be effective, the incentive has to be large enough to generate interest among salespeople.

Sales contests are often part of incentive compensation. A sales contest needs to have (1) clearly defined, specific objectives, (2) an exciting theme, (3) a reasonable probability of rewards for all salespeople, (4) attractive rewards, and (5) effective promotion and follow-through.

Nonfinancial incentives can play an important role in a firm's compensation system. Opportunities for salesperson promotion and advancement, recognition programs, and other forms of nonfinancial incentives can be effective motivators. For recognition programs to be effective, the salesperson's peers and superiors must be made aware of his or her outstanding performance. This can be done through recognition at a sales meeting, publicity in the local press, or announcements in the company newsletter, among other ways.

Because all salespeople cannot possibly be promoted into sales management positions, some companies have dual career paths to maintain the motivating potential of promotion and advancement. One path leads to positions in the sales management hierarchy, while the other leads to greater responsibilities in sales positions, such as a larger territory or key account position.

Expense accounts can enhance a salesperson's overall compensation. Three common ways to handle salesperson expenses are direct reimbursement, limited reimbursement, and no reimbursement.

The sales manager must determine an appropriate mix and level of compensation for salespeople that maximizes the compensation plan's motivational value, is fair, and is consistent with the firm's resources.

Key Terms

compensation plan
salary
incentive pay
commission
bonus
quota
sales contests
benefits
nonfinancial incentives
variable commission rate
draw
perquisites (perks)
expense accounts

Role Play

Before You Begin

Before getting started, please go to the appendix of Chapter 1 to review the profiles of the characters involved in this role play, as well as the tips on preparing a role play.

Characters Involved

Rhonda Reed

Justin Taylor

Setting the Stage

Upland Company uses a limited reimbursement plan for salesperson expenses. Basically, salespeople submit receipts monthly to Rhonda for all allowable and reasonable expenses. Rhonda reviews these and forwards them to the home office for processing and payment. Annually, Rhonda provides each salesperson a budget for expenses based on mutually agreed-upon needs. Salespeople receive a small bonus for finishing the year within their budget. It's not unusual for a salesperson's expenses to exceed budget for a given month—though several months of exceeding budgeted expenses would be problematic.

Over the past four months, Rhonda has noticed a marked upward trend in Justin Taylor's expenses. Not only are his average monthly expenses running 23 percent higher than those of anyone else in District 10, but also his expenses for last month are 32 percent higher than his average monthly expenses just six months ago. This has put the whole district's expense budget in the red year-to-date, and the home office has noticed. Rhonda has set up a meeting with Justin to discuss this and develop a plan to reduce his expenses so they are more in line with the budget and with the other reps in the district.

Note: Rhonda sent Justin an e-mail about this problem two months ago. He replied that he would watch expenses more closely. Last month she talked to him about it in person while riding with him to call on an account, but he did not seem concerned and continually shifted the conversation to how well his sales were going for the year.

Rhonda Reed's Role

Rhonda wants to ask questions to find out exactly why Justin's expenses are so high. She does not want to squelch his motivation, as he is an outstanding performer and in fact is leading the district in sales increase year-to-date at 22 percent. However, she needs to counsel him and help him develop a set of objectives and action plans to get his expenses back in line. She knows Justin wants to move into management with Upland and sees this meeting as a coaching opportunity to help him learn more about expense control—a critical sales management function.

Justin Taylor's Role

Although Justin has done a great job selling to his customers this year, he has lost control of his expenses. This has not been intentional. He is not cheating or doing anything unethical. He simply is not keeping good tabs on his expenditures versus his budget. He comes into the meeting ready to focus on what a great year he is having in sales, and when Rhonda focuses the conversation on his expense problem, he claims his big sales increase should offset any expense overruns. He will not veer from that position until Rhonda does a good job of coaching him.

At the end of the encounter, he and Rhonda must have set specific objectives and action plans to correct the problem.

Assignment
Work with another student to develop a 7- to 10-minute coaching session between Rhonda and Justin on these issues. Be sure to play the parts in accordance with the guidance above. This should not be a "you are in trouble" session, but instead a "here's a learning and professional growth opportunity" session.

Discussion Questions

1. We know that the use of selling teams, sometimes including both salespeople and other employees, to accomplish relationship selling is common practice today. As with individual salespeople, the success of these teams depends in part on the reward systems used to motivate and recognize performance. How would you develop a compensation plan that motivates members of a selling team? How can you ensure the plan is fair for everybody involved?

2. The Ruppert Company needed to build market share quickly. To motivate sales growth, Ruppert installed a straight commission compensation plan: The more the sales reps sold, the more they made. This strategy seemed to work. Sales volume climbed and the Ruppert Company captured more market share. After two years, sales growth flattened out and Ruppert began to lose market share. Sales reps continued to earn $85,000 to $90,000 on average in commissions through developing and penetrating current key accounts in their territories. Studies showed the sales force was not overworked and further territory penetration was clearly possible. What do you think was happening?

3. When OfficeSolutions, a software producer, went into business, it needed to establish market share quickly. To accomplish this, it decided to pay the sales force a straight commission. After two years, the company had a large base of business, but customers began to complain that salespeople were not spending enough time with them on postsale service and problem solving (important relationship-selling activities). The salespeople said they did not make any money on problem solving and would rather spend their time finding new customers. What's more, salespeople spent little or no time selling the new products on which OfficeSolutions was staking its future. They said they could sell the old products more easily and earn more money for both themselves and the company. How might the company rework its compensation plan to begin to resolve this issue?

4. When designing sales compensation plans, it is important to meet the relationship-selling objectives and at the same time reward people who meet those objectives. How would you design sales compensation plans to match the following different company objectives and sales environmental situations?

   a. The company has a high revenue growth objective in a sales environment characterized by frequent product introductions, boom markets, and a loose competitive structure.

   b. The company has a protect-and-grow revenue objective in a sales environment characterized by slow growth, many competitors, and few product introductions. The firm's primary source of differentiation is its excellent sales force.

c. The company's objectives are to have overall revenue growth and sell a balanced mix of products. The sales environment has multiple customer markets, many product groups, high-growth and low-growth products, and high and low sales intensity.

d. The company's objective is to maintain revenue and have new-account sales growth (that is, conversion selling by taking customers from the competition). The sales environment is a moderate to slow-growth marketplace.

5. Sales contests, although very popular, raise questions like these: Don't sales reps simply shift into the contest period sales volume that would have occurred anyway? How can everyone be equally motivated when certain territories have a built-in edge because of customer and market characteristics? Won't the contest backfire if people feel they haven't had a fair chance to win? Will all reps participate with equal enthusiasm when there can be only a few winners? Respond to each of these objections.

6. A sales manager says, "You can never hold enough sales contests for your salespeople. The more the merrier. They are guaranteed to increase your business." Evaluate this statement.

7. Things are tough at Morgan, Inc. For the last several months, sales reps, who are paid on a commission basis, have barely covered their monthly personal expenses. To help the sales force through these tough times, Morgan executives decided to introduce monthly draws. Sales reps whose commission earnings fall below a specified monthly amount receive a special loan, or draw, against commissions. When sales and commissions improve, the reps will repay the cash advance from future earnings. Under what conditions will this plan help Morgan achieve its sales strategy? Under what conditions is it likely to fail? (Hint: Think about what might happen in the future in terms of sales volume.)

8. Assume you are taking a job in relationship selling right out of college. What would be your own ideal compensation mix? Why?

9. What are the pros and cons of placing ceilings on salesperson incentives? If you were a sales manager, would you ever advocate incentive ceilings? If so, in what situation(s) and why?

10. Veteran salespeople can pose unique challenges in terms of compensation. Why? How would you design a compensation plan that would motivate a veteran sales rep?

Ethical Dilemma

Jack Trimble (vice president of sales for New World Technologies) is hesitating. He knows he has to make the call, but he's unsure what to tell Lupe Gonzalez, a veteran salesperson at New World. Lupe has just had the most successful year of her career. Indeed, she got the largest order of anyone in the history of the company. For two years she had been calling on Lockwood Jones Industries, one of the largest military contractors in the world, with very limited success. Although the company had placed small orders for a few products, Lupe had been unable to get a large order.

Recently, however, Lockwood Jones was awarded a huge contract from the Pentagon for a new jet fighter. The company's vice president for purchasing told

Lupe it was going to make New World the primary supplier of several key components. He also mentioned that New World was chosen because it has the extra capacity to handle the contract—the biggest single contract ever received by New World. Lupe believes her hard work in cultivating the relationship with Lockwood Jones has paid off big for New World, and she's expecting a substantial incentive reward.

Although Jack is thrilled with Lupe's success and knows she will very likely win "salesperson of the year," he is also faced with a difficult problem. While the sales force is paid a salary (which averages nearly $100,000 per person across the entire sales force), every year a bonus is awarded based on hitting sales targets. The bonus uses a pool of money set aside at the beginning of the year by upper management. This process was created to help management budget for expenses in any given year. The size of the bonus pool is announced at the beginning of each year and all the reps know they are working toward a piece of it.

In the 20 years of the company's existence, this process has worked well. New World has experienced steady growth and everyone in the company looks forward to the bonus at the end of the year. However, Lupe's success in landing the big order from Lockwood Jones has thrown the bonus system into chaos! Based on the existing formula for calculating bonuses, Lupe's share would equal 90 percent of the total bonus pool, or $450,000. No one anticipated the size of the order from Lockwood Jones, and Jack is faced with an incentive system that does not take into account the implications of such success.

The company has 10 salespeople, including Lupe. All of them managed to hit their sales target for the year. While Jack intended to raise the bonus pool by 10 percent to accommodate everyone's success, he knows it is impossible to adjust the pool enough to award Lupe the full amount she expects. In addition, although Lupe has worked hard, there is a sense that she was simply in the right place at the right time. Finally, Jack believes the rest of the sales force would react very negatively to Lupe receiving such a large bonus.

On the one hand, Lupe has won the largest single contract in the history of the company and deserves a huge bonus based on the existing bonus pool formula. On the other hand, the bonus pool system will not accommodate such a large payout to one person. In addition, is it fair to give Lupe the full amount when she has benefited in large part because the company simply had excess capacity?

Questions

1. What should Jack do to resolve this situation? How should he explain it to Lupe, the rest of the sales force, and his superiors?

2. If you were Lupe, how would you feel if you did not receive the full expected amount?

Mini Case

MedTech Pharmaceuticals

CASE 13

DOUG: "Now that it looks like we are going to get approval on these two new cancer drugs, we need to get a sales force out there selling them for us and we need to do it quickly."

HAROLD: "I agree. We've put so much time and effort over the last three years into developing the drugs, conducting the clinical trials, and getting them through the FDA approval process that we forgot to consider what would happen when that approval came through. We have to make sure the sales force has the right incentive to see a lot of doctors and generate sales. Our window of opportunity for these drugs is only seven years, so we have to maximize our return during that time."

BECKY: "Based on my experience with other sales organizations, paying our sales force based solely on commission should generate the sales we're looking for. Salespeople love to make money, and if they know that the more they sell the more they'll make, we'll be in good shape."

DOUG: "Good idea, Becky. Harold, put together a sales organization and start assembling your sales force. With FDA approval expected within the next six weeks, we'll need to move quickly."

With that conversation as the backdrop, MedTech Pharmaceuticals was in business. MedTech began when Doug Reynolds left his position as a university research fellow to start a new company. Doug's work as a molecular biologist gave him an idea for a new cancer treatment compound that could be used to treat the deadliest form of skin cancer, melanoma. This new drug can treat melanoma without surgery (which is the typical treatment for this type of cancer). Doug also speculated that a different variation of the drug compound would treat a more common but less deadly type of skin cancer called basal-cell carcinoma. Doug thought that these new drugs would be in great demand in the future because as baby boomers age, many will be afflicted with skin cancer.

Based on the promise shown by this new drug, Doug was able to secure venture capital financing to develop the compound and submit it for approval by the Food and Drug Administration. To facilitate the development and approval process, Becky Smith was hired from another pharmaceutical company because of her expertise in conducting clinical trials and responding to FDA inquiries about the effects of the drug on patients. Harold Moran was hired to be the business manager. When the conversation above took place, Harold was the only person in the company with the expertise to develop a sales force that could successfully introduce the products.

Four Years Later

In the four years since MedTech received FDA approval, it has employed a sales force of 150 representatives organized geographically across the United States, calling on oncologists and dermatologists whose primary specialty is treating skin cancer. Each sales rep reports to one of 10 sales managers. The sales managers all report to Harold. Sales of the new drugs have been good but have not met the company's expectations. Several of the sales managers have mentioned to Harold that a regular program of sales contests would create more excitement among the sales force and provide greater motivation to increases sales. Harold's response is always, "The salespeople are getting paid 100 percent commission. That should be enough incentive for them to generate more sales."

The sales managers also have mentioned that reimbursing sales reps for entertainment expenses would allow them to compete on a level playing field, since most pharmaceutical companies reimburse physician entertainment expenses. MedTech currently provides a $250 per month car allowance and another $50 per month for incidental expenses such as parking, tolls, and making copies of sales information to leave with doctors. This reimbursement plan was implemented four years ago when the sales force began, and neither the dollar amounts nor the types of expenses reimbursed have changed since.

In light of the disappointing sales numbers and the impending expiration (in three years) of the company's patent on the two drugs, Harold has been listening to his sales managers more closely. He's concerned that a number of the salespeople may leave the company to pursue other opportunities. Consequently, he is considering changes to the overall compensation program at MedTech Pharmaceuticals.

Questions

1. Discuss the advantages and disadvantages of MedTech Pharmaceuticals paying employees on a straight commission basis. What specific changes would you recommend Harold make to the compensation program? Why?
2. What do you think of Harold's opinion about sales contests? Are contests an appropriate incentive in this situation? Why or why not?
3. Design a sales contest that MedTech can implement to generate enthusiasm among the sales force and increase sales for the company. Describe the contest's objective, its theme, how many of the reps should be winners, and what types of rewards the contest should provide.
4. What are the differences between direct and limited expense reimbursement plans? Which type of plan do you think Harold should use with MedTech's sales force? Justify your response.

selling environment

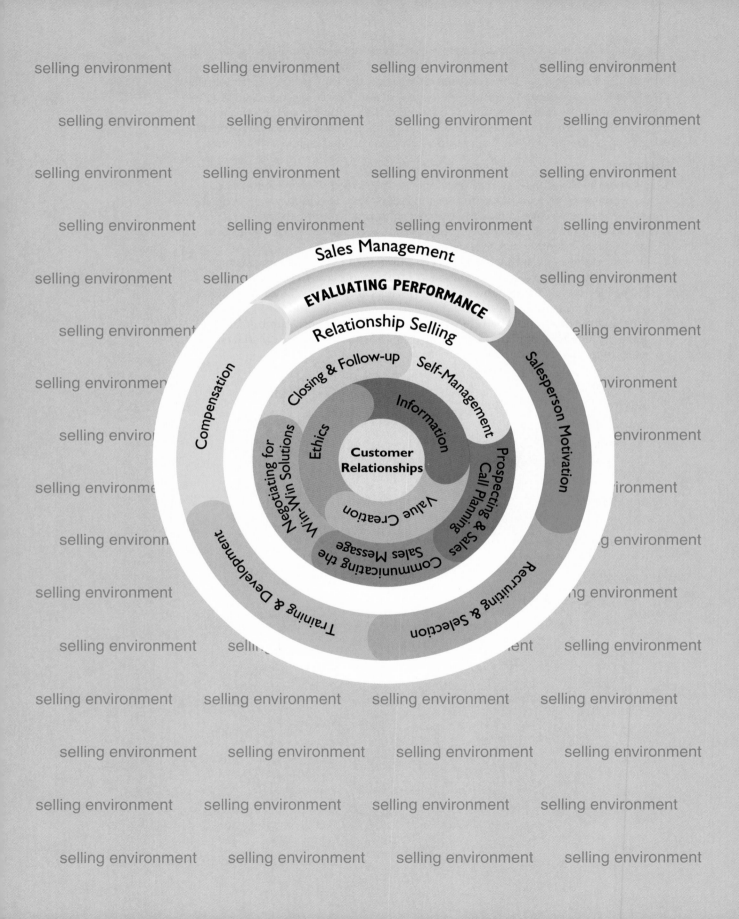

Sales Management

EVALUATING PERFORMANCE

Relationship Selling

Compensation

Salesperson Motivation

Recruiting & Selection

Training & Development

Closing & Follow-up

Self-Management

Prospecting & Sales Call Planning

Communicating the Sales Message

Negotiating for Win-Win Solutions

Ethics

Information

Value Creation

Customer Relationships

14 chapter

Evaluating Salesperson Performance

Learning Objectives

Performance evaluations should be a process that provides a forum for dialogue between a salesperson and the sales manager, focused on future professional development and performance success. To successfully execute a performance review, sales managers must have a strong working knowledge of different measures of performance that are appropriate to a particular selling situation. Then they must conduct the appraisal in a manner that allows the salesperson to build on current strengths and proficiencies and make performance improvements where warranted.

After reading this chapter, you should be able to

- Explain the difference between performance and effectiveness.
- Identify objective measures of salesperson performance, both output and input.
- Use ratio analysis as an objective approach to salesperson performance measurement.
- Discuss key issues related to subjective measurement of salesperson performance and the forms that might be used to administer such an evaluation.
- Understand how a sales manager can make the performance review process more productive and valuable for the salesperson.
- Explain the benefits of 360-degree feedback.

expert advice

Expert: Gerald J. Bauer

Company: President of Bauer & Associates, a sales training and consulting firm. Before starting his own firm, Jerry had a distinguished career with DuPont Company, retiring in 1999 as Sales Competency Leader.

Business: Besides his own sales consulting practice, Jerry is a member of The Sales Educators, LLC (TSE). The members of TSE recently released a book titled *Strategic Sales Leadership: BREAKthrough Thinking for BREAKthrough Results* (Thompson, 2006). (Visit Jerry at www.TheSalesEducators.com.)

Education: BBA, Marketing, University of Toledo, 1964, and MBA, Marketing, University of Toledo, 1965.

From your experience, what are the two or three things about the process of evaluating salespeople that tend to cause the most problems if they are not executed well, and why is each a potential problem?

First, what a shame it would be to waste the valuable opportunity afforded by the salesperson performance evaluation process to coach and develop a sales team by turning what should be the positive experience into a negative situation! Prior planning is one thing that can help a sales manager assure that this process is the beneficial activity it is supposed to be. That planning needs to start early on with a sales manager sharing his or her vision with the sales team and making sure everyone on the team clearly understands what the performance expectations are.

Second, goals should be set mutually and agreed on for buy-in. The performance targets should cause the salesperson to stretch to reach them, but be realistic and attainable. Striving for and then reaching goals is highly motivational; however unreasonable goals create the opposite response. The goals set need to be measurable regardless of whether they relate to sales results, knowledge enhancement, skill building, cost controls, or other areas of performance. The measurement aspect sets the stage for the performance review by providing benchmarks to use when discussing how the salesperson did versus his or her goals.

Third, the actual performance review meeting should be kept positive by emphasizing the success that the salesperson has had. There should be *no surprises* because feedback should have been provided incrementally throughout the period under review. Thus, the meeting should include a summary of previous points made and an update of the current status of goal attainment and professional development.

How should a sales manager balance objective data about a salesperson's performance (for example—calls, orders, volume, profit, etc.) with subjective information (for example—selling skills, account management, relationship with buyers, etc.) when developing a performance evaluation?

It is necessary for a sales manager to balance objective data with subjective information as both give insights into sales success. Sales competency is a blend of effectiveness, efficiency, and productivity. Effectiveness depends on the salesperson's time management, behavioural choices, and priorities. Efficiency is how well the salesperson does the job. This depends on what knowledge and skills they possess, how motivated they are, and what internal support they have. Productivity (meaning results produced) encompasses many standard sales output measures. Given these three elements, competency has to be looked at both objectively and subjectively.

Of course, these elements leading to sales success are intertwined and some are easier to measure than others. Ultimately, a combination of objective and subjective inputs makes up the basis for the evaluation discussion. A great approach to evaluating salesperson performance is one that fully takes into account the role the salesperson has played, through both customer interactions and nonselling behaviors, in achieving the mutually agreed-on goals.

Performance versus Effectiveness

As you heard from Gerald Bauer in his Expert Advice, the process of evaluating the performance of salespeople is very important. A key issue in this process is the distinction among the concepts of behavior, performance, and effectiveness.[1] Although role perceptions, aptitude, skill level, and motivation level are directly linked to performance (as discussed in Chapter 10), they are directly linked to behavior as well.

Behavior refers to what salespeople do—the tasks on which they expend effort while working. These tasks might include calling on customers, writing orders, preparing sales presentations, sending follow-up communication, and the like. These are the sales activities discussed in Chapter 2.

Think of **performance** as behavior evaluated in terms of its contribution to the goals of the organization. In other words, performance reflects whether a salesperson's behavior is good or bad, appropriate or inappropriate, in light of the organization's goals and objectives. Note that behavior and performance are both influenced by relevant sales activities, which depend on the types of sales jobs in question.

Before we discuss salesperson evaluation further, let's also distinguish between performance and effectiveness. By definition, **effectiveness** refers to some summary index of organizational outcomes for which an individual is at least partly responsible. Examples include sales volume, market share, profitability of sales, and customer retention rate. The crucial distinction between performance and effectiveness is that the latter does not refer to behavior directly. Rather, it is a function of additional factors not under the individual salesperson's control, including, for example, top management policies, sales potential or difficulty of a territory, and actions of competitors.

It is generally agreed that salespeople should be evaluated solely on those phases of sales performance over which they exercise control and should not be held responsible for factors beyond their control. If a company's method of measuring salesperson performance is to result in valid comparisons, yardsticks for objective or subjective evaluation must distinguish between factors within a salesperson's control versus those outside his or her control. Leadership 14.1 presents a classic theory of motivation, attribution theory, that is quite relevant to this managerial dilemma.

One could argue that a sales manager's careful specification of performance standards by territory should eliminate inequities across territories. For example, percentage of quota attained should be an acceptable measure of performance because quotas supposedly consider variations in environmental factors across territories. True, a comparison of salespeople's percentage of quota attained is a better measure of their performance than a comparison that simply looks at each rep's level of absolute sales or market share—assuming the quotas were done well. However, that is a big assumption. Sometimes quotas are arbitrary and not based on an objective assessment of all the factors that facilitate or constrain a salesperson's ability to make a sale. This is especially true if quota development relies too heavily on historical trends and not enough on emerging trends in a given sales territory.

Even when quotas are done well, the measure "percentage of quota attained" still omits much about a salesperson's performance. For one thing, it ignores the profitability of sales. Sales reps can be compared with respect to profitability, or the return they produce on the assets under their control. It is difficult to establish quotas that accurately consider the many factors affecting the sales a rep should be able to produce in a territory, but determining the appropriate standards of profitability for each territory is even more difficult.

Leadership 14.1

Attributions and Salesperson Performance Evaluation

Evaluating the performance of a salesperson is all about the sales manager attributing causes of that performance. That is, managers seek out *why* a salesperson's effectiveness is diminished or enhanced so they can take appropriate reinforcing or remedial actions. This process of attributing causes of outcomes has been studied extensively under the rubric *attribution theory,* an approach quite relevant to sales management practice.

Psychologist Fritz Heider developed the cornerstone concept that evaluators tend to operate as "native psychologists" when they observe and analyze the behavior of others. He classified variables evaluators use to interpret the actions of others into three categories: (1) performance variables (i.e., task success, or effectiveness); (2) environmental variables (task difficulty and luck); and (3) person, or dispositional, variables (ability and effort). Heider proposed that evaluators assess performance based on the following relationships among these factors:

1. Ability = Task difficulty ÷ Effort
2. Performance = (Ability × Effort) ± Task difficulty

Based on equation 1, if two salespeople put forth the same amount of effort, the one who performs the more difficult task is expected to have the greater ability. Also if two salespeople accomplish the same task with equal levels of performance, the one who expends less effort is expected by the rater to have the higher ability. Based on equation 2, a sales manager's perception of a salesperson's performance is a function of ability times effort, plus or minus the effects of differing task difficulty.

In the context of salesperson evaluation, Heider's concept of task difficulty may be easily translated to territory difficulty, which is important because rarely (if ever) in professional selling are two territories equal in all respects. Therefore, sales managers must adjust performance ratings by taking into account the differences in territory difficulty among the salespeople they supervise.

Unfortunately, sales managers often neglect this adjustment. A phenomenon known as the *fundamental attribution error* predicts that evaluators will systematically ignore contextual or background information (such as differences in territories among salespeople). Instead their ratings will be based on "person" factors such as perceived ability and effort. Heider proposed that background situational (contextual) information is less salient to evaluators than is person (appraisee) information, and is analogous to the Gestalt concept of .figure against ground. In the context of salesperson evaluations, such thinking suggests that an evaluation bias may arise in which sales managers focus on dispositional factors, such as the salesperson's ability and effort (the "figure") and ignore contextual factors (the "ground"), such as territory difficulty and luck.

Sales organizations must work hard to guard against this form of evaluation bias. Assuming equal performance, over time a salesperson who is evaluated equally or lower than a peer whose territory is less difficult may become dissatisfied and feel unfairly treated, resulting in a very effective salesperson leaving the company. Firms must train their sales managers to consider all contextual and person factors when making their evaluations. By doing so, managers can avoid the fundamental attribution error.

Sources: Thomas E. DeCarlo, Sanjeev Agarwal, and Shyman B. Vayas, "Performance Expectations of Salespeople: The Role of Past Performance and Casual Attributions in Independent and Interdependent Cultures," *Journal of Personal Selling & Sales Management* 27 (Spring 2007), pp. 133–47; Andrea L. Dixon, Lukas P. Forbes, and Susan M. B. Schertzer, "Early Success: How Attributions for Sales Success Shape Inexperienced Salesperson's Behavioral Intentions," *Journal of Personal Selling & Sales Management* 25 (Winter 2005), pp. 67–77; Andrea L. Dixon and Susan M. B. Schertzer, "Bouncing Back: How Salesperson Optimism and Self-Efficacy Influence Attributions and Behaviors Following Failure," *Journal of Personal Selling & Sales Management* 25 (Fall 2005), pp. 361–69; Greg W. Marshall, John C. Mowen, and Keith J. Fabes, "The Impact of Territory Difficulty and Self versus Other Ratings on Managerial Evaluations of Sales Personnel," *Journal of Personal Selling & Sales Management* 12 (Fall 1992), pp. 35–47.

Even if good sales and profit standards could be developed, the problem of evaluating salespeople would not be solved because neither measure incorporates activities that may have no short-term payout but still have substantial consequences to the firm in the long run. These include the time devoted to laying the groundwork for a long-term client relationship, particularly when developing a potentially large account. Other activities that often go unmeasured are building long-term goodwill for the company and developing a detailed understanding of the capabilities of the products being sold. Thus, other measures beyond sales and profits are needed to evaluate salesperson performance more directly.

These other measures fall into two broad categories: (1) objective measures and (2) subjective measures.[2] **Objective measures** reflect statistics the sales manager can gather from the firm's internal data. These measures are best used when they reflect elements of the sales process. **Subjective measures** typically rely on personal evaluations by someone inside the organization, usually the salesperson's immediate supervisor, of how he or she is doing. Subjective measures are generally gathered via direct observation of the salesperson by the manager but may involve input from customers or other sources.

Objective Measures of Performance

Objective measures fall into three major categories: (1) output measures, (2) input measures, and (3) ratios of output and/or input measures. Exhibit 14.1 lists some of the more common output and input measures, and Exhibit 14.2 provides some commonly used ratios.

EXHIBIT 14.1 Common Output and Input Measures Used to Evaluate Salespeople

Output Measures	Input Measures
Orders	Calls
Number of orders	Total number of calls
Average size of orders	Number of planned calls
Number of canceled orders	Number of unplanned calls
Accounts	Time and time utilization
Number of active accounts	Days worked
Number of new accounts	Calls per day (call rate)
Number of lost accounts	Selling time versus nonselling time
Number of overdue accounts	Expenses
Number of prospective accounts	Total
	By type
	As a percentage of sales
	As a percentage of quota
	Nonselling activities
	Letters to prospects
	Phone calls to prospects
	Number of formal proposals developed
	Advertising displays set up
	Number of meetings held with distributors/dealers
	Number of training sessions held with distributor/dealer personnel
	Number of calls on distributor/dealer customers
	Number of service calls made
	Number of overdue accounts collected

Source: *Churchill/Ford/Walker's Sales Force Management*, 9th ed., by Mark W. Johnston and Greg W. Marshall (New York: McGraw-Hill, 2009), p. 443. Reprinted by permission of the McGraw-Hill Companies.

EXHIBIT 14.2 Common Ratios Used to Evaluate Salespeople

Expense Ratios

- Sales expense ratio $= \frac{\text{Expense}}{\text{Sales}}$
- Cost per call ratio $= \frac{\text{Total costs}}{\text{Number of calls}}$

Account Development and Servicing Ratios

- Account penetration ratio $= \frac{\text{Accounts sold}}{\text{Total accounts available}}$
- New-account conversion ratio $= \frac{\text{Number of new accounts}}{\text{Total number of accounts}}$
- Lost account ratio $= \frac{\text{Prior accounts not sold}}{\text{Total number of accounts}}$
- Sales per account ratio $= \frac{\text{Sales dollar volume}}{\text{Total number of accounts}}$
- Average order size ratio $= \frac{\text{Sales dollar volume}}{\text{Total number of orders}}$
- Order cancellation ratio $= \frac{\text{Number of canceled orders}}{\text{Total number of orders}}$
- Account share $= \frac{\text{Sales person's business from account}}{\text{Account's total business}}$

Call Activity and/or Productivity

- Calls per day ratio $= \frac{\text{Number of calls}}{\text{Number of days worked}}$
- Calls per account ratio $= \frac{\text{Number of calls}}{\text{Number of accounts}}$
- Planned call ratio $= \frac{\text{Number of planned calls}}{\text{Total number of calls}}$
- Orders per call (hit) ratio $= \frac{\text{Number of orders}}{\text{Total number of calls}}$

Source: *Churchill/Ford/Walker's Sales Force Management*, 9th ed., by Mark W. Johnston and Greg W. Marshall (New York: McGraw-Hill, 2009), p. 447. Reprinted by permission of the McGraw-Hill Companies.

The use of outputs, inputs, and ratios to measure salesperson performance is a recognition of the nature of the relationship-selling process. As you have learned, some sales processes, especially those that contribute to securing, building, and maintaining long-term relationships with profitable customers, can take months or years. Within the relationship-selling process, salespeople engage in activities with (or in pursuit of) the prospect or buyer. The manager can measure those activities and compare them with results for each stage. By examining this performance evidence, the manager can pinpoint areas for improvement by each salesperson or identify changes needed in the sales strategy to align it with how buyers want to buy.

Output Measures

Output measures show the results of the efforts expended by the salesperson. They include information about orders and various account measures.

Orders. The number of orders each salesperson secures is often used to assess the rep's ability to close sales. Although the number of orders is important, their average size is equally so. Having many small orders suggests the rep is spending too much time calling on small, low-potential customers and not enough time calling on large, high-potential customers.

Another related measure is the number of canceled orders. A salesperson who loses a large proportion of total orders to cancellation may be using high-pressure tactics in sales presentations rather than engaging in relationship selling.

Accounts. The various account measures provide a perspective on the equity of territory assignments and also on how the salesperson is handling the territory. Attention to these measures can help the sales manager overcome the tendency to discount territory difficulty information (as discussed in Leadership 14.1).

One popular measure focuses on the number of active accounts in the salesperson's customer portfolio. Various definitions of an active account are used. For example, it may be any customer that has placed an order in the past six months or in the past year. Contrasting the number of active accounts is one way to compare a salesperson's performance from year to year.

Closely related to this yardstick is the number of new accounts a salesperson develops in a given time. Some companies even establish new-prospect quotas that allow a ready comparison of performance to standard in this area of evaluation.

Like the number of new accounts, the number of lost accounts can be a revealing statistic, since it shows how successfully the salesperson is maintaining relationships with the established accounts in the territory. Still other account measures by which salespeople can be compared are the number of overdue accounts, which might indicate how well the salesperson follows company procedures in screening accounts for their creditworthiness, and the number of prospective accounts, which assesses the salesperson's ability to identify potential target customers.

Input Measures

Many objective measures of performance evaluation focus on the efforts sales reps expend rather than the results of those efforts. These efforts are **input measures** of performance.

Input measures are important for two key reasons. First, efforts or desirable behaviors are much more directly controllable than results in the short term. If a rep's sales fall short of quota, the problem may lie with the person, the quota, or a change in the environment. On the other hand, if the number of calls a salesperson makes falls short of the target, it is clear that the problem lies with the individual.[3]

Second, in relationship selling there is often a time lag between inputs and outputs. A particularly large sale may be the result of several years of effort. Thus, focusing on the efforts (behaviors) themselves lets the sales manager evaluate and coach the salesperson during the relationship-selling process into making changes that can improve the output (results).

Calls. The number of current customer and/or prospect calls is often used to decide whether a salesperson is covering the territory properly. The number of calls on each account is also an important factor in the design of territories. Sales calls are a time-sensitive resource with a finite supply. The time available to make them evaporates if it is not used.

As you have learned, CRM systems integrate customer contacts by salespeople into their information collection, analysis, and reporting. Contact management software like GoldMine automates the call report process. The salesperson can input information about each call into a record established for each account. This information can be summarized by the software for a report available to the sales manager by e-mail or the Web. If the CRM software resides on a shared network, the sales manager can access the information directly. Such technological advances minimize the time spent preparing paperwork and help salespeople maximize their time in front of buyers. They also aid sales managers greatly in performance evaluation.

Time and Time Utilization. The number of days worked and the calls per day (call rate) are routinely used by many companies to assess salespeople's efforts since the product of the two quantities provides a direct measure of the extent of customer contact. If a rep's customer contact is low, the manager can look separately at the components to see where the problem lies. Perhaps the salesperson has not been working enough because of extenuating circumstances, a situation that would show up in the number of days worked. Or perhaps the rep's total time input was satisfactory, but he or she was not using that time wisely and consequently had a low call rate.

Comparing salespeople's division of time among sales calls, traveling, office work, and other duties offers a useful perspective. For the most part, the firm wants salespeople to maximize face-to-face customer contact and minimize unproductive time. **Telecommuting,** or working from a home office, is not new in the field of professional selling and can certainly reduce travel time. Through necessity (e.g., no company facility in the salesperson's headquarters city) or convenience, many reps maintain their primary office in their home.

Analysis of time utilization requires detailed input on how each salesperson is spending time. Collecting and analyzing this data can be expensive (and can itself be time consuming). Some companies, however, routinely conduct such analyses because they believe the benefits outweigh the costs.

Expenses. The objective inputs discussed so far for evaluating salespeople (calls; time and time utilization) focus mainly on the extent of a salesperson's efforts. Another key emphasis is the cost of those efforts. Many firms keep records detailing the total expenses incurred by each salesperson. Some break these expenses down by type (car, lodging, entertainment, etc.). Sales managers might look at these expenses in total and/or as a percentage of sales or quota by salesperson and then use these expense ratios as part of the performance evaluation.

Nonselling Activities. In addition to assessing salespeople's direct contact with customers, some firms monitor indirect contact. They use indexes such as the number of letters written, number of phone calls made, and number of formal proposals developed.

As you've learned, in relationship selling a salesperson's activities go beyond pure selling. For example, companies that sell to retailers may ask salespeople to help retailers advertise, monitor and stock shelves, create displays, and engage in a number of other nonselling activities as part of ongoing client relationships. Firms often try to monitor the extent of these duties, using such indexes as the number of promotional or advertising displays set up, the number of dealer meetings, the number of training sessions for distributor personnel, the number of calls on dealer customers, the number of service calls, the number of customer complaints, and the number of collections on overdue accounts. Some of this information can be gathered from the salesperson's reporting system, but it is increasingly common to gain feedback on elements of salesperson performance directly from customers. This trend is discussed in a later section of this chapter on 360-degree feedback.

Ratio Measures

Just as a focus on outputs other than straight sales volume and profit can provide useful information on how salespeople are performing, so can analysis of input factors. Combining the various outputs and/or inputs in selected ways, typically in various ratios, can yield further insights.[4] Exhibit 14.2 lists some of the ratios commonly used to evaluate salespeople. They are grouped under expense ratios, account development and servicing ratios, and call activity and/or productivity ratios.

Expense Ratios. The sales expense ratio combines both salespeople's inputs and the results produced by those inputs in a single number. Salespeople can affect this ratio either by making sales or by controlling expenses. The ratio can also be used to analyze salesperson expenses by type. Thus, a sales/transportation expense ratio that is much higher for one salesperson than others might indicate the salesperson is covering his or her territory inefficiently. Or that rep may simply have a larger, more geographically dispersed territory to cover. It is important that the sales manager recognize territory difficulty differences when comparing these ratios.

The cost per call ratio expresses the cost of supporting each salesperson in the field as a function of the number of calls the salesperson makes. The ratio can be evaluated using total costs, or the costs can be broken down by elements so that ratios like expenses per call and travel costs per call can be computed. These ratios are useful for comparing salespeople from the same firm. They can also be compared with those of other companies in the same industry to assess how efficient the firm's relationship-selling effort is. Comparative data may be available from trade or professional associations and from companies like Dartnell, which gather and publish expense data and ratios.

Account Development and Servicing Ratios. A number of ratios concerning accounts and orders reflect how well salespeople are capturing the potential business in their territories. The account penetration ratio, for example, measures the percentage of accounts in the territory from which the salesperson secures orders. It measures whether the salesperson is simply skimming the cream of the business or working the territory systematically and hard. It can also help management identify both underperforming accounts and accounts that have low lifetime value.

The new-account conversion ratio similarly measures the salesperson's ability to convert prospects to customers. The lost account ratio measures how well the rep is serving the established accounts in the territory.

The sales per account ratio indicates the rep's average success per account. A low ratio could mean the salesperson is spending too much time calling on small, less profitable accounts and not enough time calling on larger ones. You could also look at sales per account ratios by class of account, which can reveal the strengths and weaknesses of each salesperson. For example, a salesperson who has a low sales per account ratio for large, high-potential accounts might need coaching in how to sell to a buying center.

The average order size ratio can also reveal the salesperson's patterns of calling on customers. A very low average order size might suggest that calls are too frequent and the salesperson could improve productivity by spacing them more. The order cancellation ratio reveals the salesperson's selling method. A very high ratio could mean the rep is using high-pressure tactics to secure orders rather than pursuing relationship-selling approaches and handling customers in a consultative manner.

A key measurement in some types of businesses, particularly those that provide supplies and raw materials, is account share, which is the percentage of the account's business that the salesperson gets. Many buyers split their business among several vendors, believing (often erroneously) that they get better service and lower prices when sellers have to compete for the business. In industries where such buying practices are prevalent, the number of accounts is less important to salespeople than the share of each account. As account share increases, economies of scale increase, raising the profit generated by the account. The measure also indicates the strength of the relationship with the account.

Call Activity and Productivity Ratios. Call activity ratios measure the effort and planning salespeople put into their customer call activities and the successes they reap. Calls per day or per total number or type of account could be used to compare salesperson activities in total. The planned call ratio could be used to assess whether the salesperson is systematically planning territory coverage or working the territory without an overall game plan. The orders per call ratio bears directly on the question of whether the salesperson's calls are, on average, productive. It is sometimes called the hit ratio or batting average, since it captures the number of successes (hits or orders) in relation to the number of at-bats (calls).

Summary of Objective Measures

As Exhibits 14.1 and 14.2 and this discussion indicate, many objective output measures, input measures, and ratio measures exist by which salespeople may be evaluated and compared. As you probably sense, many of the measures are somewhat redundant in that they provide overlapping information on salesperson effectiveness. Combining the various outputs, inputs, or ratios in different ways would yield a number of other ratios. One combination that is often used to evaluate salespeople is the following equation:

$$\text{Sales} = \text{Days worked} \times \frac{\text{Calls}}{\text{Days worked}} \times \frac{\text{Orders}}{\text{Calls}} \times \frac{\text{Sales}}{\text{Orders}}$$

or

$$\text{Sales} = \text{Days worked} \times \text{Call rate} \times \text{Batting average} \times \text{Average order size}$$

The equation highlights nicely what a salesperson can do to increase sales: increase the (1) number of days worked, (2) calls made per day, (3) level of success in securing an order on a given call, and (4) size of those orders. Thus, the equation can be used to isolate how an individual salesperson's performance could be improved. But this equation focuses on the results of the salesperson's efforts and ignores their cost. Many of the other measures we have reviewed could be combined via similar equations, but they too would probably ignore one or more elements of salesperson success. No single measure can fully capture the scope of salesperson effectiveness.

In this discussion of objective measures of performance, two essential points deserve mention. First, just as measuring straight sales volume and profit have advantages and disadvantages in evaluating salespeople, so do all these other objective measures of performance. Rather than relying on only one or two of the measures to assess performance, managers should use them in combination.

Second, all of the indexes are an aid to judgment, not a substitute for it. For example, the U.S. Army Recruiting Command (the part of the Army that sells young people on joining) once overrelied on conversion ratios (the percentage of prospects who actually ended up joining the army) to evaluate recruiters' performance. Orders were issued that sales calls of certain types had to be increased by a high percentage. The problem was that while the calls could be increased, quality could not be maintained. Recruiting effectiveness actually went down as recruiter morale declined. The comparisons allowed by the various indexes should be the beginning, not the conclusion, of any analysis aimed at assessing how well the entire sales force or individual salespeople are doing.

Subjective Measures of Performance

A useful distinction exists between the quantitative nature of objective measures of performance just discussed and the qualitative nature of the subjective performance measures discussed in this section. Quantitative measures focus on the outputs and inputs of what salespeople do; qualitative measures reflect behavioral or process aspects of what they do and how well they do it. This difference in what is being measured leads to marked differences in how objective and subjective measurements are taken and how they are used.

In many ways, it is more difficult to assess quality than quantity. Quantity measures can require a detailed analysis of a salesperson's call report, an extensive time utilization analysis, or an analysis of the type and number of nonselling activities employed. However, once the measurement procedure is set up, it typically can be conducted fairly and consistently.

When assessing qualitative performance factors, even a well-designed measurement process that is firmly in place leaves much room for bias in the evaluation. **Bias** in a performance evaluation represents a difference from objective reality, usually based on errors by the evaluator (the sales manager). Even well-designed systems rely on the personal judgment of the individuals charged with evaluation. Typically, the manager rates the salesperson on a performance appraisal form on a number of attributes, such as the following:

1. *Sales results.* Volume of sales, sales to new accounts, and selling of the full product line.

2. *Job knowledge.* Knowledge of company policies, prices, and products.
3. *Management of territory.* Planning activities and calls, controlling expenses, and handling reports and records.
4. *Customer and company relations.* The salesperson's standing with customers, associates, and company.
5. *Personal characteristics.* Initiative, personal appearance, personality, resourcefulness, and so on.

Note the mix of objective and subjective performance measures. Most formal performance evaluations of salespeople involve a combination of these two types of criteria.

Forms Used for Subjective Performance Measurement

Exhibit 14.3 shows a typical salesperson evaluation form for various subjective performance criteria. The specific evaluative criteria should match those identified as key success factors for the position. Chapter 2 provided a discussion of key success factors for sales positions. Evaluations may be completed annually, semiannually, or quarterly depending on the firm's human resource management policies. They supplement the objective performance data generated for the same time frame to provide an overall evaluation of salesperson performance.

Exhibit 14.3 is better than many in use because it contains anchors (verbal descriptors) for the various points on the scale. It also has space provided for comments, which can enhance understanding of the ratings supplied. The form contains a section for detailing needed improvements and corrective actions. All in all, the form should facilitate a constructive dialogue between a salesperson and sales manager and help the salesperson understand his or her strengths and weaknesses and develop approaches to improve performance.

The worst rating forms simply list the attributes of interest on one side and the evaluation adjectives on the other. Little description is provided, so the evaluation may be very ambiguous. Exhibit 14.4 illustrates such a poor form. Notice how it uses the same attributes as Exhibit 14.3 but treats them superficially. Of course, this form can be completed very easily since the evaluator simply checks the box for the adjective that most clearly describes his or her perceptions of the salesperson's performance on each attribute. Unfortunately, such forms are quite common in sales organizations. They work very poorly and do little to stimulate a constructive dialogue between the salesperson and sales manager. Salespeople typically receive little useful information on improving performance from them.

Problems with Subjective Performance Measurement

Common problems with performance appraisal systems that rely on subjective rating forms, particularly those using the simple checklist type, include the following:[5]

1. *Lack of an outcome focus.* The most useful type of performance appraisal highlights areas for improvement and the actions the employee must take to implement such improvements. For this to occur, the key behaviors in accomplishing the tasks assigned must be identified. Unfortunately, many companies have not taken this step. They have simply identified attributes thought to be related to performance without systematically assessing whether the attributes are key. One type of performance appraisal, called

EXHIBIT 14.3 Sample Subjective Performance Evaluation Form

SALES PERSONNEL
INVENTORY

Employee's Name ______________________ Territory ______________________
Position Title ______________________ Date ______________________

INSTRUCTIONS (Read Carefully)

1. Base your judgment on the previous six-month period and not on isolated incidents alone.
2. Place a check in the block that most nearly expresses your judgment on each factor.
3. For those employees who are rated at either extreme of the scale on any factor—for example, outstanding, deficient, limited—please enter a brief explanation for the rating in the appropriate space below the factor.
4. Make your rating an accurate description of the person rated.

FACTORS TO BE CONSIDERED AND RATED:

Factor	☐	☐	☐	☐	☐
1. Knowledge of Work (includes knowledge of product, knowledge of customers' business)	Does not have sufficient knowledge of products and application to represent company effectively.	Has mastered minimum knowledge. Needs further training.	Has average amount of knowledge needed to handle job satisfactorily.	Is above average in knowledge needed to handle job satisfactorily.	Is thoroughly acquainted with our products and technical problems involved in this application.

Comments ____

Factor	☐	☐	☐	☐	☐
2. Degree of Acceptance by Customers	Not acceptable to most customers. Cannot gain entry to their offices.	Manages to see customers but not generally liked.	Has satisfactory relationship with most customers.	Is on very good terms and is accepted by virtually all customers.	Enjoys excellent personal relationship with virtually all customers.

Comments ____

Factor	☐	☐	☐	☐	☐
3. Amount of Effort Devoted to Acquiring Business	Exceptional in the amount of time and effort put forth in selling.	Devotes constant effort in developing business.	Devotes intermittent effort in acquiring moderate amount of business.	Exerts only minimum amount of time and effort.	Unsatisfactory. Does not put forth sufficient effort to produce business.

Comments ____

(continued)

EXHIBIT 14.3 Sample Subjective Performance Evaluation Form (continued)

	☐	☐	☐	☐	☐
4. Ability to Acquire Business	Is able to acquire business under the most difficult situations.	Does a good job acquiring business under most circumstances.	Manages to acquire good percentage of customer's business if initial resistance is not too strong.	Able to acquire enough business to maintain only a minimum sales average.	Rarely able to acquire business except in a seller's market.

Comments ____

____

	☐	☐	☐	☐	☐
5. Amount of Service Given to Customers	Rarely services accounts once a sale is made.	Gives only minimum service at all times.	Services accounts with regularity but does not do any more than called on to do.	Gives very good service to all customers.	Goes out of the way to give outstanding service within scope of Company policy.

Comments ____

____

	☐	☐	☐	☐	☐
6. Dependability—Amount of Supervision Needed	Always thoroughly abreast of problems in the territory, even under most difficult conditions. Rises to emergencies and assumes leadership without being requested to do so.	Consistently reliable under normal conditions. Does special as well as regular assignments promptly. Little or no supervision required.	Performs with reasonable promptness under normal supervision.	Effort occasionally lags. Requires more than normal supervision.	Requires close supervision in all phases of job.

Comments ____

____

	☐	☐	☐	☐	☐
7. Attitude toward Company—Support Given to Company Policies	Does not support Company policy—blames Company for factors that affect customers unfavorably.	Gives only passive support to Company policy—does not act as member of a team.	Goes along with Company policies on most occasions.	Adopts and supports Company viewpoint in all transactions.	Gives unwavering support to Company and Company policies to customers

(continued)

EXHIBIT 14.3 Sample Subjective Performance Evaluation Form (continued)

					even though he/she personally may not agree with them.
	Comments ______				
8. Judgment	☐	☐	☐	☐	☐
	Analyses and conclusions subject to frequent error and are often based on bias. Decisions require careful review by supervisor.	Judgments usually sound on routine, simple matters but cannot be relied on when any degree of complexity is involved.	Capable of careful analyzing of day-to-day problems involving some complexity and rendering sound decisions. Decision rarely influenced by prejudice or personal bias.	Decisions can be accepted without question except when problems or extreme complexity are involved. Little or no personal bias enters into judgment.	Possesses unusual comprehension and analytical ability. Complete reliance may be placed on all judgments irrespective of degree of complexity. Decisions and judgments are completely free of personal bias or prejudice.
	Comments ______				
9. Resourcefulness	☐	☐	☐	☐	☐
	Work is consistently characterized by marked originality, alertness, initiative, and imagination. Can be relied on to develop new ideas and techniques in solving the most difficult problems.	Frequently develops new ideas of merit. Handling of emergencies is generally characterized by sound decisive action.	Meets new situations in satisfactory manner. Occasionally develops original ideas, methods, and techniques.	Follows closely previously learned methods and procedures. Slow to adapt to changes. Tends to become confused in new situations.	Requires frequent reinstruction. Has failed to demonstrate initiative or imagination in solving problems.
	Comments ______				

(continued)

EXHIBIT 14.3 Sample Subjective Performance Evaluation Form (concluded)

To be more effective on present job, this employee should:

1. Be given additional instruction on ____________________

2. Be given additional experience such as ____________________

3. Study such subjects as ____________________

4. Change attitude as follows ____________________

5. There is nothing more that I can do for this employee because ____________________

6. Remarks ____________________

Source: *Churchill/Ford/Walker's Sales Force Management*, 9th ed., by Mark W. Johnston and Greg W. Marshall (New York: McGraw-Hill, 2009), pp. 451–54. Reprinted by permission of the McGraw-Hill Companies.

BARS (behavioral anchored rating scale), helps overcome this weakness by identifying behaviors that are more or less effective with respect to the goals established for the person. BARS will be discussed in detail shortly.

2. *Ill-defined personality traits.* Many performance evaluation forms use personality factors as attributes. For salespeople, these attributes might include such things as initiative and resourcefulness. Although these attributes are intuitively appealing, their actual relationship to performance is open to question.[6]
3. *Halo effect.* A halo effect is a common phenomenon with any performance evaluation form. Halo means the rating assigned to one characteristic may significantly influence the ratings assigned to all other characteristics, as well as the overall rating. The halo effect holds that a sales manager's overall evaluations can be predicted quite well from his or her rating of the salesperson on the single performance dimension the manager believes is most important. Different branch or regional managers may have different beliefs about what is most important, compounding the problem.
4. *Leniency or harshness.* Some sales managers rate at the extremes. Some are very lenient and rate every salesperson as good or outstanding on every attribute; others do just the opposite. This behavior is often a function of their own personalities and their perceptions of what comprises outstanding performance, rather than of any fundamental differences in how the salespeople are actually performing. Different managers' use of different definitions of performance can undermine the whole performance appraisal system.
5. *Central tendency.* Some managers err in the opposite direction. They never or rarely rate people at the ends of the scale. They stick to middle of the road,

EXHIBIT 14.4 Poorly Constructed Subjective Performance Evaluation Form

	Poor	Fair	Satisfactory	Good	Outstanding
Knowledge of work	☐	☐	☐	☐	☐
Degree of acceptance by customers	☐	☐	☐	☐	☐
Amount of effort devoted to acquiring business	☐	☐	☐	☐	☐
Ability to acquire business	☐	☐	☐	☐	☐
Amount of service given to customers	☐	☐	☐	☐	☐
Dependability, amount of supervision needed	☐	☐	☐	☐	☐
Attitude toward company, support for company policies	☐	☐	☐	☐	☐
Judgment	☐	☐	☐	☐	☐
Resourcefulness	☐	☐	☐	☐	☐

Source: *Churchill/Ford/Walker's Sales Force Management,* 9th ed., by Mark W. Johnston and Greg W. Marshall (New York: McGraw-Hill, 2009), p. 454. Reprinted by permission of the McGraw-Hill Companies.

play-it-safe ratings. Such ratings reveal very little about true differences in performance. They can be particularly troublesome when a company attempts to use a history of poor performance as the basis of a termination decision. Some companies have instituted forced ranking systems partly to circumvent managers' leniency, harshness, or central tendency in their evaluations—but ranking systems have their own problems.

6. *Interpersonal bias.* Our perceptions of other people and the social acceptability of their behaviors are influenced by how much we like or dislike them personally. Many sales managers' evaluations of sales reps are similarly affected. Furthermore, research suggests a salesperson can use personal influence or impression management strategies on the manager to bias evaluations upward.
7. *Organizational uses influence.* Performance ratings are often affected by the use to which they will be put within the organization. If promotions and monetary payments hinge on the ratings, a manager who values the friendship and support of subordinates may be lenient. It is not difficult to imagine the dilemma of a district sales manager if other district sales teams receive consistently higher compensation increments and more promotions than his or her group. On the other hand, when appraisals are used primarily for the development of subordinates, managers tend to pinpoint weaknesses more freely and focus on what is wrong and how it can be improved.[7]

By now, it should be clear that performance evaluation is fraught with opportunities for biases and inaccuracies to creep into the process. Leadership 14.2 describes one form of potential evaluator bias—the outcome bias—in more detail. An **outcome bias** occurs when a sales manager allows the outcome of a rep's decision or series of decisions to overly influence his or her performance ratings.

Leadership 14.2

Outcome Bias in Salesperson Performance Evaluations

By nature, professional selling is focused on bottom-line results. People who are successful in sales tend to like meeting tough goals and thrive on the immediacy, regularity, and visibility of feedback on their results. Management often views results (or "outcomes") in sales as a surrogate for the behavioral side of salesperson performance. If you make your quota, you must be doing things right. But if you miss your quota, boy, are you ever doing the wrong things.

The "things" we are talking about are all the process steps that go into the job of selling. On a basic level, they are all the decisions made by the salesperson over the course of a day, week, month, quarter, and year that add up to that person's performance. (Remember, earlier in this chapter we defined performance as behavior evaluated in the context of its contributions to the goals of the organization.)

Sometimes the outcomes and the process leading to them match. For example, a salesperson has a great sales quarter and also was great at doing all the things that are part of the sales job (presentations, customer care, administration, and the like). Clearly, the sales manager should recognize and reward this achievement. In the opposite case, where a salesperson has a lousy sales quarter and also is struggling with the process elements of the job, the sales manager needs to document the poor performance and put a developmental plan in place.

But what about the mixed cases? What about the rep who has a great sales quarter but is not cutting the mustard in the day-to-day elements of the job? Maybe the favorable outcome was due to an unexpected windfall from a client, an easy territory, or some other event not directly attributable to much of anything the rep actually did to earn the business. Evaluating this salesperson favorably overall, based strictly on his performance outcome, can open a huge can of worms in a sales unit. Peers will see him as a slacker who got lucky. Finally, in perhaps the worst case of all, consider the salesperson who has a lousy sales quarter but who has done absolutely everything right. If she is evaluated as a poor performer, based strictly on the outcome, chances are the organization will lose her.

The *outcome bias* is that evaluators tend to overlook process and rate performers based on outcomes. This tendency for outcome to overwhelm process can lead to poor morale, ill will, and turnover in the sales force.

There is a school of thought in sales that claims a bias toward outcomes isn't really a bias at all. That is, salespeople know when they get into the profession that bottomline sales volume is the key to success. This perspective may be somewhat valid in straight commission selling situations. But in most of today's relationship-driven professional sales jobs, it is folly to use performance evaluation systems that ignore good (or bad) behavioral aspects of performance in favor of only the short-run bottom line. As you have learned, success in relationship selling involves a complex set of actions inside and outside the selling firm, and the true outcome of these activities may not be realized for a long time. Fortunately, most modern sales organizations understand the threat of the outcome bias and work to integrate multiple aspects of performance into the evaluation process. The BARS system discussed in this chapter is one approach.

For recent treatments on the outcome bias see: Nidhi Agrawal and Durairaj Maheswaran, "Motivated Reasoning in Outcome Bias Effects," *Journal of Consumer Research 3* (March 2005), pp. 798–805; Philip J. Mazzocco, Mark D. Alicke, and Teresa L. Davis, "On the Robustness of Outcome Bias: No Constraint by Prior Culpability," *Basic and Applied Social Psychology* 26 (2/3 2004), p. 131.

Avoiding Errors in Performance Evaluation

To guard against distortions in the performance appraisal system, many firms provide extensive training to sales managers on how to complete the forms and conduct the appraisal process. Common instructions issued with such forms include the following:

1. Read the definition of each attribute thoroughly and carefully before rating.
2. Guard against the common tendency to overrate.
3. Do not let personal like or dislike influence your ratings. Be as objective as possible.

4. Do not permit your evaluation of one factor to influence your evaluation of another.
5. Base your rating on the observed performance of the salesperson, not on potential abilities.
6. Never rate an employee on a few instances of good or poor work, but rather on general success or failure over the whole period.
7. Have sound reasons for your ratings.[8]

These admonitions can help, particularly when the evaluator must supply reasons for ratings. However, they do not resolve problems with the form's design (the selection of attributes for evaluation and how they are presented). A trend in performance appraisal directed at resolving this issue is the BARS.

BARS Systems

A **BARS (behaviorally anchored rating scale)** system concentrates on the behaviors and other performance criteria the individual can control. The system focuses on the fact that a number of factors affect any employee's performance. However, some of these factors are more critical to job success than others, and in evaluation it is important to focus on the key success factors for relationship selling as identified and discussed in Chapter 2. Implementing a BARS system for evaluating salespeople requires identifying the specific behaviors relevant to their performance. The evaluation must rate these behaviors using the appropriate descriptions.[9]

To develop a BARS system, management identifies the key behaviors with respect to performance using critical incidents. Critical incidents are occurrences that are vital (critical) to performance. Managers and sales reps could be asked to identify some outstanding examples of good or bad performance and to detail why they were good or bad.[10] The performances are then reduced to a smaller number of performance dimensions.

Next, the group of critical incidents is presented to a select group of sales personnel (perhaps top salespeople and sales managers), who assign each critical incident to an appropriate performance dimension. An incident is typically kept in if 60 percent or more of the group assigns it to the same dimension as did the instrument development group. The sales personnel group is also asked to rate the behavior described in the critical incident on a 7- or 10-point scale with respect to how effectively or ineffectively it represents performance on the dimension.

Incidents that generate good agreement in ratings, typically indicated by a low standard deviation, are considered for the final scale. The particular incidents chosen are determined by their location along the scale, as measured by the mean scores. Typically, the final scale has six to eight anchors. Exhibit 14.5 shows a BARS scale that resulted from such a process for the attribute "promptness in meeting deadlines."

A key advantage of a BARS system is that it requires sales managers to consider in detail a wide range of components of a salesperson's job performance. It must also include clearly defined anchors for those performance criteria in specific behavioral terms, leading to thoughtful consideration by managers of just what comprises performance. Of course, by nature a BARS emphasizes behavior and performance rather than effectiveness. When used in tandem with appropriate objective measures (sales and profit analyses and output, input, and ratio measures),

EXHIBIT 14.5 A BARS Scale with Behavioral Anchors for the Attribute "Promptness in Meeting Deadlines"

Level	Scale	Behavioral anchor
Very high This indicates the more-often-than-not practice of submitting accurate and needed sales reports.	10.0	Could be expected to promptly submit all necessary field reports even in the most difficult of situations.
	9.0	
	8.0	Could be expected to promptly meet deadlines comfortably in most report completion situations.
	7.0	
	6.0	Is usually on time and can be expected to submit most routine field sales reports in proper format.
Moderate This indicates regularity in promptly submitting accurate and needed field sales reports.	5.0	
	4.0	Could be expected to regularly be tardy in submitting required field sales reports.
	3.0	Could be expected to be tardy and submit inaccurate field sales reports.
	2.0	Could be expected to completely disregard due dates for filing almost all reports.
	1.0	
Very low This indicates irregular and unacceptable promptness and accuracy of field sales reports.	0.0	Could be expected to never file field sales reports on time and resist any managerial guidance to improve this tendency.

Source: *Churchill/Ford/Walker's Sales Force Management,* 9th ed., by Mark W. Johnston and Greg W. Marshall (New York: McGraw-Hill, 2009), p. 457. Reprinted by permission of The McGraw-Hill Companies.

BARS can handle subjective evaluation criteria, providing as complete a picture as possible of a salesperson's overall performance and effectiveness.

BARS systems are not without their limitations, though. For one thing, the job-specific nature of their scales suggests they are most effective in evaluating salespeople performing very similar functions. They might be good for comparing one national account rep to another national account rep or two territory reps against each other, but they could suffer major shortcomings if used to compare a national account rep against a territory rep because of differences in responsibilities in these positions. BARS systems can also be relatively costly to develop since they require a good deal of up-front time from many people.[11]

360-Degree Performance Feedback

As you learned in Chapter 2, one important attraction of CRM systems is their inherent ability to provide feedback from a wide range of constituents and stakeholders. Although much of this information is used for product development and formulation of the overall marketing message, CRM systems typically also facilitate the gathering, analysis, and dissemination of a great deal of information directly relevant to the performance of the sales force.

To take full advantage of the information generated by enterprise software such as CRM, the firm as a whole must embrace the philosophy that the customer is a customer of the *company,* not just of the individual salesperson. You have seen that the complex and often lengthy process of developing and managing customer relationships almost always involves more than just a salesperson and a purchasing agent. An effective CRM system should be gathering data at all the touchpoints where members of a selling organization interact with members of a buying organization and where members of a selling organization interact internally to build a business relationship with a customer.

Such a comprehensive information management process allows us to rethink the nature of input data for use in salesperson performance evaluation. Rather than relying on purely objective measures or on subjective measures generated by one person (the sales manager), evaluators can receive information from multiple sources. This concept, called **360-degree performance feedback,** opens the door to a new era in using the performance appraisal process as an effective tool for salesperson development and improvement.

Among the sources of feedback useful to salespeople are external customers, **internal customers** (organization members who are resources in serving external customers), other members of the selling team, any one who reports directly to the sales manager (such as sales assistants), and of course the sales manager.[12] Integrating feedback from these and other relevant sources of performance information into the formal evaluation process (and thus onto the evaluation form) can provide the impetus for a more productive dialogue between the sales manager and salesperson at performance review time.

Related to 360-degree feedback is **self-evaluation.** Sales organizations should encourage salespeople to prepare an honest assessment of their own performance against the established objective and subjective performance criteria. This should be prepared *before* the formal performance review session with the sales manager.[13] The best sales organizations use this process to begin setting sales unit goals for the next period and especially to establish a professional development program to help move salespeople toward the fulfillment of their personal goals on the job.

You learned in Chapter 13 that intrinsic rewards like feelings of accomplishment, personal growth, and self-worth are among the most powerful motivators. Allowing salespeople to have direct input by establishing personal growth goals on the job, and then institutionalizing the achievement of those goals via the formal performance evaluation process, goes a long way toward providing a workplace atmosphere where they can realize their intrinsic rewards.

It is important to involve salespeople directly in all phases of the performance appraisal process. When appraisals provide clear criteria whose development included input by salespeople, and the appraisals are perceived as fair and are used in determining rewards, salesperson job satisfaction increases. The critical determinants of appraisal effectiveness are not purely criteria-driven. They are largely determined by appraisal process factors that managers can influence, such as buy-in by those being appraised and fairness of the appraisal process.[14]

An old adage in human resource management holds that if an employee is surprised by anything he or she is told during a formal performance review, the manager is not doing a very good job. Performance evaluation should not be one cathartic event that happens once or twice a year. Such a view can cause great trepidation from both employees and managers and often leads managers to procrastinate in conducting the review and minimize the time spent with the employee during the review.

Great sales organizations use the performance evaluation process to facilitate *ongoing* dialogue between salespeople and their managers. A key goal should be to facilitate professional and personal development by providing salespeople the feedback and tools they need to achieve their goals in the job. To make this happen, sales managers must carry on the dialogue beyond just the periodic formal appraisal event into day-to-day communication with salespeople. Importantly, this developmental perspective on performance evaluation requires sales managers to not just give feedback but also listen and respond to feedback and questions from the salespeople.

Ultimately, sales organizations need to work toward developing a **performance management system,** which requires a commitment to integrating all the elements of feedback on the process of serving customers. The result is performance information that is timely, accurate, and relevant to the firm's customer management initiative.[15] The pieces of the performance puzzle are integrated in such a way that the salesperson does not have to wait on the manager for a formal validation of performance. Instead, under a performance management system approach, salespeople take the lead in goal setting, performance measurement, and adjustment of their own performance.[16] The concept of performance management is analogous to Total Quality Management (TQM) approaches that advocate the empowerment of employees to take ownership of their own jobs and conduct their own analyses of performance against goals, creating a culture of self-management. To successfully implement a performance management system, sales managers must shift their leadership style to that of a partner in a mutually shared process.

Summary

Performance and effectiveness are different concepts. Performance is a salesperson's behavior evaluated in terms of its contribution to the goals of the organization. Effectiveness is an organizational outcome for which a salesperson is at least partly responsible, usually examined across a variety of indexes.

Salespeople may be evaluated based on objective and subjective criteria. Objective measures reflect statistics a sales manager can gather from a firm's internal data and other means. They may be categorized as output measures (the results of the efforts expended by salespeople) and input measures (the efforts they expend achieving the results). Objective measures also may take the form of ratios that combine various outputs and/or inputs.

On the other hand, subjective measures typically rely on personal evaluations, usually by the sales manager, of how the salesperson is doing. Managers should pay attention to both objective and subjective measures in evaluating salespeople.

A variety of potential pitfalls exist in performance measurement, especially regarding subjective measures. These problems often take the form of various errors or biases in the evaluation, which result in an inaccurate performance appraisal that the salesperson rightly perceives as unfair. Sales organizations and their managers must take great care to conduct the performance evaluation process as fairly and accurately as possible. BARS systems aid in this process.

In addition, 360-degree feedback in the performance review, including a strong component of self-evaluation by the salesperson, can greatly improve the usefulness of the performance evaluation process.

Key Terms

behavior
performance
effectiveness
objective measures
subjective measures
output measures
input measures
telecommuting
bias
outcome bias
BARS (behaviorally anchored rating scale)
360-degree performance feedback
internal customers
self-evaluation
performance management system

Role Play

Before You Begin

Before getting started, please go to the appendix of Chapter 1 to review the profiles of the characters involved in this role play as well as the tips on preparing a role play.

Characters Involved

Rhonda Reed

Zane Cleary, regional sales manager for Upland Company. Zane is Rhonda's direct supervisor and reports to the vice president of sales, Leslie Skipper. Upland has four regions in the United States, each containing 15 to 20 districts.

Setting the Stage

Leslie Skipper recently announced that Upland will be undertaking a full review of its salesperson performance evaluation process. A committee has been named to lead this initiative, including all four regional sales managers and four select district managers (one from each region). Because Rhonda is very highly regarded within the organization, she has been named to the committee.

Leslie has charged the group with designing the best possible performance evaluation system for salespeople at Upland without regard to "how it has been done in the past." In two weeks, the committee will hold its first formal meeting at the home office to kick off the discussions. Zane Cleary has scheduled a trip to Rhonda's city this week so they can develop some ideas and notes before the big meeting.

Rhonda Reed's Role

Rhonda needs to come to the meeting with Zane prepared to discuss what might comprise an ideal performance evaluation system for Upland. She reviews material on objective and subjective performance measures as well as the concept of 360-degree feedback. It will be important for her to discuss various measurement options with Zane, consider the pros and cons of each as well as their applicability to Upland's particular situation, and come up with some clear goals that Upland would like to accomplish through its salesperson performance evaluation process.

Zane Cleary's Role

Zane wants to go into the big committee meeting at the home office prepared to share and support the ideas that he and Rhonda develop now. He will remind Rhonda that they can start with a clean slate to develop and recommend a great salesperson performance evaluation process for Upland without regard to how it has been done in the past.

Like Rhonda, Zane needs to come to the meeting prepared to discuss what might comprise an ideal performance evaluation system for Upland. He too reviews material on objective and subjective performance measures as well as 360-degree feedback. It will be important for him to discuss various measurement options with Rhonda, consider the pros and cons of each as well as their applicability to Upland's situation, and come up with some clear goals that Upland would like to accomplish through its salesperson performance evaluation process.

Assignment

Work with another student to prepare a 15- to 20-minute role-play dialogue for the meeting between Rhonda and Zane. Be sure to cover the issues outlined and reach a conclusion that includes the necessary deliverables for the big meeting at the home office. To do this successfully, you will need to review carefully the material in Chapter 14.

Discussion Questions

1. Kevin Harrison, sales rep for Allied Steel Distributors, had an appointment with his sales manager to discuss his first year's sales performance. Kevin knew that the meeting would not go well. One of Allied's major accounts had changed suppliers due to problems with Kevin. The purchasing agent claimed the so-called personality differences were so serious that future business with Allied was not possible. Kevin knew these "personality differences" involved his unwillingness to entertain in the same style as the previous sales rep, who often took the purchasing agent and others to a local topless bar for lunch. The rep told Kevin that this was expected and if he wanted to keep the business, it was necessary. Besides, tickets to pro basketball games didn't count anymore.

What are the short- and long-range implications of this type of customer entertaining? What would you do in a similar situation? How should Kevin's sales manager react?

2. The sales manager for a large corporation notices an irregular decrease in the sales of a particular sales representative. The rep, normally in very high standing, has of late failed to achieve her quota. What can the sales manager do to determine whether the slump in the sales curve is the rep's responsibility or due to things beyond her control?

3. Given the following information from evaluations of the performance of different sales representatives, what can you conclude about why the reps are not achieving quota? (Assume each is not making quota.)

   a. *Rep 1:* Achieved goals for sales calls, phone calls, and new accounts; customer relations are good; no noticeable deficiencies in any areas.

   b. *Rep 2:* Completed substantially fewer sales calls than goal. Many phone calls, but primarily with one firm. Time management analysis shows the sales rep spends a disproportionately large amount of time with one firm. New accounts are low; all other areas good to outstanding.

c. *Rep 3:* Number of sales calls low, below goal. Telephone calls, letters, proposals all very low and below goal. Evaluation shows poor time utilization. Very high amount of service-related activities in rep's log; customer relations extremely positive; recently has received a great deal of feedback from customers on product function.

4. Is sales just a numbers game, as one sales manager claims? She believes that all you have to do is make the right number of calls of the right type, and the odds will work in your favor. Make 10 calls, get one sale. So to get two sales, make 20 calls. Is this the right approach? Why or why not?

5. Jackie Hitchcock, recently promoted to district sales manager, faced a new problem she wasn't sure how to resolve. The district's top sales rep is also the district's number one problem. Brad Coombs traditionally leads the company in sales but also in problems. He has broken every rule, bent every policy, deviated from guidelines, and been less than truthful. Jackie knew Brad had never done anything illegal, but she was worried that something serious could happen. Brad also does not prepare call reports on time, fails to show up at trade shows, and doesn't attend sales training programs.

How should Jackie handle this problem? How does a sales manager manage a maverick sales rep? Specifically, how can the performance evaluation process help Jackie deal with Brad?

Ethical Dilemma

Terri Jensen is reviewing the semiannual customer satisfaction scores for the sales force at Planet Plastics. As eastern region vice president of sales, she had played an important part in getting senior management to support using customer satisfaction surveys as part of the compensation package for each salesperson. These surveys were initially criticized by the sales force, but over the last two years they have come to see the scores as a successful part of the salesperson evaluation process. Customers appreciate the opportunity to provide feedback, and salespeople realize the benefits of keeping their customers satisfied—*and* 25 percent of their incentive compensation is tied to these customer satisfaction reports.

However, as Terri looks at the reports she notices a disturbing problem. Jason Zaderhorn, a young salesperson in Nashville, received very low scores from his largest customer, Mercury Manufacturing. These numbers mean that Jason will not be eligible for any of the compensation tied to customer satisfaction this year. Terri knows why Jason's scores are so low. Jason e-mailed her a month ago and later called about a serious problem at Mercury. The director of purchasing in Mercury's Nashville plant had called Jason into his office and said that if Planet Plastics wanted to continue as the lead plastics supplier for Mercury, there would need to be a "special arrangement." Jason knew at once the purchasing director meant some form of bribe.

Planet Plastics has always held to the highest ethical standards. While Jason said he would check with his boss, he knew that Planet would not participate in bribes just to keep the business. Terri affirmed Jason's perspective in a phone call. Jason told the purchasing director that Planet felt it deserved the business based on performance and would not be involved with any "special arrangements." (He was careful not to use the inflammatory word "bribe" with the purchasing director.)

Mercury is Planet's second largest customer worldwide. Jason is responsible for several of its facilities in the Nashville area, but Mercury has business around the world and Planet has been its supplier for 10 years. This is a difficult situation. Terri knows why Jason's customer satisfaction scores are low, but if she explains why to senior management at Planet, it will get back to Mercury's facilities around the world. This could put the entire account at risk.

On the other hand, Jason has done well on other accounts, and it is not fair to withhold his bonus based on the feedback from this one customer. If Terri does give Jason the bonus, how will she explain it to the executive vice president of sales—who just happens to be coming into her office later today?

Questions

1. What should Terri Jensen tell the EVP of sales?
2. Should Jason get a bonus? If so, how might it be calculated?
3. How should Jason, Terri, and Planet Plastics respond to Mercury?

Mini Case

CASE 14

American Food Processors

Jamie Walker, regional vice president of sales for American Food Processors (AFP), is looking at the performance numbers of his sales force for the past year. He is starting to get that sinking feeling he gets every year at this time. Once again he has to evaluate the performance of his sales force, and he is not looking forward to the exercise. The problem is that Jamie really likes all of his sales reps as people. Because of that, he would like to use more subjective criteria in evaluating them. He thinks they all do a good job, and many of them have extenuating circumstances that just don't show up in the objective performance data the company requires him to use.

Jamie knows from having been a sales rep himself for eight years before getting into sales management that various things come up each year that can drastically affect a salesperson's territory. A large customer may go out of business, a competitor may place renewed emphasis on gaining accounts in a certain territory, or the economy may simply be poor for some customers. Any one of these events or many others can significantly impair a salesperson's performance, and the rep has little to no influence on these events. Nonetheless, AFP's evaluation process for the time being is numbers driven. Jamie will have to get to work calculating the required ratios and rank ordering his sales reps before holding his annual performance review meetings with each rep next week.

In looking at the performance data, Jamie immediately sees an example of why objective performance information by itself is not the best way to evaluate a sales force. The standard number of days any representative could work in his or her territory for the year was 240 (52 weeks/year × 5 days/week − 10 holidays − 10 travel and meeting days). Since Steve Rogers has been with the company for just over a year, he gets only one week of vacation. However, Marti Edwards combined her two weeks of vacation with six weeks of maternity leave when her baby was born. Such discrepancies in the number of days worked affects the evaluation process, but going strictly by the numbers doesn't allow for any consideration of those extenuating circumstances. Jamie also notices that Rick Randall, who was originally on his way to having a breakout year, barely exceeded quota. One of Rick's largest customers went bankrupt nine months into the year, and he had a hard time recovering from that setback.

TABLE 1 Current Year Sales Performance Data

Sales Rep	Previous Year's Sales	Current Year's Sales	Current Sales Quota	Total Number of Accounts
Steve Rogers	$480,000	$481,000	$575,000	1,100
Adam Murphy	750,000	883,000	835,000	1,600
Vicki Doyle	576,000	613,000	657,000	1,150
Rick Randall	745,000	852,000	850,000	1,350
Brenda Palmer	765,000	860,000	850,000	1,300
David Chen	735,000	835,000	825,000	1,400
Marti Edwards	665,000	670,000	720,000	1,600
Kim McConnell	775,000	925,000	875,000	1,700

Sales Rep	Number of Orders	Annual Sales Expenses	Number of Calls	Number of Days Worked
Steve Rogers	780	$ 9,300	1,300	235
Adam Murphy	1,970	12,300	1,800	223
Vicki Doyle	1,020	7,500	1,650	228
Rick Randall	1,650	11,000	1,700	230
Brenda Palmer	1,730	11,300	1,750	232
David Chen	1,790	11,500	1,750	220
Marti Edwards	960	10,800	1,550	200
Kim McConnell	1,910	12,800	1,850	225

As Jamie continues to ponder the task before him, he knows that the other three regional sales VPs are working on the same assignment. He also begins to realize (as he does every year) that there are as many extenuating circumstances as there are salespeople and that considering them all when evaluating performance would be an impossible task. Maybe looking at only the numbers and ratios is the fairest method after all.

Questions

1. Using the information provided in Table 1, rank Jamie's sales representatives from best to worst by calculating and considering the following ratios: sales growth, sales to quota, sales per account, average order size, sales expense, calls per day, and orders per call (hits).
2. Suppose you are Jamie Walker and you're holding the annual review meeting with each of these sales reps. What recommendations will you give to the four lowest-ranking reps to improve their sales?
3. What are some of the limitations of using only ratios to evaluate members of AFP's sales force? How could Jamie improve the performance evaluation process so that other information is considered? If Jamie could convince AFP to consider other performance information, what other information do you recommend he use?

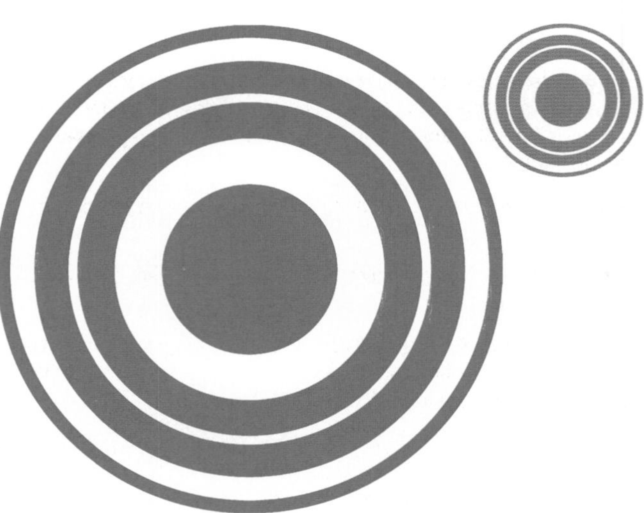

Glossary

A

Account attractiveness the degree to which a customer is desirable to the company, such as, generating new business.

Account analysis estimating the sales potential for each customer and prospect in the territory.

Account call rates a calculation of the number of times a particular account is called on in a given time (week, month, or year).

Account priorities goals and objectives for individual customers.

Active listening carefully monitoring the dialogue with the customer, watching for buying signals (verbal and nonverbal).

Activities professional priorities that relate to activities and include goals such as number of new accounts, number of sales call per week or month, and sales-to-expense ratio.

Activity priorities goals and objectives for specific sales related activities (i.e., number of new accounts).

Adaptive selling the altering of sales behaviors during a customer interaction or from one situation to another based on information the sales rep gathers about the nature of the selling situation.

Advantage a particular product/service characteristic that helps meet the customer's needs.

Alternative choice close gives the prospect options (neither of which is not to buy at all). It focuses on making the choice between viable options—options the prospect is most likely to accept.

Approach the first part of the sales presentation. It is a transition point from the greeting to the main body of your presentation, where the primary sales message will be delivered to the customer.

Assessment approach a sales strategy in which you ask the customer to complete a set of questions, collect the data, analyze the information, and make a presentation based on your analysis.

Assumptive close a closing technique in which a salesperson assumes the buyer accepts the sales presentation and the sale will be successfully completed.

Attitude a state of mind or feeling with regard to a person or thing (or product or service).

Autonomy the degree of independence the salesperson can exercise in making his or her own decisions in the day-to-day operation of the job.

Average cost of a sales call has been estimated to be as much as $242, depending on the industry. This cost is increasing by about 5 percent per year.

B

Balance sheet close, also known as **t-account close**–gets the salesperson directly involved in helping the prospect see the pros and cons of placing the order by creating a list of "Reasons for Buying" and "Remaining Questions" on paper.

BARS (behaviorally anchored rating scale) an approach to performance appraisal directed at resolving problems related to the selection of attributes for evaluation and how they are presented on the form.

Basic control unit the fundamental geographic area used to form sales territories—county or city, for example.

Behavior refers to what salespeople do—that is, the tasks on which they expend effort while working.

Benefit is the favorable outcome to the buyer from the advantage found in the product feature.

Benefits are designed to satisfy the salesperson's basic need for security and include medical and disability insurance, life insurance, and a retirement plan.

Bias refers to the degree to which performance evaluations differ from objective reality, usually based on errors by the evaluator (in our case, the sales manager).

Bird dogs, or spotters are people who come into contact with an unusually large number of people in the course of their daily routine. Salespeople use bird dogs as their eyes and ears in the marketplace.

Bonus a payment made at the discretion of management for achieving or surpassing some set level of performance.

Bounce-back occurs when a salesperson turns a customer concern into a reason for action. The bounce-back is effective in many different situations (appointment setting, negotiating, and closing).

Brand equity the value inherent in a brand name in and of itself.

Bribe a financial present given to a buyer to manipulate his or her purchase decision.

Business climate a set of unwritten norms and rules that influence the behavior of individuals. Every organization has a business climate. See also *corporate culture.*

Business ethics moral principles and standards that guide behavior in the world of business. The purpose of such principles and standards is to define right and wrong behavior for salespeople. See also *ethics.*

Business-to-business (B2B) market (previously called *industrial selling*)—the sale of goods and services to buyers who are not the end users. Relationship selling is much more predominant in the B2B market than the B2C market.

Business-to-consumer (B2C) market the sale of goods and services to end-user consumers (retail selling).

Buying center all the people who participate in purchasing or influencing the purchase of a particular product. Buying center members include initiators, users, influencers, gatekeepers, buyers, deciders, and controllers.

Buying signals verbal and nonverbal cues that the customer is ready to make a commitment to purchase.

Buy-now close also sometimes referred to as the **impending event** close or standing-room-only close, creates a sense of urgency with the buyer that if he or she doesn't act today, something valuable will be lost.

C

Call frequency the number of times the salesperson calls on certain customers or classes of customers (for example, retail stores with less than a certain amount of sales in a given period). It is expressed as so many times per week, month, and year.

Call reluctance occurs when salespeople resist prospecting because (of all the activities required in successful relationship selling) it is the one that involves making cold calls. Salespeople must overcome call reluctance.

Career priorities priorities that deal with what kind of sales career one wants to have over time.

Caveat emptor or **("Let the buyer beware")** adage defined the 20th-century sales model. It was generally considered the buyer's responsibility to uncover any untruths in the seller's statements.

Centers of influence people who are in a position to persuade a salesperson's potential customers.

Closing the sale obtaining a commitment from the prospect or customer to make a purchase. It is one of the most important sales call goals.

Code of ethics formulated through learning a sense of right and wrong. Employees make ethical decisions using two ethical frameworks, their own personal code of ethics and the company's ethical code.

Cold calls, also referred to as **canvassing**—telephoning or going to see potential prospects in person without invitation.

Collusion occurs when competing companies get together and fix prices, divide up customers or territories, or act in a way to harm a third party (often another competitor or a customer).

Commission a payment based on short-term results, usually a salesperson's dollar or unit sales volume.

Compensate for deficiencies moving the customer from focusing on a feature your product performs poorly to one in which it excels.

Compensation all monetary rewards professional salespeople receive.

Compensation plan is the method used to implement the reward structure in an organization.

Competitor defamation harming a competitor by making unfair or untrue statements about the company, its products, or the people that work for it.

Competitor obstruction the practice of impeding competitor access to a customer.

Conferences events held by the sales organization to provide a forum for prospecting. Conferences typically combine information sessions with social outings and are usually held in attractive locations.

Confidentiality the sharing of sensitive information between salespeople and customers, an important aspect of relationship selling.

Consultative selling the set of skills, strategies, and processes that works most effectively with buyers who demand, and are willing to pay for, a sales effort that creates new value and provides additional benefits beyond the product.

Corporate culture developed through establishment of a well-defined mission together with a successful corporate history and top management's values and beliefs. Corporate cultures shape employee attitudes and actions and help determine the plans, policies, and procedures salespeople and their managers can implement.

Cultural differences occur through a manifestation of a specific set of norms, accepted behaviors, and beliefs created by every culture.

Customer advocacy a customer is satisfied, loyal, and willing to spread the word that he or she is pleased with you.

Customer benefit approach a sales technique that involves starting the presentation with a solution to at least one of the customer's problems, creating an instant win–win situation.

Customer-centric firms that put the customer at the center of everything that happens both inside and outside the organization.

Customer complaints concerns raised by the customer about some aspect of the relationship. They may involve service problems, the salesperson's performance, pricing concerns, product quality, or any other issue that creates a problem for the customer.

Customer delight exceeding customer expectations to a surprising degree, is a powerful way to gain customer loyalty.

Customer loyalty when salespeople give customers many reasons not to switch to competitors. Your value proposition must be strong enough to move customers past mere satisfaction and into a commitment to you and your products for the long run.

Customer mindset the salesperson's belief that understanding and satisfying customers, whether internal or external to the organization, is central to doing his or her job well. It is through this customer mindset that a customer orientation comes alive within a sales force.

Customer orientation the importance that a firm places on customers. Customer-oriented organizations instill an organizationwide focus on understanding customer requirements, generate an understanding of the marketplace, disseminate that knowledge to everyone in the firm, and align system capabilities internally so that the organization responds effectively with innovative, competitively differentiated, satisfaction-generating products and services.

Customer relationship management (CRM) a comprehensive business model for increasing revenues and profits by focusing on customers. CRM uses advanced technology to maximize the firm's ability to add value to customers and develop long-term customer relationships.

Customer satisfaction the degree to which customers like the product, service, and relationship.

D

Daily event schedule one of the basic elements in a good time management plan. It involves a daily to-do list with specific tasks.

Data mining sorting the information warehoused in a database to learn more about current and potential customers.

Data warehouse a comprehensive, customer-centric approach to handling customer data and transforming it into useful information for developing customer-focused strategies and programs.

Deception occurs when a manager and/or salesperson are not being totally honest with each other.

Defamation harming a competitor by making unfair or untrue statements about the company, its products, or people who work for it. See also *libel* and *slander*.

Defer is postponing the customer concern until salespeople have had the chance to explain other material.

Demarketing a process that a company may engage in during periods of shortage that may involve a part or all of its product line. The process seeks to reduce demand in the short run.

Derived demand demand for goods and services derived from the customers' demand for the goods or services it produces or markets.

Development a long-term road map or career track for a salesperson so he or she can realize professional goals.

Direct close the most straightforward closing approach, in which the salesperson simply asks for the order.

Direct denial an immediate and unequivocal rejection of a customer statement.

Direct marketing a promotional vehicle that might include direct mail, telemarketing, electronic marketing via Web site or e-mail, and other means that seek a direct response from customers.

Directories published books of contacts (available from a variety of sources) that can serve as lead generators.

Dishonesty providing false or deliberately inaccurate information to customers.

Draw an advance of money to a salesperson in months when commissions are low to ensure he or she will always take home a specified minimum pay.

E

Educational institutions refer to colleges and universities and include both four-year and two-year organizations.

Effectiveness refers to some measure of organizational outcomes for which a salesperson is at least partly responsible.

Effort the core of motivation. That is, motivation may be thought as the amount of effort a salesperson chooses to expend on each activity or task associated with the job.

80:20 rule eighty percent of a company's business comes from twenty percent of its customers.

Electronic training methods deliver training using CD-ROM or other types of technology.

Empathy a salesperson's identification with and understanding of the buyer's situation, feelings, and motives.

Employee benefits part of a compensation package designed to satisfy the salesperson's basic needs for security. They typically include medical and disability insurance, life insurance, and a retirement plan.

Employment services companies that specialize in the placement of individuals in jobs. Some companies focus on certain types of jobs, like sales, and others are general employment agencies.

Endless chain referral occurs when the salesperson asks an open-ended question during each customer contact in an effort to gather the names of potential prospects, who in turn will provide more leads.

Enterprise resource planning (ERP) software that links bid estimation, order entry, shipping, billing systems, and other work processes.

Enterprise selling the set of skills, strategies, and processes that work most effectively with strategically important customers who demand an extraordinary level of value creation from a key supplier. The primary function of enterprise selling is to leverage the sales organization's corporate assets to contribute to the customer's strategic success.

Ethics moral principles and standards that guide behavior. Importantly, social values set the standards for ethical behavior. A particular action may be legal but not ethical.

Expectancy the salesperson's estimate of the probability that expending effort on a task will lead to improved performance on some dimension.

Expectancy theory of motivation provides the framework for motivating salespeople.

Expense account a formal reimbursement plan for travel, lodging, meals, entertainment, and other expenses incurred by sales reps in the field.

External customers the people and companies a salesperson sells to outside his or her own company. See also *internal customers.*

External environment, or **macroenvironment** the issues that arise outside the control of the selling organization. Examples include the Federal Reserve raising interest rates or the government regulating a product. See also *internal environment.*

External sources for recruits include people in other firms (who are often identified and referred by current members of the sales force), educational institutions, ads, and employment agencies.

Extrinsic rewards the rewards bestowed on the salesperson by people or organizations outside the individual, most notably the company. See also *intrinsic rewards.*

F

FAB an acronym that stands for features, advantages, and benefits. By applying the FAB approach, salespeople can make the company's products and services relevant for the customer.

Feature is any material characteristic or specification of the company's products and services.

Firing a customer a rather harsh way to express the idea that a customer does not generate enough profit, thus needs to find alternative sources or channels for products needed.

Follow-up one of the most important ways to add value through excellent service after the sale. Effective follow-up is one way that salespeople and their firms can improve customer perceptions of service quality, customer satisfaction, and customer loyalty and retention rates.

Formula presentation a prepared outline that directs the overall structure of the presentation but enables the salesperson to gain customer feedback and adjust the presentation. A formula presentation is highly structured but increases customer interaction by soliciting more information.

4 Ps of marketing product, place or distribution, price, and promotion. They are also known as the marketing mix.

G

Gift a nonfinancial present.

I

Inbound telemarketing gives prospects a way to receive more information from the sales organization via the telephone.

Incentive pay is the compensation paid by commission or bonus that direct salespeople's efforts toward specific strategic objectives during a given time period.

Incentives financial as well as nonfinancial rewards. Nonfinancial incentives include recognition programs, promotions to better territories or to management positions, or opportunities for personal development.

Indirect denial is less threatening than a direct denial and involves agreeing with the customer and validating their objection before explaining why it is untrue or misdirected.

Industrial selling an old term for business-to-business (B2B) selling. See *business-to-business marketing.*

Input measures objective measures of performance that focus on the efforts sales representatives expend rather than the results of those efforts.

Instrumentalities are the salesperson's estimates that improved performance will lead to attaining particular rewards.

Integrated marketing communications (IMC) ensures that all the messages about a company and its products are consistent.

Internal customers people within a firm who may not have direct external customer contact but who nonetheless add value that will ultimately benefit the people and companies that buy the firm's products and services. See also *external customers.*

Internal environment, or **organizational environment** are issues that arise inside the company and are controllable by the firm. Examples include hiring more support staff or improving quality control. See also *external environment.*

Internal marketing marketing inside a firm to provide a consistency of messages among employees and show that management is uniform in supporting key strategic themes.

Internal sources for recruits consist of people already employed in other departments within the firm.

Intimate space the space within two feet of a person. This space is reserved for family and close friends. Salespeople who violate this space are considered rude and even offensive.

Intrinsic rewards the rewards inherent to satisfaction derived from elements of the job or role itself. The salesperson bestows intrinsic rewards on himself or herself. See also *extrinsic rewards.*

J

Job analysis determines what activities, tasks, responsibilities, and environmental influences are involved in the job.

Job description used to develop a statement of job qualifications, which lists and describes the personal traits and abilities a person should have to perform the tasks and meet the responsibilities involved.

Job enlargement the fact that the sales role today is broader and contains substantially more activities than it once did.

Job qualifications are the personal traits and abilities a person should have to perform the job.

Job satisfaction refers to all the characteristics of the job that sales reps find rewarding, fulfilling, and satisfying. Job dissatisfaction refers to aspects they find frustrating and unsatisfying.

Junk mail unsolicited mass direct mail that many customers throw away.

K

Key account one of a firm's largest customers (especially one with a buying center) whose potential business over time represents enough dollars and entails enough cross-functional interaction among various areas of both firms to justify the high costs of the team approach. Key accounts generally have a senior salesperson as the key account manager (KAM).

Key success factors the various skills and knowledge components required to perform the sales role successfully. Identifying these key success factors in relationship selling is the first step in recruiting and selecting good salespeople.

L

Lead the name of someone who might have the potential to buy from the sales company. See also *prospects.*

Libel defamation in which unfair or untrue *written* statements materially harm the reputation of a competitor or the personal reputation of anyone working for it.

Life priorities personal priorities that deal with basic choices in life.

Lifetime value of a customer an estimate of the present value of the stream of future profits expected over a customer's lifetime of purchases.

M

Margin refers to profit made by the firm.

Market potential combines historical data and market research results with feedback from salespeople to estimate the potential sales for all similar products in a given area.

Marketing concept an overarching business philosophy where companies turn to customers for input in making strategic decisions about what products to market, where to market them, how to get them to market, at what price, and how to communicate with customers about the products.

Marketing mix the 4 Ps of marketing, is the tool kit marketers use to develop marketing strategy (product, place or distribution, price, and promotion).

Matrix organization an organization of direct reports and supporting internal consultants who bring their collective expertise to bear for a client.

Memorized presentation a very structured presentation that focuses on the product and is based on the memorization of specific canned statements and questions. Companies and salespeople who adopt a memorized presentation strategy, believe they can make a compelling argument for the product without spending time learning more about the customer's problems and needs.

Mentors managers in sales organizations who work with their salespeople to enhance their effectiveness during sales presentations and help them improve their skill sets.

Metropolitan statistical area (MSA) an integrated economic and social unit with a large population nucleus.

Minor point close occurs when the salesperson focuses the buyer on a small element of the decision. The idea is that agreeing on something small reflects commitment to the purchase and lets the salesperson move forward with the deal.

Modified rebuy where a customer wants to modify the product specs, prices, or other terms it has been receiving from existing suppliers and will consider dealing with new suppliers to make changes.

Motivation refers to an individual's choice to initiate action on a certain task, expend a certain amount of effort on that task, and persist in expending effort over a period of time.

N

Need analysis occurs when a firm determines the best solution to the customer's requirements by combining knowledge of the company's products and services with the recognition of customer needs. The salesperson must make the analysis quickly, often during the presentation.

Need identification involves questioning customers to discover their needs.

Need satisfaction occurs when the salesperson presents the company's solution (products and services) to a customer's needs.

Need satisfaction presentation a sales presentation in which the focus is on customers and satisfying their needs. As much as 50 to 60 percent of the first half of the presentation is spent asking questions, listening, and determining the customer's real needs.

Negotiation a process in which a sales organization works with customers to develop a win–win solution to their problems. It is at the heart of the relationship-selling process.

Networking using contacts—personal, professional, everyone a sales rep meets—to develop leads.

New-task purchase occurs when a customer is buying a relatively complex and expensive product or service for the first time.

Nonfinancial incentives incentives in addition to financial compensation such as opportunities for promotion or various types of recognition for performance like special awards and citations.

Nonverbal communication communication that does not involve words, such as someone's facial expressions, posture, eye contact, gestures, and even dress.

O

Objections concerns that some part of a product offering (solution) does not fully meet the buyer's need. The objection may be over price, delivery, terms of agreement, timing, or myriad other potential elements of a deal.

Objective measures of salesperson performance reflect statistics the sales manager can gather from the firm's internal data. These measures are best used when they reflect elements of the sales process. See also *subjective measures.*

On-the-job (OJT) training individual instruction (coaching) and in-house classes held close to where the salesperson is working, such as district sales offices.

Opportunity rate the proportion of salespeople promoted into management in a year.

Organization of critical information ability to organize and create a system for easy access to information critical to effective time management.

Organizational citizenship behaviors encompass four basic types of activities: (1) sportsmanship, (2) civic virtue, (3) conscientiousness, and (4) altruism.

Outbound telemarketing involves making unsolicited phone calls to leads in an attempt to qualify them as prospects.

Outcome bias occurs when a sales manager allows the outcome (rather than the process) of a decision or a series of decisions made by a salesperson to overly influence his or her performance ratings.

Output measures objective measures of performance that represent the results of efforts expended by a salesperson.

Out supplier a potential supplier that is not on a buyer's approved vendor list. An out supplier's objective is to move the customer away from the automatic reordering procedures of a straight rebuy toward the more extensive evaluation processes of a modified rebuy.

P

Perceived risk for a firm when buying a particular product—affects the makeup and size of the buying center. It is based on the complexity of the product and situation, the relative importance of the purchase, time pressure to make a decision, and the degree of uncertainty about the product's efficacy.

Perceived role ambiguity occurs when a salesperson lacks sufficient information about the job and its requirements.

Perceived role conflict arises when a salesperson believes that the demands of two or more of his or her role partners are incompatible.

Perceived value whether or not something has value is in the eye of the beholder—the *customer.*

Performance behavior evaluated in terms of its contribution to the goals of the organization. Performance has a normative element reflecting whether a salesperson's behavior is good or bad, appropriate or inappropriate, in light of the organization's goals and objectives.

Performance gap the difference between what a salesperson promised and what he or she delivers to a buyer. Performance gaps result in customer complaints.

Performance management system integrates all the elements of feedback on the process of serving customers so that performance information is timely, accurate, and relevant to the customer management aspects of the firm.

Perquisites (perks) might include higher compensation, a better automobile, better office facilities, and the like to provide incentives for top salespeople to move into more advanced sales positions.

Personal interviews structured and unstructured, the most common method of selecting salespeople and the one sales managers consider most helpful.

Personal priorities what's really important to a given individual. See also *professional priorities.*

Personal space the space of two to three feet around a person. It should not be violated except for a handshake.

Persuasive communication hoping to convince someone to do something or win someone over to a particular course of action.

Preapproach planning the sales call before actually making the initial approach to set the appointment.

Price discrimination the practice of giving different prices or discounts to different customers who purchase the same quality and quantity of products and services.

Problem-solving presentation approach considered the most complex and difficult sales presentation strategy. It is based on a simple premise that the customer has problems and the salesperson is there to solve them by creating win–win solutions.

Product demonstration a sales presentation for a product (like a car) for which demonstrating the product is a critical part of the presentation.

Professional priorities an individual's goals and objectives for his or her work life and career. See also *personal priorities.*

Promotion mix, or **marketing communications mix** includes personal selling, advertising, sales promotion, public relations and publicity, and direct marketing.

Prospects leads who meet certain criteria to qualify as potential customers. Prospects are considered to be a set of *very likely* potential customers.

Prospecting pursuing leads that you hope will develop into customers as a way to fill your pipeline of future business.

Public space the space greater than 12 feet around a person. It is the most accessible space around the customer.

Q

Qualifying the prospect the process of analyzing a lead to see if the person meets the criteria to be a prospect.

Question approach asking customers questions in the approach to involve them right from the start and get customer feedback to position you for success in the presentation.

Quota the minimum requirement a salesperson must reach to earn a bonus. Quotas can be based on goals for sales volume, profitability of sales, or various account servicing activities.

R

Reciprocity the practice of suppliers buying from one another.

Referral occurs when an existing customer sends business to his or her salesperson.

Rejection not the way a salesperson should take the failure to get an order or close a deal. Such outcomes are not personal rejections.

Relationship selling has the central goal of securing, building, and maintaining long-term relationships with profitable customers. Relationship selling works to add value through all possible means.

Repeat purchase, or **straight rebuy** occurs when a customer buys the same product under the same circumstances again and again. It tends to be much more routine than new-task purchase or modified rebuy.

Restraint of trade forcing a dealer or other channel member to stop carrying its competitors' products as part of its arrangement with the dealer.

Retail selling involves selling goods and services to end-user consumers for their own personal use.

Retention rate how long a salesperson or company keeps customers.

Return on customer investment how much time, money, and other resources are invested in a customer divided by how much the company earns from that customer's purchases.

Reward mix relative emphasis placed on salary versus commission or other incentive pay and nonfinancial rewards.

Role accuracy the degree to which the salesperson's perceptions of his or her role partners' demands are accurate.

Role playing a popular technique in which the sales trainee acts out a part, most often a salesperson, in a simulated buying session.

Routing schedule the plan for reaching all customers in a given time period and territory.

S

Salary a fixed sum of money paid at regular intervals.

Sales contests get reps to compete for prizes like vacations and clothes. They encourage extra effort aimed at specific short-term objectives.

Sales management the way the various aspects of relationship selling are managed within the salesperson's firm.

Sales potential the share of total market potential a company expects to achieve.

Sales presentation the delivery of information relevant to solving the customer's needs. It often involves a product demonstration.

Sales pressure the pressure exerted on the salespeople. It is one of the ethical issues in the relationship between managers and salespeople. Management should define clear sales goals without threatening undue pressure.

Sales territory an area defined by the company that includes customers or potential customers for the salesperson to call on. It is often designated geographically.

Sales training analysis investigates the training needs of a sales force and results in a plan for management to conduct a training program designed to benefit a particular salesperson or, more likely, an entire sales force.

Selection procedure a process that results in hiring the best sales rep from the available pool of applicants.

Self-evaluation means salespeople prepare an assessment of their own performance against the established objective and subjective performance criteria. This is part of 360-degree performance feedback and should be done before the formal performance review session with the manager.

Selling center brings together individuals from around the organization (marketing, customer service, sales, engineering, and others) to help salespeople do their jobs more effectively.

Service recovery a well-handled follow-up to customer problems that solidifies long-term customer relationships.

Silence a closing tool in which a salesperson sits back, stays quiet, and lets the customer talk.

Single-source supplier only one vendor used by a firm for a particular good or service to minimize the variation in quality of production inputs.

Slander defamation in which unfair or untrue *oral* statements materially harm the reputation of a competitor or the personal reputation of anyone working for it.

Slotting allowances fees retailers charge sales organizations for guaranteed shelf space. They cover the cost of setting up a new item in their IT system, programming it into inventory, and ultimately distributing it to stores.

Social responsibility the responsibility a company has toward its stakeholders: customers, employees, shareholders, suppliers, the government, creditors, and a host of other entities, who expect the company to act in an ethical manner.

Social space the space from 4 to 12 feet, often the space between customer and salesperson in a personal sales presentation.

Solution selling a relationship-selling approach in which the salesperson's primary role is to move the buyer toward visualization of a solution to his or her problem (need).

Spam junk e-mail. Many e-mail users (especially business users) filter spam out of their inboxes before they even view the messages.

SPIN strategy a comprehensive selling approach based on a series of four questions about the situation, problem, implication, and need payoff.

Stall occurs when customers ask for more time because they wish to delay the final decision for several reasons.

Straight rebuy occurs when a customer reorders an item he or she has purchased many times. See also *repeat purchase.*

Strategic partnerships formal relationships where companies' assets are shared for mutual advantage.

Subjective measures of salesperson performance typically relies on personal evaluations by someone inside the organization, usually the salesperson's immediate supervisor. They are generally gathered via direct observation but may involve input from customers or other sources. See also *objective measures.*

Summary-of-benefits close a relatively formal way to close by going back over some or all of the benefits accepted, reminding the buyer why those benefits are important, and then asking a direct closing question (or perhaps ending with a choice or some other method).

Supply-chain management the way firms manage every element in the channel of distribution. Firms that have excellent supply-chain management add a great deal of value for customers.

T

Team selling these structures commonly make the salesperson responsible for working with the entire selling team in order to manage the customer relationship.

Telecommuting working from a remote or virtual office, often at home, and seldom traveling to company offices.

Telemarketing selling by telephone. It is a support provided to salespeople by many firms and may be outbound, inbound, or both. Recent legislation limits outbound telemarketing.

Tenacity sticking with a task, even through difficulty and adversity.

Territory management plan defines where and how customers will interact with the company, in order to maintain the right relationship with its customers. It involves designing and monitoring the territory and tapping its full potential.

360-degree performance feedback solicits information for performance evaluation simultaneously from multiple sources, such as external customers, internal customers, selling team members, sales assistants, the sales manager, and the salesperson him- or herself.

Time management plan a schedule of goals based on identification of personal and professional priorities.

Touchpoints various points at which a firm has contact with its prospects and customers for the purpose of acquiring, retaining, or cross-selling customers. Examples include a call center, salesperson, distributor, store, branch office, Web site, or e-mail.

Trade shows major industry events in which companies doing business in a particular industry gather together to display their new products and services.

Training generally focuses on building specific skill and knowledge sets needed to succeed in a job.

Transactional selling the approach of conducting business as a series of discrete transactions. Transactional selling creates its value by stripping costs and making acquisition easy.

Trial close at any time during the sales process, the salesperson tries to close upon detecting one or more buying signals. The buyer may or may not actually be ready to commit. If commitment is achieved, it is considered *the* close. If commitment is not achieved, the trial close can uncover buyer objections that must be overcome. A trial close can involve any of the closing methods discussed in the book.

Trial offer an offer that allows the customer to use a product (perhaps in a small quantity) without a commitment to purchase.

Trust a belief by one party that the other party will fulfill its obligations in a relationship.

Turnover the number of people who leave the organization in a given time period (usually one year). Turnover is often expressed as a percentage (those who leave versus the total salesforce).

U

Uniform Commercial Code a group of regulations that defines the legal implications of selling. Consisting of nine articles and modified by each state, the UCC sets out the rules and procedures for almost all business practices in the United States.

Utility the want-satisfying power of a good or service.

V

Valence for performance the salesperson's perception of the desirability of improving performance on a given dimension.

Valence for rewards are the salesperson's perceptions of the desirability of receiving increased rewards as a result of improved performance.

Value the net bundle of benefits derived by the customer from the product you are selling.

Value-added selling works to add value through all possible means. Examples include better customer service, enhanced product quality, or improved buyer–seller communication. A value-added selling approach changes much of the sales process to a relationship approach.

Value chain envisioned by Michael Porter of Harvard to identify ways for a selling firm to add customer value.

Value proposition the communication of value, which is the net bundle of benefits that the customer derives from the product you are selling.

Variable commission rate pay relatively high commissions for sales of the most profitable products, sales to the most profitable accounts, or sales of new products.

Virtual office a location outside the company's offices where a salesperson works from (often his or her home).

W

Weekly/monthly planning calendar is one of the basic elements in a good time management plan. Salespeople use it to create lists with specific tasks they wants to accomplish in longer periods of time.

Word of mouth a powerful source of leads that have a strong chance of resulting in qualified prospects.

Work/family conflict a lack of balance between work and family life, usually involving work encroaching on family.

Workload analysis a determination of how much work is required to cover each sales territory.

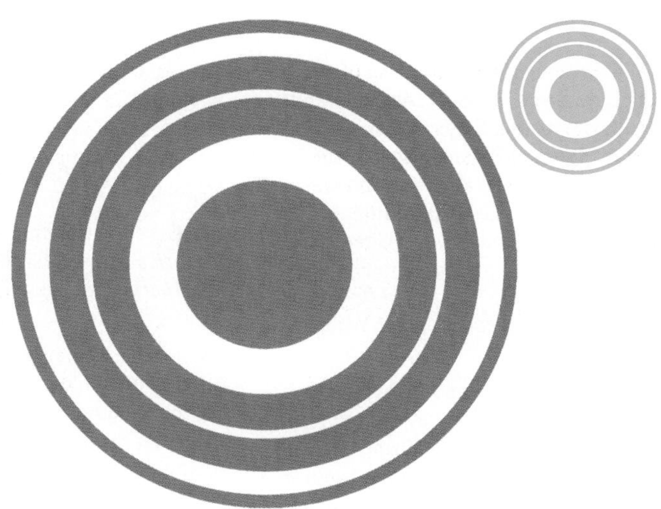

Endnotes

CHAPTER 1

1. Benson P. Shapiro, Adrian J. Slywotsky, and Stephen X. Doyle, *Strategic Sales Management: A Boardroom Issue,* Case #9 (Cambridge, MA: Harvard Business School, 1994), pp. 1–23.

2. Karen Norman Kennedy, Felicia G. Lassk, and Jerry R. Goolsby, "Customer Mind-Set of Employees Throughout the Organization," *Journal of the Academy of Marketing Science* 30 (Spring 2002), pp. 159–71.

3. Neil Rackham and John DeVincintis, *Rethinking the Sales Force: Redefining Selling to Create and Capture Customer Value* (New York: McGraw-Hill, 1999).

4. Tom Reilly, "Relationship Selling at Its Best, *Industrial Distribution* 95 (September 2006), p. 29; Tom Reilly, *Value-Added Selling: How to Sell More Profitably, Confidently, and Professionally by Competing on VALUE, Not Price* (New York: McGraw-Hill, 2003).

5. Sean Valentine and Tim Barnett, "Ethics Code Awareness, Perceived Ethical Values, and Organizational Commitment, *Journal of Personal Selling & Sales Management* 23 (Fall 2003), p. 359; Jennifer Gilbert, "A Matter of Trust," *Sales & Marketing Management,* March 2003, pp. 31–35.

6. Michael T. Bosworth, *Solution Selling: Creating Buyers in Difficult Selling Markets* (New York: McGraw-Hill, 1995).

7. Kenneth B. Yap and Jillian C. Sweeney, "Zone-of-Tolerance Moderates the Service Quality-Outcome Relationship," *Journal of Services Marketing* 21 (Issue 2, 2007), pp. 137–48; Valarie Zeithaml, A. Parasuraman, and Leonard L. Berry, *Delivering Quality Service: Balancing Customer Perceptions and Expectations* (New York: The Free Press, 1990).

8. Mark P. Leach, Annie H. Liu, and Wesley J. Johnston, "The Role of Self-Regulation Training in Developing the Motivation Management Capabilities of Salespeople," *Journal of Personal Selling & Sales Management* 25 (Summer 2005), pp. 269–81; Mrugank V. Thakor and Ashwin W. Joshi, "Motivating Salesperson Customer Orientation: Insights from the Job Characteristics Model, *Journal of Business Research* 58 (May 2005), pp. 584–92; John P. Campbell and Robert D. Pritchard, "Motivation Theory in Industrial and Organizational Psychology," in *Handbook of Industrial and Organizational Psychology,* ed. Marvin D. Dunnette (Chicago: Rand McNally, 1976), p. 65.

9. Greg W. Marshall, Daniel J. Goebel, and William C. Moncrief, "Hiring for Success at the Buyer–Seller Interface," *Journal of Business Research* 56 (March 2003), pp. 247–55.

10. William L. Cron, Alan J. Dubinsky, and Ronald E. Michaels, "The Influence of Career Stages on Components of Salesperson Motivation," *Journal of Marketing* 52 (January 1988), pp. 78–92; William L. Cron, "Industrial Salesperson Development: A Career Stage Perspective," *Journal of Marketing,* Fall 1984, pp. 41–52.

11. Jerome A. Colletti and Mary S. Fiss, *Compensating New Sales Roles: How to Design Rewards That Work in Today's Selling Environment,* 2nd ed. (New York: AMACOM, 2001).

12. HR Chally Group, *The Chally World Class Excellence Research Report: The Route to the Summit* (Dayton, OH: HR Chally Group, 2007).

13. Leonard L. Berry, *On Great Service: A Framework for Action* (New York: The Free Press, 1995).

CHAPTER 2

1. This classic line of research on job satisfaction of salespeople was initiated by Gilbert A. Churchill, Jr., Neil M. Ford, and Orville C. Walker, Jr., in the article "Organizational Climate and Job Satisfaction of the Sales Force," *Journal of Marketing Research,* November 1976, pp. 323–32. Measurement approaches and study results within this domain have remained relatively stable for nearly 30 years.

2. Nic Sale, "The Way We Will All Work," *Global Telecoms Business* (July/August 2007), p. 1.

3. Julia Chang, "Desperately Seeking Sales Stars," *Sales & Marketing Management* 158 (October 2006), pp. 45–47.

4. Greg W. Marshall, Daniel J. Goebel, and William C. Moncrief, "Hiring for Success at the Buyer–Seller Interface," *Journal of Business Research* 56 (April 2003), pp. 247–55.

5. Dawn R. Deeter-Schmelz, Daniel J. Goebel, and Karen Norman Kennedy,

"What Are the Characteristics of an Effective Sales Manager: An Exploratory Study Comparing Salesperson and Sales Manager Perspectives," *Journal of Personal Selling & Sales Management* 28 (Winter 2008), p. 7; Stephen B. Castelberry and C. David Shepherd, "Effective Interpersonal Listening and Personal Selling," *Journal of Personal Selling & Sales Management,* Winter 1993, pp. 35–49.

6. Bulent Menguc and Seigyoung Auh, "Creating a Firm-Level Dynamic Capability through Capitalizing on Market Orientation and Innovativeness," *Journal of the Academy of Marketing Science* 34 (Winter 2006), pp. 63–73; Rosemary P. Ramsey and Ravi S. Sohi, "Listening to Your Customers: The Impact of Perceived Salesperson Listening Behavior on Relationship Outcomes," *Journal of the Academy of Marketing Science* 25 (Spring 1997), pp. 127–37.

7. George R. Franke and Jeong-Eun Park, "Salesperson Adaptive Selling Behavior and Customer Orientation: A Meta-Analysis," *Journal of Marketing Research* 43 (November 2006), p. 34; Barton A. Weitz, Harish Sujan, and Mita Sujan, "Knowledge, Motivation, and Adaptive Behavior: A Framework for Improving Selling Effectiveness," *Journal of Marketing* 50 (October 1986), pp. 174–91.

8. William C. Moncrief III, "Selling Activity and Sales Position Taxonomies for Industrial Sales Forces," *Journal of Marketing Research* 23 (August 1986), pp. 261–70.

9. Greg W. Marshall, William C. Moncrief, and Felicia G. Lassk, "The Current State of Sales Force Activities," *Industrial Marketing Management* 28 (January 1999), pp. 87–98.

10. William A. O'Connell and William Keenan, Jr., "The Shape of Things to Come," *Sales & Marketing Management,* January 1990, pp. 36–41.

11. Michelle Marchetti, "The Cost of Doing Business," *Sales & Marketing Management,* September 1999, p. 56.

12. O'Connell and Keenan, p. 38.

13. Julie Hill, "The Tale of the Tablet Computer," *Presentations,* February 2002, p. 13.

14. *Presentations* Web site (www.presentations.com), June 2003.

15. Derek A. Newton, *Sales Force Performance and Turnover* (Cambridge, MA: Marketing Science Institute, 1973), p. 3.

16. Donald W. Jackson, Jr., Janet E. Keith, and Richard K. Burdick, "Purchasing Agents' Perceptions of Industrial Buying Center Influence: A Situational Approach," *Journal of Marketing,* Fall 1984, pp. 75–83.

17. P. Fraser Johnson and Michiel R. Leenders, "Building a Corporate Supply Chain Function," *Journal of Supply Chain Management* 44 (July 2008), pp. 39–52; Richard G. Jennings and Richard E. Plank, "When the Purchasing Agent Is a Committee: Implications for Industrial Marketing," *Industrial Marketing Management* 24 (November 1995), pp. 411–19.

18. Frank Jacob and Michael Ehret, "Self-Protection versus Opportunity Seeking in Business Buying Behavior: An Experimental Study," *Journal of Business & Industrial Marketing* 21 (Issue 2, 2006), p. 106; V. W. Mitchell, "Buy-Phase and Buy-Class Effects on Organizational Risk Perceptions and Reductions in Purchasing Professional Services," *Journal of Business and Industrial Marketing* 13 (1998), pp. 461–71.

19. Jennings and Plank.

20. Mark A. Moon and Susan Forquer Gupta, "Examining the Formation of Selling Centers: A Conceptual Framework," *Journal of Personal Selling & Sales Management,* Spring 1997, pp. 31–42.

21. Geoffrey Brewer, "Lou Gerstner Has His Hands Full," *Sales & Marketing Management,* May 1998, pp. 36–41.

22. Louis V. Gerstner, Jr., *Who Says the Elephant Can't Dance? Inside IBM's Historic Turnaround* (New York: HarperBusiness, 2002).

23. Donald W. Barclay and Michele D. Bunn, "Process Heuristics in Organizational Buying: Starting to Fill a Gap," *Journal of Business Research* 59 (February 2006), p. 186. Wesley J. Johnston and Jeffrey E. Lewin, "Organizational Buying Behavior: Toward an Integrative Framework," *Journal of Business Research* 35 (January 1996), pp. 1–15.

24. The Data Warehouse Institute, Industry Study 2000 Survey, p. 1.

25. http://www.Pricewaterhouse Coopers.com.

26. Ronald S. Swift, *Accelerating Customer Relationships: Using CRM and Relationship Technologies* (Upper Saddle River, NJ: Prentice-Hall PTR, 2000), p. 42.

27. Stanley A. Brown, ed., *Customer Relationship Management: A Strategic Imperative in the World of E-Business* (Toronto: John Wiley & Sons Canada, 2000), pp. 8–9.

28. Swift, pp. 39–42.

CHAPTER 3

1. Bill Brooks, "Ten Ways to Add Value and Defeat Price Objections," *American Salesman* 50 (November 2005), pp. 3–4.

2. Lewis Hershey, "The Role of Sales Presentations in Developing Customer Relationships," *Services Marketing Quarterly* 26 (Issue 3, 2005), p. 41.

3. David W. Cravens and Nigel F. Piercy, *Strategic Marketing,* 9th ed. (New York: McGraw-Hill/Irwin, 2009).

4. Roger D. Blackwell, *From Mind to Market* (New York: HarperBusiness, 1997), pp. 182–83.

5. Hershey, p. 41.

6. Michael E. Porter, *Competitive Advantage* (New York: Simon & Schuster, 1985).

7. Frederick F. Reichheld, *Loyalty Rules! How Leaders Build Lasting Relationships in the Digital Age* (Cambridge, MA: Harvard Business School Press, 2001).

8. David A. Garvin, "Competing on the Eight Dimensions of Quality," *Harvard Business Review,* November/December 1987, pp. 101–9.

9. Rosemary P. Ramsey and Ravipreet S. Sohi, "Listening to Your Customers: The

Impact of Perceived Salesperson Listening Behavior on Relationship Outcomes," *Journal of the Academy of Marketing Science* 25 (Spring 1997), pp. 127–37; John Swan and Johannah Nolan, "Gaining Customer Trust: A Conceptual Guide for the Salesperson," *Journal of Personal Selling & Sales Management,* November 1985, pp. 39–48.

10. Valarie A. Zeithaml, Mary Jo Bitner, and Dwayne D. Gremler, *Services Marketing: Integrating Customer Focus across the Firm,* 4th ed. (Chicago: McGraw-Hill/Irwin, 2005).

11. David A. Aaker and Erich Joachimsthaler, *Brand Leadership: Building Assets in the Information Society* (New York: The Free Press, 2000).

12. Barton A. Weitz, Stephen B. Castleberry, and John F. Tanner, *Selling: Building Partnerships,* 5th ed. (New York: McGraw-Hill/Irwin, 2003).

CHAPTER 4

1. William T. Ross and Diana C. Robertson, "A Typology of Situational Factors: Impact on Salesperson Decision Making about Ethical Issues," *Journal of Business Ethics* (September 2003), pp. 213–25; Willem Verbeke, Cok Ouwerkerk, and Ed Peelen, "Exploring the Contextual and Individual Factors on Ethics Decision Making of Salespeople," *Journal of Business Ethics* 15 (1996), pp. 1175–87.

2. O. C. Ferrell, John Fraedrich, and Linda Ferrell, *Business Ethics: Ethical Decision Making and Cases,* 7th ed. (Boston: Houghton-Mifflin, 2008), p. 7.

3. Jennifer Gilbert, "A Matter of Trust," *Sales & Marketing Management,* March 2003, p. 32.

4. Thomas N. Ingram, Raymond W. LaForge, and Charles H. Schwepker, Jr., "Salesperson Ethical Decision Making: The Impact of Sales Leadership and Sales Management Control Strategy," *Journal of Personal Selling & Sales Management* (Fall 2007), p. 301; Frank Sonnennberg, "Trust Me . . . Trust Me Not," *Journal of Business Strategy,* February 1994, pp. 14–16; and Fredrick Trawick, John Swan, Gail McGee and David Rink, "Influence of Buyer Ethics and Salesperson Behavior on Intention to Choose a Supplier," *Journal of the Academy of Marketing Science,* Winter 1991, pp. 17–23.

5. Michael Bendixen and Russell Abratt, "Corporate Identity, Ethics and Reputation in Supplier-Buyer Relationship," *Journal of Business Ethics* (November 2007), pp. 69–75; Fredrick Trawick, Fred Morgan, and Jeffery Stoltman, "Influence of Buyer Ethics and Salesperson Behavior on Intention to Choose a Supplier," *Journal of the Academy of Marketing Science,* Winter 1991, pp. 17–24.

6. Dawn Myers, "You Get What You Give So Make it Good," *Promotional Products Business,* June 1998, pp. 105–11.

7. Erin Strout, "Are Your Salespeople Ripping You Off?" *Sales & Marketing Management,* February 2001, pp. 56–62.

8. Betsy Cummings, "An Affair to Remember," *Sales & Marketing Management,* August 2001, pp. 50–57.

9. Rowena Crosbie, "Who Defines Ethics in Your Organization," *Industrial and Commercial Training* (2008), pp. 181–98; Charles Schwepker, O. C. Ferrell, and Thomas Ingram, "The Influences of Ethical Climate and Ethical Conflict on Role Stress in the Sales Force," *Journal of the Academy of Marketing Science* 25 (Spring 1997), pp. 106–16.

10. Scott John Vitell and Anusorn Singhapakdi, "The Role of Ethics Institutionalization in Influencing Organizational Commitment, Job Satisfaction, and Esprit de Corps," *Journal of Business Ethics* (August 2008), pp. 343–55; Charles Schwepker, "Ethical Climate's Relationship to Job Satisfaction, Organizational Commitment and Turnover Intention in the Salesforce," *Journal of Business Research* 54 (2001), pp. 39–52.

11. Carolyn Hotchkiss, "The Sleeping Dog Stirs: New Signs of Life in Efforts to End Corruption in International Business," *Journal of Public Policy and Marketing* 17 (Spring 1998), pp. 108–21.

12. Joel E. Urbany, Thomas J. Reynolds, and Joan M. Phillips, "How to Make Values Count in Everyday Decisions," *MIT Sloan Management Review* (Summer 2008), pp. 75–87; O. C. Ferrell, Thomas N. Ingram, and Raymond W. Laforge, "Initiating Structure for Legal and Ethical Decision in a Global Sales Organization," *Industrial Marketing Management,* 2000, Vol. 29, no. 6, pp. 555–64.

13. John F. Veiga, Timothy D. Golden, and Kathleen Dechant, "Why Managers Bend the Company Rules," *The Academy of Management Executive* (May 2004), pp. 84–97; Debbie LeClair, O. C. Ferrell, and Linda Ferrell, "Federal Sentencing Guidelines for Organizations: Policy Issues for International Marketing," *Journal of Public Policy and Marketing* 16 (Spring 1997), pp. 27–37.

14. Douglas B. Grisaffe and Fernando Jaramillo, "Toward Higher Levels of Ethics: Preliminary Evidence of Positive Outcomes," *The Journal of Personal Selling & Sales Management* (Fall 2007), pp. 355–68; Thomas G. Brashear, James S. Boles, Danny N. Bellenger, and Charles M. Brooks, "An Empirical Test of Trust-Building Processes and Outcomes in Sales Manager–Salesperson Relationships," *Journal of the Academy of Marketing Science* 31, no. 2 (Spring 2003), pp. 189–200; and Willem Verbeke, Cok Ouwerkerk, and Ed Peelen, "Exploring the Contextual and Individual Factors on Ethical Decision Making of Salespeople," *Journal of Business Ethics* 15 (Fall 1996), pp. 1175–87.

CHAPTER 5

1. Philip Kotler and Kevin Keller, *Marketing Management,* 13th ed. (Upper Saddle River, NJ: Prentice Hall, 2009).

2. John Boe, "Six Powerful Prospecting Tips," *American Salesman* 52 (October 2007), pp. 23–25.

3. John J. Bowen, Jr., "Relationship Marketing," *Advisor's Edge* 8 (June 2005), p. 37.

4. Ralph Kisiel, "Dealers Discover Social Networking Sites: MySpace, YouTube, Others Help Reach Sales Prospects," *Automotive News* (February 4, 2008); Jon Swartz, "Social Networking Sites Work to Turn Users into Profits," *USA Today* (May 12, 2008).

5. Jennifer Gilbert, "The Show Must Go On," *Sales & Marketing Management,* May 2003, p. 14.

6. Frank Belschak, Villem Verbeke, and Richard P. Bagozzi, "Coping with Sales Call Anxiety: The Role of Sales Perseverance and Task Concentration Strategies," *Journal of the Academy of Marketing Science* 34 (Summer 2006), pp. 403–18; Willem Verbeke and Richard P. Bagozzi, "Sales Call Anxiety: Exploring What It Means when Fear Rules a Sales Encounter," *Journal of Marketing* 64 (July 2000), pp. 88–101.

7. Robert McGarvey, "Ice Cubes to Eskimos," *Entrepreneur,* August 2000, pp. 68–76.

CHAPTER 6

1. Pradeep Bhardwaj, Yuxin Chen, and David Godes, "Buyer-Initiated vs. Seller-Initiated Information Revelation," *Management Science* (June 2008), pp. 1104–15; Marvin A. Jolson, "Broadening the Scope of Relationship Selling," *Journal of Personal Selling & Sales Management,* Fall 1997, pp. 75–88.

2. Patricia Fripp, "Power Pitching," *Business Forms, Labels & Systems,* (November 20, 2006), p. 14; Tad Simons, "Study Shows Just How Much Visuals Increase Persuasiveness," *Presentations,* March 1998, p. 20.

3. Lillian H. Chaney and Catherine G. Green, "Effective Presentations," *American Salesman* (June 2004), pp. 22–28; Tony L. Henthorne, Michael S. Latour, and Alvin Williams, "Initial Impressions in the Organizational Buyer–Seller Dyad: Sales Management Implications," *Journal of Personal Selling & Sales Management,* Summer 1992, pp. 57–65.

4. Julie Hill, "Nail Your First Three Minutes to Avoid Going Down in Flames," *Presentations,* February 1999, p. 28.

5. Dan Hill, "Emotionomics, Winning Hearts and Minds," *American Salesman,* March 2008, pp. 12–14; Erika Rasmusson, "The 10 Traits of Successful Salespeople," *Sales & Marketing Management,* February 1999, p. 34.

6. Author interview with financial consultant, June 2003.

7. Edward C. Bursk, "Low Pressure Selling" *Harvard Business Review,* July/August 2006, pp. 150–65; Dorothy Leeds, "The Art of Asking Questions," *Training and Development,* January 1993, p. 58.

8. Neil Rackham, *SPIN Selling,* (New York: McGraw-Hill, 1988) and Huthwaite, Inc. Web site (www.huthwaite.com), June 2003.

9. Tanya Drollinger, Lucette B. Comer, and Patricia T. Warrington, "Development and Validation of Active Empathetic Listening Scale," *Psychology & Marketing* (February 2006), pp. 161–79; John Stewart, *Bridges Not Walls: A Book about Interpersonal Communication,* 8th ed. (New York: McGraw-Hill, 2001).

10. John Boe, "Customers for Life," *American Salesman* (June 2008), pp. 3–7; James Champy, "Selling to Tomorrow's Customer," *Sales & Marketing Management,* March 1999, p. 28.

11. Bill Brooks, "How to Present Your Product with No Resistance," *American Salesman* (November 2006), pp. 27–31; Sarah Lorge, "Selling a Product That's Ahead of Its Time," *Sales & Marketing Management,* July 1999, p. 15.

CHAPTER 7

1. Tom Batchelder, "A More Human Approach to Sales," *American Salesman* (June 2008), pp. 7–13; Tom Riley, "Step Up Your Negotiating Success," *Personal Selling Power,* April 1990, p. 40.

2. Micheal Soon Lee, "10 Common Negotiating Mistakes That Cost You Thousands," *American Salesman* (September 2007), pp. 25–29; Joe F. Alexander, Patrick L. Schul, and Denny E. McCorkle, "An Assessment of Selected Relationships in a Model of the Industrial Marketing Negotiation Process," *Journal of Personal Selling & Sales Management* 14 (Summer 1994), pp. 25–39.

3. *Webster's Online Dictionary* (www.m-w.com), January 2009.

4. Marvin Jolson, "Broadening the Scope of Relationship Selling," *Journal of Personal Selling & Sales Management* 17 (Fall 1997), pp. 75–88.

5. www.wired.com, January 2009.

6. Kim Sydow Campbell, Lenita Davis, and Lauren Skinner, "Rapport Management during the Exploration Phase of the Salesperson-Customer Relationship," *Journal of Personal Selling & Sales Management* (Fall 2006), pp. 359–73; Judy A. Wagner, Noreen M. Klein, and Janet E. Keith, "Selling Strategies: The Effects of Suggesting a Decision Structure to Novice and Expert Buyers," *Journal of the Academy of Marketing Science* 29 (Summer 2001), pp. 289–306.

7. Joanne Lynch and Leslie de Chernatony, "Winning Hearts and Minds: Business-to-Business Branding and the Role of the Salesperson," *Journal of Marketing Management* (February 2007), pp. 123–37; Kenneth Evans, Robert E. Kleine, Timothy D. Landry, and Lawrence A. Crosby, "How First Impressions of a Customer Impact Effectiveness in an Initial Sales Encounter," *Journal of the Academy of Marketing Science* 28 (Fall 2000), pp. 512–26.

8. Krongjit Laochumnanvanit and David H. B. Bednall, "Consumers' Evaluation of Free Service Trial Offers," *Academy of Marketing Science Review* (January 2005), pp. 1–17; Julie Johnson, Hiram C. Barksdale, and James S. Boles, "The Strategic Role of the Salesperson in Reducing Customer Defection in Business Relationships," *Journal of Personal Selling & Sales Management* 21 (Spring 2001), pp. 123–34.

CHAPTER 8

1. Roger Fisher, William Ury, and Bruce Patton, *Getting to Yes: Negotiating Agreement without Giving In,* 2nd ed. (New York: Penguin Books USA, 1991).

2. Sean Dwyer, John Hill, and Warren Martin, "An Empirical Investigation of Critical Success Factors in the Personal Selling Process for Homogeneous Goods," *Journal of Personal Selling & Sales Management* 20 (Summer 2000), pp. 151–59.

3. James W. Pickens, *The Art of Closing Any Deal: How to Be a Master Closer in Anything You Do* (New York: Warner Books, 2003).

4. Tom Reilly, "Salespeople: Develop the Means to Handle Rejection," *Personal Selling Power,* July/August 1987, p. 15.

5. Pickens, pp. 263–95.

6. Stephan Schiffman, *Getting to "Closed"* (Chicago: Dearborn Trade Publishing, 2002).

7. Greg W. Marshall, Daniel J. Goebel, and William C. Moncrief, "Hiring for Success at the Buyer–Seller Interface," *Journal of Business Research* 56 (April 2003), pp. 247–55.

8. Valarie A. Zeithaml, Mary Jo Bitner, and Dwayne D. Gremler, *Services Marketing: Integrating Customer Focus across the Firm,* 4th ed. (Chicago: McGraw-Hill/Irwin 2005).

9. Frederich F. Reichheld, "Loyalty and the Renaissance of Marketing," *Marketing Management* 2 (1994), pp. 10–21.

CHAPTER 9

1. Google Web site (www.google.com), January 2009.

2. Michael Guld, "Effectively Manage Your Multi-Tasking Day," *American Salesman* (July 2008), pp. 25–29; Renee Zemanski, "A Matter of Time," *Selling Power,* October 2001, pp. 80–82.

3. Dave Kahle, "Salespeople: Position Yourselves with Power," *American Salesman* (November 2007), pp. 14–21; William Kendy, "Time Management," *Selling Power,* July 2000, pp. 34–36.

4. Jim Morgan, "Customer Information Management (CIM): The Key to Successful CRM in Financial Services," *Journal of Performance Management* (May 2007), pp. 47–66; Daniel Tynan, "Leveraging Your Needs," *Sales & Marketing Management,* December 2003, p. 23.

5. TerrAlign Web site (www.terralign.com), January 2009.

6. County and City Data Book (www.census.gov), January 2009.

7. PRIZM Web site found at (www.claritas.com), January 2009.

8. Judy A. Siguaw, Sheryl E. Kimes, and Jule B. Gassenheimer, "B2B Sales Force Productivity: Applications of Revenue Management Strategies to Sales Management," *Industrial Marketing Management* (October 2003), pp. 539–51; Andris A. Zoltners and Sally E. Lorimer, "Sales Territory Alignment: An Overlooked Productivity Tool," *Journal of Personal Selling & Sales Management* 20, no. 3 (Summer 2000), pp. 139–50.

9. Mark W. Johnston, and Greg W. Marshall, *Sales Force Management,* 9th ed. (New York: McGraw-Hill, 2009), p. 163.

10. *Ibid.,* p. 166.

11. *Ibid.*

CHAPTER 10

1. Mark W. Johnston, and Greg W. Marshall, *Sales Force Management,* 9th ed. (New York: McGraw-Hill, 2009), p. 201.

2. C. Fred Miao and Kenneth R. Evans, "The Impact of Salesperson Motivation on Role Perceptions and Job Performance—A Cognitive and Affective Perspective, *Journal of Personal Selling & Sales Management* (Winter 2007), pp. 89–106; Jeffrey K. Sager, Junsub Yi, and Charles M. Futrell, "A Model Depicting Salespeople's Perceptions," *Journal of Personal Selling & Sales Management* 18, no. 3 (Summer 1998), pp. 1–22.

3. Thomas E. DeCarlo, R. Kenneth Teas, and James C. McElroy, "Salesperson Performance Attributions Process and the Formulation of Expectancy Estimates," *Journal of Personal Selling & Sales Management* 17, no. 3 (1997), pp. 1–17.

4. Bill Brooks, "Self-Management and Character, *American Salesman* (February 2006), pp. 19–22; Rene Y. Darmon, "Where Do the Best Sales Force Profit Producers Come From?" *Journal of Personal Selling & Sales Management* 13, no. 3 (1993), pp. 17–29.

5. Joseph O. Rentz, C. David Shepherd, Armen Taschian, Pratibha A. Dabholkar, and Robert T. Ladd, "A Measure of Selling Skill: Scale Development and Validation," *Journal of Personal Selling & Sales Management* (Winter 2002), pp. 13–22; Siew Meng Leong, Paul S. Busch, and Deborah Roedder John, "Knowledge Bases and Salesperson Effectiveness: A Script Theoretic Analysis," *Journal of Marketing Research* 26 (May 1990), pp. 164–78.

6. Francie Dalton, "Motivating the Unmotivated," *American Salesman* (June 2007), pp. 6–10; Audrey Bottjen, "Incentives Gone Awry," *Sales & Marketing Management,* May 2001, p. 72.

7. Michael W. Pass, Kenneth R. Evans, and John L. Schlacter, "Sales Force Involvement in CRM Information Systems: Participation, Support, and Focus," *Journal of Personal Selling & Sales Management* (Summer 2004), pp. 229–42; Nicholas G. Paparoidamis, "Learning Orientation and Leadership Quality: Their Impact on Salespersons' Performance," *Management Decision,* (July 2005), pp. 1054–64; Arthur Baldauf, David W. Cravens, and Nigel F. Piercy, "Examining Business Strategy, Sales Management, and Salesperson Antecedents of Sales Organization Effectiveness," *Journal of Personal Selling & Sales Management* 21, no. 2 (Spring 2001), pp. 109–22; Ken Grant, David W. Cravens, George S. Low, and William C. Moncrief, "The Role of Satisfaction and Territory Design on Motivation, Attitudes, and Work Outcomes of Salespeople," *Journal of the Academy of Marketing Science,* Spring 2001, pp. 165–78.

8. TerrAlign Web site (www.terralign.com), January 2009.

9. Michael Segalla, Dominique Rouzies, Madeleine Besson, and Barton A. Weitz, "A Cross-National Investigation of Incentive Sales Compensation," *International Journal of Research in Marketing* (December 2006), pp. 419–30; William A. Weeks, Terry W. Loe, Lawrene B. Chonko, Carlos Ruy Martinez, and Kirk Wakefield,

"Cognitive Moral Development and the Impact of Perceived Organizational Ethical Climate on the Search for Sales Force Excellence: A Cross-Cultural Study," *Journal of Personal Selling & Sales Management* (Spring 2006), pp. 205–21; Donald W. Jackson, Stephen S. Tax and John W. Barnes, "Examining the Salesforce Culture: Managerial Applications and Research Propositions," *Journal of Personal Selling and Sales Management* 14, no. 4 (Fall 1994), pp. 1–14.

10. James S. Boles, John Any Wood, and Julie Johnson, "Interrelationships of Role Conflict, Role Ambiguity, and Work-Family Conflict with Different Facets of Job Satisfaction and the Moderating Effects of Gender," *Journal of Personal Selling & Sales Management* 23, no. 2 (Spring 2003), pp. 99–113.

11. *Ibid.*

12. Jeffrey K. Sager, Junsub Yi and Charles M. Futrell, "A Model Depicting Salespeople's Perceptions," *Journal of Personal Selling & Sales Management* 18, no. 3 (Summer 1998), pp. 1–22.

13. Dee K. Knight, Hae-Jung Kim, and Christy Crutsinger, "Examining the Effects of Role Stress on Customer Orientation and Job Performance of Retail Salespeople," *International Journal of Retail & Distribution Management* (2007), pp. 381–99; Theresa B. Flaherty, Robert Dahlstrom and Steven J. Skinner, "Organizational Values and Role Stress as Determinants of Customer-Oriented Selling Performance," *Journal of Personal Selling & Sales Management* 19, no. 2 (Spring 1999), pp. 1–18.

14. Peter Sowden, "What Motivates Me," *Sales & Marketing Management,* May 2003, p. 22.

15. Subhra Chakrabarty, Diana T. Oubre, and Gene Brown, "The Impact of Supervisory Adaptive Selling and Supervisory Feedback on Salesperson Performance," *Industrial Marketing Management* (June 2008), pp. 447–60; Farrand J. Hartenian, J. Hadaway, and Gordon J. Badovick, "Antecedents and Consequences or Role Perceptions: A Path Analytic Approach," *Journal of Applied Business Research* 10 (Spring 1994), pp. 40–50.

16. Fernando Jaramillo, Jay Prakash Mulki, and Paul Solomon, "The Role of Ethical Climate on Salesperson's Role Stress, Job Attitudes, Turnover Intention, and Job Performance," *Journal of Personal Selling & Sales Management* (Summer 2006), pp. 271–90; Eli Jones, Donna Massey Kantak, Charles M. Futrell, and Mark W. Johnston, "Leader Behavior, Work-Attitudes, and Turnover of Salespeople: An Integrative Study," *Journal of Personal Selling & Sales Management* 16, no. 2 (Spring 1996), pp. 13–23.

17. Mark P. Leach, Annie H. Liu, and Wesley J. Johnston, "The Role of Self-Regulation Training in Developing the Motivation Management Capabilities of Salespeople," *Journal of Personal Selling & Sales Management* (Summer 2005), pp. 269–81; Susan M. Keaveney, and James E. Nelson, "Coping with Organizational Role Stress: Intrinsic Motivational Orientation, Perceived Role Benefits, and Psychological Withdrawal," *Journal of the Academy of Marketing Science* 21 (Spring 1993), pp. 113–24.

18. Jerry Unseem, "A Manager for All Seasons," *Fortune,* April 30, 2001.

19. Tara Burnthorne Lopez, Chistopher D. Hopkins, and Mary Anne Raymond, "Reward Preferences of Salespeople: How Do Commissions Rate?" *Journal of Personal Selling & Sales Management* (Fall 2006), pp. 381–99; Susan K. DelVecchio, "The Quality of Salesperson Manager Relationship: The Effect of Lattitude, Loyalty and Competence," *Journal of Personal Selling & Sales Management* 18, no. 4 (Winter 1998), pp. 31–48; Vincent Alonzo, "Perks for Jerks," *Sales & Marketing Management,* February 2001, pp. 38–40.

CHAPTER 11

1. Kenneth R. Evans, John L. Schlacter, Roberta J. Schultz, and Dwayne D. Gremler, "Salesperson and Sales Manager Perceptions of Salesperson Job Characteristics and Job Outcomes: A Perceptual Congruence Approach," *Journal of Marketing Theory and Practice* (Fall 2002), pp. 30–45; Thomas Rollins, "How to Tell Competent Salespeople from the Other Kind," *Sales & Marketing Management,* September 1990, pp. 116–18, 145–46.

2. Diane Coutu, "HBR Case Study: We Googled You," *Harvard Business Review* (June 2007), pp. 37–45; Thomas Rollins, "How to Tell Competent Salespeople from the Other Kind," *Sales & Marketing Management,* September 1990, pp. 116–18, 145–46; See also Timothy J. Trow, "The Secret of a Good Hire: Profiling," *Sales & Marketing Management,* May 1990, pp. 44–55.

3. Richard L. Griffith, Tom Chmielowski, and Yukiko Yoshita, "Do Applicants Fake? An Examination of the Frequency of Applicant Faking Behavior," *Personnel Review* (2007), pp. 341–61; Kevin M. McNeilly and Frederich A. Russ, "Does Relational Demography Matter in a Personal Selling Context," *Journal of Personal Selling & Sales Management* 20, no. 4 (Fall 2000), pp. 279–88; Sanjit Sengupta, Robert E. Krapfel, and Michael A. Pusateri, "An Empirical Investigation of Key Account Salesperson Effectiveness," *Journal of Personal Selling & Sales Management* 20, no. 4 (Fall 2000), pp. 253–61.

4. Carole Ann King, "Frustration Mounts as Recruiting Gets Harder," *National Underwriter,* March 19, 2001, pp. 6–7.

5. David Ice, "Looking to Hire New Reps?" *Agency Sales* (January 2008), p. 7; Jim Pratt, "Recruiting Talented Sales Associates," *Transaction World Magazine,* May 2001, (www.transactionworld.com).

6. Brian P. Matthews and Tom Redman, "Recruiting the Wrong Salespeople: Are the Job Ads to Blame?" *Industrial Marketing Management* (October 2001), pp. 541–59; Marianne Matthews, "If Your Ads Aren't Pulling Top Sales Talent . . .," *Sales & Marketing Management,* February 1990, pp. 73–79.

7. Dana Mattioli, "How to Minimize Chances the Boss Will Learn You Are

Looking," *Wall Street Journal* (Eastern edition), August 21, 2007, p. B.6; Marianne Matthews, "If Your Ads Aren't Pulling Top Sales Talent . . .," *Sales & Marketing Management*, February 1990, pp. 73–79.

8. Michael A. Wiles and Rosann L. Spiro, "Attracting Graduates to Sales Positions and the Role of the Recruiter Knowledge: A Re-examination," *Journal of Personal Selling & Sales Management* (2004), pp. 39–52; Audrey Bottjen, "The Benefits of College Recruiting," *Sales and Marketing Management*, April 2001, p. 20.

9. Alan J. Dubinsky, Rolph E. Anderson, and Rajiv Mehta, "Selection, Training, and Performance Evaluation of Sales Managers: An Empirical Investigation," *Journal of Business-to-Business Marketing*, 1999, pp. 37–51; E. James Randall and Cindy H. Randall, "Review of Salesperson Selection Techniques and Criteria: A Managerial Approach," *International Journal of Research in Marketing* 7 (1990), pp. 81–95.

10. Donald M. Truxillo, Talya N. Bauer, Michael A. Campion, and Matthew E. Paronto, "A Field Study of the Role of Big Five Personality in Applicant Perceptions of Selection, Fairness, Self, and the Hiring Organization," *International Journal of Selection and Assessment* (September 2006), pp. 269–81; Neil M. Ford, Orville C. Walker Jr., and Gilbert A. Churchill Jr., "Selecting Successful Salespeople: A Meta-Analysis of Biographical and Psychological Selection Criteria," *Review of Marketing*, ed. Michael J. Houston (Chicago: American Marketing Association, 1988), pp. 90–131.

11. Myron Gable, Charles Hollon, and Frank Dangello, "Increasing the Utility of the Application Blank: Relationship between Job Application Information and Subsequent Performance and Turnover of Salespeople," *Journal of Personal Selling and Sales Management*, Summer 1992, pp. 39–55.

12. Philip L. Roth, Chad H. Van Iddekinge, Allen I. Huffcutt, Carl E. Eidson, Jr., and Mark J. Schmit, "Personality Saturation in Structured Interviews," *International Journal of Selection and Assessment* (December 2005), pp. 261–81; Jo Ann Greco, "Natural Selection: Finding the Perfect Salesperson," *Realtor Magazine Online*, August 1, 2002.

13. "In the Workplace: Unusual Hiring Techniques," *Business World* January 5, 2000, p. 1; William Keenan Jr., "Who Has the Right Stuff?" *Sales & Marketing Management*, August 1993, pp. 28–29.

14. Joe Mullich and Shari Caudron, "Cracking the Ex-files," *Workforce Management* (September 2003), pp. 51–54; Arthur Bragg, "Checking References," *Sales & Marketing Management*, November 1990, pp. 68–71.

15. Margaret Jenkins and Richard Griffith, "Using Personality Constructs to Predict Performance: Narrow or Broad Bandwidth," *Journal of Business and Psychology* (December 2004), pp. 255–70; Seymour Adler, "Personality Tests for Salesforce Selection: Worth a Fresh Look," *Review of Business*, Summer 1994, pp. 27–31.

16. Robert P. Tett and Neil D. Christiansen, "Personality Tests at the Crossroads: A Response to Morgeson, Campion, Dipboyes, Hollenbeck, Murphy, and Schmitt," *Personnel Psychology* (Winter 2007), pp. 967–94; Marvin A. Jolson and Lucette B. Comer, "The Use of Instrumental and Expressive Personality Traits as Indicators of a Salesperson's Behavior," *Journal of Personal Selling & Sales Management* 17, no. 1 (Winter 1997), pp. 29–43.

CHAPTER 12

1. Frank Cespedes, *Organizing and Implementing the Marketing Effort: Text and Cases* (Reading, MA: Addison-Wesley, 1991), pp. 87–88.

2. Annual Report for Cisco Systems, 2009, online at www.Ciscosystems.com.

3. Rebecca Aronauer, "The Classroom vs. E-Learning," *Sales and Marketing Management* (October 2006), p. 21; Mark McMaster, "A Tough Sell: Training the Salesperson," *Sales & Marketing Management*, January 2001, p. 42.

4. Jean C. Mowrey and Scott Hull, "Beyond Training," *Pharmaceutical Executive*, April 2001, pp. 108–22.

5. Alfred Pelham, "Sales Force Involvement in Product Design: The Influence on the Relationships Between Consulting-Oriented Sales Management Programs and Performance," *Journal of Marketing Theory and Practice* (Winter 2006), pp. 37–56; Judy A. Wagner, Noreen M. Klein, and Janet E. Keith, "Selling Strategies: The Effects of Suggesting a Decision Structure to Novice and Expert Buyers," *Journal of the Academy of Marketing Science* 29, no. 3 (Summer 2001), pp. 289–306.

6. Andrew B. Artis and Eric G. Harris, "Self-Directed Learning and Sales Force Performance: An Integrated Framework," *Journal of Personal Selling & Sales Management* (Winter 2007), pp. 9–21; "What's the Problem with Sales Training?" *Training Today*, March 1990, p. 16.

7. Kathleen McLaughlin, "Training's Top 50 Edward Jones," *Training Magazine*, March 2001, p. 20.

8. Adel I. El-Ansary, "Sales Force Effectiveness Research Reveals New Insights and Reward-Penalty Patterns in Sales Force Training," *Journal of Personal Selling & Sales Management* 13, no. 2 (Spring 1993), pp. 83–90.

9. Erika Rasmusson, "Training Goes Virtual," *Sales & Marketing Management*, September 2000, p. 48.

10. Johnson Controls Web site (www.jci.com), January 2009.

11. Caterpillar, Inc., Web site (www.caterpillar.com), January 2009.

12. Jack Falvey, "Forget the Sharks: Swim with Your Salespeople," *Sales & Marketing Management*, November 1990, p. 8.

13. Verizon Web site (www.verizon.com), January 2009.

14. Education Development Center (www.edc.org), November 2008, and Kevin Dobbs, "When Learning Really Happens," *Sales & Marketing Management*, November 2000, p. 98.

15. Elana Harris, "Stars in the Making," *Sales & Marketing Management*, March 2001, p. 61.

16. Kevin Dobbs, "Training on the Fly," *Sales & Marketing Management,* November 2000, pp. 92–98.

17. "Industry Report 2007," *Training Magazine,* October 2008, found at www.trainingmag.com.

18. Ashraf M. Attia, Earl D. Honeycutt Jr., and M. Asri Jantan, "Global Sales Training: In Search of Antecedent, Mediating, and Consequence Variables," *Industrial Marketing Management* (April 2008), pp. 181–201; Robert C. Erffmeyer, K. Randall Russ, and Joseph F. Hair, Jr., "Needs Assessment and Evaluation in Sales-Training Programs," *Journal of Personal Selling & Sales Management* 11 (Winter 1991), pp. 17–31.

CHAPTER 13

1. Bruce Talgan, "Real Pay for Performance," *Journal of Business Strategy,* May/June 2001, pp. 19–22.

2. Leslie M. Fine and Janice R. Franke, "Legal Aspects of Salesperson Commission Payments: Implications for the Implementation of Commission Sales Programs," *Journal of Personal Selling & Sales Management,* Winter 1995, pp. 53–68.

3. C. Bram Cadsby, Fei Song, and Francis Tapon, "Sorting and Incentive Effects of Pay for Performance: An Experimental Investigation," *Academy of Management Journal* 50 (April 2007), p. 387; James W. Walker, "Perspectives on Compensation," *Human Resource Planning* 24 (June 2001), pp. 6–8.

4. Arun Sharma, "Customer Satisfaction-Based Incentive Systems: Some Managerial and Salesperson Considerations," *Journal of Personal Selling & Sales Management,* Spring 1997, pp. 61–70.

5. Joel Silver, "Building an Effective Sales Incentive Program," www.saleslobby.com, January 2002.

6. *Ibid.;* Audrey Bottjen, "Incentives Gone Awry," *Sales & Marketing Management,* May 2001, p. 72.

7. Karen Renk, "The Age-Old Question: Case vs. Merchandise?" *Occupational Health & Safety,* September 2002, pp. 60–62.

8. *Ibid.*

9. Mark McMaster, "Personalized Motivation," *Sales & Marketing Management,* May 2002, p. 16.

10. Cengiz Yilmaz and Shelby D. Hunt, "Salesperson Cooperation: The Influence of Relational, Task, Organizational, and Personal Factors," *Journal of the Academy of Marketing Science,* Fall 2001, pp. 335–57.

11. Ajay Kalra, Mengze Shi, and Kannan Srinivasan, "Salesforce Compensation Scheme and Consumer Inferences," *Management Science* 49 (May 2003), p. 655; Arun Sharma and Dan Sarel, "The Impact of Customer Satisfaction Based Incentive Systems on Salespeople's Customer Service Response: An Empirical Study," *Journal of Personal Selling & Sales Management,* Summer 1995, pp. 17–29.

12. Tará Burnthorne Lopez, Christopher D. Hopkins, and Mary Anne Raymond, "Reward Preferences of Salespeople; How do Commissions Rate?" *Journal of Personal Selling & Sales Management* 26 (Fall 2006), p. 381; S. Scott Sands, "Ineffective Quotas: The Hidden Threat to Sales Compensation Plans," *Compensation and Benefits Review* 32 (March/April 2000), pp. 35–42.

13. Kemba J. Dunham, "Back to Reality: To Lure Workers, Dot-Coms Are Having to Focus on Something Besides Options, Such as Salaries," *Wall Street Journal,* April 12, 2001.

CHAPTER 14

1. V. Kumar, Rajkumar Venkatesan, and Werner Reinartz, "Implications of Adopting a Customer-Focused Sales Campaign," *Journal of Marketing* 72 (September 2008), p. 50; Charles E. Pettijohn, Linda S. Pettijohn, and A.J. Taylor, "Does Salesperson Perception of the Importance of Sales Skills Improve Sales Performance, Customer Orientation, Job Satisfaction, and Organizational Commitment, and Reduce Turnover," *Journal of Personal Selling & Sales Management* 27 (Winter 2007), p. 75; Ramon A. Avila, Edward F. Fern, and O. Karl Mann, "Unraveling Criteria for Assessing the Performance of Salespeople: A Causal Analysis," *Journal of Personal Selling & Sales Management* 8 (May 1988), pp. 45–54; and Richard E. Plank and David A. Reid, "The Mediating Role of Sales Behaviors: An Alternative Perspective of Sales Performance and Effectiveness," *Journal of Personal Selling & Sales Management* 14 (Summer 1994), pp. 43–56.

2. Sven A. Haugland, Igunn, Myrtveit, and Arne Nygaard, "Market Orientation and Performance in the Service Industry: A Data Envelopment Analysis," *Journal of Business Research* 60 (November 2007), p. 1191; Bernard Jaworksi, Vlasis Stathakopoulos, and Shanker Krishan, "Control Combinations in Marketing: Conceptual Framework and Empirical Evidence," *Journal of Marketing* 57 (January 1993), pp. 57–69.

3. David W. Cravens, Thomas N. Ingram, Raymond W. LaForge, and Clifford E. Young, "Behavior-Based and Outcome-Based Salesforce Control Systems," *Journal of Marketing* 57 (October 1993), pp. 47–59.

4. Lee Froschheiser, "Unlock the Power and Potential of Your Team," *American Salesman* 53 (May 2008), p. 5; Alan Test, "Selling Is Still a Numbers Game," *American Salesman* 38 (June 1993), pp. 10–14; and Pete Frye, *The Complete Selling System* (Dover, NH: Upstart Publishing Co., 1992).

5. Benton Cocanougher and John M. Ivancevich, "BARS Performance Rating for Sales Personnel," *Journal of Marketing* 42 (July 1978), pp. 87–95.

6. Arun Sharma, Michael Levy, and Heiner Evanschitzky, "The Variance in Sales Performance Explained by the Knowledge Structures of Salespeople," *Journal of Personal Selling & Sales Management* 27 (Spring 2007), p. 169; Lyndon E. Dawson, Jr., Barlow Soper, and Charles E. Pettijohn, "The Effects of Empathy on Salesperson Effectiveness," *Psychology and Marketing* 9 (July/August 1992), pp. 297–310; and

Neil M. Ford, Orville C. Walker, Jr., Gilbert A. Churchill, Jr., and Steven W. Hartley, "Selecting Successful Salespeople: A Meta-Analysis of Biographical and Psychological Selection Criteria," in *Annual Review of Marketing,* ed. Michael J. Houston (Chicago: American Marketing Association, 1987), pp. 90–131.

7. Cocanougher and Ivancevich, "BARS Performance Rating," p. 89.

8. Greg W. Marshall, John C. Mowen, and Keith J. Fabes, "The Impact of Territory Difficulty and Self versus Other Ratings on Managerial Evaluations of Sales Personnel," *Journal of Personal Selling & Sales Management* 12 (Fall 1992), pp. 35–47.

9. Cocanougher and Ivancevich, "BARS Performance Rating," pp. 90–99.

10. Mary Jo Bitner, Bernard H. Booms, and Mary Stanfield Tetreault, "The Service Encounter: Diagnosing Favorable and Unfavorable Incidents," *Journal of Marketing* 54 (January 1990), pp. 71–84.

11. Roger J. Placky, "Appraisal Scales That Measure Performance Outcomes and Job Results," *Personnel* 60 (May/June 1983), pp. 57–65.

12. Scott Wimer and Kenneth M. Nowack, "13 Common Mistakes Using 360-Degree Feedback," *Training & Development* 52 (May 1998), pp. 69–78.

13. "Give Yourself a Job Review," *American Salesman,* May 2001, pp. 26–27.

14. Charles E. Pettijohn, Linda S. Pettijohn, and Michael d'Amico, "Characteristics of Performance Appraisals and Their Impact on Sales Force Satisfaction," *Human Resource Development Quarterly* 12 (Summer 2001), pp. 127–39.

15. William Fitzgerald, "Forget the Form in Performance Appraisals," *HR Magazine* 40 (December 1995), p. 134.

16. Helen Rheem, "Performance Management: A Progress Report," *Harvard Business Review,* March/April 1995, p. 11.

Name Index

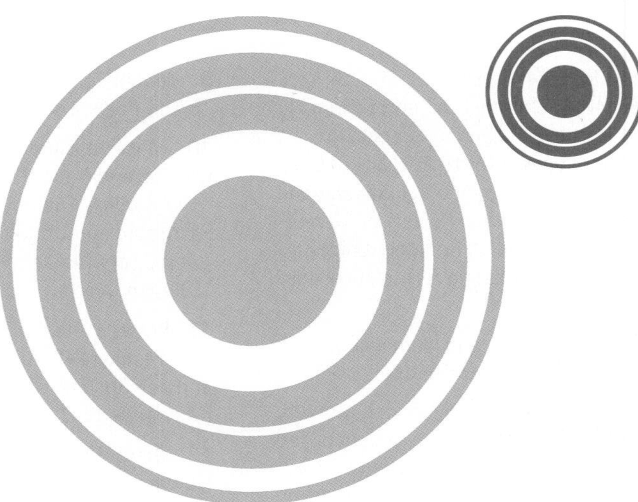

F

G

H

I

J

K

L

M

N

O

P

R

S

T

U

V

W

Y

Z

Subject Index

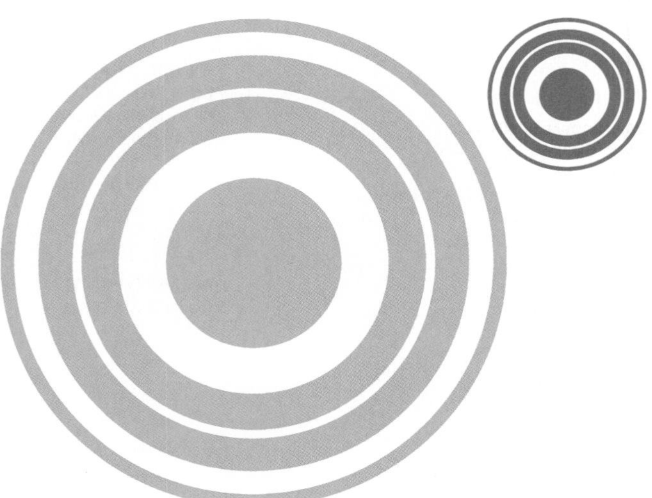

A

B

C

D

E

F

M

N

O

P

Q

R

S

T

U

V

W

X

Z